ANCIENT INDIAN TRADITION & MYTHOLOGY

Translated by
A BOARD OF SCHOLARS

And Edited by
Prof. J.L. SHASTRI

VOLUME 15

ANCIENT INDIAN TRADITION AND MYTHOLOGY SERIES

[PURĀṆAS IN TRANSLATION]

Volumes Released

ŚIVA 1-4
LIṄGA 5-6
BHĀGAVATA 7-11
GARUḌA 12-14
NĀRADA 15-19
KŪRMA 20-21
BRAHMĀṆḌA 22-26
AGNI 27-30
VARĀHA 31-32
BRAHMA 33-36
VĀYU 37-38
PADMA 39-48
SKANDA, PARTS I-XXI, 49-69

Volumes Under Preparation

SKANDA, PARTS XXII-XXIII, 70-71
VĀMANA 72-73
BHAVIṢYA
BRAHMAVAIVARTA
DEVĪBHĀGAVATA
KĀLIKĀ
MĀRKAṆḌEYA
MATSYA
VIṢṆU
VIṢṆUDHARMOTTARA

THE NĀRADA-PURĀNA

PART I

Translated and Annotated by

DR. G.V. TAGARE

MOTILAL BANARSIDASS PUBLISHERS
PRIVATE LIMITED • DELHI

Reprint: Delhi, 1995, 2010
First Edition: Delhi, 1980

ISBN: 978-81-208-0347-3

MOTILAL BANARSIDASS
41 U.A. Bungalow Road, Jawahar Nagar, Delhi 110 007
8 Mahalaxmi Chamber, 22 Bhulabhai Desai Road, Mumbai 400 026
203 Royapettah High Road, Mylapore, Chennai 600 004
236, 9th Main III Block, Jayanagar, Bangalore 560 011
Sanas Plaza, 1302 Baji Rao Road, Pune 411 002
8 Camac Street, Kolkata 700 017
Ashok Rajpath, Patna 800 004
Chowk, Varanasi 221 001

UNESCO COLLECTION OF REPRESENTATIVE WORKS—*Indian Series*
This book has been accepted in the Indian Translation Series
of the UNESCO Collection of Representative Works,
jointly sponsored by the United Nations Educational,
Scientific and Cultural Organization
(UNESCO) and the Government of India

Printed in India
By Jainendra Prakash Jain at Shri Jainendra Press,
A-45 Naraina, Phase-I, New Delhi 110 028
and Published by Narendra Prakash Jain for
Motilal Banarsidass Publishers Private Limited,
Bungalow Road, Delhi 110 007

PUBLISHER'S NOTE

The purest gems lie hidden in the bottom of the ocean or in the depth of rocks. One has to dive into the ocean or delve into the rocks to find them out. Similarly, truth lies concealed in the language which with the passage of time has become obsolete. Man has to learn that language before he discovers that truth.

But he has neither the means nor the leisure to embark on that course. We have, therefore, planned to help him acquire knowledge by an easier course. We have started the series of *Ancient Indian Tradition and Mythology* in English Translation. Our goal is to universalize knowledge through the most popular international medium of expression. The publication of the Purāṇas in English translation is a step towards that goal.

PREFACE

The present volume contains the *Nārada Purāṇa* Part I (Chapters 1-41 completing the first Pāda in English translation). This is the fifteenth volume in the series of fifty volumes, which we have planned on *Ancient Indian Tradition and Mythology*.

The project of the series was envisaged and financed in 1970 by late Lala Sundarlal Jain of Messrs Motilal Banarsidass. Hitherto fifteen volumes of the series, including the present one (that is, four volumes of the *Śiva Purāṇa*, two volumes of the *Liṅga Purāṇa*, five volumes of the *Bhāgavata Purāṇa*, three volumes of the *Garuḍa Purāṇa* and the present volume of the *Nārada Purāṇa*) have been published and released for sale.

The present volume, like all other volumes, is encyclopaedic in character. It deals with miscellaneous topics such as religion, philosophy, Veda and its ancillaries—Śikṣā, Kalpa, Vyākaraṇa, Nirukta, Chandas and Jyotiṣa. In *Śikṣā* it describes the rules of pronunciation of Vedic and Classical Sanskrit and the rules regarding music. In *Kalpa* it deals with the Nakṣatra, Veda, Saṁhitā, Āṅgirasa and Śānti kalpas. In *Vyākaraṇa*, it gives a general idea of the subject. In *Chandas* it prescribes rules for Sanskrit and Prākṛta, Vedic and Classical metres by the method of *Prastāra*. In Jyotiṣa it explains the essentials in detail. While dealing with the Purāṇas, it describes the contents of the Purāṇas which help us to ascertain the interpolations of the later period. Among the general topics, it describes Vratas and Tīrthas in details and exhaustively.

In the Sectarian grouping of the Purāṇas, the Nārada Purāṇa is classified as a Vaiṣṇava Purāṇa on the basis of the fact that among the deities glorified in this Purāṇa, Viṣṇu holds the supreme position, though laudatory references to other deities — Śiva, Śakti, etc. are also made. In his obvious partiality for Vaiṣṇavism, Nārada gives special treatment to Rādhā and Kṛṣṇa, even prescribes a hymn of 1000 names in their eulogy and proclaims special importance of Ekādaśī Vrata in honour of Viṣṇu. He is the first to mention Rāma, Kṛṣṇa, Nṛsiṁha and other incarnations in connection with Tāntric practices.

The variety of topics is very interesting but it is marred as sometimes it is couched in expression that needs elucidation — a task which could not be accomplished by a mere translation. Hence, a provision has been made for the notes, which are attached to each chapter, separately, and not put at the foot of a page as has been the practice hitherto. We hope the reader will not feel embarrassed by this shift.

The translation is based on the Sanskrit text of the *Nārada Purāṇa* published by Messrs Kṣemarāja Śrīkṛṣṇadāsa, Veṅkaṭeśvara Press, Bombay. This text, constructed on the collation of mss and supported by the evidence of citations found in the Smṛti granthas, is fairly accurate.

We have included abbreviations in this part and they will be repeated in successive parts with such additions as are inserted in the notes in those parts. The Glossary and the General Index to the complete Purāṇa will be appended to the last part.

Acknowledgment of obligation

It is our pleasant duty to put on record our sincere thanks to Dr. R. N. Dandekar and the authorities of the UNESCO for their kind encouragement and valuable help which render this work more useful than it would otherwise have been. We are extremely grateful to Dr. Tagare who in the storm and stress of his pressing occupations has snatched time for this national work. The exhaustive Introduction, the lucid translation and explanatory notes are, in fact, monumental contributions in the field of Indology. We must also thank Shri T. V. Parameshwar Iyer for his valuable assistance in the preparation of Translation, and express our gratitude to all those who offered suggestions for improving the same.

—Editor

CONTENTS

ABBREVIATIONS

Common and self-evident abbreviations such as ch (s)—chapter (s), p—page, pp—pages, v—verse, vv—verses, Ftn—footnote, Hist. Ind. Philo—History of Indian Philosophy are not included in this list.

ABORI —*Annals of the Bhandarkar Oriental Research Institute*, Poona.

AGP —S. M. Ali's *The Geography of Purāṇas*, PPH, New Delhi, 1973.

AIHT —*Ancient Indian Historical Tradition* F. E. Pargiter, Motilal Banarsidass (MLBD), Delhi.

AP —*Agni Purāṇa*, Guru Mandal Edition (GM), Calcutta, 1957

AV —*Atharva Veda*, Svadhyaya Mandal Aundh.

Bd.P. —*Brahmāṇḍa Purāṇa*, MLBD, Delhi 1973.

Bh.P —*Bhāgavata Purāṇa*, Bhagavat Vidyapeeth, Ahmedabad.

Bm.P. —*Brahma Purāṇa*, GM, 1954

Bnr. —*Bṛhan-narādiya*—Pt. Hrishikesh Shastri, Chowkhamba, 1975.

Bs.P. —*Bhaviṣya Purāṇa*, Vishnu Shastri Bapat, Wai

Bv.P. —*Brahma Vaivarta Purāṇa*, GM, 1955-57

CC —*Caturvarga Cintāmaṇi* by Hemādri.

DB. —*Devi Bhāgavata*, GM, 1960-61.

De or *GDAMI*—*The Geographical Dictionary of Ancient and Mediaeval India*—N. L. De, Orienta Reprint Delhi, 1971.

Dh.s. —*Dharma Sūtra* (preceded by the author's name such as Gautama).

ERE —*Encyclopaedia of Religion and Ethics*—Hastings.

GP. —*Garuḍa Purāṇa*, Ed. R. S. Bhattacharya, Chowkhamba, Varanasi 1964.

GS. —*Gṛhya Sūtra* (Preceded by the name of the author such as Āpastamba).

HD —*History of Dharma Śāstra* by P. V. Kane, G.O.S. class B6.

IA —*The Indian Antiquary*

IHQ —*The Indian Historical Quarterly.*

KP —*Kūrma Purāṇa,* Venkateshwar Press Edt. Bombay also Kashirāj Trust Edt., Varanasi 1971.

LP. —*Liṅga Purāṇa,* GM, 1960.

Mbh —*Mahābhārata,* Gita Press, Gorakhpur v.s. 2014.

MK. —*Mārkaṇḍeya Purāṇa.*

MN. —*Mahābhārata Nāmānukramaṇi,* Gita Press, Gorakhpur v.s. 2016

Mt.P. —*Matsya Purāṇa,* GM, 1954.

MW —Monier Williams—*Sk.-English Dictionary,* MLBD, Delhi, 1976.

NP —*Nāradiya or Nārada Purāṇa,* Venkateshwar Press, Bombay.

PCK —*Bhāratavarṣiya Prācina Caritra Kośa*—Siddheshwar Shastri Poona 1968.

Pd.P. —*Padma Purāṇa,* GM., 1957—1959.

PE *Puranic Encyclopaedia* by V. Mani, English, MLBD, Delhi, 1975.

PJ —*Purāṇa* (Journal of the Kashirāj Trust) Varanasi.

PR or PRHRC—*Puranic Records on Hindu Rites and Customs*—R. C. Hazra, Calcutta, 1948.

ṚV —*ṚG Veda,* Svadhyaya Mandal, Aundh.

Śat. Br. —*Śatapatha Brāhmaṇa.*

SEP —*Studies in Epics & Purāṇas* by A.D. Pusalkar, Bharatiya Vidya Bhavan, (BVB), Bombay.

SG or SGAMI—*Studies in the Geography of Ancient & Mediaeval India*—D. C. Sircar MLBD, Delhi, 1971.

SKD —*Śabda-Kalpa-Druma—Raja* R.K. Dev., Chowkhamba, Varanasi.

Sk.P. —*Skanda Purāṇa,* GM. 1960-65.

SM —*Sādhana Mālā*—B. Bhattacharya, GOS, Baroda, 1928.

SMC —*Smṛti Candrikā*—Devanna Bhatta.

Smr. —*Smṛti* (preceded by the author's name or simply by the author's name e.g. Manu Smr. or Manu. All GM editions in the Smṛti-Sandarbha, 1952-57).

Sv.P. —*Śiva Purāṇa,* Pandit Pustakālaya Kashi v.s. 2020.

Va.P.	—*Vāyu Purāṇa*, GM, 1959.
Vm. P.	—*Vāmana Purāṇa*, Kashiraj Trust, Varanasi.
VP.	—*Viṣṇu Purāṇa*, Gita Press, Gorakhpur, v.s. 2026.
VR	—*Vālmīki Rāmāyaṇa*, Gita Press, v.s. 2020.
VRK	—*Vālmīki Rāmāyaṇa Kośa*—Ramkumar Rai, Chowkhamba Varanasi.
Yaj	—*Yājñavalkya* (*Smṛti*), etc.
YSP	—*The Yoga Sūtras of Patañjali* by J.H. Wood.

NĀRADA PURĀṆA (NOTES)
PURĀṆAS—ABBREVIATIONS

1. AP — Agni Purāṇa
2. Bh.P. — Bhāgavata Purāṇa
3. Bd.P. — Brahmāṇḍa Purāṇa
4. Bm.P. — Brahma Purāṇa
5. Bs.P. — Bhaviṣya Purāṇa
6. BVP — Brahma Vaivarta Purāṇa
7. GP. — Garuḍa Purāṇa
8. HP. — Harivaṁśa Purāṇa
9. KP — Kūrma Purāṇa
10. LP — Liṅga Purāṇa
11. MBH — Mahā-Bhārata Purāṇa
12. Md.P — Mārkaṇḍeya Purāṇa
13. Mt.P — Matsya Purāṇa
14. NP. — Nārada or Nāradīya Purāṇa
15. Pd.P — Padma Purāṇa
16. Sk.P. — Skanda Purāṇa
17. Sv.P — Śiva Purāṇa
18. Va.P — Vāyu Purāṇa
19. Vh.P — Varāha Purāṇa
20. VMP — Vāmana Purāṇa
21. VP — Viṣṇu Purāṇa

INTRODUCTION

I. THE NĀRADĪYA PURĀṆA (NP.) AND ITS PLACE IN THE EVOLUTION OF THE PURĀṆA LITERATURE

i. *The Ur-Purāṇa* :

The term Purāṇa, though variously derived,[1] originally meant 'old' and was used as an adjective in the *Ṛgveda* (ṚV.). It developed the connotation 'something handed down from old times', 'a collection of old legends' by the time of the *Atharvaveda* (AV.) wherein it is used as a noun. Its use in the singular number in the sense of a tract of literature consisting of some ancient traditional lore in the AV[2] testifies to the existence of some collection of legends or an *Ur-Purāṇa* in the days of the AV. The institution of sacrifice needed some such collection of legends for narration on certain days (called *Pāriplava*) during the course of a sacrifice of long duration is clear from the prescription in the *Śatapatha Brāhmaṇa* (*Śat. Br.*) which calls upon the reciter to assert that the Purāṇa is the Veda and recite it.[3]

That there was such an *Ur-Purāṇa* in ancient times has been endorsed by Purāṇas in their mythological way. States the *Nāradīya Purāṇa* (*NP.*)

'There was only one Purāṇa (at the beginning of) every Kalpa. It was one hundred crores (of verses ?) in extent and that Purāṇa was the source of all Śāstras.[4]

1. For example :

Purāṇavaṁ bhavati "What was new in ancient times" Yāska-*Nirukta* III. 27, *Purāanati* 'That which breathes (existed) in the past (*Vāyu* P. I. 203)., *Purā* (*Pūrvasmin kāle*) *bhavam* (*Pāṇini* 4.3.23, 2.1.4).

2. AV. XI. 7.24; XV.6.10-11.

In AV.XI.8.7., the designation *Purāṇa-vit* 'Knower of Purāṇas' merely testifies to the existence of *Purāṇa* at that time but not the number of *Purāṇas*.

**Ṛcaḥ sāmāni chandāṁsi Purāṇaṁ yajuṣā saha/ucchiṣṭāj jajñire ...*

(AV.XI.7.24)

Tam itihāsaś ca Purāṇaṁ ca gāthāś ca nārāśaṁsīś cānuvyacalan/

(AV.XV.6.10-11)

3. Śat. Br. XIII.4.3.12-13.

4. NP.I.92.22.23.

The Matsya Purāṇa (Mt. P.) is more explicit.

'God Brahmā 'remembered' Purāṇa (*sg. no.*) before all other Śāstras. It is after that all the Vedas proceeded from his mouths. Purāṇa was only one at the beginning.[5]

As the mention of 'Purāṇa' in the sg. no. in AV is corroborated by the traditional belief in Purāṇas in the existence of one, single *Ur-Purāṇa*, this tradition need not be regarded as 'purely imaginary', though the mythical origin of Purāṇas is fictitious.

But the Purāṇas accept the theory of the human authorship and the compilation of the first Purāṇa is attributed to Kṛṣṇa Dvaipāyana, the 'arranger' (Vyāsa) who is credited to have compiled this Purāṇa from the floating mass of orally transmitted legends (*ākhyāyikās*), tales or anecdotes (Upākhyānas) gnomic or *Subhāṣita*-like verses (*gāthās*) and description of the Kalpa-epochs.[6] If as is traditionally believed, this compiler be the same sage who arranged the scattered — traditional *mantras* into *Vedic Saṁhitās*, he is located on a sober datation to the middle of the 10th cent. B.C.[7]

ii. *The Mūla Purāṇas* :

The VP. informs us that Vyāsa taught this Purāṇa—compilation to a disciple who could thrill his audience (*Roma-harṣaṇa*) with his narration. As the Purāṇa was to be recited during the leisure period of sacrificial sessions, Romaharṣaṇa must

---

5. Mt.P.53.3-4.

Also *vide* the *Vāyu* (Vā. P.) I-60-61, Brahmāṇḍa (Bd.P.) (I.1.40-41), *Padma* (Pd.P) V.1.45.52.

6. *ākhyānaiś cā'pyupākhyānair gāthābhiḥ kalpaśuddhibhiḥ|*
Purāṇa-saṁhitāṁ cakre purāṇārtha-viśāradaḥ ||
Viṣṇu P. (VP) III.6.15

Endorsed in the *Vāyu* I.60.21. The Bd. P., P.I.1.8-11 establishes the relation between the composer of the heavenly Purāṇa and its human adapter as follows : Brahmā → Vasiṣṭha → Parāśara → Jātūkarṇya → Dvaipāyana (Vyāsa).

7. S. K. Chatterji—*Selected Writings*—P. 140 (Vikas, Delhi 1978) Ray Chaudhari locates king Parīkṣit in 900 B.C. (*Political History of India from the Accession of Parīkṣit to the Extinction of the Gupta Dynasty P.* 9) also Pargiter, A I H T. P. 54 fn. 1.

have tried to make it interesting with additions, modifications etc. It thus became a revised and enlarged edition of Vyāsa's Purāṇa and this came to be looked upon as an independent Purāṇa. Romaharṣaṇa taught it to his six disciples out of whom Akṛtavraṇa of Kāśyapa *gotra*, Sāvarṇi of Somadatta clan and Suśarmā of Śaṁśapāyana *gotra* composed their own *Purāṇa-Saṁhitās*.[8]

Thus the *Purāṇa Saṁhitā* of Vyāsa proliferated into four *Saṁhitās*, viz). that of Romaharṣaṇa which through his son Ugraśravas continued independently and the three ones revised (and enlarged ?) by his three disciples mentioned above. The four *Saṁhitās* were the basic ones — *Pūrva-Saṁhitā* (*Vāyu.* II.61.58), or *Mūla-Saṁhitā* (Bh.P.XII.7.7) or *Ādi-Purāṇas* (Mt. P. 164.16). The *Vāyu* tells us that all these *Saṁhitās* consisted of four parts (*catuṣ-pādāḥ*); they dealt with the same subject matter but were distinguished from one another in readings. All of them consisted of 4000 verses except that of Suśarmā (Śāṁśapāyana) which consisted of 8600 verses.[9]

The four *Pādas* of these original purāṇas are called (1) *Prakriyā*, (2) *Anuṣaṅga* (3) *Upodghāta* and (4) *Upasaṁhāra*. The *Bd.* and *Vāyu*, the oldest of the Purāṇas follow the *Mūla-Purāṇas* in this division. The NP. also has four Pādas (in part I*) (1) Chs. 1-41, (2) Chs. 42-62, (3) Chs. 63-92, and (4) Chs. 93-125. As the Part II of the NP. is apocryphal, the original NP. seems to follow the old tradition of four *Pādas*.

These original Purāṇas are not now extant but their

8. *VP.III*.6. 16-18.

vide *Bhāgavata P.* (Bh. P.) XII.7.5.7; *Vāyu* II. 61.56-58 mentions the *gotras* of these as follows :

Name of the disciple	: *Gotra*
Sumati	—Atri
Akṛtavraṇa	—Kāśyapa
Agnivarcas	—Bhāradvāja
Mitrāyu	—Vasiṣṭha
Sāvarṇi	—Somadatta
Suśarmā	—Śāṁśapāyana.

9. *Vāyu.* II.61.

*The *Pādas* are originally named as *Bhoga, Mokṣa, Kriyā* and *Caryā*, though the printed edition gives (1) Prathama, (2-4) Bṛhadupākhyāna as the names of these sections.

authors — Romaharṣaṇa, Sāvarṇi, Kāśyapeya and Śaṁśapāyana are the interlocutors in various Purānas.[10]

What could have been the contents of the *Mūla-Purāṇas* is anybody's guess. But as Purāṇas served the needs of sacrificial ritual, the ten cycles of legends to be recited on *Pāriplava* days as laid down in the *Śat. Br.*, *Āśvalāyana Śrauta Sūtra* (Aś. ŚS) may be regarded as the topics therein. They are as follows :

1. King Manu Vaivasvata and his subjects (human beings).
2. King Yama Vaivasvata and his people (Pitṛs).
3. King Varuṇa Āditya and his subjects, the Gandharvas.
4. King Soma Vaiṣṇava and his subjects, the Apsaras.
5. King Arbuda Kādraveya and his subjects, the serpents.
6. King Kubera Vaiśravaṇa and his subjects, the Rākṣasas.
7. King Asita Dhanva (or Dhanvan) and his subjects, the Asuras.
8. King Matsya Sammada and his people, the water-dwellers.
9. King Tārkṣya Vaipaśyata (or Vaipaścita) and his subjects, the birds.
10. King Dharma, Indra and his subjects, the gods.[11]

To these may be added the ancient Vedic legends forming the background of the *Ākhyāna Sūktas* (e.g. Purūravas and Urvaśī), cosmological hymns like the *Nāradiya Sūkta* and similar statements in ancient works like the AV. XI.7.24, XV.6.10-11, eulogistic legends composed by bards in honour of the royal sacrificer or patron leading to descriptions of the heroic exploits, conquests, donations granted by royal families. Pargiter rightly concludes "that the original Purāṇa dealt with ancient traditions about gods, *ṛṣis*, kings, their genealogies and famous deeds.[12]

---

10. For example : Śāvarṇi (Vāyu 1.21.1) Kāśyapeya (Vāyu I.56.1-2, 57.86-88, Bd. P.II. 15.1. etc.) vide Pargiter A I H T, P. 23 ft. notes.

Mahābhārata (Mbh.) and Purāṇas quote a number of old verses with some such remarks 'they say' 'It is said'. These verses presumably belonged to the older Purāṇas.

11. R. C. Hazra — The Aśvamedha, the common source of the origin of the Purāṇa Pañca Lakṣaṇa. ABORI. 1955, pp. 122.3.

12. *Pargiter — A I H T, p. 36.

These topics later developed in the famous five characteristics (*pañca lakṣaṇas*) of *Purāṇas* viz. original creation (*Sarga*), re-creation after deluge (*Pratisarga*), genealogy (*Vaṁśa*), *Manvantaras* and accounts of dynasties of kings and sages (*Vaṁsānucarita*). But Pargiter's presumption that the *Ur-Purāṇa* had all the characteristics of later Purāṇas is not adequately substantiated and hence not acceptable.[13]

What may be the period of the proliferation of the *Ur-Purāṇa* in four *Mūla-Purāṇas* ? Even if Ugraśravas, Sāvarṇi and others are regarded as the direct disciples of Romaharṣaṇa whom Vyāsa taught his *Purāṇa-Saṁhitā*, for the establishment of four different traditions of these Purāṇas as independent *Mūla-Purāṇas* a period of at least one century from Vyāsa would be necessary. If the normally acceptable date of Vyāsa is 950 B.C., the *Mūla-Purāṇas* may be assigned to *circa* 850 B.C. as the probable date of their recognition as independent (though related) *Mūla-Purāṇas*. The use of *Purāṇāni* (in the Plural number) in the *Taittirīya Āraṇyaka* II-10, in Manu III. 232 and Yaj. III. 189 indicate that the number of Purāṇas then was 3 or more. VP's statement of being based on Mūla Purāṇas (III.6.19) shows that these existed at least upto the 3rd cent. A.D.

iii. *Purāṇam Pañca-Lakṣaṇam* :

As stated above, the five characteristics, viz., *Sarga* (creation), *Pratisarga* (Re-creation after dissolution), *Vaṁśa* (genealogy), *Manvantaras* and *Vaṁśānucarita* (Saga of the dynasties of kings and sages) came to be looked upon as *sine qua non* of Purāṇas. Not merely *Amara Siṁha* (5th cent. A.D.) in the *Amara-kośa* but Purāṇas themselves (e.g. AP. 1.14, BD.P.I 1.37.38, GP. I.215.11, KP.I.1.12, Mt.P. 53.65, SK.V.1.37) have endorsed this *Pañca-lakṣaṇa* definition of Purāṇas, viz.,

sargaś ca pratisargaś ca vaṁśo manvantarāṇi ca /
vaṁśyānucaritaṁ caiva purāṇam pañca lakṣaṇam //

This enumeration of characteristics of Purāṇas is not strictly a definition as it does not record the *differentia* of Purāṇas; nor is there any invariable concomitance. On the

13. *vide Kirfel — *Purāṇa Pañcalakṣaṇa* — Intro : A view accepted by Kane — HD. V. ii, p. 853.

contrary, as noted by Pusalkar "Pañca-lakṣaṇa occupies as insignificant part (about 1/40) of the extant Purāṇas."[14]

The analysis of the contents of the Mahāpurāṇas in NP. I. Chs. 92-109 (and annotations thereon) shows that the extant Purāṇas (with the exception of VP. and KP.) generally do not conform to the Pañca-lakṣaṇa definition (*vide infra* NP. and the five characteristics of Purāṇas). The problem is : why Purāṇas have been associated with the five characteristics in public mind though many of them do not conform to them and some Purāṇas such as the Bh.P. and NP.II.82.30, (unsuccessfully) claim themselves to have ten characteristics — and even when they incorporated much more material than could be covered in the "Ten characteristics."

A review of the evolution of Purāṇas shows that from the days of *Kauṭalīya Arthaśāstra* (c. 300 B.C.)* to the days of Viṣṇu Purāṇa (100-300 A.D.), the five characteristics from Sarga (creation) to *Vaṁśānucarita* (the saga of the dynasties of kings) were probably prominent in the then current Purāṇas and the *Pañcalakṣaṇa* definition became permanently associated with Purāṇas — even in the minds of the (non-conformist) authors of the Purāṇas themselves.

iv. *Dharma-Śāstra and Purāṇas*

By the 5th cent. B.C., there was probably some increase in Purāṇas which came to acquire titles and included some materials on Dharma Śāstra. The *Āpastamba Dharma Sūtra* (Ap. Dh. S.) quotes from some *Bhaviṣyat Purāṇa*, which states that performers of Vedic injunctions become the seed (i.e. Progenitors or Prajāpatis) of the new creation after Pralaya.[15] Ap. Dh. S. quotes from another (un-named) Purāṇa, the view of Prajāpati that food offered unasked and if its gift is unannounced

---

14. Studies in Epics and Purāṇas (SEP.), p. 23.

**vide* Kane — HD. V. ii. 818-819 and his conclusion about the existence of Purāṇas resembling the extant ones before the Mahābhārata (*ibid.*, p. 821).

15. *punaḥ sarge bījārthā bhavantī'ti Bhaviṣyat Purāṇe*
—Ap. Dh. S. II.9.24.6

This implies the existence of the feature *pratisarga* as well as the inclusion of *Dharmaśāstra* in the then *Bhaviṣyat Purāṇa*. For the injunction mentioned cf. *Yājñavalkya Smṛti* (Yāj). III. 184.186 which echoes the wording of the Āp. Dh. S.

is acceptable (even from a sinner); if it be rejected, the *manes* (Pitṛs) of the rejector do not accept food from him for fifteen years nor does the fire carry his offering to gods.[16]

Āpastamba quotes another Purāṇa which states that house-holders performing sacrifices and desiring progeny undergo births and deaths while those who remain celibate throughout their life (renouncing *saṁsāra*) become immortal.[17]

Āpastamba summarises the view of another Purāṇa wherein he enunciates the right of self defence stating that no sin is incurred if a person attacked by another with the object of injuring, kills the attacker.[18]

v. *Dharmaśāstra in the Nārada Purāṇa*

It will be thus found that matters on Dharmaśāstra began to be incorporated in Purāṇas since the 5th cent. B.C. We find that the following topics of Dharmaśāstra are treated in the NP : *Tīrthas* — Holy places (I.12), *Pūrta* (e.g. temple-building, works for public well-being) and *Dānas* 'religious gifts' (I.13), duties of *Varṇas* 'castes' and *Āśramas* 'stages in life', sins, penances, funeral rites (I.14), *Vratas* 'vows' (I.chs. 17-23), *Varṇāśrama-dharma*, funeral rites, penances or *prāyaścittas*, *tithis*, major and minor sins (I.chs. 24-30), *Varṇāśramadharma* (I.31-32 and ch. 43), Initiation, the methodology of *Mantraśāstra* and worship

16. *atha purāṇe ślokāvudāharanti—*
udyatām āhṛtām bhikṣām purastād apraveditām/
bhojyāṁ mene prajāpatir api duṣkṛta-kāriṇaḥ//
na tasya pitaro'śnanti daśa varṣāṇi pañca ca/
na ca havyaṁ vahatyagnir yas tām abhyadhimanyate//
—Ap.Dh.S.I.6.19.13

Quoted *verbatim* in Manu IV 248-249.

17. *aṣṭāśīti sahasrāṇi ye prajām īṣirarṣāyaḥ/*
dakṣiṇenāryamṇaḥ panthānaṁ te śmaśānāni bhejire//
aṣṭāśīti sahasrāṇi ye prajāṁ neṣirarṣayaḥ/
uttareṇāryamṇaḥ panthānaṁ te'mṛtatvaṁ hi kalpante//
ityūrdhvaretasāṁ praśaṁsā/
Āp. Dh. S. II.9.23.3-6

Cf. Vp. II.8.93, *Vāyu* II.50.214.

18. *yo hiṁsārtham abhikrāntaṁ hanti manyur eva manyuṁ spṛśati na tasmin doṣa eti purāṇe—*
Ap. Dh. S. I.10.29.7

Cf. Manu VIII. 350-351, Mt. P. 226. 115-118. *Vṛddha-Hārīta* IX. 34.50.

(I.chs. 64-68, I chs. 82-91), *Vratas* (I.chs. 110-124). The II part though apocryphal deals with the importance of religious vows (chs. 1-37) and glories of *Tīrthas* 'holy places' (chs. 39 & to the end.)

To these may be added the scrappy description of the terrestrial globe (I. ch. 3), the contents of 18 Mahāpurāṇas (NP.I.92-109) which is very important from the Purāṇa literature point of view and brief resumé of each of the Vedāṅgas, *viz. Śikṣā, Kalpa, Vyākaraṇa, Nirukta, Chandas, Jyotiṣa* (NP. I. chs. 50-57).

The NP. is thus a Purāṇic encyclopaedia.

(vi) *The Purāṇa in Modern Indian Languages* :

As a matter of fact, there was an unbounded and unrestrained scope for the Purāṇas to expand. Indians being a mixed people synthesized their traditional Aryan, Dravidian, Austric and Mongoloid beliefs, folk-lore, dogmas and rituals into Purāṇas. And when Sanskrit ceased to be understood by the masses, they wrote Purāṇas in modern Indian languages, e.g. the *Mānasa Purāṇa* in Assamese and Bengali, the *Ḍāṅgavai Purāṇa* in Marathi, the Śaivite *Periya-Purāṇam* in Tamil.[19]

To sum up :

1. There was a collection of ancient legends or an *Ur-Purāṇa* at the time of the AV. and the credit of its being the arranger (Vyāsa) is given to Kṛṣṇa Dvaipāyana (Circa 950 B.C.).
2. The Ur-Purāṇa developed into four *Mūla* or *Ādi Purāṇas* by Circa 850 B.C.
3. By the time of Āpastamba (C. 500 B.C.) Purāṇas having names like *Bhaviṣyat* existed and in addition to the usual characteristics like *Sarga, Pratisarga,* matters pertaining to *Dharma Śāstra* were found in them.
4. By the time of *Kauṭaliya Arthaśāstra* (C. 300 B.C.) the Paurāṇika Sūta came to be substituted by an officer of the state with the Purāṇa portfolio. Dr. Kane presumes that those Purāṇas were similar in characteristics with the extant ones.

---

19. vide S. K. Chatterji — *Purāṇa Apocrypha Select Writings*, pp. 121-138.

5. The Mūla Purāṇas seem to have survived till the time of the *Viṣṇu Purāṇa* (100-300 A.D.). The VP. retained the *Pañcalakṣaṇa* structure in tact.
6. As the Purāṇas were associated with *Pañca-lakṣaṇas* for about 5 or 6 centuries, even the Purāṇa authors who did not conform to that structure, have incorporated the *Pañca-lakṣaṇa* definition of Purāṇa in their own works — a fact recorded by Amara Siṁha (5th cent. A.D.) in his Sk. lexicon (*Amara Kośa*).
7. Purāṇas went on developing and incorporating copious material on *Dharmaśāstra* and some from other branches of knowledge in encyclopaedic *Purāṇas* like the *Nārada*, *Garuḍa* and *Agni*. But the mediaeval writers on *Dharma Śāstra* treated them like Smṛtis and quoted them as authorities on matters pertaining to Dharma (such as *Vrata*, *Tīrtha*, *Prāyaścitta*, *Varṇāśrama-dharma* and others).
8. The tendency of Purāṇa writing continued even in Modern Indian languages.

The NP. however, belongs to the Sk. stage. Hence, we consider it as per *pañca-lakṣaṇa* criterion of Mahāpurāṇas.

II. THE NĀRADĪYA AS A MAHĀPURĀṆA :

Mediaeval Writers on Dharma-Śāstra quote from two similar-sounding and equally authoritative Purāṇas viz. *Nārada* or *Nāradīya* (NP.) and *Bṛhan-nāradīya* (Brn. P.). Out of them the NP. is a Mahāpurāṇa and Brn. is an *Upa-purāṇa* and as the adj. *Bṛhat* shows, it is later than the NP. The Brn is a small work of about 3600 verses and 38 chapters.[20] It is a sectarian (Vaiṣṇava) work and though Nārada is the speaker, the criteria of *Pañca-lakṣaṇa* is not applicable to it. The NP. is a *mahāpurāṇa* traditionally supposed to contain 25000 verses (though the printed text of Veṅk, edt. has 18550 verses — 13144 in NP. Part I and 5406 in Part II). Maybe due to the synthesis of Aryo-Dravidian cultures as suggested by S. K. Chatterji,[21] the number eighteen became favourite with ancient Indians. The Vāyu Purāṇa mentions a part stage of ten Purāṇas but gives no

---

20. Edited by Hrishikesha Shastri, 2nd Edition Chowkhamba, Varanasi, 1975.

21. S. K. Chatterji — *Select Writings*, p. 123.

details. But soon the number of Purāṇas came to be stated as eighteen though actually nineteen Purāṇas are enumerated.[22] Even the *Upa-purāṇas*, (minor Purāṇas) the actual number of which exceeds one hundred* are also stated to be eighteen.

The NP. gives the following list of Purāṇas[23] (Mahā-Purāṇas) :

1. Brahma	2. Padma	3. Viṣṇu
4. Vāyu	5. Bhāgavata	6. Nārada
7. Mārkaṇḍeya	8. Agni	9.. Bhaviṣya
10. Brahma-Vaivarta	11. Liṅga	12. Varāha
13. Skanda	14. Vāmana	15. Kūrma
16. Matsya	17. Garuḍa	18. Brahmāṇḍa

This list with slight variations is repeated in many other Purāṇas such as the *Viṣṇu* III. 6.21-23, *Liṅga* I.39.61-63, *Matsya* 53.11 ff, *Padma* IV.100.51-54, *Bhaviṣya* I.1.61-64, *Mārkaṇḍeya* 134.7-11, *Bhāgavata* XII 13.4-8 and the *Devī Bhāgavata* I.32.

The variations are about the inclusion of the *Śiva* P. for the *Vāyu* P. and the rank of the NP. in the list of Purāṇas. The NP. gives itself the 6th place which is confirmed by other Purāṇas like VP. III 6.21-23, MK.P. 134 7-11, while it is ranked as the 7th in the list of Purāṇas in KP. I.13-15 and LP.I.39.61-64. Though the NP. is included as a (Mahā)-Purāṇa in the Purāṇa-lists of most other Purāṇas, the list in the *Bhaviṣya* P. III (*Pratisarga*) iii.28.10-14 does not mention the NP. and the Brahma-Vaivarta (Br. V). Alberuni gives two lists of Purāṇas, the one being the same as in the VP., but the second list omits the NP., Bh.P. and Pd.P.[24] The list of Purāṇas with Kavīndrācārya (1600-1650 A.D.) omits the NP. and substitutes the *Nandi* Purāṇa instead.[25]

The NP. consists of two parts — *Pūrvārdha* and *Uttarārdha*. The Pūrvārdha seems to be the original NP. as, like old Purāṇas, it is divided into four Pādas and concludes with a *Phalaśruti* (merit accruing from listening to the NP.). The *Phalaśruti* indicates that the NP. ends there. The Mt.P. 53.23 AP. 272.8, and

22. KP. I.1.13-15.

*R. C. Hazra — *ABORI* XXI. 38-62 and *Upa-purāṇas* I., p. 24, note 24.

23. NP. I. 92.26-28.

24. E. C. Sachau — *Alberuni's India*, Vol. I, p. 131 ff.

25. G.O.S. 1921 PJ VII.2., pp. 339-340.

Skanda VII. i-2-43 say that the NP. was declared by Nārada with reference to events in the Bṛhat-Kalpa in 25000 verses.* In the present NP., Nārada is the listener while his four brothers, Sanaka, Sanandana, Sanatkumāra and Sanātana are the speakers and there is no reference to Bṛhat-Kalpa. The Brn. though an Upa-Purāṇa has *Nārada* as the speaker but makes no mention of Bṛhat-Kalpa and the whole of Brn. is textually the same as NP. chs. 1-41. The statements of other Purāṇas about the interlocutors, Kalpa of reference and the textual identity between NP. part I and Brn. indicate that there must have been an older (and different) NP. which was the source of the extant NP. and Brn.

Now let us see how far the *Pañcalakṣaṇa* definition is applicable to the extant NP.

(i) *Sarga* (creation of the universe)

The NP. is a Vaiṣṇava Purāṇa; as such it attributes the ultimate credit of creation, destruction, etc., of the Universe to Mahā-Viṣṇu. The NP., however, records the following theories of creation :

1. The Popular Purāṇic Trinity Theory.
2. The Śākta-Sāṅkhya Theory.
3. The Mānasa or Bhṛgu theory quoted from Mbh. Śānti. ch. 182.

1. *The Trinity Theory* :

Mahāviṣṇu divided himself into three forms according to *guṇas*; Brahmā characterised by *Rajo-guṇa* was created from the right side of Mahā-Viṣṇu for the creation of the Universe; from the middle (chest) appeared Rudra, characterised by *Tamo-guṇa*, for the destruction of the Universe. While Viṣṇu (a lower grade deity than Mahā-Viṣṇu) characterised by *Sattva-guṇa* was originated from his left side for the maintenance and protection of the Universe.[26]

**yatrāha nārado dharmān bṛhat-kalpāśritān iha/*
pañca-viṁśa (°*śat-*) *sahasrāṇi nāradīyaṁ tad ucyate//*

26. NP. I.3.3-4.

2. *The Śākta-Sāṅkhya Theory* :

The other theory gives all credit to the *Parā śakti* (the Supreme Power) of Mahāviṣṇu. It is of the nature of existence and non-existence (*bhāvābhāvarūpā*). It is variously called Vidyā, Avidyā, Umā, Lakṣmī, Bhāratī, Girijā, Ambikā, Durgā, Bhadrakālī, Caṇḍī, Maheśvarī, Kaumārī, Vārāhī, Aindrī, Śāmbhavī, Brāhmī, Māyā.

The NP. emphasizes the fundamental unity of the divine power under different nomenclature. This power manifests itself into three forms — *Prakṛti*, *Puruṣa* and *Kāla* (Time) when *Prakṛti* is agitated the principle called *Mahat* is produced. The process is as follows : *Prakṛti*→*Mahat*→*Ahaṁkāra* (Cosmic ego) → Five *Tanmātras* (subtle elements) and (subtle) sense-organs → (*Mahā*) *bhūtas* (Five gross elements, viz., *Ākāśa* (the sky or ether), *Vāyu* (air, wind) *Agni* (Fire), *Jala* (Water) and *Bhūmi* (the earth) — each element arising out of the previous one. After the creation of the earth, god Brahmā created beings characterised by *Tamoguṇa* (e.g. insects, birds, beasts and other non-human beings), by *Sattvaguṇa* (Devas — gods in heaven) and by *Rajo-guṇa* (viz. human beings). He created progenitors like Dakṣa and others who populated the world.[27]

2. *The Mānasa or Bhṛgu Theory* :[28]

The eternal ageless God called Mānasa at first created *Mahat* from which was evolved *Ākāśa* (ether), the support of all *Bhūtas*. The evolution here differs from the traditional one. From Ākāśa is evolved water, from water arose fire and wind and the earth is the product of fire and wind. The unmanifest Mānasa (Viṣṇu) created the lotus from which was born Brahmā, the embodiment of Vedas, also known as *Ahaṁkāra*. The earth is the lotus for the Brahmā form of Mānasa and Mount Meru is its pericarp. Mānasa created mentally all the subjects.

The first theory is a popular Purāṇic way of attributing the functions of creation, protection and destruction to the Trinity whose mutual identity and one-ness with the Brahman is always emphasized.

---

27. NP. I.3.6.36. The verse after 36 enumerates the worlds (*bhuvanakośa*).

28. Ibid., I.42. 7-40. This is borrowed from Mbh.-Santi 182-11-33.

The second theory which appears with some modifications in the VP. (I.2.4, 5 etc.), Bh.P. (III Skandha) and with some difference in KP.I.4 employs the doctrine of transformation (*Pariṇāmavāda*) typical of the *Sāṅkhya*[29] system of thought to explain the evolutionary process. The philosophic aspect of this theory cannot be discussed here.[30]

The third theory is a quotation from *Mbh. Śānti.* 182.11-38. How far the credit of this is to be given to the NP. is doubtful. But as NP. claims it as its part, this theory seems alternatively acceptable to the NP.

2. *Pratisarga*

As compared with other Purāṇas like Bh.P., KP., NP. gives a meager description of *Pratisarga* when Mārkaṇḍeya was shown the *Pralaya* by Viṣṇu (NP.I.5.20 ff.). But that is the description of the *Naimittika pralaya.* Other Purāṇas like Bh.P., KP.II.45 describe the four types of Pralayas, viz. *Nitya* (everyday — disappearance of the world in the dark), *Naimittika* (at the end of the Kalpa), *Prākṛta* (At the end of god Brahmā's life when every thing is destroyed and *Prakṛti* attains equilibrium of the *guṇas*), *Ātyantika* — merger of the individual soul in the Para Brahman due to attainment of the Supreme spiritual knowledge. The NP. gives the duration of Viṣṇu's sleep, viz., two Parārdha years in one verse[31] while Mārkaṇḍeya floated on the waters of the deluge and states that Viṣṇu assumed the form of Brahmā and re-created the Universe.

The treatment of *Pratisarga* in the NP. is quite scrappy.

3. *Vaṁśa* (Genealogy)

Genealogies of gods or sages are not recorded in the NP. This characteristic is not applicable to the NP.

4. *Manvantaras* :

Though *Kāla* (Time) has been regarded as beginningless and endless and the evolutions and dissolutions of the Universe per *Kalpa*-periods have been going on, since time immemorial,

---

29. For details *Tattvakaumudī of Vācaspati on the Kārikās of* Īśvarakṛṣṇa

30. For this, vide S. Bhattacarya's *The Philosophy of Srīmad Bhāgavata* I, pp. 285-307.

31. NP. I.5.31.

an empirical attempt is made by man to measure Time. We find tabular statements of units of time in the Vedāṅga Jyotiṣa, in Smṛtis (e.g. Manu I.64), Purāṇas (like the Bh. P.III. 11.310, KP. I.5.6-19, Mt. P. 142.4, Vāyu 50.169) and Secular works like *Kauṭalīya Arthaśāstra* II.20.41). Though there is a general consensus regarding the names and duration of these units of Time, there are some differences regarding the duration of Kṣaṇa and Yāma.[32]

Purāṇas regard one human year as one day of gods, so one divine year = 360 human years.

As Kane shows, the theory of Yugas and Kalpas began to take shape in the 3rd cent. B.C. and was fully developed in the first centuries of the Christian era.[33]

The NP. enumerates Kṛta, Tretā, Dvāpara and Kali as the four Yugas and this set of four Yugas (inclusive of the 'twilight period' — *Sandhyā+Sandhyāṁśa* — preceding and following a Yuga) is 12000 divine years.[34] At another place the NP. gives the following durations of each yuga :[35]

Kṛta	: 1728,000	Tretā	: 1296,000
Dvāpara	: 864,000	Kali	: 432,000

human years.

It will be seen that though some *Purāṇas* (e.g. Vāyu I.57. 22-28, KP.I.5.9-13) give the duration of these Yugas in 'divine years', they do not differ much from each other.

NP. has given the further division of time units as follows :[36]

12000 Divine years = 1 *Divya-yuga* (Divine Yuga)

1000 Divya Yugas = 1 day of Brahmā (or the period of 14 Manus.

71 divya-yugas = 1 Manvantara.

2 Parārdhas—Brahmā years = one day or night of Viṣṇu.

Description of Yugas

The NP. I.41.6 ff. gives the description of the nature of four Yugas. The close similarity (even Textual) in these

32. vide Annotation No. 90 for details.
33. HD. III.888-890.
34. NP. I. 41.4-5.
35. Ibid., I. 54.61-62.
36. Ibid., I. 5-21-31.

descriptions as found in *Mbh. Vana.*149.11-38, Vāyu 32 and 57-58 LP.39, Mt.p. 142-144, KP.I.30 shows that probably some Ādi-Purāṇa contained the nucleus of this description. Briefly the following are the characteristics of different Yugas.

Kṛta was an age of equality. All persons were contented, pious. The Veda was undivided. People followed the duties of their respective stages of life with no ulterior motive. Lord Nārāyaṇa was white in complexion and Dharma (whom Manu equated with a bull in VIII.16) was stable on four legs. In the Tretā age Dharma became pale and three-footed. Hari became red-complexioned. People engaged themselves in meditation and performance of sacrifices. They were truthful but a bit distressed. In Dvāpara, Dharma became two-footed and Hari became yellow in complexion. Veda-saṁhitā became divided. People had taken to Adharma.[37] And their span of life became shorter.

Description of the Kali Age

The dismal, harrowing 'Predictions' about the social, political, economic and religious disintegration and reversal of previous order in the NP. I.41.21-89 deserve comparison with similar 'predictions' about the state of society in the Kali Age in Mbh. Vana. chs. 188, 190, Brahma P. chs. 229-230, LP.I.40, Bh.P.XII.2, VP.VI. chs. 1-2 KP.I.30, Vayu, chs. 58, Mt.P. 143.32-88. These descriptions agree not only in the details of contents but even in the text of many verses. This points to some common source — some *Ādi-purāṇa* — of the closely similar descriptions or 'predictions'.

About social disintegration, the NP. states, "Kali is a sinful age. All castes will give up their prescribed rites and duties; all will be like Śūdras; Brāhmaṇas will desist from Vedic studies and follow psuedo-religion. Brāhmaṇas will 'sell' Dharma and the Vedas and will accept gifts from the unworthy. Brāhmaṇas will sell wine, take food from Śūdras and go to Śūdra women.

The Śūdra dynasties like Nandas, and Mauryas ruled over the land. Naturally there was the dominance of Śūdras and servility of Brāhmaṇas. As NP. puts it, :

37. dharmādharmau samau syātām/ NP. I. 41.19

"Śūdras will pretend to be Brāhmaṇas, study the Vedas and preach Dharma. They will disguise as Brāhmaṇas and deceive people. Brāhmaṇas will intermarry, serve Śūdras and lower castes and even carry the dead bodies of Śūdras. Kings will be of Mleccha tribes. They will be greedy and will squeeze money from the people by top-heavy taxation."

There was the dominance of Buddhism and Jainism. As NP. puts it : "Heretics (Buddhists and Jainas) would denounce the Vedas, condemn *Āśramas* (stages in life) and walk nude or wearing ochre-coloured garments. Their woman are faithless; women maintain themselves by prostitution.

When Kṛṣṇa (Viṣṇu) turns black in complexion, nobody will think of God. Women will imitate courtesans, sell their virtue. There will be droughts and famines. Average human span of life will be 16 years and girls will give birth to children at the age of five.

Only the devotees of Viṣṇu or Śiva will be immune from the effects of Kali Age."

R. C. Hazra shows that such was the condition in the Indian Society before 200 A.D.[38]

4. *Manvantaras*

We have seen above that one day of god Brahmā extends to 1000 *Divya-yugas* during which 14 Manus rule. Every Manvantara has a new set of a Manu, Manu's sons, an Indra, Devas and Seven Sages.[39] NP. gives the following names of Indras and gods.[40]

	Manu	*Indra*	*Gods*
1.	Svāyambhuva	Śacīpati	Yāmas.
2.	Svārociṣa	Vipaścit	Pārāvatas & Tuṣitas

38. PRHC, Part II, ch. 1, pp. 193-215.

39. vide VP. III. chs. 1 & 2, Bh. P. VIII, chs. 1,5,13.
KP. I. 51.4-5, 53.29-31; Vāyu, ch. 62.

Also cf. *Manus saptarṣayo devā bhūpālāś ca manoḥ sutāḥ/*
manvantare bhavantyete śakrāś caivādhikāriṇaḥ//
—VP. III.2.48

To these officers Bh. P. adds Hari's part incarnations.
(Bh. P. XII.7.15)

40. NP. I.40-20-23 gives the list of 14 Manus and vv. 24-35, their sets of Indras and Devas.

	Manu	*Indra*	*Gods*
3.	Uttama	Suśānti	Sudhāmans, Satyas, Śivas and Pratardanas.
4.	Tāmasa	Śiva	Sūtas, Pāraharas, Sutyas and Sudhīs.
5.	Raivata	Vibhu	Amitābhas and others.
6.	Cākṣuṣa	Manojava	Aryas and others.
7.	Vaivasvata	Purandara	Ādityas, Vasus, Rudras and others.
8.	Sūryasāvarṇi	Bali	Aprameyas, Sutapās and others.
9.	Dakṣa Sāvarṇi	Adbhuta	Pāra and others.
10.	Brahmasāvarṇi (-ka)	Śānti	Suvāsanas.
11.	Dharmasāvarṇi- (-ka)	Vṛṣa	Vihaṅgamas and others.
12.	Rudrasāvarṇi	Ṛbhu	Harinābhas,
13.	Rocamāna	Divaspati	Sutrāmās, etc.
14.	Bhautya	Śuci	Cākṣuṣa and others.

The Manus, Indras and Devas of different Manvantaras possessed equal refulgence, prosperity and prowess.[41]

There is a consensus of the Purāṇas regarding the number and names of Manus, though there are some differences about the names of future Manus. Thus, Mt. P. gives the names of the future Manus as follows:[42]

Sāvarṇa, Raucya, Bhautya, Merusāvarṇi, Ṛta, Ṛtudhāma and Viśvaksena — while the *Brahma* P.[43] gives the following list, of future Manus : Sāvarṇi, Raibhya, Raucya and Merusāvarṇa.

Kalpa

Like all Purāṇas, NP. states that the present Manvantara is Vaivasvata in the Śveta-Vārāha Kalpa. But it does not give the list of Kalpas nor does it mention matters belonging to Bṛhat Kalpa. But Mt. P. chs. 53 and the Vāyu P. chs. 21, 22 give the list of Kalpas and the Purāṇas pertaining to them.

41. NP. I. 40.18-19.
42. Mt. P. 9.30-38.
43. Brahma P. 5.5 & 6.

5. *Vaṁśānuvarṇana*

The NP. is not interested in giving the genealogies of kings belonging to the Solar and Lunar races. It describes the episodes and information regarding the reigns of the following kings from the Solar race :

Bāhu — Sagara — Asamañjasa — Aṁśumān — Dilīpa — Bhagīratha (NP.I. 7 & 8) ; Sudās and Saudāsa alias Kalmāṣapāda (NP.I.ch.9) — Daśaratha — Rāma (and his three brothers) — NP. I.73.

Only three kings from the Lunar race are mentioned, viz., Sumati (I.ch.20), Dharmakīrti (I.ch.23) and Jayadhvaja (I.ch.39). As compared with Kṛṣṇa or Sahasrārjuna, these kings of Lunar race are insignificant if not fictitious.

It will thus be found that the definition *Purāṇam Pañcalakṣaṇam* is not applicable to the NP. In fact, it claims to be a Purāṇa of ten characteristics in its apocryphal part :

Nāradīyam purāṇaṁ tu lakṣaṇair daśabhir yutam |

— NP.II.82.30.

But the ten characteristics are not spelt out. Nor the ten *lakṣaṇas* of the Bh.P. are applicable to the NP. In fact, the author of the NP. is interested in the *Dharma-Śāstra* rather than the traditional characteristics of Purāṇas.

III. THE SOURCES OF THE NĀRADĪYA AND ITS PROBABLE DATE

As the NP. calls itself 'a compilatory work' (*Saṁhitā*),[44] its sources are numerous and its date or rather the dates of its parts depend on the dates of its sources. The NP. is mainly divided into two parts, — the first containing four Pādas and the second containing the glorification of the Ekādaśī vow and the story of Rukmāṅgada. The first part is, according to the NP. itself, the complete *Nārada Purāṇa*. It calls itself "consisting of four Pādas" (*catuṣpādasamāyuktam* — NP.I.125.26) in the *Phala-śruti*.

Being a Purāṇa — an *Upabṛṁhaṇa* of the Vedas — it draws heavily upon Vedic literature — the philosophical hymns like the *Puruṣa Sūkta* (RV.X.90), the Ākhyāna Sūktas, stories from

44. NP. I. 62.77, 79; II.82.34, 35.

Brāhmaṇas and the *Mantras* of *Upaniṣads*. It is obviously post-Vedic. Moreover, like other Purāṇas, it fully utilised traditional gnomic verses — *gāthās* or *subhāṣita*-like verses — current in the Indian Society since ancient times, as many of these *gāthās* are found in old Sk., Pāli and Prakrits. The Mbh. and Purāṇas many times use the words "It has been said," "So they or the wise say" indicating that such verses are quotations and quote them. These are found in secular works like the *Pañca Tantra* or *Hitopadeśa* or collection of verses under *Śatakas* or 'a treasury of Subhāṣitas'. It is difficult to fix the date of a work on the basis of these gnomic verses as their authorship or source is many times obscure. The NP. has absorbed a number of verses from *Smṛtis* like Manu, Yāj. NP. I.14 is the same as the *Laghu Yama Smṛti*.

The Bnr. and NP Part I (chs. 1-41) are textually the same. Though the adj. *Bṛhan* — in Bnr. shows that it is later than the NP., it is not later than the extant NP. but than the one to which the Mt. P. 53.23, the Sk.P. VII; 1.2.43 and AP. 272.8 refer as one narrated by Nārada with reference to the Bṛhat-Kalpa[45] — which the extant NP. is not. The Bnr. is an *Upa-purāṇa* and the extant NP. is the borrower from the Bnr.[46] Naturally the date of NP. Part I (chs. 1-41) is later than that of the Bnr. Govindānanda (1500-1540 A.D.) quotes Bnr. 7.14, 25-27 in his *Kaumudī* works viz. *Śuddha-Kriyā* — *Varṣa-Kriyā* and *Śrāddha-kriyā*, Raghunandana (1520-1575 A.D.) quotes Bnr. 7.14,22, and 24 in his *Smṛti-tattva*. Śūla-pāṇi (1375-1440 A.D.) quotes Bnr. ch.16 in his *Vrata-Kāla-Viveka*. Hence, Bnr. cannot be later than 1350 A.D. The Bnr. and NP. are mentioned as separate works in the *Bṛhad-dharma Purāṇa* (after 1250 A.D.), in the Bengal version of the Uttarakhaṇḍa of *Śiva Purāṇa* (circa 1200 A.D.) and the Orissan-*Ekāmra Purāṇa* (circa 1000-1100 A.D.). Hence, the Bnr. may be assigned 1050 A.D. at least. The Viṣṇu Śakti theory in the Bnr., crediting her with power of creation and destruction of the Universe and her various forms such as Lakṣmī, Durgā, Bhāratī and her identification with Prakṛti and Māyā (Bnr. 3-6, 9, 15, 16 etc.), shows that the Bnr. is posterior to Āgamas. The doctrine of Advaita and Māyā in

---

45. *yatrāha nārado dharmān bṛhat-kalpāśritān iha/*
pañca-viṁśa (o śat-AP.) sahasrāṇi nāradīyaṁ taducyate//

46. R. C. Hazra — PRHRC, p. 127.

(Bnr. 31.57ff) shows Bnr's acquaintance with the Advaita teacher Śaṅkara (788-820 A.D.). Thus the date of the composition of the Bnr. appears to be circa 850 A.D. Hence, the date of NP. Part I (chs. 1-41) is probably somewhat later i.e. circa 900-950 A.D.

3. *The Mahābhārata and the Viṣṇu Purāṇa*

From the comparison given below between NP.I. chs. 42, 43, 44 and 45 with Mbh. Śānti.[47] chs. 183, 192, 194, 195, 218 and 219 will show that NP. borrowed a great deal from the Mbh.

Topics	*NP.I.*	*Mbh. Śānti*
Evolution of the Universe-Sāṅkhya theory	42.7-40	182.1-38
Evolution of (gross) elements	42.41-57	183-1 ff.
Nature of the gross elements	42.58-98a	184.1-44
Nature of the vital airs and gastric fire	42.98b-113	185-1-17
Doubts about the existence of the Jīva	43.1-15	186.1-15
The Jīva exists and is eternal.	43.18-49	187.1-31
Creation of *Varṇas* (castes)	43.50-62	188.1-20
Code of conduct for *Varṇas*	43.63-81a	189.1.18
The greatness of truth, etc.	43.81b-98	190.1-16
Duties of Āśramas — of celibates and householders	43.99-119	191.1-18
Duties of Vānaprasthas and Sannyāsins	43.120-127	192.1-6
The excellence of the northern region	44.1-20	192.7-25
Disquisition on Spiritual knowledge	44.22-82	194.1-63
Dhyāna-Yoga	44.83-105	195.1-22
Existence of the eternal soul	45.2.-49	218.2-49
Mokṣa-dharma	45.50-87	219.2-28, 44-52
Story of Śuka. (Many verses common in the NP. & Mbh.)	58-62 NP. I	323-333 VP.*
The story of Khāṇḍikya etc.	46, 47	VI. 5.56 ff. & chs. 6, 7
The story of Jaḍa Bharata (and Ṛbhu and Nidāgha)	48, 49	II. 13.13ff & chs. 14,15,16

47. Gita Press, Gorakhpur V. S. 2014.
*Gita Press, Gorkhpur V.S. 2036

The NP. is ascribed to the 3rd cent. A.D. The present text of the Mbh. is assigned to 400 A.D., so this part of the NP. is later than 400 A.D.

4. *The Vedāṅgas*

The chapters on the *Vedāṅgas* are derived from different sources and as such needs be assigned different dates. The chapter on Śikṣā (phonetics) in the NP. (I.50) deals not only with the correct pronunciation of Vedic and classical Sk. but treats of vocal and instrumental music also. As many of the terms and points of information are found in the *Sthānāṅga* Sūtra of the Śvetāmbara Jainas, this section need not be considered as late as the 11th cent. work — *The Saṅgīta Makaranda* of one Nārada (of the 11th cent. A.D.), but it is obviously later than Bharata's *Nāṭya Śāstra* (400 A.D.). The source of NP.'s treatment of music needs more investigation, though the *Nāradīya śikṣā* may be one.

The chapter on Kalpa (vedic ritual) (NP.I.51) deals with the following *Kalpas* — *Nakṣatra K.*, *Veda K.*, *Saṁhitā K.*, *Āṅgirasa K.* and *Śānti K.* and not with the *Śrauta*, *Gṛhya* and *Dharma Sūtras* as of old. Moreover, according to the NP., these Kalpas belonged to every branch of the Veda though in ancient times they formed a part of the *Caraṇa Vyūhas* of the *Atharva Veda*. This innovation is due to Kumārila Bhaṭṭa (8th cent. A.D.) and as such the chapter may be assigned to the latter half of the 9th cent. A.D.

The chapter on *Vyākaraṇa* (Grammar), though not a systematic treatment based on Pāṇini's *Aṣṭādhyāyī* shows that it is not based on Kātantra but on Pāṇini, probably after the revival of studies in Pāṇini after Bhartṛhari (7th cent. A.D.). This chapter may be assigned to Circa 700-750 A.D.

The GP. and AP. do not treat *Nirukta*. The NP. gives a popular statement of that erudite work of Yāska but its immediate source is the Vaidikī Prakriyā of Paṇini's *Aṣṭādhyāyī* (the order of the Sūtras being similar to that in Bhaṭṭoji Dīkṣita's *Siddhānta Kaumudī*. Its date (though post-Yāska) cannot be precisely stated. But we are on surer grounds with regard to chapters on *Jyotiṣa* (chs. 54-56). The profuse quotations from the *Sūrya-Siddhānta* (6th cent. A.D.) in the chapter on *Gaṇita*, those from Varāha-mihira's *Bṛhajjātaka* (6th cent. A.D.) in the portion of *Jātaka* and those from *Nāradīya Saṁhitā* (4th cent. A.D.) in the *Saṁhitā* portion of the NP. show that the chapters on *Jyotiṣa* (Astronomy) cannot be earlier than the middle of the 7th cent. A.D. The three verses common to Bhāskarācārya's *Lilāvatī* (12 cent. A.D) may be probably from a common source from which NP. borrowed them.

Though other encyclopaedic Purāṇas like the GP. and the AP. treat *chandas* (metrics) in details, its treatment in the NP. is succinct and different, but its date is uncertain.

Thus the chapters on the Vedāṅgas are presumably compiled between the 7th and the 9th cent. A.D.

The third part of the NP. deals with sects like Pāśupata, Śākta and Tantrism in general. The Pāśupata in the NP. regards Bindu as a Pāśa (I.63.22 and later), but Mādhava in the *Sarvadarśana-saṅgraha* does not mention it to be so in the sections on Nakulīśa-pāśupata, Śaiva and the Pratyabhijñā (प्रत्यभिज्ञा) *darśanas*. The Pāśupata in the NP. may be an old stage of the *darśana* discussed in a late (14th cent. A.D.) work like the *Sarvadarśana saṅgraha*, but that does not help to fix the date, though 8th cent. A.D. proposed by H. P. Sastri is not improbable. But more interesting and chronologically more helpful is the Rādhā cult in chs. 82-90. In the NP. there is a phenomenal exaltation of an anonymous cowherd woman of the Bh.P. to the position of the topmost deity of whom great goddesses like Mahālakṣmī and Durgā are but part-incarnations (*aṁśāvatāras*) and whose *Sahasra-nāma* eulogy is sung by the great god Mahādeva and the Tāntric procedures of *Mantras* and *Yantras* of whose sixteen incarnations occupy a place of honour in the NP. It must have taken some 2-3 centuries after the Bh.P. As the Bh.P. is mentioned in the *Nandi Sūtra* of the Śvetāmbara Jain canon, it must be located at least in the latter half of the 5th cent. A.D. Thus the date of the chapters on the Rādhā cult may be assigned to the 8th cent. A.D. Hazra, however, assigns the chapters I.64-68, 82-91 and the chapters on Vratas I.110-124 as "late interpolations" without assigning a probable date or period. This exaltation of Rādhā provided a sound background for Gauḍīya Vaiṣṇavism for the other circumstantial evidence about the author of the NP. shows that he belonged to the eastern part of India — probably the Bengal-Orissa region.

Allied with the Rādhā cult, we have the Śakti cult under different names (chs. 85), Yakṣiṇī *mantras* (pertaining to an incarnation of Mahā Sarasvatī), *mantras* pertaining to Bagalā and other incarnations of Mahālakṣmī (ch. 86) and the procedure about four *mantras* of Durgā (ch. 87), to which may be added the *Kavaca* and *Sahasra-nāma* of goddess Lalitā (ch. 89).

It must have been a hey-day of Tantrism as the NP. gives not merely Śākta and Śaiva Tantrism (ch. 91) but the so-called *Bhāgavata Tantra* in the NP. includes cults such as (1) Vaiṣṇavism (with special emphasis) and (2) Śākta (3) Śaiva (4) Pañcāyatana (i.e. a group of Viṣṇu, Śiva, Devī, Gaṇeśa and Sūrya), (5) Rāma group (wherein Hanūmān, the monkey-lieutenant of Rāma, receives much more importance than both Rāma and Lakṣmaṇa) and the Kārtavīrya *mantra* and planet-worship.

As is well-known Tantrism was practised by Hindus, Buddhists and Jainas and there is much in common in their Tantric rites. East India—especially Bengal and Assam—were the centres of Tantrism for centuries. But between 8th to 11th cent. A.D. Tantrism was very popular. We shall not be much wrong if we assign early part of the 11th century as the time and East India (especially the Bengal-Orissa area) as the place of composition of these chapters.

(6) *The Mahāpurāṇas*

As shown elsewhere (and in the annotations) chs. 92-109 show that the contents of the *Purāṇas* and the technical names of the sections of the *Purāṇas* in the NP. are different from those in extant *Purāṇas*. The extant *Purāṇas* were practically completed by the 10th cent. A.D. These chapters from the NP. showing an earlier version of the purāṇas must be earlier at least by half a century or so.

Here ends the 4th Pāda and the original NP. In ch. 125 named as *Purāṇa mahimā*, all interlocutors disperse and vv. 25-30 describe when and how the NP. should be recited and the fruit accruing therefrom. Sūta also departs to see Vyāsa. Thus ends the NP. itself.

(7) *NP. Part II*

In the *Uttarārdha* of the NP., there is no Nārada either as a speaker or a listener. It is Vasiṣṭha who expounds the greatness of *Ekādaśī Vrata* to King Māndhātā and the story of Rukmāṅgada and Mohinī covers chs. 1-37. Though this part has no direct connection with Part I, these *dramatis personae* are mentioned as narrators in the *Caturvarga-cintāmaṇi* (1260-1270 A.D.) by

Hemādri, in the *Smṛti-Candrikā* by Devaṇṇabhaṭṭa (1200-1225 A.D.). Aparārka (1100-1130 A.D.) quotes two verses from NP. II on the *Ekādaśi Vrata*. The above evidence shows that even the II part of the NP. was composed before 1100 A.D.[48]

It will thus be seen that the NP. I was probably compiled between 700-1000 A.D. while NP. II was appended by the 11th cent. A.D.

Dr. P. V. Kane[49] assigns 700-1000 A.D. while Dr. R. C. Hazra,[50] 875-1000 A.D., as the period of compilation of the NP.

IV. THE VEDĀṄGAS IN THE NP. (Chs. 50-57)

The Vedāṅgas are the 'limbs' or accessories of the Veda which help the proper understanding, recitation and sacrificial application of the Vedas. They include the following exegetical sciences : *Śikṣā* (phonetics), *Kalpa* (ritual), *Vyākaraṇa* (grammar), *Nirukta* (etymology), *Chandas* (metrics) and *Jyotiṣa* (astronomy).[51] These are compared to the following limbs of the Veda: the nose, the hands, the mouth, the ears, the feet and the eyes.

1. *Śikṣā*

The traditional list of *Vedāṅgas* assigns the first place to *Śikṣā* or instruction given for the correct pronunciation, accentuation, etc. of the Vedic text. Its oldest mention is found in the *Taittirīya Upaniṣad* (I.2) and the oldest text dealing with them are the *Prātiśākhyas*.

The NP. deals with not only the rules of correct pronunciations of (Vedic and classical) Sanskrit but also with the science of music—vocal and instrumental. The importance of this section of the NP. becomes obvious when we find AP. summarising the *Pāṇinīya Śikṣā* practically in Pāṇini's words.[52]

According to Nārada, *Svara* (accent) is important in *Śikṣā*. In chanting *ṚK*, *Gāthās and Sāma-mantras*, *the Svarāntara* pertaining to ṚK (*Arcika*) is one, to Gāthās (*Gāthika*) is two, while that related to Sāma-mantras (*Sāmika*) is three. The *Arcikasvara* is used in chanting *Kaṭha*, *Taittirīya*, *Ṛgveda* and *Sāma*

48. Kane HD I.ii, p. 753.
49. Ibid. V. ii. p. 893.
50. R. C. Hazra — PRHRC, pp. 184-185.
51. NP. I. 50.9-12.
52. vide AP. ch. 336.

Veda Saṁhitās. The Ṛgveda may be chanted in *Gāthika* and *Sāmika Svaras* as well.[53]

In the *Vāṅmaya* (every day speech) the pronunciation is from (1) the chest (*uras*), (2) the throat (*kaṇṭha*), and the head (*śiras*) These three are known as *Savanas*.

The *Svaras*, low (*nīca*), medium (*madhya*) and high (*Ucca*) have their sources from *uras*, *kaṇṭha* and *śiras* respectively, and the seven notes (*sapta-svaras*) in the *Sāmaveda* also are produced from these. The *Ārcika svaras* are classified as *Udātta*, *Anudātta* and *Svarita*.[54] From physical (*pārthiva*) point of view, the *svara* is classified as *ucca*, *madhyama* and *saṅghāta*. Out of seven *Svaras*, the third, the first and the sixth (*kruṣṭa*) are used by *Āhvarakas*, the four svaras from second to the fifth by Taittirīyas, all the seven *svaras* by Sāmavedins and the second and the first *svaras* by Tāṇḍins, Śātapathas and the Vājasaneyins.

Vocal Music

Although one is tempted to compare this section of the NP. with Nārada's *Saṅgīta Makaranda*, the latter being later in date (11th. cent. A.D.) cannot be the source of the NP. The NP., however, quotes verses from 50.44 ff from an older work with the words : *bhavanti cātra ślokāḥ*.

The Svara-Maṇḍala

The *Svara-maṇḍala* consists of seven *svaras*, three *grāmas* (gamut), twentyone Mūrchanās (melodies) and fortynine *tānas* (protracted tunes). The seven *svaras*[55] are : Ṣaḍja (*Sa*), Ṛṣabha (*Rṣ*), Gandhāra (*Ga*), Madhyama (*Ma*), Pañcama (*Pa*), Dhaivata (*Dha*) and Niṣāda (*Ni*). They are regarded as originating from the throat (*kaṇṭha*), head (*śiras*), nose (nāsika), chest (*uras*), conjointly from chest, head and throat, forehead and the last from all these combined (*sarva-sandhija*) respectively. These correspond to the cry of a peacock (*Mayūra*), a bull (*Go*), a goat (*Aja*) a heron (*Krauñca*), a cuckoo in spring (*puṣpa-sādhāraṇakāle kokila*), a horse (*Aśva*) and an elephant (*Kuñjara*). They were first sung by Agni, Brahmā, Soma,

53. NP. I. 50. 15-23.
54. Ibid., I. 50.23-26.
55. Ibid., I. 50.30-109.

Viṣṇu, Nārada, and (the last two by) Tumburu respectively. The *Ṣaḍja* pleases gods, *Ṛṣabha* sages, *Gandhāra* manes (*pitṛs*), *Madhyama* Gandharvas, *Pañcama* gods, sages and *pitṛs*, *Niṣāda* Yakṣas and *Dhaivata* all living beings (*bhūtas*). Strangely enough castes are associated with these *svaras*. For example, *Pañcama*, *Madhyama* and *Ṣaḍja* are supposed to have been presided over by Brāhmaṇas. The importance of these *svaras* (of *sāman*) for sustenance of all beings is emphasised by Nārada.[56]

Grāmas

The three *Grāmas* are Ṣaḍja, Madhyama and Gandhāra and they are supposed to have been produced respectively by *Bhūrloka* (the earth), *Bhuvar-loka* (the firmament) and conjointly from *Svarloka* and *Abhra* (heaven and clouds). *Grāma-rāgas* are due to the special position of Svaras (NP. I.50.32a-34a.)

Mūrchanās

Mūrchanās (melodies) are classified as pertaining to gods, manes (*pitṛs*) and sages. Those pertaining to gods are : 1. Nadī, 2. Viśālā, 3. Sumukhī, 4. Citrā, 5. Citravatī, 6. Mukhā and 7. Bālā. Those belonging to *Pitṛs* are 1. Āpyāyinī, 2. Viśvabhṛtā, 3. Candrā, 4. Hemā, 5. Kapardinī, 6. Maitrī, and 7. Bārhatī. The Mūrchanās of sages are : 1. Uttaramandra in Ṣaḍja, 2. Abhirūhatā in Ṛṣabha; 3. Aśvakrāntā in Gandhāra 4. Sauvīrā in Madhyama, 5. Hṛṣīkā in Pañcama, 6. Uttarā in Dhaivata and 7. Rajanī in Niṣāda.

Gandharvas sing the Mūrchanās of gods, Yakṣas use those of *Pitṛs* and men, those of sages (NP.I.50.35-41).

It is for proper Vedic studies that the NP. seems to have discussed the science of music in *Śikṣā*. Some of the instructions to students are interesting. Good teeth being essential, he recommends the twigs of Mango, *Bilva*, Apāmārga (*Achyranthes aspera*) etc. for brushing the teeth. He advises the use of *Triphalā* powder mixed with salt for good digestions and clear pronunciation. He advises to inhale (sandal ?) smoke and take in ghee. The student should recite the first seven Mantras in *Mandra* and then in his usual tone.[57]

---

56. *Sarvāṇi khalu bhūtāni dharyanti sāmikaiḥ svaraiḥ||* —NP. I. 50.109a.

57. Ibid. I. 50.207ff.

In spite of this discussion, he confesses that even expert musicians like him, Tumburu, Viśvāvasu and Gandharvas have a limited knowledge of Śikṣā[58] and what he stated is only a pointer (*diṅ-mātra*) in the matter.[59]

Musical Instruments

Nārada described only two instruments — *Viṇā* (a lute) and *Veṇu* (a flute). A Lute is either wooden (*Dāravī*) or human (*Gātravatī*) and the latter is to be used in singing Sāmans.[60]

Nārada gives the correspondence between the notes of the flute and those of Sāman. The Madhyama of a *Veṇu* (flute) is the first *Svara* of Sāman. Thus the 2nd, 3rd, 4th, 5th, 6th and 7th *svaras* of Sāman are the Gandhāra, Ṛṣabha, Ṣaḍja, Dhaivata, Niṣāda, and Pañcama *svaras* on the flute[61] respectively.

Unexpectedly here are two verses on *chandas*. The one gives the characteristics of *Āryā* (a *mātrā-vṛtta* with 12, 18, 12 and 15 *mātrās* per foot) and the rest Vipula (I.50.199-200).

2. *Kalpa*

This oldest tract of Sūtra literature deals with the (Vedic) ritual and was classified as *Śrauta*, *Gṛhya* and *Dharma Sūtras* according to the subject matter. The Kalpa in the NP. is divided into (1) *Veda*, (2) *Saṁhitā*, (3) *Āṅgirasa*, (4) *Śānti* and (5) *Nakṣatra*. The *Veda Kalpa* deals with performance of rituals with chanting of *mantras* from the *Ṛgveda*. *Saṁhitā Kalpa* describes the deities, metres (*chandas*) and *ṛṣis* of the mantras; *Āṅgirasa Kalpa* deals with the six specific acts (*karmas*) pertaining to sorcery (*abhicāra*). *Śānti Kalpa*, as the name suggests, describes the rites to ward off calamities caused by gods (*divya*), beings on the earth (*bhaumika*) and from the sky (*āntarikṣa*). *Nakṣatra Kalpa* deals with planets and stars (I.51.1-8). The NP. ascribes these *Kalpas* for every branch of the Veda though in ancient times they formed the part of the *Caraṇa Vyūhas* of the Atharva Veda.

The NP. describes the domestic rites and rituals under *Nakṣatra Kalpa* whrein we are given the purification of the plot

58. NP. I. 50.206.

59. Ibid., I. 50.237.

60. The details of recital of Sāmans given from verse 79 ff. show that *Gātravatī* lute stands for human body or voice.

61. Ibid., 50.59-60.

of ground, placing of fire upon the altar (*Vedi*), arrangement of sacrificial materials, Gaṇeśa worship, propitiation of planets and *pitṛkalpa* i.e. performance of *Śrāddha* (NP.I.51.9 ff). The NP. draws heavily from the Yāj. smṛti ch. I in this chapter.

3. *Vyākaraṇa*

Vyākaraṇa or the science of grammar was developed for understanding the Veda and the earliest specimens of which are found in stray observations in the Āraṇyakas, the *Uṇādi-sūtras* (on formation of nouns from roots) and Phiṭ-sūtras (dealing with accents), Paṇini's *Aṣṭādhyāyī* being the only representative of such exegetical works. Out of the encyclopaedic Purāṇas, AP. gives the most exhaustive treatment of Sk. grammar in 11 chapters (chs. 349-359). It is an epitome of *Kumāra vyākaraṇa*.[62] GP. devotes two chapters (chs. 203-204) which show that Kātantra's grammar was its basis.[63]

According to Nārada, grammar is the mouth of the Veda (NP. I.52-1) and it discusses the following topics : (1) the seven case-endings, (2) Declension of nouns (in three genders), (3) *Kāraka* (cases), (4) *Saṁhitās* or *Sandhis*, (5) *taddhita* (nominal formation), (6) *compounds* (Samāsa), (7) *Tiṅ Vibhakti* (conjugation of verbs).

NP.'s presentation of grammar is popular and not scientific. He only gives examples and does not bother about Paṇini's rules.[64] It is possible that this section was written after Pāṇini was made popular by Bhartṛhari's *Vākyapadīya*, in the 7th cent. A.D.

4. *Nirukta*

Nirukta gives the etymology of Vedic words. The NP. considers it to be the ear of the Veda (Śrotrāṅga). It classifies Vedic roots into five categories, viz. those with *Varṇāgama* (addition of a syllable), *varṇaviparyaya* (Metathesis), *varṇa-vikāra* (change in the syllable), *Varṇa-nāśa* (Haplology), *Saṁyoga* (joining of letters) and he gives *haṁsa, siṁha, gūḍhotmā, pṛṣodara* and *bhramara* as the instances of these respectively (NP.I.53.1-5). As noted above, on p. 21 NP. further points out the difference in the

62. AP — A study, pp. 138-146.

63. R. S. Bhattacharya — GP — intro., p. 31.

64. NP. I.53.91-95 for Avyayībhāva compounds. But verses 2-24 are a versified form of the Sūtras of Pāṇini quoted in *Kāraka Prakaraṇa* of the *Siddhānta Kaumudī*.

declension and conjugation of Vedic and classical Sk. as in Pāṇini's *Vaidikī Prakriyā.* The roots are divided in ten groups (*gaṇas*) like *bhvādi, adādi* and the groups have 1006, 73, 22, 140, 32, 157, 25, 10, 52, 136, roots respectively. These are again classified according to their *padas* (e.g. *Parasmaipada*) and accents (e.g. *Udātta, Anudātta, Svarita*) (NP.53.16-76).

As all words are *Siddha* (derived), the study of their original form (*Prakṛti*), the morphology (*Pratyaya*), the augment (*Āgama*) should be undertaken (NP.I.53.70-86).

As compared with Yāska's work, NP. gives only a concise popular presentation containing a few illustrations. But the other two encyclopaedic Purāṇas (AP. & GP.) have not treated this topic at all.

5. *Jyotiṣa* (*Astronomy*)

Unfortunately no work of Vedic antiquity on Jyotiṣa proper has come down to us, except the references in the *Saṁhitās* and *Brāhmaṇas* (especially of the Yajurveda).[65]

Out of Purāṇas, AP. (some twenty chapters from 121ff) and GP. chapters 58-62 deal with Astronomy. GP. like NP. states that this science was composed by god Brahmā in 4,00,000 verses[66] — a figure popular with Purāṇa-writers. The treatment of this science in the NP. is more scientific and exhaustive. This science has three branches —*Gaṇita* (Astronomical calculations), *Jātaka* (Horoscopy) and *Saṁhitā* (Astrology, omens, etc.).

Gaṇita deals with (1) arithmetical operations (*Parikarma*), (2) calculation of the motions of planets, (3) place, direction, times of the *grahas*, (4) lunar and solar eclipses, (5) the time of the rising and setting of the sun, (6) the elevation of lunar cusps and (7) conjunction of planets.[67]

The arithmetical operations in the NP. are the same as in Bhāskarācārya's *Līlāvatī.* This is *not* to suggest that the NP. is the borrower even though three verses in the *Līlāvatī* (47, 48, 135) are found in the NP. (54.28, 29, 45).

The astronomical portion from the NP. except (4), (5), (6), and (7) is the same as in the *Sūrya-Siddhānta.* Though 186 verses of this portion are common to the NP. and the *Sūrya*

65. *Vedic Age,* BVB. Bombay P. 482.
66. GP. I.59.1; NP. I.54.2.
67. NP. I. ch. 54.

Siddhānta, both the works might be independent borrowers from a common source.

The *Jātaka* portion of the NP. (ch. 55) and Varāhamihira's *Bṛhajjātaka* are practically identical in contents though textually the verses cannot be so claimed.

But the *Saṁhitā* portion in the NP. (ch. 56) is a digest of the *Nārada Saṁhitā* and the fact that in the 755 verses of the NP. we find about 300 quotations from the *Nārada Saṁhitā* shows how the NP. is indebted to the *Nārada Saṁhitā*, though the possibility of a common source cannot be ruled out.[68]

6. *Chandas* (*Metrics*)

Literature comprising the Vedāṅga on metrics is meagre. The AP. gives a detailed summary of the *chandas śāstra* in chs. 328-335.

As compared with AP. and GP. NP.'s treatment of metrics in 21 verses is brief (*Kiñcillakṣaṇa*). Naturally, it is merely an outline of the Vedic and classical metres, (including the syllabic (*Varṇa*) and the *mātrā* varieties. He explains the eight syllabic feet (*gaṇas*) and the variation of *laghu* and *guru* syllables (short and long), in them. He also explains the *Sama* (even-footed), *Ardha-sama* and *Viṣama* types of metres and the 26 classes of *chandas* depending on the number of syllables from one to twentysix per *pāda* (feet) of a regular metre. A metre in which the *pāda* exceeds 26 syllables is called a *Daṇḍaka* having names like Caṇḍa, Vṛṣṭi, etc. (I.57.1-10).

It is by a variation in the distribution of *laghu* (short) and *guru* (long) syllables that a great variety of new, subordinate metres takes place (I.57.14-21).

V. THE NĀRADA PURĀṆA AND TANTRISM

Tantrism has a special importance in the NP. It devotes 29 chapters (NP.I.63-91) to Tantrism. After hearing the discourse on *Mokṣadharma* in the 2nd *pāda* of the NP. (I.chs.45-49

68. Dr. K. Damodaran Nambiar has traced all the quotations in the three branches of Jyotiṣa to the *Līlāvatī*, the *Sūrya Siddhānta* and the *Nārada Saṁhitā*, vide PJ. Jan.1974, pp. 103-112 of his dissertation on the *Nārada Purāṇa*.

and 59-62), Nārada asks Sanatkumāra about the Bhāgavata Tantra or the Mahā Tantra whereby one can realize Viṣṇu (I.63.8-10). Sanatkumāra gives a comprehensive discourse which covers Pāśupata-darśana (I.63), procedure of initiation (I.64), the *Pādukā-mantra* and the procedure of its chanting (I.65), procedure of chanting the *Gāyatrī Mantra* and performance of the Sandhyā-prayer and worship of one's deity (I.66,67), system of worship and chanting the Mantra of Gaṇeśa (I.66), of Mahā Viṣṇu (I.70), of *Pīṭhadevatās* and of Hayagrīva (I.72), of Lakṣmaṇa and Rāma (I-73) and of Hanūmān (I.74). Hanūmān receives more attention than Rāma, for we are told about his exploits (I.79), the lighting of lamps before Hanūmān (I.75) and the protective hymn (*kavaca*) of Hanūmān (I.78) and also the *mantra*, lamp-lighting and *Kavaca* of Kārtavīrya Arjuna (I.76, 77).

NP. gives also the *Yantravidhi* in addition to the procedure regarding *mantra-japa* of planets (I.69) (such as the Sun, the Moon, the Mars, the Mercury, the Jupiter and the Venus), of Nṛsiṁha (I.71).

The Rādhā cult is more enthusiastically propagated, as in addition to propitiation by Kṛṣṇa-mantra (I.80,81) and the *Rādhā-kṛṣṇa-sahasra-nāma* narrated by god Śiva to Nārada (I.82), we are informed of the *mantras* of the five Prakṛtis — rays or portions of Rādhā (I.83) and the procedure regarding the *mantras* and *yantras* of the sixteen incarnations of Rādhā (I.88). Allied with it is the Śakti cult under different names like Mahākālī, Mahālakṣmī and Mahāsarasvatī as can be seen from procedures about the *mantras* of Devī (I.85), Yakṣiṇī mantras, Yakṣīṇī being an incarnation of the deity of speech (I.85), *mantras* regarding goddesses Bagalā and others (regarded as incarnations of Mahā-lakṣmī) (I.86), the procedure about the four *Mantras* of Durgā (I.87), the *Kavaca* and *Sahasranāma* of Lalitā (I.89). Lastly the eulogy (*stotra*) and the procedure about the *mantras* of god Śiva (Maheśvara) receives attention (I.91).

Thus the *Bhāgavata Tantra* in the NP. includes :

1. Vaiṣṇava (with special emphasis), (2) Śākta; (3) Śaiva, (4) Pañcāyatana (Viṣṇu, Śiva, Devī, Gaṇeśa and

Sūrya), (5) Hanūmat and other (e.g. Kārtavīrya *mantra*, planet-worship) cults.[69]

It seems that this part was composed in the hey-day of Tantrism (700-1000 A.D.) when Hindus, Buddhists and Jainas enthusiastically followed the Tantra form of worship.[70] The synthetic tendency in Brahmanic Tantras as the inclusion of these diverse cults under the Bhāgavata Tantra shows post-Śaṅkara (After 800 A.D.) period of the composition of this part.

Though NP. glorifies the Bhāgavata Tantra as the great and the best Tantra[71] leading to attainment (of the realisation) of Viṣṇu[72], conducive to the accomplishment of people's desires[73] and 'revealing all gods', it is careful to emphasize that the first priority to one's duties according to one's caste and stage of life (*varṇāśrama-dharma*)[74] be given; 'one should never neglect them even mentally' even after getting initiation (*dīkṣā*).[75]

Importance of Mantra

In Tantrism much importance is attached to *Mantra* or incantation of a formula sacred to a deity. The NP. regards the two syllables in *mantra* as signifying 'omniscience' (*man*) and protection or liberation from Saṁsāra (*tra*).[76] *Mantras* are classified as Male, female and neuter according as they are concluded with the sound *hum* or *phaṭ* (masc) *dviṭh* or *svāhā* (Fem.) and *namaḥ* (neut). The male deities preside over man-

---

69. NP. I.92.233-235.

70. Vide Hazra PRHRC, pp. 260-264. He concludes : "Due to the great spread of the Tantric cult among the Hindus and the Buddhists, the Tantric elements made their way into the Purāṇas in a greater degree as the interpolations in the works were later."

71. *mahā-tantraṁ tvayā proktaṁ sarva-tantrottamottamam* /
—NP. I.92.2

72. Ibid., I. 63. 112-13.

73. Ibid., I. 91.231.

74. *sva-varṇācāra-tatparaḥ* Ibid., I. 63.113.
tasmāt tu dīkṣitaḥ kuryān nitya-naimittikā-dikam//
Ibid., I.63.118

75. *nija-varṇāśramācārān manasā 'pi na laṅghayet* / Ibid., I. 63.114

76. *mananaṁ sarva-veditvaṁ trāṇaṁ saṁsāryanugrahaḥ*/
mananāt trāṇa-dharmatvān mantram ityabhidhīyate//
Ibid. I.64.3

tras while Vidyās are presided over by female deities and they are recommended in six kinds of Karmas. Mantras are classified as pertaining to fire (Āgneya) when they are R-ending or are used with *Oṁ* or *Svāhā* and as pertaining to the moon (*Saumya*) when associated with Bhṛgubīja (*Saṁ*) and Pīyūṣabīja (*Vaṁ*). The *Āgneya mantras* are 'awakened' when one's breath flows through the right nostril (*Piṅgalā*) and the *Saumya mantras* awakened when the breath flows through the left nostril (*Iḍā*) and all mantras become active when the breath flows through both (called *Suṣumṇā*).[77] The *Āgneya mantras* are to be used in evil or cruel acts and *Saumya mantras* for mild ones. The *mantras* are again classified as *Śānta* (Quiescent), *Jñāna* (knowledge-giving) and *Raudra* (Terrific). A *Śānta mantra* can be transformed into Raudra mantra by adding *huṁ* or *phaṭ*.[78]

As Defective mantras are ineffective in protecting the *Sādhaka* and give no *Siddhi* even if muttered for one crore of Kalpas (I.64.60) the NP. enumerates the defects of *mantras*[79] and explains the meaning of the technical defects as given below.[80]

If a defective mantra is muttered while one is seated on the Yonimudrāsana (a *Siddhāsana*-like posture), it becomes effective. (vv. 60-62)./

Technical term for the defective mantra[80]	Characteristics
Chinna (broken)	: A mantra associated or dissociated with *Vahni-bīja* or conjoined with a vowel (*svara-sahita*) at its beginning, middle or end. It may recur three to five times (verse 21).
Ruddha (obstructed)	: (A mantra) having two *bhūmibījas* (*Laṁ*) in the beginning, middle or end. (verse. 22).
Śakti-hīna (weak)	: A mantra having three *Oṁkāras* and Varṇas (Huṁ) is 'Lakṣmī'. Bereft of these is *Śakti-hīna*, (v. 23).

77. NP. I. 64.4-9.
78. Ibid., I. 64.12-13.
79. Ibid., I. 64.14-19, 20-58.
80. Defective Mantras and their characteristics. (NP. I. 64).

Procedure of Initiation[81]

(i) *Suitability of the Pupil*

Before a pupil is initiated into a particular *mantra*, the most popular method to test the suitability of the pupil to receive that *mantra* is to draw an esoteric diagram —generally a square divided into 16 equal squares. The first line of four squares is to be filled by the first four letters of the alphabet — *a*, *ā*, etc. The fifth letter is to be written in the South-east corner of the square and in this way all the squares are consecutively filled by letters of the alphabet in their usual order. The first letter of the *mantra* is to be given and the first letter of the name of the pupil to be initiated in the *mantra* are located in this square. The counting of the squares is clockwise. It begins from the square where the first letter of the pupil's name stands. If both the initial letters (of the pupil's name and of the *mantra*) come in the first square of the first row, the mantra is *Siddha* (completely achieved). If the initial letter of the mantra is found in the squares of the second row (from the row of squares containing the first letter of the pupil's name, the mantra is *Sādhya* (worth accomplishing). If the intial letter of the mantra be in the third row, the mantra is *susiddha* (already mastered) but if in the fourth row, the mantra is hostile (*ari*). If the initial letters of both the *mantra* and of the pupil come in the first, second, third and fourth squares of the first row, the *mantra* is regarded as *Siddha-Siddha*, *Siddha-Sādhya*, *Siddha-Susiddha* and *Siddhāri* in due order. If they come in the four squares of the second-row, the mantra is respectively *Sādhya-Siddha Sādhya-Sādhya*, *Sādhya-Susiddha and Sādhyāri*. If in the squares of the third row, the *mantra* is looked upon as *Susiddha-Siddha*, *Susiddha-Sādhya*, *Susiddha-Susiddha* and *Susiddhāri*, respectively and if they both are in the fourth row, the mantra is *Ari-siddha*, *Ari-Sādhya*, *Ari-Susiddha* and *Ari-ari* respectively.

Mantra Siddhi

The *Siddha-Siddha* mantras become accomplished and effective when the prescribed number of their chantings is

81. NP. I.65.

duly completed. Twice that number of chantings is required in the case of *Siddha-Sādhya, Sādhya-Siddha, Sādhya-Susiddha, Susiddha-Siddha mantras*. A *Sādhya-Sādhya* mantra takes a long time for mastering while *Susiddha-Susiddha* becomes immediately effective. But *Ari* types of mantras are dangerous. If *Siddhāri* and *Susiddhāri* is chanted, it destroys the chanter's household; *Sādhyāri mantra* destroys his relatives; *Ari-Siddha*, his sons; *Ari-Sādhya*, his daughter; *Ari-Susiddha*, his wife and *Ari-Ari*, the chanter himself.[82]

Deity-wise classification

Mantras are also classified according to deities, viz : (1) Rāma-mantras (2) Kṛṣṇa-mantras (3) Rādhā-mantras (4) Śākta-mantras (5) Sūrya-mantras (6) Gaṇeśa mantras (7) Śiva mantras. Out of these, Vaiṣṇava mantras are the excellentmost (*Sarvottamottamāḥ*). Out of them, the Rāma-mantras[83] are crorefold greater in efficacy (*koṭi-koṭi-guṇādhikāḥ*). Out of Rāma-mantras that of six-letters (*ṣaḍakṣara*) is of the greatest efficacy.[84]

(ii) *Procedure of Initiation*

The initiation of the mantra (*mantra-dikṣā*) is as per following procedure :

1. The pupil to pay obeisance to the *guru's* (spiritual teacher's) wooden sandals (*pādukās*) and having worshipped him with cloth, ornaments, etc., to request him to initiate him in the mantra.

2. After entering the sacrificial place (*yajña-maṇḍala*) the *guru* utters *Astra mantras* to drive out all evils and prepares a mystical diagram (*maṇḍala*) called *Sarvatobhadra*. Having worshipped the fire-god along with ten *kalās* (digits), he places a pot before him and performs a sacrifice to the twelve *kalās* of the sun-god. He chants the main mantra of *viloma-mātṛkās* and filling the pot with pure water worships the sixteen digits of the moon-god in the pot. Covering the pot with two garments, he puts in it herbs, nine jewels and tender sprouts of *Panasa*

82. NP. I. 65.12-16.
83. Ibid. I. 91.233-234.
84. Ibid. I. 73.2.

(Jackfruit-tree), *Āmra* (Mango), *Aśvattha* (pippala), *Vaṭa* (banyan) and *Bakula* (*Mimusops elengi*) and thus worships the deity to be propitiated (*iṣṭa-devatā*) . The *guru* seats the pupil on the sacred altar, sprinkles water over him, places the sprouts on the pupil's head. Chanting one hundred and eight times the *Mūla mantra* in his mind, the *guru* sprinkles water over him. The pupil performs *ācamana* (sipping of water), puts on new clothes, bows to his *guru*, sits in front of him. The *guru* places his right hand on the pupil's head and repeats the *mantra* eight times in the ear of the pupil. The pupil bows down to the *guru* and the *guru* blesses him with all the desirable objects (health, wealth, fame, etc.). After paying respects and *dakṣiṇā* (religious gift) to his *guru*, the pupil returns home and worships his deity in the 'Pañcāyatana' set-up (In this set-up the main deity, say Viṣṇu, is in the middle and the remaining four gods like the sun-god, Devī, Gaṇeśa, Śiva[85] are around him.

Yogic significance of the mūla vidyā :[86]

This knowledge of the Supreme (*Mūlavidyā*) is practised by 'waking up' the *Kuṇḍalini* and leading her through *Suṣumṇā nāḍī* upto the *Sahasrāra kamala* in the crown of the head where Kuṇḍalinī is to be submerged (*sam-magnī-kṛiya*) in the reservoir of nectar thereof.[87] In directing how the *kuṇḍalinī* is to be taken from one *cakra* (*nerve-plexus* ?) to another, NP. describes each *cakra* or Lotus with its petals and the *bījas* on them, the deity presiding over the particular *cakra* and what amounts to *Japa* is to be dedicated to that deity. For example, the first *Cakra* is a lotus of four petals with four *bījas*, viz. *va, śa, ṣa*, and *sa*. Its presiding deity is Gaṇeśa with *pāśa* (a noose), *aṅkuśa* (a goad), *Sudhā pātra* (a vessel of nectar) and *modaka* (sweetmeat of a particular type) in his hand. A *japa* for 600 times is prescribed for this deity. The cakras are (1) *Mūlādhāra*, (2) *Svādhiṣṭhāna*, (3) *Maṇipūra* (4) *Anāhata* (5) *Viśuddha*, (6) *Ājñā* and the description in the NP. tallies with those given in texts on Yoga. After concentrating on the supreme Soul there, the *Kuṇḍalinī* should be brought back to its original place at *Mūlādhāra Cakra*.

85. NP. I. 65.19-47.
86. Ibid., I. 65.67 ff.
87. Ibid., I. 65.72.

Every person breathes 21600 times per day. Basing the Mantra-chanting on one's breathing is called *Ajapā-Gāyatrī* or *Haṁsa-Gāyatrī* and the pupil should determine to perform it.

WORSHIP

In describing the ideal, pure life of such an initiated pupil, the NP. chalks out a programme or a time-table from getting up at dawn[88], during the course of which worship of the deity occupies an important place. The deity may be represented by a *Yantra*, a Śālagrāma, a jewel, an image of gold, silver, etc. or a Bāṇaliṅga. As a *Yantra* has special place in Tantrism, a few words about it are necessary.

YANTRA

A *Yantra* is a geometrical diagram engraved on a hard medium like a stone or a metal or painted on a paper with *mantrabījas* inscribed therein. "It is a development or product of *mantra* and the deity implied in the *mantra*. The deity worshipped on a Yantra becomes immediately propitious."[89] A *Yantra* may resemble a *maṇḍala* as an outward figure, but a *maṇḍala* can be employed in the worship of any deity, while a *yantra* is specifically meant for a particular deity for a special purpose.

The NP. describes the preparation and the efficacy of some *yantras* such as :

1. *Trailokya-mohana-yantra* is to be inscribed on a white *Bhūrja patra* (a leaf of the birch tree). If duly worshipped, it helps one accomplish one's desired objects.[90]
2. [91]*Nārasiṁha-yantra* is to be inscribed on a metal (gold or copper) — gives success, influence and protection.
3. [92]*Sarva-vaśaṅkara yantra* (giving ability to control all).
4. [93]Kālāntaka (destroyer or preventer of death) to be inscribed on a *Bhūrja* leaf.

---

88. NP. I. 66.
89. *Yantram mantra-mayam proktaṁ devatā mantra-rūpiṇī*
Yantre ca pujitā devī sahasaiva prasīdati || — *Kulārṇava Tantra* VI. 85.
90. NP. I. 71.86-89.
91. Ibid. 71.91-96.
92. Ibid. 71.96.98.
93. Ibid. 71.98-99.

5. [94]*Yantra-rāja* (the king of Yantras).
6. [95]*Hanumadyantra* is to be drawn on a leaf of a palm or a birch tree.

WORSHIP

As idol-worship was in vogue before the time of Pāṇini[96] and the Gṛhyasūtras[97], its discussion in the NP. is natural. According to it, worship confers accomplishment of the desires of the worshipper (*Sādhakā' bhīṣṭa-siddhidā*[98]). The NP. classifies worship as follows :

1. *Āturī* : Performed by a sick person. He should look concentratedly at the idol (of the sun) and offer flowers while muttering the prescribed mantras.
2. *Sautikī* : During the period of mourning or delivery of a near relative woman, only mental worship during this period of impurity is prescribed.
3. *Trāsī* : While under intimidating circumstances or duress, the devotee is to offer worship with whatever material is available.
4. *Sādhanābhāvinī* : If material of worship is not available even leaves or fruits will do. Nay even mental worship is advised.
5. *Durbodhī* : Worship by the ignorant, the aged and by women.[99]

The NP. recommends the Pañcāyatana system of worship in which the group of deities, viz. Viṣṇu, Śiva, Devī, Gaṇeśa and the sun-god are to be worshipped together, the main deity to be worshipped occupies the central position and the remaining four surround that deity.[100] This obviously points out to post-Śaṅkara (800 A.D.) period.

In different regions in India different methods of worship and articles for it are found, and they have a sanction both

---

94. NP. 73.35-38.
95. Ibid. 74.62.70, 74.172-176.
96. Pāṇini IV. 1.54.
97. For example, Āpastamba XX.1-3.
98. NP. I.67.1.
99. Ibid., I. 67.124-140.
100. Ibid., I. 65.43-47.

textual and that of custom. Special instructions in the NP. regarding worship are noted :

1. A disfigured (crooked, burnt, distorted, etc.) idol should not be worshipped.[101]
2. Simultaneous worship of two conch-shells, two *cakra-śilās*, two idols of the Gaṇeśa or of the sun-god and of three idols of Śakti in a house is not advisable.[102]
3. According to NP. *Arghya* is a mixture of flowers, unbroken rice-grains (*Akṣata*), barley, ends of *Kuśa* grass, sesame, mustard, sandal paste and *Dūrvādala* (young and tender leaves of grass), while *Ācamanīya* is water mixed with Japāpuṣpa, Kaṅkola and cloves (lavaṅga).
4. Vessels of conch-shells are prohibited for the worship of the sun-god and Śiva.[103]
5. Red clothes are to be offered to Śakti, the sungod, and Gaṇeśa, yellow to Viṣṇu and white to Śiva.[104]

The deities and the special flowers to be offered to them are also mentioned in the NP., but being of little interest it is passed over.

The details of the worship of a deity right from the drawing of a *maṇḍala* upto its end when the *Tīrtha* is to be sipped and the *Naivedya* to be partaken of is given in NP. I.67 (for which *vide* the translation and annotations of that chapter).

Special Tantric Procedures :

The NP. belonged to the age when Tantrism (Hindu, Jain, Buddhist) was popular and widely practised. The very fact that the NP. devotes 29 chapters to Tantrism and prescribes both right and even abominable 'left' practices (*Vāmācāra*) gives credence to the theory that the author of the NP. belonged to East India as the eastern states like Assam, Bengal and Orissa were noted for such practices since olden times. The NP. records the following types of Tantric *Ṣaṭ-karmas* :

---

101. NP. I.67.33.
102. Ibid. 67.120-121.
103. Ibid. 67.27-29.
104. Ibid. 67.56.

1. *Pauṣṭika* (bringing peace and prosperity or propitiatory).
2. *Vaśya* (Helpful in controlling others).
3. *Stambhana* (Paralysing the other party).
4. *Vidveṣa* (creating animosity).
5. *Uccāṭana* (expulsion, extirpation).
6. *Māraṇa* (Annihilation, killing).

Durgā confers these powers if she is propitiated in the prescribed way (I.87.22-30). A number of Mantras (of various deities) have this efficacy. It may appear strange, but even an auspicious deity like Hanūmān is credited to give these evil powers, if propitiated in the special Tantric procedure (I.73.40-45). The Kārtavīrya Mantra was supposed to endow the initiated with the above-mentioned powers (I.76.30-34).

1. *Pauṣṭika* : There are auspicious practices like chanting of Śānti Mantras, worship of deities, performance of a *homa*, taking of medicines. A number of *mantras* with the technique of its *Japa*, *homa*, worship, etc. are given in this section, in connection with the propitiation of various deities e.g. for god Gaṇeśa (ch. 68) planets including the sun-god (ch. 69) etc. Muttering of *mantras* while preparing medicines had magic effects) such as a barren woman giving birth to a son. (ch. 68.81-84). The *mantras* of the deities had a healing effect; for example repetition of the Lakṣmaṇa *mantra* a hundred thousand times heals the patient from veneral diseases (ch. 73.158-160). The chanting of Hanūmān *mantra* 900 times at night for ten days and performance of Homa has the efficacy of curing the trouble of goblins, planetary troubles and diseases (I.74.17-19).

2. *Vaśya or Vaśikaraṇa* (Bringing under control). Flowers seem to be an important factor in charming others and influencing them. If Lakṣmaṇa *mantra* is chanted one hundred thousand times followed by a homa with ten thousand lotuses, it enables a man to marry a girl of his liking (NP. I.73.166-67). If one offers different types of lotuses to god Gaṇeśa, one is able to influence royal personages like the king or the queen (NP. I.68.37). If one thousand *Kumuda* (night blossoming lotuses) are offered as Homa while muttering the Viṣṇu mantra,

all kings come under one's control (70.200). While chanting Nṛsiṁha, the sacrificer can control the whole world.[105]

3. *Stambhana* (the magical power of stupefying or paralysing). If while muttering the Nṛsiṁha *Mantra*, flowers of the Madhūka (*Bassia Latifolia*) tree and pieces of *Dhātrī* (*emblica officinalis*) are offered, one attains the power of stupefying others.[106] Even a minor deity like Mātaṅgeśvarī if propitiated with a Homa of a mixture of salt and turmeric powder, can grant this magical power.[107]

4. *Vidveṣa* (creating discord)

For attaining this power the procedure is a bit elaborate. For example, for attaining this power from the gracious good Hanūmān, one should draw a *Yantra* on the hide of a donkey and chanting the *mantra* of Hanūmān, one should perform a *homa* with Hayamāra (Nerium tinctorium) flowers.[108]

5. *Uccāṭana* (Extirpation)

In order to extirpate terrible goblins and spirits causing epilepsy (*apasmāra*), one should mutter the *Jvālā-mālinī-mantra* one hundred thousand times and worship Nṛhari with the performance of a Homa with cow's ghee.[109] If the deity Hanūmān is to be propitiated for this purpose, one hundred thousand chantings of the deity's *mantra* and ten thousand *Āhutis* of sesame in fire are recommended. Thereby the haunting devil yells loudly and frees the haunted person.[110] If the deity is lord Kṛṣṇa, the *mantra* describing Hari attacking the hostile forces with fiery arrows, is to be chanted one thousand times every day, for the period of a week. When the total of seven thousand chantings is completed, the enemy is extirpated in a week.[111]

6. *Māraṇa* (Total annihilation)

A number of *mantras* of various deities is credited to have this power. Even the *mantra* of a king Arjuna Kārtavīrya, if chanted and a *Homa* with mustard, garlic, Ariṣṭa (*Sapindus*

---

105. NP. I. 71.83.
106. Ibid. I. 71.84.
107. Ibid. 1.87.153.
108. Ibid. I. 73.42, 74.55.
109. Ibid. 71.100-106.
110. Ibid. 75.98-104.
111. Ibid. 80.274-276.

emarginatus) and cotton is performed gives such a power.[112] Durgā, if propitiated by 'left-hand practices' (*Vāmācāra*) confers this power.[113]

Black magic and left hand practices

These records in the NP. show that the author must be hailing from East India as the states of Assam and Bengal were the strongholds of these immoral and obscene rites practised by the Hindus and the Buddhists. It may be the 'twilight speech' (*Sandhyā Bhāṣā*) of the Siddhas of ancient times who camouflaged their spiritual experience and procedures by using terms with apparent un-gentlemanly significance. But if that be not the case in the NP. some of the specimens quoted in the footnote[114] are not complimentary to the then standard of morality.

VI. RELIGIOUS SECTS IN THE NĀRADA PURĀṆA

After the discussion of Tantrism in the NP. and on its background, some important religious sects may briefly be noted.

---

112. NP. I. 76.30-31.

113. Ibid., I. 87.25-30.

114. I refer here only to one chapter pertaining to goddess Kālī (I.85):

If one wants the power of speech he should gaze at the female organ and chant Kālīmantra for 10,000 times (20). If he performs the *japa* at midnight in a cemetary, in a naked condition, letting down his (matted hair), he attains all *Siddhis* or (Supernormal powers) (21). If he sits naked on the chest of a dead body in a cemetary and while chanting the Kālī *mantra*, worships the goddess with one thousand *Arka* (calotropis Gigantea) flowers sprinkled with his own semen, the person becomes a king ere long (22-23). If one concentrates his attention on the female organ in the monthly course and mutters the Kālī *mantra* awhile, he certainly becomes a fascinating poet (24). If he meditates upon Mahākālī fighting with Mahākāla, while he himself is having sexual intercourse, and performs even one thousand chantings of the *Kālī mantra* he becomes just like another god Śaṅkara (25-26).

The whole section is abominable. Let me conclude with one instance of the practice of offering *bali* to the goddess which is supposed to give supernatural power.

The aspirant is to sit on a corpse (at night) on the 8th or 14th of the dark half of the month. It may be in a cemetary, or a temple but a lonely place. While looking, touching or 'going' (cohabiting) a woman, he should offer as *bali* a person killed in a battle or a babe of six months only. (70-72).

The use of wine, fish and flesh in worshipping female deities was quite common (I.90.2').

The Pāñca-rātras and Vaiṣṇavism

The aversion of the writers on Dharma Śāstra against this originally non-Vedic sect and its final acceptance and amalgamation into Vaiṣṇavism cannot be discussed here for want of space. But since the 3rd cent. A.D. (the approximate date of the *Viṣṇu Purāṇa*), Purāṇas accepted Pāñcarātra as their own and all Vaiṣṇava Purāṇas including the Bhāgavata have accepted it. The elaborate form of the Pāñcarātra worship and the Tantric procedures have been prescribed by the NP. for the propitiation of all deities, irrespective of their being Vaiṣṇavites, though NP. shows them to be born of Viṣṇu — Kṛṣṇa or Rādhā.

Vaiṣṇavism

The NP. being a Vaiṣṇavite Purāṇa, identifies Mahā-Viṣṇu with the *Para Brahman*. He is the God of gods, the *Ādi-deva* (the first God), the *Śabda-brahman* and of the form of spiritual sound (*nāda-rūpa*) and consciousness (*Cidrūpa*).[115] He is imperishable (*akṣara*), infinite (*ananta*), the Lord of the Universe (*Viśveśvara*) and the Veda incarnate.[116] Gods Brahmā, Viṣṇu and Śiva are the manifestations of Mahā-Viṣṇu for the creation, protection and dissolution of the universe.[117]

The NP. knows the usual ten incarnations of Viṣṇu.[117a] but deals with only three, viz. Nṛsiṁha,[118] Rāma[119] and Kṛṣṇa,[120] though strangely enough that is in the context of Tantrism and, curiously Hanūmān is given more importance[121] than Rāma and the anonymous cowherdess of the Bh.P. is assigned the position of a Supreme goddess.[122] This development of the Rādhā-cult shows the comparatively recent date of this section.

Just as God Mahā-Viṣṇu manifests himself in the Trinity

115. NP. I.; 63.7; 33.154.

116. Ibid., I. 25.64; 31.62; 13,153154.

117. Ibid., I. 3.3-5; 31.62-71.

117a. Vide the *Daśāvatārākhya Vrata* (Ibid., I. 119.14-19).

118. Ibid., I.71.

119. Ibid., I.73.

120. Ibid., I.80. Rāma with his three brothers, is a four-fold incarnation. N.P. I. 79. 1.

121. Ibid., I.74, 75, 78, 79.

122. Ibid., I.chs. 82 ff.

of Brahmā, Viṣṇu (a lesser deity than Mahā-Viṣṇu) and Śiva Kṛṣṇa — an incarnation of Mahā-Viṣṇu is credited with creating Nārāyaṇa from the left side of his body, Brahmā from his navel and Śiva being his (left) half and these three gods are appointed by Kṛṣṇa with the functions of creation, protection and destruction of the Universe — functions assigned to the Trinity of gods in the Mbh. and other Purāṇas.

The special feature of the NP. is the application of *Tāntrika* rites to incarnations of Viṣṇu such as Nṛsiṁha, Rāma and Kṛṣṇa and the Super-goddess treatment given to Rādhā (as the highest deity in the Tantra form of worship, with other deities like Mahā-lakṣmī, Durgā holding a secondary place). even though Mahālakṣmī was born from Rādhā and Durgā from Kṛṣna (NP. I 83. 13-29). The Supreme importance of the Ekādaśī Vrata and the influence of Pāñcarātra school are undeniable.

Śaivism

The NP. though a Vaiṣṇava purāṇa, regards Śiva as Viṣṇu's alter-ego who fulfils the desires of all.[123] Viṣṇu does not spare even goddess Pārvatī for talking lightly of Śiva.[124] King Bhagīratha propitiated god Śiva[125] and secured the descent of the Gaṅgā. The NP. describes the Tāṇḍava dance of Śiva before Jaimini.[126] The glory of the worship of Śivaliṅga (NP. I.79) and the ascription of many holy places to Śiva (NP.II. 74) shows the great regards paid to that deity. Out of the family of Śiva, Gaṇeśa has a special place in the Tantra form of worship, with special Mantras and Gaṇeśa Gāyatrī, etc. He is the chief of Gaṇas, remover of obstacles, brilliant as the rising sun, is the creator and destroyer of the universe. In addition to his usual description of elephant-headedness, etc., he is regarded as a Dvija. An elaborate worship *Japa*, etc. in the Tantric way is detailed in NP. I. 68.

Pāśupata

The NP. though Vaiṣṇavite, gives a more detailed treatment to the *Pāśupata darśana* than do the so-called Śaivite

123. NP. I.16.71-74.
124. Ibid., I. 79.217-226.
125. Ibid., I. 16.78-103.
126. Ibid., I. 74.

Purāṇas. It insists on the observance of the *Varṇāśrama-dharma*, Yoga and Bhakti.

According to the NP. (I.63.13-124) the Pāśupata school regards *Paśupati* (Lord Śiva), *Paśu* (an animal i.e. the *jīva*) and *Pāśa* (bondage) as three fundamentals. Pati i.e. Lord Śiva is all in all about the universe and he grants salvation despite the karmas of the *Paśu*. *Paśus* are classified into three : *Kala* (tainted with *mala* or ignorance), *Talapākala* (possessing *mala* and *karmans*), and *Sakala* (affected by *mala*, *māyā* and *Karma*) — the last suffers from transmigration in Saṁsāra. Unlike later Śaivism, NP. holds that there are five Pāśas each resulting from *mala* (ignorance), *Karman*, *Māyā* (delusion), *tirodhāna-śakti* (obscuring power) and *Bindu* (the last being the special *pāśa* in the NP.). All these pāśas can obscure the powers of the *paśu*, viz. the powers of vision, knowledge, action and *bindu-śakti* — the power of attaining Mokṣa. The Supreme soul (*Paramātman*) is constituted of *Sat* (being, existence), *cit* (consciousness) and *Ānanda* (spiritual bliss). It is the Śaiva Tejas endowed with powers of knowledge and action.

When the *Bindu-pāśa* is reinforced with *Cit*, it becomes endowed with *Jñāna-Kriyā-Śakti*. Though the NP. enumerates many Tattvas (principles) like Śiva, Śakti, Vidyā, (knowledge), Kāla (Time), there is only one Tattva called Śiva (*Śivākhya*) which possesses all Potencies (*Śaktis*). He blesses his devotees with the same form as himself (*Śiva-Sāmānya-rūpa*) endowed with bliss and salvation. *Ś*iva is the *Kartā*, Māyā, the Upādāna (material cause) and his śaktis, *Karaṇa* (the Instrumental cause). *Kalā*, *Kāla niyati Vidyā*, *rāga*, *Prakṛti* and *Guṇas* are the Products of Māyā wherewith the universe is created.

The NP. advises all to cut asunder the Pāśas by following *Varṇāśramadharma* and practice of Yoga and Bhakti, by getting oneself initiated in Pāsupata Tantra.

3 *Śāktism*

According to the NP. Rādhā is the chief deity — *Śakti* — in Śāktism. She is ever associated with Lord Kṛṣṇa. Mahā-Lakṣmī, Mahāsarasvatī, Durgā, Sāvitrī, Devī, etc. are her part incarnations (*aṁśāvatāras*)[127] or aspects of Rādhā. Rādhā was born from Kṛṣṇa's person and lives resplendently

127. NP. I.-83.10-32.

in the Goloka. Rādhā is the Primordial Nature] (*Mūla Prakṛti*), the goddess of all gods and is known as the Ilusive Power of Viṣṇu (*Viṣṇumāyā*), Kṛṣṇa-māyā, the mother of god Brahmā (*Vairāja-janani*). Although she has thirtytwo attendants, her two friends Candravatī and Lalitā are chief and are the heads of two groups of goddesses.[128]

Mahālakṣmī and Śrī

Goddess Mahālakṣmī was born from the left side of Rādhā. She is fair in complexion, bedecked in jewels and seated in a lotus.[129] Mahālakṣmī assumed the form of Śrī in a previous Kalpa to destroy demons like Mahiṣa. She dwells in the Aravinda forest. She is the goddess of wealth and is represented as seated in a lotus, being sprinkled by four elephants with nectar. She wears a silk Sari and a crown and her hands represent the *Vara* (gifting a boon) and *Abhaya* (protection from fear) *mudrās* and holds a garland and a lotus in the other two hands.[130]

Though Mahālakṣmī is herself an incarnation, her incarnations are the three-eyed goddesses Tripurā (NP. I. 86.3, 16-17) Annapūrṇeśī (I. 86.63-69) and the formidable goddess Bagalāmukhī (I. 86.82-88). Bagalā is represented to be of golden complexion, wielding in her arms a thunder-bolt, a noose (*pāśa*), a hammer (*mudgara*) and wearing a moon on her forehead. These incarnations show influence of or synthesis with Śaivism.

Durgā

This most important Śaivite (and Śākta) goddess with a crescent moon on the forehead and one thousand hands was (according to the NP.) born from Kṛṣṇa's person and was given to Śiva in marriage (I. 83.17-19, 27-29). Creating a special region (*Devī-loka*) for herself, she continues to perform penance and has three incarnations per day and is the main cause of creation (I. 83.70-78).

Durgā has taken the following incarnations :

(1) *Chinnamasta-Ramā* — a terrific deity with broken head, disheveled hair and drinking her own blood (I. 87.1-8).

128. NP. I. 83.44-47; 88.7-15.
129. Ibid., I. 83.50-53.
130. Ibid., I. 58-60.

(2) *Tripura-bhairavī* — A three-eyed goddess wearing a red garment and a garland of skulls; with two hands she expresses boon-giving (*Vara*) and protective (*Abhaya*) *mudrās* and has a rosary of beads and *Vidyā* in the other two hands. She has the refulgence of a thousand suns (I. 87.41-62).

(3) *Mātaṅgī* — This hideous goddess is black, and has profuse hair with a crescent-moon on the forehead. She is bedecked with ornaments of conch-shells and represented to be intoxicated and playing on a lute (I. 87.100-130).

(4) *Dhūmāvatī* — A wicked fierce widow like deity with lean body, long breasts, scattered hair, broken teeth and pale complexion. She is ever hungry and thirsty but is seated in a chariot with a heron on her flag. She destroys enemies (I.87.156-160).

The Śākta influence on the Kṛṣṇa-born Durgā is obvious. But it is Rādhā and not Durgā who is the main deity of Śāktism in the NP.

Sarasvatī

Another important Kṛṣṇa-born deity is Sarasvatī. She is born from Kṛṣṇa's mouth. She is white in complexion, with a face like the full-moon, holding a lute and a book in her hands and is seated on a white swan. Kṛṣṇa sent this goddess of speech to Vaikuṇṭha for the company of *Lakṣmī-Nārāyaṇa* (I. 83.30-31, 96-97).

The incarnations of Sarasvatī are three :—

(1) *Mahāsarasvatī* — In appearance she is like Sarasvatī. She lived in the Himālayas for killing demons Śumbha and Niśumbha. After accomplishing her task she entered the Mānasa lake (I. 84.78-84).

(2) *Kālikā* — NP. regards Kālikā as Sarasvatī's incarnation. She is dark in colour and wields a sword and a skull in two hands and while the other two express *Vara* (Boon-giving) and *Abhaya* (Protection) (NP. I.85 1-7).

(3) *Tārā* — A three-eyed deity, blue in complexion, with a crescent moon on her forehead but is seated on a dead body (I. 85.35-41).

Sāvitrī : According to the NP., this goddess was born along with Brahmā from Kṛṣṇa's umbilical region. She is bright as a thousand suns and the *Vedas* are born from her (*Brahma-Yoni*). She has three incarnations in three parts of the day — at dawn, noon and the dusk (as described in the *Sandhyā*-Prayers of three times) and is thus associated with Brahmā, Rudra and Viṣṇu (I. 83.20-22; 109-117 and also vide I. 27.44-58).

Devī

The NP. calls her the mother of the universe (*Jagadambikā*), the greatest Śakti of Śiva, creator of the whole universe. With a smile eternally playing on her countenance, this three-eyed goddess, lustrous like the rising sun, wears the Moon on her forehead. She wields a noose (*Pāśa*) and a goad (*aṅkuśa*) in her two hands and expresses *Vara* and *Abhaya* with the other two (I. 84.1-17).

VII. RELIGION AND PHILOSOPHY IN THE NĀRADA PURĀṆA

A good deal of ground concerning religion and philosophy in the NP. has been covered in the previous two sections. Only a few remaining points will be briefly noted :

Varṇāśramadharma

The NP. is a staunch supporter of *Varṇāśrama dharma*. Endorsing the social application of the concept of the Cosmic Man in the *Puruṣa Sūkta* (RV.X.90) and the insistence on the maintenance of that order in the Mbh.[131], the NP. repeats the duties of *Varṇas* (castes) and *Āśramas* (stages in life) in I.14, I. (chapters 24-30 also 31-32 and 43). Though the NP. waxes so eloquent on the importance of Tantrism in twentynine chapters (I.63-91), it warns that even after getting initiated, one should never even mentally transgress one's *Varṇāśramadharma*.[132] The social disintegration described in the 'predictions' about the Kali age was a historical reality to Purāṇa writers.[133] Hence, all Purāṇas insisted on the observance of the *Varṇāśramadharma*.

The NP. is, however, aware of the classless stage of society in ancient times. It quotes Mbh. *Śānti* 188.10-20 as the *rationale*

131. Mbh. Śānti. 57.15.
132. NP. I. 63.114.
133. R. C. Hazra — PRHRC pp. 193-227.

of the division of society into Varṇas as being due to the moral deterioration of the people.[134] It, however, assures that by observing one's prescribed duties one becomes a *Muni*[135] (sage) and by neglecting them he should be known as a heretic (Pāṣaṇḍa).[136] These duties need not be elaborated here as the *Ācāradharma* is detailed in Smṛtis, Mbh. *Śānti*. chs. 189, 192 and 193 and are repeated many times in the NP. (I.14, I.chs. 24-30, 31, 32, 43).

Cosmogony :

In cosmogony the NP. follows the Sāṅkhya Vedānta theories as given in the *Mbh. Śanti*. chapters 182-184. (vide *sarga* above).

About other points :

The existence and eternal nature of the Jīva[137] is stated in the NP. in the words of the Mbh. *Śānti*. 187.1-31. It is by the practice of Yoga that one realizes the nature of the soul, its distinctness from the body, its transmigration due to his Karmas, its non-relation to pleasure and pain.[138] The teaching of *Mokṣadharma*, viz., the soul's difference from the eleven sense-organs (5 organs of actions and 5 cognitive senses+1 mind), its unrelatedness to actions (*Karmas*) whether Sāttvic, Rājasic or Tāmasic, the necessity of controlling sense organs and performance of acts disinterestedly (*niṣkāmakarma*)[139] is the same (even textually) as that in the *Mbh. Śānti*. 219.2-28, 44-52.

Yoga (*NP. I.* 33)

According to the NP., Yoga is of two types — Karma Yoga and Jñāna Yoga. A follower of the Karma Yoga worships god *Viṣṇu*, observes *Vratas* and listens to Purāṇas. Observance of the five *Yamas* like non-violence, truth, kindness and renunciation of jealousy are common to both the Yogas.[140] By both the

134. NP. I. 43.56-63.
135. Ibid., I.24.30.
136. Ibid., I. Chs. 14, 24-30.
137. Ibid., I. 43.18-49.
138. Ibid., I. 45.78-84.
139. Ibid., I. 45.50-87.
140. Ibid., I. 33.31-36.

Yogas, one can realize the identity of the *Para* and *Apara* Ātmans.[141] It is the Māyā which creates diversity in the nature of the soul. An aspirant after *Mokṣa* should destroy the delusion by means of Yoga.[142]

The NP. discusses the eight steps of Yoga (the *aṣṭāṅga* Yoga). The NP. follows Patañjali in the treatment of Yoga, though there are minor differences such as addition of *Akrodha* and *Anasūyā* (Absence of anger and jealousy) in Yama (the 1st. *Yogāṅga*) and *Haripūjana* (specifically of Viṣṇu and not Patañjali's vague (*Īśvara-praṇidhāna*) and *Sandhyopāsanā* in the *Niyamas*,[143] (The 2nd *aṅga* of Yoga). It appears that the 30 *Āsanas* (physical postures) recommended in the NP. 33.12-15 were popular at the time and region of the author of the NP.

According to the NP., breath-control (*Prāṇāyāma*) may be *sa-bīja* or *nir-bīja* (i.e. accompanied or non-accompanied with the mental pronunciation or muttering of the *mantra*). If so accompanied it is *sa-garbha* and more effective.[144] *Dhyāna* (meditation) is perfect concentration on God or chanting *Praṇava* (OM) while meditating on Nārāyaṇa, as the *Praṇava* is the combination of the Trinity of gods, viz., Brahmā, Viṣṇu and Rudra — nay, as a matter of fact of the *Brahman*[145] itself. Due to contemplation, the Yogī acquires *vicāra*, *vitarka* and *viveka* and gradually attains *Nirvāṇa*.[146]

The whole course of Yoga is again succinctly retold later in the dialogue of Keśidhvaja and Khāṇḍīkya in NP.I.47. It shows that it is the Vaiṣṇavite Yoga with Vedantic basis.

Bhakti Yoga

The NP. is eloquent in describing the efficacy and greatness of *Bhakti*. It is the prime cause and life-giving force of all *Siddhis* (NP. I.4.3-4)—a veritable wish-yielding cow (*Kāmadhenu*). The *Parābhakti* destroys all sins like a conflagration burning down the forest of sins. A devotee of Viṣṇu attains success in life here and liberation from Saṁsāra hereafter (NP. I. 1.78-79)—

141. NP. I. 33.57.
142. Ibid., I. 33.37-72.
143. Ibid., I. 33.87.
144. Ibid. I. 33.119.
145. Ibid. I. 33.153-160.
146. Ibid. I. 44.83-105.
(A quotation from Mbh. Śānti. 195.1-22)

even the worship of Viṣṇu's devotees leads to the region of Viṣṇu and he who repeats the name of Viṣṇu is honoured by gods (NP. I. 3.53-56). Such *Bhakti* is achieved through association with god's devotees if one has the good luck or merits to his credit (NP. I. 3.53-56).

The NP. classifies *Bhakti* on the basis of *guṇas*, viz., *Sattva*, *Rajas* and *Tamas*, as follows :

1. *Tāmasī-bhakti* of a low (*adhamā*) nature : By this Viṣṇu is worshipped in order to destroy others.
2. *Tāmasī-bhakti* of a middle (*Madhyamā*) type : Dishonest worship of Nārāyaṇa like the love of a lewd woman (*svairiṇī*) to her husband.
3. *Tāmasī-bhakti* of the excellent (*Uttamā*) type : A competitive type of *Bhakti*, when a person jealously competes with others in performance of *Bhakti*.
4. *Rājasī Bhakti*—The lowest type (*adhamā*) : Worship of Hari for getting wealth, grains, prosperity.
5. *Rājasī Bhakti* of the middle (*madhyamā*) : Worship of Viṣṇu for gaining fame and popularity.
6. *Rājasī Bhakti* of the best type : Worship of Hari for securing *salokatā mukti* (residence in Hari's region).
7. *Sāttvikī Bhakti* — The lowest type : Worship of Hari for destruction of one's sins.
8. *Sāttvikī Bhakti* — The middle type : Service to Hari as per his will.
9. *Sāttvikī Bhakti* — Uttamā : Voluntary service (*Dāsya Bhakti*) to Viṣṇu to please him.
10. *Uttamottamā* : The most excellent: the Devotee realises himself to be Viṣṇu and the universe is within him.[147]

In the next chapter (NP. I.16) the NP. gives another threefold classification depending on the states of the mind.

1. *Śraddhā-Bhakti* — the devotee realises that the Universe (including himself) is Viṣṇu. Viṣṇu is the cause of everything. He is to be worshipped as per prescribed rules.

2. *Samatā-Bhakti* — The devotee realizes that Viṣṇu is omnipresent in all beings and nothing is different from him.

3. *Śānti Bhakti* — The state of mind when the devotee regards friends and foes alike and faces with pleasure whatever comes to him.[148]

147. NP. I. 15.138-151.
148. Ibid., I. 16.31-35.

VIII. THE INTERPRETATIONS OF 'BHAGAVAT' and 'BHĀGAVATA'

As *Bhagavān* is the object of the Bhakti, the NP. gives different interpretations of the term *Bhagavān*.

1. *Bhagavān* : The *Brahman* which is inexpressible in words is called *Bhagavat* for the purpose of worship (in the *Bhakti* cult).
2. An artificial interpretation of each syllable in *Bha-ga-vat*.
   Bha = (1) the knowable, (2) the knower.
   Ga. = (1) the creator.
   (2) the father of *Āgamas* (*Āgama-pitā*)
   Bhaga = The six excellences from Prowess to Renunciation.
   Va = That in whom the *bhūtas* reside and whom he prevades.
3. One who knows both *Vidyā* and *Avidyā*, the creation and destruction of *bhūtas* and one endowed with entire knowledge, power, prosperity, prowess and brilliance.[149]

Bhāgavatas

Though the word *Bhāgavata* is derived from *Bhagavat*, the NP. paints an ideal devotee in I.5.46-76. *Bhāgavata* is applied to both Śaiva and Vaiṣṇava devotees. He is self-controlled, quiescent, interested in listening to the *Sat-kathās* (stories about the gods as in Purāṇas), is devoted to the name of the Lord, performances of sacrifice, doing works for public welfare, observes the *Ekādaśi Vrata* and performs *Karmas* for God.

IX. THE DHARMA ŚĀSTRA

The NP. is specially interested in *Dharma Śāstra*. It discusses in details topics like *Dāna* (religious gifts I.13), *Prāyaś-citta* (expiatory rites), *Tithis*, *Śrāddha*, (I.chs. 24-30), *Vratas* 'religious vows' (I. chs. 17-23) II, chs. 1-37, *Tīrthas* 'sacred places' (I. 12 II.39).

It closely follows the injunctions in Smṛtis and other Purāṇas. It also elaborates the doctrine of *Karmavipāka* which holds out hopes of redemption even to the worst sinners. There

149. NP., I. 46.12-23.

is very little that can be claimed as the original contribution of the NP. except the decisions about the day of Ekādaśī and such other matters of special interest to Vaiṣṇavas.

The NP. (and the Bnr) are treated as authorities on the Dharmaśāstra and are frequently quoted as authorities by such great mediaeval writers like Devaṇṇa Bhaṭṭa, Hemādri, Mādhavācārya, Vācaspati Miśra and others.

X. THE NP. AND THE MAHĀPURĀṆAS

NP. chapters 92-109, are very important, as they give some idea about the contents of the Mahāpurāṇas before the final redaction of the NP. (in the 10th cent. A.D.). As the annotations to the above chapters show, the contents and divisions in the present published Purāṇas are different from those given in the NP. The extant Purāṇas differ from the NP. in the following respects :

1. The total number of verses recorded in the NP. and the actual number of verses in the extant Mahāpurāṇas. For example the NP. (and AP. Brv. Vāyu, and Bh.P. itself) gives 18000 as the total number of verses in the Bh.P. but actually the Gītā Press edition of the Bh.P. contains 14,579 verses.[150]
2. The nomenclature of different parts of the Purāṇas as given in the NP. is different in their extant versions. For example, the Vāyu Purāṇa states (in 103.44) that it has the following four *Pādas* (sections) (1) *Prakriyā* (2) *Anuṣaṅga* (3) *Upodghāta* and (4) *Upasaṁhāra* and calls itself a *four-footed* Purāṇa. But the NP. gives *Pūrvabhāga* and *Uttarabhāga* as the divisions of the Vāyu (*vide* NP.I.95.7).
3. The details of contents given in the NP. and those found in the extant Purāṇas are different. There are both additions and deletions. For example, NP. I.92.34 mentions the story of Rāma in the contents of the Br.P. but it is not found in the printed (G.M.) edition of the same. So also NP. I. 95.7-15 mentions the Revā Māhātmya in the Vāyu but the printed texts (both Anandashram and Guru Mandal

150. For other such differences vide NP. Part IV annotations, Nos. 13, 28, 17 etc.

editions) do not give these chapters.* A number of such differences show that the texts of Purāṇas available to the author of the NP. were different than those in the extant Purāṇas. But all the additions to the extant versions of the Purāṇas (as compared with the NP.) need not be considered 'spurious' simply because it is not mentioned in the NP. It is the MSS-evidence which is more important in deciding the genuineness of certain verses or portions of a Purāṇa rather than its inclusion or exclusion in the NP. NP. Part II is definitely a later interpolation and 'spurious' even though the last redactor of the NP. interpolated a few verses (NP. I. 97.11-18) to legitimise NP. Part II.[151]

XI. THE AUTHOR

The author of the present *Nārada Purāṇa* is not Nārada. He is simply a listener to the discourses of his brothers Sanaka, Sanandana and others. At the end of NP. Part I, he departs and goes finally to Nārāyaṇa (NP. I. 125.6-24). The author or the last redactor of the present work may be presumed to be some Vyāsa who opts to observe silence about himself.

There are, however, some indications in the NP. itself which supply some clues about his sub-caste, region, time, etc. as follows:

1. NP. I. 27.38-67 give the details about *Sandhyā* (twilight prayer) which every twice-born has to perform. The details of the *Sandhyā* show that the author of the NP. was presumably a Mādhyandina Brāhmaṇa, a follower of the *Kātyāyana Sūtra* (vide annotation no. 331 and 332).

2. NP. I. 28 deals with the rite of *Śrāddha*. We find that the NP. and the *Kātyāyana Śrāddha Sūtra* use the same full Mantras, prescribe the repetition of the word *Madhu* thrice in addition to the *Gāyatrī* and *Madhumatī* verses, prescribe the recital of the same texts while Brāhmaṇas are being fed, and agree

*Also Revā Khaṇḍa of 232 chs. and *caturaśītī-liṅga-Māhātmya* 84 chs. in the SKP., Lalitā Episode of 40 chs. in Bd.P. are not mentioned in the NP.

151. The differences between the contents of extant Purāṇas and those recorded in the NP. are discussed in the annotations of chs. 92-109.

with each other in many details. The procedure of Śrāddha observed by Mādhyandina Brahmins of Bengal is similar to that given in the NP. (probably because Raghunandana's *Yajurvedi-Śrāddha-tattva* which they follow in Bengal is based on Kātyāyana's *Śrāddha-Sūtra*). The similarity regarding the procedure of *Śrāddha* may perhaps be due to the author's being a Mādhyandina Brahmin and resident of the Eastern region (Bengal-Orissa).

3. As noted above in the section on the NP. and Tantrism, the NP. propagates enthusiastically the Rādhā Cult. The anonymous cowherdess in the Bh.P. is the highest deity here. Śiva recites her *Sahasra-nāma* (I.82). The five *Prakṛtis* are but rays of Rādhā (I.83). This exaltation of Rādhā provides favourable background for the subsequent development of Gauḍīya-Vaiṣṇavism.

4. The NP. shows a high popularity of Tantrism especially of the 'left hand' (*Vāmācāra*) cult. As remarked in the same section, the eastern states of India, viz., Bengal, Assam and Orissa were ths strong-holds of Vāmācāra practices both in Brahmanical and Buddhist Societies.

5. The importance of Rādhā in the 'Left hand' practices, the procedure regarding the *Mantras* and *Yantras* of the sixteen incarnation, of Rādhā (NP. I.88) and the Rādhā-Kṛṣṇa relations in the NP. might be the back-ground of Sahajīya Vaiṣṇavism and other obscure religious cults that thrived in Bengal and other adjacent areas in the mediaeval times.

6. Sections in Purāṇas in the NP. (for example those of the *Padma Purāṇa*) agree with those given in the Bengal MSS of that Purāṇa (vide note no. 13 on NP. I.93).

The evidence given above tends to show that the author of the NP. was probably a Mādhyandina Vaiṣṇava Brahmin from the eastern states — probably the Bengal-Orissa area.

XII. CONCLUDING REMARKS

The translation of the NP. is based on the text in the Venkateshwar Press edition Bombay (Śaka 1845) = A.D. 1923 the only available edition of the NP. Unfortunately the editors of that text did not consider the syntactic aspect of the text. An Anuṣṭubh verse with three lines i.e. six feet, is common in Purāṇas; they should have added one line of *Anuṣṭubh* from the next verse to an otherwise incomplete sentence, so that the whole chapter would have been smoothly readable. In the interest of completing the sentences, I had to bring together the (b) and (a) lines of consecutive but different verses (e.g. 29b-30a) and translate them. A. S. Gupta in the edition of the Kūrma *Purāṇa* has many times added two pādas (one line from the next *anuṣṭubh* verse to such verses and his edition of the Kūrma Purāṇa as compared with that of the Veṅkaṭeśvara Press of the same Purāṇa is more readable.

This translation is faithful to the text of the Venkateshwar Press edition of the NP. — emendations are rarely attempted and evidence for their adoption is recorded in annotations.

CHAPTER ONE

The Dialogue between Sūta[1] *and the Sages*

1. *Om*, obeisance to the holy preceptors. *Om*, bow to Lord Gaṇeśa.[2] *Om*, salutations to glorious Lord Vāsudeva.[3] *Om*, after making obeisance to Nārāyaṇa[4] as well as to Nara,[5] the most excellent among men, and also to goddess Sarasvatī,[6] one should begin the recitation of *Jaya*[7] (the *Nārada Purāṇa*).

Om, obeisance to Veda-Vyāsa.[8] I bow to Upendra (Lord Viṣṇu), who abides (permanently) in Vṛndāvana[9] and is the shrine of Bliss unto Indirā (goddess Lakṣmī); who abounds in compassion and is greater than the greatest and whose form constitutes the highest Bliss.

2. I worship that Supreme primordial Lord whose form is the purest Consciousness (*cid-rūpa*); who is the greatest (of all beings), and whose parts called Brahmā, Viṣṇu, and Maheśa (Śiva) are (the deities) who accomplish (the cycle of creation, maintenance and destruction of) the world.[10]

3. Śaunaka[11] and other noble-souled sages, the expounders of the *Brahman*, performed a penance in the great forest named Naimiṣa,[12] with a desire to attain Final Liberation.

4. They had conquered their sense-organs; had full control over their diet; they were saintly persons of truthful exploits. With greatest devotion, they worshipped the eternal, primordial Viṣṇu.

5. They were above jealousy and were conversant with all holy rites. They were devoutly engaged in blessing the world and had no feeling of my-ness (sense of personal possession). They were devoid of egotism and their minds revelled in the transcendental *Ātman*.

6. They had renounced all passions and longings and were sinless; they were endowed with self-control and other good qualities. With matted hair and the hide of black-antelope as

their upper garments, they led a celibate life (Lit. they observed the vow of celibacy).

7. They eulogised the Supreme *Brahman*, the eye of the universe. All of them were of equal prowess. They were the knowers of the meaning and reality of the sacred scriptures. They performed penance in the Naimiṣa forest.

8. Some of them worshipped the Lord of sacrifices by performance of sacrifices; others worshipped the Deity, the Embodiment of spiritual knowledge, by means of the path of knowledge; some worshipped Nārāyaṇa with devotion *par excellence*.

9. Desirous of understanding the means of righteousness, wealth, love and Final Beatitude (the four *Puruṣārthas*), those excellent noble-minded (high-souled) sages met in a congregation.

10. The sages of sublimated sexuality numbered twenty-six thousand. It is impossible to enumerate the disciples and the pupils of their disciples.

11. Those sages of sanctified souls (through meditation), of great prowess, met together. Devoid of passion and jealousy, they desired to do (something) to bless the world.

12. (The questions that made them ponder were :) What are the sacred places of pilgrimage (*kṣetra*), and the shrines or holy places (near the banks of sacred rivers, lakes, etc.) — the *tirthas* — ? How is liberation (from Saṁsāra) achieved by men distressed in their minds by worldly miseries (of three kinds).

13. How is the devotion of men unswervingly directed towards Hari ? By what means can one achieve the fruit of the three types of activities (viz. mental, verbal and physical) ?

14. On seeing the sages eagerly intent on asking him (these questions) in this manner, the intelligent Śaunaka spoke these words with palms joined in reverence, and bowing down with humility.

Śaunaka said :

15. In the holy hermitage of *Siddhāśrama*,[13] there lives Sūta, the most excellent of all the *Paurāṇikas* (exponents of the *Purāṇas*). With different types of sacrifices, he worships Janārdana of universal form.

16. That great sage, the son of Romaharṣaṇa, the

quiescent disciple of Vyāsa knows this completely. He is the propounder of the Purāṇa texts. So the tradition goes.

17. On seeing piety and religious rites being (progressively) reduced (in quantity and quality) from *Yuga* to *Yuga* (successively) the slayer of Madhu (Lord Viṣṇu), assuming the form of Veda-Vyāsa classifies the Vedas.

18. O Brāhmaṇas, we have heard that the sage Veda-Vyāsa is Nārāyaṇa himself. And Sūta has been initiated into all sacred texts directly by Vyāsa.

19. Sūta has been instructed and initiated by that intelligent Veda-Vyāsa. He does know all the Purāṇas. There is none competent than he (in this respect) in this world.

20. In this world, he is the only knower of the import of all Purāṇas. He is intelligent, omniscient and quiescent. He knows the path of righteousness leading to final liberation as well as the entire corpus of (the theory and practice of) the paths of action and devotion.

21. O prominent sages, the sage Vyāsa has, for the benefit of the universe, expounded, in the Purāṇas all those topics that constitute the essence of the Vedas, the Vedāṅgas[14] (the ancillary subjects pertaining to Vedas) and the scriptures.

22. Sūta is indeed an ocean of knowledge. He proficiently knows the real nature of (and the exact truth about) everything. Hence, we shall ask him. So said Śaunaka to the sages.

23. Then all those delighted sages embraced Śaunaka, the most excellent of those conversant with the realm of speech. "Well-spoken. Well-advised", said they (to express their approval).

24. Thereafter, those sages went to the holy Siddhāśrama in the forest. It abounded in groups of deer. It was graced with the residence of sages (living therein).

25. It was beautified with charming trees and creepers (full of abundant) flowers and fruits, and was spotted with lakes of crystalline water and was inhabited by persons warmly hospitable to guests (and strangers arriving there).

26. They (the sages of the Naimiṣa forest) saw the son of Romaharṣaṇa worshipping the infinite unvanquished Lord Nārāyaṇa, by means of the *Agniṣṭoma*[15] sacrifice.

27. Suitably honoured by Sūta, those sages of well-known powers, remained there in the hall of sacrifice, awaiting the concluding rites of ablution (*Avabhṛtha*).

28. Afterwards, when Sūta, the excellent-most of all *Paurāṇikas* completed the rites of Avabhṛtha ablution, those residents of the Naimiṣa forest asked him, as he seated himself comfortably.

The sages said :

29. O strict observer of religious vows we who ought to be hospitable to you as hosts, have come here as your guests. However, be pleased to honour us duly by means of homage in the form of charitable gift of perfect knowledge.

30. Whereas the heaven-dwelling gods live by drinking the nectarine juice from the digits of the moon, the earth-dwelling gods (the *Brāhmaṇas*) do so by drinking the nectarine juice of the perfect knowledge exuding from your mouth, O sage.

31.* (Who is that lord) by whom all this (the universe) was created, who is the support of all this, who is the Soul of all this, in whom, O dear one, everything is well established and in whom everything will get dissolved ?

32.* By what does Viṣṇu become propitiated ? How is he worshipped by men ? What is the code of conduct of life for the people in the various castes and walks of life ? How is the guest to be worshipped ?

33. What is that whereby the holy rites shall be fruitful? What is the means of salvation for men? What is achieved by men through devotion ? And of what nature is devotion ?

34. O Sūta, the most excellent of all sages, explain these things, dispelling every doubtful factor. Who is not keenly desirous to hear the nectarine words of yours ?

Sūta said :

35. Listen ye all, O sages. I shall recount what is desired by you. This has been narrated to the noble-souled Nārada by those sages the chief of whom was Sanaka.[16]

(*Better if 31 and 32 are taken together. This (31) verse then becomes a sort of an adjectival clause describing Viṣṇu in the next verse).

36. This *Purāṇa* named after Nārada is on a par with the Vedas in regard to its import (*artha*). It is destructive of all sins It wards off the influence of all evil planets.

37. It is conducive to piety and destructive of the effects of evil dreams. It yields as fruits worldly pleasures as well as salvation. Containing narratives of Nārāyaṇa, it is the cause of everything blessed and auspicious.

38. It brings about piety, wealth, love and liberation.[17] It is highly efficacious as it yields unprecedented merit as its fruit. Listen to it with great concentration.

39. One may be defiled by great sins[18] or subsidiary ones.[19] But on hearing this divine *Purāṇa* pertaining to sages and ascetics, one shall regain purity.

40. On reading a single chapter of this *Purāṇa* one shall attain the benefit of (the performance of a) horse-sacrifice.[20] Similarly, on reading two chapters, one attains the spiritual rewards of performance of *Rājasūya*[21] sacrifice.

41-42. O Brahmins, by reading three chapters one attains the same merit as a man who takes bath in the waters of the Yamunā on the full-moon day in the month of Jyeṣṭha with the moon in the constellation Mūla, who observes fast with great purity, at Mathura and who duly worships Kṛṣṇa.

43-44. I shall explain (one thing more) very well. Even as I recount, listen well. A man who listens to ten chapters of this (*Purāṇa*) with feelings of earnest devotion, shall attain to the region of Brahmā and stay therein. He will be freed from sins accumulated in the course of ten thousand births. He shall be followed by a ten million members of his family.

45-48a. No doubt or hesitation need be entertained in this matter that he will attain the final beatitude. This is more blessed than the most blessed. It is pre-eminently the best of all sanctifying things. It is meritorious and destructive of (the effects of) evil dreams. O Brahmins, this must be listened to, assiduously. A man of faith who reads at least a verse or even half of a verse is immediately absolved of heaps of great sins. Since this is the secret of all secrets, it must be narrated only to good men. This must be made to be read in front of Viṣṇu, in the presence of Brahmins, in a holy place or shrine.

48b-49a : One shall not narrate this excellent *Purāṇa* to persons engaged in injuring the cause of Brāhmaṇas and to those persons who are religious-hypocrites like (proverbial) cranes (which are supposed to pretend meditation till a fish comes within their reach).

49b-50. This, being the means to liberation from *saṁsāra*, should be recounted to those who are devoted to the pious course of life and whose mind (*ātman*), with lust and other noxious qualities eschewed out, revels in the devotion to Viṣṇu. For Viṣṇu comprises within himself all gods and destroys the agonies and applications of those who remember him.

51-52. He is favourably disposed towards his pious devotees, O Brāhmaṇas. He becomes pleased only with devotion and nothing else. A man is freed from sins if he glorifies or remembers Viṣṇu's name even without faith. He attains to the Eternal region (*Vaikuṇṭha*) the unchanging region. Madhusūdana (the destroyer of the demon Madhu) is like the big forest conflagration unto the terrible jungle of worldly existence.

53. He quickly destroys all the sins of those who remember him, O excellent ones. This excellent Purāṇa which indicates that meaning and purpose should be listened to.

53a. By listening to it or reading it one is able to annihilate all sins.

53b-55. Only he who, with a devoted mind, is inclined to listen to this Purāṇa, has really accomplished his objects in life (*Kṛta-kṛtya*) and can be regarded as adept in understanding and interpreting all the scriptural precepts. O Brahmins, I consider that whatever merits are earned or austerities performed by him, are really fruitful.

56. (Unless one has a fund of merits) it is not possible for him to have devout inclination towards listening to God's stories or Purāṇa. Those good men who are the benefactors of the universe, are engaged in stories about the Supreme Spirit.

57a. The wicked or evil persons are exclusively devoted to sinful activities and are engaged in censure and quarrels.

57b-58. O excellent Brahmins, the merits (if any) earned by those vilest of men who (i) attribute laudatory nature to Purāṇas (or) (ii) who allege that the Purāṇas are merely laudatory passages (*Artha-vāda*)[22] become exhausted. (For the *Purāṇas* are really the means of eradication of all binding actions.

59. A person who speaks of *Purāṇas* as being *arthavāda*,

falls into hell.[23] O excellent Brahmins, men duly pursue and attain other objects of worldly pleasure.

60-61a. But persons who are deluded do not do the same for accomplishing the *Purāṇas*. O excellent Brahmins, *Purāṇas* must be listened to with great devout feelings by the person who desires to accumulate merits without strain (trouble or exertion).

61b-62. Undoubtedly the sins incurred earlier by that person who feels inclined to listen to the *Purāṇas* are destroyed. Even while the Purāṇas exist, if a person, compelled by sins, feels drawn towards other *gāthās* (folk songs and fables) and is attached to them, he faces downfall.

63. A man engaged in associating himself with the good, worshipping the deities, and narrating or listening to noble stories of God as well as in imparting beneficial instructions, goes to the highest region of Viṣṇu. After death, he attains a brilliance comparable to that of Acyuta.

64. Hence, O prominent Brāhmaṇas, listen to this holy meritorious *Purāṇa* named after Nārada. On hearing this, a man becomes free from old age, rebirth, etc. His mind becomes stabilised in Acyuta.

65. The Purāṇa is excellent and highly pre-eminent. It grants the desired boons. By its own lustre, it has sanctified all the worlds. By remembering the primordial Deity that bestows the cherished objects, a man attains the state of salvation.

66. O Brahmins, he creates, protects and annihilates the universe by assuming different bodies of Brahmā, Viṣṇu and Īśa. By contemplating in one's mind that primordial Lord the transcendental Ruler, one attains liberation.

67. He who is devoid of all such (varieties based on ignorance) and alternatives such as name, caste (birth), etc., who is the greatest among the great beings, who transcends the greatest, who is comprehensible only through the *Vedānta* and who reveals himself unto his devotees, is highly praised by all *Purāṇas* and *Vedas*.

68. Hence, that Lord of the worlds, the cause of liberation, the Eternal, Slayer of Mura[24] is competent to be worshipped. By remembering the great mystic secret, the cause of attain-

---

Can we not take it as one sentence thus "Hence by remembering that Lord...whose worship is sufficiently efficacious...a man crosses...existence" ?

ment of the Puruṣārthas (objectives) a man crosses the ocean of worldly existence.

69. This should be recited only to righteous persons, the faithful ones and to ascetics devoid of passion, and to persons seeking salvation.

70. It should be recited in a holy place, in good assembly, in the temples in sacred places and sacred spots (near the bank of a holy river or lake) and in the presence of the gods (or images of gods) and the Brahmins.

71. Those who relate this excellent narrative in a place defiled with crumbs and other remnants of food are cooked in the terrible hell[26] all the long while till the dissolution of the world.

72. He who though infatuated, hypocrite and devoid of devotion, falsely pretends to listen to this Purāṇa is also similarly *cooked* in the everlasting terrible hell.

73-74. The man who carried on conversation with others in the middle of a holy discourse (about the Lord), goes to the terrible hell. Hence, O leading Brahmins the narrator and the listener should pay single-minded attention. This is the eternal path of righteousness. One without concentration of the mind does not understand anything.

75. Hence, one shall imbibe the nectarine story of Hari with concentration of mind. How can a man of confused mind appreciate the holy story ?

76-78. What happiness is achieved in the world by a man of confused intellect and mind? Hence, one shall eschew all desires which are the cause of misery and meditate on Lord Viṣṇu with the perfect concentration of the mind. If the eternal Lord Nārāyaṇa is somehow remembered even by a sinful person, he shall undoubtedly be delighted. Fruitful indeed is the life of that man who entertains highest devotion to Lord Nārāyaṇa, the eternal Lord of the universe. Salvation is as if just on the palm of his hand within his reach.

79. O excellent Brahmins, there is verily (absolutely) no doubt in this that the four objectives of human efforts, viz. Puruṣārthas of Virtue, Wealth, Love and Liberation are achieved by those who are devoutly attached to Hari.

NOTES

1. *Sūta* :

This term signifies a caste-name as well as a profession. As a caste, *sūta* is the *pratiloma* offspring born of a *Kṣattriya* male and a Brahmin woman *vide* the *Dharma Sūtras* of Gautama (4.15), Baudhāyana (1.9.9), and Viṣṇu (16.6) and the *Smṛtis* of Manu (10.11) and Yājñavalkya (1.93). *Kauṭilīya Arthaśāstra*, however, carefully distinguishes between the two. It states : *Kṣattriyāt sūtaḥ.| Paurāṇikas tvanyaḥ Brahma-Kṣattrād viśeṣaḥ* | (3.7.28-29) "The child born from a *Kṣattriya* man (and a *Brāhmaṇa* woman) is *sūta*. But Sūta — the reciter of *purāṇas* is different and is superior to Brāhmaṇas and Kṣattriyas.

According to Va.P. (1.60-61), god Brahmā compiled the *Purāṇas* before 'breathing out' the Vedas and the duty of preserving them (*Purāṇas*) was entrusted to Sūta who was mysteriously born out of the first sacrifice. As Vaṁśīdhara on Bh.P. 1.1.5 points out : as Sūta was born of fire (sacrificial fire)he was *ipso fact* a Brāhmaṇa. Sages like Śaunaka and others heard the Vedas in the form of the Bh.P. because he was a Brāhmaṇa for "a Śāstra is not to be heard from a low caste. Such hear ing is unacceptable like drinking milk from a pot of dog's hide". This Sūta, the reciter of the NP. is positively a Brāhmaṇa as can be gathered from his description as the performer of Vedic sacrifices and other details given in NP. 1.1.15-28. The fact that Śaunaka along with other Brāhmaṇa sages approaches him for enlightenment, is an evidence of his being a Brāhmaṇa. This Sūta is a direct disciple of Vyāsa (*sūtas tu Vyāsa-śāsitaḥ* | v. 18 & v. 19 later). This means that his name should be *Ro*(*Lo*) *ma-harṣaṇa*, most probably a title meaning "One who makes the hair of the members of his audience, stand on their ends, by the recitation of Purāṇas" : Va.P. (1.1.16) states :

lomāni harṣayāñ cakre śrotṛṇām yat subhāṣitaiḥ |
karmaṇā prathitas tena loke smil-Loma-harṣaṇaḥ | |

The word *Romaharṣaṇi* if emended as *Romaharṣaṇa* gives appropriate sense and does not offend the metre here or in v. 25 below.

2. *Gaṇeśa* :

Literally "The lord or controller of *gaṇas* (which is variously interpreted as *Pramatha-gaṇas* or goblin attendants of god Śiva, or evil spirits presiding over troubles or hindrances). He is also known as *Vighna-rāja* (the ruler over impediments or difficulties). Hence, he is always invoked with a prayer at the beginning of every work big or small and of any nature, be it the writing of a book or constructing a building. He is regarded as a son of god Śiva and Pārvatī or only of Pārvatī who created him of herself alone. His image is elephant-headed. This is a substitute of his original head which was cut off by Śiva for not allowing him to see Pārvatī. BV.P. reports that Gaṇeśa was originally very beautiful and out of pride for her child, Pārvatī invited everyone to see him and Śani (the presiding deity of the planet Saturn) was one of them. He was very unwilling to see, as he knew the consequences of his seeing. But not daring to displease goddess Pārvatī he looked at the child's face through the corner of his left eye. And lo ! The child's head fell off and remorsefully Śani withdrew his glance immediately. As Bv.P. puts it :

Śaneś ca dṛṣṭi-mātreṇa ciccheda mastakam mune /
cakṣur nivārayāmāsa tasthau namrānanaḥ Śaniḥ / /

BV.P.-III *Gaṇapati-khaṇḍa.* 12.6

Viṣṇu killed an elephant with his discus Śudarśana and fixed his head on that of Pārvatī's child (BV.P.III. 12.10-20) who subsequently became known as Gajānana 'Elephant-headed god'. A cycle of legends has accumulated around the god Gaṇeśa which is treated not merely as a part (e.g. *Gaṇapati khaṇḍa* in BV.P.) of a *Purāṇa*, but there are two *Upa-purāṇas* on that God, viz. the *Gaṇeśa Purāṇa* and the *Mudgala Purāṇa.* There Gaṇeśa is the Para-Brahman himself who incarnates in this world for protection of the world as stated in BG. 4.7-8. The *Gaṇeśa Gītā* attributed to god Gaṇeśa (which forms a part of the *Gaṇeśa Purāṇa*) reminds one of the BG. at every step. He is one of the five principal deities of Neo-Hinduism (the others being gods Śiva, Viṣṇu, Sūrya or the Sun-god and goddess Śakti or Pārvatī). There is a cult of this god known after him as *Gāṇapatyas.* Gaṇeśa images are found all over India and Greater India upto Japan and if Chaman Lal is correct (in his *Hindu America*) even in Central America. He is worshipped by Hindus both of the 'right' and 'left' form of worship and even by the Buddhists especially under the influence of Tantrism. Attempts are made to trace him to the Vedic period in the *Brahmaṇas-pati sūkta* (RV. 2.23.1 also Tait. S. 2, 3, 14, 3). Though Brahmaṇas-pati and Gaṇapati are connected with speech, 'elphant-headed-ness' is not the characteristic of that Ṛg-vedic deity, though both have some names (e.g. *Gaṇapati*) common. The elephant-headed god is expressly mentioned in the *Maitrāyaṇī Saṁhitā* (2.9.1) as follows :

tat-karaṭāya vidmahe, hasti-mukhāya dhīmahi /
tan no dantī pracodayāt / /

Tomes have been written on this god. An encyclopaedic dictionary in many volumes called *Gaṇeśa Kośa* in Marathi is available. As he is the god of learning, he is invoked at the beginning of all literary productions. Even Vyāsa employed him as the writer of the Mbh : (Mbh.Ādi. P. 1.75-79) Gaṇeśa is thus always saluted at the beginning of every Brahmanical literary work in ancient and mediaeval India.

3. *Vāsudeva* :

The deity that pervades the universe. The word is derived from $\sqrt{}$*vas*+ *bāhulakāt uṇ* — *vāsu / vāsuś ca devaś ca /* The omnipresence of this deity is emphasised in many Purāṇas. e.g. V.P.

sarvatrāśau samastaśca vasatyatreti vai yataḥ /
tataḥ sa Vāsudeveti vidvadbhiḥ pari-gīyate / /

— V.P. 1.2.

sarvāṇi tatra bhūtāni vasanti paramātmani /
bhūteṣvapi ca sarvātmā Vāsudevas tatah smṛtaḥ / /

— V.P. 6.5.80

So in Mbh. V.70.3 :

vasanāt sarva-bhūtānāṁ vasutvād deva-yonitaḥ |
Vāsudevas tato vedyo bṛhatvād Viṣṇur ucyate ||

Many scholars hold the view that Vāsudeva, the Yādava hero, the cowherd boy Kṛṣṇa in Gokula, and the great philosopher exponent of the *Bhagavad Gītā* are one and the same person (Cf. K. M. Munshi : *Glory that was Gurjara Deśa* I, pp. 111-27) Historicity of Vāsudeva Kṛṣṇa is generally agreed. A comparison between the tenets of Ghora Aṅgirasa, the preceptor of Kṛṣṇa the son of Devakī in *Chāndogya* Upa. (3.16-19) and Vāsudeva Kṛṣṇa's in the BG., shows great affinity between the two. Vāsudeva Cult was in vogue at the time of Pāṇini, Megasthenes and Ardha Māgadhī Jain canon. It was pro-Vedic and earlier than the non-Vedic *Pañcarātra* system of Nārāyaṇa, though ultimately they amalgamated into one : Bhāgavatism. But before doing that the Vāsudeva cult or Bhāgavatism had to accept the doctrine of Vyūhas (Emanations) and absorb it in its doctrine of Incarnation (*avatāra-vāda*), treat *Viṣṇu Purāṇa* as their own along with the *Bhagavad Gītā* and adopt the worship of Lakṣmī. Bhāgavatism, however, sticks to its specific *mantra* : *Om namo bhagavate Vāsudevāya* and does not accept the Pāñcarātra *mantra* : *Om namo Nārāyaṇāya*. Hence all sacred texts of Bhāgavatism present obeisance to Lord Vāsudeva. For more details about Vāsudevism vide Intro. to the Bh. P. Pd.P. Uttara Khaṇḍa derives Vāsudeva from his father Vasudeva (*Vasudevasya jātosau Vāsudevaḥ sanātanaḥ |*) but generally most of the Purāṇas keep Vasudeva in the background. The identification of Vāsudeva and Nārāyaṇa was completed before the epic period. Thus K.P.I. 48.69 describes the sleeping Viṣṇu :

Sa eva paramaṁ Brahma Vāsudevaḥ sanātanaḥ |
śete Nārāyaṇaḥ śrīmān māyayā mohayan jagat ||

4. *Nārāyaṇa* :

The derivation : "A deity whose residence is (in) on the waters". The standard quotation to support this is :

āpo nārā iti proktā āpo vai nara-sūnavaḥ |
ayanaṁ tasya tāḥ pūrvaṁ tena Nārāyaṇaḥ smṛtaḥ ||

— Manu 1, 10 and many purāṇas, also Mbh. Vana. 192.3.

Here the word 'Water' (*āpaḥ*) is used in the sense of primeval matter out of which the universe is formed. *Śatapatha Br.* 6.1.1.9 states : *sā idaṁ sarvam āpnod yadidaṁ kiñ ca | yad āpnot tasmād āpaḥ |* (As the chief deity of the Pāñcarātra system, Nārāyaṇa was out of Vedic fold. But the process of synthesis set in, and he was identified with Vāsudeva and Viṣṇu :

Nārāyaṇāya vidmahe, Vāsudevāya dhīmahi |
tan no Viṣṇuḥ pracodayāt ||

— *Maitrāyaṇī Saṁhitā* (ibid)

It is possible that he was the god of sea-faring people (probably of Dravidians). His being a sea-god is testified in the Buddhist *Avadāna Śataka* where a merchant's wife goes to fulfil her pledge (about safe voyage) to the god Nārāyaṇa whose temple was on the sea shore. The four Emanations (Vyūhas) of Nārāyaṇa viz. Vāsudeva, Saṅkarṣaṇa, Pradyumna and Aniruddha is the central concept of the *Pañcarātrins*. (MBH. *Śānti*. 339.19-76) The anthropomorphic figure of Nārāyaṇa, the serpent coils that form his bed, and the waters on which this serpent floats, are triune manifestations of the single divine, imperishable cosmic energy underlying and inhabiting all the forms of life. In The *Purāṇas* and the Mbh. (e.g. 6.65.52) we are told that Viṣṇu sleeps on Śeṣa, Viṣṇu is Śeṣa, and Śeṣa is the form of the Supreme Being. Thus the fusion of Viṣṇu and Nārāyaṇa was complete long before the Epics.

In the Bh.P. 2.7.6 and Mbh. *Śānti*. 334-.9-12, he is the son of Dharma and Dakṣa's daughter Mūrti and was the brother of Nara. The MBH. adds that the Lord manifested Himself in four forms — Nara, Nārāyana, Hari and Kṛṣṇa, out of them Nārāyaṇa and Nara practised penance in a gold chariot at Badarikāśrama :

Kṛte yuge mahārāja purā svāyambhuventare |
Naro Nārāyaṇas' caiva Hariḥ Kṛṣṇaḥ Svayambhuvaḥ | |
teṣāṁ Nārāyaṇa-Narau tapas-tepatur avyayau | |
Badaryāśramam āsādya śakaṭe kanakāmaye | |

Mbh. Śānti. 334.9.10.

Another derivation in Mbh.5.70.10 suggests that the god is called Nārāyaṇa as he is the resort of all people.
(*narāṇām ayanāc cāpi tato Nārāyaṇah smṛtaḥ*)
(For more details vide Introduction : *The Viṣṇu concept*)

5. *Nara* :

An ancient sage, brother of Nārāyaṇa, performed penance for thousands of years at Badarikā (Mbh. Vana. 40.1) Alongwith Nārāyaṇa he fought with Asuras on the side of Devas on the Amṛta issue and was entrusted with its protection (*Mbh. Ādi*. 19.19-31). Arjuna is said to be the Lord's incarnation (vide *Nārāyaṇa* above). *Devī Bhāgavata* / IV. chs. 5 & 6. confirms the relation between Nara and Nārāyaṇa and their penance at Badarikāśrama for 1000 years, and adds that when Indra tried to disturb their penance by deputing heavenly damsels, Nārāyaṇa created Urvaśī and presented it to Indra. When despite that the damsels refused to return, Nārāyaṇa got enraged and was pacified by Nara by referring to the fight for Amṛta. He is an eternal associate of Nārāyaṇa. He represents the eternal spirit, the Supreme Man.

6. *Sarasvatī* :

The goddess of speech, always invoked at the beginning of every Purāṇa and in Mbh. also a tradition faithfully observed by later Indian writers down to modern times. She is evolved out of the Vedic minor deity *Vāc*. BV.P.-*Brahma-khaṇḍa* 3.57 clearly identifies her with *Vāc* and she is the inspiring deity of poets and is of pure Sattva, by nature :

Vāg-adhiṣṭhātṛ-devī sā kavīnām iṣṭa-devatā |
śuddha-sattva-svarūpā ca śānta-rūpā Sarasvatī | |

She is regarded as one of the five Potencies of the Lord at the beginning of the world (BV.P.-*Gaṇeśa-khaṇḍa* 40.61.-7). In RV.X.125 she describes herself as a companion of all gods supporting gods like Indra, Agni, etc. and as bending Rudra's bow against Asuras. In the *Śatapatha Br.* 3.2.4.3-6 she helps in the barter for Soma from Gandharvas where she outwits the Gandharvas after securing Soma from them. In *Nighaṇṭu* 5.5. she is a deity of the atmosphere and probably Yāska identifies thunder as the *Vāc* of the middle region (*Nirukta* 11.27). She is regarded as the embodiment of literature as her body consists of *Om*, vowels and consonants — at least, that form of Sarasvatī appeared before Yājñavalkya when he received the Veda from the Sun-god (Mbh.Śānti. 318.14). As Mt.P. states she is the deity to be propitiated for proper grasp of Vedas, all Śāstras, and arts like dancing, music, etc. Here this is the traditional invocation as per practice of all *Purāṇas*.

7. *Jaya* :

Originally this verse was used at the beginning of the Mbh. where *Jaya* signifies the *Mahābhārata*. But after its adoption by all the *Purāṇas*, it comes to mean the *Purāṇa* which adopts it for the invocation of Nārāyaṇa and Nara. The BS.P. states : "Eighteen Mahāpurāṇas, Rāmāyaṇa, *Dharma Śāstra* works of Viṣṇu and others, the holy texts of *Śiva-dharma* and the fifth Veda *Mahābhārata* are called 'Jaya'.

> *aṣṭādaśa-purāṇāni Rāmasya caritaṁ tathā |*
> *Viṣṇu-dharmādi-śāstrāṇi Śiva-dharmaś ca Bhārata | |*
> *kārṣṇyañ ca pañcamo Vedo yan-Mahā-Bhāratam smṛtam |*
> *jayeti nāma eteṣām pravadanti manīṣiṇaḥ | |* BS.P. 1.5

8. *Veda Vyāsa* : *Vedaṁ vyasyati-pṛthak karotī'ti | vi+*as+aṇ) Vyāsa.*

The classifier of the Veda. His other synonyms are : Dvaipāyana (The island-born-Satyavatī, his mother gave birth to him on an island in the river), Pārāśarya (Son of sage Parāśara), Vyāsa, Bādarāyaṇa (the author of the *Śārīraka Sūtras* of Vedānta, prob. from his place of residence). VP. states that god Viṣṇu assumed the form of Vyāsa and classified the Vedas

> *Vedam ekam catur-bhedaṁ kṛtvā śākhā-śatair Vibhuḥ |*
> *karoti bahulam bhūyo Veda-Vyāsa-svarūpa-dhṛk | |*

His life is closely associated with the Kaurava-Pāṇḍava family, first as the father of their fathers and then in most of the important events in their lives. *Vyāsa-vana* (Mbh. *Vana.* 83.93), *Vyāsa-sthalī* (Mbh. *Vana.* 83.96-98) both places associated with his name are in and near Kuru-kṣetra. This shows that his major part of life was spent in that area.

NP.I. 1.17-18 confirm the belief tht Vyāsa was God Viṣṇu himself who classified the Vedas for righteousness, progressively eroded as yugas passed. The Mbh. composed by him is the digest of all Vedas and *Śāstras.* (MBH. Ādi-1.17-21 and later vv. 54-74). Bh.P. was the last work which, as advised by Nārada, gave him mental peace. All the Purāṇas, Mbh. and *Brahma Sūtras* are ascribed to him. He had written on all the subjects under the Sun. *Vyāsocchiṣṭaṁ jagat sarvam* is a well-deserved compliment to him.

9. *Vṛndāvana* :

Still well-known by the same name. It is in U.P. A sacred place of all Hindus irrespective of Vaiṣṇavism. It is named after Vṛndā which according to BV.P. *Kṛṣṇa-janma-khaṇḍa-Ch.* 17, was the name of the daughter of King Kedāra. She was the incarnation of Lakṣmī. Sage Durvāsas gave her the *Hari-mantra.* She performed penance for 60,000 years and sought Viṣṇu as her husband. The forest place where she performed the penance, came to be known as *Vṛndāvana* :

Vṛndā yatra tapas tepe tat tu Vṛndāvanaṁ smṛtam /

BVP. *Kṛṣṇa-janma-khaṇḍa* 17.204.

In the same chapter, Nārāyaṇa states that Vṛndā is one of the 16 synonyms of Rādhā (*Kṛṣṇa Vṛndāvanī Vṛndā Vṛndā-vana-vinodinī* / ibid 17.21.b). The forest of Rādhā (with Kṛṣṇa) came to be called Vṛndāvana.

In the *Devi-bhāgavata* 7.30.69, Vyāsa gives a list of *Śakti-pīṭhas* (Specially holy shrines of goddess Śakti) out of which Vṛndāvana is one and is associated with Rādhā.

Rukmiṇī Dvāravatyā tu Rādhā Vṛndāvane vane /

The Bh.P. *Skandha* X gives many details of Vṛndāvana which are shown by guides to pilgrims today.

10. *Loka-sādhakāḥ* :

When Kṛṣṇa is identified with Para-Brahman, the gods in charge of the creation, maintenance and destruction of the universe, naturally become his functionaries in carrying out the cycle of the creation etc. of the universe, and as such are called the servants (entrusted to accomplish the routine of this universe); and they are merely the rays of Lord Kṛṣṇa.

11. *Śaunaka* :

According to *Mbh. Ādi.* 1.19 and *Anuśāsana* 30.65 he was the son of Śunaka of Bhṛgu clan. In Mbh. he is shown to be the performer of a sacrifice of 12 years duration in the Naimiṣa forest (see below), and the Sūta, Ugraśravas (son of Vyāsa's disciple Roma-harṣaṇa) came to visit him. In NP.I. 1.3-14, Śaunaka practised austerities in the Naimiṣa forest and when he was asked some problems of world-interests by sages, he led them to Sūta at *Siddhāśrama* (see below *Siddhāśrama*).

12. *Naimiṣāraṇya* :

It is modern Nimsar at a distance of 20 miles from Sitapur and 45 miles to the Nirth-West of Lucknow. Nimsar is a railway station on the former Oudh-Rohilkhanda Railway. It is so called because Lord Viṣṇu destroyed the Asura army there, within the twinkling of the eye (*nimiṣa*). Sridhara on the Bh.P. 1.1.4 quotes from the VR.P. the etymology of this word as follows :

evam kṛtvā tato devo muniṁ Gauramukhaṁ tadā /
uvāca nimiṣeṇedaṁ nihataṁ Dānavaṁ balam / /
araṇyesmins tatas tvetam Naimiṣāraṇya-sañjñitam /
bhaviṣyati yathārthaṁ vai Brāhmaṇānāṃ viśeṣakam / /

The other more popular spelling is *Naimiśa* as is explained as a place where the felly of the wheel mentally created by god Brahmā, fell off. He instructed that to be a holy place where sacrifices, penance, etc., may be fruitfully performed. Va.P. 1.2.8 states :

bhramato dharma-cakrasya yatra nemir aśīryata /
karmaṇā tena vikhyātaṁ Naimiśam muni-pūjitam / /

This is quoted *verbatim* in Bd.P. 1.2.8. The Devī Bh. P. 1.2.28-32 gives the same etymology and adds that Kali has no entry (i.e. influence) in that forest.

There seems to be another Naimiṣāraṇya (probably near the Kuru region) mentioned in *Chāndogya* Upa. 1.2.13, also in *Kāṭhaka Saṁhitā* 10.6, *Tāṇḍya Mahābrahmana* 25.6.4. But the Naimiṣāraṇya in Purāṇas was on the banks of the Gomatī i.e. in U.P. which is Nimsar. Rāma performed his horse-sacrifice at that place :

> *yajña-vāṭaś 'ca sumahān Gomatyā Naimiśe vane |*
> *ājñāpyatām mahābāho tad hi puṇyam anantaram ||*
> — V.R. 7.91.15.

it was also the place of Sītā's second ordeal in which she disappeared in the earth. (V.R.7. Sarga 97)

13. *Siddhāśrama* :

Many places called Siddhāśrama are mentioned in the Purāṇas e.g. One near Buxar in Shahabad district is connected with god Vāmana (his birth-place); another in Gujarat near Dvārakā where Kṛṣṇa and Rādhā were reunited acording to BV.P. *Śrī-Kṛṣṇa-janma-khaṇḍa*, Ch. 124.2-8

> *aṁśena devo devībhī Rukmiṇyādyābhir eva ca |*
> *prayayau Dvārakāṁ ramyāṁ tasthau Siddhāśrame svayam | |* etc.

But the Siddhāśrama in NP. is significantly described as to be *yuktaṁ sarobhir acchodaiḥ* (spotted with the lakes of crystalline, translucent water). The specific mention of *acchoda* lake shows that this *Siddhāśrama* must be on the bank of the *Acchoda* lake which is in Kashmir. It is now called *Acchavata* and is at a distance of 6 miles from Mārttaṇḍa.

14. *Veda-vedāṅga-śāstra-vit* :

Though a common traditional adjective, it covers the entire syllabus of former eminent Pandits. Vedas are four : Ṛg, Sāman, Yajus and Atharvan. The *Vedāṅgas* are six : 1. *Śikṣā* — "The science of proper articulation and pronunciation" of particular Veda, (2) *Kalpa* — "The ceremonials and rituals pertaining to that Veda", (3) *chandas* "The science of prosody", (4) *Vyākaraṇa* "Grammar" (5) *Nirukta* "Etymological explanations of Vedic words", (6) *Jyotiṣ* 'Astronomy'. These are ancillary to Vedas for the correct pronunciation and interpretation of the text and the correct application of Mantras in the Vedic ceremonials. *śāstra* from √*śās*-'to teach, to instruct'—*Uṇādi* 4.158 *ṣṭran* i.e.-*stra*, showing a manual or treatise teaching a subject systematically. According to Mt.P. 1.3.5 *śāstras* like *Mīmāṁsā*, *Nyāya* etc. came out of Brahmā's mouth after Veda, Vedāṅgas and Purāṇas. But unorthodox *Śāstras* like Pāśupata, Nakulīśa, Bhairava (tantra), being outside the Vedic fold should not be studied (A.P.)

> *vāmaṁ pāśupataṁ yogaṁ nakulaṁ caiva bhairavam |*
> *asevyam etat kathitaṁ Veda-bāhyaṁ tathetarat | |*

15. *Agniṣṭoma* :

It is a kind of Soma sacrifice. This was regarded as being born out of the first mouth of god Brahmā :

> *Gāyatrīṁ ca ṛcaṁ caiva trivṛt-soma-rathāntare |*
> *Agniṣṭomaṁ ca yajñānāṁ nirmame prathamān mukhāt | |*
> — Bd.P. 1.2.8.50

Va.P. 2.9.49 reads :

Agniṣṭomaṁ ca yajñānāṁ nirvame prathamān mukhāt |

It is a part of Jyotiṣṭoma. It is to be performed in the Spring. Study of the Vedas and being an *agni-hotrin* are the two pre-conditions of eligibility to perform this sacrifice. The main material is Soma and the deities invoked are Indra, Vāyu, etc.

16. *Sanaka-mukhyaistu* :

By the four mentally-created sons of Brahmā viz., Sanaka, Sananda (na), Sanātana and Sanatkumāra, of which Sanaka was the first to be enumerated. In Bh.P. 3.12. 4, 5 god Brahmā created these sons and ordered them to procreate. They transcended the path of *karma* and were perpetually celibate. They disobeyed Brahmā and followed the path of Liberation from *Saṁsāra*. Time had no power over them. They looked five years old. This child-like appearance deceived Jaya and Vijaya, Viṣṇu's attendants who did not allow them to see Viṣṇu. Being enraged they cursed them to be demons but assured them that Lord Viṣṇu will redeem them and they will rejoin their previous posts. Thus they were born as Hiraṇyākṣa, Hiraṇya-kaśipu and Lord Viṣṇu had to incarnate as Varāha and Nṛsiṁha to relieve them from their demonic birth. It is worth noting that in the Mbh., it is Sanatkumāra who is more active in propagating Vaiṣṇavism and not Sanaka. Even in NP.I. 2.1 sages ask Sūta where Nārada met Sanatkumāra, in spite of the seniority of Sanaka as mentioned here. They are always found in each others' company and are sometimes called collectively 'Kumāras' (Boy-sages). In *Kāśī khaṇḍa* we are told that they generally live in *Janaloka*. More description about them is given in the next chapter (vv. 3-5).

17. *Puruṣārtha* :

Principal objectives or goals in human life. Mādhava defines them as *puruṣair arthyate iti* (that after which men aspire (*Sarvadarśana-saṅgraha*). They are four in number : 1. *Dharma*—righteous behaviour, 2. *artha* — wealth, 3. *kāma* (Desires or love not superseding righteousness or *dharma* — BG.7.11), *Mokṣa* — Liberation from *Saṁsāra*. To this mediaeval Vaiṣṇavas added *Bhakti* (Devotion unto the Lord) as the fifth *puruṣārtha*. Manu advises all to strive for these energetically;

etac caturvidhaṁ vidyāt puruṣārtha-prayojanam |
asya nityam anuṣṭhānaṁ samyak kuryād atandritaḥ | |

— Manu S.7.100

An advice endorsed by all *Smṛti*-writers and *Purāna*-compilers.

18. *Mahā-pātaka* :

Smṛti-writers regard the commission of the following acts as very heinous crimes, viz., Murder of a Brāhmaṇa, liquor-drinking, theft, adultery with one's preceptor's wife and complicity in these acts :

Brahma-hatyā, surā-pānaṁ steyaṁ gurvāṅganāgamaḥ |
mahānti pātakānyāhus tat-saṁsargaś ca taiḥ saha | |

— Manu 11.54

Also vide Yājñavalkya 3.227, *Viṣṇu-Dharma Sūtra* 35.

The rigour about *saṁsarga* (association) with a sinner is modified by later *Nibandha-kāras*. (Kane—*Hist. Dh. Śāstra* III.944).

19. *upa-pātakas* :

Minor sins. *Smṛtis* differ as to which are minor sins, and hence their lists differ in details. Manu and other writers give about 49 acts as minor sins. Most of them are anti-social in nature, e.g. abandoning one's parents or preceptor, adultery or incest, selling of one's wife or children, etc. The *Smṛtis* have provided different types of atonements (*prāyaścittas*) for these sins. The *prāyaścittādhyāya* is a common feature between Smṛtis and many *Purāṇas*.

20. *Vāji-medha or Aśva-medha* :

It is a sort of a *Soma-yāga* for absolute victory and only kings could perform it. It is the "king of sacrifices" as *Śatapatha* Br. 13.2.2.1 puts it. Its spiritual description *Oṁ Uṣā va aśvasya medhyasya śiraḥ*/ etc. is very famous, but is a later sublimation. Originally, even in the time of RV., the horse was killed for the sacrifice. Hence its name *aśva-medha.* But the orgy that was later associated with it in later Vedas, is absent in RV. It appears to be an Indo-European rite as Romans had their "October horse" similar in many details to ours. The *Upaniṣads* have spiritualised sacrifices, of which the spiritualization of the horse-sacrifice is quoted above. It appears that since the Aśvamedha of the Pāṇḍavas, this sacrifice was going out of vogue. Pali and Ardha Magadhi canons do not mention any Horse-sacrifice at the time of Buddha or Mahāvīra. It is after the revival of Hinduism that Hindu kings like Puṣyamitra (180 B.C.), Vākāṭaka Pravarasena I, etc. took fancy to perform this sacrifice. Muslim invasions from the 10th century became an effective check on the imperial sacrifices like Aśvamedha and Rājasūya.

21. *Rājasūya* :

A great sacrifice to be performed by a universal monarch (with the participation of tributary princes) at the time of his coronation, as a mark of his undisputed sovereignty *rājā vai rāja-sūyeneṣṭvā bhavati* as *Śatapatha* puts it. It is described in details in the *Vājasaneyī Saṁhitā Adhyāya* 9. *kāṇḍikas* 35 to *Adhyāya* 10. *Kāṇḍikās* 30. Yudhiṣṭhira's Rājasūya is described in *Mbh. Sabhā* Chs. 35-45 (In fact it starts with the expression of his desire for the great sacrifice fit to be performed by uncontested sovereigns *Mbh. Sabhā.* 13.30). In it *abhiṣecanīya* is the principal rite. In it the king is bathed with waters brought from seventeen sources in seventeen vessels of *udumbara* wood. It also fell in disuse. But curiously enough the Jain king Khārvela is credited to have performed a Rājasūya sacrifice (E.I. Vol.XX.79).

22. *arthavāda* :

It is a statement usually recommending a *vidhi* or ritual by stating the good arising from proper observance and evils befalling by its omission, and also adds historical instances to support its view. The *Mīmāṁsakas* have been discussing this topic of *arthavāda* 'Declamatory texts' for many generations. Thus Gadādhara in *Śaktivāda* states that according to Prabhākara the *Arthavāda* texts cannot be regarded as trustworthy. This view is accepted by NP. and hence its denunciation of those persons who regard *Purāṇas* as *Arthavāda.* But on this question of reliability of *artha-vāda* its trustworthy and useful character has been established (vide—Ganganath Jha — *Pūrva-Mīmāṁsā in its Sources*, pp. 179-81.

23. *Naraka* :

A place where retribution for sins is suffered. The number of such places is different. According to Śaṅkara *Br. Sūtra* 3.1.15, the hells are 7 in number. Manu 4.88-90 and Yājñavalkya believe in 21 hells, but their names differ. Bh.P. 5.26 enumerates 28 hells. According to RV. 4.5.5. and 7.104.3, a hell is a subterranean dark pit. Atharva Veda believes hell to be inhabited by ogresses and dissolute women. The list of sinners to be sent for a particular sin to a particular hell differs from Purāṇa to Purāṇa, e.g. Pd.P. *Svarga-khaṇḍa* 34, *Pātāla khaṇḍa* 48, Vp.2.6.7.32 BV.P. *Prakṛti khaṇḍa* ch.s 27 & 28. The descriptions in the *Garuḍa*, *Mārkaṇḍeya* (12.3-39) are terrible and are meant as deterrents against sinful acts.

24. *Murāri* :

Mura was the name of demon in charge of protecting the border of king Bhaumāsura (Naraka) of Prāg-jyotiṣapura. He screened Bhaumāsura's kingdom by planting 6000 nooses around that border. But Kṛṣṇa cut them all with his discus Sudarśana and killed the demon Mura (Mbh. *Sabhā*. 38.29 ff). According to Bh.P. 10.59.4-11, Mura was a demon of five heads who feeling secure about the defence of Naraka's capital, was deeply asleep in water. Kṛṣṇa cut the wire-defence by his sword, roused the demon from sleep by blowing his conch and severed his heads by his discus Sudarśana. Hence, he came to be known as Murāri.

CHAPTER TWO

Eulogy of Lord Viṣṇu

The sages enquired :

1. How did Sanatkumāra relate everyone of the religious duties to Nārada, the noble-souled sage ? How did these two come together ?

2. O Sūta ! In what place did those two expounders of the *Brahman* stay ? Where did they sing the songs of (the glories of) Hari ? Narrate that to us.

Sūta replied :

3. Sanaka and other great-souled (sages) were the mental sons[1] of god Brahmā; they were free from egotism or 'I-ness.' All of them observed perpetual celibacy.

4. I shall recount their names :— They were Sanaka, Sanandana, holy lord Sanatkumāra and he who is remembered as Sanātana.

5. They were devotees of Viṣṇu. These noble-souled sages were engaged in the meditation of *Brahman.* They resembled a thousand suns (in brilliance). They were desirous of salvation and were highly truthful.

6. O Brāhmaṇas ! Once (while) they started towards their desired destination, the peak of Meru[2] (to attend) god Brahmā's assembly, they saw on their way, the river Gaṅgā, originating from Lord Viṣṇu's foot (*Viṣṇu-padī*).[3]

7-8. On seeing it, they were about to take their bath in the waters of the Sītā[4] (a branch of the Gaṅgā). O excellent Brāhmaṇas ! In the meantime, the celestial sage Nārada came there. On seeing his elder brothers about to take their bath, he bowed to them with his palms joined in reverence. With great devotion and love, he invoked the names of the Slayer of Madhu.[5]

9-11. "Obeisance to you, O Nārāyaṇa, O Acyuta, O Ananta (Infinite one), O Vāsudeva, O Janārdana, O Lord of sacrifices, O Yajña-puruṣa[6], O Kṛṣṇa, O Viṣṇu, O Padmākṣa

(Lotus-eyed god), O Kamalā-kānta (Consort of goddess Lakṣmī), O Gaṅgā-janaka (the Proginator of the Gaṅgā), O Keśava, O Kṣīroda-śāyin (O Lord who couches in the milky ocean), O god of gods, O Dāmodara,[7] I bow to you. O Śri-Rāma,[8] O Viṣṇu, O Narasiṁha,[9] O Vāmana,[10] O Pradyumna,[11] O Saṅkarṣaṇa,[12] O Vāsudeva, O Unborn god (*Aja*), O Aniruddha,[13] O God of spotless splendour, O Murāri (Enemy of Mura), you save us perpetually from apprehensions."

12. Uttering the names of Hari in this way, and bowing down to the sages, his elder brothers, he (Nārada) sat along with them, and took bath with great pleasure.

13-14. All the five of them performed ablutions in the waters of the Sītā that dispel sins of the people, and performed the *tarpaṇa* [14]rites with reference to gods, sages and manes (*pitṛs*). They were absolved of their sins. O Brāhmaṇas! They came up (from the river) and performed the twilight prayers, and their other prescribed duties. They then held various discussions and discourses based on the attributes of Nārāyaṇa.

15. When the sages had completed their sacred rites on the beautiful banks of the Gaṅgā, Nārada put these questions in the course of various discourses and narratives.

Nārada said :

16. O excellent sages, all of you are omniscient. You are exclusively devoted to the Lord. All of you are the spiritual lords of the universe, highly blessed and eternal.

17. O learned sages ! You are engaged in the (spiritual) uplift of the worlds, and entertain friendliness towards the indigent and the wretched. Hence, I (humbly) entreat you to relate the characteristics of the Lord.

18. How is Lord Hari realized — Hari, by whom the entire universe consisting of the mobiles and immobiles, is created, and the waters from whose feet constitute the holy Gaṅgā ?

19. How do the threefold religious acts of men become fruitful ? O honour-bestowing ones ! (Be pleased) to expound the characteristics of the perfect knowledge and penance.

20. How is the worship of a guest to be performed whereby

Viṣṇu becomes propitiated ? O lords ! Be gracious unto me. It behoves you to relate precisely and in details, these and other similar things considered to be mystic secrets, bringing satisfaction unto Hari.

Śaunaka said :

(Nārada begins the eulogy of Viṣṇu)

21. Obeisance to the Supreme Lord, who is greater than the greatest. He is immanent in the greater and the lesser beings. He is both endowed with attributes and still devoid of attributes (*saguṇa* and *nirguṇa*). Salutations unto Him.

22. Hail to the Lord devoid of Māyā;[15] Obeisance to the Deity termed *Ātman*, the possessor of the deluding Potency called *Māyā* and who constitutes the universe. I bow to the Lord of *yogins*, identical with *Yoga* and comprehensible through *Yoga*. Salutations to Viṣṇu.

23. Obeisance to the Perfect Knowledge, to one who can be realized through perfect knowledge, to the sole cause of all knowledge, to the Lord of perfect knowledge, to the Deity identical with *Jñeya* (object of knowledge). *Jñātṛ*, (the knower) and the *Vijñāna-sampad* (riches of perfect knowledge).[16]

24. Obeisance to the meditation, to the one comprehensible through meditation, to him who dispels the sins of the meditator, to the Lord of meditation, to the intelligent one, and to one who represents the identity between the *dhyeya* (object of meditation), *dhyātṛ* (the subject, the person who meditates).

25. I always bow down to that unborn primeval, real, truthful Lord of prayer, whose energy and power inspire the sun, moon, fire, the creator of the gods, the demigods known as Siddhas, Yakṣas and the Asuras, and the groups of serpents.

26. I take resort to that unborn Lord who assumes the form of Brahmā, and creates the worlds, who alone is the protector (of the worlds) assuming the forms of Brāhmaṇas and Viṣṇu, and who assumes the body called Rudra for dissolving the world, at the end of the *Kalpas*, and then lies (in the form of a small child) licking (the big toe of) his foot.

27. I seek refuge in that primordial Deity Viṣṇu — the Lord who shines in his region called *Para* (the transcendental),

that Lord by reciting whose name, the mighty leader of elephants[17] was released from the terrible grip of the crocodile (I seek refuge in that primordial Viṣṇu).

28. He assumes the form of Śiva in regard to those possessing devotion unto Śiva; he assumes the form of Viṣṇu for the sake of those who are sanctified by meditation upon Hari. Ever and anon, I seek refuge in him alone, who causes physical bodies in accordance with the previous conception.

29. I bow always unto that son of Vasudeva who slew Keśin[18] and Naraka,[19] who, even as a boy lifted up a mountain[20] by means of the tip of his hand, and the God who habitually removes the burden of the Earth.

30. I salute to that unborn Lord who, incarnated in the terrific form of the Man-lion (from the pillar), tore up the chest of the demon (Hiraṇyakaśipu), as hard as the rock, and who protected Prahlāda, his own devotee.

31. I pay obeisance to that Supreme Primeval Person designated as the Self (*ātman*), who is embellished by means of the ether, etc., who is ever unsullied, Eternal and incomprehensible; who (though) the creator of the universe, is devoid of activities.

32. I worship that First Principle, the Soul (*ātman*) who stays as undivided one, with all his different forms, viz., Brahmā, Indra, Rudra, the fire-god,[21] the wind-god and the categories or classes of beings e.g. the mortals, demigods, like Gandharvas and Yakṣas, Asuras and gods (*devas*).

33. I have sought asylum in that from which all this (universe) became distinct, and was originated, sustained and in which it will get dissolved afterwards.

34. I have resorted (for refuge) to him who stands in the form of the universe, and appears to be involved in and attached to the world but who, in reality, is not attached at all, and is perfect.

35. I seek refuge in him who, though stationed in the heart (as *antarātman*), is not cognised by those whose selves or minds are deluded by Māyā, and who is the supreme-most and the purest of all.

36. I seek shelter in him who is of the nature of the perfect knowledge. He shines forth everywhere to those who refrain from all attachments, and whose souls or minds revel in the path of meditation.

37. When there was an impediment at the time of churning the ocean for the sake of nectar, he held the mount Mandara[22] on his back, for the welfare of the gods. I seek refuge in that Tortoise.[23]

38. With his pointed and curved fang, the Infinite Being lifted the earth from the ocean, and stabilised this entire universe. I bow down to that Boar.[24]

39. Desirous of protecting Prahlāda,[25] he tore up the rock-like hard chest of the demon Hiraṇyakaśipu and killed him. I pay obeisance to that Nṛsiṁha (Man-lion).

40. Having secured the gift of land from the son of Virocana (i.e. Bali), with two paces he covered the entire universe upto the region of god Brahmā, and handed over the same to gods. I bow down to that Ajita (the unconquered Lord).

41. Due to the crime committed by Kārtavīrya Arjuna of the Haihaya[26] clan, he destroyed, for twenty-one times, the race of Kṣatriyas. I bow down to that son of Jamadagni.[27]

42. He manifested himself in four forms (4 sons of Daśaratha). Surrounded by monkeys, he killed the army of the demons (Rākṣasas). I bow down to that Rāmacandra.

43. Assuming (lit. by resorting to) the two forms (viz. Śrīkṛṣṇa and Balarāma), he removed the burden of the earth and (ultimately) destroyed his own family. I worship that Śrīkṛṣṇa.

44. People of the three worlds beginning with the Earth see within their souls that pure Lord who is delighted within himself. I worship that Ruler of the universe who is resplendent and pure,[28] devoid of impurities.

45. Having massacred all the impure sinners by means of his sharp-edged sword,[29] at the end of the Kali Age, he re-established the *Dharma* at the beginning of the Kṛta Age. To him I salute.

46. I resort to him whose these and other innumerable forms are impossible to be enumerated by him (i.e. by any person) even in millions of years, O Pāṇḍavas. I worship him.

47. Even great sages, gods, demons (*Asuras*) and Manus[30] cannot[31] fully comprehend the greatness of his name. How can I, an insignificant person, worship him (with full realisation) ?

48. Even by hearing his name, men who have committed great sins attain sanctity. How can I, a weak-minded person of mean intellect, eulogise him (adequately) ?

49. If somehow or other (by a lucky chance) the sinners manage to glorify or hear his name, they become purified and the purified ones attain Liberation (from Saṁsāra).

50. I seek refuge in that deity of the form of perfect knowledge whom Yogins, freed from sins, perceive after stabilising their individual soul (*ātman*) in the (supreme) *ātman*.

51. The *Sāṁkhyas*[32] (followers of the path of knowledge) perceive Hari of perfect *ātman*, in everything. I worship that Ageless, Eternal (hence the First) Deity who is of the nature of perfect knowledge.

52. I salute Lord Hari who is immanent in all living beings, is quiescent, omniscient (perceiver of everything), who has thousands of heads[33] and who is very real (of positive existence).

53. I worship that unaging Supreme Ruler who stands the breadth of ten fingers above the universe of both past and the future, whether mobile or immobile.[34]

54. Again and again do I pay obeisance to that unborn mystic Deity, who is minuter than the minutest and greater than the greatest,[35] and the secret-most among the secrets.

55. I salute the Supreme Person, the Ruler of the universe who bestows his own region if he be meditated upon, remembered, worshipped, heard of or even bowed to.

56. As Nārada eulogised the great Lord thus, those great sages like Sanandana and others, with eyes bedimmed with tears of joy, became highly delighted, in the company of Nārada.

57. He who gets up early in the morning and reads this hymn to the Supreme Person (Viṣṇu) gets his soul purified of all sins, and attains to region of Viṣṇu (Vaikuṇṭha)

CHAPTER TWO

Eulogy of Lord Viṣṇu

1. *Mānasāḥ Sutāḥ* :

Spiritual sons. These are collectively called *Sanakādi* (Sanaka and others). When they were created they were asked by god Brahmā to procreate the world, but they, being *sāttvic* incarnations, adopted the path of perpetual celibacy and devotion unto Lord Viṣṇu. These should be distinguished from another group of *mānasa putras* (mental sons) of god Brahmā who became the progenitors of the world. According to *VP.* 1.7.4.5, they are Bhṛgu, Pulastya, Pulaha, Kratu, Aṅgiras, Marīci, Dakṣa, Atri and Vasiṣṭha. *Mbh Ādi* 5.10 and 66.4 delete Bhṛgu, Dakṣa and Vasiṣṭha and give only six mental sons.

2. *Meru-Śṛṅga* :

The peak of mount Meru, the site of god Brahmā's abode, Manovatī. The city is situated on the main peak or rather plateau (middle) of the Meru and 10,000 yojanas in square-area. The *Mt.P.*, ch. 113, states that Meru (or Sumeru) is bounded on the North by *Uttara Kuru,* on the South by *Bhārata Varṣa*, on the West by *Ketu-māla* and on the east by *Bhadrāśva.* Scholars regard Pamirs as Meru (K. L. Daftari — *Astronomical Method : Application to the chronology of Ancient India*, pp. 196-98, V. S. Agrawala — *Mārkaṇḍeya Purāṇa — Eka Sāṁskṛtika Adhyayana*, p. 139; S. M. Ali — *The Geography of the Purāṇas* 63-64) Dr. Harsha's ingenious identification of Mt. Altai ('A Mount of gold' — in Mongolia) with 'Meru, the Homeland of Aryans' in *Vishveshwarānanda Bhārata-Bhāratī*, Hoshiarpur, 1964 and accepted by Baldev Upadhyay in *Purāṇa Vimarśa*, pp. 319-20, deserves consideration.

3. *Viṣṇupadī Gaṅgā* :

According to Bh.P. 5.17.1-3, when Lord Viṣṇu, in his Vāmana incarnation, manifested his cosmic form and raised his left foot to cover the heavenly regions in the second step, he let the upper crest of the shell of the cosmic egg (*brahmāṇḍa*) go cracked by the nail of the big toe of his left foot, and through that opening rushed in the water covering the cosmic egg externally. The stream of water washed the feet of the Lord and was designated *Bhagavatpadī.* After a period of thousands of *yugas*, she descended on the top of the celestial regions called *Viṣṇupada*, where Dhruva, the son of Uttānapāda meditates on the Lord (*Bh.P.*5.23). It is due to her association with the feet of Lord Viṣṇu and its first descent on *Viṣṇupada* that Gaṅgā is known as *Viṣṇupadī*. In *Brahma-Vaivarta P. Prakṛtikhaṇḍa* 11.127-140, we are told that Gaṅgā went to Vaikuṇṭha by *Rādhikā mantra*, and by Viṣṇu's order flowed out of the lotus-feet of Viṣṇu. Hence, she is called *Viṣṇupadī*.

nirgatā Viṣṇu-pādābjāt tena Viṣṇupadī smṛtā | *ibid.* 140.

4. *Sītā* :

The Tārim-yarkand river called *Sītā* by Chinese (e.g. Hiuen Tsang) V. S. Agrawala identifies it with the Oxus (*Mārkaṇḍeya P.*, p. 139). N. L. De remarks, "From the names of the places mentioned in the *Brahmāṇḍa P.* ch. 57 through which the Sītā flows, its identification with the Jaxartes appears to be correct (GDAMI 1.187).

5. *Madhu-dviṣ* :

The enemy-slayer of Madhu, an epithet of god Viṣṇu. Madhu and Kaiṭabha were demon-brothers who stole away the Vedas from god Brahmā, while Lord Viṣṇu was in his *yogic* trance (sleep). Brahmā sought Viṣṇu's help. Viṣṇu sought a boon from Madhu and his brother Kaiṭabha of killing them (*Mbh. Vana.* 203.30). Viṣṇu killed him by placing him on his lap. Hence, Viṣṇu came to be known as *Madhusūdana* (slayer of Madhu). *Devī Bhāgavata* X.11 supports the M*bh*. information of their birth from ear-wax, and their power due to the boons received from Devī, the rest is the same as in the M*bh*.

6. *Yajña Puruṣa* :

Lord Viṣṇu, the presiding deity of all sacrifices. In Bh.P. 2.7-11, He is described as 'sacrifice incarnate (for whom sacrifices are performed), and an embodiment of Vedas, the Soul of all deities. Vedas are his breath.

7. *Dāmodara* :

(I) One who is tied with a rope round the waist. Owing to complaints about his mischiefs by cowherdesses of Gokula, Lord Kṛṣṇa was so tied to a wooden mortar by his foster-mother, Yaśodā (Bh.P. 10.9.13-14). Hence (Kṛṣṇa's or Viṣṇu's epithet), also HV.63-14-26.

(II) One who is approachable through intellect enriched by Self-Control and such other means (*damādi-Sādhanena utkṛṣṭā matir yā, tayā gamyate iti Dāmodaraḥ*.

(III) One who carries universes in his abdomen

(III) *dāmānī lokanāmāni tāni yasyodarāntare*
ten Dāmodaro devaḥ — Śaṅkara on *Viṣṇusahasranāma*

8. *Śri Rāma* :

The Seventh incarnation of Viṣṇu. The Hero of Vālmīki's epic the *Rāmāyaṇa*. The son of Daśaratha for whose word he exiled himself for fourrteen years, to a forest. He was an ideal king, a paragon of virtues.

9. *Narasiṁha* :

The fourth incarnation of god Viṣṇu. For saving the world from the tyranny of the demon-king Hiraṇyakaśipu, and for protecting his devotee Prahlāda, the demon-prince (Son of Hiraṇyakaśipu), the Lord manifested himself through a column in a half-lion-half-man form, and killed him on his own lap with his claws (thereby observing all the conditions of immortality in the boon conferred on him by god Brahmā). After killing Hiraṇyakaśipu and blessing Prahlāda, he disappeared. For details vide Bh.P. 7.8.18-33, *Mbh.Sabhā.* 38.29.

10. *Vāmana* :

Vedic Viṣṇu, the Sun-god and his three giant steps are famous in RV. 1-22.17, 18, etc. *Śatapatha* 1-2.5-7 is probably the source of the Purāṇic Vāmana episode in Purāṇas, He is the fifth incarnation of Viṣṇu. To re-instate Indra to his post in the celestial world, which was occupied by the pious demon king Bali, Viṣṇu was born of Kaśyapa and Aditi. As a short boy (Vāmana) whose investiture of thread was just performed, he went to Bali who was then performing a sacrifice on the bank of the Narmadā, and begged for three paces of land. Bali's preceptor Śukra saw through this ruse of Viṣṇu and opposed the gift. Bali was adamant. And as soon as Bali formally completed the gift with water, Viṣṇu suddenly manifested his cosmic form. He occupied the earth in one step, and the heavens in the second, and asked Bali space for the third step. King Bali, the great devotee of Viṣṇu offered his head for the third step. Viṣṇu pushed Bali down to the nether world where he was however provided with all the affluence of the celestial world. But Indra found the throne of the heaven vacant and occupied it.

—*Bh.P.* 8.19, *Rām. Bāla.* 29
Mbh.Sabhā 38.29, *Padma P.* vol. V
Uttarakhaṇḍa 'ch. 240.

11. *Pradyumna* :

According to *purāṇas* he is the god of Love burnt by god Śiva for disturbing his penance. He was then born as the son of Kṛṣṇa and Rukmiṇī. As the epithet is applied to Lord Viṣṇu, it implies his manifestation (*Vyūha*) as *Pradyumna* (*Bh.P.* 12.11.21), detailed in the *Pañcarātra āgamas*. He represents *ahaṁkāra* (Ego, 'I'-ness), and is the witness of the dreamless state of sleep. This is the *Bhāgavata* concept. According to the *Ahirbudhnya saṁhitā*, the difference between Prakṛti and Puruṣa starts in the Pradyumna stage. He actuates men to perform work (*Ahirbudhnya* 55.18). He is an intramundane *vyūha* and also a *vibhava* (incarnation) of Vāsudeva. It must in the *āgamic* sense that this epithet is applied to Viṣṇu.

12. *Saṅkarṣaṇa* :

N. of Balarāma, Kṛṣṇa's elder brother who in his embryonic stage was transferred from Yaśodā's womb to Rohiṇī's.

garbha-saṅkarṣaṇāt taṁ vai
prāhuḥ Saṅkarṣaṇam bhuvi / *Bh.P.* 10.2.13.

But his identification with Viṣṇu is a *Pañcarātra* concept which regards him as a manifestation (*Vyūha*) of Viṣṇu

Vāsudevaḥ Saṅkarṣaṇaḥ Pradyumnaḥ puruṣaḥ svayam !
Aniruddha iti Brahman mūrtivyūho'bhidhīyate ! !

Bh.P. 12.11.21.

The *Bh.P.* regards them as mere *mūrti-vyūha* or a part incarnation. With the *Pāñcarātra Āgama*, however, Saṅkarṣaṇa is an important *vyūha* and also a *vibhāva*. *Saṅkarṣaṇa* carries in him the whole of the universe, as if it is an atom. He is the support of the universe (*aśeṣa-bhuvanādhāra*). All the Śāstras have been produced by him and in him they disappear at the end of the universe (*Ahirbudhnya* 54.16).

13. *Aniruddha* :

The N. of a grandson of Kṛṣṇa and the son of Pradyumna, the romantic lover of Uṣā, the daughter of Bāṇāsura ((*Mbh. Sabhā.* 38) His identification with Viṣṇu, god Brahmā being born out of the lotus sprouted from his naval is accepted in *Mbh.Bhīṣma* 65.71; *Śānti.* 340.30-31. As noted above, the *Bh.P.* accepts him as a *mūrti-vyūha* — part incarnation of Viṣṇu. But his identification with Viṣṇu and its use as Viṣṇu's epithet is a Pāñcarātra concept wherein Aniruddha is both a *vyūha* (manifestation) as well as a *vidyeśvara*. There are some conflicting statements about the functions of Aniruddha in the *Lakṣmī Tantra, Viṣvaksena saṁhitā*, but to the *Purāṇa* writer, Aniruddha being a *vyūha* was probably enough to use it as an epithet of Viṣṇu. For details vide O.Schrader — *Intro. to the Pañcarātra.*

14. *Tarpaṇa* — (rites)

One of the five daily *yajñas* to be performed by men, in which libations of water to the gods, sages and the deceased ancestors are offered by mentioning their names.

tarpaṇaṁ ca śuciḥ kuryāt pratyahaṁ snātako dvijaḥ |
devebhyaśca ṛṣibhyaśca pitṛbhyaśca yathākramam || — *Śātātapa*

15. *Māyā*

The illusion by virtue of which one considers the unreal universe as really existent, and as distinct from the Supreme Spirit. Lord Viṣṇu is above this illusion. Hence. he is called *amāya* (devoid of — transcendental to — *Māyā*), But *Māyā* is regarded as the deluding Potency of Viṣṇu. Hence, he is called the Lord of Māyā (*Māyin*) as well, in this verse. In the *Varāha P.*, the presiding deity of the earth asks Viṣṇu to describe His Māyā potency to her. In reply Viṣṇu recounts in details how the whole universe works under the influence of his Māyā. It is also called *yoga-Māyā* resorting to which Kṛṣṇa (Viṣṇu) participated in the *rāsa* in the *Bh.P.* 10.30-31. *Pañcadaśī* 6.122-141 describes the Vedāntic concept of Māyā (as succinctly stated at the beginning). God Viṣṇu is not affected by the Māyā. Hence the epithet 'amāya'.

16.

In an advanced spiritual stage, the triad of the knower, knowledge and the object of knowledge or the meditator, meditation, and the object of meditation loses the distinctness of these components, and is realized as one. This is known as *Tripuṭi-nirāsa*. Here, all these trinities are merged in Viṣṇu and hence regarded as identical with Lord Viṣṇu.

17. *Gajendra*

King Indradyumna, the Pāṇḍyan king, born in the family of Svāyambhuva Manu, was a great devotee of Viṣṇu. While engaged in meditation during retirement from kingship, he did not notice the arrival of sage Agastya who, being enraged, cursed him to be an elephant. When he, as a king-elephant, entered the lake near mount Trikūṭa, a crocodile which was previously a Gandharva called Hūhū and was cursed to be a crocodile, caught hold of his leg. The elephant wanted to extricate its leg, but could not do so, despite a struggle for 1000 years. At last, finding all his strength exhausted and that he would be dragged into the water and meet death, he appealed to Lord Viṣṇu who relieved him by killing the alligator with his discus Sudarśana and both the elephant and the crocodile got absolved from their curses. This episode from Bh.P. 8 chs 2-4 is mentined here.

18. *Keśin*

A demon, follower of Kaṁsa; he possessed the po wer of 10,000 elephants. At the instance of Kaṁsa, he assumed the form of a horse and attacked Kṛṣṇa, and was killed by Kṛṣṇa at a place now known as Keśighāṭ at Vṛndāvana (UP.) *VP*.5.16. — *MBH.Sabhā*, ch. 38. In *Mbh. Āśvamedhika* 69.23, Kṛṣṇa declares to have killed Keśin as per *dharma*.

19. *Naraka alias Bhaumāsura*

A valiant *asura* — son of the goddess presiding over the earth. He was a king of Prāgjyotiṣa (Assam). He carried away and kept in confinement 16000 princesses and daughters of *siddhas*,, *asuras*, etc. He attacked the celestial region and defeating Indra carried away the ear-rings of Aditi, and the white umbrella, insignia of Indra's sovereignty. Indra appealed to Kṛṣṇa at Dvārakā. Kṛṣṇa, along with his queen Satyabhāmā, rode on Garuḍa, flew to Naraka's capital and slew him. He installed his son Bhagadatta on the throne at Prāgjyotiṣa, and released the 16000 princesses who subsequently married him. *Bh.P.* 10 dh.59., *V.P* 5.29

— *HV.* (*Harivaṁśa*) — *Viṣṇu Parva* ch. -63, *Mbh. Sabhā* 38, also *Udyoga* 48, 80-84.

20. *Gotram*

Mount Govardhana, 18 miles from Vṛndāvana in Mathurā district. In the village known as Paitho, Kṛṣṇa is said to have lifted up the mountain on his small finger, and held it as an umbrella over the heads of inmates of Nanda's Vraja and the cattle, to protect them from the deluge like rain-showers sent by Indra, to punish them for not offering him his annual sacrifice. The story is detailed in the following :

Mbh. Sabhā 41.9, *udyoga* 130.46

VP.5.Ch.11, *HV. Viṣṇu P.* ch. 18, *Bh. P.* 10.25

21. In the 1st half of this (No. 32) verse, in *Brahmendra-Rudrānilavāyumartya*: the underlined word be emended as anala instead of the present *anila* 'wind', as the word is followed by *vāyu* and *anila-vāyu* is tautologous.

22. *Mandāra*

The mount that was used as a churning-rod for churning the ocean, for obtaining nectar (*amṛta*) (*Mbh.Ādi* 18-6-8, 13, 16-21, *Bh.P.* 8.5-10). It is now identified with a hill two or three miles to the north of Baṁsī, in the Bānkā sub-division of Bhāgalpur District. It is an isolated hill of about 700 feet height with a groove all round the middle, to indicate the impression of the coil of serpent Vāsuki. This groove is artificial and bears the marks of *chisels*.

23. *Kūrma* (A Tortoise)

The second, out of ten chief incarnations, of Viṣṇu. At the time of churning the ocean for getting the nectar, gods and demons/used the mount Mandāra as the churning-drill and serpent Vāsuki as the churning-rope. But mount Mandāra having no fixation of the bottom, began to sink down. God Viṣṇu then assumed the form of a tortoise with a back 100,000 *yojanas* in extent, got under the sinking mountain and lifted it up, and supported it till the nectar was churned out.

—*Bh.P.* 8.7.8-10, *Agni* P.3. *VR.Bāla* 45 (*sarga*).

24. *Varāha*

In Vedic Literature, Varāha is a manifestation of Prajāpati (*Tait. Saṁhitā* 7-1-5-1, *Tait. Br.* 1.1.6, Śatapatha 14.1.2.11) But in Purāṇas the Boar is an incarnation of Viṣṇu. This is usually regarded as the third, out of the ten main incarnations of Viṣṇu, (*AP.—Agni Purāṇa*-Ch.4), but according to the *Bh.P.*

1.3.7, it is the second incarnation which Viṣṇu, the presiding deity of sacrifices, undertook for lifting up the earth which sank down to the nether-world — *rasātala* (*Bh.P.*3.13.15), but *AP.*4.2 states that the killing of demon Hiraṇyākṣa is the main purpose. *Bh.P.* 3.13.18-45 describes the fight between Varāha and Hiraṇyākṣa in which the demon was killed, but he killed the demon as he came in the way of lifting up the earth, and stabilising it in its proper position. (also *Mbh. Sabhā*, ch. 38). MP. in ch. 5.247-48 details the symbolism of this incarnation. The description of *yajña-varāha* (in *MP.* 248. 67-73) beginning with *Vedapādo yūpa-daṁṣṭraḥ Kratudantaś citīmukhaḥ*, etc. has its echoes in *VP.* 6.16.23, *Bd.P.* — *Prakriyā Pāda* 5.9-23, *Bm.P.* 213.33.7 and even in *Smṛtis* like the *Viṣṇu Smṛti* 1.3-9. The image of *yajña-Varāha*, at Vihāra (ancient *Varāhanagara*), 8 miles from Vijāpur, N. Gujarat, shows the influence of the concept till 1000 A.D. Mahā-Varāha images at Udayagiri cave ...(circa 400 A.D.), at Bādāmī (Bijapur Dist. Karnataka) of the 7th cent. A.D., and at the Daśāvatāra cave at Ellora (circa 800 A.D.), show the hold of this *avatāra* on popular mind. It must, however, be noted that originally *yajña-varāha* is a Vedic concept with profound meaning with reference to Vedic cosmogony, though Purāṇa-writers draped it differently with their imagination, and a correspondence between the elements of sacrifices and the parts of Varāha's body is established.

25. *Prahlāda* or *Prahrāda*

Son of demon Hiraṇyakaśipu and Kayādhū. When Hiraṇyakaśipu went to perform penance, gods attacked his kingdom and Indra carried away Kayādhū who was pregnant, but Nārada rescued her and gave her asylum in his hermitage. It was while dwelling here that Prahlāda, in his mother's womb, was given instructions in spiritual matters (*Bh.P.* 7.7 10-16). He was sent by his father to Śukra's son for education, but he became a staunch devotee of god Viṣṇu — the enemy of their family. While testing the progress of his son, Hiraṇyakaśipu discovered this (*Bh.P.* 7.5.23-32), and used torture to correct him (*Bh.P.* 7.5.37-44; *VP.* 1.17.32-53, also ch. 18 to 20). In the final interview, Hiraṇyakaśipu asked Prahlāda if god Viṣṇu was the pillar of the audience hall, and Viṣṇu manifested himself as a Man-Lion from within, and killed Hiraṇyakaśipu. Prahlāda was crowned as the king. Vāmana P. chs. (7 & 8) describe his pilgrimage to Puṣkara, and fight with sages Nara and Nārāyaṇa and defeat by Nārāyaṇa. He is regarded as a great devotee of Lord Viṣṇu — *mahābhāgavata* (*Bh.P.* 6.3.20). When Viṣṇu incarnated as Vāmana and manifested his cosmic form to put down his grandson Bali, he praised Vāmana (*Bh.P.* 8.23.6). In the *Mbh.* also, he is a respectable figure. According to *Bh.P.* 5.18.7, he spends his remaining days as a devotee of god Viṣṇu as Man-Lion in the Harivarṣa — (*Bh.P.* 5.18.7).

26. *Haihaya—Sahasrārjuna.*

This refers to king Arjuna, the son of king Kṛtavīrya of the Haihaya clan—a branch of Yadus. According to *Bh.P.* 9,23.24-27, he was the lord of the entire earth. 'No other ruler of the earth can reach Arjuna's status in performance of sacrifices, munificent donations, *yogic* powers, scholarship, military victories'. He was a disciple of Datta who conferred on him 1000 arms, and thus he came to be known as *Sahasrārjuna.* (*Bd.*P.44). He ruled at Māhiṣmatī (Mod. Maheśvara) on the right bank of the Narmadā in M.P. He defeated Rāvaṇa and kept him a captive. His glorious rule is described in *Bd.P.*58, *Mbh.Vana.*115, *Anuśāsana* 29.

The hereditary rivalry between Bhṛgus and Haihayas for supremacy in Western India, culminated in the raid of Jamadagnī's hermitage for the possession of Kāmadhenu (a wish-yielding cow) (*Bd.P.*chs 67-70, *Bh.P.*9,23. 24-28, *Mbh. Vana* 116.19-21). In a lightening reprisal, Paraśurāma killed Arjuna in a surprise attack near Māhiṣmatī—an act— strongly disapproved by Jamadagni (*Bh.P.*9.15.38-41).

The mention of annihilation of Kṣatriyas for 21 times in the above verse is a mythological representation of the struggle between Bhṛgus and Haihayas. Paraśurāma discomfited the Haihayas a number of times, but after his retirement, the Bhṛgus withdrew from Central and Western India and shifted to the North.

27. *Jāmadagnya* (Paraśurāma)

Paraśurāma, the son of Jamadagni of the Bhṛgu clan. A great military leader of his times. In the hereditary feud between Bhṛgus and Haihayas in which Jamadagni was killed, Paraśurāma defeated the Haihayas 21 times, which is inflated as "the annihilation of the Kṣattriya race for 21 times" (*Mbh. Ādi.*64.4, *Vana* 117. etc. *Bd.P.*ch.83. etc.) It appears that he was dissuaded from his ruthlessness by his elderly clansmen and he performed a sacrifice at Samantapañcaka (Kurukṣetra) where he gave to Kāśyapa as a gift, all the land conquered by him. Kāśyapa requested him to go out of the donated lands and find out for him some new place. He seems to be the first explorer of the land between the Western Ghats and the Arabian-sea, as people from Northern Koṅkaṇa to Kerala claim him as such. He finally retired to mount Mahendra—Eastern Ghats probably to *Mahendra malei* near Ganjam. After retirement, he had a scuffle with Rāma for breaking Śiva's bow (*Mbh. Vana.* ch.9) and with his disciple Bhīṣma for his refusal to marry Princess Ambā abducted by him.

He is popularly regarded as the 6th incarnation of Viṣṇu though he is called the 16th in the *Bh.P.* 1.3.20; 9.15.13. They suppose that he is one of the seven eternally living persons (*cirajīvin*). Also vide *M.P.*47, *V.P.* 4-7, 4-11.

28. Here *nirmala* and *Śuddha* are not tautological, God is both resplendent (*nirmala*) and pure (unmixed) despite his being *antarātman* the Inner Soul and Controller' of all, as mentioned in the 1st half.

29. This refers to Viṣṇu's future (the 10th) incarnation called Kalki who will terminate the Kali age by massacring all sinners, re-establish *dharma* and pave the way for the Golden Age (*Kṛta yuga*). He will be born in a place called Śāmbhala, as a son of a Brāhmaṇa Viṣṇuyaśas (*Bh.P.*1.3.25, *AP.*ch.16.8-10).

30. *Manu*

The mythical progenitor and Law-giver of the human race and the first sovereign of the entire world. His reign or life-span extends to 71 *Caturyugas* or roughly (71 × 36,00000 = 2566,00000 human years) V. Mani—*Purāṇic Encyclopaedia*, p. 482. But in *Siddhānta-śiromaṇī* on *Kālamāna*, *manvantara* = 30,67,20.00 human years. He is helped by seven sages, gods, Indra and his sons or kings. There are-14 Manus whose reigns taken together make one day or *kalpa* of god Brahmā. The fourteen Manus are as follows :

(1) Svāyambhuva, (2) Svārociṣa, (3) Auttami, (4) Tāmasa, (5)Raivata, (6) Cākṣuṣa (7) Vaivasvata (the present Manu) (8) Sāvarṇi, (9) Dakṣa-sāvarṇi, (10) Brahmasāvarṇi, (11) Dharmasāvarṇi, (12) Rudra-sāvarṇi, (13) Deva-Sāvarṇi, and (14) Indrasāvarṇi (*Bh.P.*8.13; *V.P.* 3.1, 3.2.)

31. Syntactically a defective verse for lack of a finite verb. The meaning is obvious. Hence 'cannot' is supplied to make the sentence complete.

32. *Sāṁkhya*

Used in the epic sense 'Path of knowledge' as in the *BG.*II *Sāṁkhya yoga.* It is the theistic Sāṁkhya Philosophy that is implied here. It may be noted that at the worst the Sāṅkhyas are Agnostic and not Atheist, as about God the *Sūtra* says 'God is not proved logically' (*Iśvarāsiddheḥ*/and not *Īśvarābhāvāt*/)

33-34. Echoes of the text of the *Puruṣa Sūkta*,viz.

Sahasra-Śīrṣā puruṣaḥ sahasrākṣaḥ sahasrapāt /
sa bhūmim viśvato vṛtvā atyatiṣṭhad daśāṅgulam //

RV.X.90.1

35. cf. *Kaṭha Up.* 2.20, *Śvet. Up.* 3.20.
Mahānārāyaṇa 8.3, *Kaivalya Up.* 20.

CHAPTER THREE

The Description Of The Sphere Of The Earth And Of Bhārata

Nārada enquired :

1. How did the Omnipresent Primordial Deity create Brahmā and others, formerly ?[1] O Sanaka, narrate this unto me, since your worship is omniscient.

Śrī Sanaka narrated :

2. Nārāyaṇa is imperishable and Infinite. He is omnipresent and unsullied. This entire universe consisting of the mobile and immobile beings is pervaded by him.

3. At the time of the first creation,[2] the self-luminous great Viṣṇu constituting the universe, presided over a differentiation in the *guṇas*, and created the three forms of the deities.

4-5. Formerly, the Lord created god Brahmā from the right part of his Person, for the purpose of creation (of the worlds), O sage; from the middle, he created Īśāna (the Master) called Rudra, who causes the dissolution of the universe. For the sake of protecting this universe, he created the immutable Viṣṇu from his left side. Some designate that imperishable Primordial Lord by the epithet Śiva, some by the name Viṣṇu (the Eternal Truth), while some call him Brahmā.

6. Viṣṇu's Supreme Śakti[3] (Energy) stimulating the process of the universe is both positive and negative (existent and non-existent) in nature, and is described 'Vidyā-avidyā' (Spiritual Knowledge and Ignorance or Nescience).

7. When the universe appears as distinct and separate from Great Viṣṇu, that is the accomplishment (effect) of Nescience which is the cause of misery.

8. O Nārada, when the conditioning factors such as the knower, the knowable etc. fuse together, and cease to exist,

the knowledge or comprehension of the oneness of everything (in the universe) i.e. the existence of only one entity, viz., Brahman, is called Vidyā (spiritual lore).

9. Thus the Māyā of the great Viṣṇu, if seen as distinct and separate from him, bestows (i.e. involves one in) the worldly existence, but if realized with the consciousness of non-difference from him, it brings about the destruction of the Saṁsāra (or metempsychosis).

10. The entire universe of the mobile and immobile beings, has been originated from Viṣṇu's (illusive) potency. All these things whether they move or not are different from it.

11. Just as, by means of the conditioning factors (such as a pot, a room) the ether differs (as the ether conditioned by the pot, etc.), so also the entire universe appears different through the conditioning factor of *avidyā* (Nescience).

12. O Sage, even as Lord Hari pervades the entire universe so also does his (potency), just as the burning capacity of a (heated, fiery) coal manifests itself by pervading its substratum.

13. Some call this potency (*Śakti*), Umā,[4] others call it Lakṣmī, still others call it Bhāratī, Girijā and Ambikā.

14-15. The great sages designate her as Durgā, Bhadrakālī, Caṇḍī, Māheśvarī, Kaumārī, Vaiṣṇavī, Vārāhī, Aindrī, Śāmbhavī, Brāhmī, Vidyā (spiritual knowledge), Avidyā (Nescience), Māyā (The illusive potency of the Lord) and *Parā Prakṛti* (The Supreme Primordial Nature).

16. *Śeṣaśakti* is Viṣṇu's transcendental power, the cause of creation, etc. of the universe. It pervades the universe in its 'manifest-cum-unmanifest form', and abides therein.

17. One of these is the cause of creation, maintenance and dissolution, viz., *Prakṛti* (The Primordial Nature), *Puruṣa, Kāla* (Time), *Vidhi* (abidance of the opportune time or fate) and *sthiti* (steadiness or continuance in one state).

18. All this (universe) has been created by the deity assuming the form of Brahmā, but it is (authoritatively) stated that the Supreme Deity transcends him and is eternal.

19-22. The God who protects is called the Eternal Deity. The Lord who protects is the *Puruṣa*, greater than and beyond the worlds. What is greater than and beyond him is the highest imperishable region. (He is called) *akṣara* (the imperishable), *Nirguṇa* (devoid of attributes), *Śuddha* (pure), *Paripūrṇa* (perfect, complete) and *Sanātana* (eternal). The greatest being is called *Kālarūpa*. He is greater than the greatest, worthy of being meditated upon by *yogins*. He is the greatest *ātman*, the greatest bliss, devoid of all conditioning factors. He can be realised only through perfect knowledge. The greatest Being has Existence, Knowledge and Bliss for his physical bodies.

23. Although he is the greatest and the purest, He is accompanied by the Ego, and is then called *dehin* (the embodied soul) by persons of confused mind. Alas, the deception of Ignorance !

24. That greatest and purest Lord, on being differentiated through Sattva etc., assumes the forms of three Deities, and causes Creation, Sustenance and Dissolution.

25. The deity who is the creator of the universe is Brahmā. The deity from whose umbilical lotus Brahmā came out is the *ātman*, in the form of Bliss. O sage, none except him is so.

26. He is the immanent Soul. He pervades the universe. He is the Cosmic witness. He is unsullied, The great Īśvara abides both as different and non-different.

27. His *śakti* is the great *māyā*, the trustworthy upholder of the universe. In view of its being the material cause of the universe, it is called *prakṛti* by scholars.

28. Of Viṣṇu who was exerting for creation of the the worlds, at the time of the primordial creation, there evolved three-fold forms, viz. *Prakṛti* (primordial matter), *Puruṣa* and *Kāla* (Time-spirit).[5]

29. What men of purified souls perceive as the pure highest, resplendent asylum called Brahman, is the supreme region of Viṣṇu.

30. The pure, imperishable, infinite Maheśvara in this way assumed the form of Kāla (Time spirit), and with a form constituted of and affording support to *guṇas* (modifications of Prakṛti e.g. *sattva* etc.) the omnipresent Lord became the primary creator of the world.

31. When *prakṛti* became agitated[6] through the Lord of the world called Puruṣa, the principle of *Mahat* became manifested. Therefrom evolved the *Buddhi* (Intellect) from which originated the *Ahaṁkāra* (Cosmic Ego).

32. From the Cosmic Ego were evolved the subtle primary elements called the *tanmātras* and the subtle sense organs. All the gross elements were evolved out of the *tanmātras* for the creation of the universe.

33. Of the elements, viz., the ether, air, fire, water and the earth the former becomes the cause of the latter one, in the due order, O Nārada, the son of the lotus-born god Brahmā.

34. Thereafter, Lord Brahmā, the creator of the universe, (at first) created the *tāmasa* beings[7], viz., the sub-human beings such as creatures, beasts, birds, deer, etc.

35. Considering that the *Deva-sarga* (the creation of celestials) was non-productive and fruitless, god Brahmā the eternal lotus-born deity, conceived of and created the *Mānuṣa-sarga* (the creation of human beings).

36. Thereafter, he created Dakṣa and other sons who were exclusively devoted to the task of creation. All this entire universe including gods, demons and human beings, is occupied through these sons.

37. The following seven regions[8] are stationed above : (above the earth) *Bhūḥ, Bhuvaḥ, Svaḥ, Mahaḥ, Jana, Tapas* and *Satya* (each one is above the other).

38-39. There are seven nether worlds,[9] each below the other, viz., Atala, Vitala, Sutala, Talātala, Mahātala, Rasātala and Pātāla. He created the guardians of the worlds also, for all these regions.

40. He duly created the principal (seven) mountains and rivers in each of these worlds, and assigned specific means of livelihood befitting the residence of the respective worlds.

41. The mountain Meru, the resort of all gods, is located at the centre of the surface of the earth. The Lokāloka mountains[10] form the farthest end (limit) of the earth. In between them are the seven seas.

42. O, prominent Brāhmaṇas ! There are seven continents[11] and each continent has its own (chain of) principal mountains, and well-known rivers flowing therein, and the people thereof resemble the immortals i.e. gods.

43. The names of the continents are : *Jambū, Plakṣa, Śālmala, Kuśa, Krauñca, Śāka,* and *Puṣkara.* All of them are regions (traversed by) gods.

44. These seven continents are surrounded by seven

oceans,[12] each having (for its liquid content) salt water, sugarcane juice, wine, ghee, curds, milk and sweet water.

45. These continents and oceans should be understood (to have dimensions) in this manner : the latter one is double the former one in extent, and the same with the Lokāloka mountains.

46. The continent which is to the north of the salt sea, and to the south of the mountain Himālaya should be known as *Bhārata Varṣa* — the Indian continent. This continent confers the fruit of all actions.

47. O Nārada ! People perform three types of holy acts here, the fruit thereof is enjoyed in the following order : enjoyment of desired pleasures, land and affluence.

48. If any act whether auspicious or inauspicious is performed in Bhārata, the fruit thereof, being of a perishable nature, is enjoyed by the creatures elsewhere (in the other worlds).

49-51. Even today the celestials desire to secure birth in the *Bhārata-varṣa.* They think, "Great, auspicious, pure and everlasting merit has been accumulated by us. When shall we get the opportunity of being born in the *Bhārata varṣa,* where we shall attain to the supreme region (i.e. liberation) thanks to the great merits. Through charitable gifts or performance of different kinds of sacrifices or various types of penances, we shall attain to Lord Hari, the Ruler of the Universe, of eternal bliss and free from ailments."

52. O Nārada ! There is no one else in all the three worlds comparable in merits to that person who, after being born in Bhārata, is devoted to the worship of Viṣṇu.

53. A person habitually glorifying Lord Hari or a person beloved of his devotees or one who is eager to render service to the great persons, is worthy of being bowed down by the heaven-born gods.

54. A person delighting in the worship of Lord Hari or his devotees or a person regularly partaking of the leavings of the food of the devotees of Hari, attains to the highest region of Viṣṇu.

55. He who constantly utters the names of Viṣṇu, such as Nārāyaṇa, Kṛṣṇa, and Vāsudeva, and who is quiescent and devoted to non-violence, etc., is also worthy of being saluted by the foremost ones of gods.

56. It is traditionally remembered (i.e. laid down in *Smṛtis*) that he who constantly remembers (and mutters the divine names) *Śiva*, *Nīlakaṇṭha* and *Śaṅkara*[13] and is always engaged in doing good to all living beings, deserves to be worshipped by the celestials.

57. One devoted to his preceptors, a person meditating on Śiva, a man engaged in performing the duties prescribed for his own stage of life, one devoid of jealousy and one who is pure, is worthy of being adored by leaders of gods.

58. One who is a benefactor of Brāhmaṇas, one who cherishes faith (in the duties prescribed for) *varṇas* (classes in society and their duties), one who is ever devotedly engaged in propounding the Vedas, should be regarded as one who sanctifies all persons who sit in the same row to dine with him.[14]

59. A person who looks upon the pair of the Lords of gods consisting of Nārāyaṇa and Śiva equally without any discrimination, should always be saluted by god Brahmā. What need be said of persons like us ? (We must definitely worship him).

60. A person who has established perfect control over his senses and organs, is celibate, refrains from slandering others and invariably abstains from having any possession (or acceptance of monetary gifts), is, O Nārada, worthy of being worshipped even by gods.

61. One who is averse to such censurable acts as stealing, is full of gratefulness, is a man of purity and truthful speech and takes delight in rendering help to others, deserves to be worshipped by gods and demons.

62. He whose mind and intellect are inclined to listen to the exposition of the *Vedas* and the *Purāṇas*, and is keen in associating with the righteous persons, deserves respect and salutations from excellent ones amongst the gods.

63. Association with such persons be established by us — with persons who perform such and other sacred rites with perfect faith, in this continent of Bhārata.

64. If anyone, despite being a Brāhmaṇa, does not begin any one of these sacred or holy activities, he is a man of wicked actions, dullard in mind, and none else is more insensible than he.

65. Even after being born in Bhārata, a person who is

totally averse to the performance of righteous acts, is like a person who prefers a pot of poison spurning aside the jar of nectar.

66. O sage, a person who does not sanctify himself by performing religious rites prescribed in the *Vedas* and the *Smṛtis* is the leader of sinners, confounder of his own self.

67. O prominent sage ! After attaining birth in the land of holy rites (i.e. Bhārata), if one does not abide by the path of righteousness (*dharma*), he is decried as the meanest of all, by knowers of the *Vedas*.

68. He who eschews auspicious rites and acts and performs evil deeds is (like a person who) abandons (the milk of) the wish-yielding cow (*Kāmadhenu*) and seeks the milk-like exudation from the sun plant (*arka*).

69. O leader of Brāhmaṇas ! In this way even the inhabitants of heaven like god Brahmā and others who are afraid of the termination of their period of enjoyment of pleasures, praise the land of Bhārata.

70. Hence, the excellent subcontinent of Bhārata should be regarded as exceedingly meritorious. It is accessible with great difficulty even to gods. It bestows the fruits of all holy rites and actions.

71. In the three worlds, there is no one comparable to that person who diligently attempts to perform good and righteous acts in this holy land.[15]

72. A man who is born in this land and who attempts to destroy and exhaust the balance of his actions in previous birth, is Lord Hari himself in the guise of a man. There is no doubt about this.

73. One who is desirous of attaining the highest worldly benefits or fruits, should vigilantly perform righteous and holy acts. If an act is performed, after dedicating with devotion the fruit thereof unto Lord Hari, that fruit is said to be ever lasting.[16]

74. If one is devoid of any desire for the fruits of actions, one shall not cause any such acts to be done. He should dedicate a pious and religious act (to Lord Hari) by saying, "May Lord Hari be hereby pleased with me".

75. All the worlds upto and including the region of god Brahmā are the bestowers of rebirth. But a person who has

no desire for the fruit even of meritorious acts, attains to the highest region namely *Mokṣa* — Liberation from *saṁsāra*.

76. It is just for the propitiation of the Lord of the Universe, that one should perform sacred rites and actions prescribed in the Vedas as per his stage in life (*āśrama*). One who is desirous of renouncing all *karmas* altogether including even those prescribed for his *āśrama* (stage of life), attains to the Eternal Region.

77. Irrespective of one's desire for obtaining the fruit thereof, one should perform the holy rites in accordance with the injunctions laid down in the *śāstras* (for performance of sacred acts). One who is fallen from the conduct of life (performance of duties) befitting the stage of his life, is called "a fallen fellow" by wise persons.

78. A Brāhmaṇa devoted to righteous conduct shines forth with Brahmanical splendour. O Nārada ! Lord Viṣṇu also is propitious to him who is endowed with devotion.

79. If, after being born in the continent of Bhārata a person does not redeem himself, he is tortured in the terrible hell as long as the moon, the sun and the stars shine.

80. Real *Dharma* has Vāsudeva as the highest object. Penance is to be solely devoted to Vāsudeva. Perfect knowledge refers to Lord Vāsudeva and Lord Vāsudeva is the ultimate goal.

81. The entire Universe including the mobile and the immobile beings, from god Brahmā down to a clump of grass, is identical with Lord Vāsudeva. There is nothing else other than he.

82. He alone is god Brahmā, the Creator of the Universe as well as god Rudra, the destroyer of *Tripuras* (Three Cities). He alone has assumed the forms of gods, demons, and sacrifice. He alone constitutes this *Brahmāṇḍa* (Cosmic Egg). There is nothing else that is separate and distinct from him.

83. There is nothing else greater than he. There is nothing more minute or more immense than he.[17] All this wonderful Universe is pervaded by him. One should bow down to that Lord of gods, worthy of being praised.

CHAPTER THREE

The Descriptions of the sphere of the earth and of Bhārata

1. The description of the creation of the universe is the 1st characteristic of all Purāṇas. The famous verse enumerating 5 characteristics of Purāṇas :

Sargaśca prati-sargaśca vaṁśo manvantarāṇi ca /
Vaṁśānucaritaṁ ceti purāṇam pañca-lakṣaṇam //

is found with slight modifications in *V.P.*3.6.25, *A.P.*1.14, *BS.P.* (*Bhaviṣya Purāṇa*) 2.5, *M.P.*64, *Bd.P.-Prakriyā* 1.38 etc. Naturally after eulogizing god Viṣṇu, (*NP.* is a Vaiṣṇava Purāṇa), the *NP.* opens with the 1st topic, viz. creation of the universe, although the chapter is designated by the author as 'The description of the earth and that of Bhārata'.

2. Though NP. as a Vaiṣṇava Purāṇa, treats Viṣṇu, as the Supreme Brahman, the theory of the evolution of the universe is strongly influenced by the Sāṅkhya theory of evolution. It is, of course, the Theistic Sāṅkhya and not the Agnostic. In the Primary Creation, the credit of the differentiations of three *guṇas*, the modes of Prakṛti, into *sattva*, *rajas* and *tamas*, is given to the All-Pervading Viṣṇu who created the functionaries or Agents of the Creation, sustenance and destruction of the Universe, viz. Brahmā, Viṣṇu and Rudra from himself. Vide vv.4 & 5 below.

3. The *Vaiṣṇavī Śakti* (the Supreme potency of Lord Viṣṇu) is the real force that stimulates the process (creation, etc.) of the universe. It is noteworthy that the Purāṇa author regards *Vidyā* (Spiritual Knowledge) and *Avidyā* (Nescience) as both sides of the same coin as it were. This potency of the Lord is called by various names such as Umā, Lakṣmī, etc. vide vv. 13-15 below. And also of *BVP-Kṛṣṇa-Janma-Khaṇḍa* 118.35 where Śakti (Pārvatī) tells the Śaiva pantheon : 'I am Mahālakṣmī in Vaikuṇṭha, Rādhā in Goloka, Śivā in the region of Śiva, and Sarasvatī in the abode of god Brahmā.'

4. Although the *purāṇa*-writer appears to give synonyms of *Vaiṣṇavī śakti*, he is actually describing or summarizing the various aspects of this potency. Thus Māyā emphasizes the illusive power, *Vidyā*, the Spiritual Knowledge, *Avidyā*, Nescience, *Parā Prakṛti*, the Supreme Primordial nature, and the *Śaktis* of various gods like Brāhmī, Aindrī, etc. are given to emphasize that whatever feats these gods achieve are due to the motive force of Viṣṇu.

5. *Kālaḥ svabhāvo niyatir yadṛcchā, etc.—SV.Up.*1.2

N.P. broadly follows the concept of Time, as delineated in the *Bh.P.* e.g. 3.10.11 ff, 3.26.18ff. etc. According to the *Bh.P.*, Time is the Supra-phenomenal Reality. It pre-exists creation. Its primary function is to disturb the equilibrium of the *guṇas* of *Prakṛti* and thus set in motion the process of creation. It is a complex concept and appears to be a mixture of three aspects—God, the Power of God and the Time sequence. Time as a power of motivation does not simply stop with disturbing the equilibrium of the tri-partite matter (*guṇa-mayī ātma-māyā*), but pursues the creative process at every stage. If God is the agent-cause of creation, Time is the efficient cause. Creation takes place through the force or operation of Time. It is classified as : (i) *Prākṛta* (material) (ii) *Vaikṛta* (elemental) and (iii) *Prākṛta-Vaikṛta* (mixed, material-cum-elemental). The Bh.P. states that the following 10 types of creations are brought about by the motive-force of *Kāla* :

I. *Prākṛta* : (i) *mahat,* (ii) *ahaṁkāra* (ego), (iii) *tanmātras* (subtle sense-organs), (iv) External sense-organs, (v) presiding deities of senses and the mind, (vi) *avidyā* (with its five 'knots').

II. *Vaikṛta* : (i) vegetations (ii) animals (iii) human beings.

III. *Prākṛta-Vaikṛta* : (i) Divinely human souls, e.g. Sanatkumāra, etc. It is called *Kaumāra sarga.*

V.P. 5.1-25, *MK* P. 47 and other *Purāṇas* enumerate 9 (nine) types of creations as follows :

I. *Prākṛta*: (i) *Brāhma* vide *mahat* of the Bh.P. (ii) *bhūta* vide *tantmātras* of the Bh.P. (iii) *Vaikārika* corresponds to (iv) & (v) of *Prākṛta* creation of the Bh.P.

II. *Vaikṛta* : (i) *mukhya* or *Tāmasa* creation of immobiles and immovables :

mukhyā vai sthāvarāḥ smṛtāḥ /—V.P.1.5.21

(ii) *tiryak*—(birds and beasts) (iii) *deva* (celestial beings) (iv) *mānuṣa* (human beings) (v) *anugraha*—(both *Sāttvika* and *Tāmasa*) vide VP. 1.5.24.

About this II-v *MK.P.* 47.28 and *Vāyu P.* 6.57 state :

Pañcamo'nugrahasargaś caturdhā sa vyavasthitaḥ /
viparyayeṇa śaktyā ca tuṣṭyā siddhyā tathaiva ca //

Bh.P. & other *purāṇas* agree about the 3rd type of creation.

6. This is the *Prākṛta* creation.

7. This is the *Vaikṛta* creation, *vide* 65 above.

8. These seven *lokas* represent the different parts of the upper half of the Cosmic Man's (*Virāja-Puruṣa's* body. Vedic cosmogony as found in the *Puruṣa* (RV.X.90), *Nāsadīya* (RV X. 129) and *Hiraṇyagarbha* (RV.X.121) *sūktas* presuppose cosmic water, Viṣṇu, the primordial creator and three worlds : *Pṛthvī*, *Antarikṣa* and *Dyau*—the earth, intermediate space and the sky. *Bh.P.* adopted these three worlds as *bhū*, *bhuva* and *Svar* respectively. But the still upper regions *mahar*, *jana*, *tapas* and *satya* is a later—*purāṇic*—contribution. Even *Bh.P.* has vague idea about these four upper regions. They are separated from the lower three worlds by a boundary mountain *Lokālokācala* which shuts out the light of the sun and other luminaries to these higher four worlds.

These seven *lokas* are also regarded as the 'planes' of existence, the lowest being over terrestrial globe (*bhū*) and the highest, *satya*—the region of god Brahmā.—Bh.P.5.22 *V.P.* 2.7, *Vāyu* 50.

9. These represent the lower part of the body of the Cosmic Man. These regions are below our earth and do not receive the light of the Sun (*Bh.P.* 5.24.11). In *Atala* lives Bala, the son of Maya. *Vitala* is the region of god Śiva with His divine Consort Bhavānī. In *Sutala* reigns Bali with Lord Viṣṇu as his door-keeper. *Mahātala* is the region of serpents and Rasātala, that of Daityas, Dānavas and Paṇis. *Talātala* is the residence of Maya, under the protection of god Śiva. The last of the nether-world is *Pātāla,* the kingdom of Vāsuki, the serpent king. All these regions are held together by *Saṅkarṣaṇa* (The principle of gravitation (*Bh.P.*5.ch.24 & 5.25.1). To regard Mexico as Pātāla and identify the *Mayas* thereof with demon Maya of Purāṇas is only a

clever theory of Chamanlal in *Hindu America* though it must be conceded that he made out a good case for it. *Bh.P.*5.24, *VP.* 2.7, *Vāyu* 50.1-48.

10. *Lokāloka mountain* :

This mountain is the dividing range between *Loka* i.e. regions illuminated by the Sun and other heavenly bodies and *Aloka*—those regions like *mahar, jana, tapas* and *satya* which do not receive such light. It is beyond the 'sea of sweet water' and encircles it. All the seven great continents and seven oceans etc. lie between Mount Meru and Lokāloka mountain—the distance between them being twelve and half crores of *yojanas*. The tract beyond the ocean of 'fresh water' upto Lokāloka mountain is 'a land of gold shining like a sheet of mirror. Nothing that goes or is dropped there ever returns'. God Brahmā has posted four big elephants, viz. *Ṛṣabha, Puṣkara, Vāmana* and *Aparājita* in four cardinal points beyond that mountain, for retaining the stability of the world—*Bh.P.*5.20.34-39.

11. *Seven Continents* :

The dominant cosmographical conception of the *Purāṇas* is that of the earth consisting of seven concentric island-continents (*saptadvīpā Vasundharā*). Each continent has its own chain of principal mountains, river-systems. The names of these continents, as enumerated in the next (43rd) verse, are : *Jambū, Plakṣa, Śālmala, Kuśa, Krauñca, Śāka* and *Puṣkara*. This order of *dvīpas* is found also in *VP.*2.4, *Bh.P.*5.20 but *M.P.* 121, 122, *AP.* 108.1-3 differs, though all begin with *Jambūdvīpa*. The following is briefly the Purāṇic conception of these *dvīpas* :

(1) *Jambū dvīpa* with mount Meru or Sumeru at the centre and surrounded by the ocean of *Lavaṇa* (salt water). It is identified with India and the land around it as *Bhārata varṣa*—a prominent part thereof is 'to the north of the salt sea and south of the Himālayas' (*NP.* 1.3.46 below) and the glorification of this holy land from vv.47-72 below leaves no doubt that India is the land so praised.

(2) *Plakṣa*—Surrounding the *Lavaṇa* ocean and surrounded by the ocean of *Ikṣu* (sugarcane juice).

(3) *Śālmali*—Surrounding the *Ikṣu* ocean and surrounded by the ocean of *Surā* (wine); probably *Chaldea—chal-dia*<*śālmali dvīpa* : Ancient region SW Asia on the Euphrates and Persian Gulf (*Webster—College Dict. P.* 1106), if the derivation recorded by N.L. De in *GDAM I*, p.175 be correct. But the rivers *Nirvṛtti* and *Vitṛṣṇā* mentioned by him in *Brahmāṇḍa P.* Ch.53 are not traced in Jagdish Shastri's new edition (Motilal Banarsidass, Delhi) either at ch.19 describing *Plakṣadvīpa* or ch. 53 as mentioned by De at the corresponding ch. therein.)

(4) *Kuśa*—Surrounding the *Surā* ocean and surrounded by *Sarpis* (Ghee) ocean. *Purāṇas* state that the source of the Nile is in a lake in the *Kuśa dvīpa*. It is, of course, a region in Africa. Ancient Persian inscriptions mention a country called 'Kusha' and its people 'Kushiya' "There is no doubt that Kusha was situated in North East Africa beyond Egypt" D. C. Sircar—*GAMI* P. 25. Probably it is Ethiopia.

(5) *Krauñca*—Surrounding *sarpis* ocean and surrounded by the ocean of *Dadhi* (curds).

(6) *Śāka*—Surrounding the Dadhi ocean and surrounded by the ocean

of Milk. It is obviously the land of Śakas or Scythians of the Greeks. Dr. Ray Choudhary identifies it with Seistan (<Śākasthāna) in Eastern Iran, the land of the Māgi and of the Mihira cult and its inhabitants. The *Maga-dvijas* worshipped *Sūrya-rūpadharo Hariḥ*. There had been three settlements of Śakas—modern Mesopotemia, Helmund in Eastern part of Iran and Seistan. D.C. Sircar weighs the evidence and states, "Śaka-dvīpa in the original Purāṇic conception...is the Śaka settlement in the Oxus and Jaxartes valleys in Central Asia" (*GAMI*. P. 25).

(7) *Puṣkara*—Surrounded by *Surā sāgara* 'A portion of Central Asia commencing from the north of the Oxus including Western Tartary. Perhaps it has preserved its name in Bhushkara or Bokhara'—N.L. De *GADMI*, p. 163.

It will be seen that though the idea of concentric islands is poetic, there is some geographical reality about some lands in these Purāṇas. This conception of *sapta-dvīpā vasumatī* is as old as Patañjali (187-151 B.C.) and has strongly influenced Jain works like *Tiloya pannatti* : *GAMI*, pp. 22-24.

12. Seven Seas surrounding these island continents are traditionally mentioned as in v.44-B.

laveṇekṣu-surā-sarpir-dadhi-kṣīra-jalaiḥ samam /

i.e. seas consisting of (1) Salt water, (2) Sugar-cane juice (3) wine, (4) ghee, (5) curds, (6) milk and (7) sweet water. N.L. De locates them as follows :

(1) *Lavaṇa* (salt water) : The Indian Ocean surrounding *Jambū dvīpa* or India.

(2) *Ikṣu*—(Sugar cane juice). *Ikṣu* is another name for the Oxus (*V.P.* 2.4.66 mentions this as a river). De explains, "Here the river is taken as a sea."

(3) *Surā* (wine)—Corruption of the sea of Sarain, another name for the Caspian sea and it formed the Southern or south-eastern boundary of *Kuśa dvīpa*.

(4) *Sarpis* or *Ghṛta* (Clarified butter)—It is a corruption of the Erythraen sea or the Persian Gulf and formed the boundary of Śālmali-dvīpa or *Chaldia* i.e. Assyria.

(5) *Dadhi*—(curds) : The sea of Aral, *Dadhi* is Sanskritisation of *Dahi* (*Dahae*) the name of a Scythic tribe which lived in the upper Jaxartes and evidently on the shores of this lake, it formed the boundary of *Krauñca dvīpa*.

(6) *Kṣīra* (Milk) : It is a corruption of Shirwan sea, as the Caspian sea was called, and it formed the northern boundary of *Śāka dvīpa*.

(7) *Jala i.e. Svādujala* (sweet water)—Perhaps a corruption of *Tchadun*, a river in Mongolia forming a boundary of or flowing through *Plakṣa dvīpa*—*GDAMI*, p. 179.

Rivers and seas were formerly designated by the same word. Hence some rivers came to be understood as 'seas' in Purāṇas. The extent of some seas like the Caspian and the Aral were different (much larger than at present) in ancient times. But the unanimous tradition in Purāṇas shows a race-memory and not a geographer's report of an expedition. The above is enough to show that geography in Purāṇas is not all imagination, but had some basis in reality.

13. Though NP. is a *purāṇa* of the Viṣṇu group, it does not show the bitterness of later Vaiṣṇavas against Śiva. On the contrary, it advocates the oneness of Śiva and Viṣṇu both being the forms of *Para-Brahman*. vv.4-5 above state

that the trinity—Brahmā, Viṣṇu and Rudra are the forms of Nārāyaṇa or Mahāviṣṇu. This is the breadth of outlook consistently shown by the *N.P.*

14. *Paṅkti-pāvanaḥ* : *Paṅkti* is a row of diners. The *Dharmaśāstra* prohibits sitting in the same *paṅkti* with undeserving persons. But some highly religious persons sanctify the row of diners by sitting with them in the same row for dining. The 'sanctifiers of rows of diners' are persons who know the 6 *aṅgas* of the *Veda*, who have studied the *Jyeṣṭha-sāman*, who have enkindled the *Nāciketa fire*, who know the three *madhu* verses, who have studied the text called *trisuparṇa*, who maintain 5 fires, have taken ceremonial bath after finishing Vedic studies (*snātaka*), know the *mantras* and *Brāhmaṇas* of their respective Veda, who have studied *Dharma-śāstra* and who are born of a woman married in the Brāhma form. *paṅkti-pāvanaḥ ṣaḍaṅga-vij jyeṣṭha — sāmikas tri-ṇāciketas tri-madhus tri-suparṇaḥ, pañcāgniḥ snātako mantra-brāhmaṇa-vid dharmajño brahma-deyānusantānaḥ* ||

—*Gautama dh.Sū XV*. 29.

In this *jyeṣṭha-sāmaka* is the reciter of *udu tyam* (RV.I.50.1) and 'citram' (R. I.115.1) which constitute the *sāman* of the *Talavakāras*. (Haradatta on *Gaut.* above).

The *nāciketa fire* is described in Tait.Br.III.11.7 & 8 and *Kaṭha Up.* I. 1.17-18.

Tri-madhu is the reciter of RV.I.91-6-8 each of which begins with the word *madhu*. It can, however, be claimed that this term refers to the knower of *madhu-vidyā* mentioned in *Śatapatha BR*.IV.1.5.18 and *Br.Up.* II.5.16. But this *vidyā* does not explain the word *tri* in *tri-madhu*. *trisuparṇa* are the *anuvākas* of *Tait.Ar.Q*.48-50 *brahmaetu mām, madhu etu mām* etc. in this side of the country, but Haradatta alternately suggests the 3 verses in RV. X.114. 4-6 (*ekaḥ Suparṇaḥ*, etc.)

The topic is discussed in *Baudhāyana Dh. Sū.* II.8.2, *Āpastamba Dh.Sū.* II.7.17 21-22, *Manu* III. 184-86, versified *Śaṅkha. Smṛti* 14.1-8 *MBh. Anuśāsana* 90.34, *Vāyu P.* chs. 79 & 83, and other Purāṇas which give long lists of such 'sanctifier Brāhmaṇas'. The list in NP.I.3.57-58 above is already covered in the above-mentioned works.

15. The glorification of Bhārata in the above verses is common to a number of Purāṇas e.g. *Bm.P.* 27.2, 70.21-24, 143.8-11, *VP.* 2.3.2, 22-26. The common verses in these *Purāṇas* suggest that they belong to some ancient common source

16. Verses 73-76 advocate *Niṣkāmakarma-yoga*, NP. insists that a person should perform all the religious rites etc. prescribed for his particular social class (*varṇa*) and stage of life (*āśrama*) in *śāstras*, without coveting for its fruit but should dedicate it to the Lord. *As BG* 9.27 says whatever one does should be dedicated to Me (the Lord).

yat karoṣi yad aśnāsi yaj juhoṣi dadāsi yat |
yat tapasyasi Kaunteya tat kuruṣva madarpaṇam ||

As Śaṅkara, the great *advaitin* happily put it in his famous hymn *parā pujā* (the supreme worship)

yad yat karma karomi tat tad akhilaṁ Śambho tavārādhanam |

'Whatever act I do, Lord Śiva, each and everything of it is thy worship.'

17. An echo of *upaniṣadic mantra*

aṇoraṇīyān mahato mahīyān etc. —*Kaṭha* 2.2—,2.20, *Śvet. Up.* 3.20 *mahānārāyāṇa* 8.3, *Kaivalya* 20.

CHAPTER FOUR

Anecdote of Mārkaṇḍeya[1]

Sanaka said:

1. All pious rites performed with religious faith confer blessings in accordance with one's cherished desires. Every thing is achieved through faith. It is through faith in him that Hari is propitiated.

2. Acts of devotion should be performed devoutly (and with reverential faith). All holy rites should be performed with devotion. O excellent Brāhmaṇa ! Holy rites lacking in faith never become fruitful.

3. Just as the light (of the sun, etc.) is the cause of the activities of creatures, so also, devotion is the ultimate cause of all *Siddhis*[2] (complete accomplishments of objects or acquisition of super-human powers).

4. Just as water is regarded to be the enlivening factor in all the world, similarly, devotion is laid down (i.e. regarded) as the life-inspiring force in all *Siddhis* (spiritual attainments).

5. Just as all creatures live by resorting to the earth (as their support), so also, one should accomplish all objects by taking recourse to devotion.

6. A person endowed with *Śraddhā* (earnest faith) attains the *Puruṣārtha* — the end of human life — called *Dharma* (righteousness); the possessor of *Śraddhā* secures wealth; the desire for enjoyment (*Kāma*) — the third objective of human life, is realized through faith, and a man of faith attains salvation (*Mokṣa*).

7. O Excellent Sage ! Lord Hari is not pleased with charitable gifts, austere penances or sacrifices with sumptuous monetary gifts, should these acts be devoid of devotion.

8. Charitable gifts of heaps of gold as huge as the mount Meru, and donated billions of times — if they be devoid of devotion — result only in wastage of wealth.

9. The penance performed without devotion is but the desiccation of the body. The offering of oblations to gods in sacrificial fire, if it be without devotion, is fruitless like the oblations consigned to ashes.

10. Whatever sacred rite, howsoever insignificant it may be, if performed with faith, certainly becomes the bestower of perpetual happiness.

11. O Brāhmaṇa ! A thousand horse-sacrifices or any other holy rite enjoined in the Vedas, (in fact) everything is fruitless, if it is performed without devotion.

12. Devotion to Hari is the highest blessing to men. It is remembered (in sacred texts) to be comparable to a *Kāma-Dhenu*[3] (Wish-yielding heavenly cow). Alas ! The pity of it is that, when it (such a wish-yielding cow) is available, ignorant fools gulp and quaff the poison of *saṁsāra* (worldly existence).

13. O Son of Aja (God Brahmā) ! The following constitute the cream and quint-essence of this terrestrial existence which is otherwise worthless :—association with the devotees of Lord Hari, devotion to him and forbearance.

14. O Brāhmaṇa ! Know that devotion, charitable gifts and other holy acts are futile in the case of people whose minds are defiled with jealousy, and that Lord Hari is still further away from them.

15. Hari is far off from them who are greatly distressed to see the affluence of others, those whose minds revel in hypocritical religious activities, and those engaged in wrong and futile actions.

16. Hari is still further away from those who falsely interpret the *Dharma* to those who inquire about the highest religious duties, and from those whose minds are not devoted to religious and virtuous acts.

17. *Dharma* (the path of righteousness) is laid down by the *Vedas*.[4] The *Vedas* are identical with the Supreme Deity Nārāyaṇa. Hence, Hari is far off from those who have no faith in the *Vedas*.

18. If the days in the life of a person simply come and go without his performance of righteous acts, such a man is like the bellows of a blacksmith which mechanically inhales and exhales the air, and is not a living being. (The man simply breathes but does not lead a real life).

19. O Son of god Brahmā ! The principal aims in human life or *Puruṣārthas,* viz. *Dharma,* (righteousness), *Artha*— (wealth), *Kāma* — (love) and *Mokṣa* (liberation) are realized only by men of faith and not otherwise.

20. He who, without infringing his prescribed code of conduct, is engrossed in devotion to Hari, goes to the abode of Lord Viṣṇu which is visualized only by the seers.

21. O leader of sages ! He who performs religious rites befitting the stage of his life as enjoined by the Vedas, and who is wholly absorbed in contemplating Hari, attains the highest region.

22. *Ācāra* (good and righteous conduct of life) is the source of *Dharma,*[5] of which Lord Viṣṇu, the Imperishable, is the Master. God Hari is always worshipped by those who observe the righteous conduct befitting their *āśrama* (stage of life).

23. A person fallen from the course of conduct prescribed for his stage of life, should be regarded as an apostate even though he might have mastered the *Vedas,* the *Upaniṣads* and the ancillary subjects of the *Vedas,* for he is excluded from holy rites (or duties laid down in the *śāstras*).

24. Although a person is solely devoted to Lord Hari or is wholly engaged in contemplating him, he is called an apostate or fallen from the religious path, if he swerves from the prescribed code of conduct laid down for his stage of life (*āśrama*).

25. O excellent Brāhmaṇa ! Neither the Veda nor devotion unto Hari or to the great god Śiva, sanctifies the confounded fellow who has fallen from his *ācāra* (the prescribed code of behaviour).

26. O Brāhmaṇa ! Pilgrimage to holy places, ablutions in sacred waters or performance of sacrifices of different types, cannot save one who has forsaken his *ācāra* (righteous conduct).

27. Heaven is attained through *ācāra*; happiness is derived through observing the code of righteous conduct; Liberation from *saṁsāra* is secured through *ācāra.* What is there which is not obtainable through *ācāra* ?

28. O excellent Sage ! Reverential devotion is laid down as the primary cause of all *ācāras, yogas* and even of devotedness to Hari.

29. Lord Viṣṇu bestows the desired objects and fruits only

when worshipped with devotion. Hence, adoration of God is glorified as the mother of all the worlds.

30. Just as all creatures come to life by resorting to their mother, so also all righteous persons live by taking recourse to pious devotion.

31. If a person endowed with the course of conduct befitting his *āśrama*, is also devoted to Lord Hari, O son of god Brahmā, there is no one equal to such a person in the three worlds.

32. Holy rites fructify through devotion. Hari is pleased with holy rites. Perfect knowledge dawns when he is pleased, and Liberation from *saṁsāra* is attained through perfect knowledge.

33. Piety is generated by contacts with the votaries of the God and such contacts are secured by men, thanks to the merit accumulated in the previous births.

34. Saintly people abiding by the rules of conduct to be observed by men according to their respective castes and stages in life, and ardently desirous of engaging in the devotion of God, and free from passions and other blemishes, are the preceptors of the world.

35. Association with saintly souls, the greatest achievement, cannot be secured by people who are not self-possessed, O Brāhmaṇa. If it be acquired at all, it should be known as being due to the merits earned in previous births.

36. Associations with the good take place in case of a person, when the sins accumulated earlier, have been completely annihilated; otherwise it does not come about.

37. During the day time, the Sun dispells the external darkness by means of the clusters of his rays, but saintly persons remove the internal darkness of ignorance at all times by means of the streams of light, in the form of wise sayings.

38. Few and rare are the persons who are eagerly desirous of being devoted to the Lord in this world. Perpetual peace accrues to him who comes in contact with such persons.

Nārada enquired :

39. What are the characteristics of the *Bhāgavatas* (devotees of the Lord) ? What holy acts do they perform ? What regions do they attain to ? Narrate to me everything (about these) precisely.

40. You are indeed the real devotee of the discus-bearing Lord of gods, the divine consort of goddess Lakṣmī. There is no one else better qualified and competent than you to recount this.

Sanaka said :

41. Listen to that esoteric secret which the Lord of the Universe confided to the intelligent Mārkaṇḍeya, as he (the Lord) woke up from his *yogic* slumber, O *Brāhamaṇa.*

42. That Supreme-most refulgent god Viṣṇu is the Eternal Lord of the Devas. He is the Creater of the Universe as well as the pervader of the same, and has assumed the forms of Śiva (destroyer of the Universe) as well as Brahmā (the creator of the Universe).

43-44. At the end of the *yugas*, he manifested himself in an immensely huge form as *Rudra* and swallowed up the whole Universe as one morsel. When the whole Universe became a vast sheet of cosmic water after the destruction of the mobile and immobile creation, the Lord, the only residual soul Hari, lies on the leaf of a banyan tree. The hairs over his body are embellished by innumerable lotus-born deities (Brahmās) and others.

45-46. The god sanctifies every one by means of the cool water of the *Gaṅgā* issuing out of his big toe. The Lord is subtler than the subtlest, yet he assumes an immense form and swallows the Universe.

46. Endowed with all Super-human potencies (*Śaktis*), he lay resting on the leaf of a banyan tree. At that spot stood the highly blessed devotee of Nārāyaṇa, the sage Mārkaṇḍeya who was observing all the sports of the great Lord.

The sages said :

47. O Sage ! Formerly, we heard that in that terrible period (of Universal deluge) when the mobile and immobile creation had already perished, it was Lord Hari alone who remained there.

48. When the whole Universe had become one single cosmic ocean and when all the mobile and immobile beings were annihilated, how is it that he (Mārkaṇḍeya) alone was spared by god Hari who had swallowed everything.

49. O Sūta ! Exceedingly great is our curiosity in this regard. Who will forsooth get lethargic and idle at the opportunity of imbibing the nectar of the glory of Lord Hari ?

Sūta replied :

50-51. There was a highly blessed sage well-known by the name Mṛkaṇḍu. He performed an austere penance at the important sacred place known as Śālagrāma,[6] the great holy centre. For the duration of ten thousand *Yugas*, he repeated the sacred mystic syllable *Om*, observing fast all the while. He exercised forbearance, control over his sense-organs, and practised truthfulness (in thought, word and deed).

52. Looking upon all living beings as his own *ātman* (self), he performed that great penance entertaining no desire for worldly pleasures, and was solicitous for the welfare of all creatures, and held his sense-organs under control.

53. Afraid of his penance, Indra and all other gods sought refuge in the highest god Nārāyaṇa who is free from all ailments.

54. After reaching the northern shore of the Milky Ocean, the residents of the celestial region eulogised Lord Viṣṇu, the god with a lotus in his navel, the Supreme Lord of all gods, and the preceptor of the universe.

The gods submitted :

55. O Nārāyaṇa, the imperishable, infinite Lord, the protector of those who seek asylum in you, do protect us who, being afraid of Mṛkaṇḍu's penance, have sought refuge in you.

56. Victory to the Supreme Lord of the chiefs of gods ! Victory to the wielder of the conch (*Pāñcajanya*), and the mace *Kaumodakī* ! Hail to you whose form is the Universe and who is the cause of the *Brahmāṇḍa.* (the cosmic age or the Universe).

57. Obeisance to you the Lord of gods. We bow to you the sanctifier of the worlds. Hail to you the Lord of the Universe and the witness of the Universe.

58. Obeisance to you who are comprehensible through meditation. Hail to you who are the object of contemplation. Obeisance to you whose form is contemplated and who is the witness of meditation.

59. Obeisance to you the slayer of the Demon Keśin and the destroyer of Madhu. Hail to you the great *ātman* (the

Supreme soul) who assume the form of the earth, etc. and whose form is sentience itself.

60. Hail to the eldest (eternal) God, the pure and attributeless one, yet whose nature is *guṇa*. Obeisance to you who are devoid of form yet who possess your own form and manifest yourself into many forms.

61. Obeisance to the Lord friendly to Brāhmaṇas. Hail to you, O Kṛṣṇa,[7] the protector and benefactor of cows and Brāhmaṇas. Hail to you Govinda, the benefactor of the Universe.

62. Bow to Hiraṇya-garbha.[8] Obeisance to the Lord who assumes the form of god Brahmā and others. Hail to you who manifest yourself in the form of the sun and other gods. Obeisance to you, the enjoyer of the oblations of food offered to gods and deceased ancestors (*havya* and *kavya*).

63. Obeisance to the Eternal Deity worthy of respect. Hail to you whose form constitutes perpetual bliss. Bow to you who destroy the distress of those who remember you. Obeisance to you again and again."

64. On hearing the eulogy sung by the *devas*, Lord Viṣṇu, the Divine Consort of goddess Lakṣmī, the wielder of the conch (*Pāñcajanya*), discus (*Sudarśana*) and the mace (*Kaumodakī*) manifested himself to them.

65-67. On seeing him, the multitude of gods made obeisance to him — the Lord whose eyes resembled the petals of a full blown lotus, whose lustre equalled the combined effulgence of a hundred million suns, whose person was bedecked all over with ornaments, whose chest was characterised by *Śrīvatsa* (a curl of golden hair on Viṣṇu's bosom), who was being eulogised by great sages and was surrounded by his prominent attendants (*Pārṣadas*). The brilliance of the *devas* was eclipsed by the majestic lustre of the Lord. With great joy, they bowed down to him laying themselves prostrate before him, touching the ground with eight parts of their bodies.[9]

68. The Lord who was propitiated, addressed *devas* in a voice deep and majestic like the rumbling of clouds. thus giving delight to Indra and other *devas* who bowed down to him.

The Lord said :

69. O gods ! I do understand your mental agony caused

to you by the penance of Mṛkaṇḍu. But that sage is the foremost one among the saintly people and will not trouble you.

70. O excellent gods ! Whether endowed with affluence or bedevilled by adversities, the good shall by no means cause any harm unto others even in dreams.

71. Himself being harassed continuously by enemies called the 'worldly pleasures,' how can the highly intelligent one be hostile towards others, instead of protecting himself.

72. How can the excellent one who is himself ever molested by three types of distresses (originating from the physical body, the external world and extra-mundane sources), be competent (or inclined) to trouble others ?

73. He who always troubles others mentally, verbally or physically, and who is always in the grip of passions, etc. is called a person of confounded mind.

74. The man who renders service to the world even at the risk of his life, and is devoid of rivalry or jealousy, is said to be an excellent man both here and hereafter.

75. A person troubled with fear or with suspicion is always miserable and a fearless or nonsuspicious person shall always be happy. Return to your abodes and rest assured that he will not play false to you.

76-77. I am the Protector of you all. Be happy and sport about as you please." After granting this boon to them, the Lord with the beauty and lustre of the *atasī* flowers (a blue flower) vanished there immediately even as the gods were simply gazing on. Delighted in their minds, all the multitudes of gods returned to the celestial world whence they had come.

78-79. Being pleased and propitiated in his mind, Hari revealed himself to Mṛkaṇḍu. Mṛkaṇḍu was surprised to see the formless Supreme Brahman, the self-luminous unsullied Acyuta resembling the *atasī* flowers in complexion and clad in yellow garments, holding in his hands divine weapons.

80. Opening his eyes from meditation, he (Mṛkaṇḍu) saw in front of him, Lord Hari of pleasing appearance, the quiescent creator of the world possessing and radiating lustre all around the world.

With his hair standing on their ends on his body, with tears of joy welling up in the eyes, Mṛkaṇḍu prostrated himself like a staff in front of the Eternal Lord of gods.

82. Washing the feet of the Lord with tears of delight and joining together his palms over his head, he began to eulogise.

Mṛkaṇḍu said :

83. Obeisance to the Supreme Lord who is the Paramātman, the great self. Hail to you who are greater than the greatest and transcendental (to everything else). Bow to you whose greatness is unfathomable and who redeem your devotees from enemies and are the most eminent one.

84. I worship the supreme Deity, the ruler of the Universe worthy of being praised — the Deity who is devoid of false notion such as name, caste,etc., and whose form is opposed to and unconnected with such defects as *śabda* (words) and who, though possessed of many forms, is unsullied by them.

85. I worship the Eternal Lord of all, the ancient Person knowable through the Upaniṣads (*Vedānta*), whose form is the universe itself (including god Brahmā and others), who is beyond comparison and who is merciful to his devotees.

86. I bow down to that great holy Deity who redeems his devotees from *saṁsāra*, and who reveals himself to those who are free from all blemishes, those completely absorbed in meditation, those free from desires and those who have no delusion.

87. I bow down to the merciful great Lord Viṣṇu, the destroyer of the distress and mental agony of those who remember him, the protector of those who seek refuge in him, worthy of being served by the universe and the asylum of the world."

88. Being thus praised by that great sage, god Viṣṇu, the wielder of conch (*Pāñcajanya*), discus (*Sudarśana*) and the mace (*Kaumodakī*) was highly pleased.

89. Embracing the sage with all his four long arms, the Lord said with great pleasure, "O Sage, a strict observer of religious vows ! Seek any boon.

90. O sinless sage ! I am delighted by your penance as well as this hymn of praise. Choose whatever boon you have cherished in your mind, O highly virtuous sage."

Mṛkaṇḍu said :

91. "O God of gods ! O Lord of the universe ! I am certainly satisfied and have all my objects achieved by your

manifestation to me, since it is remembered (in *śāstras*) that your vision is impossible to those who are devoid of merit.

92-93. I perceive you whom even god Brahmā and others cannot see. Even the *yogins* who have fulfilled their vows, are extremely righteous, are initiated (in sacrifices or sacred lores), are devoid of passions and jealousy, cannot perceive you. I now visualise you who are the highest resort. What other boon should I choose? O Janārdana, O Preceptor of the universe, I am perfectly satisfied with this vision only.

94. O Acyuta ! Even by mere remembrance of your name persons with heinous sins, attain to your highest region, what then after getting your audience and a view ?"

The glorious Lord said :

95. O Learned Brāhmaṇa ! What you spoke is true. I am really pleased with you. Never can my vision be fruitless.

96. Learned men always say, "God Viṣṇu treates his devotees as members of his family." I shall bear it out. My devotees would not utter what is untrue.

97. Hence, being propitiated by your penance, I shall become your son. He (my incarnation) will be endowed with all good qualities. He will be handsome and long-lived.

98. The family in which I incarnate, attains salvation. O excellent sage ! What is there that cannot be achieved in the three worlds, if I am pleased.

99. After addressing thus, the Lord of *devas* vanished then and there, even as the sage was watching. The sage Mṛkaṇḍu completed his penance.

CHAPTER FOUR

The Ancedote of Mārkaṇḍeya

1. The story of the immortal sage Mārkaṇḍeya and his vision of Viṣṇu as an infant lying on a banyan leaf on the cosmic waters of the great deluge that submerged the universe, is common to many *Purāṇas*, e.g. *Bh.P.* 12 chs. 8, 9, 10 *Mbh. Vana*—a whole sub-*parvan* chs. 182-231 devoted to Mārkaṇḍeya's dialogues with Yudhiṣṭhira. Out of them, chs 188-89 contain the story of the deluge. His conquest of death is described in *Bh.P.* 4.1.45, *Pd.P.—Sṛṣṭi-Khaṇḍa*, ch. 33 & *Narasiṁha P.* ch. 7.

2. *Siddhis—super human powers* also called *vibhūtis*; PYS (*Pātañjala Yoga Sūtra*) 3.45 enumerates the following 8 super-normal or mystic powers :

1. atomization (*aṇimā*),
2. levitation (*laghimā*)
3. *magnification* (*mahiman*)
4. *extension* (*Prāpti*). A yogi can touch the moon with his finger-tip.
5. efficacy—non-obstruction to desires (*Prākāmya*)
6. mastery of elements (*Vaśitva*)
7. sovereignty over the creation (*īśitva*)
8. capacity to determine (the course of) things (*sarva-kāmāvasāyitā*)

Vyāsa and Vācaspati Miśra elaborate the details of these Supernormal powers in *Yogabhāṣya* and *Tattva-vaiśāradī* coms. respectively.

The belief in the acquisition of such powers is common to Buddhists, Jainas and the followers of different *Tantras* and still survives in Indian masses.

3. *Kāmadhenu* :

A mythical wish-yielding cow. She was one of the jewels i.e. important finds that came out, when gods and demons churned the ocean, for obtaining nectar (*amṛta*). (*Bh.P.* 8.8.1) *Mbh.Ādi* 18.36 ff.) *Bh.P.* calls her *Havirdhānī* (probably from her function in sacrifices), while M*bh.* gives *Surabhi* as her name. She is regarded as Dakṣa's daughter who married Kaśyapa (*VP*.1.15), and gave birth to a cow called Nandinī which the sage Vasiṣṭha retained as his own (*Mbh.* 98.8-9). Jamadagni had a Kāmadhenu called *Havirdhānī* which Sahasrārjuna carried away per force to Māhiṣmatī. But the fact that Havirdhānī did not defend herself, and prevent the raid on Jamadagni's hermitage, as Nandinī did against Viśvāmitra (*Mbh-Ādi* 174.22-43 also *Śalya* 40.21-22) shows her powerlessness. In addition to Havirdhānī (which should be distinguished from Surabhi and Nandinī) there appear to be more Kāmadhenus in *purāṇas* (e.g. one at Varuṇa's sacrifice). Surabhi is regarded as the progenitor of all cows. She performed penance and was given permanent residence in *Goloka* (*Mbh.Anuśāsana* 83.29-39).

4. Cf. *Vedoktaḥ paramo dharmaḥ* / *Mbh. Anu.* 141.65. The sources of religion are : *Śruti*, *smṛti* and *śiṣṭācāra* (The *vedic* texts, the *smṛti* compilations and the code of conduct followed by *śiṣṭas* or leaders of the society). As *Baudhāyana Dh.Sū* : 1.1-4. states :

upadiṣṭo dharmaḥ prati-vedaṁ—smārto dvitīyaḥ /
tṛtīyaḥ śiṣṭāgamaḥ (शिष्टागमः) —a view endorsed by *Mbh. Vana.* 207.83, *śānti.* 354.6.

5. Cf. *ācāraḥ prathamo dharmaḥ*. In fact, the whole of *dharma-śāstra* revolves round the *ācāra* (code of conduct) of all *varṇas* (classes of societies) and *āśramas* (the stage of life of the individual). Hence, in ancient *smṛtis* like Manu and Yājñavalkya, we find sages requesting Manu and Yājñavalkya to impart instructions in the *ācāra-dharmas* (code of conduct) of *varṇas* & *āśramas*. For example *Yājñavalkyasmṛti* opens with the request :

varṇāśrametarāṇāṁ no brūhi dharmān aśeṣataḥ / 1.1

Cf. Manu 1.2

The whole discourse from vv.22-31 emphasizes the importance of *ācāra* (code of conduct), prescribed for the *varṇas* and *āśramas*—classes in society and stages of one's life.

6. *Śālagrāma* :

A place situated near the source of the Gaṇḍak. It is mentioned in the *Padma P.—Pātāla khaṇḍa* ch.78 and *Bh.P.* 5.7.8. (as Pulahāśrama) and in *BV.P.*2.13. The short course of Gaṇḍaka near Muktināth is called Śāligrāmī, as the bed abounds in black pebbles called *śāligrāma*.

7. The epithets Kṛṣṇa, Govinda are used for addressing God Viṣṇu as the Vedic god and the historical hero (Vāsudeva Kṛṣṇa) came to be fused long before the NP. and other *purāṇas* were written.

8. *Hiraṇya-garbha* :

Originally this epithet was used for god Brahmā who was born from the cosmic golden egg. But it is used to designate Viṣṇu as he was the father or procreator of that 'golden egg'—Hiraṇya-garbha—*sambhūti-kāraṇaṁ hiraṇmayam aṇḍaṁ yad-vīrya-sambhūtam, tadasya garbha iti Hiraṇyagarbhaḥ* /—Śaṅkara on *Viṣṇusahasranāma*, *verse* 57.

9. *aṣṭāṅgair avanīm gatā* :

The usual concept of a respectful obeisance consists of prostration of the following eight limbs of the body—two feet, two knees, two palms, chest and head, on the ground. But the real concept requires the laying down of the mind or intellect, speech and sight as well.

Jānubhyāṁ ca tathā padbhyām pāṇibhyām urasā dhiyā /
śirasā vacasā dṛṣṭyā praṇāmo'ṣṭāṅga īritaḥ //

quoted in *ASD*, p. 67

CHAPTER FIVE

The Description of Mārkaṇḍeya's Life[1]

Nārada said :

1. O Brāhmaṇa sage ! Be pleased to narrate to me how the glorious Lord became the son of Mṛkaṇḍu and what Hari did after being born in the family of Bhārgava.

2. It is heard mentioned in the *purāṇas* that Mārkaṇḍeya, the long-lived sage, perceived the *māyā* of Viṣṇu, at the time of Deluge (dissolution of the world).

Sanaka replied :

3. Listen, O Nārada. I shall narrate to you this ancient story about the sage Mārkaṇḍeya which is closely connected with devotion to Viṣṇu.

4. At the conclusion of his penance, the excellent sage Mṛkaṇḍu entered the householders' stage, and gladly performed the duties prescribed for householders. He was self-controlled, quiescent and contented.

5. His wife was pure, attentive and always devoted to her husband. She was chaste and true to her husband in thought, word and deed.

6. At the proper time, she conceived in her womb the child born of a ray of the majestic lustre of Hari. At the end of the tenth month, she gave birth to an exceedingly brilliant son.

7. On seeing the son endowed with all auspicious characteristics, that sage was extremely delighted. He caused all the prescribed post-natal auspicious rites[2] to be performed in accordance with the *śāstric* injunctions.

8-9. The boy grew up there like the moon in the bright half of the month, O prominent Brāhmaṇa. He invested the boy with the sacred thread, in his fifth year. With great joy, he imparted instructions to him in the *Vedic* lore and in scriptures on *dharma*. "O son ! The Brāhmaṇas should always be paid respects when seen. As per sacred precepts, the practice has been enjoined and observed.

10. After worshipping the sun with offerings of libation of water (with joining together of palms i.e. performing *Sandhyā-vandana*) thrice a day, *Vedic* rites should be performed with due attention to the study of the *Vedas*.

11. Hari should always be worshipped through observance of celibacy and performance of penance. All forbidden acts such as conversation with the wicked (or on improper topics) should be avoided.

12. One should always associate oneself with saintly persons engaged in devotion to Viṣṇu. One should never entertain hatred or hostility to any one and one should perceive activities conducive to the welfare of all.

13-15. O son ! Performance of sacrifices, Vedic studies and granting of charitable gifts should always be carried on by you." Ordered thus by his father, Mārkaṇḍeya, the prominent sage, abided by the path of righteousness, constantly contemplating on Hari. The highly fortunate (or the illustrious) sage was compassionate, a lover of *dharma* or piety. He was self-possessed and true of word. His splendour was like that of the Sun. He was self-controlled, quiescent, deeply learned and wise, and proficient in the knowledge of the true nature of *Brahman*.

16. He performed a great penance that gave delight to Lord Acyuta. The Lord of the universe was propitiated by the intelligent Mārkaṇḍeya.

17. Acyuta conferred on him the boon of being competent to compose a *purāṇa saṁhitā*[3] (known as the *Mārkaṇḍeya Purāṇa*)[3] Hence, the sage Mārkaṇḍeya is remembered as Nārāyaṇa.

18-20. He was long-lived. He was also a great devotee of the discus-bearing Lord of *devas* (Viṣṇu). O Brāhmaṇa, when the universe was converted into one vast sheet of Cosmic water, Janārdana did not absorb him in himself in order to show to him his prowess. The learned son of Mṛkaṇḍu, endowed with devotion to Viṣṇu, floated like a shattered dry leaf in that extremely terrible mass of water. As long as Hari lay there in his yogic slumber, Mārkaṇḍeya too remained there.

21-23.[4] I shall now describe to you the extent or the duration of that period. Listen to it, as I recount it : The time unit *kāṣṭhā* is made up of fifteen times winking of eyes (*nimeṣas*). O son of god Brahmā, thirty *kāṣṭhās* should be known as making one *kalā* (eight seconds). A *Kṣaṇa* (four minutes) should be known as made up of thirty *kalās*. Six *kṣaṇas* constitute a *ghaṭikā* (twenty-four minutes). Two *ghaṭikās* constitute one *muhūrta* (forty-eight minutes). Thirty *muhūrtas* constitute a day (of twenty-four hours). Thirty days or two fortnights make one month.

24. Two months constitute one *ṛtu* (a season). Three such *ṛtus* make one *ayana*. (time from one solstice to another). Two such *ayanas* make one year, which constitutes one complete day (day and night) of *devas*.

25. They say that the *Uttarāyaṇa* (northward transit of the sun) is the day of gods, and *Dakṣiṇāyana* (southward transit of the sun) is their night. A human month is said to be one day of the *pitṛs* (manes).

26. The day of the *pitṛs* is from one new moon day to another (lit. when the sun comes into contact with the moon). A thousand celestial years constitute the period of a *kalpa*, and twelve *yugas* constitute one *yuga* of gods.

27. Two thousand divine yugas make two *brāhma kalpas* and according to human calculations, seventy-one divine *yugas* constitute a *manvantara*.

28. O sage, fourteen such *manvantaras* make one day of god Brahmā. The extent of the night is declared to be the same as that of the day.

29-30. O leading Brāhmaṇa, at that time, all the three worlds perish. Listen to the extent of time according to human calculations. O sage, a thousand cycles of four *yugas* make one day of Brahmā. Similarly, the months and the years of god Brahmā should be known (calculated).

31. O Brāhmaṇas, according to his calculations the period of two *parārdhas* should be known as one day of Viṣṇu. The period of night is also said to be of the same extent.

32. In the middle of that terrible deluge of water, the son of Mṛkaṇḍu lay like a withered leaf for that period. He was sustained by the spiritual potency of god Viṣṇu. He stood near Hari meditating on the Supreme Soul.

33. When the proper time came, the Deity, waking up from *yogic* slumber, assumed the form of god Brahmā and created this universe, consisting of the mobile and immobile beings.

34. Noticing the recession of water and the creation of the universe, the son of Mṛkaṇḍu was surprised as well as was extremely delighted. He saluted the feet of Hari.

35. With palms joined in reverence over his head, the great sage Mārkaṇḍeya eulogised the Deity whose body iṣ constituted solely of perpetual bliss. He praised him in desired and desirable, appropriate words.

Mārkaṇḍeya said :

36. I bow unto Janārdana, the God with thousands of heads, Nārāyaṇa, free from ailments, Vāsudeva, who needs no other support, himself being the support of all.

37. I pay obeisance to Janārdana who is beyond all measures (immeasurable), who is un-aging and eternal, whose person consists of pure perpetual bliss, who cannot be specifically pointed out, and whose nature surpasses imagination.

38. I bow unto Janārdana who is imperishable, who is the Eternal Supreme Being, universal-eyed (Omnipresent and *Omniscient*) who is the source of the universe, who is quiescent and who constitutes all principles (enumerated by *Sāṅkhyas*).

39. I pay my deep respects to Janārdana, the ancient *Puruṣa,* the master of all super-human potencies, the sole receptacle for all perfect knowledge and whose form is greater than the greatest.

40. I bow to Janārdana who is the highest splendour, the greatest abode, whose region is the holiest and suprememost and who is both multiformed and single.

41. I bow unto Janārdana who is existence or entity, knowledge and bliss *incarnate*; whose region is higher than the highest; who is the most pre-eminent, eternal Deity.

42. I pay respects to Janārdana who is endowed with attributes as well as is transcendental to them; who is quiescent and beyond the deluding potency *Māyā* and yet is its (*Māyā's*) master; who is formless yet has many forms.

43. My obeisance to that Janārdana, the primordial Deity, the Ruler of the universe, who creates, preserves and annihilates it.

44. O great Lord ! Embodiment of Supreme bliss, who are compassionate to those who seek refuge. O Ocean of

mercy ! Be pleased to save me, O Lord, who are beyond the comprehension of the mind. My obeisance to you."

45. Lord Viṣṇu, the preceptor of the universe, the wielder of conch, discus and mace, addressed Mārkaṇḍeya with great pleasure, as the prominent Brāhmaṇa Mārkaṇḍeya was thus eulogising him.

The Lord said :

46. Those who are the devotees of the Lord in this world, those whose minds are devotedly directed towards the glorious Lord, are called the *Bhāgavatas* (devotees of the Supreme Lord). Undoubtedly, I am always pleased with them and I protect them.

47. O excellent Brāhmaṇa ! It is I alone who, assuming the forms of devotees, protect the world in that guise. concealing my direct personality.

Mārkaṇḍeya said :

48. What are the characteristics of real Bhāgavatas ? By performance of which holy rites are they born ? I am extremely eager to hear this.

The Lord said :

49. O Excellent sage, listen to the characteristics of the *Bhāgavatas*. It is impossible to recount in details their capacity and prowess; even in a hundred million years.

50. The excellent *Bhāgavatas* are those who are the benefactors of all living beings, are devoid of jealousy and covetousness, who are quiescent and who exercise self-control.

51. Those who do not trouble others mentally, verbally and physically and those who are disposed to renounce their possessions and property (or those who refrain from accepting gifts), are regarded as *Bhāgavatas*.

52. The devotees of Viṣṇu as well as those who are devoutly attached to listening to the stories of the pious and who are of *sāttvic* temperament — all these are excellent *Bhāgavatas*.

53. Those excellent men who serve their parents regarding them (respectable) like the sacred river *Gaṅgā* and god Śiva, the ruler of the universe,are excellent *Bhāgavatas*.

54. Those who are engaged in the worship of gods and

those who are helpmates or assistants in that worship, and those who appreciate the worship on seeing it, — all are excellent *Bhāgavatas*.

55. Those who are intent on serving the observers of religious vows and ascetics, and those who abstain from reviling others and entertaining contempt for them, are indeed excellent *Bhāgavatas*.

56. Those excellent men who speak words beneficial to others and those who appreciate the merits of others in the world are indeed (regarded) as *Bhāgavatas*.

57. Those excellent persons who perceive all living beings like their own *ātman* and those who are equally disposed towards enemies as well as friends, are indeed excellent *Bhāgavatas*.

58. Those who propound the sacred scriptures (*dharma-śāstras*) and those who are keen on making truthful statements and who render service to pious men, are indeed excellent *Bhāgavatas*.

59. Those who give exposition of the *purāṇas*, those who listen to them and those who are devotees of the narrators of the *purāṇas* are indeed excellent *Bhāgavatas*.

60. Those persons who constantly render service to cows and Brāhmaṇas, and those who are interested in the pilgrimage to holy places, are indeed excellent *Bhāgavatas*.

61. Those men who rejoice on seeing the prosperity of others, and those who are devoted to the repetitions of the name of Hari, are excellent *Bhāgavatas*.

62. Those who are interested in laying out parks and groves, those who maintain lakes in good repairs, and those who dig wells and tanks, are excellent *Bhāgavatas*.

63. Those who get big lakes and tanks constructed, those who build temples and those who are engaged (in repeating in undertone) the *Gāyatri mantra*[5] are excellent *Bhāgavatas*.

64. Those who feel overjoyed on hearing the names of Hari and appreciate the same and those who get their hair standing on the ends through joy, all over their body (at the mention of Hari's name), are indeed excellent *Bhāgavatas*.

65. Those men who bow down on seeing the grove of *Tulasi*[6] (basil) plants, and those who embellish their ears with Tulasī twigs are indeed excellent *Bhāgavatas*

66. Those men who are delighted on inhaling the

fragrance of the *Tulasī* plant, or the soil at its root, are indeed excellent *Bhāgavatas*.

67. Those who are engaged in conducting their lives according to their injunctions prescribed for their particular *āśrama* (stages in life), those who reverently receive and worship guests, and those who explain the meaning of the *vedas*, are indeed excellent *Bhāgavatas*.

68. Those to whom god Śiva is dear, those who are devoted to Śiva, and those who revel in worshipping the feet of Śiva, and those who wear the *tripuṇḍra* mark (three horizontal parallel lines of ashes) on their foreheads, are indeed prominent *Bhāgavatas*.

69. Those who repeat the names of Hari as well as of god Śiva, the Supreme *ātman*, and those who are bedecked with *Rudrākṣa*-beads[7] are indeed excellent *Bhāgavatas*.

70. Those who worship the great god Śiva by means of sacrifices, with liberal sacrificial fees to the priests, or adore Hari the same way with great devotion, are indeed excellent *Bhāgavatas*.

71. Those who expound the scriptures as known (to them to the best of their knowledge) to others and those who appreciate and assimilate only the good qualities everywhere, are indeed known as Bhāgavatas.

72. Those who regard god Śiva the great ruler of the world, and Viṣṇu the Supreme Soul, with equal attitude, are indeed spoken as *Bhāgavatas*.

73. Those who take delight in performing sacrificial rites in honour of Śiva and those who revel in the repetition of the *mantra* with five syllables (viz. *Om Namaḥ Śivāya*) and those who are engaged in contemplating god Śiva are indeed excellent Bhāgavatas.

74. Those who are engaged in serving waters to the thirsty, and those who are intent on catering the gifts of cooked food (to the hungry), and who observe the *ekādaśi* vow (consisting of complete fast and meditation on the eleventh day of each fortnight, as prescribed in the *Śāstras*) are indeed eminently good *Bhāgavatas*.

75. Those who take delight in gifting away cows and those who are interested in getting virgins married (at their own cost) and those who perform holy rites dedicating the fruits thereof unto me, are indeed excellent *Bhāgavatas*.

76. O Brāhmaṇa sage, some of the categories of *Bhāgavatas* have been mentioned by me here. It is impossible to recount them wholly even in hundreds and millions of years even by me.

77. Hence, O prominent Brāhmaṇa ! You also be well-behaved for all time to come, offering refuge to all beings, being a friend unto them, exercising self-control and ardently interested in *dharma*.

78. Until the end of this *yuga*, practice *dharma* in all respects, and be engaged in the meditation of my form (*mūrti*). You will thus attain to the highest *nirvāṇa*[8] (liberation).

79. After granting the boon thus to his devotee, the son of Mṛkaṇḍu, the Lord of the *devas*, the ocean of mercy, vanished then and there.

80. Mārkaṇḍeya, the extremely blessed sage, was always engrossed in devotion to Hari. He practised the great *dharma* and duly performed sacrifices.

81. He performed a great penance in the highly sacred place Śālagrāma. After wiping of all the hoarded *karmas* (actions and their consequences) by means of meditation, he attained the great *nirvāṇa*.

82. Hence, a person who adores Hari, the benefactor of all creatures, undoubtedly attains whatever is mentally desired by him.

Sanaka said :

83. O excellent Brāhmaṇa ! In this way the greatness of devotion unto the Lord, about which a query was made by you, has been completely recounted by me in details. What else do you wish to hear.

CHAPTER FIVE

The Description of Mārkaṇḍeya's Life

1. The present chapter gives only a glimpse of Mārkaṇḍeya's life, viz, the vision of the end of the world and of god Viṣṇu as an infant lying on the leaf of a banyan tree, floating on the cosmic ocean. The object of this chapter is to detail, to Nārada, the characteristics of a true devotee of Viṣṇu in reply to his question in *Supra* 4.39-40. Though Mārkaṇḍeya is called 'a long-lived sage' in this ch. (v.2), the *Bh.P.* tells us that he was destined to die in boyhood, but he propitiated god Śiva and secured the life of 14 *kalpas* from him. (*Bh.P.* 4.1.45). The *Mbh.* shows him to have close contacts with Pāṇḍavas. The name of his wife was Dhūmorṇā (*Mbh.Anu.* 146.4.).

2. *Jātakaṁ kārayāmāsa maṅgalaṁ vidhipūrvakam* /

The term *Jātaka* seems to be used in the sense of *jātakarma* as required by the qualifying adjectives *maṅgala* (auspicious) and *vidhi-pūrvaka* (according to *Śāstric* injunctions). It is a rite of hoary antiquity as it is mentioned in *Tait. Saṁhitā* II.2.5.3-4. It was a common rite supported in various *Gṛhya-sūtras* e.g. *Āpastamba* 15.1.7, *Āśvalāyana* I.15.1-4, *Khādira* II.2.32-34, *Pāraskara* I 16, *Hiraṇyakeśi* II.3.2 II.4-5 and others. They differ *inter se* in minor details, but the main idea is to ensure the longevity and prosperity of the child by invoking divine grace. Thus, according to *Āśvalāyana*, the father, while giving ghee and honey with gold rubbed in it (probably in a golden spoon), utters the *mantra* investing the child with Veda (wisdom) and longevity (of hundred years). He touches the child's shoulders muttering the *mantras* to make them hard and powerful. A secret name is to be given to the child (by the father) on the very day of the birth of the child.

The original form and procedure has changed over the centuries and is influenced by custom in different states of India. The 'naming ceremony' has assumed a great importance now-a-days, and other formal rites e.g. *homa*, *aṁsābhimarṣaṇa* (touching the child on the shoulder, etc.) have been practically relegated to the past.

3. This implies the *Markāṇḍeya Purāṇa*. It is in the form of a conversation between Jaimini, the disciple of Vyāsa, and Mārkaṇḍeya, in which Mārkaṇḍeya solves some of the problems about the *Mahābhārata*, raised by Jaimini. It is a small work of 137 chapters (about 9000 verses). According to European scholars, it is an ancient and important work. The life and teachings of Madālasā, *Durgā saptaśatī* are some of the specially important topics in it. It was translated into English by Pargiter in the Bibliotheca Indica series Calcutta, 1888-1905.

4. There appear to be some divergent views about the calculation of time. Thus, the *Bh.P.* 3.11.5-8 gives the following measures of time :

2 *paramāṇus* = 1 *aṇu*;
3 *aṇus* = 1 *trasareṇu*;
3 *trasareṇu* = 1 *truṭi*;

100 *trutis*	=	1 *vedha*;
3 *vedhas*	=	1 *lava*;
3 *lavas*	=	1 *nimiṣa*;
3 *nimiṣas*	=	1 *kṣaṇa*;
5 *kṣaṇas*	=	1 *kāṣṭhā*;
15 *kāṣṭhās*	=	1 *laghu*;
15 *laghus*	=	1 *nāḍikā* (or *ghaṭikā*); .
2 *naḍikās*	=	1 *muhūrta*
6 or 7 *nāḍikās*	=	1 *yāma* or *prahara*

The *NP*. gives the following measures :

15 *nimiṣas*	=	1 *kāṣṭhā*
30 *kāṣṭhās*	=	1 *kalā* (= 8 seconds)
30 *kalās*	=	1 *kṣaṇa* (= 4 minutes)
6 *kṣaṇas*	=	1 *ghaṭikā* (= 24 minutes)
2 *ghaṭikās*	=	1 *muhūrta* (= 48 minutes)
30 *muhūrtas*	=	1 *day* (24 hours)
15 days	=	1 *pakṣa*
2 *pakṣas*	=	1 month=1 day of *Pitṛs*
2 months	=	1 *ṛtu* (season)
3 *ṛtus*	=	1 *ayana*
2 *ayanas*	=	1 year=1 complete day of gods, (*uttarāyaṇa* being the day-time and *dakṣiṇāyana* the night of gods)
1000 years of gods	=	1 *kalpa*
12 human *yugas*	=	1 *yuga* of gods
2000 celestial *yugas*	=	2 *Brāhma kalpa*
71 divine *yugas*	=	1 *manvantara*
14 *manvantaras*	=	1 day of god Brahmā 1000 *caturyugis* (cycles of 4 *yugas*) of men (?)
2 parārdhas	=	1 day of Viṣṇu (i.e. 12 hours of Viṣṇu)

Siddhānta-Śiromaṇi, a standard work on old astronomy, gives the calculation in human years (in *kāla-mānādhyāya*) as follows :

18 *nimeṣas*=1 *kāṣṭhā*; 30 *kāṣṭhās*=1 *kalā*; 30 *kalās*=1 *ghaṭi*; 2 *ghaṭis* or 60 *kalās*=1 *muhūrta* ; 60 *ghaṭis* =30 *muhūrtas*= 1 day (24 hours) ; 15 days= 1 *Pakṣa* ; 2 *pakṣas* =1 month ; 6 months=1 *ayana* (*dakṣināyana*=the night of gods; *uttarāyaṇa*=the day of gods)

2 *ayanas*=1	year	=	1 complete day of gods.
30 (human)	years	=	1 month of gods.
360 (human)	years	=	1 year of gods.
96000? (human)	years	=	1000 years of gods (?) It is 360,000 human years ?
43,20,00,0	years	=	*caturyugī* (a cycle of 4 yugas)
30,67,20,00	years	=	1 *manvantara* (or 71 *caturyugī*)
4,29,40,80,000	years	=	14 *manvantaras*
2,59,20,000	years		the twilight-time between the *manvantaras*
4,32,00,00,000	years	=	1 day of god Brahmā.

The night of god Brahmā is of the same duration.

It will be noted that the NP. and some other Purāṇas do not take into account the Twilight period of *manvantaras* and there is some confusion of terminology in *Bh.P.* & *NP.* Thus *kṣaṇa* in NP. is a bigger unit than *kāṣṭhās*, while in the *Bh.P.* 5 *kṣaṇas* make a *kāṣṭhā*. There is some confusion in the Bh.P. about the duration of *yāma* (3 hours) which is equated with 6 *or* 7 *ghaṭikās*. A critique of the 'astronomy' in *purāṇas* & *siddhānta śīromaṇi* and other works is beyond the scope of this note.

5. It is perhaps the most famous *Ṛc* in praise of the Sun god :

tat savitur vareṇyaṁ bhargo devasya dhīmahi dhiyo yo naḥ pracodayāt |

RV. 3.62.10, *Tait.S.*1.5.6.4, 4-1.11.1; *Vāj.S.*3.35, 22.9

and in a no. of Vedic works vide Bloomfield: *Vedic Concordance*, p. 392. It is designated as *Sāvitrī* or *Gāyatrī* throughout Vedic and Sanskrit literature.

6. *Tulasī* or the Basil plant.

This fragrant plant is regarded as the most beloved to god Viṣṇu. It is regarded as Mahālakṣmī, the divine consort of Viṣṇu who assumed the form of this plant.

According to *Devī Bhāgavata*, goddess Mahālakṣmī, in response to King Dharmadhvaja's penance, incarnated as his daughter 'Tulasī', and herself performed penance for obtaining Lord Viṣṇu as her husband, but was destined to become the wife of Kṛṣṇa's *aṁśa* Sudāman (who was then born as Śaṅkhacūḍa) for some time. Śaṅkhacūḍa was invincible because of Tulasī's chastity. Viṣṇu sent god Śiva to fight with Śaṅkhacūḍa, and himself went in the form of Śaṅkhacūḍa to Tulasī. Unsuspecting, she consented to her husband's wish for intercourse, but finding difference in his sexual approach, she jumped and before she could curse that imposter, Viṣṇu manifested himself and explained to her that Śaṅkhacūḍa who was Sudāman cursed by Rādhā, is now redeemed of the curse, and returned to Goloka, and that now she should give up her body transforming it into the river Gaṇḍaka (?) and *Tulasī* plant and return to Vaikuṇṭha. Since then the Tulasī plant is dear to Viṣṇu (*Devībhāgavata* 9—chs.17-75). She is called *Tulasī* as she was matchless (*Ibid.*9.25.24), and she is regarded as "the purifier of the universe", and "bestower of devotion to Hari and final emancipation" (*Ibid.*9 25.43). In *Pd.P. Kriyā yogasāra khaṇḍa*, ch.24, we have the glorification of the Tulasī sung in the exaggerated way of purāṇas as "absolvent of all sins", "healer from all ailments" (ibid.24.26) "yielding all wishes" (ibid 24.45), etc.

7. *Rudrākṣa*—Elaco carpus seed.

It is an instance of how popular etymologies became *purāṇic* stories. The word consists of two words *Rudra* & *akṣa* (eye). According to *Devī Bhāgavata* 11.4.7-10, god Śiva explains to Nārāyaṇa : "when gods approached me to kill Tripura, I sat contemplating, with my eyes open for 1000 divine years, how to kill him. From the strain, some tears dropped from my eyes, which were transformed into *Rudrākṣas*". *Rudrākṣa* beads are sacred to *Śaivites* as *Tulasī* beads to *Vaiṣṇavites*. The various varieties and the spiritual benefits accruing from using them are elaborated in the above work—Skandha 11 chs. 4, 5, 6, 7. The final benefit being :

rudrākṣa-dhāraṇāt sadyaḥ sarva-papaiḥ pramucyate |

—ibid. 11.7.42.

One is absolved of all sins by wearing the *rudrākṣas*.

8. *nirvāṇa*

The conceptions of *nirvāṇa. vaikuṇṭha* etc. are mixed up in *purāṇas*, the main idea being the cessation of rebirth or termination of *saṁsāra, anāvṛtti* as *Br.Sū.*4.4.22 puts it. The term *nirvāṇa* occurs in BG.2.72, 5.24, 25, 26 and need not be regarded as a borrowal from the Buddhists. The Buddhist *nirvāṇa* is not 'nothingness' or 'void', but an approach to the Vedantic concept of *Mukti* (R. D. Ranade—*Vedanta, The culmination of Indian thought*, pp. 156-57. Bharatiya Vidya Bhavan, Bombay 1970.) But the *purāṇic* concept is a mixture of *Dvaita* and *Advaita* points of view, for sometimes the devotees are said to retain their individuality in Vaikuṇṭha.

CHAPTER SIX

The Glory of the Gaṅgā[1]

Sūta said :

1. On hearing the glorification of devotion unto the Lord, Nārada was pleased, and he again asked Sanaka, the master of spiritual knowledge and philosophy.

Nārada said :

2. O Master of interpreting scriptural precepts! Kindly tell me the truth as to what is the excellent-most of all the places of pilgrimage and the sacred-most of all sacred spots.

Sanaka replied :

3. O Brāhmaṇa ! Listen to this utmost secret which bestows all riches and which is the holy thing that destroys the effects of evil dreams, and the auspicious thing that is conducive to virtue and destructive of sins.

4. This should be listened to even by sages. It for-ever wards off the influence of evil planets, subdues all ailments and causes longevity.

5. Great sages say that the confluence of the Gaṅgā and Yamunā[2] is the most excellent of all sacred spots, and the most sacred of all holy places.

6. All divinities headed by god Brahmā, all sages and all Manus, desirous of acquiring merits, resort to this sacred confluence of waters, with dark and white hues.

7. The Gaṅgā should be known as a merit-giving holy river since it has its source from the feet of Viṣṇu, O Brāhmaṇa, and the Yamunā[2] is born of the Sun. Hence their confluence is bound to be very auspicious.

8. O Sage, the Gaṅgā is the most distinguished of all rivers. When remembered, it destroys the distress and absolves the rememberers of all sins and removes all harms and injuries.

9. O great sage ! The holy place called Prayāga[3] should be known as the sacred-most, and the most meritorious of all the holy spots on the earth, delimited by the oceans.

10. It was here that god Brahmā performed a sacrifice to propitiate the Lord of the goddess Lakṣmī. All sages also similarly perform different sacrifices for him.

11. The meritorious ablutions in all other sacred waters (taken together) do not deserve to be even a fraction, one-sixteenth of the merits accrued from the ablution with a drop of water of the Gaṅgā.

12. Even a man staying a hundred *yojanas* away from the Gaṅgā and uttering repeatedly the name of Gaṅgā, is also released from all sins. What then of a person who actually performs ablution in the water of the Gaṅgā ?

13. The goddess (viz. the holy river Gaṅgā) originating from Viṣṇu's feet and held over the head respectfully by the Lord of the Universe (viz. Śiva), deserves to be resorted to by sages and gods. What need be said that it should be resorted to by hapless human beings ?

14. If the sand of the Gaṅgā is applied on the forehead by excellent persons, it should be known that a brilliant (third) eye[4] will be developed there beneath a crescent moon (the devotee will have a similarity of form like god Śiva).

15. Bath taken into the Gaṅgā is highly meritorious. It is difficult to have it even to the resident of celestial regions. It bestows the *Sārūpya*[5] (similarity in form) with Viṣṇu. What more can be said to be greater than this ?

16. Even sinners taking their bath there in the Gaṅgā become absolved of all their sins. Seated in a great aerial car, they proceed ahead to the highest region (*Vaikuṇṭha*).[6]

17. By taking their bath therein (in the Gaṅgā), noble-souled persons redeem thousands of members on the sides of their father's family and mother's family, and go to the region of Viṣṇu.

18. O Brāhmaṇa ! There is no doubt in this that he who remembers the Gaṅgā attains the merit of performing ablutions in all the sacred waters and staying in all the holy places.

19. By the sight of a person who has taken a bath in the Gaṅgā, even a sinner attains to the celestial world. One should

become over-Lord of gods merely by touching my body (i.e. the waters of the Gaṅgā).

20. The mud and dust from the root of the *Tulasī* plant, the foot of a Brāhmaṇa or from the bed of the river Gaṅgā confers upon people assimilation type of *mukti-sārupyatā*—(similarity of form) with Acyuta.

21. Extremely rare indeed are the following : viz. the Gaṅgā, the Tulasī plant, unflinching devotion to Hari and devoted attachment to the expounder of the Dharmas, (among the people).

22. A man endowed with devotion, who applies over his head the dust from the feet of the expounder of the sacred *dharmas*, or the dust and mud taken from the bed of the Gaṅgā, or from the root of the Tulasī plant, attains Viṣṇu's region.

23. He who ardently desires and yearns, "When shall I go to the Gaṅgā ? When shall I see that river ?", goes to the region of Viṣṇu.

24. It is not possible even for Viṣṇu to describe adequately the greatness of the Gaṅgā even in hundreds of years. Of what use is a garrulous talk by others, O Brāhmaṇa ?

25. It is exceedingly surprising that the Māyā deludes the entire universe, and that people do fall into the hell, despite the existence of the name of the Gaṅgā.

26. The name of the Gaṅgā is glorified as one that dispels the misery of the worldly existence. Similarly renowned is the plant *Tulasī* and devotion to the expounder of Hari's glory.

27. He who mentions, even for once, the two syllables *Gaṅ-gā*, becomes completely liberated from all sins, and goes to the region of Viṣṇu.

28. He who goes within three *yojanas* (one *yojana* = 12.8 km) of the Gaṅgā, becomes absolved from all sins, and attains to the region of the Sun.

29. The river Gaṅgā is highly meritorious. If resorted to, with great devotion, when the Sun is in *Meṣa* (the sign Aries of the Zodiac) and *Tulā* (Libra, the 7th sign of the zodiac as well as in the month of *Mṛgaśirṣa*, it sanctifies the entire universe.

30-31. There are many holy rivers, viz. the Godāvarī,[7] the Bhīmarathi,[8] the Kṛṣṇā,[9] the Revā,[10] the Sarasvatī,[11] Tuṅgabhadrā[12] the Kāverī,[13] the Kālindī,[14] the Bāhudā,[15] the Vetravatī,[16] the Tāmraparṇī,[17] the Sarayū,[18] etc. Among all these rivers, the Gaṅgā is remembered (in *Smṛti* works) as the holiest of all, O excellent Brāhmaṇa.

32. Just as the Omnipresent Viṣṇu stays, by pervading the whole of the universe, similarly, the Gaṅgā is all-pervading and destroys all sins.

33. The Gaṅgā is as if a nurse unto the universe. It sanctifies the world when bathed in it, or when its waters are drunk. Thus it is *Pāvanī* (purifier). What a pity, that it is not resorted to by men !

34. Vārāṇasī[19] is well-known as the holiest of all holy centres, and the sacred-most of all sacred spots. It is resorted to by all *Devas*.

35. Only those two persons are intelligent: learned and well informed, and the men of Vedic learning by whom the word *Kāśi*[20] is frequently heard.

36. O excellent Brāhmaṇa ! Those who remember the sacred place *Avimukta*[21] (i.e. Kāśī) shake off all their sins, and proceed to the region of god Śiva.

37. A man, even if standing at a distance of hundred *yojanas* from it, remembers the holy place *avimukta*, attains to the region of no ailment i.e. *Mokṣa*, although he may be full of many sins.

38. O Brāhmaṇa ! If at the time of breathing his last, a person remembers *avimukta* (at the last moment), he is released from sins and goes to the region of god Śiva.

39. The person enjoys the merits resulting from remembering Kāśī, in the heaven. At the end of that period, he is born as the sole emperor of the earth, and then after going to Kāśī, he attains salvation.

40. What need there is of a long exposition regarding the merits of Vārāṇasī ? The fulfilment of the four-fold aims of human life (*Puruṣārthas*) is not far from those who at least take the name of Kāśī.

41. The confluence of the Gaṅgā and the Yamunā is superior even to Kāśī, O Brāhmaṇa. For, merely by having a look at it, men reach the highest goal (Liberation).

42. If ablution is performed anywhere in the Gaṅgā when the Sun is in the *Makara* (capricorn) sign of the zodiac, it sanctifies the universe by a bath in it or by drinking its water.

it takes the whole universe to the capital of heaven (Indra's city)[22].

43. Even god Śaṅkara, the benefactor of the world who assumes the form of a *liṅga*,[23] is always devoted to the Gaṅgā. How can its greatness be adequately described ?

44. The *Liṅga* assumes the form of Hari. Lord Hari assumes the form of the *Liṅga*. There is not even the slightest difference between these two. One who differentiates between these, is a person of evil intellect.

45. Only sinners, immersed in the ocean of ignorance, seek to make any difference between Hari and Śaṅkara, the glorious Lords without beginning or end.

46. They (i.e. learned men) say that Lord Hari who is the ruler of all the worlds and the ultimate cause (of all the causes), assumes the form of Rudra at the end of the *Yugas*.

47. It is Lord Rudra who protects the entire universe in the form of Viṣṇu, and creates it assuming the form of Brahmā. In the final analysis, god Śiva alone is all these three.

48. The man who differentiates between Lord Hari, god Śiva and god Brahmā, goes to the exceedingly terrible hell.

49. This is the conclusion of all scriptures that he who sees Hara, Hari and Brahmā all constituting the same deity attains the supreme bliss.

50. God Viṣṇu (Janārdana) who is omniscient and beginningless, and who is the omnipresent Lord and Creator of the worlds, is ever present there (at Kāśī) in the form of a *Liṅga*.

51. The *Liṅga* of Lord Kāśī-Viśveśvara[24] is called *Jyotirliṅga*. On seeing it, the excellent one of men merges in the supreme light of Brahman.

52. If Kāśī, the sanctifier of the three worlds, is circumambulated,[25] it is as good as the circle-ambulation of the whole earth consisting of seven continents, oceans and mountains.

53. There are spotless (brilliant) *mūrtis* (images) of Śiva or Acyuta made of metals, clay, wood or stone or their representations in paintings, etc. But Lord Hari is present in them all.

54. God Hari is present wherever there is a grove of *Tulasi* plants or where there is a cluster of lotuses, or where the *purāṇas* are being read, O Brāhmaṇa.

55. The propounder of the text of the *purāṇas* is also called Hari. Men who are devoted to them have (to their credit the merit of performing) bath in the Gaṅgā every day.

56. It is stated in *Smṛtis* that pious inclination to listen to the *purāṇas* is on a par with the ablutions in the Gaṅgā, and devotion unto the propounder is comparable to bath into Prayāga.

57. He who, by recounting the *purāṇa dharmas*, redeems and uplifts the entire world that is sunk and immersed in the ocean of worldly existence, is glorified as Hari himself.

58. There is no other sacred water like that of the Gaṅgā. There is no greater teacher than (honour, self-confidence. There is no other deity like Viṣṇu, and there is no other primary principle (or Brahman[26]) other than the spiritual preceptor.

59. Just as the Brāhmaṇa is the most excellent of all castes, or the moon is the best of all constellations, and just as the ocean is the best of all rivers, so the Gaṅgā is remembered as the greatest river.

60. There is no kinsman on a par with calmness; there is no greater penance than truthfulness : no other acquisition is greater than liberation from *saṁsāra*, and there is no other river on a par with the Gaṅgā.

61. The great name of the Gaṅgā is like a forest conflagration unto the jungle of sins. The Gaṅgā is the healer of the sickness called *saṁsāra* (worldly existence); hence, it should be resorted to with assiduity.

62. The *Gāyatrī mantra* and the river Gaṅgā both of these are remembered to be the destroyers of all sins, O Brāhmaṇa. A person who is lacking in devotion to these two, should be known as a fallen fellow, O Brāhmaṇa.

63. The Gāyatrī is the mother of all Vedic metres, the Gaṅgā is the mother of the world. Both of them are the cause of destruction of all sins.

64. If any one is favoured by Gāyatrī, the Gaṅgā too is pleased with him. Both of these possess the potency of Viṣṇu and both equally bestow desired objects as well as renown.

65. Both of them are quite pure. They are, as it were, the fructification of the Puruṣārthas (desired objectives of human life, viz. righteousness, wealth, love and liberation from *saṁsāra*).

These great and excellent ones function for conferring blessings on the world.

66. Rare indeed and very difficult to attain are the Gāyatrī, the Gaṅgā, devotion to the *Tulasī* plant and devotion of *Sāttvic* nature to Hari.

67. O ! How blessed is the Gaṅgā ! On being remembered, it destroys sins, on being seen it bestows the region of Hari. When its water is drunk, it grants *sārūpya* (similarity of form like Viṣṇu). And men who perform ablutions therein, attain the excellent region of Viṣṇu.

68. God Nārāyaṇa, the Creater of the Universe, Vāsudeva, the eternal deity, is the bestower of the fruits of all desired objects, to persons who are devoted to regular ablutions in the waters of Gaṅgā.

69. The excellent person who is sprinkled with at least a drop of water of Gaṅgā, is liberated from all sins and he attains the highest region, *Vaikuṇṭha*.

70. It is only by taking in just a drop of its water that a descendant in the family of King Sagara,[27] eschewed the state of Rākṣasa and attained to the supreme region.

CHAPTER SIX

The Glory of the Gaṅgā

1. *The Gaṅgā*

The holiest of the rivers in India. It is eulogized since Vedic times (e.g. *RV.* 10.75.5, *Tait. Ār.* 10.1.13, *Mahānārāyaṇa Up.* 5.4) The *Mbh* & *VR* are full of semi-historical legends about it e.g. Gaṅgā's marriage with king Śantanu (*Mbh. ādi.*chs 96 to 98). King Bhagīratha's success in bringing down the Gaṅgā on the earth (*Mbh. Vana.* chs 108, 109, *VR. Bāla* cantos 43, 44 *Bd.*ch.97) seems to be a saga of the attempts of 3 generations of kings of Ayodhyā to irrigate the parched plains of the U.P. in their kingdom. During the course of flowing, the river was swallowed up and allowed to flow by king Jahnu, and hence it came to be known as his daughter Jāhnavī. This is an allegorical description of the major changes in the course of the river. There are six *Jahnu-āśramas*, e.g. 1st, at Bhairavaghati near Gangotri at the confluence of the Bhāgīrathī and the Jāhnavī; the 2nd at Kanauj, the last being at Jamnagar 4 miles to the West of Nadia (De-*GDAMI* 61-62). The description of the descent of the Gaṅgā (*Bh.P.* 5.17.2-9 & *Mbh Bhīsma* 6.88-50) is a traditional memory of the land which the Indo-Aryans left behind in some ancient past, where from 'mount Meru' (prob. Pamirs), big rivers like the Sītā, the Alakanandā, the Cakṣu and the Bhadrā flowed in four directions. Geographers have now identified them and have shown that there is much truth in the racial memory couched in poetical terms in *Purāṇas* (vide N.L. De *GDAMI* under respective heads; also D. P. Misra—*Proto-history of India*).

The Gaṅgā came to be regarded so holy unanimously, due to the purity of its water, which does not deteriorate even after long storage. The scientists and engineers of the Roorkee university have experimentally shown that this is due to the presence of (1) radio-active-minerals, (2) bacteriophages and (3) metallic compounds in the river-bed which possess bacteri-cidal properties (*The Sunday Standard*, Bombay dt. 26-9-76, p.8). The ancient Hindus discovered this undeteriorating quality of the Gaṅgā water by their experience, and it has been the practice in many homes to keep vases or container of the Gaṅgā water for daily worship, and to use it to purify a dying person of sins, by pouring some drops of Gaṅgā-water in his mouth. This purity led to the belief that not only bath in the Gaṅgā or drinking a few drops of its water, but even remembering the name of the river had sanctifying influence. Most of the *Purāṇas* contain some verses or chapters on the glorification of Gaṅgā or *Gaṅgā-māhātmya*. As expected, some verses are common to many Gaṅgā-māhātmyas.

2. *Yamunā or Kālindī*

Next to the Gaṅgā, the Yamunā is regarded as the No. 2 holy river in India. It is mentioned along with the Gaṅgā since-Vedic Times (vide *Gaṅgā* above). It is regarded as the daughter of the-Sun-god and Yama's sister (*DevīP.* ch. 45). It rises in Kālinda-giri (a portion of the 'bandarapuccha'—mountain, De—*GDAMI*, p. 215), and hence is called Kālindi. The comparatively dark colour of its waters is attributed to the bath of god Śiva who, after the death of his first wife Satī, was in an excited mood, in which condition, being shot at by Kāmadeva (Cupid), became intolerably troubled and jumped into the Yamunā to extinguish the fire of his agony, changing the colour of its water to darkness (*Vāmana P.* ch. 6). The association of Kṛṣṇa's *līlās* (sports) on its banks, and his *rāsa līlā* with *gopīs* (which some believe continues unending), has immortalised the river in the hearts of Indians. It, being a very sacred river since the Vedic times, kings like Ambarīṣa, Bharata, Śantanu performed sacrifices on its bank (*Mbh. vana* chs 90, 129, 162; *Droṇa* 68.8). Its confluence with the Gaṅgā at Prayāga (Allahabad) made it a highly sacred place to Hindus.

3. *Prayāga.*

Modern Allahabad. A very sacred place due to the confluence of the two holiest rivers—the Gaṅgā and the Yamunā. The Sarasvatī is supposed to join this confluence and hence it is called *triveṇī-saṅgama.* According to *Mbh*, at Prayāga deities right from Brahmā, guardians of the world and the cardinal points (*Lokapāla, Dikpāla*), pitṛs (manes) great sages, Nāgas and even god Mahāviṣṇu are present here. If one bathes at the *triveṇī* confluence one gets the merit of performing the horse-sacrifice and the *Rājasūya* together. (*Vana* 85.70-86).

Purūravas, the son of Ilā, probably the leader of the earliest Indo-Aryan colonizers from Ilāvarta selected this then strategically important site and established his capital here. It was then called Pratiṣṭhāna—a permanent settlement. Here Nahuṣa, Yayāti, Puru, Duṣyanta and Bharata reigned (*Brahma P.* Chs 10-12). This place is now called Jhusi, and is a part of the precincts of Prayāga. This sacred place is highly praised in *Pd.P. Svarga khaṇḍa*, chs 41,42,43. *Km P.* regards this as "the most blessed, heaven-giving, auspicious, meritorious and sanctifying" of all sacred places (1.38.12), and recommends that death at Prayāga leads to the highest region (*Ibid.* V.5). There is the celebrated *Akṣaya Vaṭa* (undecaying banyan tree) in the fort which Akbar built in 1581 A.D. on the ruins of a Hindu fort. *Pd.P. Svarga* 43.11 recommends death at the foot of this tree. According to Hiuen Tsiang, people used to end their life at this banyan tree for attaining heaven. The Khairha plate of Yaśaḥ-Karṇadeva (1073 A.D.) records that king Gāṅgeya obtained release along with his 100 wives at the famous banyan tree of Prayāga.

Prāpte prayāga-vaṭa-mūlaniveśa-bandhau
Sārdhaṁ śatena gṛhiṇībhir amutra muktim

Ep. Indi.XII. 205 p.211.

Prayāga still holds powerful influence on all religious minded Hindus.

4. *The eye on the forehead*

The identification of Rudra and Fire—Sacrificial fire in later Vedic times, seems to have transferred The *Kapālāgni*, fire on the circular earthen plate for baking *Puroḍāś* which is kept near the *yajña-kuṇḍa*, to the *Kapāla* (forhead of śiva as *Kapāla* means both 'earthen plate' and 'a forehead'. But according to Purāṇas, God Śiva has three eyes, the two normal eyes are the sun and the moon, and the third eye is the Fire-god. He opens it only to destroy the enemy (like Kāmadeva) or the universe. Although popular belief attributes the opening of the third eye of fire due to the playful shutting of his two eyes by his divine consort Pārvatī. *Mbh.Anu,* 140.33-38 attributes the fire to Nārāyaṇa which after burning (a part of) the Himalaya subsided and submitted itself at Kṛṣṇa's feet. In NP. this reference is to glorify the efficacy of the application of the sand of the Gaṅgā to one's forehead as it gives the applier *sārūpya* (similarity of form) like god Śiva.

5. *Sārūpya*

This is a type or state of Liberation in which the liberated soul has the appearance or form like the deity. The Bh.P. enumerates five such types as follows :

sārṣṭi-sārūpya-sālokya-sāmīpyaikatvam apyuta /

Out of these, *sālokatā*—residence in the same region of the Deity (e.g. Vaikuṇṭha, Kailāsa), *samīpatā*—Being in the proximity of the Deity, *sarūpatā* or *sārupya*—as above, *sāyujyatā*—Intimate union or absorption into the Deity, *sārṣṭitā* or *sārṣṭya*—is the last stage consisting of equality with the Supreme Being in power and all the divine attributes of the Deity.

6. *Vaikuṇṭha*

The region of Mahāviṣṇu (Bh. P.9.4.60). The Vedic seers regarded Viṣṇu's place as supreme and glowing like an extensive 'eye' in heaven (RV. 1.22.20) and contains the eternal source of honey (RV.1.154.5). Its location was high up in the sky. The Bh.P. thinks that it is beyond the three worlds, and is endowed with innate splendour. It has elaborated and remodelled earlier ideas about the abode of Viṣṇu. The *Vaikuṇṭha dhāman* is the highest region of Viṣṇu endowed with an outer garden called-*Naiḥśreyas.* It is liberation *incarnate* and has the privilege of simultaneous revelry of all the six seasons bursting upon the wish-yielding tree. It abounds in singing birds, golden chariots, women with explosive beauty and captivating smiles yet evoking no baser passions, etc. (Bh.P.3.15. 16-22 also *vide* 2.9. 10-17). Later *purāṇas* like *Pd.P. Svarga khaṇḍa* regarded it as situated on a higher plane than the region of Brahmā and is 18 crore yojanas (=144 crores of miles) far above the earth.

bhūr-lokāt-parisaṅkhyātaḥ koṭir aṣṭādaśa prabho /

(vide *Śabda-kalpa-druma* IV.p.507). It is called *Vaikuṇṭha* as it is a stage of existence free from worldly limitations (*kuṇṭhā*).

7. *The Godāvarī*

Also called the Gautamī, as the sage Gautama brought down the Gaṅgā to redeem him from cow-slaughter. It rises in Nasik district near a village, Tryambak, famous for the *jyotir-liṅga* 'Tryambakeśvara'. Rāma, along with his consort Sītā and Lakṣmaṇa, is said to have stayed for the most part of their exile at Pañcavaṭī near Nasik (*Mbh.Vana* 277.41 also *VR.Araṇya Kāṇḍa*). Every twelfth year, when the planet Jupiter is in the Leo sign of the Zodiac, thousands of pilgrims from all parts of India flock to bathe in the Godāvarī near Trymbak and Nasik. It flows through Maharashtra and Andhra Pradesh and falls into the Bay of Bengal near Rajamahendrī.

The Mbh. regards it as one of the holiest rivers in India and bath in it confers the fruit of *go-medha* and life in the region of *Vāsuki* (*Mbh. Vana* 85.33, 88.2), and bath in the Godāvarī at *Janasthāna* (Nasik) bestows one with royal fortune (*Mbh.Anu* 25.29).

8. ***The Bhīmarathī***

Also called Bhīmarathā and Bhīmā. The Mbh regards it as one of the holiest rivers in India which absolves one of all sins (*Vana* 88.3 *Bhīṣma* 9.20). It rises near Bhīmāśaṅkara, one of the twelve *jyotir-liṅgas*, in the Western Ghats, in Poona District and joins the Kṛṣṇā near Raychur. The famous Vaiṣṇavite centre Pandharpur and the sacred shrine of Viṭṭhala is on the bank of the Bhīmarathī which, due to its crescent shape there, is called *Candrabhāgā*. Balarāma had visited this place during his pilgrimage (*Bh.P.* 10.79.12).

9. *The Kṛṣṇā*—

The river is mentioned in the *Mbh. Bhīṣma* 9.33, *Bh.P.* 5.19.18, *VR. Kiṣkindhā* 4). It rises at Mahabaleśvara in Western Ghats in Satara district, flows through Maharashtra, Karnatak and Andhra Pradeśa and falls into the Bay of Bengal at Sippelar near Masulipatam (De—*GDAMI*, p. 104). In *purāṇas* it is always associated with the Veṇā, Veṇṇā, Veṇṇī, or the Veṇvā and the *Mbh. Vana* 85.37-38 states that bath at the *devahrada* (prob. confluence) of the Kṛṣṇā and Veṇṇā confers the memory of one's previous births,

D.C. Sircar is not correct when he says, 'The Veṇvā is the modern Varṇā running between the Satara and Kolhapur districts *GAMI*. (*Studies in The Geography of Ancient and Medieval India*, p. 59).

Apart from the name of Satara dist. instead of that of Sangli for the location of the Vārṇā, the main fact remains that there is a river called the Veṇṇā in Satara district—a sister of the Kṛṣṇā as its source is the same—which joins the Kṛṣṇā in Satara district.

The late Prof. Dr. (Mrs.) Irawati Karve, from the Deccan College, Poona, told me that on sociological grounds the Kanhan and the Benna from Vidarbha have a better claim to be ancient Kṛṣṇā and Veṇṇā, as the culture of the people in the present Kṛṣṇā—Veṇṇā valley is pro-Dravidian, and the derivation Kanhan<Kṛṣṇā and Bennā<Veṇṇa is quite plausible.

10. ***The Revā***

So called because of the roaring sound created by its current while breaking its way through the Amarkantaka mountain.

> *bhitvā śailaṁ ca vipulam prayātyevam mahārṇavam* |
> *bhrāmayantī diśaḥ sarvā raveṇa mahatā purā* ||
> *plāvayantī virājantī tena Revā iti smṛtā* ||
> —*Sk.P. V. Revā khaṇḍa* 6.37-38

In fact, the major part of the *Revā khaṇḍa* naturally glorifies the Revā or Narmadā. The *Bh.P.* distinguishes between the Revā and the Narmadā (*Bh.P.* 5.19.18). *Sk.P.* (1.1.31.103, *V*.1.56.6 and I.1.18.153) reconciles this by stating that though the Revā and the Narmada were originally different, they joined together and formed the Southern Gaṅgā. It forms the traditional boundary between the North and South India (*Bh.P.* 5.19.18). It rises in the Amarkaṇṭak hills and falls into the Gulf of Cambay near Broach. Maheshwar (ancient Māhiṣmatī of king Sahasrārjuna, a *Jyotir-liṅga, Omkāra Māndhātā* , are on its bank. It is regarded as highly meritorious to go round the course of this river. *Pd.P.Svarga*.chs 17-22. glorify the Narmadā. Balarāma visited this river during his pilgrimage (*Bh.P.* 10.79.21).

11. *The Sarasvatī*

Though now practically non-existent in its pristine glory, the Sarasvatī is a very famous river from the Vedic times and is mentioned in RV. 6.61, 7.95.1-2, 10.17.7-9. From RV.7.95.1-2, it appears to be a mighty river flowing to the Arabian sea. It rises in the Sirmur hills of the Siwalik range in the Himalayas. The fountain—the source of the river—was at the foot of a *Plakṣa* (Indian fig.) tree, and it became known as *Plakṣāvataraṇa* or *Plakṣa-prasravaṇa*, now a place of pilgrimage. It emerges into the plain at Ād-Badri in the Ambala District. It disappears at Chalaur, but reappears at Bhavānī-pura; then it disappears at Balchappar, but again appears at Bara Khera. It is later joined by the Mārkaṇḍā at Urnali near Pehoa and the joint stream under the name Sarasvatī falls into the Ghaggar which is believed to have the name Sarasvatī in ancient times.

Vedic seers prayed the river for glorious treasures, and milk, and wished to stay on her banks for ever. The *Atharva veda* describes Maruts ploughing barley on its banks. The spread of Aryan culture from the land of the Sarasvatī to Kosala is symbolically described in the *Śatapatha* I.4.1.10 ff. as the carrying of sacrificial fire by Videgha Māthava to the east. The *Mbh.* and the *purāṇas* speak of its disappearance at *Vinaśana-tīrtha* near Sirsa. It is associated with sages Dadhīca (Mbh.*Vana* 100.13,) Vasiṣṭha (*Śalya* 42.29) and Vyāsa (*Bh.P.* I.1.4.15.4-15). Sacrifices were performed on its banks by kings like Matināra (*Ādi* 95.26-27), Yayāti, Nahuṣa, Puru and later by Kṛṣṇa. Vidura and Balarāma visited it as pilgrims (*Bh.P.* 3-1.22 & 10.78.18). After the death of Kṛṣṇa, his 16000 wives drowned themselves to death in the Sarasvatī (*Mbh.Svarga* 5.25). The archaeological explorations of the Sarasvatī—Ghaggar—Hakra bed proved that the Vedic and epic tradition about the Sarasvatī being once a mighty river with a continuous and perennial flow down to the Arabian Sea, is correct. According to the evidence available, the river dried up due to serious seismic disturbances towards the end of the Vedic period. The hydrographical and archaeological investigations by Suraj Bhan have shown that in the late Harappan times, the desiccation of the river had already started resulting in the shifting of her settlements to the upper valley (*The Sunday Standard*, Bombay 19-9-76). Hence the fervent prayers in Vedas not to deprive the seer of its water. Purāṇic stories of Sarasvatī carrying Vaḍavānala to the sea, and her disappearance through the fear of being touched by Ābhīras and other wild tribes.

The rejuvenation of the Sarasvatī by diverting surplus waters of the Yamunā, Rākhī and other rivers would transform the desert of Rajasthan into a granary of India.

12. *The Tuṅgabhadrā*

A tributary of the Kṛṣṇā. It is due to the confluence of two rivers, the Tuṅgā and the Bhadrā (at Kudali in Shimoga dist., Karnatak) that the river came to be called Tuṅgabhadrā. It joins the Kṛṣṇā beyond Curnool. The ancient Kiṣkiṇḍhā of Sugrīva was situated on its bank. It is also called Tuṅga-veṇī (*Mbh.Bhīṣma* 9.27) and is a very holy river (*Bh.P.*5.19.18).

13. *The Kāverī*

One of the holiest rivers in India. It rises from a fountain *Candra Tīrtha* (KP.2.37) in the Brahmagiri mountain in Coorg. Famous sacred places like

Śrīraṅgam, Trichanapalli and Kumbhakoṇam are on its banks. The Kaveri falls at *Śiva samudra* are famous for natural beauty. According to *Sk.P.* God Śiva gave this river to sage Agastya who carried it in his *Kamaṇḍalu* (a water-bowl of gourd), and while Agastya was deep in meditation at Brahmagiri, Gaṇapati, at the request of Indra, upset the bowl and secured the river for the parched region of South India. (Mentioned as a very holy river in *Mbh. Vana* 85.12 and *Bh.P.* 5.19.18).

14. *The Kālindī*

Vide Yamunā, above, Note No. 2.

15. *The Bāhudā*

Modern scholars differ on its identification. Pargiter identifies it with the Rāmagaṅgā which joins the Gaṅgā near Kanauj (His. *MK.P.*ch. 57). De regards it as Dhavalā (modern Dhumelā or Buḍhi Rāptī) a tributary of the Rāptī (*GDAMI*, p.16). The sage Likhita got his arm restored by bathing in this river; hence it is called arm-giver or *Bāhudā*—(*Mbh. Śānti*.23.39-40). Gaurī, wife of king Prasenajit was cursed by her husband and was transformed into a river called Bāhudā. Observance of fast and celibacy for one night on this river confers a godhood in heaven (*Mbh. Vana* 84.67-68; 95.4).

16. *The Vetravatī*

Modern Betwā, a tributary of the Yamunā. A river of all India importance (*Mbh.Bhīṣma* 16-19).

17. *The Tāmraparṇī.*

Also the Tāmbraparṇi, Tāmbravari. It rises in the Agastya-kūṭa mountain, and joins the gulf of Manar celebrated for pearlfishery. Pandyan king Malayadhvaja stayed after retirement from kingship here (*Bh.P.* 4.28.35, 5.19.18).

18. *The Sarayū*

The Ghagra or Gogra in Oudh on which Ayodhya was situated. The river rises in Kumaun and after its confluence with the Kāli-nadī, it is called the Śarayū or 'Ghagra'. According to Mbh, it is one of the seven streams of the Gaṅgā (*Ādi* 169.20-21). Vasiṣṭha brought it to the Mānasa lake whence it dashed forth as the Sarayū from that lake (*Anu.* 155.23-24). From a Tīrtha called *Gopratāra* in Sarayu, Rāma along with all his followers, went to His highest abode. Mere remembrance of the river sanctifies a person (*Anu.* 165.21).

19. *Vārāṇasī*

Also known as Kāśī, Avimukta-kṣetra, Mahāśmaśāna, Rudra-kṣetra or Ānandavana in Purāṇas.

It is the holiest town in India where two great religions Hinduism (Brāhmanism) and Buddhism flourished. Originally Vārāṇasī was the capital of the ancient State (*Janapada*) Kāśī and is so mentioned in the Mahāgovinda Suttanta in *Dīgha Nikāya* II.235 (also vide the *Aṅguttara Nikāya* (I.213, IV. 252, 256) and the *Bhagavatī*— XV. Uddesa I) The name is derived from the river-names the Varuṇā (Vāraṇā) and Āsī which join there, and the myth of one king Banār giving his name to Benares is an instance of popular etymology. Kāśis the early Aryan settlers, selected this then strategically important site, due to the protection afforded by the rivers the Gaṅgā, the Varuṇā and the Āsī against the hostile aboriginals, and an all the year round safe route of communications with the Aryan colonies to their West. Havel in his *Benares, the sacred city* states that Vārāṇasī might have been the centre of primitive Sun-worship, and Brāhmaṇas glorified it in all their *purāṇas* and the *Skandha purāṇa* devoted one full book (Part IV) as *Kāśī khaṇḍa* for describing all the sacred places and legends connected with Kāśī. The Buddha selected Vārāṇasī for his 1st sermon—'setting the wheel of *dharma* in motion', and the Aśokan Stūpa at Sāranāth commemorates the site of the 1st sermon of the Buddha. Pārśvanātha, the historical founder of Jainism belonged to Vārāṇasī. This glory of Vārāṇasī attracted Muslim invasions which razed to the ground its ancient glory. It, however, continued to be the centre of learning despite political and religious troubles, and great saints like Caitanya, Rāmānanda, Vallabha, Kabir, Ekanāth, Tulasīdās visited the place and settled there for some part of their life and some permanently. In the 18th century, the Marathas who controlled the Moghul rulers of Delhi, used their influence in the rebuilding of ancient shrines and religious institutions thereof, and the present temple of Viśvanātha was built bý Rani Ahilya Bai of Indore in 1777. It is hoped that Vārāṇasī may regain its ancient glory in the post-independence period.

20. *Kāśī*

Though Kāśī is identified with Vārāṇasī here, it is originally the name of a state (*Janapada*) colonised by an Indo-Aryan tribe Kāśis. Kāśi as a *Janapada* is recorded in Brahmanical, Buddhist and Jain sources as mentioned above. The Kāśī clan of Aryans seems to be allied with the Kassites who conquered Babylon in 1700 B.C., even though the Aryanisation of the region called Kāśī was at a later Vedic period. Kāśī (and its joint name *Kāśī-kosala*) often occurs in the Brāhmaṇa period. It was an independent state at the time of the Buddha, but soon after submitted to and formed a part of the empire of Magadha. As noted above Vārāṇasī was its capital but today both are the parts of the same city-complex. The author of *Skandapurāṇa* is conscious of the bigger geographical extent of Kāśī and calls that section of *Skanda Purāṇa* as *Kāśī-khaṇḍa* and not *Vārāṇasī-māhātmya* or some such name. Now, most of us regard Kāśī and Vārāṇasī as identical.

21. *Avimukta*

As per SKP.IV. (*Kāśikhaṇḍa*) i.39.71-78 God Śiva manifested himself here and did not leave the place and that the sight of the *liṅga* confers complete liberation from Saṁsāra. Hence, the significance of the name *avimuktaka*.

22. It is called *Amarāvatī*.

23. *Liṅga*

The word means 'a distinguishing mark' 'characteristic' and is used in this sense by all Brāhmaṇa and non-Brāhmaṇa *śāstric* writers e.g. Br.Sū.4.1.2 *liṅgācca*. For stating nudity as the distinguishing mark of a *Śramaṇa*, Kundakunda (in *Pravacanasāra* 3.25) says : *uvayaraṇam jiṇamagge liṅgaṁ jaha-jada-rūvam idi bhaṇitaṃ* The *Śiva-liṅga* is the symbol of the sacrificial fire ablaze. Rudra is identified with the Fire in RV.2.1.6, 3.2.5. etc. in AV.7.87.1. and in the *Tait.Saṁhitā* 5.4.3.1 etc. The 8 epithets *Śarva*, *Bhava*, *Paśupati*, etc. are common to Rudra and Agni (AV.15.5.1-7, *Śatapatha* Br.1.7.3.8). The burial of skulls of animals under some sacrificial altars explains his epithets as "dweller in crematory", "five-facedness" etc. if *Tait. Saṁhitā* 5.7.10.1 is properly explained. The *Liṅga* as a 'phallic symbol' shows the ignorance of the Vedic identification of Rudra and the Sacrificial fire. It may be noted that some female deities e.g. Madālasā, the divine spouse of Khaṇḍobā—an incarnation of god Śiva, has a *Liṅga* as her representation, along with that of her spouse Śiva or Khāṇḍobā. Śiva Liṅgas are found on the heads of gods like Viṭṭhala of Pandharpur and goddesses like Viśālākṣī. G.B. Dandage of Kolhapur in his *Rudra, Yajña āṇi Śiva-liṅga* (Kolhapur 1970) has made out a good case about the identity of Rudra and Sacrificial fire and shown the weakness of the Phallic worship theory.

24. *Kāśī Viśveśvara* :

The presiding Deity of Kāśī and the main *Jyotir-liṅga* in the 12 *Jyotir-liṅgas* in India, it is glorified very highly in the *Kāśī Khaṇḍa* (Sk.P. IV.ii.ch.99) according to which it is the *Liṅga* par excellence (ibid verse 51). It means, to the best of the knowledge of the author of *Sk.P. Kāśī khaṇḍa*, god Śiva is represented in the form a *liṅga* at this place since time immemorial. The facts are otherwise. In the 7th cent. A.D., when Hiuen Tsiang visited the place, there was an august brass statue of about 100 feet height of god Mahādeva. To quote his words : "The statue of Deva Maheśvara, made of brass, is somewhat less than 100feet high. Its appearance is grave and majestic, and it appears as though really living." The iconoclastic fervour of Muslims razed important Hindu statues, images, shrines and the stones were used to construct their mosques and buildings even as far as Jaunpur (N.L. De-*GDAMI*, pp. 23-25). The fortunes of this god had their ups and downs, as Vārāṇasī changed hands from Hindus to Buddhists, ultimately to rest for sometime with the Hindu kings of Kanauj. But the temple and the Deity suffered worst at the hands of Muslims, in spite of attempts of Hindu chiefs under Moghuls, like Raja Todarmal and Hindu religious leaders. Sikhs and Marathas sealed the fate of the Moghul empire, and a Maratha queen Rani Ahilyabai Holkar of Indore built the present temple of Kāśī Viśveśvara in 1777.

25. *Kāśī-pradakṣiṇā*

This is a religious custom to show respect to a sacred place, shrine or town in which the Deity is situated. It consists of circumambulating the sacred object showing our right side to the deity after saluting it.

prasārya dakṣiṇaṁ hastaṁ svayaṁ namra-śiraḥ punaḥ |
dakṣiṇaṁ darśayan pārśvam manasā'pi ca dakṣinaḥ ||

Kālikā and other purāṇas quoted in *Śabda-kalpa-druma* Part III.pp.273-74.

26. *tattva*=Brahman, *paramātmā*.

27. *King Sagara* SKḌ (*Śabda-kalpa-druma*) Vol.II.p. 581.

A king worth remembering at dawn and dusk (*Mbh.Anu.*165.49) Posthumous son of king Bāhuka of the Ikṣvāku dynasty who, being deprived of his kingdom by Tālajaṁghas lived in exile in a forest near the hermitage of sage Aurva. His younger wife Yādavī who was pregnant, wanted to immolate herself after Bāhuka's death, but was prohibited from doing so by Aurva who told her that, the child in her womb, was destined to be an emperor of the world. The senior queen who was issueless became jealous of her younger co-wife and administered poison to her, with a view to kill the child in its embryonic stage. But as fortune would have it, a son along with the poison (*sagara*) was born. (*Bm.P.* 2.3.48-49). The child grew up in Aurva's hermitage and presumed Aurva to be his father. The mother told him the story of her life, and Sagara determined to reconquer Ayodhyā. In the meanwhile, Vasiṣṭha and the citizens of Ayodhyā whose struggle of liberation was going on, got a leader in Sagara, and he reconquered his father's kingdom and ruled at Ayodhyā.

Sagara subdued the Tālajaṅghas and became the absolute monarch of the world. From his queen Sumati, he had a son Asamañjasa who troubled his subjects, and was exiled for that. He had 60,000 sons from the lump of flesh delivered by his second wife Keśini.

Sagara performed 99 horse-sacrifices, but when he was to perform the 100th sacrifice, Indra, being afraid of losing his position, stole the horse and kept it near sage Kapila's hermitage in the nether world. Sagara's 60000 sons traced the horse by means of its hoof-prints, and dug down to Pātāla. The horse was near the hermitage of Kapila, who was immersed in meditation. Thinking him to be the horse-thief, they attacked him only to get reduced to ashes. (*Mbh. Vana* 107.33).

Sagara retired making Aṁśumān, the son of prince Asamañjasa, as the next (*MBH. Vana* 107.64) king and performed penance for bringing down the Gaṅgā on the ashes in Aurvāśrama. (Bh.P.9.8.5-31). He was strictly Vegetarian (*Mbh.Anu.* 115.66).

CHAPTER SEVEN

The Glory of the Gaṅgā (contd.)

Nārada enquired :

1. O excellent sage ! It behoves you to relate to me who this Sagara was, and which descendant of the family of Sagara, was freed from the state of being a Rākṣasa (demon).

Sanaka narrated :

2. O prominent sage ! Listen to the pre-eminent greatness of the Gaṅgā, by mere contact with whose sacred waters, the whole dynasty of Sagara was sanctified, and attained the region of Viṣṇu, which is the excellent-most of all excellences in the world, O Brāhmaṇa !

3. In the Solar race, there was born a king named Bāhu[1], the son of king Vṛka. Exclusively devoted to righteousness in duty, he enjoyed and ruled the whole earth righteously.

4. The Brāhmaṇas, the Kṣatriyas, the Vaiśyas, the Śūdras and other living beings were established by him in their respective *dharmas* (duties). King Bāhu was (in the real sense of the term) the Lord of the subjects. (*viśāmpati*).

5. In each of the seven continents[2] (of the earth), he performed seven horse-sacrifices. He propitiated (to their heart's content) the Brāhmaṇas by means of cows, lands, gold, garments and such other gifts.

6. As per advice given in the treatises on politics, he subdued and controlled the enemies, as he pleased. He considered himself as having achieved his ambition in life by removing the troubles and miseries of others.

7. The people in his land always offered exquisite sandlewood as gifts. All the people in his kingdom were bedecked in very costly (divine) ornaments, and they were happy, O Sage.

8-9. The earth yielded rich food-grains without being ploughed. It was full of fruits and flowers. The king of the *devas* showered rain on the earth at the proper time, O excellent sage. In time of calamities, due to indulgence in unrighteousness, the subjects were protected as per *dharma* (duties of kingship).

10. Once, great arrogance which is destructive of all riches and the cause of transgressions and failures, and which was accompanied by jealousy, took possession of that king.

11. "I am the monarch, the powerful protector of all the worlds. I am the performer of great sacrifices. Who else is more worthy of being worshipped than I ?

12. I am affluent and clever. All enemies have been subdued by me. I am the knower of the principles (the real knowledge) of the Vedas, and of the ancillaries of Vedas (*Vedāṅgas*), and am expert in the science and art of politics.

13. I am invincible. Unchallengeable and unthwarted is my Lordship (Supremacy). Who else is superior to me in this world ?" As arrogance increased in him, he became also jealous of others.

14. O excellent sage ! As sequel to jealousy, passion too crept into that king. When all these possess a man, he undoubtedly goes to ruin.

15. Youth, affluence, power and authority as well as indiscretion—even one of these is sure to bring about mishaps and ruin. What then, when all these four operate collectively ?[3]

16. O Brāhmaṇa ! The jealousy that held sway over him was very great. It was antagonistic to all his worldly interests, was destructive of all his riches and even of his physical body.

17. If wealth begins to over-influence a person whose mind is affected by envy, know that it is like the fire in combination with gusts of wind which consume husk.

18. Neither here nor hereafter can there be any happiness to persons whose minds are affected by jealousy, whose conduct of life is full of hypocrisy, and who always use harsh words.

19. To men of harsh speech whose minds are possessed of jealousy, even the beloved wife, the sons or other kith and kin are enemies.

20. If anyone harbours in his mind any lustful desire on seeing another man's wife that is nothing but an axe that brings about the destruction of all his riches. There is no doubt about this.

21. O sage ! If a man wishes to attempt to bring about the destruction of his own well-being that man of crooked intellect harbours malicious thoughts on seeing the good of others.

22. O Brāhmaṇa ! If a man feels inclined to incur the loss of friendship, progeny, house, landed property, riches, food grains, etc., and cattle and other animals, he may very well indulge in jealousy all along.

23. As his mind was possessed of jealousy and he became more impudent, the powerful kings of Haihaya[4] and Tālajaṅgha[5] families became his enemies.

24. If the Lord of Lakṣmī is favourable to any one, his fortune flourishes, but if he is adverse to him, his fortune dwindles down.

25. O Nārada ! Sons, grand-sons, riches, food-grains, homestead, etc. favour one, only as long as the Lord of Lakṣmī casts favourable side-glances mercifully.

26. O prominent Brāhmaṇa ! Even the foolish, blind, deaf and stupid persons become heroic, praise-worthy and discriminating, if they are glanced at favourably by Mādhava, the Consort of Lakṣmī.

27. There is no doubt that the good fortune of a person who is contaminated with jealousy, etc., dwindles down and that particularly hatred towards all living beings is generated in his mind.

28. If a man hates continuously some one or the other, all his blessings and religious merits perish, O excellent sage.

29. Viṣṇu becomes averse to him in whom jealousy goes on increasing. After this, that person's wealth, stock of grains, lands and affluence are definitely destroyed.

30. Egotism and arrogance destroy the power of discrimination, as a consequence of which, adversities befall living beings. One should, therefore, eschew egotism.

31-32. He who becomes puffed with pride precipitates his ruin erelong. The king whose mind was possessed with jealousy put up a continuous terrible fight for the period of a month with his enemies, the Haihayas and the Tālajaṅghas in which he was ultimately defeated. He then repaired to the forest.

33. Although Bāhu was dejected, he felt great pleasure on seeing a great lake. He was then accompanied by his pregnant wife.

34. It was a great miracle that perceiving the nature or temperament of the king whose mind was possessed of jealousy, all the birds residing in the lake hid themselves.

35. While the birds were hastily entering their respective abodes, they exclaimed : "Alas ! How painful it is ! What a terrible form has come down here !"

36. Accompanied by both of his wives, the king joyously entered the lake, drank its water that gave him abundant pleasure. He, thereafter, went and rested under a tree.

37. While the king Bāhu was proceeding to the forest, the subjects, though erstwhile protected by him, exclaimed "Fie ! Fie", after considering Bāhu's evil propensities.

38. O Brāhmaṇa ! A man endowed with good qualities, whoever he may be, is worthy of being praised by every one. A person devoid of good qualities, is censured by men, though he may be possessed of all kind of riches.

39. There is nothing comparable to ignominy in this world which is as painful as death. When Bāhu went to the forest, the people of his kingdom felt much relief and pleasure, as though an inflammation of the eye had subsided.

40. O excellent Brāhmaṇa ! Censured on many occasions, Bāhu remained in the forest like a dead man, with his fame in the world destroyed, and activities cut off.

41. "There is no death like ignominy (ill-reputation); there is no enemy like anger; there is no sin like slandering and there is no intoxicating liquor like delusion.

42. There is no ill fame like jealousy; there is no fire like passions; there is no snare like attachment; there is no poison like intimate contact (sexual intercourse)."

43. Being extremely dejected, Bāhu lamented in this and many other ways. Due to mental agony as well as to old age, the limbs of his body became wasted and feeble.

44. After the passage of a great deal of time, the king Bāhu was overwhelmed with sickness, and he died in the vicinity of the hermitage of sage Aurva,[6] O excellent sage !

45. His younger wife became very miserable. After lamenting for a long time, she thought of going with him (to the other world, by immolating herself in the fire), even though she was pregnant.

46. Deeply grieving she brought the fuel herself and prepared the funeral pyre. After placing (Bāhu's body) on the pyre, she began to ascend the pyre herself.

47. In the meantime, the intelligent sage Aurva, the

receptacle of spiritual lustre, understood all this by means of his deep trance.

48. With the vision of their perfect knowledge, the noble-souled prominent sages who are cognizant of whatever exists in the three units of time—the past, the future and the present—and who are devoid of jealousy, see everything.

49. The most meritorious sage, Aurva, the store-house or treasure of brilliance accrued through penance, reached the place where the beloved wife of Bāhu was standing.

50. On seeing that she was about to ascend the funeral pyre, that leading sage spoke to her these words, based on *dharma*, O excellent sage !

Aurva said :

51. "O chaste lady ! O beloved wife of the excellent king ! Please do not proceed ahead with this risky venture. An emperor, verily the slayer of enemies, stays within your womb.

52. O blessed princess ! The following (ladies) do not ascend a funeral pyre, viz. those with infant children (depending on them), pregnant women, those whose monthly course has not yet started, and women in the menses.[7]

53. Means for expiation for Brāhmaṇa-slaughter and other sins have been mentioned by excellent men;[8] but there is no expiation for an imposter, a person who slanders, and killing a child in embryonic stage.

54. O observer of good vows ! There is no atonement for an atheist,[9] an ungrateful fellow, a person indifferent to *dharma* and a treacherous fellow.

55. Hence, O splendid lady ! It does not behove you to commit this great sin. The misery that has befallen you shall subside completely."

56. Thus advised by the sage, the chaste lady believed in his blessings. Taking up the lotus-like feet of her husband (in her hands), she lamented very much and was extremely distressed.

57. The sage Aurva who was an adept in the interpretation of scriptural texts, consoled her again, "O Princess do not cry. Later on, you will attain prosperity in due course.

58. O extremely blessed lady ! Please do not shed tears. The dead body should now be cremated by good men. Hence, controlling your grief, perform the rites befitting the occasion.

59. The god of Death is impartially alike to all, be he a learned man or a fool, an indigent fellow or a person in affluent circumstances, a wicked person or a man of good behaviour.

60-61. I consider it so in a city(?).[10] Indigence is surpassed in this respect here. Whatever is the past, ancient act (*karma*), it is directed in this world. I consider that the fate alone is the cause of this, and men are simply conditioned thereby.

62. O lady of lotus face ! All creatures have to succumb to the influence of the god of Death, whether one is even in the womb or in infancy or in youth or in old age.

63. It is Lord Govinda who destroys or protects creatures that are conditioned by and are at the mercy of their own actions. Ignorant persons super-impose a false belief on the creatures that are but casual causes.

64. Hence, O lady of pious observances, shed off your sorrow, and be happy. Perform the funeral rites of your husband. Try to be steady (in mind) through sensible discrimination and thought.

65. This physical body (of ours) is surrounded by ten thousands of miseries and ailments. It is subject to much pain and torture. It has only a semblance of happiness, but is full of sufferings. It is fettered by the bonds of actions."

66. Consoling her thus, the highly intelligent sage made her perform all the funeral rites. That gentle lady controlled her grief, bowed down to that prominent sage and said to him.

67. "What is surprising there that good men always wish for the benefits and well-being of others, as it is not for their own enjoyment that trees bear fruits on the earth.

68. He who, realising the miseries of others, enlightens them through good advice, is the veritable Lord Viṣṇu, the main-stay of *sattva guṇa*, for he is ready to render service to others.

69. He who feels miserable at the miseries and sorrows of others, and who feels delighted at the happiness of other people, is himself Hari, the Lord of the worlds, who has assumed a human form.

70. Scriptures have been heard and learnt by good men only to relieve others of their misery. It is for the destruction of the misery of every individual : So say the pious men.

71. Misery cannot affect anyone at a place where good men function. How can there be darkness when the sun shines?"

72. Speaking these and similar words, that lady performed all the other (funeral) rites of her husband, on the bank of that lake, in accordance with the instructions of that sage.

73. As the sage was standing by, the king appearing brilliant like the king of gods, rose out of the funeral pyre and ascended an excellent aerial car. After bowing down to Aurva, the leader of sages, he attained to the Supreme Abode.

74. Persons whether defiled by great sins[11] or by subsidiary types[11a] of sins, do attain to the Supreme Region when graciously glanced at by great men.

75. If a highly meritorious person looks (favourably) at the dead body or its ashes or the column of smoke (going up from the funeral pyre), the dead man attains the highest goal, O excellent one.

76. O Nārada ! After performing the funeral rites of her husband, she went to the hermitage of the sage and accompanied by her co-wife, she rendered service to him.

CHAPTER SEVEN

1. Bāhu *alias* Bāhuka (1.7.3)

A king of the solar race; The eighth descendant from Hariścandra. The Bh. P. and other Purāṇas do not attribute his loss of throne to his arrogance as in NP. (vide below VV 10-15). The Purāṇic account shows a struggle for supremacy over the Indo-Gangetic plain between the Ikṣvākus of Ayodhyā and the Yadus i.e. Haihayas from Māhiṣmatī. In that hereditary feud, Bāhu lost his throne and had to spend the rest of his life in exile—which he did in the vicinity of sage Aurva's hermitage.

2. (I.7.5). They are (1) Jambū (2) Plakṣa, (3) Śālmali (4) Kuśa (5) Krauñca (6) Śāka, (7) Puṣkara.

3. (I.7.15-30) This verse is found in other works like Hitopadeśa, Pañcatantra, etc.

In ancient India, a number of wise-sayings in a verse form, on subjects like ethics and politics (*nīti*), renunciation (*vairāgya*), right conduct (*Sadācāra*) etc. were handed down by oral transmission. These were called *gāthās* and *Subhāṣitas* and were found in practically in the same verbal form in Sanskrit, Pāli and Prākrits (with the necessary phonetic and other changes). This fund of commonsense and wisdom is the legacy of all Indians.

4. *Haihayas* (I.7.23).

The dynasty founded by Haihaya, the great-grandson of Yadu :

Yadu→Sahasrajit→Śatajit→Haihaya. Kārtavīrya Arjuna or rather Sahasrārjuna about whom the Bh.P. 9.23.25 states : "Other rulers of the earth cannot reach the status of Kārtavīrya, in point of performance of sacrifices, munificent donations, asceticism, *yogic* powers, scholarship, victories, etc., In the traditional feud between Bhṛgus who had family ties with Ikṣvākus, the rivals of Haihayas and Haihayas, belonged to this dynasty. Sahasrārjuna was killed in a surprise attack by Paraśurāma. But after Paraśurāma's retirement, Sahasrārjuna's grandson Tālajaṅgha—probably an epithet to indicate his long marches—reasserted his supremacy by inflicting a crushing defeat on Ikṣvākus of Ayodhyā, the supporters and relatives of Bhṛgus (who had already left Western India and took refuge to the North), and King Bāhuka or Bāhu of Ayodhyā spent his life in exile near the hermitage of Aurva, a sage of the Bhṛgu clan.

5. *Tālajaṅghas* (N.P.I. 7.23 & 31-32).

Tālajaṅgha was the grandson of Sahasrārjuna who recovered the original position of his kingdom. The Tālajaṅghas were comprised of five clans or groups of people : (1) Vītihotras, (2) Śaryātis (3) The Bhojas, (4) the Āvantis and (5) the Tuṇḍikeras. He conquered his hereditary enemies, the Ikṣvākus and drove out King Bāhu in exile. Their dominion stretched from the gulf of Cambay (the Bhṛgus vacated Western India before the Tālajaṅghas) to the Gangetic doab. But King Sagara, son of the exiled King Bāhu, consolidated his position, destroyed the Haihaya power completely and the glorious Māhiṣmatī was soon forgotten (Bh.P.IX.23, 9.8.5B.7.A, Pargiter A I H T. PP.267-71).

6. *Aurva* (I.7.44)

A great sage, scientist-cum-statesman of the Bhṛgu clan. He was the son of Cyavana and Āruṣī, the daughter of Manu. The Bhṛgus were an affluent, militant community. Once the Haihaya King, Sahasrārjuna was in need of money and the Haihayas approached the Bhṛgus who did pay the tax levied. But one of Haihayas being over-exacting, dug up the house of a Bhṛgu and got enormous wealth. This led to the exploration compaign of all the houses of the Bhṛgus who resisted and the Haihayas started the genocide of Bhṛgus (if we are to believe *Mbh. Ādi.*179.5.6—which is a Bhṛgu recension). All women of the Bhṛgu clan hid themselves in the caves of the Himālayas (*Ibid* 177.21). While fleeing, Āruṣī concealed her *garbha* in her thigh, but a Brāhmaṇa woman informer reported to Haihayas about Āruṣī's escape though pregnant. When Haihayas arrested her, the child came forth from his mother's thigh. Hence he was called *Aurva*—Thigh-born. The Kṣattriya pursuers became blind by Aurva's lustre. They regained their eyesight when they begged pardon. But Mbh. Ādi 177.1-6 shows that by the time the Haihayas reached Aurva and his mother, he must have been a grown up boy, expert in Vedas and the accessories, as his being in the womb for 100 years and studying the Vedas in the embryonic stage is a purāṇic way of statement. It appears that Aurva was a scientist who was then developing a fire-missile capable of destroying the world (like the Hibomb of to-day) and the very terrific glare of the missile at that stage blinded the Haihayas. But he continued his researches and to quote the *Mbh* : "With a desire to avenge the massacre of Bhṛgus, he decided upon a weapon of universal distruction" (*Ādi.* 178. 10-11). Aurva's penance (his development of a fire-missile) sent a cold shudder through the spine of 'the world' and his ancestors (i.e. senior members of the Bhṛgu clan). Like great thinkers of today protesting against the military use of atomic energy, they dissuaded him from the effort. "while I was in my mother's womb, I heard the wailing of my mothers (Bhārgava women). When Bhṛgus right from 'wombs' were massacred, nobody came to help my mothers. Then why should I spare the Kṣattriyas now ?" growled Aurva (*Mbh. Ādi.* 179-5-14). It appears that the senior Bhṛgus anyhow dissuaded him from his resolve and the fire-weapon was thrown into the sea which as submarine fire still burns the sea water (and is called *Vaḍavāgni*). *Ibid.* 179.21-2.

It appears that Aurva's hermitage was near the kingdom of Ayodhyā. The political support of Ikṣvākus and the geographical distance between Ayodhyā and Māhiṣmatī enabled Aurva to carry on his researches undisturbed.

Aurva seems to have a long life. He lived to see the destruction of the Haihayas by his great grandson (Aurva—Ṛcika—Jamadagni—Paraśurāma) Paraśurāma.

When the grandson of Sahasrārjuna, Tālajaṅgha marched against King Bāhu of Ayodhyā—for it was really a struggle for supremacy in the Indo-Gangetic plain between the kings of the Solar and Lunar Races (and the Bhṛgus, partisans of Ikṣvākus) when King Bāhu was expelled, he took shelter with-Aurva. Why Tālajaṅghas did not attack Aurva's hermitage and execute the King is a mystery. May be inefficient intelligence service, pre-occupation with the rebel population of Ayodhyā who continued resistance under the leadership of Vasiṣṭha, the communication difficulties with their distant capital Māhiṣmatī to conduct a protracted war or possibly the deterrent of Aurva's secret missiles—it is anybody's guess.

But the fact remains that Aurva could bring up Bāhu's son Sagara in his hermitage, give him the necessary training and see to it that under Sagara's leadership, the freedom-struggle of Ayodhyā resulted in the expulsion of Tālajaṅghas. King Sagara, however, ruthlessly continued his struggle till the Tālajaṅgha power was wiped out of the Indo-Gangetic plain and crushed permanently—a feat which the much-glorified Paraśurāma could not achieve. But the *Mbh. Anu.* 153.11 a Bhṛgu recension gives the credit solely to Aurva !

(1) *Mbh. Ādi.* and *Anu.* (as cited above)
(2) *Bh.P.* IX.8.8; IX.23.28.
(3) *Bmd. P.* 2.3.48.1-25

7. (I.7.52)

This verse is quoted by *Parāśara Mādhava* II.1.P.58 and *Smṛti-muktāphala* I P. 162 (where it is ascribed to Aurva) as an authority prohibiting self-immolation (*Satī*) of women under these conditions.

bāla-saṁvardhanaṁ tyktvā bālāpatyā na gacchati |
rajasvalā sūtikā ca rakṣed garbhaṁ ca garbhiṇī ||

attributed to Bṛhaspati in *Parāśara Mādhava. Smṛti-Candrikā* (on *Vyavahāra*, p. 254) regards celibate life in widowhood as superior to the rewards of self-immolation to fire.

8. (I.7.53)

Although *Brahma-hatyā* (murder of a Brāhmaṇa) is regarded as the most heinous sin (*mahā-pātaka*) and the murderer was to meet death, the *Bhaviṣya Purāṇa* states that Manu has given thirteen alternative expiatory rites for this sin : Quoted by Kullūka on *Manu* XI.72-82; *Prāyaścitta-Viveka*, p. 63. Commenting on this, Govindānanda in his com. *Tattvārtha-Kaumudī* has given the details of these 13 alternative expiations (*prāyaścittas*).

9. (I.7.54) *Nāstika* :

This term includes not merely those who deny the existence of God, but those who do not accept the authority of the Vedas. It includes Jainas, Bauddhas, Pāśupatas and such heretics. One should take bath along with the clothes if one is touched by them (*Ṣaṭ-triṁśan-mata* quoted in *Prāyaścitta-Prakaraṇa* P.110 and *Smṛti-candrikā* I.P.118). The contents of VV.54 & 55 are repeated again in Chs. 14, 15, etc.

10. (I.7.60)

Although the word *nagare vā* occurs at the beginning of verse 60, it is better to take it with verse 59 and translate "Death overtakes one or in a city".

11. (I.7.74) *Mahāpātakas* : Major i.e. very grievous sins.

NP. I.15.22 b and 23a enumerates these. They are (1) murder of a Brāhmaṇa, (2) drinking of spirituous liquor, (3) stealing, (4) defiling the bed of one's preceptor (by enjoying his wife) and (5) association with any one of the above four sinners. That chapter details what actions amount to Brāhmaṇa-slaughter, etc.

Mahāpātakas should be distinguished from *Ati-pātakas*; the former can be expiated by undergoing some severe penance, etc., but the latter is beyond redemption. In the list of *Atipātakas*, *Viṣṇu Dharma Sūtra* 34.1 includes sexual intercourse with one's mother, daughter or daughter-in-law.

11A. (I.7.74) *Upapātakas* : Minor sins.

The number of minor sins is large and varies from *Smṛti* to *Smṛti* and from time to time. Yājñavalkya enumerates fifty-one minor sins. The most important one of the minor sins is killing a cow and the expiation for all *upa-pātakas* is the same, viz. that prescribed for killing a cow. It consists of *Cāndrāyaṇa*, *Parāka*, *Gosava* (subsisting on cow's milk for one month). If minor sins are repeated, the man loses his caste and becomes fallen. (*Viśvarūpa* on *Yājñavalkya* III.229-36).

CHAPTER EIGHT

The Glory of the Gaṅgā (Contd).

Sanaka said :

1. O leading sage ! Thus, in the hermitage of Aurva, the two wives of Bāhu continued to render services with the feeling of devotion, every day.

2. O Brāhmaṇa ! After the lapse of half the year, the elder queen became evil-minded towards the good fortune of her co-wife (since she was pregnant)

3. Then poison was administered to the junior queen by the elder sinful lady.[1] But the poison was not effective, thanks to her service to the sage.

4. As she served the sage very well by scrubbing and smearing the ground (with cowdung, etc.) and other activities, the poison became digested as the effect of her holy (meritorious) acts.

5. After three more months, she, all of whose sins were wiped out due to her services (to the sage), gave birth to her son along with the poison, at a highly auspicious time.

6. O ! What sin in the world is there which association with righteous men does not destroy ? What happiness does it not give unto the men of meritorious acts ?

7. Services rendered unto the noble-souled, immediately destroyed the sins committed knowingly or otherwise or those one is compelled to do by others.

8. Even the dull attains to the state of being worshipped in this world, thanks to the association with the good, even as a digit of the moon when accepted (on his forehead) by god Śiva (became so to the world).

9. O leading Brāhmaṇa ! Indeed, association with the good always bestows on men the greatest prosperity, both here and hereafter. Hence good men are the worthiest to be worshipped.

10. O leading sage ! Who is competent to describe adequately the good qualities of the great ? It was miraculous that the poison that was administered to the child in the womb became digested (and came out after) three months.

11. On seeing the son born along with the poison, the sage, a receptacle of brilliance, performed the post-natal rites[2] and named the son *Sagara*[3] (a child with the poison).

12. The child's mother brought up the boy Sagara with great affection. The prominent sage performed the rites of tonsure[4] and the investiture with the sacred thread in the appropriate manner.

13 & 14. Observing that Sagara had outgrown the stage of early childhood, and that he was very capable, the leader of sages who was a past master in the knowledge of *mantras*, taught him scriptures (science and arts) that were befitting and essential for kingship. He granted him mastery over (the use of weapons) and miraculous missiles alongwith the requisite *mantras* (incantation of mystic formulae), O sage. Sagara was trained well by that sage Aurva.

15. The virtuous Sagara became powerful, righteous, grateful and intelligent. He possessed all good qualities. Every day he brought sacrificial twigs, *kuśa* grass, water, flowers, etc., for immense splendour.

16. On one occasion Sagara, full of modesty, and storehouse of good qualities, bowed down to his mother with palm joined in reverence and inquired.

Sagara inquired

17. "O mother ! Where is my father ? What is his name ? In which family was he born ? Kindly narrate to me all these details as I am interested in hearing about them.

18-20. Those who are devoid of father in this world, are as good as dead ones, even though they may be alive. A person whose father is alive is comparable to Kubera, the lord of wealth, even though he may be indigent. He who is bereft of both father and mother has no happiness. Just as a foolish person devoid of virtues is censured both here and hereafter, so also futile is the life (lit. birth) of a parentless orphan, of an ignorant fellow, of a thoughtless person, of a childless man, and of one immersed in debt.[5]

21. Like a night devoid of the moon, like a lake devoid of lotuses and like a woman devoid of her husband is a boy without his father.

22. A child without his father is like a creature without

a virtue, or like a householder not practising holy religious rites or like a person from *Vaiśya* community (whose main job is agriculture and tending of cows) without having any cattle or animals.

23. A child without his father is like a statement devoid of truth, or like an assembly without good men or like a penance without (the sense of) mercifulness.

24. A child without his father is like a forest without trees, or like a river devoid of water or a horse without quickness or speed.

25. O mother ! just as a man engaged in begging is considered despicable and wretched, so also a son without his father is overwhelmed by many miseries."

26. Hearing what was so far spoken by her son, the poor miserable mother sighed deeply, and in reply to his questions, she narrated to him everything as it had taken place.

27. On hearing it, Sagara flung into rage and with his eyes turned red due to fury, he immediately took the pledge: 'I shall kill the enemies one and all'.

28. After circumambulating the sage Aurva and bowing down to his mother, he set out and was given a due send-off by the sage himself.

29. Starting from the hermitage of Aurva, the pure and truthful Sagara approached with great pleasure Vasiṣṭha,[6] his family preceptor.

30. He bowed down to Vasiṣṭha, his noble-souled preceptor. He reported to him everything, although the sage had known it all through his vision of knowledge.

31. Prince Sagara acquired the miraculous missiles specially empowered by gods Indra, Varuṇa, Brahmā and Agni, through that sage (Vasiṣṭha). So also he obtained from him a sword and a bow comparable to Indra's thunderbolt.

32. Honoured by the blessings of the sage and permitted by him, Sagara paid respects to Vasiṣṭha and started immediately.

33. Only with his single bow, that heroic prince converted his enemies alongwith their sons, grandsons and followers into residents of the other world (i.e. slew them).

34. His enemies were distressed by the fire generated from the arrows discharged from his bow. Some of them perished, while others became frightened and fled.

35. Some of them lay dead on anthills with their hair dishevelled and scattered. Some of them ate grass. Even as they were naked some entered water (to hide themselves).

36. In their ardent desire to save their lives the Śakas, the Yavanas as well as other kings immediately sought refuge in Vasiṣṭha.

37. Getting the intelligence through his spies, of the approach of his enemies to his preceptor, Bāhu's son, now the conqueror of the world, promptly came to the presence of his preceptor.

38. On hearing that Bāhu's son has arrived, Vasiṣṭha reflected for a while as he wanted to save Bāhu's enemies who had sought refuge in him and also to carry out what his disciple had conveyed to him.

39. He made Śabaras[7] shave off their heads and made Yavanas wear long tresses of hair. He made Andhras retain the moustaches but shave off their heads. All these were ex-communicated from the Vedic fold.

40. On seeing that they had been made no better than dead by sage Vasiṣṭha, Sagara laughingly said to his preceptor, the store-house of penance.

Sagara said :

41. "O Sir, in vain do you try to protect these wicked persons. By all means I shall see to it, that all these fellows who deprived my father of his ancestral land are killed.

42-43. If in spite of being capable of annihilating the enemies of righteousness, one were to neglect them and look upon the entire world at first, as being one's relatives, he himself becomes the cause of total destruction. For those very wicked persons, if powerless, pretend (lit. outwardly resort to) extreme piety to be extremely righteous.

44. Alas ! All the (pseudo-) righteous acts (mentioned above) are done fraudulently to deceive others. The wicked ones are sinfully disposed by nature. So long as one's army is powerful, they behave and perform good acts or obey.

45. A person who desires to gain his own ultimate good, should not believe in the assumption of the role of servants or slaves by the enemies, in the professions of loving friendliness of prostitutes and in the innocent appearance of serpents.

46. Showing off their teeth, the wicked always indulge in jokes and pleasantries (while we are powerful). But when there is a reversal of one's power, they quickly show those very teeth (in a different way).

47. Vile persons at first (while in power) speak stern and abusive language with their tongue. But when they become powerless, they use it to speak in extremely pitiable words.

48. He who desires his welfare and he who is adept in treatises on polity, shall not believe in the outward goodness or (pseudo-) equability or equanimity of wicked persons.

49. Undoubtedly, a person who believes in the following is no better than dead :—a wicked man who (outwardly) shows submission, a friend who indulges in roguery and a wife of evil unfaithful nature.

50. Hence, verily, please do not afford protection to these persons who are like cows in (outward) appearance but are (cruel) like tigers in their deeds. After killing all these wicked persons, I shall rule over the earth with your grace".

51. On hearing his words, Vasiṣṭha, the excellent sage, was highly pleased with him. Stroking (patting) Sagara's body gently with his hands (to express his approbation), he spoke to him as follows:

Vasiṣṭha said :

52. "Well done ! Well done ! O blessed one. What you speak is the truth, O prince of noble rites. Still you will attain great peace of mind by paying heed to my words.

53. These persons who stood against your pledge have already been killed by me. Tell me, what fame can accrue to you by killing those who have already been killed ?

54. O Lord of the Earth, all creatures are fettered by shackles of their own actions. They are, however, already killed by their own sinful acts. Why do you kill them again ?

55. This is the decisive conclusion of all scriptures that the physical body produced by sins is already killed at the outset by those very sins, but the soul is impregnable because it is full and perfect.

56. Creatures are but instruments in the enjoyment of fruits of their own actions. The *karmas* are the outcome or the result of Fate (lit. have the Fate as their root). The entire universe is subject to the control of Fate.

57. Since Fate alone is the protector of the good and the chastiser of the wicked what is it that can be achieved by men who are not free (have no free will). Tell me.

58. The physical body is born through sin and it functions through sin. Why did you attempt to kill even after knowing that all this is rooted in evil ?

59. Though the soul (*ātman*) is pure, it is called the embodied one, by learned men, since it abides in the body. Hence, O king, there is no doubt in this that the physical body is rooted in evil.

60. O son of Bāhu, what renown can come to you by killing the body rooted in evil ? Thinking decisively (on these lines) O son, do not do them to death"

61. On hearing these words of the preceptor, the prince refrained from his angry venture. The sage patted his son-like disciple with his hands and consoled him.

62. Then (sage Vasiṣṭha) expert in the *Atharva Veda* performed the coronation ceremony[8] of the noble-souled Sagara with the co-operation of sages who were strict observers of religious vows.

63. He (Sagara) had two wives, Keśinī and Sumati. They were the daughters of Vidarbha of Kāśyapa's family.

64. Seeing that Sagara was well established in his kingdom the sage Aurva, the store-house of penance, came from the forest and after holding conversation with the king, returned to his hermitage.

65. On one occasion the sage Aurva who knew the *Bhārgava mantra* was requested by the two queens of that king. He granted them the boon of having children.

66. The prominent sage, the knower of the past, the present and the future, remained in meditation for a moment. Giving delight to the queens Keśinī and Sumati, he addressed them thus.

Aurva said :

67. "One of you will give birth to a single son who will keep the continuity of your race. The other will give birth to sixty thousand sons O blessed ladies; choose either of the boons for the sake of having children.

68. On hearing the words of the sage Aurva, O Nārada,

queen Keśinī chose a single son who will be the cause of perpetuation of their family life.

69. According to the boon sixty thousand sons were born of Sumati, O excellent sage, and the son of Keśinī was Asamañjas by name.

70. Asamañjas committed mischievous pranks like a mad man. On seeing him (act that way) the other sons of Sagara too became evil-minded and ill-behaved.

71. On seeing their childhood thus vitiated (by these mischievous deeds), king Sagara, the son of Bāhu, pondered over anxiously about the despicable activities of his son as brought about Fate.

72. He reflected : "Alas ! Extremely painful indeed is the association with the wicked persons. Fire is always beaten by blacksmiths for its only fault of being in contact with iron.

73. Asamañjas had a son named Aṁśumān. He was a knower of scriptures, righteous and engaged in what was beneficial to his grandfather. He was endowed with all good qualities.

74. But all the sons of Sagara committed evil deeds and harassed the people. They always created obstacles in the undertaking of holy rites of those who practised them regularly.

75. They drove off the gods (to whom oblations were offered) and partook of all sacrificial offerings duly submitted by the Brāhmaṇas.

76. They always brought by force celestial ladies like Rambhā and others dragging them by the tresses of their hair, and the sons of Sagara enjoyed them against their will.

77. Those wicked fellows were addicted to the drinking of wine. They plucked and brought the flowers of Pārijāta and other celestial trees and adorned their bodies with them.

78. Those great sinners but very powerful ones, abducted women who were well-behaved and chaste and destroyed men of good conduct. They even began fighting with their friends.

79. On seeing this, the gods, the leader of whom was Indra, became extremely distressed. They began to think deeply of the means of bringing about their destruction.

80. Taking a decision in the matter, all the *Devas* assuming disguised forms approached Kapila, the Lord of the chiefs of gods, who was at that time present in the Nether world.

81. The gods prostrated themselves on the ground before him like a staff and extolled him who was meditating in his mind on the *Ātman*, who is the very embodiment of pure and absolute bliss. They eulogised him as follows :

The gods prayed :

82. "Obeisance to you, the yogin who are absorbed and delightfully engaged in *Sāṅkhya-Yoga*; salutations to you who are Lord Viṣṇu Himself, disguised in the form of a human being, but who is all the while victorious (Jiṣṇu).

83. Bow to the devotee of the Supreme Lord; obeisance to you who are the Cause and bestower of benediction to all the world. Salutations to you who like the forest conflagration are the destroyer of the forest of *Saṁsāra*; we bow to you who are like a bridge affording protection to (the observers of) *Dharma*.

84. We bow again and again to you who are the great one totally devoid of passions and attachment. Be pleased to save us who have been afflicted by the sons of Sagara and have approached to you as a refuge for protection."

Kapila said :

85. "O excellent gods, only those who seek destruction of their own fame, power, wealth and longevity, harass the world. There is nothing surprising in this.

86. O gods, know that a person who intends to harass innocent persons in this world, is one who is engaging himself in the enjoyment of sins.

87. No doubt need be entertained in that that the Fate quickly destroys a person who continuously harrasses others physically, mentally or Verbally.

88. These sons of Sagara will meet their death in a very few days." When this assurance was given by that noble-souled sage Kapila, the heaven-dwellers bowed to him duly and returned to the celestial world.

89. In the mean-time, Sagara began to perform the *Yajña* (sacrifice) called *Hayamedha* (horse-sacrifice) with the help and guidance of Vasiṣṭha and other great sages.

90. Indra, the Lord of gods, took off the horse that was fixed for that sacrifice and placed it in the Nether world where Kapila was staying.

91. In order to find out the horse taken away by Indra with his physical body invisible, the sons of Sagara were extremely surprised and they wandered over the earth and other worlds in search of it.

92. When they could not trace the horse, they attempted to make their way to the *Pātāla*, the nether-world. And each one of them severally dug up the earth's surface to a depth of a *Yojana* (eight miles).

93. The earth dug out by them, they scattered on the shores of the ocean. All the sons of Sagara reached Pātāla through that passage.

94-96. The sons of Sagara who were perplexed and mad with arrogance searched for the horse. There they beheld the noble-souled Kapila dazzling with the lustre of ten million suns together, absorbed in meditation. And they espied the sacrificial horse near him. On seeing the sage they became very furious. With great speed they rushed at him and attacked him with the intention of killing him.

97-98. They shouted to one another : "Let him be struck down. Let him be struck. Let him be slain. Let him be killed. Let him be taken captive. Let him be quickly taken prisoner. It is he only by whom the horse is taken away and like a stork he pretends to be absorbed in meditation, showing off to be a saint. Alas ! There are wicked persons in this world who put up a great show (of saintliness)".

99-100. Shouting thus, they laughed and jeered at Kapila, the leader of sages who had exercised perfect control over his sense organs and stabilized his mind in the *Ātman*. As he was absorbed in meditation, Kapila did not notice their activities.

101. Those sons of Sagara whose death was imminent, lost their sense and kicked the sage, while others caught hold of his arms.

102. When the sage left off his trance, he was surprised (to see all this). In a deep majestic voice, he spoke to them who caused harassment to the world.

103. "The following persons lose their power of discrimination viz. those who are intoxicated with the arrogance of affluence; those who are oppressed with hunger; the passionate ones and those who are puffed with self-conceit.

104. The earth blazes internally continuously by merely being the receptacle of a treasure. What wonder is there when men blazed forth after enjoying the same ?

105. What is surprising in it, if wicked men annoy and harass the good people ? The force of the current in a river makes the trees on the bank fall down.

106. Misfortune, old age and foolishness always occur where there is wealth, youth and learning.

107. By whom can the greatness of *Kanaka* (gold) be described adequately ? Alas ! It is wonderful that similarity in name (viz. *kanaka*) makes the *Dhattura* plant (the thorn-apple tree) cause intoxication. (The word *kanaka* means *Dhattura* as well).

108. If a wicked person became endowed with affluence, that very same fortune of being affluent is destructive of the world, just as the violent gust of a wind is a friend of fire and poison that of a serpent.

109. Alas ! One blinded with the arrogance of his wealth does not see, though he may look on. If he sees wherein lies his welfare and interest, he sees properly."

110. Uttering these words, the infuriated Kapila created and discharged fire out of his eyes. The fire reduced the sons of Sagara to ashes instantaneously.

111. On seeing the fire issuing forth from the eyes of Kapila, the residents of the nether-world thought that the time of the dissolution of the universe had arrived prematurely. And they screamed out in their excess of sorrow.

112. All the reptiles and *Rākṣasas* were scorched by that fire. They entered into the ocean immediately. Indeed the fury of saintly persons is simply unbearable.

113. Thereafter a messenger of gods came to the place of the sacrifice of the king. He reported everything that had taken place to the king who was desirous of performing that sacrifice.

114. On hearing those words of the messenger the emperor Sagara, the knower of everything, became extremely glad and remarked, "The wicked ones have been tamed and subdued by the Fate.

115. Whether it be the mother or the father or the brother or the son, whoever commits a sin should be considered to be an enemy.

116. This is the decision arrived at in the scriptures—one should consider that person as the greatest enemy who is engaged in evil actions and who entertains hostility to all the people."

117. O eminent sage, Sagara did not feel sorry for the loss of his sons; for, the death of a person of evil conduct, enthuses good people.

118. Since the *Smṛti*[10] text ordains that a person who has no son is not eligible to perform a sacrifice, the king installed his grandson Aṁśumān as his son.

119. Moreover, the king, the knower of the essentials about sacrifice, deputed the son of Asamañjas with the assignment of bringing back the horse.—the son who was highly intelligent and the most excellent one among those who were skilled in speech.

120. It is reported that when he went to the entrance to that hollow chasm, he saw there pre-eminent sage Kapila, a mass of brilliance. And he prostrated himself before the sage, touching the ground with eight limbs of his body.

121. With his palms joined in reverence, he stood humbly before the sage. He addressed that eternal Lord of gods who was of quiescent and serene mind, as follows :

Aṁśumān said :

122. O Brāhmaṇa sage, kindly forgive the wicked offence committed by my uncles. Indeed, saintly persons who are engaged in rendering help to others are essentially of a forbearing nature.

123. Saintly persons show mercy even to the wicked. Indeed, the moon does not withdraw its beams of moon-light from the abode of a *cāṇḍāla*.

124. A good man, even when he is harassed and troubled, gives happiness to all. Just as the moon that is being eaten by the immortals gives the greatest pleasure and satisfaction to everyone.

125. Even when split and cut to pieces, the sandle wood renders everything fragrant. So is also a good person.

126. O Supreme Being, prominent sages, by their penance, forbearance and *ācāra* (behaviour and activities) know the excellent attributes of *puruṣottama* (Supreme Man), and they

know that you are that Supreme Person yourself born to chastise and discipline the world.

127. Salutations to you, O Brāhmaṇa sage. Obeisance to you who are the embodiment of *Brahman.* Bow to you who are by nature favourable and friendly to Brāhmaṇas and engaged in meditation on the *Brahman.*"

128. The sage who was thus eulogised by him evinced his delight on his countenance. He said, "O sinless one, I am highly pleased with you. Seek any boon of me."

129. When the sage spoke to him thus, Aṁśumān bowed down to him and requested, "Be pleased to take our ancestors to the world of Brahman".

130. Thereafter the highly delighted sage assured him, "Your grandson will bring down the Gaṅgā respectfully and lead your ancestors to the heaven.

131. The Gaṅgā, the river of holy waters, brought down by your grandson shall absolve these your ancestors of all their sins and lead them to the highest region.

132. O dear child, take this horse back so that the sacrifice can be completed". Accordingly reaching the vicinity of his grand-father, Aṁśumān related everything that happened and submitted the horse too.

133. Sagara performed his sacrifice by means of the sacrificial animal in the company of the Brāhmaṇas (sacrificial priests). He propitiated Lord Viṣṇu by performing penance and attained the region of Hari.

134. A son was born to Aṁśumān. He became famous as Dilīpa. From him was borne Bhagīratha who brought the Gaṅgā from the heaven.

135. O sage, God Brahmā who was pleased with the penance of Bhagīratha, bestowed the Gaṅgā on him. He (Bhagīratha) then began to think how to hold the water-fall of the Gaṅgā.

136. Thereafter, he propitiated god Śiva and brought the heavenly river to the earth. He helped his ancestors to go to the heaven as they became sanctified by touching the waters of the Gaṅgā.

137. A king named Sudās was born in the family of Bhagīratha. His son Mitrasaha was well-known in all the worlds.

138. That son of Sudās got the form of a Rākṣasa due to the curse of Vasiṣṭha. When the drops of the water of the Gaṅgā were sprinkled over him that king became liberated again.

CHAPTER EIGHT

The Glory of the Gaṅgā (contd.)

1. According to BN. (*Bṛhan-Nāradīya*) Aurva had one queen only with whom he spent his exile. That queen was poisoned by his enemies (Haihayas and Tālajaṅghas) and not by her cowife as in the NP. (BN.7.41-48). It was due to the merit accrued in the service of the sage Aurva, which did not kill her or the child in the embryo (BN.8.2-3).

2. *Jātakarma*—

The rites to be performed after the birth of a child. It is a very old rite, as it is mentioned in *Tait.Sam.*II.2.5.3-4. In Upaniṣadic times, it consisted of a *homa*, repeating thrice the word 'speech' in the child's ear, making it lick curds, honey and ghee in a gold spoon, giving the child its secret name (*nāma-karaṇa*), putting the child to the breast (by the mother), and addressing the mother with *mantra*. A great deal of these was dropped, and a variety of practices arose in the *Gṛhya-sūtras* and *Smṛtis*. Now-a-days some ceremonies (with little connection with *Gṛhya-sūtras*) are performed on the 5th and 6th day after birth.

3. This is a popular etymology, but is supported by *Bh.P.* IX.8.4. The Sagara-legend is very popular with *Purāṇas*, vide *Va.P.* 3.88.123-67; *Br.P.* III.Ch.s 47-55, *Śiva P.-Umā saṁhitā* 38.29-57.

4. *Caula* or *Cūḍākarma*—

The first cutting of the hair on the child's head. It is a rite the purpose of which is keeping a lock of hair. According to *Gṛhyasūtras*, it is to be performed in the third year from birth. After cutting the hair on an auspicious day, feeding of Brāhmaṇas, receiving their benedictions, the cut hair are to be so disposed as nobody can find them.

5. Are *subhāṣitas* describing the greatness of one's father.

6. *Vasiṣṭha*—

Name of the family preceptor of Sagara and other kings of the solar race. There appear at least three different persons called Vasiṣṭha : (1) The son of god Brahmā, who died at the time of the destruction of Dakṣa's sacrifice, (ii) Born from the sacrificial fire of god Brahmā and died by king Nimi's curse, and (iii) Born from a pot by Mitrāvaruṇa and a brother of the sage Agastya. In all these births the same woman—Arundhatī—took new births and married him. It is difficult to say which of these Vasiṣṭhas composed or 'saw' the Eighth Maṇḍala of the *Ṛgveda*, who carried on a feud with Viśvāmitra and who, after king Bāhuka, carried on the struggle against the Tālajaṅghas and inspired and helped Sagara to overthrow them. It seems to be a family of royal priests, loyal to kings of the solar race for many generations, and a variety of episodes in the life of these have clustered around Vasiṣṭha as if he was a single individual.

7. Out of these tribes, Śabaras were the aboriginal hill-tribe, Yavanas or the Ionians were Indo-Greeks who settled in the former NWF. province and

adjoining areas, while Andhras s probably the Pkt. form of Āndhras who were once beyond the border of Aryan India. Here their custom of cutting the hair and moustaches are recorded. *Bh.P.*IX.8 records the story of king Sagara and in verses 5B to 7A mentions Tālajaṅghas, Yavanas, Śakas, Haihayas and Barbaras as the tribes subdued by king Sagara.

8. Royal coronation was a very important solemn ceremony. Different procedures of coronation are given in the *Aitareya*, *Gopatha* and *Sāmavidhāna Brāhmaṇas* and in Purāṇas like *Brahma* and *Viṣṇudharmottara*. The *purāṇic* procedures were probably meant for Śūdra kings. The mediaeval writers tried for a synthesis of these procedures. For example, *Rājanīti Prakāśa* states that following the dictum of Śabara on Jaimini II.4.9, the coronation rite should comprehend all the different items mentioned in several Vedic texts (if not contradictory to each other) or the royal priest should follow that which is nearest to his own branch of Veda.

> (*tadevaṁ yasya purohitasya sva-śākhāvihitatvena yaḥ pakṣaḥ saṁhitas tenaiva tenābhiṣekaḥ kāryaḥ*)
>
> —*Rājanītiprakāśa*, p. 112.

The last was the easiest solution of the problem. Descriptions of the various procedures of such coronation is beyond the scope of this note.

As Vasiṣṭha's expertise in the *Atharva Veda* is mentioned here. It appears that the author of NP. implies here the procedure of coronation laid down in the *Gopatha Brāhmaṇa* which belongs to the *Atharva Veda* and prescribes *mantras* from the *Atharva Veda* for the various acts prescribed in this ceremony. (For details see *Rājanītiprakāśa*, pp. 42-43, *Rājadharma Kaustubha*, pp. 335-36).

9. Asamañjasa's pranks and his exile are confirmed in the *Mbh. Vana* 107.43 and *Śānti* 57.7-9. But *Bh.P.*IX.8.16-19 states that Asamañjasa was a *yogī*. He showed himself outwardly as being unreasonable. When he departed as an exile from Ayodhyā, he showed people that all their children were alive and returned them to their parents hale and hearty and that king Sagara was filled with remorse at his order of banishment.

10. This vague reference to *Smṛti* could not be located but in the *Mbh.Ādi.* 119.15-22 King Pāṇḍu deplores that a sonless person has no entrance in heaven even if he pleases gods with sacrifices and sages with learning.

> *na tasya lokaḥ santī'ti dharmavidbhiḥ pratiṣṭhitam* |

CHAPTER NINE

The Glory of the Gaṅgā

Nārada said :

1. How was the excellent king, the son of Sudās,[1] cursed by Vasiṣṭha ? How was he purified again by means of ablution in the drops of the waters of the Gaṅgā.

2. O brother, it behoves you to relate to me completely all these things. The episode of the Gaṅgā is conducive to the blessedness both of those who listen as well as those who relate it.

Sanaka said :

3. The son of Sudās was the knower of all Dharmas. He knew everything and was possessed of all good qualities and was pious and pure. He enjoyed the whole of the earth, giving delight to his subjects like their own father.

4. Just as this earth consisting of seven oceans[2] was protected and ruled over by Sagara in former time, he ruled over the earth and did not oppose any Dharma.

5. Blessed with sons and grand-sons,[3] endowed with all prosperity and glory, he enjoyed the earth for thirty eight thousand years and still retained his youth.

6. Enthusiastic over hunting expeditions, the royal son of Sudās entered the forest which was carefully cleared by his trustworthy ministers, along with his army.

7. Accompanied by Niṣāda hunters, he killed various groups of animals. That knower of Dharma became thirsty and came to the river Revā (Narmadā).

8. O sage, the son of Sudās took his bath there and performed the daily rites. After taking food along with his ministers, he stayed there for the night.

9. Thereafter he got up early in the morning and performed all the forenoon rites. Accompanied by his ministers, he wandered in the forest on the banks of the Narmadā.

10. Alone, the lord of the Earth wandered from one forest to the other. Keeping the bow drawn till the tip of the arrow reached his ear, he chased a deer.

11. Mounted on a horse, the king who intensely chased the deer, left his army far behind. There he saw in a cave a tiger couple engaged in sexual intercourse.[4]

12.14. He abandoned his pursuit of the deer and came in front of the tiger couple. He was conversent with the science called *Dhanurveda.* He fitted an arrow to his bow and discharged the arrow at the tigress and made her fall down with the shaft of sharp point and depressed joints (*nata-parva*). As the tigress fell down, she changed herself into hideous ogress thirty six Yojanas in length. She roared like the rumbling clouds and thunder.

14-15. On seeing his beloved wife fallen down, the tiger giant hatefully threatened the king, "I shall take revenge for this". After saying so, he vanished there. The king who was frightened in his mind, returned and rejoined his army in the forest. He reported everything that had happened and came back to his capital city.

15-18. The king, the son of Sudās, began to suspect that the demon would perpetrate something terrible. So from that time, he gave up hunting altogether, O Nārada. After a lapse of a great deal of time, the king with a happy mind began to perform a horse-sacrifice in the company of (under the direction of) Vasiṣṭha and other sages. After offering oblations to Brahmā and other gods according to the injunctions of the Śāstras and concluding the sacrifice, Vasiṣṭha and the performer of the sacrifice who had taken the final holy oblations went out.

19. In the meanwhile, the demon whose wife had been killed by the king, came there angrily in order to wreak revenge on the king

20. When the preceptor Vasiṣṭha had gone out, the demon disguised himself as Vasiṣṭha. Approaching the king at that time, he told, "I want to take food here". I desire to eat meat."[5]

21. Instantly the Rākṣasa assumed the guise of the royal cook, cooked human flesh and presented it to the king. The king held it in a vessel of gold and stood awaiting the arrival of the preceptor.

22. The humble son of Sudās respectfully served the flesh kept in that gold vessel, to the preceptor when he came there.

23. On seeing the preparation, the preceptor wondered what it was and began to reflect

24. By means of his concentration of mind (*Samādhi*), he came to know that it was human flesh "O ! How depraved in character is this king that he has served this forbidden food to me !"

25. Along with this surprise, the sage felt great indignation and annoyance. "O lord of the earth, this prohibited food has been given to me with a view to bringing about my ruin.

26. Hence, let this be your regular diet. Human flesh, the food fit only for the Rākṣasas has been given to me by you.

27. Hence, O king, assume the status of a Rākṣasa which is accustomed to this (human flesh) as the usual diet." When the preceptor uttered this imprecation to him, the son of Sudās was agitated and overwhelmed with fear.

28. Trembling with fear, he immediately submitted, "I have been so commanded by your holiness yourself !" Urged by this statement, Vasiṣṭha reconsidered the situation.

29. With his divine vision, he came to know that the king was deceived by the Rākṣasa. The king on his part took up water in his hand and was about to curse Vasiṣṭha.

30. Seeing the king enraged and attempting to curse his preceptor, his beloved queen Madayantī, a strict observer of religious vows, intervened thus.

Madayantī said :

31. "O scion of a noble Kṣatriya family, it behoves you to curb your anger. There is no doubt in this that the *Karman* which you alone have to experience, has visited upon you.

32. The stupid fellow who roars and grunts saying *HUṀ* and *TUṀ* to one's preceptor, becomes a *Brahma-rākṣasa* in a forest, in a waterless tract.

33. This is the decisive conclusion of the scriptures that those who have conquered the sense-organs, those who have controlled their irate nature and those who are engaged in serving the preceptor, go to the abode of Brahmā."

34. Dissuaded by her, the king eschewed his wrath. He appreciated the intercession of his wife. He thought to himself, "Where shall I throw this water (taken for uttering the curse."

35. It is certain that the spot where this water is sprinkled will be reduced to ashes." Thinking thus, he poured the water on his own feet, of his own accord.

36. By the mere contact of that water his feet took the variegated complexion of black and white. So, thenceforth, he became known as Kalmāṣapāda (one whose feet are black and white in complexion.)

37. The intelligent king Kalmāṣapāda was then consoled by his beloved wife. Excessively frightened in his mind, he saluted his preceptor and bowed down to his feet.

38. Resorting with palms joined with reverence, the king, an adept in political stratagems humbly submitted thus ! "O holy sir, be pleased to forgive me about everything (that has happened), but the fact of the matter is that no offence or sin has been committed by me."

39. Hearing this, the sad sage heaved a deep sigh and he censured himself for his own thoughtlessness. He said to the king."

40. "Absence of discrimination is the greatest cause of all adversities.[5a] There is no doubt about this that one who is devoid of discrimination is no better than a beast.

41. Indeed, this king had not known the mischief of the Rākṣasa. What he did was proper. It was I who was thoughtless and ignorant. Hence I committed the sin of cursing him.

42. He who is controlled by discretion and thoughtfulness—whoever he may be—invariably attains bliss. He who lacks discretion, whoever he may be, meets with the opposite of bliss."

43. After saying this to himself, the sage replied to the king, "This curse will not be permanent. It will last for twelve years.

44. Being sprinkled over with the drops of the waters of the Gaṅgā, you will give up the physical form of a Rākṣasa. Reassuming your original form, you will enjoy this earth.

45. Your sins will be dispelled through the perfect knowledge as a result of the sprinkling of the drops of the waters of the Gaṅgā. You will be solely devoted to the service of Lord Hari and will attain the highest spiritual peace."

46. After saying this to the king, Vasiṣṭha, the knower of the *Atharva Veda*, returned to his hermitage. The king also filled with grief, took up the physical form of a Rākṣasa.

47. He was particularly oppressed with hunger and thirst and was always furious. With a complexion as dark as the night in the dark fortnight, and terrific in appearance, he wandered over the tenantless forest.

48. There he killed and devoured different kinds of beasts, men, reptiles, birds and monkeys.

49. Even the ground allround became terrible and it became spotted with various colours, as it was littered with innumerable bones, bodies out of which all blood was sucked and the hairs of the dead bodies mixed with blood.

50. In the course of three seasons (i.e. six months) he rendered the land of a hundred yojanas in extent, very miserable, and then went over to another forest.

51. Even there also, he continued to eat human flesh every day. He then went to the banks of the Narmadā resorted to by the sages and Siddhas.

52. Moving about on the banks of the Narmadā, that Rākṣasa (king) who frightened all the world, happened to see a certain sage engaged in amorous sports with his beloved.[6]

53. Scorched by the fire of hunger, he rushed at the sage and caught hold of him with great force, like a hunter catching the fawn of a deer.

54. On seeing her husband struggling within the grip of the demon, the highly frightened Brāhmaṇa lady entreated to him with palms joined in reverence over her head.

The Brāhmaṇa lady prayed :

55. "O tiger among kings, save me who am now extremely frightened. Be pleased to make my desire fulfilled by restoring my beloved husband who is dearer to me than my very life breath.

56. You are not a real Rākṣasa. You are a king born of the solar race, by the name Mitrasaha. Hence protect me, a helpless woman, in this forest, devoid of human population.

57. A woman bereft of her husband, is comparable to a dead person, though she may be alive. Still, O suppressor of enemies, what more can I say about widowhood in the early age?

58. I do not know either my mother or my father. I do not know any other kinsman. My husband alone is the greatest relative unto me. He is my very life.

59. O Lord of the people, you know all the Dharmas. You know how ladies ought to make their livelihood. Hence, save me who am a woman having no kinsman and a lady (mother) having an infant child (in the arms).

60. How can I live in this tenantless forest without my husband ? O sir, I am your daughter. Be pleased to save me, by bestowing upon me my husband, as a charitable gift.

61. Highly intelligent men say:—"There never has been or there can never be in future a nobler charitable gift than that of saving one's life." Please give unto me the charitable gift of my vital breath (viz. my husband)."

62. After praying him thus, she fell at the feet of the Rākṣasa. Though implored thus by the Brāhmaṇa woman, the Rākṣasa devoured the Brāhmaṇa like a tiger devouring the fawn of a spotted antelope.

63. That chaste wife of the Brāhmaṇa lamented very much. Becoming infuriated again, she cursed the king, though he had already been cursed.[7]

64. "Inasmuch as you have forcibly killed my husband who was engaged in sexual inter-course, hence the moment you are united with a woman, you will die."

65. After cursing him thus the indignant Brāhmaṇa lady uttered another imprecation once again on him : "Since you had devoured my husband, your Rākṣasahood will be permanent."

66. On hearing these two curses uttered by her, the Rākṣasa flew in rage and was as if emitting sparks of fire due to anger.

The Rākṣasa said :

67. "O wicked woman, why have you heaped two curses on me in vain (without any reason) ? As my offence was only one, it would have been but proper to pronounce one imprecation on me.

68. O vilest of wicked woman, since you have uttered a second curse on me, you will go to the state of a female ghost (Piśācī) just now to-day, along with your son."

69. The Brāhmaṇa woman, who was cursed by him thus, immediately assumed a ghostly form. She was distressed with hunger. The terrible woman along with her son went on screaming aloud.

70. Screaming loudly in that tenantless forest, the Rākṣasa and the Piśāca woman went to the forest, on the bank of Narmadā inhabited by Rākṣasas.

71. At that place, there lived a demon who was tormented with miseries and was antagonistic to the world. He had assumed the physical form of a Rākṣasa, because he was indifferent towards his preceptor.

72. On seeing the Rākṣasa and the Piśācī coming to his banyan tree (occupied by him), the Brāhmaṇa demon (*Brahma-Rākṣasa*) already on that banyan tree said furiously:—

73. "O terrible ones, why have you both come to this abode fondly occupied by me. Certainly you must tell me for what sins of yours, you have become like this."

74. On hearing his words, the son of Sudās related to him everything that was committed by himself as well as by that lady. Thereafter he said to him thus.

Sudās's Son Said :

75. O highly blessed one, who are you ? Please tell me what was done by you before. It behoves you to relate everything to me, your friend, out of your great friendliness.

76. Indeed, that wicked-minded fellow, whoever he might be, but who deceived his friend, experiences the fruit of his sins and undergoes tortures in hell, for ten thousand *Yugas*.

77. All miseries of creatures are diminished (and disappear) at the sight of a friend. Hence, no sensible person shall practice deception on his friends."

78. O Nārada, the *Brahma-Rākṣasa*, already on the banyan tree, who was thus urged by Kalmāṣapāda, spoke these virtuous words delightfully :

The Brahma-Rākṣasa said :

79. "Formerly, I was a Brāhmaṇa in the country called Magadha. I had mastered the Vedas and was wellknown by the name Somadatta.[8] I was devoted to the practice of Dharma.

80. O blessed one, I became too much elated and arrogant due to my learning, wealth and youthful age. I showed indifference towards my preceptor and consequently I was reduced to this stage (of being a *Brahma-Rākṣasa*).

81. I am unable to derive any happiness. I am fed up with the food I take (?) since I am distressed. Formerly, hundreds and thousands of Brāhmaṇas were devoured by me.

82. Still I was tormented by hunger and thirst. I was afflicted by internal agony. I created a terror in the whole universe and I was always engaged in eating flesh.

83. Disrespect and indifference to the preceptor lead to Rākṣasa-hood in human beings. This has indeed been experienced by me. Hence, no one in prosperity shall do like-wise."

Kalmāṣapāda said :

84. "Of what nature is a preceptor as laid down in Śāstras ? Who was panegyrized by you formerly ? O friend, tell me everything. I am extremely curious and anxious to know it."

The Brahma-Rākṣasa said :

85. "There are many categories of preceptors[9]. All of them are worthy of being worshipped and honoured respectfully. O friend, listen with single-minded attention as I narrated them (viz. categories of preceptors).

86-88. They are as follows:—One who teaches the Vedas, one who explains the connection between the Vedic passage and its interpretation (i.e. the interpreter of the Vedas), the expounder of the scriptures, the exponent of the Dharmas, the instructor in moral philosophy (or politics), one who initiates in the *Mantras*, one who explains the *Mantras*, one who dispels doubts in Vedic passages, one who instructs in religious observances and vows, one who saves from dangerous situation, one who provides with food, the father-in-law, the maternal uncle, the eldest brother, the father, one who invests the sacred thread, the impregnator and the consecrator, O excellent friend.

89. These are said to be the preceptors. They deserve to be worshipped and bowed with great respect."

Kalmāṣapāda enquired :

90. "O friend, many preceptors have been mentioned by you. Who is the most excellent of all these ? Or, are all of them of equal status ? Tell me precisely."

The Brahma-Rakṣasa replied :

91-92. "Very nice ! A very good question ! O highly intelligent one. I shall explain to you what has been enquired by you of me. The narration of the glory of preceptors, listening to that glory and approbation of the same—all these accord welfare unto all. Hence, I shall explain now:—There is no doubt in this that all these are equally worthy of being worshipped at all times.

93-94. Still, however, listen to me. I shall relate to you the essential and crucial decision of the scriptures (in the matter). The teacher of the Vedas, the person who explains the *Mantras*, the father and expounder of the Dharma—these are regarded to be special types of preceptors in the *Smṛti* texts. O lord of the earth, listen as to who should be regarded as the most excellent of all these.

95-96. I shall explain unto you what has been proclaimed by the knowers of the principles and interpretations of all scriptures. That learned man who explains the *Purāṇas* along with the Dharmas which contribute to the snapping asunder of the noose of the worldly existence, is the most excellent preceptor. It is from the *Purāṇas* that one knows the various rites proper for the worship of Devas and the fruit (one achieves) of the worship of the deities.

97-98A. Hence, O king, gods and sages say that the *Purāṇas* constitute the essence of the meaning of all Vedic passages. The expounder of the *Purāṇas* is, therefore, the greatest of all the preceptors.

98B-100. The man who strives to cross the ocean of worldly existence should listen to the *Purāṇas*—so says the classifier of the scriptures (i.e. the sage Vyāsa). O king, it was he who laid down in details all the Dharmas in the *Purāṇas*. Logic or reasoning is only for the sake of arguments in dispute. Ethics or politics is the means for worldly affairs and Purāṇas indeed are conducive to the happiness both here and hereafter, O highly intelligent one.

101. The intellect (or mind) of a person who always listens to the *Purāṇas* with great devotion becomes free from impurities. He shall be devoted again to Dharma.

102. O king, thanks to listening to the *Purāṇas*, auspicious

devotion towards the Lord of Lakṣmī, is thereby engendered. The intellect of men who are the devotees of Viṣṇu is engaged in Dharma.

103-105A. Sins are destroyed due to Dharma and the knowledge becomes pure. Those who are well versed in the ancient lore say thus:—"Those who are desirous of attaining the fruits of *Puruṣārthas*, viz. *Dharma*, wealth, love and liberation from *Saṁsāra*, should listen to the *Purāṇas*." On the beautiful banks of the Gaṅgā, I heard all the topics on religion or Dharma from sage Gautama, who was omniscient and expounder of the *Brahman* or the Vedas.

105B-107. Once, I went to perform the worship of god Śiva. Although he (Gautama) was present, I did not make obeisance to him. But Gautama, the highly intelligent sage, the very receptacle of great lustre was calm. He rejoiced at the proper performance of the rites as mentioned in the *Mantras* and since Lord Śiva, the preceptor of all the universe, was worshipped by me.

108-110A. Since disrespect was shown towards the preceptor, he (Śiva) turned me into a Rākṣasa. If a person, knowingly or unknowingly, shows contempt and disrespect towards the preceptor, his intelligence, learning, wealth and all holy observances perish. O king, the learned men say that if a man renders service unto the preceptors with great respect, he is endowed with affluence.

110B-112A. I am burnt by that curse. Internally I am being consumed by the fire of hunger. O excellent king, I do not know when I shall be liberated." O prominent Brāhmaṇa (Nārada), when the Brahma-Rākṣasa residing on the banyan tree was discussing thus, the sins of both of them were dispelled, as they were engaged in discussion on the topics of Dharma.

112B-113. In the meantime, a highly righteous Brāhmaṇa came there. He was born in the land of Kaliṅga (Orissa) He was known by the name Garga.[10] He was carrying the holy water of the Gaṅgā on his shoulders. He was eulogising Lord Viśveśvara.

114-115. He was singing the names of Lord Śiva. With a thrill of joy, his hair over his body stood on their ends. On seeing the sage arrive, the *Piśāci* and the Rākṣasa rushed at him, raising their arms aloft and saying:—"Our break-fast has arrived !" But they stood away on hearing the names recited by him, as they were unable to attack him. The Rākṣasa said as follows:—

116. "O highly blessed Brāhmaṇa, salutations to you who are a noble-souled one. Thanks to the greatness of the recitation of the names of God, we, the Rākṣasas, have to stay away at a distance.

117. O Brāhmaṇa, thousands and millions of Brāhmaṇas have been formerly devoured by us. It is the covering shield of the holy names of Viṣṇu that protects you from the great fear of death.

118. O respected sir, that even we, the Rākṣasas have attained great tranquility and solace by merely listening to (his hallowing) names, is due to the greatness of Acyuta.

119. O highly blessed one, you are in every respect free from attachment and passion. Be pleased to absolve us of the heaps of sins, by making us perform the ablution with the waters of the Gaṅgā, by sprinkling it over us.

120. Wise and learned persons proclaim that he who redeems his own *Ātman* by engaging himself in service to Hari, shall redeem the entire universe.

121. Except by Hari's name which is the panacea for all terrible ills of the worldly existence, by what other means can liberation, which is so very difficult to attain everywhere, be secured ?

122. Just as a person trying to cross a river or a sea by means of a raft of iron, sinks under water, similarly, how can they who have not performed meritorious acts, redeem others ?

123. O ! The conduct of life of great men is conducive to the happiness of every one, just as the moon contributes to the delight of all.

124. O excellent Brāhmaṇa, whatever sacred and holy waters are there on the earth, they are not equal in holiness even to a particle of the waters of the Gaṅgā.

125. A drop of the water of the Gaṅgā, of the size of a mustard seed mixed with the Tulasī leaf, definitely sanctifies twentyone generations.

126. Hence, O highly blessed Brāhmaṇa, O expert one in the meanings of all scriptures, protect us, the perpetrators of sinful acts, by giving us the water of the Gaṅgā."

127. On hearing this excellent discourse on the greatness of the Gaṅgā related by those Rākṣasas, the excellent Brāhmaṇa was very much surprised.

128. (He thought) "Even in these (Rākṣasas,) there is such a devotion towards the Gaṅgā, the mother of the worlds. How much more there should be devotion of the great men of meritorious deeds who are endowed with sound perfect knowledge ?"

129. Then the excellent Brāhmaṇa mentally came to a conclusion on the *Dharma* that a devotee who is a benefactor of all living beings attains the highest region.

130. Then the Brāhmaṇa, full of mercy, sprinkled the excellent waters of the Gaṅgā mixed with a Tulasī leaf over the Rākṣasas.

131. On being sprinkled by the drops of water of the size of a mustard, those Rākṣasas gave up their Rākṣasa state and became refulgent like Devas.

132. The Brāhmaṇa lady accompanied by her son and her husband—Brāhmaṇa Somadatta—became prominent among gods resembling a hundred million suns in brilliance.

133. They were distinctly characterised by conches, discuses and the iron maces. They attained to *Sārūpya* (similarity in form) with Hari. Eulogising the Brāhmaṇa very much, they went to the abode of Hari, i.e. Vaikuṇṭha.

134. The king Kalmāṣapāda regained his own (Royal) form. On seeing those sinless Brāhmaṇas being liberated, he began to think deeply.

135. When the king was extremely distressed and miserable, a mysterious secret voice uttered in deep sonorous tone this great statement based on *Dharma* :

136. "O highly blessed king, it does not behove you to be miserable. O king, at the end of your enjoyment of pleasures, you also will attain to the highest beatitude (*Mokṣa*).

137. There is no doubt that those who have washed off their sins by means of good acts and who are engaged in devotion to Hari, attain to the highest region of Viṣṇu.

138. Those who are merciful towards all living beings, those who function along the path of *Dharma* and those who are eagerly devoted to the worship of the preceptor, attain to the highest region."

139. On hearing this utterance of Bhāratī (Goddess of speech), the excellent king attained deep mental satisfaction and tranquillity and remembered the words of his preceptor.

140. With great delight, he praised his preceptor, that Brāhmaṇa (from Kaliṅga) and Lord Viṣṇu. He narrated all his former story to that Brāhmaṇa.

141. O sage, thereafter, the king made obeisance to the Brāhmaṇa from Kaliṅga duly. Repeating the names of Viṣṇu, he immediately proceeded to Vārāṇasī.[11]

142. He took bath in the Gaṅgā there for six months and paid visits to god Sadāśiva. King Mitrasaha thereby became free from the curse of the Brāhmaṇa lady.

143. Thereafter, he went to his capital city. O excellent sage, he was then crowned by the noble-souled Vasiṣṭha. He protected his own kingdom thereafter.

144. He ruled over the entire earth. He enjoyed all worldly pleasures except that from his queen. He got a son begot by Vasiṣṭha. Ultimately the excellent king attained salvation.

145. O excellent Brāhmaṇa, it is not surprising that the man who praises the excellences of Viṣṇu and Vārāṇasī listens to them and muses over them and drinks the water of the Gaṅgā, becomes liberated from Saṁsāra.

146. Hence, O leading Brāhmaṇa, it is not possible to reach the other shore of the great glory of the Gaṅgā (i.e. to describe it exhaustively), even to the lords of gods, viz. Brahmā, Viṣṇu and Śiva.

147. Undoubtedly, by merely remembering the names of the Gaṅgā, a man becomes absolved of millions of heinous sins and attains to Brahmā's abode.

148. If the name 'Gaṅgā' is repeated even once, one is immediately liberated from all sins, and he is honoured in the region of god Brahmā.[12]

CHAPTER NINE

The Glory of the Gaṅgā

1. Saudāsa, the son of Sudās was, according to Bh.P.IX.45, the 8th descendant from Bhagīratha who brought the Gaṅgā to the earth. His real name was Mitra-saha, but he came to be known as Kalmāṣa-pāda. The legend of king Mitra-saha, better known as Kalmāṣapāda is given in details in the *Mbh.Ādi* chs. 175, 176, 181, *Śānti* 234.30 and *Anu.*137.18, in the *Bh.*P. IX.45. 20-38, *Śiva P.*—IV ch.10 and a brief reference in *VR* I.70.39-40. The legend differs slightly in different Purāṇas. The main facts as given in the *Mbh.* are as follows : Mitrasaha and queen Madayantī, a happy royal couple was ruling over Ayodhyā. On one occasion, while the king, dog-tired with the fatigue of hunting, was returning, he was confronted by a sage Śakti at a narrow pass. The quarrel arose who was to give way to whom and the enraged sage cursed the king to be a demon (*Mbh.Ādi* 175. 1-14). Vasiṣṭha's rival Viśvāmitra instigated a demon 'Kiṅkara' to possess the king and made him serve human flesh to a sage who cursed the king to be an ogre. Viśvāmitra instigated him to eat Śakti (Vasiṣṭha's son who cursed him) and the rest of the sons of Vasiṣṭha. When he approached to eat up Vasiṣṭha, he sprinkled him with water charged with a *mantra* and restored him to his original status as king of Ayodhyā (*Ādi*. 176.26). Unfortunately during his demonic state, king Mitrasaha ate up a Brāhmaṇa out of a couple at the time of their sexual intercourse. The Brāhmaṇa woman Āṅgirasī cursed him that he would meet death if he touched a woman. Hence, he had to request Vasiṣṭha to procreate a son from his queen Madayantī. The *Bh.P.* agrees with this basic episode. The *N.P.*, however, adds some spicy material and gives an interesting story.

2. *Sapta-sāgarāḥ* :

The traditional list of seven seas and their identification by N. L. De (p.179) is as follows : (1) *Lavaṇa* (salt) or the Indian Ocean, (2) *Kṣīra* (milk) —the Shirwan or the Caspian sea, (3) *Surā* (wine)—a corruption or rather Sanskritisation of the Sea of Sarain, a part of the Caspian Sea forming the south-eastern boundary of *Kuśa-dvīpa.* (4) *Ghṛta* (Ghee)—Derived from Erythraen sea or the Persian Gulf forming the boundary of *Śālmala-dvīpa* or *Chaldia* or Assyria (5) *Ikṣu* (sugar-cane juice)—*Ikṣu* is the Oxus—the river and sea having a common term—here taken as a sea. It formed the southern boundary of *Puṣkara-dvīpa* (Puṣkara—Bhushkara or -Bokhara), (6) *Dadhi* (curds) is a Sanskritisation of Dahi (Dahae), a scythic tribe living on the shore of the Sea of Aral. Hence, the Aral sea. It formed the boundary of Krauñca *dvīpa.* (7) *Svādu* perhaps a corruption of Tehadun, a river in Mongolia flowing through *Plakṣa dvīpa.* Like *Ikṣu* a river-name used for the sea—De, p. 179.

3. Saudāsa in the *Mbh.* is childless but in the *NP.*, he is blessed with sons and grandsons.

4. The episode that a couple of Rākṣasas assumed the form of tigers and were engaged in sexual intercourse and that king Saudāsa killed the female partner

and was threatened by the male-partner after assuming his demon form is an addition of the *NP*.

5. The episode that the demon assumed the form of Vasiṣṭha and requested to send human flesh to his hermitage and the king innocently sent it and got cursed is not in *Mbh.* but in the *Uttara Rāmāyaṇa* (vide *Puranic Encyclopaedia*, p. 377).

5A. Cf. *Sahasā vidadhīta na kriyām*
avivekaḥ paramāpadām padam—Kirāta. II.30

6. According to the *Mbh.Ādi* 175.40, he was Vasiṣṭha's son, Śakti who cursed him to be a demon for not giving him the way (*Ibid.* 175.13-14).

7. The Brāhmaṇa woman's imprecation and Kalmāṣapāda's counter-curse turning the lady and her child into goblins (*piśācas*) and their joint wandering have no basis in the *Mbh.* and but are *NP.*'s contribution. The *Śiva P.* however, endorses Kalmāṣapāda being cursed by a Brāhmaṇa lady but not his counter-curse to that lady.

8. The Somadatta episode is not in the *Mbh.* but it is probably *NP.*'s contribution.

9. The term *guru* connotes an elderly person. *Viṣṇu Dharma Sūtra* 32.1-2 states that the father, mother and preceptor (*ācārya*) are the highest *gurus.* Manu (II.225-32) and *Mt.P.* 210.20-27 compare them to the three sacred fires maintained by an *Agnihotrin.* Devala extends the title to five, including in them elder brother and husband. (*Smṛti-candrikā* I, p.35). In the list given here in the NP. the first eight *gurus* can be included under 'preceptor', the next two under 'maintainer' (employer, husband), the next three have traditionally the status of a father—a status extended to the last three, viz., the performer of *upanayana* which admits one to Vedic studies and of *Saṁskāras* and the progenitor.

10. The episode of Garga, a Brāhmaṇa from Kaliṅga, liberating Kalmāṣapāda and the Brāhmaṇa-Ogre Somadatta, with sprinkling of the water of the Gaṅgā has no basis in the *Mbh.* In *Mbh.* the sage Vasiṣṭha redeems him sprinkling him with water charged with *mantras.* No mention of the Gaṅgā water is in *Mbh.Ādi* 176.26-30. NP. contributes this to glorify the efficacy of the water of the Gaṅgā.

11. King Kalmāṣapāda's sojourn at Vārāṇasī for six months for redemption from the curse of the Brāhmaṇa woman is NP.'s contribution with no basis in the *Mbh.* or *Bh.P.*

12. In *NP.* II chs. 39 and 40 we find the glory of the Gaṅgā repeated and many of these verses in the Chs. on the glory of the Gaṅgā are echoed therein.

CHAPTER TEN

The Defeat of the Devas by Bali[1]

Nārada said :

1. O brother, if I am considered worthy of being blessed by you, kindly narrate to me the origin and other details of the river that is called the Gaṅgā and that has its source from the feet of Viṣṇu.[2]

Sanaka narrated :

2. O Nārada, listen. I shall relate to you, O sinless one, the source or the origin of the Gaṅgā that bestows merits on the speakers as well as on the listeners, and destroys their sins.

3. There was a certain sage, Kaśyapa, who was the father of Indra and other gods. Diti and Aditi, the daughters of Dakṣa, were his wives.

4. Aditi was the mother of all Devas or gods and Diti was the mother of Daityas. O Brāhmaṇa, those two wives of Kaśyapa and their sons vied with each other, seeking to vanquish the other.

5. The Daityas were called *Pūrvadevas*, as they had been always senior to Devas. The first Daitya, the son of Diti, was the powerful Hiraṇyakaśipu.

6. Prahlāda, the extremely noble and the righteous-most Daitya, was his son. Prahlāda's son Virocana was a great devotee of Brāhmaṇas.

7. His son was the extremely brilliant and valorous Bali. O sage, he alone was the real leader of the armies of Daityas.

8. He was endowed with great strength. He enjoyed this earth. After conquering the entire earth, he became desirous of conquering the heaven.

9. O excellent sage, his elephants were in billions. The number of his horses and the chariots came to as many. For every elephant, the number of foot-soldiers was five hundred. How can his excellent army be described adequately ?

10. His ministers were Kumbhāṇḍa and Kūpakarṇa who surpassed the leaders of millions of ministers. Bali had a hundred sons, the eldest of whom was Bāṇa. He was equal to his father in heroism and prowess.

11. Bali was actuated by a desire of vanquishing the gods. He started the campaign accompanied by a great army. Through banners and umbrellas, he reminded the people of the flashes of lightning which were the billows on the ocean in the form of the sky.

12. Arriving at the city of the slayer of Vṛtra (viz. Amarāvatī), the demon laid siege to it through Daityas, strong and vehement like lions. The thunder-bolt-bearing Indra and other gods came out of the city for fighting with them.

13. A terrible battle ensued thereafter between the gods and Daityas, with shouts like thunders of clouds at the end of the universe, mixed with the sounds of big drums.

14. In that extremely terrible battle, Daityas discharged volleys of arrows on the army of Devas. The gods too retaliated like-wise on the army of Daityas.

15. Yelling sounds and shouts came up from both the armies (such as 'Kill', 'Tear', 'Hit', 'Split', 'Annihilate', 'Strike down', etc.

16-17. The whole world was filled with various sounds such as the sounds of conches, whistling arrows,[3] kettle-drums, the roaring sound of the shouting demons, the creaking of the chariots, the hissing of the arrows, the neighing of horses, the trumpeting of the elephants and the twanging sound of the bow-strings.

18. Beholding the fire that originated from the mutual friction of the shafts discharged by gods and Asuras, the whole universe regarded it as an untimely *Pralaya* (the dissolution of the world).

19. The army of the enemies of gods, wielding a stream of refulgent weapons shone like the night over-cast with clouds with streaks of lightning flashing across.

20. In that war, the agile, active and valorous gods, by means of their arrows, smashed to smithereens the huge boulders of mountainous rocks, hurled by the Asuras.

21. Some of them confronted the elephants with their elephants, the chariots by means of their chariots, the horses

with other horses. Some hit them with the handles of maces and iron bars.

22. Some of them, on being hit with *Parighas* (Iron clubs), fell into the marsh of blood. Some of them whose vital breath had come out i.e. (died), occupied the aerial cars.

23. Those Daityas who were forcibly killed by the gods in the battle, assumed the forms of *devas* and rushed at demons.

24. Then the extremely terrible hosts of demons who became infuriated on being beaten soundly by the gods, hit back gods by means of various kinds of weapons (such as)

25-27. Rocks, *Bhindipālas* (a cubit-long wooden club), swords, axes, *tomaras*, (Javelins), *Parighas* (Iron clubs), daggers, spears, discus, pointed poniards, pestles, goads, plough-shares, *Paṭṭiśas* (a spear with sharp points) *śaktis*, stones, *Śataghnis* (a cylinderical piece of wood studded with iron pikes and capable of killing hundreds of people), nooses, mailed fists, tridents, pointed iron spikes and pounding rods. The battle grew more and more tumultuous and fierce through the confrontation between the chariots, horses, elephants and foot-soldiers.

28. The gods hurled various kinds of weapons at Daityas. In this way, the extremely terrible battle continued for eight thousand years.

29. When the army of Daityas became powerful, the defeated heaven-dwellers abandoned their celestial region in great fright and fled precipitately.

30-33. The defeated gods disguised themselves as human beings and wandered over the earth. The son of Virocana, Bali, was devotedly attached to Nārāyaṇa. He enjoyed the three worlds without any obstruction to his overlordship. His prosperity flourished. The mighty Daitya desirous of propitiating Viṣṇu, performed many horse-sacrifices. He discharged the duties of Indra in the heaven as well as those of the guardians of cardinal points. The king of Daityas began to partake of oblations offered in all various sacrifices performed by Brāhmaṇas for propitiating Devas. On seeing her sons in such a plight Aditi, the mother of Devas, became distressed.

34-35A. She thought to herself, "I am staying in vain", and then she went to the mountain Himālaya. Wishing for the prosperity of Indra and the defeat of Daityas, she who was devotedly attached to meditation on Hari, performed a severe penance.

35B-38A. While performing the penance she did it in the sitting posture for some time and then performed it while in a standing posture. For a long time, she stood on only one leg. Thereafter, she stood on the tip of her feet. For some time her diet was fruits. Thereafter, she subsisted on the withered leaves fallen down from trees. Then she lived only on water. Afterwards she gave up food altogether and subsisted on air only. She began to meditate on the Supreme Ātman through her individual Ātman. She contemplated on the Deity, the embodiment of existence, knowledge and bliss. O Nārada she performed the penance for one thousand divine years.[4]

38B-41. On hearing of that unending penance of Aditi, Daityas, expert in their science of creating illusions, assumed the form of Devas as per command of Bali. They approached Aditi and said, "O mother, why do you perform this penance desiccating your body. If Daityas come to know of this, great misery may befall us. Leave off this (penance) causing so much misery and drying up your body. Learned men do not approve of a meritorious act which requires to be achieved only with very great difficulty and troubles. Those who are eager to achieve *Dharma* should assiduously preserve and take care of their body.

42. Those who neglect their body are the slayers of *Ātman*. O fortunate and blessed lady, stay here happily. Please do not cause grief to us, your sons.

43-45A. O mother, undoubtedly those who are devoid of their mothers are no better than dead, whether they be cows or other animals or even trees. None of these derives any happiness without their mother. Whether one is an indigent fellow or an ailing one, or one in exile in a foreign land, one derives the greatest joy at the mere sight of one's mother.

45B-46. One may perhaps develop aversion to food, water, richs, etc. and even to lovely women. But there is none who turns his face away from his mother. If one has neither a mother nor a chaste wife devoted to religion (righteousness) and loyally attached to her husband at home, he should rather betake himself to the forest.

47. A person devoid of his mother is like the righteous path of life devoid of devotion to Nārāyaṇa, or like wealth which is not enjoyed in any decent manner or like house-hold without a wife or a son.

48. Hence, O gentle lady, save us who are your sons and who are extremely distressed".

Even though she was thus importuned by Daityas, Aditi did not get disturbed from her trance.

49. When Daityas found that in spite of their speech to her, Aditi was still absorbed in meditation on Hari, they were extremely infuriated and wanted to kill her.

50. Due to fury, their eyes turned red. They roared like clouds at the end of the *Kalpa* (when the universe is dissolved). By the gnashing of the tips of their curved fangs (in anger), they created fire which burnt down the forest instantaneously.

51-52. The forest extended to a hundred *Yojanas*. It was teeming with various kinds of living beings. The very same fire burnt Daityas who had gone there to destroy Aditi.

Only Aditi, the mother of gods, remained alive. She had been meditating on Acyuta (Viṣṇu) for hundreds of years. She was protected by the *Sudarśana* discus of Viṣṇu who killed Daityas and took pity on his own devotees.

CHAPTER TEN

The Description of the Defeat of Devas by Bali

1. The legend of Bali, his generosity, truthfulness, valour and nobility of character overshadow the greatness of Viṣṇu who deceived him by begging three feet of land as a pigmy, and assuming a cosmic form, pressed him down to the nether world, is very popular with Purāṇas. We find it is *Mbh.*III.272. 61-76, *Bh.P.*VIII.chs. 15, 18 to 23, *AP.* 4.5-11, *Bd.P.*2.73.75-87, *AP.*I.41. 79-103, *KP* I.16.1-69, *Va.P.* 36.74-86, to mention a few. The transformation of the Vedic sun-god Viṣṇu into Purāṇic Trivikrama and its fusion with Bali legend is interesting.

It is significant that practically for every generation of Diti, the exterminator is some form of Viṣṇu. Thus Hiraṇyākṣa : Varāha, Hiraṇyakaśipu : Nṛsiṁha, Bali : Vāmana, Bāṇa : Kṛṣṇa—these pairs indicate a stubborn resistance of Diti's family to the descendants of Aditi's family—the socalled 'gods'—probably a historical family feud in days of yore.

This legend is given here to glorify the Gaṅgā. While God Viṣṇu, in his Trivikrama form, tried to cover the heavens, his toe-nail struck against the outer crust of the universe and from the crack created by the toe-nail, rushed in the cosmic waters that envelop this universe. That is the source of the Gaṅgā which flowed down Viṣṇu's feet. (vide *infra.* I.11. 179-182).

2. As indicated there, the attribution of a heavenly source to the Gaṅgā is a part of the racial memory of Indo-Aryans, who still remembered in a legendary form, their stay in the Meru (Pamir) region. S.M. Ali in the *Geography of the Purāṇas,* describes graphically the geneses of the 'descent of the Gaṅgā and why the Gaṅgā came to be called *Tripathagā.* His conclusions are as follow :

"It will be realised from the above discussion that the Purāṇas intend to bring out three stages in the evolution of the Gaṅgā :

(i) They connect it with the heavens by comparing and identifying it with the Milky Way. This is the celestial stage.

(ii) As the snow falls on the high mountains they identify the snow cap of High Asia which covers its high range and its central knot, the Pamirs, the Gaṅgā is just a cover or belt of snow and ice at this stage. This is the Gaṅgā at its 'snowy stage'.

(iii) From this common source i.e. The Pamirs, the snowy Gaṅgā melts and divides itself into the four main rivers of Asia which radiate in different directions. The Gaṅgā at this stage becomes a stream or rather four streams of water.

The Purāṇas have thus rolled the accounts of the glaciers of Asia, the rivers of Asia and their origin into one, in a simple but colourful statement, which is repeated practically in all the Purāṇas.

—*The Geography of the Purāṇas*, pp. 63-64.

This description explains to some extent the legend of the descent of the *Gaṅgā* (*Gaṅgāvataraṇa*), in various Purāṇas.

3. Probably the correct reading must be *śaṅkha-dundubhi-niddhvanaiḥ* and not *śara* — as the *Śaṅkha* and *dundubhi* are sounded together in fighting and the sound of arrows (*bāṇa-kreṅkāra*) is mentioned below and its mention would be superfluous. It is probably the slip of the scribe of the MS in Devanāgari script where instead of शंख, the scribe must have written शंर or शर, in the previous case, the editor of that MS. emended शंर as शर. This is my guess about the correct reading as the venkateshwar edition records.

4. One year of human beings (360 days) constitutes one day of gods. Thus one year of gods or divine year = 360 years of men. So Aditi performed penance for 1000 divine years or 360,000 human years.

CHAPTER ELEVEN

The Glory of the Gaṅgā : The Origin of the River

Nārada said :

1. You have mentioned, my brother, an extremely miraculous incident. How did that forest fire spare Aditi and burnt all Daityas in a moment ?

2. Be pleased to tell me in details about the immense inherent strength of Aditi that caused this special surprise. Indeed, prominent sages and good men are always engaged in tendering advice to others.

Sanaka replied :

3. O Nārada, listen to the greatness of those who revel in devotion to Hari.[1] Is there any person who is capable of harassing saintly persons engaged in the meditation of Hari ?

4. Gods Brahmā, Hari, Śiva and others, Siddhas and prominent leaders of sages — all stay permanently at the residence of a person who is engaged in devotion to Hari.

5. O highly blessed Nārada, Lord Hari is enshrined in the hearts of his devotees who are serene-minded and are always engaged in repeating his name. Need it be said that he abides in the hearts of those who are engaged in contemplating on him ?

6. Lakṣmī, the goddess of wealth, and all the deities stay only there, where a person is engaged in Śiva's[2] worship or where one devoted to the worship of Viṣṇu, resides.

7. Neither a fire nor a tyrant nor a thief can molest any person devoted to Viṣṇu's worship. Nor is he affected by diseases.

8. Neither ghosts nor evil spirits nor the Kūṣmāṇḍa (evil spirits), evil planets, nor the goblins that attack children nor Ḍākinīs (witches) nor Rākṣasas can dare to trouble a worshipper of Acyuta.

9. Those Bhūtas, Vetālas (goblins and genii) and others, who take delight in afflicting others, take to flight from the residence of an excellent devotee engaged in the worship of Hari and Lakṣmī.

10. All the sacred places and Deities stay there only, where a person who has subdued his sense-organs, or one who is a benefactor unto all, or one who is devoted to *Dharma* and holy rites, stays.

11. All fortunes and blessings are found at that place only where *yogins* stay even for a moment or a half. That spot is a holy place and that is a real penance-grove.

12. All troubles disappear at the mere utterance of Hari's names. What need be said of those who propitiate him through eulogies, worship or through meditation ?

13. O Brāhmaṇa, in this way, the whole forest along with Asuras was consumed by the fire. But Aditi was not even scorched, since she was protected by the discus of Viṣṇu.

14. Thereupon, the gracious-looking Lord with a pleasant countenance, and eyes large like the petals of a lotus, revealed himself just in front of her, wielding in his hands a conch, the discus Sudarśana, and the mace Kaumodakī.

15. Illuminating various quarters with the lustre of his refulgent teeth which appeared slightly as he smiled gently, and touching the beloved wife of Kaśyapa with his holy hand, the Lord said:

The glorious Lord said :

16. "O mother of Devas, I am pleased with you, by virtue of your propitiation through performance of penance for a long time. You are exhausted. You will certainly be blessed with good fortune.

17. Seek any boon that you cherish in your heart and I shall grant it to you. O gentle Lady, you need not be afraid. Good fortune will certainly come to your lot."

18. The mother of Devas who was thus addressed by the discus-bearing Lord of the gods bowed to him, and eulogised the Lord, the bestower of happiness unto all people.

Aditi prayed :

19. "Salutation to you O Janārdana, the Lord of the chiefs of Devas, O omnipresent one, you are the cause of the functioning of the world through *Sattva* and other *Guṇas*.

20. I bow to you who have innumerable forms and are still a formless one, to you who are the Supreme Soul.

Salutations to you who comprise all forms within yourself. Obeisance to you who possess all excellences and are still without an attribute.

21. I bow to you, the Lord of the worlds, the embodiment of Supreme spiritual knowledge. Salutations to the Deity ever favourably disposed to good devotees. Obeisance to you who are of auspicious nature.

22. For the achievement of desired object, I bow unto that Lord, the Primordial Person whose incarnated forms are worshipped by prominent sages.

23. I bow down to that Cause of the universe, the Controller of Māyā, yet devoid of Māyā (i.e. not influenced by her) whom the Śrutis do not know and who is beyond the comprehension of sages.

24. I salute to him whom all pay obeisance, who is of a mysteriously surprising vision; who is the cause of the removal of Māyā, whose form constitutes the whole of the universe, and who is the cause of the universe.

25. I offer obeisance unto the consort of Kamalā (the Goddess Lakṣmī). People who bow to his feet (*lit.* whose forehead is saved by the service rendered to the filaments of his lotus-like feet) attain the highest *Siddhi* (*Mokṣa*).

26. God Brahmā and other Devas do not comprehend his glory, but he is very close to his devotees. I salute that close associate of devotees.

27. Though he himself is absolutely unattached and companionless, the Lord who is the ocean of mercy, blesses with his contact, people who have renounced all association and attachment, and who are calm and quiet. I bow to him.

28. I salute to the Lord of sacrifices; one who is the very rite of performance of sacrifices; one who is established in the rites of sacrifices; one who bestows the fruit of sacrifices; one who enlightens people about the sacrificial rites.

29. I bow down to that Lord, who is the witness unto all the universe. By uttering his name, even Ajāmila,[3] the sinning soul, instantaneously attained to the Supreme region (Vaikuṇṭha).

30. Mahādeva is a form of Hari and Janārdana is in the form of Śiva. Thus, that Lord is the leader of the world. I bow down to that preceptor of the universe.

31. I bow to the Leader of all, the noose of whose Māyā binds and restrains Brahmā and other lords of gods who, therefore, do not know his essential, Supreme nature.

32. I salute to that witness of perfect wisdom who appears to be stationed far away, though (actually) he is enthroned in the lotus of the heart of *Yogins*. his very presence is beyond the scope of cognition by means of valid knowledge.

33. Obeisance unto that Lord from whose mouth was born the Brāhmaṇa, from whose arms, came forth the Kṣattriya; from whose thighs was born the Vaiśya and from whose feet the Śūdra was born.

34. From whose mind was evolved the moon, from whose eyes the sun was born, from whose mouth Agni the fire God and Indra came forth, from whose Prāṇa (vital breath) the wind-god was born.[4]

35. I bow to the Lord who is the embodiment of the Ṛk, Yajus and Sāman (Vedas), whose *Ātman* has permeated the seven notes of the musical scale.[5] I bow to you again and again—you whose form is comprised of six *Aṅgas*.[6]

36. O Lord, you are Indra, Pavana (the wind God), Soma (the moon God), you are Īśāna, you are the annihilator (of the world); you are Agni (the fire God) Nirṛti, (the Deity of death); you are Varuṇa, the Lord of the seas and also Divākara, the sun-god.

37. The celestial residents, the immobile beings, *Piśācas*, Rākṣasas, mountains, Siddhas, Gandharvas (Heavenly musicians), the rivers, earth and oceans — all these are your manifestations.

38. You alone are the Lord of the worlds; wherever you are, you are greater than the greatest; everything exists within your person; O Lord, my obeisance be to you for ever.

39. O protector of the helpless ! O omniscient Lord ! O Lord, who comprise within your body all living beings right upto the Lord of gods. O Janārdana, protect my sons who are harrassed by Daityas".

40. Eulogising him thus and bowing again and again unto the Lord, the mother of the Devas spoke with palms joined in reverence, and tears of joy drenching her bosom.

41. "O Lord of Devas; O the first cause of everything, it behoves you to bless me. Be pleased to grant unto my

sons, the heaven-dwellers, prosperity, freedom from nuisance and troubles.

42. O indwelling soul of the world ! One immanent in the universe ! O omniscient ! Supreme Lord ! What is unknown to you, O Lord of Lakṣmī ? What is it that you make me long for (is already known to you) ?

43. I shall, however, tell you what appeals to my mind. O Lord of Devas, I have become as if bereaved of my sons. The existence of my sons is in vain and futile, as they are harassed by Daityas.

44. I do not wish to cause any harm unto Daityas, since they too are my sons.[7] O Lord of gods, without killing them, bless my sons with fortune and prosperity."

45. The Lord of the chiefs of Devas who was thus addressed again, became delighted. O Brāhmaṇa, he respectfully addressed the mother of Devas in words giving her delight.

The Lord said :

46. O gentle lady ! I am pleased with you. May good betide you. I shall, therefore, be your son, since O goddess, affection towards sons of one's co-wife is rare.

47. Men who read and recite this prayer composed by you will never be deficient in excellent riches and sons.

48. He who treats his own son as well as that of another person with equality, will never experience sorrow, due to separation or bereavement of his son. This is the eternal Dharma."

Aditi said :

49. "O Lord, I am unable to bear you (in my womb)—you who are the Supreme First Person, the greatest Being with innumerable cosmic eggs constituting the hair on your body; you, the Lord of all, the cause or creator of the world.

50. O Lord, how can I bear that Supreme chief of the leaders of gods, whose prowess even the Śrutis and all the deities cannot comprehend.

51. O Lord, you are the Puruṣottama (the Supreme Person), the eternal Lord (hence unborn), minuter than the minutest and greater than the greatest.[8] How can I bear you ?

52. How does that Lord, the very remembrance of whose name liberates a man, vitiated by great sins, deserve the birth among the rustic and the unrefined ?

53. May this incarnation of yours, O Lord, be like that of your other incarnations, like the boar, the fish. Who can comprehend your activities, O Lord of the universe?

54. I bow down to your lotus feet. I am devotedly attached to the remembrance of your names. O Lord, I contemplate exclusively on you. Do as you please."

Sanaka Said :

55. On hearing the words uttered by her, Janārdana, the Lord of Devas, granted to the mother of gods the boon of fearlessness (and security from dangers). He addressed her the following words:

The glorious Lord said :

56. "O highly blessed Lady, there is no doubt about the truth that has been uttered by you; however, O auspicious lady, I shall tell you the secret of secrets.

57. My votaries who are devoid of passionate attachment and hatred and are devoutly attached to me, who are devoid of jealousy and are free from hypocrisy, do perpetually bear me.

58. Those who are disinclined to cause injury to others, who are interested and engaged in devotion to Śiva, and who are intensely devoted to the listening of my stories, perpetually bear me.

59. O gentle Lady, even those chaste women who love their husbands like their very vital breath, and are exclusively devoted to their husbands and have eschewed malice and rivalry, perpetually bear me.

60. He who renders service to his parents, is a devotee to the preceptor, who likes to receive and serve guests, and who is benefactor unto the Brāhmaṇas, perpetually bears me.

61. Those who always take delight in visiting holy places, who are engaged in associating themselves with saintly people, and who are habitually obliging and favouring other people—all these perpetually bear me.

62. Those who are interested in helping others, those who

are not desirous of the wealth of another person and who cherish no illicit desire when other men's wives are concerned—these bear me perpetually.

63. Those who always worship with Tulasī plant, those who are attached to the names of the Lord and those who carefully protect cows—all these bear me perpetually.

64. Those who desist from accepting monetary gifts, those who do not take food at another man's house and those who make gifts of food and water to the needy, do perpetually bear me.

65. O gentle Lady, you value your husband like your own vital breath; you are virtuous and you take delight in the welfare of all living beings. Hence, I shall assume the state of being your son and fulfil your desire."

66. After addressing thus to Aditi the mother of Devas, the Lord of the chiefs of Devas gave her the necklace from his neck and blessed her with fearlessness and protection from danger, and vanished.

67. The mother of the gods, the daughter of Dakṣa, bowed to the consort of Lakṣmī with extremely delighted mind and went back to her own abode.

68. Thereafter, the highly blessed Aditi, who was extremely glad and was respected all over the world, in due course of time gave birth to a son whom the whole world paid obeisance.

69. He was named Vāmana. He was holding a conch and a discus, in his hands. He was quiescent. He shone in the middle of the lunar sphere. The pot of nectar and curds mixed with cooked rice were in his hands.

70. He was Lord Viṣṇu himself resembling thousand suns in brilliance. His eyes were like a full blown lotus. He was adorned with all ornaments and was clad in yellow garment.

71. Realising that Hari who was worthy of being eulogised and was the sole leader of all the worlds, had manifested himself accompanied by hosts of sages, Kaśyapa was overwhelmed with joy. With palms joined in reverence, he bowed to him and began to praise him.

Kaśyapa prayed :

72. "I pay obeisance again and again to the cause (the creator) of all the worlds. I bow again and again to the protector

of the entire universe. I salute again and again to the leader of immortal beings. Obeisance to the destroyer of Daityas.

73. Obeisance, obeisance to one who is the beloved of his devotees. Salutations to him who is beloved of the good people. I bow again and again to the annihilator of the wicked. My bow to the lord of the universe.

74. Salutations to Vāmana, the cause of the universe. Obeisance to Nārāyaṇa of infinite prowess. I bow to the wielder of the discus (Sudarśana), the sword (Nandaka), the mace (Kaumodakī) along with the Śārṅga bow. Obeisance be to that Supreme Person.

75. Salutations to the resident of the ocean of milk. Obeisance to one enthroned in the lotus-like heart of the pious. Obeisance to the Lord of immeasurable splendour of luminaries like the sun, etc. I bow again and again to the God glorified in holy stories.

76. I pay obeisance to him whose eyes are the sun and the moon. Salutations be to you, the bestower of the fruits of sacrifices. Salutations to the god who is the resplendent embodiment of sacrifice. Obeisance to you the lover of saintly persons (or beloved of saints).

77. Obeisance to the Primary Cause of the creative factors of the universe. Salutations to him who is beyond the range of sound, etc. Bow to you the bestower of divine bliss. I bow again and again to one who abides in the minds of his devotees.

78. Obeisance to you the dispeller of darkness (of ignorance). Salutations to you the supporter of the mount Mandara (at the time of churning the ocean for nectar). Bow to you who are designated as *Yajñavārāha* (Boar incarnation representing *Yajña*).[9] Salutations to the slayer of Hiraṇyākṣa.[10]

79. Obeisance to you who have assumed the form of a divine dwarf (Vāmana). Salutations to the annihilator of the Kṣattriya race (i.e. Paraśurāma).[11] I bow to you the suppressor of Rāvaṇa (i.e. Śrī Rāma). Obeisance to the elder brother of cow-herd Nanda's daughter (i.e. Śrī Kṛṣṇa).

80. O consort of goddess Lakṣmī, Obeisance to you. Salutations to you, the bestower of happiness. I bow again

and again to you, the destroyer of the distress of those who remember you.

81. O Lord of sacrifices, O receptacle of sacrifices, O destroyer of obstacles to sacrifices, O embodiment of Yajña, O sacrificer incarnate, I worship you whose person is constituted of the various parts of Yajña."

82. Thus eulogised, Vāmana, the Lord of the earth, the sanctifier of the worlds, laughingly spoke thus, enhancing the delight of Kaśyapa.

The glorious Lord said :

83. "O dear father who are worshipped by gods, I am pleased with you. You will be blessed with good fortune. Ere long, I shall accomplish for you all your desires.

84. In the two previous births of mine, I had been a son unto both of you. Similarly, in this birth also I shall achieve what is excellent happiness for you."

85. In the meantime, the Daitya Bali began a great sacrifice of long duration with the help of his preceptor Kāvya (i.e. Śukra) and other great and prominent sages.

86. In that sacrifice, Viṣṇu accompanied by Lakṣmī had been invoked by the sages, the expounders of the *Brahman* or the *Vedas*, in order to accept the sacrificial offerings.

87. Taking leave of his mother and father, that Brāhmaṇa bachelor Vāmana, went over to the great sacrifice of the supremely affluent Daitya, that was being performed.

88. Vāmana, favourably disposed towards his devotees, fascinated the world with his smile. He was Hari himself who had come as if to take part of the sacrificial oblations offered by Bali, directly.

89. Hari is always present in the heart of persons endowed with devotion, irrespective of whether his votary is evil-minded or good-natured, whether he is insentient or benevolent.

90. On seeing Vāmana coming, the sages, blessed with the vision of spiritual knowledge, knew him to be Lord Nārāyaṇa. They stood up (to show him respect), along with the other members of assembly.

91. Having come to know of this, the preceptor of Daityas said to Bali in privacy. Indeed wicked men commit

many acts without judging (estimating correctly) their own strength and weakness.

Śukra said :

92. "O gentle-natured Lord of Daityas, Viṣṇu who in the form of Vāmana (Dwarf) is born as the son of Aditi, will deprive you of your riches and glory.

93. O Lord of Asuras, he will pay a visit to your sacrifice. Nothing should be given to him by you. O learned one, please listen to my advice.

94. One's own intellect is conducive to happiness. Particularly so is the intellect (i.e. intellectual guidance) of the preceptor. The intellect of an enemy is destructive and a woman's intellect causes complete destruction (lit. dissolution).

95. He who is the benefactor of one's enemy should be especially killed straightway."

Bali replied :

96. "O preceptor, you should not tender such an advice which is contrary to the path of virtue. If Viṣṇu himself partakes of oblations or gifts, what can be better than that?

97. Learned men perform sacrifices for the purpose of propitiating Viṣṇu. If he personally comes and partakes of oblations offered, who can be superior to me on this earth?

98. If anything is given to Viṣṇu, even by an indigent person, O preceptor, that is the greatest of charitable gifts. That gift which is so given, becomes ever-lasting in its benefits.

99. Even when simply remembered with great devotion, the Supreme Person sanctifies the rememberer. By whomsoever he is worshipped, he awards to him the highest state of existence i.e. *Mokṣa*.

100. Even when remembered by evil-minded persons, Hari dispels their sins, just as the fire even if touched unwillingly, (invariably) does burn.

101. If the two syllables HA-RI stay at the tip of the tongue, that man attains the region of Viṣṇu from which the return to *Saṁsāra* is very difficult (impossible).

102. Wise men say that he who constantly meditates on Govinda, without passionate attachment, etc. (to the worldly objects), goes to Viṣṇu's abode.

103. O highly blessed preceptor, if oblations are offered to the fire or to Brāhmaṇa with devotion to Hari, Viṣṇu becomes delighted with it (viz. oblations offered to fire or the gift given to a Brāhmaṇa.)

104. I am performing this excellent sacrifice for the propitiation of Hari. If Hari himself comes to it, I am undoubtedly satisfied and have accomplished my objects."

105. Even as the Lord of Daityas was speaking thus, Viṣṇu who had assumed the form of a Dwarf, entered the sacrificial hall that was charming (and resplendent) due to the consecrated fire.

106. On seeing Vāmana who had the refulgence of ten million suns and who was extremely handsome, Bali stood up suddenly and greeted him with palms folded in reverence.

107. He offered him a seat. After washing the feet of the Lord in the form of Vāmana, he (sprinkled the water of washing) over his own head and on the heads of other members of his family. He derived great joy thereby.

108. After duly offering *Arghya* (respectful offerings given to a distinguished guest) to Viṣṇu, the abode of the universe, Bali was greatly delighted. All the hairs over his body stood on their ends and tears of joy welled up in his eyes.

Bali said :

109. I have accomplished the purpose of my birth to-day. It is to-day that my sacrifice has become fruitful. My life has also become fruitful to-day. Undoubtedly, I have achieved the goal of human life and I am contented.

110. Extremely rare (opportunity of the) shower of nectar which never goes waste, has come to my lot. By your very arrival a great festival has been accomplished without entailing any strain.

111. There is no doubt in this that all these sages have also achieved their goal in life. Whatever penance they have formerly performed, has become fruitful to-day.

112. I am blessed and contented. I repeat that I am really blessed and contented. Undoubtedly, I have achieved the purpose of my life. Hence, obeisance unto you. Salutations unto you. Repeated bows to you.

113. I think that I should carry out your behest with your

own permission. O Lord, command me who have been fired with great enthusiasm."

114. Thus urged by that Daitya who was consecrated (for the sacrifice), Vāmana said laughingly:—"Give unto me as much space as can be measured by my three steps, in order to stand in and perform the penance."

115. On hearing it, Bali said : "You have not requested for a kingdom. Not even a village or a city or even wealth has been requested for by you. What have you done ? (what a gift you have requested !)."

116. On hearing it, Viṣṇu who bears all bodies (by pervading them) said to Bali as if with a view to create detachment in him who was about to be deposed from his kingdom.

The glorious Lord said :

117. "O Lord of Daityas, listen to me. I shall tell you the great secret of secrets. Please tell me what can be realised through riches in the case of those who have eschewed all worldly contacts and attachment.

118. Think over this that I am the Inner Controller in all living beings. O Daitya, all these things existing in the universe are within me. Tell me what can be achieved by others (i.e. objects or gifts).

119. What can be realised by means of other external riches in the case of those who are devoid of attachment and hatred, who are quiescent and have eschewed Māyā and who are embodiment of eternal bliss ?

120. To those who perceive all living beings like their own *Ātman* (Self), to those whose minds are quite serene and to those to whom everything is non-different from the *Ātman*, who is the giver and what can be given ?

121. It is the decisive conclusion in all Scriptures that this Earth is subject to the control of the Kṣatriyas. All the people who abide by their behests, achieve the greatest happiness.

122. O Bali, the revenue of one-sixth part of the entire produce should be given to the king even by sages. This Earth should be granted to the Brāhmaṇas with special efforts.

123. The greatness of the charitable gift of land[12] cannot be adequately described, as such a kind of gift has never been

offered before (in the past) nor will it ever be so (in future). Undoubtedly a donor of lands attains the Supreme *Nirvāṇa* (Emancipation from *Saṁsāra*).

124. By giving a small piece of land to a Brāhmaṇa who is well versed in the Vedas and maintains the sacrificial fires, the donor attains Brahmaloka (region of Brahman), return from which is difficult.

125. A donor of lands is said to be a giver of all. A giver of lands will attain emancipation from *saṁsāra*. It is to be known as the highest type of religious gift.[13] It absolves the donor of all sins.

126. Even if one is vitiated by five great sins or even by all kinds of sins, one is absolved from them by gifting away ten cubits of land (*hasta*=24 *Aṅgulas* or 18 inches).

127. He who bestows a charitable gift of land on a deserving person, shall attain the fruit of all kinds of charitable gifts. There is nothing in the three worlds which is equivalent to a charitable land grant.

128. O Bali, even in hundreds of years, I shall not be able to describe adequately the meritorious benefits of a person who donates lands to a *Brāhmaṇa* who has no means of livelihood.

129. O Lord of Daityas, he who gives in charity even a small piece of land to a person who has no means of subsistence, but who is interested in the worship of the Lord, is undoubtedly Viṣṇu himself.

130. There is no doubt in this that he, by whom a piece of land with a flourishing crop of sugarcane, wheat, pulses, areca palm and other trees is donated, is Lord Viṣṇu *incarnate*.

131. By donating even a small piece of land to an indigent Brāhmaṇa who has no means of livelihood and who is burdened with a big family, one shall attain *Sāyujya* (identity) with god Viṣṇu (by being absorbed into his divine essence).

132. By giving a piece of land sufficient for sowing one *āḍhaka*—full of grain to a Brāhmaṇa who is interested in divine worship, one attains the benefit of performing ablution in the holy Gaṅgā for three days.

133-134. Listen to the benefit one derives by giving a *droṇikā* of land (i.e. a piece of land sufficient to sow a *droṇa* or four *āḍhakas* of grain) to a Brāhmaṇa who is devoid of any means of subsistence and who is engaged in saintly conduct of life. Such a person attains that enormous merit which a man obtains by performing hundreds of ablutions in the Gaṅgā, pilgrimage to a hundred sacred places and performance of a hundred horse sacrifices.

135. I shall explain to you the merit that accrues to a person who gives a *Khārikā* of land (i.e. land sufficient for sowing 16 *droṇas* of grain) to an indigent Brāhmaṇa. Please be attentive to it, even as I relate it to you.

136. He, the donor, shall obtain that fruit which one obtains after performing thousands of horse sacrifices and hundreds of *Vājapeya* sacrifices on the bank of the holy Gaṅgā.

137. The gift of a land is glorified as a great gift[14] — a gift which surpasses all other kinds of donations. It subsides (i.e. absolves the donor of) all the sins and confers on him the benefit of liberation from *saṁsāra*.

138. O Lord of Daitya clans, listen to me as I shall relate to you an ancient anecdote in this connection. A person who listens to this with faith, shall obtain the merit of donating lands.

139. O Bali, formerly in the Brāhma Kalpa, there was a highly intelligent and excellent Brāhmaṇa by name Bhadramati. He was indigent and had no means of livelihood.

140. All scriptures have been ever heard (i.e. learnt) by that Brāhmaṇa who was expert in the knowledge of the Vedas. All the *Purāṇas* and treatises on the *Dharmaśāstra* had been mastered by him.

141. He had six wives, viz. Śruti, Sindhu, Yaśovatī, Kāminī, Mālinī and Śobhā.

142-143. O excellent Asura, from these wives he begot two hundred and forty sons. All of them suffered from perpetual starvation. On seeing his sons and wives starving with hunger and himself feeling the poignancy of hunger, the indigent Bhadramati lamented loudly with all his sense-organs afflicted and famished with hunger.

144. "Fie upon this life devoid of good fortune ! Shame upon that life wanting in wealth ! Fie upon that life which is wanting in virtue ! Fie upon that life which is devoid of good name !

145-147. Pity the life of a man bereft of prosperity and

burdened with a number of children ! Alas ! Virtues, gentleness, scholarship, nobility of birth—all these do not shine in a man immersed in the ocean of destitution. Beloved wives, sons, grandsons, brothers, kinsmen and disciples—nay, all men forsake the man devoid of wealth. Only the fortunate one irrespective of his being a Brāhmaṇa or a Cāṇḍāla, is respectfully honoured.

148-149. A poor man is condemned in the world like a dead body. Alas ! If a person is endowed with wealth, he is hailed as a kind man though he may be ruthless; though he be deficient in all good qualities, he is still considered to be endowed with all virtues; though he be foolish, he is still regarded as a scholar. One is undoubtedly praiseworthy only if one is endowed with the virtue of being rich.

150. Alas ! Indigence is certainly miserable. Still more grievously painful is the wishful expectation (of getting something from others). Men overwhelmed with false wishful expectations (from others) experience everlasting misery.

151. Those who are the slaves of wishful expectations are the bondsmen or helots of the entire world. But the whole world submits to those who have subdued their wishful (but false) hopes.

152. Honour is said to be the everlasting wealth of great men in the world. If honour is ruined by the enemy called "hopeful expectation", one is faced with poverty.

153. Even an expert in the interpretation of all scriptural texts appears to be a fool if he is poverty-stricken. Who can rescue those persons in the grip of the great crocodile called "pennylessness" ?

154. O misery ! O misery ! Poverty itself is a great misery. There too, if one has numerous wives and sons, it is all the more painful."

155. After lamenting thus (lit. saying this) Bhadramati, the master of all scriptural topics, mentally thought about other religious rites (efficacious in) bestowing prosperity.

156. He came to the decision that charitable gift of lands is the most excellent of all charitable gifts. He who consents to a charitable gift, is as good as one who has formerly given it.

157. *Dāna* or a charitable gift is the greatest merit or virtue that enables one to reach (his destination). It bestows the fruit

of all cherished desires. The gift of lands is glorified as the best of all *dānas*.

158-159. After making a gift of land, a man obtains whatever is most desirable to him". O Bali, after deciding thus, the intelligent and self-possessed Bhadramati went to the city named Kauśāmbī,[15] along with his wives and children. He approached the leading Brāhmaṇa thereof named Sughoṣa who was endowed with affluence. O Bali, he then requested Sughoṣa for a plot of land extending to five cubits (*hastas*).

160-162. Observing that he was a man burdened with a large family, Sughoṣa, who was virtuously inclined, honoured him with a delighted mind and addressed him thus : "O Bhadramati, I feel I have achieved my objectives in life. My life is fruitful. O Brāhmaṇa, thanks to your blessings, my family has become sanctified". After saying these words and honouring him suitably, the highly intelligent and virtuous Sughoṣa donated to him a plot of land extending to five cubits (*hastas*).

163-165a. (The *mantra* to be uttered at the time of donation) "The holy earth belongs to Viṣṇu. The Earth is protected by Viṣṇu. Thanks to the gift of this earth, may lord Janārdana be pleased with me". Sughoṣa conceived that excellent Brāhmaṇa to be Viṣṇu and worshipped him with the (above) *Mantra* and granted him that much land, O lord of Daityas !

165b-167. The Brāhmaṇa Bhadramati gave the piece of land as requested by that intelligent one who was a Brāhmaṇa devotee of Hari, well-versed in the Vedas and had a large family to support. Due to the merit accrued from the gift of the land, Sughoṣa along with ten million members of his family, attained Viṣṇu's abode on reaching which one ceases to worry and grieve. O Bali, since he sought glory and prosperity, Bhadramati also stayed in Viṣṇu's abode for ten thousand *yugas* along with the members of his family.

168-170. Similarly, he stayed in the region of Brahmā for ten thousand crores of *yugas*, and he attained the abode of Indra where he stayed for five *kalpas*. Thereafter, he came back to the Earth. He was endowed with every affluence, he was highly blessed. He could even remember his previous births. He enjoyed all excellent pleasures. Thereafter, O Daitya, Bhadramati became free from all desires. Devotedly attached to Viṣṇu, he gave his lands unto the Brāhmaṇas who had no means of livelihood.

171-172. Lord Viṣṇu became pleased with him. He conferred upon him all excellent rites and blessed him along with ten million members of his family, by bestowing upon them the highest emancipations from *saṁsāra*. Hence, O Lord of Daityas, interested in all holy rites, give unto me a plot of land measuring three steps. I shall perform penance there for the sake of salvation."

173b-176a. The delighted son of Virocana, thereafter, took up a pitcher filled with water[16] to grant the land to Vāmana[17] in the guise of a religious student. Viṣṇu, the omnipresent, realised that *Kāvya* (Śukra) was obstructing the flow of water (from the spout of the pitcher). He, therefore, introduced the tip of the Kuśa grass that was in his hand into the spout of the pitcher. At the tip of the blade of the *darbha* grass, there was the never-failing great weapon pertaining to Brahmā (*Brahmāstra*). It had the lustre of ten million suns. It was very fierce and was desirous of plucking the eye of Kāvya.

176b-177. "O preceptor, Bhārgava, see the gods or the demons with a single eye (probably implying "Look at them impartially")", so commanded the tip of the *darbha* grass which resembled a weapon. Bali granted Viṣṇu as much land as could be measured in three spaces.[18]

178. Viṣṇu that Soul of the Universe began to grow in size till he reached the abode of Brahmā. Hari who contains the Universe in his own person measured the world in two paces.

179-180. The refulgent Lord covered all the Regions delimited by the semi-spheroidal crust of the region of Brahmā. The outer crust of the egg of the Universe pierced by the tip of his tow was split into two.[19] Through it, the cosmic water enveloping the outer crust of the egg of the universe, rushed in many torrential currents and washed the feet of Viṣṇu — water that thereby became pure and sanctified the world.

181. The water was enveloping the egg of Brahmā (that is the Universe) from outside. It rushed in jets of currents. That water was extremely sacred and it sanctified god Brahmā and other gods.

182. It was served and resorted to by the seven sages (*The Ursa Major*). Then it fell on the top of mount Meru.

183. On seeing this miraculous phenomenon, gods of whom Brahmā was prominent, the sages and the Manus were overwhelmed with ecstatic delight and they eulogised him.

The gods said :

184. "Obeisance to the great Īśa (The Ruler of the Universe) whose form is the Supreme Self; Salutations to him who transcends the transcendents; bow to him that assumes the highest form; salutations to the Ātman of Brahmā. Obeisance to him whose Soul and Intellect take delight in the *Brahman*; bow to him whose activities are invariably unobstructed.

185. O great Īśa, the highest bliss, O Supreme *Ātman*, greater than the greatest. Obeisance to you the indwelling soul of all; O embodiment of the Universe, who are beyond the pale of valid means of knowledge, we bow to you.

186. Obeisance to you who (being immanent in the Universe) have eyes all round; salutation to you who have arms and heads all round; bow to you who course everywhere.

187. Thus eulogised by Brahmā and others, the great Viṣṇu granted the boon of fearlessness to the heavendwellers and the Eternal Lord of devas was over-joyed.

188. Due to Bali's inability to grant land for one more step, he imprisoned Bali, the son of Virocana. Thereafter, knowing that he was dedicated unto him, he (Viṣṇu) gave him (Bali) the dominion in the nether world called *Rasātala* for his residence. The Lord who is ever under the control of his devotees, became his (Bali's) doorkeeper.

Nārada said :

189. "What diet was assigned by Mahāviṣṇu to the son of Virocana, in the terrible region of Rasātala which is dangerous due to the fear of serpents ?"

Sanaka replied :

190-191. The oblations consigned to the fire without proper chanting of the *Mantras*, whatever is given to a non-deserving person, black magic for obtaining the means of enjoyment, what is consigned to the sacred fire, whatever is given in charity or holy rites performed by persons in an impure state—in fact all acts, etc. which bring about one's downfall—all these deserve to be Bali's means of enjoyment.

192. In this way god Viṣṇu gave the nether world called Rasātala to Bali along with all his Asuras. Offering fearlessness (a secure place) to all gods, Viṣṇu granted them heaven.

193. While he was being worshipped by the groups of immortals (gods), eulogised by great sages and sung about by Gandharvas, he once again resumed the form of the divine Dwarf (Vāmana).

194. Witnessing this great deed, the sages, the expounders of the *Brahman*, smiled at one another and bowed to the Supreme Person (*Puruṣottama*).

195. Lord Viṣṇu, the Soul abiding in all living beings, who had assumed the state of a Dwarf (Vāmana) fascinated the entire world and repaired to forest for performing penance.

196. Of such sanctifying power is the goddess Gaṅgā who originated from Viṣṇu's feet. By merely remembering her, one is liberated from all sins.

197. Whoever reads or listens to this narrative of the glory of the Gaṅgā, in a temple or on the banks of the river, shall obtain the fruit of the performance of a horse-sacrifice (*Aśvamedha*).

CHAPTER ELEVEN

The Glory of the Gaṅgā : The Origin of the River

1. *Bhakti* or devotion is a favourite topic of Purāṇa-writers. In *NP*.I.4.1-42, I.15.39-40, *Bh.P*.III. 29.1-45, XI.5.1-52, *KP*.II.11.68-106 etc. we find *Bhakti* is highly extolled.

2. Although the NP. is regarded as a Vaiṣṇava Purāṇa, we find that Śiva worship is also glorified and Śiva and Viṣṇu are regarded as identical (*vide* verses 30, 58 below). The same is found in the so-called Śaivite Purāṇas. The authors of Purāṇas emphasize that the *Brahman* is one, and Śiva, Viṣṇu etc. are its designations or manifestation, and hence are equal or identical—a continuation of the Vedic Thought—*ekaṁ sad viprā bahudhā vadanti* /.

RV.I.164. 46c. *AV*.IX.10.28c.

3. Ajāmila, according to *Bh.P*. VI chs. 1-3, was an extremely sinful Brahmin of Kānyakubja. At the time of his death, he uttered the name 'Nārāyaṇa' with the intention of calling his son. But this utterance of the name of God saved him and he attained to Vaikuṇṭha. The story of Ajāmila is always mentioned as an instance of the efficacy of God's name.

4. A Purāṇic paraphrase of the *Puruṣa-sūkta* *RV*.X.90.12 & 13. The *mantras* are repeated in *AV*.XIX.6.6-7 *Vāj.Saṁ*. 31.11-12. The *Sūkta* has been paraphrased in other Purāṇas also, vide *Bh.P*. II.ch.6.

5. The notes of the Indian musical scale or gamut are seven. They are inumerated in the *Amara Kośa* as follows :

niṣādarṣabha-gāndhāra-ṣaḍja-madhyama-dhaivatāḥ /
pañcamaś cetyamī sapta tantrīkaṇṭhotthitāḥ svarāḥ //

In common parlance they are stated as : *sā, re, ga, ma, pa, dha, nī.*

6. The six accessories (of the Vedas) are as follows : *Śikṣā* (phonetics), *Kalpa* (rules of rituals), *Vyākaraṇa* (Grammar), *nirukta* (etymology), *Chandas* (prosody), *jyotiṣa* (astronomy).

7. Aditi was Diti's sister and both the sisters married to Kaśyapa. Hence Diti's sons—Daityas—are Aditi's sons (i.e. step-sons) as well.

8. The expression *aṇoraṇīyān*, etc. was very popular in *upaniṣads* and found in *Kaṭha* 2.20, *Śvet*. 3.20, *mahānārāyaṇa* 8.3, *Kaivalya* 20. The continuity of Vedic Sūktas, Upaniṣadic *mantras* in *purāṇas* testify to the continuity of Vedic tradition (thought, expression, passages, etc.) during the Purāṇic age.

9. Originally *yajña-varāha* is an entirely Vedic concept having a profound meaning with reference to Vedic cosmogony. The *VaP*. first adopted it from *Tait.Brāh*. 1.2.13 (Sāyaṇa) and included it in the *Sṛṣṭi-varṇana*. The *Mt.P*. elaborated it at the fag end in ch. 238 where the correspondence between the various elements of sacrifice or *Yajña* and the different limbs of the body of *Varāha* as an animal, are mentioned.

There is a Yajña-Varāha image of 10th cent. A.D. at Vihāra (ancient Varāhanagara) 8 miles from Vijāpur in North Gujarat.

10. Here Kaśyapa bows to the previous incarnations of Vāmana (Viṣṇu), viz. the divine tortoise, the boar-incarnation who while uplifting the earth from the bottom of the ocean, killed demon Hiraṇyākṣa and the Man-Lion who tore up Hiraṇyakaśipu with his claws. The *NP.* wrongly names Hiraṇyākṣa whom Varāha killed, but the adjective *vidārakāya* implies the Man-Lion incarnation, who killed Hiraṇyakaśipu with his claws.

Yajña-varāha :

11. The author of the NP. makes Kaśyapa to pay obeisance to the future incarnations of Viṣṇu, viz. Paraśurāma, Rāma and Kṛṣṇa.

12. The gift of land has been highly praised as the most meritorious, from ancient times. Aparārka (pp.368-70) quotes many verses from the *Viṣṇudharmottara*, the *Āditya Purāṇa* and *Matsya Purāṇa*, KP.II.26.15 and states that there is no gift comparable to the gift of the land. Verses pertaining to land-grant are common not only in Purāṇas or Smṛti works but are recorded on inscriptions and copper-plates of such grants all over India, (vide Kane-*Hist. Dhs.* vol.II.ii., pp. 1271-77).

atidāna—

13. According to *Vasiṣṭha Smṛ.*29.19 gifts of cows, land and learning (*Sarasvatī*) are the supreme *dānas* (*atidānas*). *Mbh.Anu.* 62.2 however, regards gift of land as *atidāna.*

14. Cf. *ati-dānāni sarvāṇi pṛthivīdānam ucyate* |

Mbh.Anu. 62.2

15. Kauśāmbī—Modern Kosam, a village on the left bank of the Jamuna about 30 miles to the west of Allahabad. Formerly it was the capital of King Udayana of Vatsadeśa.

16. According to *Āpastamba Dharma S.* II.4.9.9-10 the donor has to pour water on the hands of the donee—

sarvāṇyudaka-pūrvāṇi dānāni |

17. According to the legend of Viśvakarman Bhauvana narrated in the *Aitareya Br.* 39.7, and *Śatapatha Br.* XIII.7.1. 13-15, a king is not to gift land. When Viśvakarman was about to give away the earth to his sacrificial priest Kaśyapa, the earth manifested herself and strongly protested against it saying no man should give away land and threatened him that she would plunge herself in water and render his promise of gift fruitless :

na mā martyaḥ Kaścana dātum arhati |
Viśvakarman Bhauvana mā didāsitha ||
nimaṅkṣyé'haṁ salilasya madhye
moghas ta eṣa kaśyapāya Saṅgaraḥ ||

This foresight and prudence in restrictions on landgrants were later not respected, and not only Pauranic Kings like Bali and Hariścandra, but historical persons vied with each other in donating lands, villages, etc., as can be seen from inscriptions, copper plates, *sanads*, etc.

18. This act of Bali is criticised even in *subhāṣitas* warning against excesses of good things :

ati-dānād Balir baddhaḥ...
ati sarvatra varjayet |

Smṛti texts have been very emphatic in prohibiting gifts causing detriment to the family. Thus Manu (XI.9) condemns charity causing misery to the members of his family as false *dharma.*

Śaktaḥ para-jane dātā svajane duḥkhajīvini /
madhvāpāto viṣasvādaḥ sa dharmapratirūpakaḥ //

Yājñavalkya II.175 prescribes that no detriment to one's family be caused by one's gifts.

It can be argued that grant of three paces of land to a dwarf (*Vāmana*) was ridiculously insignificant and Bali never anticipated that the boy will be a cosmic person. But Śukra gave him clear warning that Viṣṇu was coming as Vāmana to deprive him of his kingdom. In the *Bh.P.* VIII.20.15 Śukra calls him an obstinate learned-fool who transgresses the order of his *guru* and curses him—rather predicts his fall.

Mahā-Viṣṇu might be physically a cosmic person pervading the heavens in one step, but morally Bali is much taller than Viṣṇu.

19. The story of Bali is introduced to explain how the Gaṅgā flowed into the universe, became pure by washing Viṣṇu's feet and descended on the mount Meru. For the actual phenomenon even at present vide S.M. Ali's account in *Geography in the Purāṇas,* pp. 63-64.

CHAPTER TWELVE

A dialogue between god Dharma and King Bhagīratha

Nārada inquired :

1. The great glory of the Gaṅgā has been heard. It is desirable, as it destroys all sins. Now, dear brother, tell me the characteristic of charitable gifts as well as of the persons deserving the same.[1]

Sanaka replied :

2. A Brāhmaṇa is the greatest preceptor of all classes in the society. Charitable gifts should be given to him by one who is desirous of securing perpetuation of the fruit of his charitable gifts.

3. Without any fear or reservation, a Brāhmaṇa should accept charitable gifts from all, but neither a Kṣatriya nor a Vaiśya should ever accept a charitable gift or a donation.

4. Whatever is given to one who is of a fiery temper or is sonless or is addicted to hypocritical conduct of life and one who avoids his righteous duties and acts prescribed for his caste and state in life, becomes futile.[2]

5. Whatever is donated to a person indulging in adultery with another man's wife or to one who covets the wealth of another person, or to one who is an astrologer in name only (an imposter), is useless.

6. Whatever is given in charity to a man whose mind is prejudiced with jealousy or to an ungrateful person, or to a cheat or to a person who officiates as a priest at the sacrifice of an unauthorized and ineligible person, is fruitless.

7. Whatever is given to one who is a perpetual beggar, or to one who is violent and wicked or to a vendor of liquors, is profitless.

8. Whatever is given to a person who sells the *Vedas* (teaches after receiving fees for teaching) or one who sells the *Smṛtis* (i.e. charges fees for giving the rulings from *Smṛtis*) or to

one who makes money by performing holy rites, is valueless, O Brāhmaṇa !

9. Whatever is donated as a charitable gift to a person who makes a living by singing songs or one whose wife is an unchaste slut or a person who harasses others, becomes useless.

10. Whatever is given to the following persons is unproductive of merits : viz. one who makes a living by sword (a person belonging to the military profession); one who earns his livelihood by preparation of ink (or clerical profession) an idol worshipper by profession,[3] the village priest and a washerman.

11. Whatever is given to one who works as a cook for another, to a poet or to the remover of an ailment or to one who eats prohibited food, is futile.

12. Whatever is given in charity to one who habitually partakes of Śūdra's food or to one who cremates the corpses of Śūdras or to one who takes food prepared by an unchaste woman, becomes futile.

13. Whatever is donated in charity to one who sells the name of Viṣṇu (i.e. accepts money for the *japa*, etc. of Viṣṇu) or to one who has given up the performance of *Sandhyā* prayers and to one who is (as it were) burnt by acceptance of monetary gifts from evil men, is unproductive.

14. Whatever is given to one who sleeps during the day or to one who indulges in sexual intercourse during day time or to one who takes food at the time of twilight (both the dawn and the dusk) is ineffectual.

15. Whatever is donated in charity to a person vitiated by great sins or by one who is excommunicated by his kinsmen and relatives or to a person who is a *Kuṇḍa*[4] (an adulterine son of a woman by another person while her husband is alive) or by a person who is a *gola*[5] (the bastard son of a widow) is fruitless.

16. Whatever is given to a rogue or to a person who has married before his elder brother's marriage or one who has taken his share of ancestral property before his elder brother or an erring fellow or a henpecked husband or an extremely wicked person, is unproductive of merit.

17. Whatever is given to one who partakes of meat and wine or to a lecherous libertine, or by a greedy person or to a thief or to a treacherous back-biter, is valueless.

18. O excellent Brāhmaṇa, one should neither give any gift nor accept any donation from those who are engaged in sinful activities or those who are always censured by good people. O Nārada, a charitable gift must be given with special efforts to one who is engaged in good and noble activities.

19. That *dāna* (charitable gift) is excellent which is offered with faith, after dedication unto Viṣṇu and requested for by a deserving person.[6]

20. O Nārada, the gift that is offered to a deserving person with a desire to get its benefit either in this world or in the next, is remembered (in *Smṛti* works) to be mediocre.

21. That *dāna* is considered to be the meanest—the *dāna* or charitable gift that is offered with hypocrisy or for causing injury to others or is given in violation of the scriptural injunctions in the matter or to an undeserving person, and by an infuriated person or by a person lacking in faith.

22. The lowest type of charitable gift is only for the satisfaction of merely an act of giving (oblation?). The mediocre *dāna* is for achieving selfish ends and the excellent type of *dāna* is for the propitiation of Lord Hari—so say excellent experts in the knowledge of Vedas.

23. Charitable gifts, enjoyment and destruction—these are the three ways of going away or spending of wealth.

24. The riches belonging to a person who neither gifts it away nor enjoys it himself, are the causes of his ruin. O Brāhmaṇa, wealth is that the fruit of which is *Dharma* and *Dharma* is that which propitiates god Viṣṇu.

25. Do not trees lead a life? They live in this world for the sake of others, for they oblige others by providing them with their roots and fruits.

26-27. If men do not help others they are (no better than) dead, O prominent Brāhmaṇa. Those men who do not render service to others physically, mentally, by word of mouth or through money, should be considered as the most sinful persons. O Nārada, listen attentively to an ancient anecdote which I shall narrate to you in this connection.

28. In that story the characteristics of *dāna* (and other righteous deeds) have been described along with the greatness of the Gaṅgā, which destroys all sins.

29-30. It is in the form of a dialogue between king Bhagīratha and god Dharmarāja, as it is conducive to merit.

Formerly, there was a king named Bhagīratha, born in the lineage of Sagara. He ruled over the entire world consisting of seven continents, along with seven oceans. He was always engaged in righteous acts. He was truthful and very brave.

31. He was good-looking like the god of Love. He constantly performed sacrifices. In courage he was equal to the Himālaya and in piety (*Dharma*) he was equal to god Dharmarāja (god of Death). He was very intelligent.

32. He was richly endowed with all auspicious characteristics, O sage. He was an expert in all scriptural matters. He had all riches and prosperity. He gave delight to every one.

33. He was specially solicitous in offering hospitality to guests, and was engaged forever in the worship of Lord Vāsudeva. He was very valorous and a receptacle of good qualities. He was friendly, merciful and intelligent.

34. Having come to know that Bhagīratha was a king of this nature, god Dharmarāja became delighted. O excellent Brāhmaṇa, on one occasion he came down to see him.

35. The king greeted and honoured god Dharmarāja who had come to him, in accordance with the injunctions laid down in the scriptures (for receiving a distinguished guest). Dharmarāja who was pleased with him addressed him as follows :

God Dharmarāja said :

36. O king, you are the most excellent among the knowers of righteousness. You are famous in the three worlds. On hearing about your fame, Dharmarāja himself has come to see you personally.

37. Gods, fond of your excellent qualities, wish to see you, a truthful monarch engaged in the path of good and the welfare of all living beings.

38. O king, good qualities, saintly people and deities abide there where fame, morality or righteousness and affluence reside.

39. O highly blessed king, your conduct of life is splendid and exemplary. Your qualities such as striving for the welfare of all living beings, etc. are difficult to be found even in people like me".

40. When god Dharmarāja said this, Bhagīratha bowed down to him. Delighted yet overcome with a sense of modesty, he submitted to him in soft refined words.

Bhagīratha submitted :

41. "O Lord, the knower of all *Dharmas* (righteous duties), you are an impartial witness to everything. Filled with divine grace for me, be pleased to explain what I ask of you.

42. How many types of *dharmas* (sacred duties) are there? What regions are reserved for persons who are righteous habitually? How many kinds of tortures are there and to whom are they meted out?

43. Who are the persons to be honoured by you and who are to be chastised? O highly blessed one, it behoves you to mention all this in details."

Dharmarāja explained :

44. "Well done, O highly intelligent one, very well done. Your intellect is unblemished and powerful. I shall explain to you factually in details what are the righteous acts and what are the evil ones. Listen to it with faith and devotion.

45. *Dharmas* (righteous duties) have been proclaimed as being of various kinds. They are the bestowers of meritorious worlds. The tortures too are declared to be numerous and are very terrible to be viewed.

46. It is not possible to describe in details the examples of virtues and evils in hundreds and ten thousands of years. Hence, I shall mention them succinctly.

47. The gift of the means of livelihood to Brāhmaṇas is glorified as highly meritorious. Similarly, what is given unto a knower of spiritual lore is of ever-lasting benefit.

48. Listen to the meritorious benefits attained by one who bestows means of livelihood upon a scholar of scriptural texts who is burdened with a large family or upon a Vedic scholar blessed with all good qualities and stabilises him.

49. The twice-born donor accompanied by ten million members of his family on his mother's side and on his father's side, will enter Viṣṇu's abode and rejoice there for a period of a *Kalpa*.

50. Particles of dust on the earth can be counted. Drops of rain can be enumerated. But the benefits of providing Brāhmaṇas with means of livelihood cannot be estimated even by the Creator (god Brahmā).

51. A Brāhmaṇa is glorified as the embodiment of all deities. Who is competent to recount the merits of a person who provides him with the means of livelihood ?

52. He who is always a benefactor to Brāhmaṇas, has performed all sacrifices (i.e. he attains the same benefits as one who performs all sacrifices). He gets the credit of performing ablutions in all sacred waters and all types of penance have been performed by him.

53. He too who induces another to provide Brāhmaṇas with means of livelihood saying 'Give', attains the same merit as that of the donor. What need is there to expatiate on it ?

54. If a person constructs a lake or causes it to be dug through others, it is not possible to enumerate the merits of that person even with a span of life extending to a period of hundred years.

55. Even if a single wayfarer drinks the water of that lake, there is no doubt that all the sins of the digger of that lake are wiped out.

56. If a man is able to retain water on the surface of the earth, even for a single day, he will be absolved of all sins and shall reside in heaven, for a hundred years.

57. A person who associates himself with the work of digging a lake, according to his capacity, attains the fruit of the same (i.e. digging it himself), so also does the person who is glad at it or who persuades persons to do it.

58. If a man throws out of the tank mud of the size of a white mustard, he stays in the heaven for a hundred years, liberated from millions of sins.

59. O excellent king, the eternal Śruti states that if the deities or preceptors are pleased with any one, he shall derive the merit of digging lakes.

60. In this connection, O excellent king, I shall narrate to you a mythological anecdote on listening to which, one is undoubtedly liberated from all sins.

61. In the Gauḍa land, there was a very famous king

named Vīrabhadraka. He was very valiant and learned. He was ever worshipful to Brāhmaṇas.

62. He was a follower of the code of conduct as prescribed in the *Vedas* and *Smṛtis* or scriptural texts and those handed down by family traditions. He increased his circle of friends. His queen named Campakamañjarī was a highly fortunate lady.

63. The great ministers of that king thought and pondered over what should be or should not be done. They always came to a decision in matters of *Dharmas* through *Dharmaśāstras*.

64. If a person, without consulting the *Śāstric* texts, gives a decision in matters of expiation (of sins), medical diagnosis, or astrological topics, he is called a Brāhmaṇa-slayer in *Smṛtis*.

65. Coming to this conclusion in his mind, the king always used to listen to the holy Dharmas as proclaimed by Manu and other *Smṛti*-writers, in accordance with injunctions.

66-67a. While the king was ruling that country according to *Dharma* (Śāstric rules of government), there was no person prone to injustice or mean in his kingdom. That realm of the king became equal to the celestial world, as it was being administered through *Dharma*. It was auspiciously blessed with good king.

67b-69. One day, the king went into a great forest for hunting. Surrounded by ministers and others he wandered till midday. Due to ill-luck, he did not get any game. He became tired. O king, surrounded by men, he chanced to see a lake. On seeing that dried up lake he thought.

70. "By whom and wherefor has this lake been built on an elevated piece of land ? How can there be water here so that he, the king and his associates may survive ?"

71. O excellent king, then it occurred to him to dig it further. By digging a pit to the depth of a cubit (about 18 inches), he found water.

72. By drinking that water the thirst of the king and that of the minister Buddhisāgara was quenched.

73-74. The minister Buddhisāgara, an expert in matters regarding *Dharma*, submitted to the king : "O king, formerly this lake had plenty of rain water. Today, I am inclined to build a strong embankment round it. May it please your majesty and grant me the permission for the same, O sinless Lord."

75. On hearing these words of the minister, the excellent king was highly delighted and the king himself undertook to construct it.

76-77. He entrusted that very minister with the work of that auspicious task. Then, at the behest of the king, the highly meritorious and gifted Buddhisāgara joyously attempted to convert that lake into a sea (i.e. a big lake) extending it to fifty *Dhanus*. (1 *dhanu* = 4 *hastas* or about 6 feet) all round.

78. Having constructed the lake deep with water and with a strong embankment of stones all round he reported the matter to the king in details.

79. O king, thereafter, all the thirsty way-farers roaming in forest (and beasts of the jungle as well) got splendid, translucent water for drinking from that lake.

80. One day, when his span of life in the world ended, that minister Buddhisāgara died. O lord, he came to my region, since I am the ruler and chastiser of the worlds.

81. Citragupta, the accountant of the deeds committed by men, was asked by me about him (the minister). He reported to me everything that he did during his life time.

82. He himself was the advisor in meritorious activities to the king. Hence, he deserved to ride in the *Dharma*—aerial chariot.

83. O king, when this was reported by Citragupta, Buddhisāgara was commanded by me to get into the aerial car called *Dharma*.

84. Then, after some time, O king, the ruler Vīrabhadraka died and came to my abode. With joy, he bowed to me.

85. O king, all the deeds done by him were completely inquired of by me. The merit accruing from the construction of the lake was reported by Citragupta.

86-87. Now please listen how the king was properly enlightened by me : "O king, formerly on the ridge of the sand dume, a quail had dug up with its beak and water to the depth of two *aṅgulas* (finger-breadths) had come up. Then after some time, O excellent king, a boar dug it up with its snout to the depth of a cubit (18 inches).

88-89. Then, on another occasion, it was made to extend to two *hastas* by this *Kāli* (a black heron.) O great king, in that dug up lake, water remained for two months. It was drunk by small wild animals which were afflicted with thirst.

90-93. O king, observer of holy vows, thereafter, at the end of three years, it was dug up to a depth of three *hastas* (cubits) by this elephant and more water sprang up. The water that stood there for three months (was drunk up) by the residents and animals roaming in the forest. Your honour visited that spot after the water had been completely dried up. O king, after digging to a depth of *hasta*, water rose up and it stood for a month. Then O king, on the advice of the minister you caused it to be dug up to an extent of 50 *dhanus* (about 300 feet). It abounded in water. The great lake was made more durable with bank built up of stones. Trees were planted all round rendering great help to all people.

94. O lord of the Universe, these five have got into the aerial car called *Dharma*, thanks to their respective merit. You too, get into it."

95. O king, on hearing this statement of mine, that king got into the aerial car as the sixth one, sharing equal amount of merit with them.

96. Thus, everything connected with the meritorious benefit accruing from constructing the lake has been narrated to you. After this, one is liberated from sins committed from birth till death.

97. The man who devoutly listens to and reads this discourse, derives all the merit that is credited to one for constructing a lake.

CHAPTER TWELVE

A dialogue between god Dharma and King Bhagīratha

1. *Dāna* or charitable gifts have been eulogized from Vedic times as can be seen from a number of *Dāna-Stutis* in the *Ṛg-veda* (Vide RV. I.125, V.61, VII.18.22-25 etc.). According to Manu I.86 (and the same verse is found in Parāśara I.23, *Mbh. Śānti* 232.28 & *Va.P.*8.65-66) *Dāna* or gifts constitute the main special feature of religious life in the present, Kali yuga (*dānam ekaṁ Kalau yuge* /). A number of *Purāṇas* have discussed this topic of *Dāna* e.g. *A.P.*209-213, *Bm.P.* 81-91, 205-206.

The *NP.* discusses this topic in the present chapter and in *infra* chs 31 and *Uttarārdha* Chs 41-42. Although a number of verses on this topic are common in Purāṇas, Smṛtis and the Mbh., a comparative table of these verses is beyond the scope of a note. Only occasionally common verses are noted.

2. Gives a list of persons unfit to receive gifts. The list of these unworthy persons includes characterless Brāhmaṇas, hypocrites, ignorant of Vedas, Brāhmaṇas who sell the Vedas or officiate at the sacrifices of ineligible persons covetous, shirkers of Brahmanic vows, etc. We find these disqualifications are repeated in *Smṛtis* e.g. *Manu* 4.193-200, *Bṛhad Yama* III.34-36 and *Mbh.Vana* 200.5-9.

Dāna given to these persons is futile. *It is due to the influence of Pkts. that we find that the gen. is used for dative case in Purāṇic Sk.*

3. *Devala, also Devaloka*

A Brāhmaṇa who maintains himself by attending upon or worshipping an image in a temple on a salary-basis or by appropriating what others offer to the deity. Manu.III.152 says that such Brahmins should not be invited for *Śrāddha.* It may be noted that the qualifications (or disqualifications of a Brāhmaṇa for invitation to *Śrāddha* or for donating gifts are practically the same.

4-5. The meaning of *Kuṇḍa* and *Golaka* given in the translation is based on Manu III.174.

para-dāreṣu jāyete dvau sutau Kuṇḍa-Golakau /
patyau jīvati Kuṇḍas syān mṛte bhartari Golakaḥ //

Yājñavalkya I. 222 and Manu III.154 hold that this irregular progeny should not be invited to *Śrāddha* also. There is a similarity in the eligibility for invitation for *Śrāddha* and acceptance of *dāna.*

6. Cf. BG. 17.20-22.

180. The story of Vīrabhadraka which is probably a contribution of the NP. to the legends glorifying *dāna*, is properly speaking the propagation of the meritorious nature of *Pūrta*. Pūrta includes dedication of deep wells, oblong large wells and tanks, temples, distribution of food and maintenance of public gardens :

vāpī-kūpa-taḍāgāni devatāyatanāni ca
anna-pradānam ārāmaḥ pūrtam ityabhidhīyate //

Mbh. quoted by Aparārka, p. 290.

CHAPTER THIRTEEN

A Discourse on Dharma

Dharmarāja said :

1. Listen to the meritorious benefit to a person who himself builds or pursuades others to build a temple of either Śiva or Hari.[1]

2. There is no doubt that he (such a builder) will stay in lord Viṣṇu's region for three *kalpas* in the company of a hundred thousand and ten million members of his family on his mother's side as well as on his father's side.

3. Listen to the extent of merit, if a man builds the shrine with mud and clay. I shall now recount it.

4. Taking up a brilliant divine body and travelling by an excellent aerial car, he will stay in Viṣṇu's region for three *kalpas*. Entertain no doubt about this.

5. Listen to me even as I recount, the extent of merit if a person constructs the shrine (of Śiva or Viṣṇu) with earthen materials.

6. He will assume a lustrous, divine body and ride in an excellent heavenly car. After staying in Viṣṇu's region for three *Kalpas*, he will then proceed to the capital of god Brahmā.

7-8. After staying there for two *kalpas*, he will reside in the celestial world for the period of one *kalpa*. He will afterwards be born in the family of Yogins and be merciful (to all). Adopting the *Yoga* pertaining to Viṣṇu, he will attain eternal emancipation from *saṁsāra*. If a man builds the temple with wood, meritorious benefit twice this, will accrue to him.

9. If he builds the temple in brick, the meritorious benefit is three times that of building the temple with earthen material. If it is built with stones, the benefit is four times and if the shrine is constructed with crystal slabs, the benefit should be known to be ten time.

10-13. If the temple is built of copper (sheets and ingots), the meritorious benefit is hundred-fold and if it is built of gold, the merit that accrues to him is ten million times (that of constructing the shrine of clay).

(10b.) If a person looks after the temple, a lake or a village, O king, his meritorious benefit is hundred times that of the builder. If a person looks after the temple by scrubbing or sweeping with a broom, smearing it and sprinkling water or embellishing it with devotion, he derives infinite merit. Those who perform meritorious deeds in return for salary or without any remuneration go to Viṣṇu's eternal region perpetually. O king, the merit in digging a small artificial lake is stated to be half the merit of digging a big lake containing lotuses.[2]

14. The merit accruing from digging a well is one-fourth and that of a tank should be known as equal to that of a lotus pond. O king, the meritorious benefit in digging a canal is said to be hundred times greater than that of constructing a tank.

15. A rich person should build up a tank with stones (stone embankment) and a poor man should build it with an earthen bank. But the lotus-born god Brahmā says that the merit derived by them both is equal.

16. People who know the *Vedas* say that if a prosperous, affluent person gifts away a whole city and an indigent fellow donates a plot of land extending to a hand (18 inches), both of them have equal meritorious benefit.[3]

17. If a rich man constructs a big tank which may cause much benefit and an impoverished person digs a well, the merit in both the cases is declared to be equal.

18. A person causes a hermitage to be built—a hermitage that is of great use to many creatures, he goes to god Brahmā's world along with three generations of family.

19. O king, if a cow or a Brāhmaṇa or any one stands in the shed even for half a moment, the builder thereof is taken to heaven.

20. O king, those who lay out parks and gardens, those who construct temples and those who dig lakes and build up villages (human settlements) are worshipped along with Hari.

21. Listen, O king, to the rewards of merit accruing to those who lay out flower gardens for the benefit of all people or for the worship of deities.[4]

22. With ten million members of his family, he stays in the celestial region and enjoys himself as many years as there are flowers and fruits there (in the flower garden).

23. Those who construct a compound-wall round them and those who make thorny hedges around them, proceed to god Brahmā's abode and stay there for seventy one *yugas* or one *kalpa*.

24. O Lord of men, listen to me as I relate to you the blessings that await those who plant Tulasī[5] (the basil plant), O king.

25. O king, for a period of a hundred *kalpas* and more, he will stay at the feet i.e. in the region of Nārāyaṇa, accompanied by seventy million members of his family from his mother's side as well as from his father's side.

26. Listen to the reward of merit got by one who wears the *Ūrdhva-puṇḍra* (a vertical mark on the forehead) with the mud taken from the root from the Tulasī plant or the paste of *Gopīcandana* (a species of white clay said to be brought from Dvārakā and used by Viṣṇu's worshippers for marking the forehead), or the sandal-paste or mud taken from Citrakūṭa or that from the bed of the Gaṅgā.

27. Such a person rides in an excellent aerial car and goes to Viṣṇu's abode. He enjoys himself there while his praise is being sung about, by hosts of Gandharvas and Apsaras.

28. As many of the sins grevious like that of Brāhmaṇa-slaughter are dispelled , as the leaves that fall at the root of the Tulasī plant.

29. A man who sprinkles at least a handful of water on the Tulasī plant, shall stay along with god Viṣṇu, the dweller in the milky ocean, as long as the moon and the stars shine.

30. He who gives a tender leaf of the Tulasī plant to Brāhmaṇas, goes to god Brahmā's abode (*Satyaloka*) accompanied by three generations of his family.

31. He who offers in worship the leaves of the Tulasī plant on the Śālagrāma[6] (stone) will stay in Viṣṇu's abode (*Vaikuṇṭha*), till the time of the dissolution of all living beings.

32. He who makes a thorny hedge all around or builds a wall encompassing (a garden of flowers), rejoices in Viṣṇu's abode in the company of twentyone generations of his family (usually ten predecessors plus himself plus ten successors).

33. O lord of men, he who worships the lotus feet of lord Hari by means of the tender leaves of the Tulasī plant, does not ever return from the region of Viṣṇu.[7]

34. He who performs the ablution of Hari with milk on the full moon day or on the *Dvādaśī* (twelfth) day (both of the dark and bright half of the month) enjoys himself in the region of Viṣṇu, accompanied by ten thousand members of his family.

35. He who bathes lord Keśava (Viṣṇu) with a *prastha* measure of milk, lives in god Viṣṇu's city (Vaikuṇṭha), accompanied by ten crores of the members of his family.

36. The man who bathes Viṣṇu with a *prastha* of ghee on the *Dvādaśī* (twelfth) day, O king, attains the type of liberation called *Sāyujyatā* (identity with the deity) along with ten million members of his family.

37. He who performs the ablution of Viṣṇu on the *Ekādaśī* (eleventh day in each half of the month) with *Pañcāmṛta* (sweet mixture of milk, sugar, curds, ghee and honey) attains *Sāyujyatā* (identity) with Viṣṇu, accompanied by millions of the members of his family.

38. Listen to the fruit attained by the excellent person which performs the ablution of god Viṣṇu with the water taken from the tender coconut fruit on the *Ekādaśī* (eleventh), *Dvādaśī* (twelfth) day or the full moon day, O excellent king.

39. Such a person shall be liberated from the sins accumulated during the course of ten (previous) births. He rejoices along with Viṣṇu and two hundred members of his family, O excellent king.

40. O king, he who bathes the lord of gods (i.e. Viṣṇu) with sugar-cane juice shall attain to Vaikuṇṭha (Viṣṇu's region) along with a hundred thousand ancestors.

41. By bathing lord Govinda with water mixed with flowers as well as with scented water and worshipping lord Hari with devotion, a person will attain the region of Viṣṇu.

42. He who bathes Mādhava (the consort of Lakṣmī) with water filtered and purified with a piece of cloth, becomes liberated from all sins and rejoices with Viṣṇu.

43. He who bathes Hari with milk, etc., when the sun is in transit (from one sign of zodiac to another), stays in Viṣṇu's region along with twenty one generations.

44-49. Listen to the reward for the merit accruing from bathing lord Viṣṇu with milk, ghee, curd, or honey on the ollowing occasions :

On the *Aṣṭamī* (eighth day) or the fourteenth day in the

bright half of a month, on the full moon day, on the *Ekādaśī* day, on a Sunday, on the *Dvādaśī* (twelfth) day, and on the *Pañcamī* (fifth day of the two halves of the month), during the period of the lunar or the solar eclipse, on the anniversary of *Manvantaras* and the beginnings of *Yugas*, etc., when the Moon has partially risen (*Ardhodaya*), when the Sun accompanies the constellation *Puṣya*, when the plane t Budha (Mercury) is with the constellation Rohiṇī, when the planet Saturn is in the constellation Rohiṇī, when the planet Mars is in the company of the constellation Aśvinī, on Saturdays, when the planet Venus is in conjunction with Mṛgaśiras (the Orion) or the Revatī constellation, when the planet Mercury is with Anurādhā, when the Sun accompanies Śravaṇa, when the Moon is in Śravaṇa, when Bṛhaspati (the planet Jupiter) is in conjunction with constellation Hasta, when there is Budhāṣṭamī day or the Mercury is in conjunction with the constellation Āṣāḍhā or on other auspicious days. Such a person must be quiescent, pure and restrained in speech.

50. He accomplishes the merit of performing all sacrifices O King. Being absolved of all sins, he will stay in Lord Viṣṇu's city (Vaikuṇṭha) with twenty-one generations of his family.

51. While staying there, he attains perfect spiritual wisdom which is rarely accessible even to *Yogins*. O king, he attains liberation from *Saṁsāra* from which it is difficult to return (to the cycle of births and deaths).

52. By bathing god Śiva with milk on the fourteenth day of the dark half of the month or on a Monday, a person shall attain liberation called *Sāyujyatā* (identification) with Śiva, O King.

53. By bathing Śiva devotedly with the juice of a tender coconut fruit on the *Aṣṭamī* (eighth day) of the half of the month or on a Monday, one attains absorption in Lord Śiva.

54. By bathing god Śiva with ghee or honey on the eighth or the fourteenth day in the bright half of the month a person attains equality with him, O Lord of the Earth.

55. By bathing god Viṣṇu or god Śiva with Sesamum oil one attains the *Sārūpya* (similarity of form) with the respective deity, along with seven of his ancestors.

56. He who bathes Śiva devotedly with sugarcane juice

will stay in the region of god Śiva for the period of a *Kalpa*, along with seven generations.

57. O blessed one, listen to the meritorious benefit attained by one who bathes the *Liṅga* idol of god Śiva with ghee on the *Dvādaśī* day in the bright half of month of Kārttika when god Viṣṇu arises from his slumber of four months, as I describe it to you.

58. He will be liberated, O king, from the sins committed in ten thousand previous births. The man shall uplift the members of his family numbering to ten million and he will attain Śivahood.

59. O king, after worshipping Viṣṇu with fragrant flowers on the day sacred to Viṣṇu (i.e. eleventh or the twelfth day in the dark and bright half of the month), he will be liberated from the sins accumulated in the course of ten thousand births and proceed to his region (*Vaikuṇṭha*).

60. The person who worships god Viṣṇu or god Śiva with lotus flowers, goes to Viṣṇu's abode accompanied by ten million members of his family.

61. By worshipping god Hari with the *Ketakī* flowers and god Śiva with the *Dhattūra* flowers at night, one will be absolved from sins and will abide in god Viṣṇu's city (Vaikuṇṭha) for a *Yuga*.

62. O great king, by offering Campaka flowers to lord Hari in worship and *Arka* (the Sun-plant) flowers to god Śaṅkara, one will attain the *Salokatā* type of *mukti*, i.e. residence with the respective deity.

63. By offering *Guggula* (a fragrant gum resin) along with ghee to god Śaṅkara or Viṣṇu, with great devotion, the man is liberated from all sins.

64. By offering a lamp filled with sesamum to god Viṣṇu or Śaṅkara, a man attains all cherished desires, O best of kings.

65. He who offers a lamp filled with ghee to god Śaṅkara or Viṣṇu will be liberated from all sins. He will attain the merit of performing ablution in the Gaṅgā.

66. O king, listen to the benefit of offering a lamp with oil crushed from the oil seeds at the village or elsewhere to Lord Mahā-Viṣṇu or Śiva.

67. He becomes free from all sins. He is blessed with all

prosperity and glory. He attains residence in the region with the respective deity, along with twentyone generations of his family.

68. By offering edible and sweet dishes liked most by one, to god Śiva or to Viṣṇu, one attains to the respective region of the deity (propitiated with food), along with forty members of his family.

69. A person who offers things that he likes most, to a Brāhmaṇa, goes to Vaikuṇṭha (god Viṣṇu's abode) from which it is impossible to return to the world of mortals.

70. O king, a person who kills a child in the embryo becomes pure through a charitable gift of gold. But there has never been a charitable gift like that of cooked food nor will it ever be like it.

71. A person who bestows (as a charitable gift) cooked food is said to be a bestower of life; a bestower of life is the bestower of everything. Therefore, O excellent king, a bestower of cooked food attains the merit of charitable gift of everything.[8]

72. It has been decisively stated in the scriptures that a bestower of cooked food goes to the abode of god Brahmā along with ten thousand members of his family, and that he never returns therefrom to this world.

73. It has been declared by expounders of the Vedas that as the gift of water gives immediate satisfaction, it should be regarded as superior to the gift of cooked food, O best of kings.

74. The lotus-born deity (Brahmā) states that whether a person is defiled by great sins or by subsidiary ones, a bestower of water is absolved from them all.

75. They say that the physical body is born of food. The wise people know that the vital breath is also created from food. Hence, O lord of the earth, the bestower of food should be known as the bestower of vital breath.

76. Whatever charitable gift produces satisfaction, yields the benefit of accomplishing all cherished desires. Hence, O king, there is no other gift in the world equal to that of the cooked food.

77. O jewel among kings, all the persons born in the family of a bestower of food, up to the thousandth scion or

descendant do not see the hell. Hence, a bestower of food is the most excellent one.

78. The man who devotedly massages the feet of an uninvited and unexpected guest is one who takes bath in all sacred rivers with the ablution in the Gaṅgā at the outset (which is the best of them).

79. O great king, he who offers to Brāhmaṇas oil for oil bath, has to his credit the merit of taking holy ablutions in the Gaṅgā for one hundred and eighth times and more.

80. A person who lovingly protects ailing Brāhmaṇas, shall stay in the city of god Brahmā for one *Yuga*, accompanied by ten million members of his family.

81. O protector of the earth, if any one protects an indigent fellow or an ailing person, lord Viṣṇu becomes pleased with him and grants him his cherished desires.

82. He who looks after and saves an ailing person either by thought, word or deed, attains to all desires aspired after by him and he becomes devoid of all sins.

83. O protector of the earth, he who gives residential accommodation to a Brāhmaṇa, is blessed by the Lord of gods who becomes pleased with him and grants him heavenly world.

84. He who gives a milch cow to a Brāhmaṇa who knows (the Vedas goes to the abode of *Brahmā* which is extremely difficult for others to attain.[9]

85. O scholar, I am not competent to describe adequately the meritorious benefit derived by a person who gifts away a milch cow even after accepting it as a charitable gift from others

86. He who gives as a charitable gift, a tawny-coloured milch cow to a Vedic scholar is Rudra himself. He is devoid of all sins, O king.

87. It is impossible to enumerate, even in hundreds of years, the merit of a person who gives an *Ubhayato-mukhī* cow (i.e. when she is on the point of giving birth to a calf and thus has two mouths—hers in front and that of the calf which is being born) to a Brāhmaṇa who is a Vedic scholar.

88-90a. O king, listen to the meritorious benefit (of offering protection), I shall tell you factually. On one side of the balance are all the sacrifices with sumptuous fees and on the other side is the act of protecting a living being who is frightened.

O protector of the earth, he who protects a terrified Brāhmaṇa is like one who has taken bath in all sacred rivers and has initiated himself in all sacrifices.

90b-93a. A person who gives clothes goes to Rudra's abode. A person who gives a virgin girl in marriage[10] attains to the region of *Brahmā*; the person who gifts gold goes to Viṣṇu's heaven (*Vaikuṇṭha*) accompanied by all the members of his family. He who bedecks a virgin girl in rich ornaments and gives her in marriage to a knower of spiritual lore, goes to the region of god Brahmā, accompanied by a hundred members of his family.

93b-94a. Listen to the merit achieved by a person who lets loose a bull for the propitiation of Śiva on the full moon day either in the month of Kārttika or Āṣāḍha O king. He becomes absolved of sins accumulated in the course of seven births and assumes the form of Rudra. With seventy generations of his family, he rejoices along with Rudra.

94b-96a. He who lets loose a buffalo after marking it with the *Liṅga* of Śiva, never happens to go to the world of tortures (the hell), O best of kings. He who makes the gift of a *Tāmbūla* (the leaf of piper-betel together with powder of areca nut, catechu, etc. for chewing) according to his ability gets longevity, fame and prosperity from Viṣṇu who becomes pleased with him.

96b-98. The bestower (as charitable gift) of milk, ghee, honey or curds is honoured in the heavenly world for ten thousand divine years, O excellent king. The giver of sugar-cane goes to the abode of Brahmā. The bestower of fragrant scent yields meritorious benefit as the bestower goes to Brahmā's region. One who gives jaggery and sugar-cane juice (as charitable gift) goes to the milky ocean.

99. He who gives water to soldiers, goes to the excellent world of Sun god. By giving away instructions in learning (free of any fees in return), a man attains to the *Śāyujya* type of liberation with Lord Viṣṇu.

100. The gift of learning,[11] the gift of a plot of a land and the gift of a cow are the most excellent of charitable gifts. They lift the donor from the hell through *Japa* (repeating the name of God), vehicles and milk.

101. Among all gifts the gift of *Vidyā* (lore) is of specially

distinct merit. By the gift of *Vidyā* one attains identity with Viṣṇu, O excellent king.

102. A person giving the charitable gift of fuel is liberated from the subsidiary type of sins. The gift of *Śālagrāma* stone is glorified as a great gift.

103-104. By giving it (Śālagrāma), one attains salvation. The gift of *Liṅga* is also such as by giving which one attains that meritorious benefit which a man obtains by gifting away ten million cosmic eggs. By the gift of *Śālagrāma* stone, the meritorious benefit is twice this.

105a. It is wellknown that god Viṣṇu assumes the form of *Śālagrāma* stone.

105b-106a. O Lord of men, the man who makes charitable gifts of mansions, certainly attains the benefit of taking bath in the Gaṅgā.

106b-107. O excellent king, by the gift of gold to the accompaniment of precious stones and jewels one attains worldly pleasures and salvation, since it is mentioned as a *Mahādāna*. By the gift of rubies a man attains the highest *Mokṣa*.[12]

108. A person attains to the *Dhruva loka* (the region of the Pole star) by the gift of diamonds; one goes to a celestial world and Rudra's region by the gift of coral (*Vidruma*).

109. One goes to the region of the Moon god by the gift of a vehicle or through the *gift* of pearls. A giver of *Vaiḍūrya* (Lapis lazuli) or *Puṣpa-rāga* (Topaz) goes to the region of Rudra.

110. By gifting away topaz, one enjoys happiness everywhere. O ruler of the earth, a person who bestows horses attains nearness to horses (?) for a long time.

111. By means of the great gift of an elephant, one will obtain his cherished desires. Through the gift of a vehicle, one attains heaven seated in a heavenly aerial car.

112. A person who gifts a she-buffalo undoubtedly overcomes pre-mature death. By giving grass and fodder freely to cows, one attains to the region of Rudra.

113-114a. O lord of the earth, one who gives salt as charitable gift, attains to the region of god Varuṇa. Persons who are engaged in the conduct of life according to the rules of discipline of their own stage of life, those interested in the welfare of all living beings, those who are devoid of hypocrisy, and free from jealousy, go to the region of Brahmā.

114b-115a. Persons who are interested in imparting instructions to others, are devoid of passionate attachment, free from the sense of rivalry and those who are engaged in the worship of Hari's feet, go to the abode of Lord Hari.

115b-116a. Those who are engaged and take delight in associating themselves with saintly people, who always perform good and holy acts, are averse to slandering others, go to the region of Hari (*Vaikuṇṭha*).

116b-117a. Those who are always benevolent to Brāhmaṇas and cows, those who desist from physical contact with other men's wives, do not go to the abode of Yama.

117b-118a. Those who have conquered their sense-organs, have perfectly controlled their diet, have forbearance towards cows and those whose character is good and bear patience towards Brāhmaṇas, go to the region of Hari.

118b-119a. Those who maintain sacrificial fires, render services to their preceptors and those women who are interested in serving their husbands, do not undergo worldly sufferings.

119b-120a. Those who are always engaged in worshipping the deities, who are ever engrossed in repeating the names of Hari, and those who refrain from accepting charitable gifts, attain the highest region.

120b-121a. O best of kings, those who cremate dead bodies of Brāhmaṇas who have no claimants or heirs, always obtain the meritorious benefit of performing thousands of horse sacrifices.

121b-123a O lord of men, listen to the benefit of worshipping a neglected *Liṅga* which lies unworshipped, with *Bilva* leaves, flowers, fruits or water without elaborate adoration. Such a worshipper, seated in an aerial car and eulogised by bevies of heavenly damsels and groups of celestial singers, goes to the presence of Śiva.

123b-124a. By bathing the *Liṅga* with only a handful of water, O lord of earth, one undoubtedly attains to the merit of a hundred thousand horse sacrifices.

124b-125a. O lord of the people, the intelligent and learned person who worships the *Liṅga* of Śiva devoid of adoration for a long time, by means of flowers, will attain the benefit of ten thousand horse-sacrifices.

125b-126a. By worshipping a deserted unworshipped *Liṅga*, by offering foodstuffs, edibles, and fruits, one attains the *Sāyujya* type of liberation (identity with god Śiva) from which there is no return to this world.

126b-127a. O jewel among men, a scion of the Solar race, a person who worships the idol of Viṣṇu which lies unadored for a long time, even with water, attains residence in the region of Viṣṇu.

127b-128a. The intelligent person who sweeps a temple clean attains residence in Viṣṇu's mansion for as many *yugas* as the particles of dust he has swept.

128b-129a. The man who joins together a shattered crystal *Liṅga*[13] is freed from sins accumulated in the course of a hundred births, O jewel among the kings.

129b-130a. O king, the person who sprinkles with water, a plot of land in the temple extending at least *Go-carma**[14] one hundred and fifty *hastas* in length and breadth attains heaven.

130b-131a. He who sprinkles the ground in the temple with scented water, stays in the vicinity of the lord for as many *kalpas* as there are drops of water in sprinkling.

131b-132a. He who besmears the abode of the deity (the *sanctum sanctorum*) with mud or red chalk (metallic substances), uplifts ten million members of his family and attains equality with Lord Viṣṇu, the slayer of demon Madhu.

132b-133a. A man who over-spreads the abode of the Lord with powdered rock or draws the symbols of *Svastika*, etc. with coloured powder gains merit which is infinite.

133b-134a. O king, I am not enthusiastic in enumerating, even in the course of hundreds of years, the merit of a person who makes arrangement for lighting in the temple.

134b-135a. For a person who makes lighting arrangement (in the *sanctum sanctorum*) of god Viṣṇu or Śaṅkara, the merit of the performance of horse-sacrifices per every movement is not difficult to get.

135b-136a. He who bows down on seeing Śaṅkara or Viṣṇu worshipped, attains the abode of Viṣṇu (*Vaikuṇṭha*) and enjoys himself for ten thousand *yugas*.

---

* One of the definitions of *Go-carman* :
daśa-hastena vaṁśena, daśa-vaṁśān samantataḥ |
pañca cābhyadhikān dadyād etad go-carma ucyate ||

—*Vasiṣṭha Saṁhitā.*

136b-137. O king, after making one circumambulation of the goddess, seven circumambulations to the Sun-god, with three of god Vināyaka and four round the temple of Viṣṇu, one attains the region of the respective deity and rejoices there for one hundred thousand *yugas*.

138. He who, with feelings of devotion, circumambulates god Viṣṇu, a cow, a Brāhmaṇa, reaps the benefit of a horse-sacrifice at each step.

139. He who worships and bows down to the *Liṅga* of god Maheśvara at Kāśī,[15] has no further duty (left for performance) and he has no further existence in this world.

140. By circumambulating god Śiva in the reverse order, in accordance with injunction, a man does not fall off from heaven, thanks to the Grace of Śaṅkara.

141. By eulogising the lord of the Universe, Nārāyaṇa who is free from all ailments, one obtains the cherished desires even whatever he wishes to mentally.

142. O lord of the earth, he who dances or sings in the temple with great devotion, attains to liberation and stays in the region of Rudra.

143. Persons who play on musical instruments in the precincts of the temple, go to god Brahmā's region seated in the swan-shaped aerial car.

144. Those who clap their hands or beat the cymbals in the shrine of gods, become absolved of all sins, and for a period of ten thousand *yugas*, occupy a heavenly car (and move in the skies).

145. Even god Śiva himself is incompetent to describe adequately the merits of those who sound bells in the temple.

146. Listen to the meritorious benefit accrued to those who propitiate the Lord of gods by beating and playing upon different kinds of drums like *bheris* (kettle-drums), *Mṛdaṅgas*, (tabors), *Paṭahas* (war drums), *Murajas* (a kind of tabor) and *Ḍiṇḍimas* (small drums).

147. In association with the bevies of celestial damsels, they are honoured with the fulfilment of all their cherished desires; having attained the heavenly world, they rejoice there for five *Kalpas*.

148. The man who blows a conch in the temple of a deity becomes purged of all sins and rejoices with Viṣṇu, O king.

149. A man beating the cymbals to time or sounding the bell-metal-gong in Viṣṇu's temple is given absolution from all sins and will attain the region of Viṣṇu.

150. God Viṣṇu who is the Lord, witness to all, is the embodiment of knowledge and is absolutely pure, when delighted, confers fully the entire benefit of all religious rites.

151. O lord of the earth, all the righteous duties and holy rites do become fruitful merely by remembering the discus-bearing Lord of *Devas* (i.e. Viṣṇu).

152. He is the Supreme Soul, Lord of the Universe, the bestower of the fruits of all holy actions. He is remembered always by the performers of holy rites. He is the destroyer of all distress and gloom. Whatever is done with him in view, is capable of being infinitely multiplied in its efficacy.

153. All righteous acts are Viṣṇu; all fruits thereof are Viṣṇu; all holy rites are Viṣṇu ; Lord Viṣṇu alone is the enjoyer of fruits and rites; that which is to be done is Viṣṇu; the instruments of doing such acts are Viṣṇu. There is nothing different and separate from him.[16]

CHAPTER THIRTEEN

A Discourse on Dharma

1. *devāyatanaṁ yas tu*, etc.

After discussing the *pūrta-dharma* regarding the construction of a water-tank, god Dharma-rāja takes up in between the topic of foundation of temples (*devāyatana*) in verses 1-13a. According to *Atri-smṛti* even a Śūdra is entitled to *pūrta-dharma*

adhikārī bhavec chūdraḥ pūrte dharme na vaidike

—*Atri Smṛ*. 46

The same right has been claimed for women to claim property (or cash) to spend on *pūrta* acts, by Vijñāneśvara :

Yajña-śabdasya dharmopalakṣaṇa-paratve strīṇām api pūrta-dharmādhikārād dhana-grahaṇaṁ yuktam'

—*Mitākṣarā on Yājñavalkya Smr*. II.114.

The topic on *dāna* has been again discussed in NP. *infra*-I.31 and II.41-42.

In the NP. the discussion on building and conservation of temples is very brief. For details vide *AP*.38-106.

2. Though tanks and water-reservoirs are known since the Ṛgvedic times, the merits of dedicating such tanks is given in *Dharma Sūtras* (vide *Viṣṇu* Dhs. 91.1-2). The procedure of dedicating water-reservoirs to the public has been variously described in *Āśvalāyana Gṛhya pariśiṣṭa* IV.9, *MP*.ch.58 and *AP*. ch.64. These *pūrta dharmas* came to be looked upon as efficacious to confer worldly pleasures and emancipation from *saṁsāra*, while sacrifices bestowed only worldly pleasures.

bhukti-mukti-pradam pūrtam, iṣṭam bhogārtha-sādhanam /

—*Kālikā purāṇa* (quoted in-*Kṛtyaratnākara*)

NP. mentions here different types of reservoirs : *taḍāga*, *kāsāra*, *kūpa*, *vāpī*. The relative dimensions of these reservoirs may be presumed from the amount of merit accruing from them, though NP. (in verse 17 here) proclaims equality in merit for digging a *taḍāga* by a rich person and a *Kūpa* by an indigent person. A *Kūpa* is a well 5 to 50 cubits in length or diameter. *MP*. 153.512 gives the following relative dimensions of other reservoirs as under :

A *Vāpī*=10 *Kūpas*

a *hrada* (a deep lake or reservoir)=10 *Vāpīs* (*daśa-kūpa-samā vāpi, daśa-vāpī-samo hradaḥ*)

According to *Vasiṣṭha Saṁhitā*, a *Puṣkariṇī* is upto 400 cubits in length and 5 *Puṣkariṇīs*=1 *Taḍāga* (quoted in Raghunandana's *Dāna-Kriyā-Kaumudī*).

There being no corresponding terms in English, Sk. terms (with explanations) are retained in the translation.

Kulyā—a canal.

3. Although NP. limits itself to the capacity of the donor in these verses, as a matter of fact, it is the fundamental principle of *dāna-vāda* that merit accruing from *dānas* depends upon the mental attitude, the capacity of the donor and

morality observed in acquiring the thing donated. Aparārka quotes Devala : 'Even if the whole earth acquired by dishonest means be gifted without proper faith or to an unworthy person, one does not secure that much merit as is secured by gifting a handful of vegetables to a worthy person with devout faith.

anyāyādhigataṁ datvā sakalām pṛthivīm api |
Śraddhā-varjam apātrāya na kaṁcid bhūtim āpnuyāt ||
Pradāya śāka-muṣṭiṁ vā śraddhā-bhakti-samudyatām |
mahate pātra-bhūtāya sarvābhyudayam āpnuyāt ||

4. cf. Hemādri-Dāna-Khaṇḍa (pp. 1029-55).

On planting trees, dedication of gardens, also vide *AP*. 70, *MP*. 59 for the procedure of dedicating trees and gardens.

5. *Tulasī* or the basil plant has special sacrosanctity in Viṣṇu worship. In the *Tulasī Māhātmya,* we are told that planting, maintaining, seeing or touching this plant absolves one of all sins :

ropaṇam pālanaṁ sevāṁ darśanaṁ sparśanaṁ tu yaḥ |
Kuryāt tasya praṇaṣṭaṁ syāt sarva-pāpaṁ dvijottama
—*Pd.P.* IV.22.4.

The same *Purāṇa* (VI. *uttara-khaṇḍa* chapters 3-16), gives the story of demon Jālandhara whose queen Vṛndā became the *Tulasī* plant. *Devi bhāgavata* IX *Skandha* chs 15-24 gives a similar story but there *Tulasī* is the consort of Śaṅkhacūḍa (Kṛṣṇa's friend Sudāman cursed by Rādhā) and Mahāviṣṇu violated her chastity which led to Śaṅkhacūḍa's death. Tulasī gave up her body which became the river Gaṇḍak and her hair the Tulasī plant. (*Ibid* IX.24.30-31).

It may be noted that these are later legends. Since Vedic times we have been regarding varieties of Indian fig trees like *Nyagrodha* (Banyan- *Ficus Indica*—a *Kṣīravṛkṣa*), *Udumbara* (the Indian fig tree, *Ficus Glomerata*), *Aśvattha* (the Pippal tree) and *Plakṣa* (*Ficus Infectoria*) as sacred trees. vide (*Tait. Saṁ.*III.4.84). Early Purāṇās also are silent about the glory of *Tulasī.* NP. directs here that after taking one's bath, one should make a verticle mark of a line or lines on the forehead with the earth at the root of the *Tulasī* plant. The materials for marking *Puṇḍra* on the forehead as given in verse 25 here are repeated in *Br.P.* as quoted in *Smṛti Candrikā* I.p.115.

Gopikā Candana or *Gopī-candana* in v.26 is the soft white earth from Dvārakā. It is specially recommended at the time of performing *Śrāddha* :

Dvārāvatyudbhavaṁ gopī-candanaṁ Veṅkaṭodbhavam |
sāntarālam prakurvīta puṇḍraṁ Haripadākṛtim ||
Śrāddha-kāle viśeṣeṇa kartā bhoktā ca dhārayet
—*Vṛddha-Hārīta* VIII.67-8.

6. *Śālagrāma*—

This black piece of stone containing fossil ammonite is found in the Gandak near about its source. It is that portion of the Gandak within half a mile of Mukti Maṭha which abounds in such stones (De, p. 174 and *Muktinātha*, p. 133). *Vṛddha-Hārīta Smṛ.* 8.183-189 states the importance of this worship which, due to its reference in the *Śārīra bhāṣva* I.2.7, I.2,14, must be pretty old. The varieties of *Śālagrāmas* are given in *AP*. Ch. 46 and its procedure of worship in the next (*AP*.ch.47) chapter.

7. These verses describe the procedure of worshipping gods Viṣṇu and Śiva. *Viṣṇudharmasūtra* ch. 65 shows the earliest method of Viṣṇu-worship. But image-worship (both at home and in public temples) became very popular in the mediaeval times. There is a vast literature on this topic. The major sixteen *upacāras* outlined in these verses are elaborately dealt with (and with variations depending on the deity worshipped), in that literature. The main stages are *āvāhana* (invoking the deity), *āsana* (offering a seat to the deity), *pādya, arghya* (offering water to wash feet and hands), *ācamanīya* (water for sipping), *snāna* (bath), *vastra* (offering garments and) *yajñopavīta* (the sacred thread), *gandha* (besmearing with fragrant sandalpaste, etc.), *puṣpa* (offering of flowers—especially those specially liked by the deity as mentioned in the verses of *NP.*), *dhūpa* (incense-burning), *dīpa* (waving lights in front of the deity), *naivedya* (offering of edibles, food, sweet dishes, fruits, etc.), *namaskāra* (laying one's self prostrate before the deity), *Pradakṣiṇā* (circumambulating the deity with one's right side towards the deity) and *visarjana* (taking leave of the deity). Works like the *Pūjāprakāśa* (pp.97 ff) give many details and varieties in these, *vide Bh.P.* XI.27 for the procedure of worship called *Kriyāyoga.*

8. The *dharma-śāstra* is liberal about the free gift of food, clothes and other bare necessities of life. They waived the rules of eligibility or gift-worthiness of the donee in these cases :

annācchādana-dāneṣu pātraṁ naiva vicārayet /

—*Viṣṇudharmottara* quoted in *Dānamayūkha*, p. 5,

The merit accruing from the gift of food, water, care of ailing persons and such other humanitarian acts is extolled in most of the *purāṇas, Smṛtis* and the *Mahābhārata.*

9. Gifts of cows have been mentioned (and eulogised) since the days of the *Ṛgveda* e.g. RV.I.126.3 (Kakṣīvat receiving 60,000 cows), RV.VIII.5.37 (Kaśu Caidyas gift of 10,000 cows). *Smṛtis* regard cows as one of the best *gifts* (*uttama dāna*)—Devala quoted by Aparārka, pp. 289-90, Vasiṣṭha (29.19) calls it an *atidāna*—a gift superior to the gifts of all other things. *Purāṇas* wax eloquent (as in the case of *NP.* here) and consequently a number of verses are found common in many *Purāṇas*, on *go-dāna.*

10. Giving of girls in marriage to Brāhmaṇas as a gift, was in vogue since Vedic times : *vide* RV. I.126.3, VII.18.22, VIII.68.17, etc. This custom was current in the Smṛti and Purāṇa periods.

11. The gift of education or learning has been regarded as the gift *par excellence* in the Smṛtis. Cf.

trīṇyāhur ati-dānāni gāvaḥ pṛthvī Sarasvatī /
ati-dānaṁ hi dānānāṁ vidyādānaṁ tato'dhikam //

—*Vasiṣṭha* XIX.19.

12. The lists of free gifts is very extensive in other *Purāṇas* also. Thus *Mt.P.* ch. 83 and 92 speaks of 10 kinds of '*Meru*-gifts' i.e. of heaps of corn, salt, jaggery, gold, sesame, cotton, ghee, precious stones, etc. *Smṛtis* and *purāṇas* also speak of gifts of animals such as buffaloes, horses, elephants, useful articles like umbrellas, shoes, etc.—many times the same verses occur in different works.

13. Re-establishment of broken *liṅgas* and the procedure for the same, is described in the *AP* chs 67 and 103 and it has been elaborated later in the *Dharma*

Sindhu III *Pūrvārdha*. The Kirāḍu Inscription (Epi.Ind.XX App.56 No. 381) mentions the re-instalment of an image (broken by Turuṣkas), in Saṁvat 1235 by the wife of Tejapāl, an officer of the Chāhamānas, feudatories to king Bhīmadeva of Aṇahillapāṭaka. Reconsecration of images and reconstruction of temples (damaged or polluted) has *śāstric* sanction and historical precedents. The reconsecration of Lord Somanātha temple after Indian Independence, needs emulation in the cases of other ancient shrines.

14. *Go-carma-mātraka* :

Land measuring *go-carma*. *Go-carma* is variously defined. (1) According to Bṛhaspati, it is equal to 10 *nivartanas* and one *vartana* or *nivartana* is 30 (square) rods (a rod=10 cubits).

daśa-hastena daṇḍena triṁśad daṇḍau ni-vartanam /
daśa tānyeva vistāro go-carmaitan mahāphalam //

—*Br.Smṛ.*8 also *Śātātapa* I.15.

The only v.l. in Śātātapa is *svarga-loke mahīyate* instead of go-carmaitan *mahāphalam* in *Bṛhaspati Smṛti.*

(2) In the next verse, it is defined as a piece of land in which a thousand cows with their calves and bulls will comfortably accommodate themselves.

savṛṣaṁ -go-sahasraṁ ca yatra tiṣṭhatyatandritam /
bāla-vatsa-prasūtānāṁ tad go-carma iti smṛtam //

—*Ibid* 9.

For other definitions of *go-carma* vide—*Hemādri Vratakhaṇḍa caturvarga cintāmaṇṇi* I.pp.52-53.

15. It is noteworthy though the *NP.* belongs to the Vaiṣṇava group, the author pays equal regard to Śiva. In fact, all the *Purāṇas* irrespective of their supposed groups, regard Brahmā, Viṣṇu, Śiva or Śakti as the designation of Brahman.

16. This is the highest stage in *Bhakti* and *Vedānta*. This is the realization of the Upaniṣadic truth (everything is Brahman) expressed in *sarvaṁ khalvidam Brahma.*

CHAPTER FOURTEEN

Directions Regarding Dharma and Propitiatory rites[1]

Dharmarāja said :

1. I am now expounding the holy *dharma* proclaimed in the *Vedas* and the *Smṛti*-texts with reference to the different castes in a serial order, O best of kings. Please listen to it with great attention.

2. I shall mention the atonement to the person who, while taking food, touches an impure or a fallen person or a *Cāṇḍāla*, either out of anger or due to ignorance.[2]

3. Such a person shall perform bath three times a day (*triṣavaṇa snāna*) either for three days or for six days. A Brāhmaṇa becomes pure by sipping *pañca-gavya* (the five products of the cow taking collectively, viz. milk, curds, clarified butter, urine and cowdung).

4. Some times fecal matter may trickle down through the anus of a Brāhmaṇa as he takes food. I shall tell you the means of purification in that case. I shall also mention the means of purification when he is defiled by eating the remnants of food (*ucchiṣṭa*) or through some other cause.

5. The Brāhmaṇa shall at the outset perform the *śauca* (cleansing his hind part). Afterwards he shall perform the *ācamana* rite (sipping of water with names of Viṣṇu at each sip). He shall then observe a fast for a day and night. He then becomes pure after taking in the *pañcagavya*.

6. If a person passes urine while swallowing food or if one passes urine (immediately) after taking food, he shall observe fast for a day and night. He shall then perform the *Homa*, offering oblations of ghee into the fire.

7. If a Brāhmaṇa were to become impure at the time of taking food, he shall place that mouthful of food somewhere on the ground, and take his bath, after which he shall attain, purity.

8. If he happens to eat that mouthful, he becomes pure only by observing a fast. If he takes the entire food in his impure condition, he shall be impure for three days.

9. If while taking food, one vomits, he should repeat the *Gāyatrī Mantra* three hundred times, if he is sick, or three thousand times if normal in health. Repetition of the *Gāyatrī Mantra* is the greatest expiation.

10-12a. When a Brāhmaṇa is touched by *Cāṇḍālas* and the pariah (those who cook and eat dog's flesh) or when he answers calls of nature (of urinations and evacuations of bowels), he shall repeat the *Gāyatrī Mantra* for three days. One who is defiled by partaking the *ucchiṣṭa* food, after taking food, shall repeat the *Gāyatrī Mantra* for six days. If a person born in the lowest caste touches a woman in her menses or one who has given birth to a child (during the period while she is regarded impure), the purity of the woman touched, is regained in three days—so says Śātātapa.[3]

12b-13a. If a woman in her menses is touched by dogs, or by a man of the lowest caste or a barbarian or by a crow, she shall observe fast and remain clean. By taking her bath at the proper time, she becomes pure.

13b-14. If two women in their menses per chance touch each other, they become pure by observing *Brahma-kūrca* (a penance in which the woman is to fast for twenty-four hours, then sip *Pañcagavya* for purification). If a person is touched by a person defiled by eating *ucchiṣṭa* and fails to take bath immediately thereafter, he is also purified by *Brahma-kūrca*.[4]

15. If a person indulges in sexual intercourse during the prescribed nights after the menses and if conception is suspected, he shall take bath. If he cohabits with his wife on nights other than the prescribed ones, the purificatory rite is the same as in the case of urination or evacuation of the bowels.

16. Both husband and wife, if united in the act of sexual intercourse, become unclean. As soon as the woman gets up from the bed, she becomes pure, but the man remains unclean.

17. If, out of wickedness, a woman does not render physical service to her husband, she must be punished by abandoning her for twelve years, without giving her financial assistance.

18. Persons forsaking their kinsmen who are fallen, shall be punished with *Uttama-sāhasa*[5] (the highest monetary fine viz. one thousand *Paṇas*). Only the father may be considered as fallen but never the mother.

19. If a man attempts to commit suicide by hanging himself with a rope, etc., he shall be fined two hundred *Paṇas*, if he does not die. If he dies he (i.e. his body) must be besmeared with materials (like ghee) which are considered holy for sacrificial oblations.

20. His friends and sons should be fined one *paṇa* each. Thereafter, they shall perform expiatory rites as prescribed in the scriptures.

21-22. Those who intend to give up their bodies but turn back from water, fire, halter (by means of which they wanted to commit suicide), those, who revert from the stage of *sannyāsa* and those who are thus fallen from (accomplishing their death) by means of observing fast or from taking poison or from jumping down from precipice and those who desire to kill themselves with a weapon but are not killed) these *Pratyavasitas*[6] (fallen—reversionists) are beyond the commerce or contact of the public and they become pure by the observance of *Cāndrāyaṇa*[7] penance or two *Tapta-Kṛcchras*.[8]

23. The sinner who reverts from two such attempts (of suicide), becomes fallen. Such a fallen person becomes pure from the dark sin by observing two *Cāndrāyaṇa* penances and by gifting a cow or a bull thereafter.

24. On being touched by dogs, jackals, monkeys, etc., and by men or women except at the time of sexual act, one shall take bath whether it be day, twilight or night. He becomes pure immediately after the bath.

25. If anyone inadvertently eats the food of a *Cāṇḍāla*, he shall subsist only on food prepared from barley-flour mixed with cow's urine, for half a month, whereby he becomes pure.

26. If any twice-born person burns a cowpen or sets the abode of a Brāhmaṇa to fire and if any one cuts off the rope and cremates (without official post-mortem, etc.) the body of a person who died by hanging himself, shall perform expiatory penance called *Kṛcchra*.

27. If anyone knowingly eats the food of *Cāṇḍālas* and *Pulkasas* (two lowest castes) or kills a woman, he shall expiate himself by performing half a *kṛcchra*[9] penance. If it is done unknowingly, he shall perform two *Cāndrāyaṇa* penances.

28-29a. A person who takes food from the *Kāpālakas*[10] (the followers of a forbidden sect), one who indulges in sexual act with their women, a Brāhmaṇa who co-habits with a forbidden woman, one who takes in wine or eats cow's meat (beef), shall perform the expiatory penance called *Tapta-kṛcchra* and the *Maurvi-homa*[11] (the *homa* performed during the thread ceremony). He, thereby, becomes pure.

29b-30a. Those who commit great sins,[12] particularly the first four, become pure by entering fire or by staying near a great sacrifice.

30b-31a. If this is done secretly,[13] the man shall, for a period of one month, repeat the *Aghamarṣaṇa*[14] hymn while standing in the water. He will thereby become pure.

31b-33a. The following seven castes are regarded as the lowest born (*Antyajas*),[15] viz., the washerman, the leather-worker (cobbler and the shoe-maker), the dancer or actor, the worker in bamboos (*Buruḍa*), the sweeper (*Medas*), the fisher-men, and the *Bhillas*. He who knowingly takes the food from these or cohabits with their women or drinks their beverages or accepts monetary gift from them, shall perform a half-*kṛcchra* penance. If these things are done unwittingly, he shall perform two *Cāndrāyaṇa* penances.

33b-34a. If one has sexual intercourse with one's mother, preceptor's wife, daughter, sister or daughter-in-law, one shall enter fire.[16] No other purificatory rite is enjoined (for such sins).

34b-35a. If one cohabits with the queen, an ascetic woman or one's own nurse or a woman of a higher caste or of one's own *Gotra*, one shall undergo two *kṛcchra* penances.[17] The sin is the same whether these ladies belong to one's father's *gotra* or the mother's *gotra*.

36-37a. If one cohabits with another man's wife he shall perform the *kṛcchrārdha* or the *Sāntapana*[18] expiatory penance. Brāhmaṇas dispell the sin caused by the carnal approach to a prostitute, in a similar manner, by drinking for five nights water containing *Kuśa* grass which is extremely heated but once (?).

37b-38a. A Brāhmaṇa who commits the sin of defiling the preceptor's bed, shall perform the *Vrata* in accordance with scriptural injunctions. Some recommend (this punishment) to one who kills a cow or to a religious student who violates the vow of continence.[19]

38b-39a. He who makes a cow fall down by beating it with a stick, shall perform the expiatory penance called *Go-vrata*[20] twice.

39b-40a. A stick as stout as the thumb, as long as an arm, not dry and having leaves, is called a *Go-daṇḍa*, a stick for beating a cow).

40b-41a. If the cows are made to fall and those cows are pregnant, one shall perform the *Kṛcchra* penance (one per life harmed). This is the atonement for the slaughter of a cow.

41b-42a. If a cow dies when it is being bound or restrained or when its sickness is aggravated, he is smeared with the cause of that sin.

42b-44a. There is no need for any expiation, if the cow, after having fallen or having become unconscious when struck with a stick, gets up and walks six or seven, five or ten steps, or takes a mouthful of grass, or drinks water. Similarly when the cow dies of sickness, there is no expiation.

44b-46a. If cows are struck and killed with (a piece of wood,) a lump of clay or a stone, the expiatory penances are as follows according to respective implement (of striking). If they are killed with a piece of wood, the expiation called *Sāntapana* is to be performed. If they are killed with lumps of clay, *Prājāpatya*[21] expiatory rite is to be performed. If they are killed with stones, *Tapta-kṛcchra* penance is to be performed. If they are killed with any other weapon, the expiatory penance called *Atikṛcchra* is to be undergone.

46b-47a. One should give medicines, oils and ghee, and regular food to cows and Brāhmaṇas. If, while these are being given, any mishap takes place, there is no need for any atonement.

47b-48a. There is no atonement necessary (if any calamity befalls) while drinking the oil or the medicine or while eating solid medicines or during the process of (surgically) removing a thorn or a splinter or any extraneous substance lodged in a body.

48b-49a. When the calves are tied up with ropes round their neck for the purpose of administering any medicines, there is no need of any expiation. If cows and calves are restrained[22] or bound and shut up in the evening for the sake of protection, there is no blemish, or sin.

49b-50.a When the penance is prescribed, the steps in tonsure are : one-fourth of the hair is to be removed first;

in the second stage mustaches are removed; in the third stage all the hair except the tuft of hair is to be cut. (In the case of full penance) all hairs are to be cut off.

50b-51a. (In the case of women) all the hair of the head should be held up and only the tresses upto two *aṅgulas* are to be cut off.[23] This is proclaimed as the tonsure of head in the case of women, in the *Smṛtis*.

51b-52a. Shaving of the head is not to be practised in the case of women nor should they sit in the *Vīrāsana* pose. They should not be made to reside in the cowpens nor are they to observe the *vrata* of following the cow.[24]

52b-53a. The king or the prince or a Brāhmaṇa who is well read in *Śāstras* shall order them to undergo expiatory penance without removing the hair from their head (tonsure is essential in the case of men before such expiations).

53b-54. He should enjoin twice the expiatory observance for the preservation of their hair, and if twice the number of expiatory penances are performed, *dakṣiṇā* for the same should be double.

55a. (In case double *dakṣiṇā* is not given and the hair of the head are preserved) the sin of the killer is not dispelled; and the giver of such a *dakṣiṇā* goes to hell.[25]

55b-56a. Those who lay down expiatory penances not enjoined in the *Vedas* or *Smṛtis* are the obstructers of *dharma*. The king should duly punish them.

56b-57a. But the king shall not inflict pain on them or harass them being deluded by passion. Their sin will increase hundred-fold and envelop him only.

57b-58a. After the expiatory penance has been completely performed he (the ex-sinner) shall feed Brāhmaṇas and give them twenty cows and one bull as a *dakṣiṇā*.

58b-59a. If the cows, etc. are affected by worms born in festering wounds and infested by flies,[26] he should undergo the expiatory penance called *Kṛcchrārdha* and give *dakṣiṇā* according to his capacity.

59b-60a. After performing the expiatory rites and feeding excellent Brāhmaṇas, he should give them a *Māṇika**[27] (a weight of gold). Then they shall gain purity.

---

* *Māṇika* is a misprint for *Māṣaka* found in the *Laghu Yama Smṛti* verse 63 from which the quotation is taken here. *Māṣaka* = weight of 8 *Guñjā* seeds.

60b-61a. If one is touched by persons belonging to *Cāṇḍāla* and *Śvapaca* castes, ablution (for purification) is enjoined even at night, but he shall not stay there with those low castes, at night, he will regain purity immediately after taking bath.

61b-62a. If unknowingly a person had been careless enough to stay there (with low castes) at night, his sin is increased a hundred-fold.

62b-63a. On being touched by the rays of the stars that rise and planets that are above, he shall perform ablution in water.

63b-64a. Earth of the following seven types shall not be taken : that which is within the water, that from an anthill, that from the rats' hole, that from a barren land, that from the main highway, that from the cremation ground and that which is left after the purificative rite (after the nature's call) has been performed.

64b-65a. *Iṣṭa* and *Pūrta* rites[28] shall be performed by a Brāhmaṇa assiduously. Through the *Iṣṭa* rite one attains heaven and through the *Pūrta* rites one attains *Mokṣa.*

65b-66a. *Iṣṭa* (performance of sacrifices, etc.,) is dependant on the expenditure of money.[29] *Pūrta* includes (works of public welfare such as) the digging of tanks, etc.

66b-67a. He who repairs and maintains parks, temples, wells, tanks, lakes and particularly procession with idols of gods attains the benefit of *Pūrta dharma* mentioned before.

67b-68. (In the preparation of *Pañcagavya*[30] the following ingredients should be taken). The urine of the white cow should be collected; similarly, the dung of the black cow; the milk of the copper-coloured cow should be taken; for curds, the milk of a white cow, and for ghee, the milk of a tawny-coloured cow should be taken. All these are destructive of great sins.

69-70a. All these articles (should be purified) separately by means of *Kuśa* grass and the holy water of the sacred rivers. They should be drawn up and brought while repeating *Praṇava* (the syllable *Om*), they should be stirred and drunk while repeating the syllable *Om.*[31]

70b-71a. Water mixed with *Kuśa* grass should be held in a cup of the leaves of the *Palāśa* tree or in an auspicious copper vessel or in a cup of the leaf of a lotus plant or in an earthen vessel[32] and then drunk.

71b-72. When one is already defiled by a *Sūtaka*[33] (impurity due to the birth of a child) and another case of *Sūtaka* befalls, there is no fault or defilement of the second *Sūtaka*. One is purified along with the first one. That which is born is purified along with what is born and that which is dead along with what is dead.

73. If there is any abortion even in the first month, a three day pollution is observed.

74. After observing as many days of pollution as there had been months of pregnancy, in the case of abortion, one gets purified. The chaste lady becomes purified after the monthly course when the flow of blood ceases, and she takes her bath.

75-76. A woman is separated from her family *Gotra* after the seventh step (in the *Saptapadī*) has been taken during the marriage ceremony. Water libations and *piṇḍa* offering to her should be made in the name of the *Gotra* of her husband.[34]

76. The *uddeśya* (object in view) in every *piṇḍa* at the time of offering the *piṇḍas* should be offering them both in the names (of the husband and the wife) to the six (ancestors, viz., father, grand-father and the great grand-father along with their wives) three *piṇḍas* should be offered. Thus the person who offers it, does not become deluded.

77. The mother is fed along with her husband (i.e. the father of the performer of the *Śrāddha*)[35] along with gods, the same way also the grand-mother and the great grand-mother are fed along with their husbands,[36] in the *śrāddha*.

78. One shall perform the hospitable greeting to one's father and mother every year. He shall perform a *śrāddha* without reference to the gods and offer one *piṇḍa*.

79. There are five types of *Śrāddhas* which should be known by wise men. They are (1) *Nitya* (daily and obligatory *Pitṛ-yajña*) (2) *Naimittika* (occasional, for example after the birth of a son) (3) *Kāmya* (for attaining desired object e.g. performance of *Śrāddha* with *Kṛttikā* or *Rohiṇī* as the constellation of the Moon, for attaining heaven or progeny) (4) *Vṛddhi Śrāddha* (*Śrāddha* performed when something specially noteworthy and beneficial to the family has taken place), and the last one is the (5) *Pārvaṇa Śrāddha* i.e. A *Śrāddha* performed on the new moon day or other *parvas* or festive occasions.

80. A man shall offer three *piṇḍas* at the time of the eclipse of the planet, during the transit from one sign of the zodiac to another, and at the time of the festival occasion of *Mahālaya parvan* but only one single *piṇḍa*, on the death anniversary.

81. An unmarried vergin is not treated as separate in regard to the *piṇḍa*, *gotra* and the *sūtaka* (pollution due to the birth of a child). She moves away from her original *gotra*, when the *mantras* of marriage rites are recited.

82. A girl attains the *sūtaka*, *piṇḍas* and rites of libation in accordance with what she obtains in the caste of the husband who marries her.

83. After the marriage has taken place, on the night of the fourth day, she attains unity and identity with her husband in regard to *piṇḍa*, *gotra* and *sūtaka*.

84. The collection of bones should be made by the benevolent kinsmen usually on the first, second, third or the fourth day.[37]

85. The collection of bones has been permitted to be made on the fourth, fifth, seventh or the ninth day for the people of four castes, in that serial order.

86. If on the eleventh day, a bull is let loose on behalf of the dead man, the dead man is liberated from the world of ghosts. He is honoured in the heavenly world.

87. One should stand in the water coming up to his umbilical region and meditate thus within his heart, "May my ancestors come and accept these water libations from these folded palms of mine".

88. He shall join his two palms (in the form of a cup) and fill them with water. Lifting the joint palms upto the height of a cow's horn, he should pour the water in the middle of the water in the tank, etc.

89. He should stay in the water facing the South and throw up the water into the atmosphere. The abode of the *Pitṛs* (manes) is the Ether as well as the southern quarter.

90. Waters are said to be groups of *Devas*. Waters also constitute the groups of *Pitṛs*. Hence, water should be offered by one who wishes the welfare of *Pitṛs*.

91. Water is heated by the rays of the Sun during the daytime; during the night, it is sanctified by the rays of the stars and

the winds and by both during the dawn and dusk. Hence, waters are always sacred.[38]

92. Water is always pure by nature and if its pollution through contact with impure things is beyond one's ken. Water is always sacred whether it is in a pot or on the ground.

93. It is in water that oblations of water should be offered to the deities and the *pitṛs*. A careful and intelligent person shall offer it on the ground to those who are dead but not cremated or consecrated.

94. At the time of *Śrāddha* and *homa*, one shall offer the libation of water with one hand. During the *tarpaṇa* rite one shall offer the libation with both hands. This is the arrangement for the religious rites.[39]

CHAPTER FOURTEEN

Directions regarding Dharma and Śānti

1. The present chapter is a complete, practically word to word, incorporation of the *Laghu Yama Smṛti* (LYS) with some parallel verses from the *Yama Smṛti.* The difference between NP and LYS is that in the NP., the narrator of the *dharmas* or to be more accurate, the expiatory penances for different sins, is Dharma-rāja, the god of Death, but in LYS, Yama is a sage, a Law-giver and the object of LYS is proclamation of different expiatory rites for different kinds of sins (*nānāvidha-prāyaścitta-varṇanam*).

It is beyond the scope of the present note to explain the concept of sin which has been adequately discussed in Hasting's *Encyclopaedia of Religion and Ethics* (Vol.XI. *vide* 'sin'). It shows that the concept of sin varies from religion to religion, region to region and age to age. The use of words like *āgas, agha, drugdha, enas, aṁhas, durita,* in the *Ṛgveda* shows that the concept of sin was already developed in those times (also *vide* A.B. Keith *The Religion and Philosophy of the Veda and Upanishads* 245-9, 264-8, 310-12, etc.)

The words *prāyaścitti* and *prāyascitta* stand for the act of expiation and are found since the Vedic period. It is, however, the latter form (*prāyaścitta*) which gained popularity and is widely used in the *Dharma-śāstra* literature (in *Smṛtis, purāṇas,* etc.). The word *prāyaścitta* is variously defined—the most popular connotation is "that whereby the *citta* (the mind) of the repentant is generally (*prāyaḥ*) free (from the oppressive sense of guilt) by the *parṣad* (assembly of Brāhmaṇa *paṇḍitas*).

Prāyaśaś ca samaṁ cittaṁ cārayitvā pradīyate /
Parṣadā kāryate yat tu prāyaścittam iti smṛtam //
(a *Smṛti* quotation in *Parāśara Mādhava* II.1.p.3)

The idea that a sin can be wiped out by *Prāyaścitta* gave rise to a vast literature from the time of *Dharmasūtras* down to the medieval *nibandha-kāras* (writers on *Dharma-śāstra*). Gautama and Vasiṣṭha in their *Dharma-sūtras, Manu Smṛ.* XI.44-265, *Yājñavalkya Smṛ.* III 205-327, (LYS or the present chapter already mentioned), *Bṛhad-Yama Smṛ.* 182 verses, *AP.* ch.s 168-74; *KP.Uttarārdha* 30-34 to mention a few, deal with these expiatory penances.

2. The theory of untouchability though not satisfactorily traceable to the Vedas, came to be accepted by the time of *Smṛtis* and *Purāṇas.* And it did not depend on birth alone.

The idea is that by taking bath one washes off symbolically, the mental pollution caused by the touch of certain men connected with unclean vocations, holders of anti-Vedic views (like Bauddhas, Cārvākas, etc.), extra-Indian invaders (like Turuṣkas), uncultured hill-tribes, a women in menses or immediately after delivery, corpses, unclean animals like pigs, dogs etc. Man has practised against man unjustifiable discriminations like residential segregation, exclusion from public institutions, disenfranchisement, etc. all over the world, including advanced western societies. This is not to defend the *Purāṇic* statements about expiation, but to put them into proper historical perspective.

3. *Śātātapa*—N. of a Smṛti-writer. This quotation however could not be traced in the *Śātātapa Smṛ.* (*Gurumandal Edt.*) These verses have been quoted from LYS.

4. *Brahma-kūrca*

Normally this expiatory rite is enjoined to a man. Such a man is to observe a fast for the whole day and night on a day (particularly on a full moon day) and then drink *Pañcagavya*, the next morning

> *ahorātroṣito bhūtvā paurṇamāsyāṁ viśeṣataḥ* /
> *Pañcagavyaṁ pibet prātar brahmakūrcavidhiḥ smṛtaḥ* //
>
> —Jābāla quoted in *Prāyaścitta Viveka*, p. 515.

But in taking the separate ingredients of *Pañcagavya*, the man has to consecrate them with Vedic *mantras* and utter those *mantras* (such as the *Gāyatrī*) while taking them in (*samantrakaṁ saṁyujya samantrakam eva pañcagavyaṁ pīyate tadā brahma-kūrca ityākhyāyate*—*Mitākṣarā* on *Yājñ Smṛ.* III.314). Women were not eligible to utter *vedic mantras*. Hence, here a twentyfour hours fast broken by sips of *Pañcagavya* seem to be implied, as women are treated as *Śūdras* (being ineligible to utter Vedic *mantras*), and śūdras were allowed to take *Pañcagavya* without Vedic *mantras.*

> *Strīṇāṁ caiva tu śūdrāṇām patitānāṁ tathaiva ca* /
> *Pañcagavyaṁ....dātavyaṁ mantra-varjitam* //
>
> —*Devala Smṛ.* 61

also vide *Parāśara Smṛ.* XI.3 & 27.

5. *Uttama-sāhasa*

Nārada defines *sāhasa* as an offence committed out of pride for one's strength (*sahas*-strength)

> *sahasā kriyate karma yat kiñcid bala-darpitaiḥ* /
> *tat sāhasam iti proktaṁ saho balam ihocyate* //

He divides *sāhasa* into three categories :

(1) *Prathama* (2) *Madhyama* and (3) *Uttama.*

The last includes offences like killing by poison or weapons and rapes on another persons' wives (XIV.5) and the punishment for this is death, confiscation of property, expulsion, amputation of the organ (XIV.7) and even if the offender survives, he was to be excommunicated (XIV.10). Manu and Viṣṇu lay down the highest fine. Thus for idol-breaking the king is to fine the culprit 500 *Paṇas* and make him re-instate it at his cost (*Manu* IX.285).

As the LYS. verse 19 shows the text of the *NP.* here should be emended as *tyajantyo'patitān* as the original *tyajantyo patitān* makes no sense. For according to *Dharmaśāstra*, a fallen relative (even one's own father and never the mother as stated in the next line) is to be abandoned.

6. *Pratyavasita*

In ancient India, the right of death, civil or physical was exercised by persons who wanted to free themselves from worldly life by adopting *sannyāsa-āśrama* or by giving up their life by fast, drowning in water, self-immolation, etc. But persons who declared their desire to renounce life, were to shrink back at the last stage or revert from *sannyāsa* to the householder's stage of life, they were called *pratyavasita*. The text hereof which is a quotation from LYS. 22 & 23 (and *Bṛhad Yama Smṛ*. verses 3 & 4) classifies the *pratyavasitas* in categories according to the mode or means they proclaimed to adopt to embrace death.

7. *Cāndrāyaṇa*

This observance is an expiatory penance as well as the means of increasing one's fund of merits. When it is for expiation of sins, it is to be preceded by tonsure. As the name indicates, any act (here taking in morsels of food) varying directly with the increase or decrease of the digits of the moon is *Cāndrāyaṇa* (*candrasyāyanam ivāyanaṁ caraṇaṁ yasmin karmaṇi hrāsa-vṛddhibhyāṁ tac cāndrāyaṇam—Mitākṣarā* on *Yāj.Smṛ*.III.323). This is a very ancient type of penance as it is noted by Pāṇini (V.1.72). As Baudhāyana (III.8.33) notes it, since ancient times there were two varieties of this *Vrata*, viz., *Yava-madhya* (large in the middle and tapering at both the ends like the grain of *yava* (barley) and *pipīlikā-madhya* (slender in the middle like an ant and bigger at the ends). The first (*Yava-madhya*) type is as follows :

On the first day of the bright half of the month, one morsel of food is to be taken and the number of morsels are to be increased one per day so that on the full moon day one is to eat fifteen morsels. And in the dark half one morsel per day is to be reduced, till he observes complete fast on the New Moon day.

In the second variety, the *pipīlikā-madhya*, the observer begins on the first day of the dark half of the month and eats 14 morsels till on the New Moon day he observes complete fast and then from the first day of the bright half of the month he goes on increasing his food intake as one, two, three, etc. according to the *tithis* so that on the full moon day, he eats fifteen morsels.

Some more varieties are added by later writers on *Dharma-śāstra*. The *Cāndrāyaṇa* is prescribed when no other specific penance is prescribed (*Yājñāvalkya Smṛ*. III.326).

8. *tapta-kṛcchra-dvayena vā*

As an alternative to *Cāndrāyaṇa* two *tapta-kṛcchra* penances are prescribed. Normally this is prescribed for Brāhmaṇas who sell things or animals which should not be sold by them, such as sesame, sesame-oil, curd, salt, cooked food, slaves, etc. There are different views about its observance. Thus according to *Manu* XI.214, *Śaṅkha Smṛ*. 18.4, *Parāśara Smṛ*. 18.4 and *AP*.171.6-7. This penance consists of a period of twelve days comprising four sub-periods of three days each. In this, the penitent has to drink hot water, hot milk, hot ghee for three days each and then for the last subperiod of three days, he is to observe complete fast inhaling hot atmosphere (Hence the adjective *tapta* in the name of this penance).

tryaham uṣṇam pibed āpas tryaham uṣṇam payaḥ pibet |
tryaham uṣṇam ghṛtam pītvā vāyu-bhakṣī tryaham bhavet ||

—*AP*. 171.6-7

Manu specifically insists on breathing hot air (XI.215). According to *Mitākṣarā* (*Yājñavalkya* III.317), this duration of 12 days is prescribed for great sins, while that of 4 days, viz., taking in hot milk, ghee and water for the first three days and complete fast in the fourth day is meant for minor sins.

tapta-kṣīra-ghṛtāmbūnām ekaikaṁ pratyaham pibet |
eka-rātropavāsaśca tapta-kṛcchras tu pāvanaḥ ||

cf. *Yājñavalkya Smṛ.* III.317 —*Devala Smṛ.*84.

9. *Kṛcchārdham ācaret* :

Contact with women of lower castes was strongly condemned as a sin. If the sin is committed unknowingly, the expiation is of a milder nature, viz. *Ardhakṛcchra*, while two *Cāndrāyaṇa* penances are prescribed for deliberately committing this sin. *Ardha-kṛcchra* is a variety *of Kṛcchra*. It is to be observed for six days as follows : Food is to be taken only once at day time for one day, only once in the evening on the second day, taking food for two days without asking for it and complete fast on the last two days.

Sāyam-prātas tathaivekaṁ dina-dvayam ayācitam |
dina-dvayaṁ ca nāśnīyāt kṛcchrārdhaṁ tad vidhīyate ||

—*Āpastamba Smṛ.* IX.41-42.

It is also called *pāda-kṛcchra*—one fourth of *Kṛcchra* penance (*Yājñavalkya* IX.318)

10. *Kāpālikānna-bhoktṝṇām* is a misprint for *Kāpālikānna*° etc. as attested in LYS 29. *Kāpāla* or *Kāpālika* is the follower of a Śaiva sect (of the left-hand order) characterised by wearing skulls of men in the form of a garland, and eating and drinking from them. Any contact with them was looked upon with abhorrence and contempt. Hence, this restriction and proposed expiation.

11. *Maurvīhoma* v.l. *mauñjī-homa* in LYS.30 is the *homa* (sacrificial rite) performed at the ceremony of the investiture of the sacred thread (*upa-nayana*).

12. *mahāpātaka-kartāraḥ*

Those who commit great sins. 'Great sins' or *Mahāpātakas* are as follow : (1) Slaying a Brāhmaṇa (2) Wine-drinking (3) Theft (4) defiling one's preceptor's bed (wife) and (5) association with a person who committed any of the above four sins.

brahma-hatyā surāpānaṁ steyaṁ gurvaṅganā-gamaḥ |
mahānti pātakānyāhus tat-saṁsargaśca pañcamam ||

—*Manu* XI.55

In the next chapter (NPI.15.22b and 23a), the above is paraphrased as follows :

brahmahā ca surāpī ca steyī ca guru-talpagaḥ |
mahāpātakinas tvete tat-saṁsargī ca pañcamaḥ ||

Later on, what acts are equivalent to each of these great sins is expounded in the rest of that chapter.

13. *rahasya-karaṇo* :

Probably a misprint for *rahasya-karaṇe* as attested in LYS 32.

14. *aghamarṣaṇa-sūktam* :

RV.X.190 is regarded as an expiatory *Sūkta* for washing out sins.

15. *rajakaś carmakāraśca saptaite'ntyajāḥ smṛtāḥ* |

The term *antyaja* connotes lowest castes like Cāṇḍālas (vide *Manu* IV.61). Different lists of "low castes" are found in *Smṛtis* but this verse is found in *Atri* 199 and is attributed to *Āpastamba* in *Mitākṣarā*. The low castes enumerated above are as follows : (1) *rajaka* (washerman), *carma-kāra* (artisan in hides), *naṭa* (acrobats like *Kolhāṭīs* in Maharashtra), *buruḍa* (worker in bamboos)

Kaivarta (fishermen), *meda* (sweepers) and *bhilla.* According to *Śūdra-kamalākara medas* are sweepers.

It is noteworthy that in the medieval India, guilds of some of these had risen in social status. Works like *Vīra-mitrodaya* (*Vyavahāra,* p.12) testify to the verticle social mobility in Hindu society.

16. These are *ati-pātakas* for which there is no expiation except self-immolation in fire.

17. *Kṛcchra-dvaya* :

Two *Kṛcchra* penances. *Kṛcchra* is a general term for different penances. From *Sāma-vidhāna Brāhmaṇa,* (I.2.1-4), Gautama (26.1-6) and *Āpastamba,* (I.9.27.7) it seems to be a penance of 12 days duration. In this, the penitent is to eat sacrificial food for three days by day only (fasting at night), then for the next three days he is to fast during day time and eat at night only. Then for the next three days, he should eat when (sacrificial) food is offered to him, without his asking for it, and then should observe complete fast on the last three days.

athātas trīn kṛcchrān vyākhyāsyāmaḥ /
haviṣyān tryaham anaktāśyadivāśī, tatas tryahaṁ tryaham
ayācita-vratas tryahaṁ nāśnāti kiñcaneti kṛccha-dvādaśarātrasya vidhiḥ /
—*Āpastamba Dh.Sūtra* I.9.27.7

18. *Kṛcchrārdhaṁ tapanam* but LYS 37 reads
Kṛcchraṁ Sāntapanam.

Sāntapana, *Mahā-Sāntapana*, *Ati-Sāntapana* are penances of the same category in which the duration is different but subsistence on the cow's urine, dung, milk, curds, ghee and Kuśa water interspersed with complete fasts are the common factors. Thus, according to *Bṛhad-Yama Smṛ* I.13 (*Manu* XI.213), *Sāntapana* lasts for two days. On the first day, the penitent drinks the above ingredients and on the next day observes complete fast.

go-mūtraṁ gomayaṁ kṣīraṁ dadhi-sarpiḥ kuśodakam /
ekarātropavāsaśca kṛcchraṁ sāntapanaṁ smṛtam //

For *Mahā-sāntapana,* the observer drinks separately for six days in succession, the above six ingredients and observes a fast on the seventh day (*Devala* 82, *Atri* 118-119). Yama proclaims *Mahā-sāntapana* for fifteen days, when each of the ingredients (cow's urine, dung, etc.) are taken as food for three days consecutively. *AP.* 171.8-10 proclaims *Mahāsāntapana* as lasting for 18 days and also of 21 days.

Kṛcchrā'tikṛcchrapayasā divasānām ekaviṁśatim /
tryahābhyastam athaikekam atisāntapanaṁ smṛtam //

19. *Avakīrṇinaḥ*—

Avakīrṇin—a religious student who has committed an act of incontinence (such as sexual intercourse) against his vow of celibacy. For his donkey-like act he was to expiate by offering an ass to Nairṛti (*Yājñavalkya* II. 280) *Manu* XI. 123-24 however calls upon such a sinner to put on a donkey-hide, and beg for food in seven houses proclaiming his violation of oath.

20. *Go-vrata*:

The observance to stay among cows, act like them, bathe in cow's urine and subsist on cow-dung. The observer is not to sit, eat or drink unless cows have done so. The duration of this observance is one month.

21. *Prājāpatya* is a *Kṛcchra* penance when the noun *Kṛcchra* is not qualified by any adjective like *ati-*, *tapta-*, *mahā-* etc. (*Smṛti-śāstreṣu nirupa-padasya kṛcchra-śabdasya prājāpatya eva prācuryeṇa prayogāt, kṛcchram iti prājāpatyam iti Devala-smaraṇāc ca.* —*Parāśara Mādhava* II. Part 1 p.30.

The duration of this penance is twelve days or consecutive four periods each of three days, in which there is respectively (i) eating once by day (and fast at night), (ii) eating once by night only, (iii) eating once only unsought for (sacrificial) food and (iv) complete fast for the last three days :

tryaham prātas tryahaṁ sāyaṁ tryaham adyād ayācitam /
tryaham paraṁ ca nā'śnīyāt Prājāpatyaṁ caran dvijaḥ //

Manu XI.212

There are three more varieties or permutations of this penance.

22. *Roṣa-bandhayoḥ* a misprint for *rodha-bandhayoḥ, vide* LYS.52.

23. This is the practice for *Veṇī-dāna* (giving of tresses) of women. It seems that complete tonsure of women (whose husbands are alive) practised at Tirupati (Andhra Pradesh), is not taken into account or that custom might have come into vogue in the post-NP. period.

24. This shows that women were probably exempted from *Go-vrata.*

25. The line *pāpaṁ na kṣīyate hantur dātā ca narakaṁ vrajet* by itself is incomplete and cannot be construed with 55b which is connected with 56a. The LYS 58a supplies the missing line which runs as follows :

dviguṇaṁ cenna dattaṁ ca keśāñśca pari-rakṣayet /

To which in natural sequence runs NP I.14.55a quoted above (=LYS 58b).

26. *Krimibhis tṛṇasambhūtair*—a misprint for *Kṛmibhir vraṇa-sambhūtair vide* LYS. 62.

27. *Suvarṇa-manikam* a misprint for *suvarṇamāṣaka vide* LYS. 63. *māṣaka*—a wt. of gold variously equated with the weight of 8 or 10 *guñjā* seeds.

28. *iṣṭāpūrta*—

We have previously noted the evolution of the concept *iṣṭāpūrta* since the Vedic period. Here two *purāṇic* difinitions are quoted :

Iṣṭa consists of maintenance of sacred fire, performance of penance, truthfulness, Vedic studies, honouring a guest and performance of *vaiśvadeva,* while *Pūrta* includes dedication of tanks, wells, temples, maintenance of centres of free food distribution, and of public gardens. *Iṣṭa* leads to the celestial region. while *Pūrta*, to *Mokṣa.*

vāpī-kūpa-taḍāgāni devatāyatanāni ca /
anna-pradānam ārāmaḥ pūrtaṁ dharmaṁ ca muktidam //
agnihotraṁ tapaḥ satyaṁ Vedānāñ cānupālanam /
ātithyaṁ vaiśvadevañ ca prāhur iṣṭañ ca nākadam //

AP. 209.2-3.

Atri Smr. 43-44 are the same as the above verses. As already noted NP. implies the same by this term.

29. *Vittakṣepo* in NP. a misprint for *vittāpekṣam* vide LYS 69.

30. The colours of cows from whom urine, dung, milk, etc. are to be obtained for preparing *pañca-gavya* are differently given in some *smṛtis*. For example, Parāśara proclaims that the urine, dung, milk, curd and ghee should be of cows respectively of dark, white, copper-like, dark-red and tawny colour :

go-mūtraṁ kṛṣṇa-varṇāyāḥ śvetāyā gomayaṁ haret |
payaścā tāmra-varṇāya raktāyā dadhi co'cyate ||

31. The verses in NP. do not clarify the method of preparing *pañca-gavya.* The following is the method in brief :

"According to *Atri.*299 dung, urine, ghee and milk were to be respectively 1, 2, 4 and 8 parts and curds also 8 parts. When mixing the ingredients, urine is taken with sacred *Gāyatrī*, cowdung with *gandha-dvārām* (*Tai.Ar.*X.1), milk with *āpyāyasva* (*RV.*I.91.16), curds with *dadhikrāvṇo* (*RV.*IV.39.6), ghee with *tejosī śukram* (*Vājasaneyi Saṁh.* 22.1) and *Kuśa* water with *devasya tvā* (*Ait. Brā* 37.3). The *pañca-gavya* thus prepared is to be placed near the fire, then it is to be stirred to the accompaniment of *āpo hi ṣṭhā* (*RV.*X.9.1-3) and then with the mantra *mā nastoke* (*RV.*I.114.8) is to be repeated over it. It may be then offered into fire with green *darbhas*, not less than seven, to the accompaniment of *Irāvatī* (*RV.*VII.99.3), *idam Viṣṇur* (*RV.*I.22.1) *mā-nastoke* (*RV.* I.114.8) and the *śaṁvati* verse (RV.X.9.4) and then the remainder is to be drunk by the preparer with the verse in Parāśara XI.37"

—Kane *Hist. of Dharma Śāstra* II.ii.p.774.

32. This verse properly enumerates the kinds of vessels in which *pañca-gavya* is to be prepared (vide *Parāśara Mādhava* II.1 p.434, where Prajāpati is quoted). But here the vessels are to be used for drinking the *Kuśodaka* (water containing Kuśa grass).

It may be noted that *paṇa-bhāṇḍe* is a misprint for *parṇa-bhāṇḍe* vide LYS 74.

33. Here begins a new topic called *Aśauca*—impure state arising on birth (*jananāśauca* or *sūtaka*) and arising out of death (*mṛtakāśauca*). Verses 71b-72 give the general rule that if both *aśaucas* are of the same kind, and the second is of the same or of lesser duration than the first, a person gets rid of them both at the end of the first. *Nirṇaya sindhu* (pp.536-540) discusses 12 alternatives of such superventions of *Aśauca*, but NP. is not interested in these details.

34. This explains *Viṣṇudharma Sūtra* : 22.32-33.

strīṇāṁ vivāhaḥ saṁskāraḥ |
saṁskṛtāsu strīṣu nāśaucam bhavati pitṛ-pakṣe |

There is no *aśauca* for the parents on the death of a married woman.

35. *Śrāddha*, according to *Br.P.* is whatever is given with faith to Brāhmaṇas for the benefit of our dead ancestors, at the proper time, place and to deserving persons in accordance with the prescribed procedure: *Śrāddhas* have been variously classified. The classification accepted in the NP is : (1) *Nitya*, (2) *Naimittika* (3) *Kāmya* (4) *Vṛddhi* and (5) *Pārvaṇa* and the terms have been explained in translation.

36. *bhartrā sahasrābdam* :

A misprint for *saha śrāddham*, vide LYS.80. *sudaivata* is *sadaivaṭa* in LYS 80.

37. There is a great divergence of views regarding the day of *asthi-sañcayana* or collection of charred bones of the cremated persons. Thus *Gd.P. Preta khaṇḍa* 5.15 prescribes the 1st, 3rd, 7th or 9th and specially the 4th by twice-born persons, a view endorsed by *Vāmana* P.14.97-98. Here NP. echoes or rather quotes LYS. 87 and 88.

38. Since the Ṛgveda, water is regarded as 'great purifier', *śucayaḥ pāvakāḥ* being the favourite phrase of all Vedic seers. Hence, it was offered to the deceased after cremation by any or all *sapiṇḍas*.

39. Cf. *Viṣṇu dharma sūtra* 23.46 and *Āpastamba* both quoted by Aparārka, p.273.

CHAPTER FIFTEEN

Bhagīratha Advised to Bring the Gaṅgā

Dharmarāja said :

1. I shall mention the different types of sins as well as the tortures (in hells) in a broad manner. Take courage and listen to them since these hells are terrible.[1]

2. I shall describe those fiery hells which accord terrible results and wherein the sinner and the wicked persons are always roasted.

3. They are[2] *Tapana*, *Vālukā*, *Kumbha*, *Mahāraurava*, *Raurava*, *Kumbhīpāka*, *Nirucchvāsa*, *Kālasūtra*, *Pramardana*.

4. The terrible *Asipatravana*, *Lālābhakṣa*, *Himotkaṭa*, *Mūṣāvasthā*, *Vasākūpa*, the river *Vaitaraṇī*.

5. *Purīṣahrada* where feces are eaten, *Mūtrapāna* where urine is drunk, *Taptaśūla*, *Taptaśilā*, *Śālmalī-druma*.

6. *Śoṇitakūpa*, the terrible, *Śoṇitabhojana*, *Svamāṁsa bhojana*, *Vahnijvālāniveśana*.

7. *Śilāvṛṣṭi*, *Śastravṛṣṭi*, *Vahnivṛṣṭi*, *Kṣārodaka*, *Uṣṇatoya*, *Taptāyaḥpiṇḍa Bhakṣaṇam*.

8. *Śiraḥśoṣaṇam*, *Marut prapatana*, *Pāṣāṇavarṣa*, *Kṛmibhojana*.

9. The tortures[3] are *Kṣārodapāna* (drinking briny water) *Bhramaṇa* (whirling), *Krakacadāraṇa* (torn off with a saw), *Purīṣalepana* (smearing with fecal matter), *Purīṣa Bhojana* (eating the fecal matter).

10. Drinking semen virile, the highly terrible scorching in all the joints, inhaling smoke, binding with nooses, hitting with different kinds of spears;

11. Lying down on burning coal, pounding with the threshing pestles, many wooden machines with which men are crushed and pared;

12. Falling and throwing up and down, belabouring with iron clubs and batons, striking with the tusks of elephants, biting through serpents.

13. Sprinkling of chill water, drinking of terrible saltish water through the nostrils and mouth, and eating of salts;

14. Cutting off the muscles, binding of the sinews, the cutting of the bones, penetration of salt water through crevices or pores on the body, eating of flesh;

15. The obnoxious feeding of bile, (forcible) feeding of phlegm, throwing down from the top of the tree and sinking in the water;

16. Forcing one to bear weighty stones, lying on thorns, getting bitten through ants and stung through scorpions;

17. Infliction of pain through tigers, jackals and buffaloes, lying in mud, filling in with foul smelling things;

18. Half-crouching on many occasions, taking in excessively bitter things, drinking of extremely hot oil and eating the most pungent thing ;

19. Drinking of astringent water, paring with heated rock, bathing in excessively hot and extremely chill water, dashing of the teeth.

20. Lying on heated iron plates and tying of weighty iron blocks. O blessed one, the tortures in the hell are these and similar ones. There are millions and millions of tortures.

21. O Protector of the Earth, I am not competent to mention in details even in a thousand years, which sinner has to undergo which torture.

22. I shall now narrate to you all those things. Even as I narrate it listen to the same.

22b-23a. The slayer of a Brāhmaṇa, a wine-addict, a thief and a defiler of the preceptor's bed—these are great sinners (*Mahāpātakins*). He who associates himself with these is the fifth among them.

A Brāhmaṇa-slayer :

23b-24a. The following five are regarded as Brāhmaṇa-slayers :[4] the splitter of rows (of persons taking dinner), one who prepares food in vain, one who always slanders Brāhmaṇas, the instigator of these (or a bad astrologer) and a seller of the Vedas.

24b-24c. These five are called the slayers of Brāhmaṇas. The person who invites a Brāhmaṇa saying, "I shall give you money and other requirements" and refuses it afterward saying "there is nothing".

25. The person who acts as obstacle or intruder to a Brāhmaṇa, while he goes to take his bath and perform worship, is called a slayer of a Brāhmaṇa.

26. One who is always engaged in censuring others, who is interested in self-conceit and self-aggrandizement and who indulges in falsehood is spoken of as a murderer of a Brāhmaṇa.

27a. A person who consents to and abets these sins is spoken of as a Brāhmaṇa-slayer.

27b-28a. A person interested in alarming and frightening others, a person who always finds faults with others and the person who indulges in arrogant behaviour is called a murderer of a Brāhmaṇa.

28b-29. A person who is always interested in accepting monetary gifts and indulges in killing living beings, a person who encourages unrighteousness is spoken of as a Brāhmaṇa-murderer. O king, thus, many sins are on par with Brāhmaṇa-slaughter.

30-34. *Wine drinking*[5]

30a. I shall succinctly tell you the sins which are on par with drinking of wine:

30b-31a. Eating of the food of attendants, resorting to prostitutes, eating of the food of fallen persons—these are declared as sins equal to drinking of wine.

31b-32a. Abandoning of worship, taking of food from the professional worshipper of idols, and indulgence of sexual intercourse with women addicted to wine—all these are equivalent to drinking of wine.

32b-33a. The Brāhmaṇa who, on being invited by a *Śūdra*, partakes of his food, should be known as a wine addict. He is excluded from all holy rites.

33b-34. That mean fellow who does the work of an attendant with the permission of a *Śūdra*, incurs a sin equal to drinking of wine. Thus many sins are proclaimed to be equal to wine drinking.

35-40a. *Theft*[6]

35-36a. I shall now mention the sins which are equivalent to the theft of gold. Listen. The theft of bulbous roots, roots and fruits, of musk and of perfumed powder, and the theft of jewels—all these are always equal to the theft of gold.

36b-37a. The theft of gold, iron, tin and bell metal, of

ghee and honey and stealing fragrant articles—all these are declared (in *Smṛtis*) to be equal to the theft of gold.

37b-38a. The taking away of areca nut, of water, of sandal and the taking away of the juice of leaves—all these are equal to the theft of gold.

38b-39a. The abandonment of the *Pitṛyajñas* (offering of libations of water, *Śrāddha*, etc.), omission of performing one's righteousness and holy rites and disrespect for the ascetic—all these are equal to the theft of gold.

39b-40a. Taking away edible things, carrying away of grains, and stealing of Rudrākṣa beads—all these are equal to the theft of gold.

40b-44. *Defiling the preceptor's bed*[7]

40b-41a. Cohabiting with one's sister or with one's son's wife, or a woman in a monthly course is equivalent to the sin of defiling the preceptor's bed.

41b-42a. Sexual intercourse with a woman of low caste, intimate association with women addicted to wine and sexual intercourse with another person's wife—all these are equal to the sin of defiling the preceptor's bed.

42b-43a. Cohabiting with the wife of one's own brother or of a friend or a woman who keeps entire trust in one, is equal to the sin of defiling the preceptor's bed.

43b-44. Performance of holy rites out of the prescribed time limit, cohabiting with one's own daughter, omission in performing righteous duties and speaking low of the holy scriptures—all these are proclaimed (in *Smṛtis*) as equivalent to the sin of defiling the preceptor's bed. These and such other acts, O king, are called great sins.

45-46. One who intimately associates himself with any of these sinners shall be equal to them. Expiatory rites for these sinful activities have been found with difficulty by great, quiescent sages through the rites of atonement, etc. O king, listen to the sins which cannot be atoned for by these expiatory rites.

47. All sins are equally leading to infernal regions. It is with very great difficulty that some way of expiating sins like Brāhmaṇa slaughter are found.

48. But there is no expiation[8] anywhere to a person who hates a Brāhmaṇa. So also, O Ruler of men, there is no

atonement for those who are ungrateful persons and those who commit breach of trust.

49-50. There is no expiation anywhere to those persons who intimately associate themselves with *Śūdra* women, whose bodies are nourished with the food of the *Śūdras* and who indulge themselves in denouncing the *Vedas*. There is no expiation here or hereafter to those who find fault with stories of saintly people.

51. Even through hundreds of expiations, it is impossible to see the redemption of that Brāhmaṇa who enters a Buddhistic shrine, even in a great emergency.

52. The Buddhists are heretics, as they are the revilers of the Vedas. Hence, a Brāhmaṇa shall not even look at them, since they are excluded from righteous holy rites.

53. A Brāhmaṇa may enter a Buddhist shrine knowingly or unknowingly. If he enters knowingly, there is no redemption at all. This is the decision of the scriptures.

54-55. Since their sins are numerous, their stay in the hell is for a period of ten million *Kalpas*. O Lord, other sins for which there is no expiation are also mentioned now. Listen to it even as I recount their stay in the hell.[9]

56. Those who have committed great sins stay in each of the hells for a *yuga*. At the end of it they come back to the Earth. They are born as donkeys in the course of seven lives.

57. Then for ten lives, they are born as dogs, getting their bodies whipped and lashed. For the period of a hundred years, they remain as worms in the fecal matter, after which they are born as serpents for twelve lives.

58. O king, thereafter, in the course of a thousand lives, they are born as deer and other animals. Then for a hundred years they are born as immobile beings. Thereafter, they take up the bodies of alligators.

59. Then for seven lives they are born as *Cāṇḍālas* who commit sinful crimes. Then, for sixteen lives they are born as *Śūdras* and other persons of the lowest castes.

60. Then for two births they remain as impoverished persons afflicted with sickness. They are intent on always in accepting monetary gifts. Again, they go back to hell.

61. Those whose minds are defiled by jealousy fall into the hell called *Raurava*. Staying there for two *Kalpas*, they are born as *Cāṇḍālas* in the next hundred lives.

62. He who says 'Don't give' in regard to cows, fires and Brāhmaṇas is born as a dog in the course of a hundred lives at the end of which he is born among the *Cāṇḍālas*.

63. Thereafter, he is born as the worm in the fecal matter and a tiger in the course of three births. At its end, he goes to the hell and remains there for twenty-one *Yugas*.

64. Listen to the results of the sinful activities of those who are engaged in slandering others, those who speak roughly and harshly and those who create obstacles in regard to charitable gifts.

65. Thieves are thrashed roundly by means of mortar and pestle. They are reduced to powder. At its end, they have to hold heated stone for three years (in the *Tapta-śilā* hell).

66-67. Thereafter, in the hell called *Kālasūtra*, for seven years, they are pared with the instrument *Kālasūtra* ('the thread of death', like the thread on the wheel with which the potter cuts off a raw earthen pot in two). Those who have misappropriated other men's wealth bewail their sinful activities, as they are being cooked in the hellish fires continuously, as a retribution of their acts.

68. Listen to the terrible hell for the tale-bearers and traducers of other men's wealth. They have to hold in their mouths red hot iron for a period of a thousand *Yugas*.

69. Their tongues are pressed and crushed by means of very terrible tongs. Without being permitted to breathe they are compelled to stay in very terrible hell (called *Nirucchvāsa*) for a period of half of a *Kalpa*.

70-72a. I shall tell you the hell of those persons who are ardently desirous of other men's wives. Copper images resembling those beautiful women are made and exquisitely embellished in ornaments. They are then heated red hot. The men are then compelled to embrace those images many times. If any one is afraid of it and runs away, he is caught hold of forcibly. Attendants announcing his sinful activities take him round all the hells in order.

72b-73. O Lord of Earth, those women who abandon their husbands and resort to others, are made to lie on beds of red hot iron and are enjoyed by men of red hot iron per force for a long time.

74. Then these women are released by them. They (the

women) are then compelled to embrace iron columns blazing like fire. They have to stand in that position for one thousand years.

75. They are then bathed in liquid caustic acid and are compelled to drink that liquid acid. At the end of it, they experience the tortures of all hells for a hundred centuries.

76. He who kills a Brāhmaṇa or a cow or a Kṣatriya or an excellent king, experiences all tortures for a period of five *Kalpas*.

77-78. Listen attentively to the resulting punishment to him who enthusiastically listens to the censure of great men. Red hot iron nails are pierced through their ears. Thereafter, hot boiling oil is copiously poured into those holes so that the ears are filled with it. He is then taken to *Kumbhīpāka* hell.

79. I shall tell you the sufferings of the atheists who turn their faces away from *Hara* and *Hari*. They will be compelled to eat salt for ten million years.

80. Then, they are scorched and fried in red hot sand in *Raurava* hell. These men of sinful acts remain in that hell for the period of a *Kalpa*. O ruler of men, in other hells also (they are tortured) like this.

81. With a thousand red hot needles they hurt and pierce the eyes of those mean men who look with wrath at Brāhmaṇas furiously.

82. Then, O excellent king, they are sprinkled with currents of liquid acid. Then, the people of evil activities are cut and pierced by means of terrible saws.

83. Listen to the terrible hell of those who commit breach of trust, those who break the bounds of decency and those who covetously yearn for other men's food.

84. They are compelled to eat their own flesh. They are being eaten by the dogs continuously. They stay in everyone of the hells for a year.

85. Listen to the treatment of those who are interested in accepting monetary gifts from others, those who practise astrology (accepting fees for the advice) and those who regularly partake of the food of professional worshippers of idols (in temples).

86. O king, those persons who are always engaged in the enjoyment of pleasures and who are defiled by their sins are

miserably cooked by means of these tortures till the end of a *Kalpa.*

87. Thereafter, they are filled with oil. They are afflicted through *Kālasūtra* (thread of Death). Thereafter, they are compulsorily bathed in liquefied acid and fed on fecal matter and urine.

88. At the end of it, they come back to Earth and are born as *Mleccha* tribes. Those who are engaged in injuring others go to the river *Vaitaraṇī.*

89. Those who have abandoned the five great sacrifices go to the hell *Lālābhakṣa.* One who abandons worship goes to the hell *Raurava.*

90. O king, listen to the fate of those who exact revenues and taxes from Brāhmaṇas and villages donated to them. They are subjected to these tortures as long as the stars and the moon shine.

91. The leading king who levies the maximum tax from the villages, experiences the tortures in the hells for five *Kalpas* along with a thousand members of his family.

92-93a. The sinner who encourages and permits increased taxation from villages of Brāhmaṇas, O king, (commits the sin as if) he has (actually) committed the murder of a thousand Brāhmaṇas. He stays in the terrible hell *Kālasūtra* for the period of two cycles of four *yugas.*

93b-94a. The great sinner who discharges semen in non-vagins (*ayonis*) as in masturbation), in those who are destitute of vulva (*Viyonis*), and uterus of animals (*Paśu-yonis*) shall fall into the hell *Reto-bhojana* (where one has to subsist on semen).

94b-95a. He then falls into *Vasākūpa* (a deep and narrow well of fat). There he stays for seven divine years. That man has semen for his diet. He becomes the most despicable man in the world when reborn.

95b-96a. The man who washes his teeth with a twig of a tree as the tooth brush, O king, on the day of fast (like *Ekādaśī*) falls into the terrible hell called *Vyāghra-Pakṣa* (and remains there) for a period of four *yugas.*

96b-97. The person who abandons his religious duties is called a heretic by learned men. He and a person who associates with him are great sinners. They fall into hells in a serial order, in the course of thousand and millions of *kalpas*.

98. Those who misappropriate the assets of the deity of a temple, those who take away the wealth of their preceptors, O king, contract sins similar to Brāhmaṇa-murder and experience similar consequences.

99. Those who take away the wealth of orphans and helpless persons, those who are hostile towards them, remain in hell for thousands and millions of *kalpas*.

100. I shall mention the fruits of sins accruing to those who engage themselves in the recitation and study of the *Vedas* in the vicinity of women and *Śūdras*. Listen to it attentively.

101. They are compelled to stand with their heads down and legs upwards. Thus, they are nailed to two pillars and are compelled to inhale smoke continuously in this posture. They stay thus for the period of year of god *Brahmā*.

102. He who discharges the impurity of his body (such as fecal matter and urine) in the water or in the premises of a temple incurs as terrible a sin as the destruction of a foetus.

103. Listen to the fruit of sins accruing to those who throw teeth, bones, hair and nails in the precincts of a divine shrine or the leavings of food into water.

104-105a. Spears are thrust into their bodies. They are crushed with plough-share. While they cry and groan piteously in their distress, they are fried and roasted in the extremely terrible (cauldron of) boiling oil. They are made highly miserable there and then they go to other hells as well.

105b-106a. He who steals the asset of a Brāhmaṇa or a scented log of sandal or aloe-wood, goes to the terrible hell and remains there as long as the moon and the stars shine.

106b-107a. O king, misappropriation of a Brāhmaṇa's assets yields sorrow and misery both here and hereafter. Here, it brings about the destruction of wealth and it leads hereafter to hell.

107b-109a. Listen to the fruit of sins accruing to a perjuror. He undergoes all these tortures as long as fourteen Indras reign. In this world his sons and grandsons perish. In the other world, he falls into *Raurava* and other hells as well, in a serial order.

109b-110. Leeches comparable to serpents are thrust into

the mouths of those men who are excessively passionate and lecherous and those who are propounders of false or heretic views. Thus, they stay for sixty thousand years. Thereafter, they are sprinkled with liquefied acid.

111-112a. Those who are devoted to flesh eating without any reason, go to the hell *Kṣāra-kardama*. From there they are dragged into the hell *Marut-prapātana* where they are trampled over by elephants. At the end of the torture therein, they come back to the Earth where they are born with deficiency in their limbs (i.e. are physically handicapped).

112b-113a. O Lord of men, he who does not cohabit with his wife during the prescribed days after the monthly menses, falls into the terrible hell *Raurava* and incurs the sin of a Brāhmaṇa-slaughter also.

113b-114a. If any one, though competent to prevent, does not prevent some one seen practising the code of conduct of others (instead of his prescribed duties), he incurs the latter's sin. Both of them fall into the hell.

114b-115a. O king, (sometimes) peop e count the sins of sinners and intimate them to others. If the accusation is true, they share it equally (with the sinners), but if the accusation is false, they incur double that sin.

115b-116. He who falsely imputes sins to a sinless person and censures him for it, falls into a terrible hell and remains there as long as the moon, the sun and the stars shine. When sinners are censured, half the number of their sins is dispelled.

117. He who takes up the vow of holy observances and abandons them without observing them completely to the end, experiences distress in the hell *Asipatra* and is reborn with defects and deficiencies in his limbs, in the world.

118. The man who puts obstacles in the observance of the holy vows that have been undertaken by others, falls into the hell *Śleṣma-bhojana* which is excessively terrible and leading to misery.

119. He who shows partiality in administering justice and in the instructions of *dharma*, has no means of redemption, even after ten thousand expiatory rites.

120. A person who partakes of forbidden food falls into the hell *Viḍ-bhojya* (wherein fecal matter is served as food) and remains there for ten thousand years. Then he is born as a *Cāṇḍāla*, where he always subsists on beef.

121. One who insults and dishonours Brāhmaṇas through harsh words, incurs the sin on a par with Brāhmaṇa-slaughter. He undergoes all the tortures of hell and is born as a *Cāṇḍāla* in the course of ten lives.

122. Expiatory rites as in the case of *Brahma-hatyā* (committal of Brāhmaṇa-slaughter) must be performed by the person who puts obstacles, when something is being offered to a Brāhmaṇa.

123. If any one steals another man's wealth and gives it away as a gift (to another person), the merit of the gift accrues to the owner of the original wealth, but the thief who steals, falls into the hell.

124. By not giving a thing after having promised it, a man falls into the hell *Lālā-bhakṣa*. O king, a person engaged in censuring ascetics falls into the hell *Śilāmātra*.

125. Those who destroy parks and gardens fall into the hell *Śva-bhojana* where they stay for twentyone *yugas*. Thereafter, they undergo all the tortures of hells in a serial order.

126. Listen to the evil destination attained by the destroyer of shrines, of lakes as well as of flower-gardens, O king.

127-128a. They undergo all those tortures in the different hells severally. Thereafter, they are born as worms in the fecal matter for twentyone *kalpas*. O king, thereafter, they undertake one hundred births in the *Cāṇḍāla* caste.

128b-129a. Even during the course of my life, I am not competent to narrate adequately the great sin of the destroyer of villages and those who burn or plunder them.

129b-130a. The tortures that the partakers of other men's leavings of food and the persons engaged in injuring friends, undergo are very severe. They suffer these as long as the moon and the stars shine.

130b-131a. Those who have ceased to perform the rites and the *yajñas* for *Pitṛs* (*manes*) and Devas, those who stay outside the part of the Vedas, are notorious as heretics. They undergo all sorts of tortures.

131b-132a. O king, thus, there are various types of tortures in regard to those who commit sins. I am not competent to ennumerate either the sinners or the tortures, O Lord.

132b-133a. Who else other than Lord Viṣṇu is capable of mentioning the number of sins, tortures or righteous duties ?

133b-134. When expiatory rites are performed in accordance with the injunctions of *Dharma Śāstras*, the mass of sins is annihilated. Expiatory rites are to be performed in the presence of the lord of Lakṣmī (Viṣṇu).

135. In case the holy rites suffer due to superfluity or omission, the waters of the Gaṅgā, the Tulasī plant, companionship with holy persons and glorification of Lord Hari (are enough to compensate).

136. (In addition to these) non-jealousy and non-violence are dispeller of sins. All holy rites dedicated to Viṣṇu are indeed fruitful.

137a. Those rites which are not so dedicated are futile as like sacrificial oblations consigned to ashes (instead of offering into the sacrificial fire).

137b-138. The *Nitya* (rites to be performed daily), *Naimittika* (rites to be performed on certain occasions) and the *Kāmya* (rites performed with the desire of achieving specific objects) as well as other means of salvation, when dedicated to Viṣṇu, become *Sāttvika* and fruitful. Devotion to Hari is the greatest destroyer of all sins of men.

139. That *bhakti* (devotion) should be known to be of ten[10] types. To the forest of sins it is like a great conflagration of fire. O excellent king, it is practised by men whose natures are characterised by *sattva*, *rajas* and *tamas*.

140. O king, if any one worships the lord of Śrī for the destruction of another, his devotion is the meanest of all *Tāmasi* type of *Bhaktis*, since there is a wicked motivation therein.

141. If any one worships Nārāyaṇa, the lord of the universe with a deceptive mind like the unchaste woman serving her husband, that Bhakti is the middling (*Madhyamā*) among the *Tāmasī* type of Devotion.

142. O lord of Earth, if, on seeing others engaged in the worship of the deity, one begins to worship Hari with a spirit of rivalry, that *Bhakti* is the most excellent among the *Tāmasī* devotions.

143. If any one endowed with ardentmost faith worships Hari, seeking wealth, grain and other things that *Bhakti* is the meanest among *Rājasī bhaktis*.

144. If any one worships Mādhava with the greatest love and affection keeping in view the attainment of worldwide fame,

that *Bhakti* is *Madhyama* (middling) among the *Rājasī bhaktis*.

145. O lord of the Earth, if any one worships Hari, keeping in view the position of *Sālokya* (state of being in the same region with the lord) that *Bhakti* is glorified as the most excellent among the *Rājasī Bhaktis*.

146. If any one worships Hari for destroying sins committed by himself and he is endowed with the greatest of faith, that *Bhakti* is the meanest among *Sāttvikī bhaktis*.

147. "This is pleasing to Hari." If with this idea a person serves Hari and is endowed with a living faith that *Bhakti* is the middling among *Sāttvikī bhaktis*.

148. O king, if any one worships Hari like a slave unto lord of Śrī, with the knowledge that it is the injunction of *Śrutis*, that *Bhakti* is the most excellent of all *Sāttvikī Bhaktis*.

149. If after glorifying a little the greatness of Hari, a man is pleased and happy in identifying himself with the Lord, that *Bhakti* is the most excellent of all.

150. If any one perceives thus : "I am the great lord Viṣṇu himself. All this universe exists in me", always know him to be the most excellent of all good men.

151. Thus the devotion of ten types is the cause for the severance of the bond of worldly existence. Even there, the *Sāttvikī Bhakti* is the bestower of all cherished fruits.

152. Hence, listen, O king, *Bhakti* to Janārdana should be pursued without any antagonism to one's duties,[11] by one who is desirous of conquering the mundane world.

153. If a man forsakes his duties and lives solely by devotion, Lord Viṣṇu is not pleased with him. Viṣṇu is pleased only with the *Ācāra* (performance of one's own prescribed duty).

154. In all the *Āgamas* (sacred literature), *Ācāra* (performance of one's prescribed course of duties) is considered as the foremost. Righteousness is born of *Ācāra* and *Acyuta* is the lord of *Dharma*.

155. Hence, Hari's devotion should be pursued consistently with abidance by one's own prescribed duty. Even the *Dharmas* of those devoid of good conduct cause unhappiness.

156. The *Bhakti* devoid of pursuance of one's own duty (prescribed by one's *dharma*) is glorified, if not proceeded with. What has been asked by you has been narrated by me.

157. Hence, worship Janārdana with full devotion to *Dharma*

(performance of the duties prescribed by *Śāstras* for you). Worship Nārāyaṇa who is minuter than the minutest, and you will attain perpetual happiness.

158. Śiva alone is Hari himself.[12] Hari alone is Śiva himself. One who sees the difference between the two is a rogue. He falls into ten million hells.

159. Hence, worship with the knowledge that Viṣṇu and Śiva are identical. One who creates difference, attains misery here as well as hereafter.

160. O lord of people, I shall tell you the purpose for which I have approached you. O intelligent one, listen with attention.

161. O king, your grandfathers who have committed sins of suicidal nature and have been burnt down by the wrath of Kapila, are staying in hell.

162. O highly blessed one, deliver them by means of the act of bringing the Gaṅgā (over their remains).[13] O lord of Earth, indeed the Gaṅgā destroys all sins.

163. O excellent king, if the hair, bones, nails, teeth or the ashes of a person are touched by the waters of the Gaṅgā one is taken to Lord Viṣṇu's abode.

164. O king, the man whose bones or ashes are cast into the Gaṅgā by his kinsmen is liberated from all sins. He goes to the abode of Hari.

165. O king, whatever sins have been mentioned to you by me are destroyed by means of sprinkling with the drops of the water of the Gaṅgā."

Sanaka said :

166. O leading sage, after saying this to the great king Bhagīratha of righteous soul, Dharmarāja vanished immediately.

167. That king was highly intelligent. He was a master of all topics in the sacred texts. He entrusted the care of the entire Earth to the ministers and went to the forest for performing penance.

168. After going to the Himālayas, he performed penance on a peak which was sixteen *Yojanas* to the West of the hermitage of Nara and Nārāyaṇa and was covered with snow.

169. By performing the penance, he brought down the Gaṅgā that sanctifies the three worlds.

CHAPTER FIFTEEN

1. *raudrā ye narakā*

The *Smṛtis*, *Purāṇas* and medieval digests on *Dharma Śāstra* declare that if sinners do not undergo an expiatory penance (*Prāyaścitta*) or are not punished by the King for their crime, fall into hell, and are born as lower animals and even after attaining human birth they become marked by mal-formations, diseases. The idea of hell is found in all ancient communities, e.g. Egyptians, Hebrews, Iranians. In the *Ṛgveda* the idea about hell is vague but it became more concrete from the time of *Atharva Veda* onwards. The gruesome descriptions of the torture in hells are described in details in *Smṛtis* and more lucidly in *Purāṇas*, a specimen of which will be found in this chapter.

2. There is a divergence of opinion about the number of hells. VP. I.6.41 enumerates seven hells: *Tāmisra* (dark), *Andha-tāmisra* (blinding dark), *Mahāraurava* (abounding in paths with heated surface (*Prāyaścitta Viveka* P.15), *Raurava*, *Asipatra-vana* (a forest full of trees with sword-blades to cut up the sinner), *Kāla-sūtra* (like a thread on the wheel with which a potter cuts off a raw earthen pot into two), and *Avīci* (Full of waves in which the sinner is every now and then submerged). At another place (II.6.2-5) it mentions 26 hells. Manu IV.88-90, AP.371.20-22, mention 21 hells. The list in Manu IV.88-90 is as follows : *Tāmisra*, *Andha-Tāmisra*, *Mahā-Raurava*, *Raurava*, *Kālasūtra*, *Mahānaraka*, *Sañjīvana* (where one is killed and revived to be killed again), *Mahāvīci*, *Tapana* (burning hot as fire), *Sampratāpana* (*Kumbhīpāka* according to some. In it, the sinner is cooked as in a cooker), *Saṅghāta* (The sinner is compressed in a place smaller than his size), *Kākola* (where the sinner is pecked and preyed on by crows), *Kuḍmala* (The sinner is bound into a bundle appearing like a bud), *Pūti-mṛttika* (of putrid stenching clay), *Lohaśaṅku* (when the sinner is pierced with iron nails), *Ṛjīṣa* (Where the sinner is schorched with boiled flour), *Panthāḥ* (Where the sinner is made to walk without break), *Śālmali* (The sinner is pricked with thorns like those of *Śālmali*—silk-cotton-tree), *Nadī* (thrown in a river like the Vaitaraṇī), *Asipatra-vana*, *Lohadāraka* (Where the sinner's limbs are cut up with iron).

The list of hells given here is practically the same as above. Here for every kind of torture, a separate hell is assigned, and the number of hells went on increasing depending on the ingenuity or imagination of the writer of *Purāṇas* to conceive new kind of torture. Ultimately these numbers increased to thousands in the GP. *Preta-Khaṇḍa* 3.3

narakāṇāṁ sahasrāṇi vartante hyaruṇānuja /

3. These describe the tortures in hells enumerated above. It is a certainly, blood-curdling description.

4. These verses describe what actions come under the 'great sin' Brāhmaṇa-slaughter. It may be noted that even a slanderer of Brāhmaṇas, or one who obstructs his religious routine, or causing a Brahmin get up from the row of a dinner or a person who abets to or consents these acts is called a Brāhmaṇa-slayer.

5. Next to Brāhmaṇa-slaughter, wine-drinking is regarded as 'a great sin' but under liquor-drinking is included eating food from a low-caste and from a professional worshipper of idols, resorting to prostitutes, working as an attendant for Śūdra.

6. Theft is regarded as a heinous crime. Here in addition to stealing of precious stones and metals, abandonment of *pitṛ-yajñas*, non-performance of one's holy duties, are regarded as equivalent to theft.

7. With the exception of Soma's adultery with Bṛhaspati's wife, we do not have other outstanding cases recorded of 'defiling the preceptor's bed'. But the NP includes under this category all cases of adultery whether with near relatives or low-caste women or with one's dependants, as also omission of doing religious duties and speaking low of the scriptures.

8. These verses include the crimes for which there is no adequate expiation for redemption. It is interesting to note that 'sins' like ungratefulness, breach of trust, entrance into a Buddhistic shrine even in times of emergency are included under 'unredeemable sins'.

9. This is a sort of a penal code supposed to be in force in the land of Yama. The principles underlying these punishments are retribution and deterrence.

10. The tenfold classification is distinct from the *nava-vidhā bhakti* or the nine modes or ways of *Bhakti*. Here the motivation whether it is dominated by *Sattva*, *Rajas* and *Tamas*—is taken as the basis.

11. Not only the NP. but other *Purāṇas* also insist on a synthesis of *Karma* (performance of duties prescribed by Śāstra's for one's class or caste and stage of life) and *Bhakti*.

12. Identity between gods Śiva and Viṣṇu is the main thesis of all *Purāṇas* irrespective of their classification as Śaivite, Viṣṇuite, etc. To them these are the names attributed to the Brahman which is the only one Reality. Hence, the futility of disputes between the advocates of Śiva, Viṣṇu, or Śakti cults.

13. The efficacy of Gaṅgā in destroying sins is repeated again in NP. *infra* II.39.30-31, 40-64. The Vedic seers, *Smṛti* and *Purāṇa*-writers, and *Nibandha*-writers are unanimous in extolling the Gaṅgā in the highest terms. A reference to works like *Tīrtha-Cintāmaṇi*, *Kalpa-taru* (on *Tīrtha*) etc. gives us numerous verses (mostly quotations) on the greatness of the Gaṅgā—which is a special theme in the NP.

CHAPTER SIXTEEN

Bhagīratha Brings down The Gaṅgā

Nārada submitted :

1. It behoves you to tell me what the Lord of the Earth Bhagīratha did after reaching the snow-capped mountain Himavān, and how he brought down the Gaṅgā.

Sanaka narrated :

2. While he was going to the mountain Himavān for his penance, O sage, the great king Bhagīratha, wearing matted hair and bark garments, reached the banks of the Godāvarī.[1]

3. There in the great forest, he saw the excellent hermitage of the sage Bhṛgu. Many antelopes were frisking about here and there in that hermitage. It was frequented by herds of elephants.

4. It was resounded with the humming sound of the hovering bees and the chirping of birds. Broods of boars wandered over it and the *Camari* deer fanned it with their bushy tails.

5. In that forest peacocks danced about and the deer and the other animals tenanted in it. Great trees had been eagerly nurtured by young girls in the families of sages.

6. It abounded richly in trees such as *Śāla*, *Tāla* (Palms) and *Tamāla*. It was embellished with fresh shoots of *Hintāla* palms. It was decorated with (various flowering plants such as) *Mālati*, *Yūthikā*, *Kunda*, *Campaka* and with *Aśvattha* trees.

7. There were many full-blown flowers. The hermitage was inhabited by groups of sages. It was reverberating with the chanting of Vedic *mantras* and the scriptural texts. The king entered that hermitage of Bhṛgu.

8. There he saw sage Bhṛgu who was resplendent like the Sun in lustre, who was surrounded by groups of disciples and was eulogising the great *Brahman*.

9. He bowed down to the leader of Brāhmaṇas by

touching his feet (and other acts of reverence). Bhṛgu accorded him hospitable reception with due honour.

10. When the formalities of reception were completed by the great sage Bhṛgu, the modest king spoke to that leading sage with his palms folded in reverence.

Bhagīratha said :

11. "O holy Sir, O knower of all *Dharmas*, O sage proficient in all scriptural topics, I am awfully frightened of worldly existence. I inquire of you what brings about men's uplift (from *Saṁsāra* to the final Liberation—*Mokṣa*).

12. O excellent sage, if I am to be blessed by you, kindly recount to me the holy acts whereby the glorious Lord becomes propitiated, O omniscient one."

Bhṛgu replied :

13. "O king, what you desire has been understood. You are the most excellent of meritorious persons. Otherwise how do you deserve to uplift the entire family of yours ?

14. If any one, whoever he may be, is desirous of uplifting his own family by means of auspicious acts, know him to be Lord Viṣṇu himself in human form, O king.

15. Listen attentively, O prominent king. I shall relate to you that holy course of conduct whereby the Lord of gods bestows on men the benefit desired by them.

16. O king, be devoted to Truth. Do not indulge in violence. Always look after the welfare of all living beings. Do not utter a lie on any account.

17. Eschew contacts with the wicked people. Entertain intimacy with the saintly persons. Be engaged day and night, in meritorious acts. Meditate upon Viṣṇu, the Eternal (Deity).

18. Perform the worship of Mahā-Viṣṇu. Attain excellent (mental) peace. Perform the *Japa* of the twelve-syllabled *mantra* (viz. *Oṁ namo bhagavate Vāsudevāya*) and the eight-syllabled *mantra* (viz. *Oṁ namo Nārāyaṇāya*). Welfare and fortune will come your way."

Bhagīratha submitted :

19. "O sage, what is regarded as the nature of the

Truth which is conducive to the welfare of all living beings ? Of what nature is falsehood said to be ? Of what nature are the wicked people ?

20. What is said to be regarded as the nature of good men ? Of what nature is merit ? How is Viṣṇu to be remembered ? Of what procedure is his worship ?

21-22a. Of what nature is quiescence said to be ? O sage, what is the eight-syllabled *mantra* ? O sage, proficient in the real nature of the truth, what is the twelve-syllabled *mantra* ? It behoves you to explain everything to me by extending your greatest favour or grace on me."

Bhṛgu said :

22b-23. "Very nice ! Exceedingly nice ! O highly intelligent one. Your intellect is unsurpassably excellent. O king, I shall explain to you every thing that I have been asked of by you. The statement of what is factually correct, the learned men call it the Truth.

24-25. Indeed, that should be uttered which is not contradictory to *Dharma*, by those solely devoted to *Dharma*. That statement which is uttered after taking into account the place and time by good men, causing no offence to the same, is called the Truth. Indeed it is non-injurious to all creatures.

26. O king, that has been proclaimed as non-violence which bestows all desires and which is ancillary to holy acts and which is opposed to all wrong actions.

27-30a. The following is proclaimed to be benevolence to all the world by persons who are adept in *Dharma*. It is, following the will of a person who discriminates between *Dharma* and *Adharma* and the statement thereof. That should be known as falsehood which is antagonistic to all benevolence and welfare. O king, those hateful and foolish persons whose intellect is always engaged in the evil path should be known as wicked men. They are excluded from all righteousness and piety. Those who follow the Vedic path, discriminating between what is virtue and what is not and those who are desirous of the well-being of all the world are glorified as good men.

30b-31a. That which generates devotion to Hari, that

which the good persons are enamoured of, and that which causes spiritual pleasure is glorified as Merit.

31b-32a. All this universe is Viṣṇu. Viṣṇu is the cause of everything. I too am Viṣṇu". It is this realization that is known as *Viṣṇu-smaraṇa* (remembrance of Viṣṇu).

32b-33a. Viṣṇu is identical with all deities. I shall worship him in accordance with the prescribed rites. It is this faith that is glorified as his Devotion.

33b-34a. Viṣṇu, the perfect and the eternal, is identical with all living beings. It is this awareness of non-difference that is glorified as *Samatā* (Equalitarianism).

34b-36a. O king, impartiality towards friends and enemies, self-control and satisfaction with what is gained by chance—is glorified as quiescence. All these have been proclaimed as the bestowers of success in the accomplishment of penance. They are the cause of the instantaneous destructions of all heaps of sins.

36b-37. O king of kings, I shall tell you the great eight-syllabled *mantra* that is destructive of all sins. It is the sole means of the achievement of *Puruṣārthas* (goals in life). It is pleasing to Viṣṇu and it bestows all super-human powers.

38-39. One shall perform the *Japa* of the *mantra Namo Nārāyaṇāya* (obeisance unto Nārāyaṇa) after prefixing the *Praṇava* (*Om*) to it. (i.e. *Om namo Nārāyaṇāya*). Firstly one shall utter *Namo Bhagavate* and thereafter *Vāsudevāya*. O great king, by prefixing the *Praṇava* to it, it (viz. *Oṁ namo bhagavate Vāsudevāya*) is called the twelve-syllabled *mantra*. O king, the efficacy of both the *mantras*—the eight-syllabled one as well as the twelve-syallbled one—is the same.[2]

40a. Their equality whether in *Pravṛtti* (active participation in worldly life) or in *Nivṛtti* (renunciation of worldly activities) has been specially taught or pointed out.

40b-43. One should meditate on Nārāyaṇa who holds, *Śaṅkha* and *Cakra*, who is quiescent and free from ailments, whose left side is occupied by Lakṣmī, who is the lord that accords fearlessness, who wears a crown and ear-rings, who shines splendidly with various ornaments and embellishments, who wears a brilliant necklace with the radiant *Kaustubha* jewel, whose chest is marked with the curl of golden hair known as *Śrīvatsa*, who wears yellow robes, who is the lord bowed down to by *Suras* and *Asuras*, who has neither beginning nor end, and who is the bestower of all desired blessings. The eternal lord is perfect and immanent. He is of the form of perfect knowledge.

44. O king, thus everything that had been asked by you has been explained. Farewell to you. Attain the fruition of your penance. Proceed ahead to derive the same happily.

45. The ruler of the Earth who was advised thus by Bhṛgu, the great sage, attained the greatest pleasure. He went to the forest for the penance.

46. He reached the Himālaya mountains. He performed a severe penance in the great holy centre Nadeśvara,[3] in a charming and meritorious spot.

47. The king took his bath three times a day. He subsisted on bulbous roots, roots and fruits. Every day he greeted and honoured the guests. He was devoted to the performance of daily fire-worship.

48. He was quiescent and benevolent towards all living beings. He was absorbed in the worship of *Nārāyaṇa*. Thrice a day, he worshipped Hari by means of leaves, flowers and holy waters.

49. Spending a great deal of time like this, he courageously meditated on lord Nārāyaṇa. Thereafter, he began to eat only withered leaves.

50. Then the exceedingly righteous king became solely devoted to *Prāṇāyāma* (Control of breath). He began to perform penance without even breathing.

51. Meditating on the infinite unvanquished lord Nārāyaṇa, the king remained without breathing for sixty thousand years.

52. A terrible fire was produced from his nostrils. On seeing it, all Devas, scorched by that fire, became excessively frightened.

53. They went over to Mahāviṣṇu. On reaching the northern shore of the milky ocean, where the Lord of the worlds abides the Prominent Devas eulogised the Lord of the chiefs of Devas who protected those who respected him and sought refuge in him.

54. Devas prayed : "We bow down to Viṣṇu the sole Lord of the worlds, the Supreme Lord who removes the distress

of all those who remember him; who is naturally pure and who is the embodiment of perfect wisdom and is spoken of as perfect in nature, by those persons knowing of it.

55. The great-souled Lord should always be meditated upon by excellent *Yogins.* He has carried out the tasks of Devas by assuming bodies out of his own will. He is the embodiment of the Universe and its primordial Lord. We bow down to him, the Supreme Person, *Puruṣottama.*

56. For the purpose of achieving the *Puruṣārthas* (goals in life), we bow down to Viṣṇu, the ancient *Puruṣa,* that Ruler (of the universe), worthy of worship, by uttering whose names the sins of wicked men get dissolved.

57. It is through his brilliance that the sun and others shine; they never transgress his commandments. We bow down to that Lord of Devas who is of the nature of *Kāla* (Time or Death) and whose form is constituted of *Puruṣārthas.*

58. The lotus-born deity (Brahmā) creates the universe; Rudra annihilates it, and the Brāhmaṇas sanctify the worlds through *Śrutis*; we seek refuge in that primordial Lord who is the receptacle of all good qualities and who is the preceptor of all.

59. We bow down to the most excellent pre-eminent Lord, who can be realized only through perfect knowledge; who is the cause of the achievement of what is desired and by good devotees; who is the enemy of *Madhu* and *Kaiṭabha*[4] and whose footrest has been worshipped by both *Suras* and *Asuras.*

60. We bow down to the Lord who has no beginning, middle or end, the unborn great (Ruler of the universe), Śiva, the cause of destruction of the darkness called the beginningless *Avidyā*—the Lord whose form is the essence of existence, knowledge and bliss and who is devoid of form, etc.

61. We bow down to Nārāyaṇa, Viṣṇu, the infinite-Īśa, the yellow-robed God, worthy of being served by the lotusborn deity Brahmā and others, the beloved of sacrifices the performer of sacrificers, the purest, the most excellent, the imperishable Deity.

62. Mahā-Viṣṇu who was thus eulogised by Indra and other gods, recounted to the gods the conduct (and antecedents) of the King-sage.

63. Thereafter, O Nārada, the unsullied Lord consoled Devas after assuring fearlessness. He then went to that place where that saintly king was performing penance.

64. The Lord, the wielder of *Śaṅkha* and *Cakra*, the embodiment of existence, knowledge and bliss and the preceptor of all worlds, revealed, himself to that king.

65-67. On seeing him, the king bent down his head and prostrated himself on the ground before the Lord whose eyes resembled the lotus, who illuminated all quarters with his brilliance, whose complexion was blue like the *Atasī* flower, who was bedecked with shining ear-rings, with glossy tresses and charming lotus-like face, who was resplendent with a brilliant crown, who wore the jewel *Kaustubha* and the *Śrivatsa* mark (on his chest), who was bedecked with garland of Sylvan flowers, whose arms were long, whose limbs were elegant and whose lotus-like feet were worshipped by the lords of worlds.

68. He was overwhelmed with ecstatic delight. With hairs standing on end and voice choked with emotion, he uttered—"O Kṛṣṇa, O Kṛṣṇa, O Kṛṣṇa, O Śrīkṛṣṇa.

69. Viṣṇu, the Immanent soul, the Preceptor of the universe, the Creator of living beings, became pleased with him. Overwhelmed with Grace, the Lord spoke thus.

The glorious Lord said :

70. "O Bhagīratha, O highly blessed one, what is desired by you will be realised. Your grandfathers will come to my world.

71. O king, with hymns according to your capacity, you should eulogise Śambhu who is another *Mūrti*[5] (form) of mine. Indeed, he will instantaneously get your desires fulfilled.

72. He accepted the moon who sought refuge in him. So propitiate god Śiva, the bestower of happiness, who is worthy of being eulogised.

73. O king, he is the deity without beginning and destruction. He is the bestower of all desired blessings. On being worshipped by you, he will immediately accomplish your welfare."

74. After saying this, the Lord of the chiefs of Devas, Acyuta, the Lord of the worlds, disappeared. And the Lord of the Earth got up, O excellent sage.

75. O excellent Brāhmaṇa, the king was surprised. He wondered, "Is this a dream or the true state of affairs. What shall I do now?"

76. Then a voice in the firmament loudly proclaimed to him as he had become perplexed—"It is clear that this is the truth. It does not behove you to worry."

77. On hearing it, the devout ruler of the Earth eulogised *Iśāna*, the cause of all and the king of all deities.

Bhagiratha said :

78. "I salute to Īśāna,[6] the lord of the universe, the destroyer of the distress of those who bow down to the Lord—the Lord incomprehensive through the valid means of knowledge, who is the embodiment of *Praṇava* (OM).

79. I bow down to Virūpākṣa, of the form of the universe, the unborn, and the eternal one, the cause of creation, sustenance and dissolution of the world, the embodiment of universe and of fierce Semen.

80. I salute that Lord who increases the nourishment, on whom the eminent Yogins meditate and who is devoid of beginning, middle and end and who is Infinite Unborn and Unchanging.

81. Obeisance to the over-lord of the worlds, who wanders, who defrauds the evil doers; obeisance be to you the blue-necked god, to the Lord of Paśus.

82. Glory to one whose form is consciousness; salute to the Lord of nourished ones; Bow to one who makes the most incompetent a competent one; obeisance to the Lord of the *Bhūtas* (Living Beings or goblins).

83. Obeisance to one armed with the Pināka bow. Salutations to the wielder of the trident in hand and to the holder of a skull in his hand; Bow to one who is the bearer of a noose and an iron club.

84. Obeisance to you who are immanent in all beings; Salutations to you, the bearer of a bell in hand; Obeisance to the Lord of five faces and to the Lord of fields.

85. Obeisance to the supporter of Earth, who is the primordial one amongst all living beings. Salutations to one who assumes innumerable forms and yet is the attributeless Great *Ātman*.

86. Obeisance to the Supreme god of *Gaṇas* (troops of demigods). Salutations to the leader of *Gaṇas* and to *Hiraṇya-garbha*; Salutations to the Lord of gold.

87. Bow to you the gold-semened one; to the gold-armed one; obeisance to one who is both the form and witness of meditation.

88-90. Salutations to you stabilised in meditation and to one comprehensible through meditation. You are the Lord by whom this entire visible Universe consisting of the mobile and immobile has been illuminated and created by assuming the forms of *Pradhāna* and *Puruṣa* in the same manner as the rain is created by the cloud. You are the Lord whom the knowers of Reality consider self-luminous, great *Ātman*, the highest eternal brilliance, the Sun unto the eyes of men.

91-92. I salute the lover of Umā, the Lord of Nandin, the blue-necked Sadāśiva, Mahādeva, the conqueror of Death, the Lord greater than the greatest; the greatest deity in the form of *Śabda-brahman*, the Cause of all. Obeisance to you, O god with matted hair. Obeisance to you, *Sadyojāta*.

93. Obeisance to the Cause of the origin of the worlds ; obeisance to the purest one ; to the eldest and to the youngest; obeisance to *Manyu* (anger). Obeisance to you the possessor of Strength. Salutations to the Lord of *Trayī* (the three Vedas), obeisance to the thread of sacrifices.

94. Obeisance to the energetic one. Salutations to the Lord of quarters; bow to Kāla of the form of Aghora; obeisance to you of fiery semen; and to the highly great-souled one.

95-96. I bow down to that formless Īśa from whom all these originated, viz., the oceans, the rivers, the mountains, the groups of Gandharvas, Yakṣas, Asuras and Siddhas, the mobile and immobile creation, the greatest and the smallest beings, the *Sat* and the *Asat* (existent and non-existent), and *Jīvas* and *Ajīvas* (the living and non-living). His lotus-like feet are bowed to by the Yogins. He is the inner *Ātman* of everything. He is the only being who is independent and is the virtue of the virtuous. To him I bow down again and again."

97. Eulogised thus, the great lord Śaṅkara, the benefactor of the worlds, appeared in front of the king who had completed his penance.

98-100. O Nārada, on seeing the Lord, the king prostrated himself at his feet on the ground, like a wooden staff. The Lord had five faces, ten arms, and the crescent moon embellishing his crest. He was three-eyed, of elegant limbs and with serpents as the sacred thread. The Lord had a wide chest and his lustre was brilliant like that of the snow-capped mountain. Elephant's hide constituted his garment. His lotus-like feet were worshipped by the Suras. After prostrating, the king suddenly got up and stood in front of Śiva with palms joined in reverence.

101-102. He bowed to Mahādeva, glorifying the name of Śaṅkara. After realising the devotion of the king, the moon-crested god Śaṅkara said to the king—"I am pleased. Choose the desired boon. I have been delighted well by you by your eulogy as well as by penance".

103. Encouraged thus by the Lord, the king was highly delighted at his heart. Reverentially folding his palms, he said to the chief lord of all the chiefs of the worlds.

Bhagīratha said :

104. "O Maheśvara, if I am to be blessed by you by granting boons, bestow the Gaṅgā for the purpose of liberating our forefathers."

Śrī Śiva said :

105. "The Gaṅgā has been given to you by me. The highest is the destination of your forefathers. Excellent salvation is granted to you." After saying this, god Śiva vanished.

106. The Gaṅgā, the sole sanctifier of the world, slipped down from the matted locks of the god Śiva with matted hair. She followed Bhagīratha sanctifying the universe on the way.

107. O sage, thereafter the goddess Gaṅgā the pure, and the remover of sins and impurities became well known in the three worlds as 'Bhāgīrathī'.

108. The Gaṅgā, the most excellent among all rivers, flowed over that land where the sons of Sagara had been burnt formerly due to their own sins.

109. As soon as the ashes of the sons of Sagara were (deluged and) swept away by the current of the Gaṅgā, they who had been submerged in the hell, with their sins washed off, were uplifted.

110. Those very same persons who were severely tortured by Yama who was reviling at them, were honoured by him later, when they were sanctified by the waters of the Gaṅgā that flowed over them.

111. After realising that the sons of Sagara had been absolved of their sins, Yama duly bowed to them and honoured them. Being much pleased in his mind, he spoke to them :

112. "O princes, you have been liberated from the exceedingly terrible hell. Be seated in the aerial car and go to the abode of Viṣṇu."

113. Thus addressed by Yama, those noble-souled sons of Sagara whose sins disappeared, assumed divine forms and attained to the region of Viṣṇu.

114. Of such powerful efficacy is the Gaṅgā that had originated from the tip of the feet of Viṣṇu. She is well known all over the worlds as the destroyer of great sins.

115. He who reads or listens to this meritorious narrative that is destructive of great sins, attains the fruit of ablutions in the Gaṅgā.

116. He who narrates this meritorious anecdote in front of Brāhmaṇas goes to Viṣṇu's abode whence there is no return to the world of mortals.

CHAPTER SIXTEEN

1. *Godāvarī-taṭam* appears to be a misprint, for neither *Mbh.*, *VR* or any other Purāṇa nor De (*Gdami*) mentions such a river in the Himālayas or associates Bhagīratha's name with that river.

2. The eight-syllabled Mantra—*Om namo Nārāyaṇāya*—is the traditional Pāñcarātra *Mantra*, while the twelve-syllabled—*Om namo bhagavate Vāsudevāya*—is the traditional *mantra* of the Bhāgavata cult. The NP. tries a synthesis of both these traditional cults by declaring the same efficacy, accruing from either *mantra* both in *Pravṛtti* and *Nivṛtti* paths.

3. Nādeśvara is the same as Bindusaras (De, p. 134). It is a sacred pool situated on the Rudra Himālaya, two miles south of Gaṅgotrī (De, p. 38).

4. There are two versions about these demon-brothers : (i) The demon—brothers Madhu and Kaiṭabha were born through two drops of water fallen, through the will of Viṣṇu, on the lotus springing from his navel. They represented the *rajo-guṇa* and *tamo-guṇa*. A glance at those drops by Viṣṇu, transformed the drops into those demons (*Mbh—Śānti* 347.25-26). They were killed by Viṣṇu in the Hayagrīva form (*ibid* 347.69-70). (ii) According to *DB* I.6.20-21, they were born out of the ear-wax that flowed out of Viṣṇu's ears while he was asleep on Śeṣa.

5. Though the NP. is a Vaiṣṇava Purāṇa, the author takes such opportunities to emphasize the identity of gods Śiva and Viṣṇu.

6. This eulogy of god Śiva has several echoes from the *Rudrādhyāya* (*TS* IV.5)—especially its *Namaka* part (*TS.* IV.5.1), as a number of phrases from that *Sūkta* are incorporated in this prayer.

CHAPTER SEVENTEEN

Narration of the Vowed Observance of Dvādaśī Day[1]

The sages said :

1. Well done O Sūta, O highly blessed one, the excellent greatness of the Gaṅgā that destroys all sins, has been related by you who have great mercy in your heart.

2. O Sūta, what did Nārada of the divine vision ask Sanaka, the excellent sage, after hearing the greatness of the Gaṅgā.

Sūta said :

3. Listen, ye all sages. I shall tell you what has been asked again by Nārada, the celestial sage, and what he (Sanaka) narrated.

4. After hearing the excellent greatness of the Gaṅgā that consisted of many narratives and mythological anecdotes, the son of Brahmā asked thus with great respect.

Nārada said :

5. O sage, the meritorious greatness of the Gaṅgā has been heard by me from you, the merciful. It is greatly blessed and all the topics therein have been unravelled. It is the essence of good deeds alone. It destroys sins and bestows the desired objects.

6. Those who are saintly, worship Viṣṇu well. They strive for themselves as well as for others. With different kinds of advices, they exceedingly enlighten the man of immature mind and make him delighted.

7. Therefore, narrate (in detail) the holy observances[2] of Hari which, when performed, make Viṣṇu delighted. The merciful Lord grants devotion to those who worship him. It is known that salvation is the female slave unto it (devotion).

8. Mukunda grants salvation to those who worship and who are devoted to holy vows (pertaining to him), worship and

meditation. Pondering over the great difficulty in serving the devotees, he does not grant the path of devotion to anyone.

9. O excellent sage, recount to me the holy rite that makes Hari satisfied whether it be active participation in worldly affairs or an act of renunciation. O bestower of honour, you are a devotee of Viṣṇu."

Sanaka said :

10. "Well done, O excellent sage, well done. You are really a devotee of Puruṣottama in view of the fact that you enquire about the observances or deeds of the wielder of the Śārṅga bow (Viṣṇu) again and again.

11. I shall expound unto you the holy observances of vows that render service to the worlds and through which Hari being propitiated, grants fearlessness (i.e. Liberation from rebirth).

12. If Lord Janārdana, whose symbol is sacrifice, is pleased with anyone, he becomes happy here and hereafter and his penance flourishes.

13. Great sages say that those who are devoted to the worship of Hari, by whatever means that may be, go to the greatest abode (*Vaikuṇṭha*).

14. A man endowed with faith, should observe fast on the *Dvādaśī* (Twelfth) day in the bright half of the Mārgaśīrṣa[3] month and worship *Jalaśāyin* (Lord Viṣṇu who lies in the Milk ocean) devoutly.

15-16. After duly washing the teeth, one should take one's bath and wear clean white cloths. O excellent sage, he should be restrained in speech. With the feeling of devotion, he should worship Hari with sweet fragrant sandal paste, smelling flowers, rice grains, incense, lamps and food offerings. He should adore Viṣṇu by saying, "Obeisance to you, O Keśava."

17. He should offer oblations of ghee and sesamum seeds into the fire one hundred and eight times. At night, he should keep awake in the vicinity of the Śālagrāma stone.

18-21a. He should perform ablution of Nārāyaṇa free from ailments, with a *Prastha* measure of milk. He should worship devoutly, Keśava accompanied by Mahālakṣmī three times (that day) in accompaniment of sages, musical instruments and by food offerings of various edibles and foodstuffs.

Again after getting up early in the morning and completing the accustomed daily routine, he should worship the Lord, as before controlling the sense organs and restraining the speech. He should be pure (in word and deed). Repeating the following Mantra, he should offer milk pudding mixed with ghee and accompanied by a coconut fruit to a Brāhmaṇa. He should offer the monetary gifts with devotion.

21b-24a. "May Lord Keśava, the slayer of Keśin, the bestower of all kinds of riches and prosperity, grant me what is desired, in view of this gift of excellent dish (the most exquisite cooked rice, i.e. milk pudding)." Afterwards he should feed the Brāhmaṇas according to his capacity. Absorbed in (the devotion of) Nārāyaṇa, he should also take food along with his kinsmen but with restraint in speech (i.e. in silence). He who performs the excellent worship of Keśava thus, with devotion, shall attain eight times the benefit of *Puṇḍarīka* sacrifice.

24b-27. On the *Dvādaśī* day in the bright half of the month of Pauṣa,[4] the devotee shall observe fast. With the purity of body and mind and keeping his sense-organs in restraint, he should worship Hari saying "Obeisance to Nārāyaṇa". He should bathe the Lord in milk and offer milk-pudding as *Naivedya* (offering). He should worship thrice (on that day) and keep awake during the night. He should duly adore Hari by means of incense, lamps, *Naivedya* (offer of high dishes), scents, fragrant and charming flowers, grasses[5]* dances, songs and musical instruments as well as hymns. He should offer *Kṛśara*[6] (a sesamum preparation) and cooked rice to a Brāhmaṇa along with ghee and monetary gifts.

28. "In view of the gift of Kṛśara and the cooked rice may Nārāyaṇa be pleased—Nārāyaṇa who is the *Ātman* of every one, and the Lord of all worlds, who is eternal and all-pervasive."

29. With the above *Mantra* he should offer the excellent gift to a Brāhmaṇa. Thereafter, he should take food himself along with his kinsmen.

**Tṛṇa is* probably a misprint for *tūrya* — a musical instrument. But the corresponding line in the *Bṛhan Nāradīya* (Upa-Purāṇa) xvi. 16 is *Nṛtyair gītaiḥ pravādyaiś ca stotraiś cāpi yajed Harim* shows that the original word is "nṛtyaiḥ."

30. If a devotee worships Lord Nārāyaṇa with devotion as per above-mentioned procedure, he shall attain the benefit of eight *Agniṣṭoma*[7] sacrifices in full.

31-32. On the *Dvādaśi* day in the bright half of the month of Māgha, he should observe fast as before, saying "Obeisance to you, Mādhava." He should offer eight oblations with ghee. With the same measure of milk as before, he should bathe Mādhava. With an attentive mind, he should worship with flowers, raw rice, grains and scents.

33. As before, endowed with great devotion, he should keep awake during the night. After finishing the morning duties, he should worship Mādhava again.

34. For the purpose of liberation from all sins, he should offer a *Prastha* measure of sesamum seeds to a Brāhmaṇa with due recital of the following Mantra and offer a cloth and the monetary gifts as well.

35. "May Mādhava, the Ātman of all living beings, the bestower of the benefits of all holy rites, grant all desires, in view of this great gift of sesamum seeds".

36. Repeating this *Mantra* he should offer it to a Brāhmaṇa. Endowed with devotion and piety, he should feed Brāhmaṇas according to his capacity, remembering Lord Mādhava.

37. O sage, he who performs the holy observance thus and offers the gift of sesamum seeds, shall attain full benefit of a hundred *Vājapeya*[8] sacrifices.

38. On the *Dvādaśi* day in the bright half of the month of Phālguna, the devotee should observe fast. The observer of this holy vow should say, "Obeisance to you, O Govinda."

39. After offering to fire one hundred and eight oblations of sesamum seeds mixed with ghee, he should bathe Govinda with the aforesaid quantity of milk. He should be pure in body and in mind.

40. He should keep awake during the night and perform worship thrice on that day. After concluding the morning routine, he should worship Govinda again.

41-43a. He should offer an *Āḍhaka* measure of cereals to a Brāhmaṇa along with a cloth and the usual *Dakṣiṇā* with (the *mantra*) "Obeisance, O Govinda, O Lord of all, O lover of cowherdess folk, O preceptor of the universe, be delighted with this gift of grains." After observing thus the holy vow, he shall be absolved of all sins. The man shall attain the full merit of *Gomedhamakha* (cow sacrifice).

43b-46. On the *Dvādaśī* day in the bright half of the month of Caitra, the devotee should observe fast and worship as before, saying, "Obeisance to You, O Viṣṇu." He should bathe Viṣṇu in milk of the same quantity as before, in accordance with his ability. O Brāhmaṇa, similarly, he should bathe the Lord in a *Prastha* of ghee with due respect. As before, the observer of the vow should keep awake during the night and perform worship. Then he should get up early in the morning and finish the daily morning duties. He should offer one hundred and eight oblations of a mixture of honey, ghee and sesamum seeds.

47-49a. Thereafter, he should offer an *Āḍhaka* measure of rice mixed with honey, ghee and sesamum seeds to a Brāhmaṇa, accompanied by the usual religious fee, uttering the *Mantra*—"May Janārdana be pleased with this gift of an *Āḍhaka* of rice grains,—Janārdana who is Mahāviṣṇu in the form of *Prāṇa* (vital breath), who is the bestower of *Prāṇa* and is the lover of everyone." By doing thus with devotion, the man shall be freed from all sins. He shall acquire the benefit of the sacrifice *Atyagniṣṭoma*[9] increased eightfold.

49b-52a. One should observe fast on the *Dvādaśī* day in the bright half of the month of Vaiśākha and with great devotion bathe Madhusūdana the Lord of Devas with milk measuring a *Droṇa*. Keeping awake during the night is obligatory, along with the worship for three times on that day. With the repetition of the *mantra* "Obeisance to you the slayer of Madhu", he should perform Homa with ghee according to his capacity. After duly worshipping Madhusūdana with oblations for one hundred and eight times, he shall be freed from sins. He shall attain the benefit of eight horse-sacrifices.

52b-57. The devotee should observe fast on the *Dvādaśī* day in the bright half of the month of Jyeṣṭha and bathe Trivikrama in an *Āḍhaka* measure of milk. Endowed with devotion he should worship, saying, "Obeisance to Trivikrama". He should offer one hundred and eight oblations with the milk pudding itself. After keeping awake during the night, he should again perform worship. Along with the usual *Dakṣiṇā*, he should offer twenty sweet fried cakes to Brāhmaṇas with the mantra, "O Lord of the Universe, O Lord of Devas, O Supreme Lord, be pleased. Accepting this present, be the bestower of what is desired by me." In accordance with his capacity, he should feed the Brāhmaṇas. He should himself take food observing restraint in speech. He who thus performs the great holy observance pertaining to Trivikrama, shall be devoid of sins and shall attain the benefit of eight *Naramedhas*[10] (human sacrifices).

58. On the *Dvādaśī* day in the bright half of the month of Āṣāḍha, one should observe fast and keep all sense organs under control. The observer of the holy vow should bathe Vāmana in milk, of the same quantity as mentioned before.

59. He should worship by saying, "Obeisance to you, to Vāmana". After offering hundred and eight oblations with ghee and the Dūrvā grass, he should keep awake during the night. He should worship Vāmana again.

60. With great piety, he should offer cooked rice with curds, to a Brāhmaṇa regularly worshipping Vāmana, along with the usual *Dakṣiṇās* and a coconut fruit.

61. "Vāmana is the bestower of intellect. He is the sacrificial priest. Vāmana is always present in the materials (of worship). Vāmana is the redeemer from this (worldly existence). Obeisance, obeisance, to Vāmana."

62. With this *Mantra*, he should offer the cooked rice with curds. In accordance with his capacity, he should feed the Brāhmaṇas. By doing thus, the devotee shall attain the benefit of a hundred *Agniṣṭomas*.

63. On the *Dvādaśī* day in the bright half of the month of *Śrāvaṇa*, the observer of the holy vow should observe fast and bathe god Śrīdhara in milk mixed with honey.

64. He should worship him saying, "Obeisance be to Śrīdhara", and offering scents, etc. in due order. O sage, he should offer one hundred and eight oblations of *Pṛṣadājya* (ghee mixed with coagulated milk).

65-67. After keeping awake at night, he should perform the worship again. Excellent milk measuring an *Āḍhaka* must be given to a Brāhmaṇa along with a cloth and the usual religious fee, together with two golden earrings : O leading Brāhmaṇa, in order to realize all the cherished desires, he should repeat the following *Mantra* : "O Lord Rāma, O Lord of

Devas, reposing in the milk ocean, O Lord of the Universe, be delighted with this gift of milk. Be the bestower of all happiness."

68. In view of its being pleasure-bestowing, the performer of the holy rite should feed the Brāhmaṇas in accordance with his capacity. By performing thus, the devotee attains the benefit of a thousand horse sacrifices.

69. On the *Dvādaśī* day in the bright half of the month of Bhādrapada, the devotee should observe fast, duly bathe Hṛṣīkeśa, the preceptor of the universe, in milk measuring a *droṇa*.

70. The man should worship saying, "O Hṛṣīkeśa, obeisance to you." He should perform the *Homa*[11] with *Caru* (a preparation of boiled rice, barley and pulse) mixed with honey offering oblations one hundred and eight times.

71. After completing the rites of keeping awake, etc., he should give to a knower of the *Ātman* one and a half *Āḍhakas* of wheat with *Dakṣiṇā* and gold according to one's capacity.

72. With the *Mantra*, "O Hṛṣīkeśa, obeisance to you, the sole cause of all worlds. Grant all happiness unto me, in view of this gift of wheat."

73. According to his capacity he should feed the Brāhmaṇas, and should himself take food with restrained speech. He shall be absolved of all sins and shall attain the benefit of *Brahmamedha*.[12]

74. On the *Dvādaśī* day in the bright half of the month of Āśvina, the devotee should observe fast. With great devotion and purity, he should bathe Padmanābha with milk.

75. He should perform *Homa* in accordance with his capacity saying, "Obeisance to you, to Padmanābha., In accordance with the injunctions, he should perform worship with sesamum seeds, cereals, barley and ghee.

76. After keeping awake during the night, he should perform worship again. He should give a *Kuḍava* (measure) of honey along with the usual *Dakṣiṇā* to a Brāhmaṇa.

77. (The *mantra* shall be)—"O Padmanābha, obeisance to you, O grandfather of all worlds, be delighted with the gift of honey. Be the bestower of all happiness."

78. He who intelligently and devoutly performs the holy vow pertaining to Padmanābha certainly attains the benefit of a thousand *Brahmamedhas*.

79-82a. On the *Dvādaśī* day in the bright half of the month of Kārttika, the devotee should observe fast. He should control all his sense-organs. Saying "Obeisance to Dāmodara" with devotional feelings, he should bathe Dāmodara with milk, curds or ghee measuring an *Āḍhaka*. He should perform a hundred and eight *Āhutis* with sesamum seeds soaked in honey and ghee. He should invariably observe the vow of keeping awake (during the night), and should be devoted to the performance of worship thrice a day. In the morning he should worship the Lord with charming lotus flowers. Again, he should perform *Homa* with one hundred and eight oblations of sesamum seeds and ghee.

82b-85. With great devotion he should give to a Brāhmaṇa, cooked rice along with five *Bhakṣyas* (side dishes of edible things). (The *mantra*) "O Dāmodara, O Lord of the universe, O cause of all causes, save me compassionately. O Lord, O protector of those who seek refuge." With this Mantra he should give the charitable gift to a Brāhmaṇa, well-versed in the Vedas but burdened with a large family. In accordance with his capacity, he must give *Dakṣiṇā* and feed the Brāhmaṇas. After performing the holy rites duly, the devotee should take food along with his kinsmen. He attains twice the benefit of a thousand horse-sacrifices.

86. O excellent sage, he who performs these cxcellent *Dvādaśī vratas* for a year, attains the highest region.

87. He who devotedly performs these rites for one or two months, attains their respective benefits as well as Hari's region.

88-90. After performing the observance of the vow for one full year, the devotee should perform the *Udyāpana* rite (formally concluding it), O leading sage, on the *Dvādaśī* day in the dark half of Mārgaśīrṣa. He should take his bath early in the morning in accordance with his prescribed course of duties, after duly cleaning the teeth. He should wear white garments and garlands with white unguents and scents. He should erect an exquisite pandal, splendid in form and square in shape. It should be fitted with bells, chowries, etc. and embellished with tinkling bells.

91-92. It must be bedecked in flowers and garlands. Canopy and banners shall add to its splendour. It should be screened with a white cloth. Rows of lamps would beautify it. In its middle a *Sarvatobhadra*[13] (an auspicious design or 'Maṇḍala' in five colours) should be made. It should be duly beautified. The devotee should place twelve jars filled with water on that platform.

93. Five kinds of precious stones[14] must be put inside the jars and all of the jars with five kinds of precious stones deposited in them, should be covered with a well-washed white cloth.

94. O Brāhmaṇa, the performer of the holy rites should devoutly make the image of Lakṣmīnārāyaṇa in gold, silver or copper.

95. The devotee with good control over his sense-organs, should place the image on the jars. Or its price or gold according to his capacity may be placed (on the jars), O excellent Brāhmaṇa.

96. In all holy rites the sensible devotee should avoid dishonesty or perfidy in money. If he commits it, his span of life, wealth and riches will dwindle down.

97. At the outset, the devotee endowed with piety should bathe Lord Nārāyaṇa who, free from all ailments, is lying on (the serpent) *Ananta*, with *Pañcāmṛta* (the mixture of five sweet things, viz. milk, curds, ghee, honey and sugar).

98. The services rendered (prostration, etc.) should be based on Keśava and other names (of Viṣṇu). He should keep awake during the night, by listening to *Purāṇas*, etc.

99. He should bring under control slumber. Observing fasts, he should subdue his sense organs. In accordance with his capacity and wealth, he should worship the Lord, thrice in a day.

100. Getting up early in the morning and finishing the routine duties of the morning, he should, through Brāhmaṇas, get offered a thousand oblations of sesamum seed while repeating the *Vyāhṛti mantras*.

101. Thereafter, he should worship the Lord with scents, flowers, etc. in the prescribed order. In front of the Lord, he should listen to the *Purāṇas*.

102. He should give cooked rice mixed with curds, milk pudding, ten *Apūpas* (sweet pies or sweet round cakes) with ghee, to twelve Brāhmaṇas along with the usual *dakṣiṇā*.

103. "O Lord of gods, O Lord of the universe, O lord

whose person is for the purpose of blessing the devotees, O Kṛṣṇa, accept the present. Be the bestower of all desired objects."

104. With this *Mantra*, he should offer gifts. With palms joined in reverence, he should pray. The performer of the *Vrata* should kneel on the ground humbly.

105. (Prayer)—"Obeisance, obeisance to you, O king of the kings of Devas. Obeisance be to you, O Lord, O receptacle of the worlds, render the fruit of my vow complete today. Obeisance be to you, O Supreme Person.'

106. Thus, he should pray to the Brāhmaṇas and to Lord Puruṣottama. He should offer *Arghya* to the Lord accompanied by Mahālakṣmī.

107. "O Lord of Lakṣmī, obeisance to you, to the resident of the milk ocean. O Lord of Devas, accompanied by Lakṣmī, accept the *Arghya*.

108. I salute Acyuta whose remembrance and the utterance of whose name makes whatever is deficient in penance, performance of sacrifice and other rites compensated immediately and made perfect and complete."

109. After having prayed thus to the Lord of Devas, the devotee should offer the image to the preceptor along with *Dakṣiṇā*.

110. Thereafter, he should feed the Brāhmaṇas according to his capacity. He should give them *Dakṣiṇās* also. Afterwards, restrained in speech, he should himself take food surrounded by his kinsmen.

111-113. In the company of learned men, he should listen to the story of Viṣṇu till evening. The man who thus observes the *Dvādaśī* vow, O Nārada, attains all desires both here and hereafter. Absolved of all sins, accompanied by twenty-one generations of his family, he goes to Viṣṇu's abode after reaching which none feels grieved.

O Brāhmaṇa, the man who listens to this excellent *Dvādaśī Vrata*, or reads it, attains the benefit of *Vājapeya* sacrifice.

CHAPTER SEVENTEEN

1. Although the colophon states *Mārga-śīrṣa-Śukla-Dvādaśī-Vrata-Kathana* as the heading of the chapter, here what is known as *Dvādaśī Vrata* is described. The *Vrata* is to start on the 12th day of the bright half of Mārga-śīrṣa and god Viṣṇu in the form of Keśava, is to be adored. The following is the list of the forms of Viṣṇu to be worshipped on the particular *Dvādaśī*.

Dvādaśī (Twelfth) *day in the bright half of the month of* :	*Special Form of Viṣṇu to be worshipped.*
1. Mārgaśīrṣa	Keśava
2. Pauṣa	Nārāyaṇa
3. Māgha	Mādhava
4. Phālguna	Govinda
5. Caitra	Viṣṇu
6. Vaiśākha	Madhusūdana
7. Jyeṣṭha	Trivikrama
8. Āṣāḍha	Vāmana
9. Śrāvaṇa	Śrīdhara
10. Bhādrapada	Hṛṣīkeśa
11. Āśvina	Padma-nābha
12. Kārttika	Dāmodara.

All these forms are according to the serial order of the twenty four names of Viṣṇu in the *Sandhyā* (twilight) prayer.

The general formula of the observance of this *Vrata* is as follows :

Observance of fast—wearing white garments after bath—worship of Viṣṇu in Keśava form with the usual materials and offerings—observance of silence during worship—offering of one hundred and eight oblations in fire—observance of vigil at night near the Śālagrāma stone—The next day, the deity to be bathed in milk (or a milkproduct)—worship three times a day along with Lakṣmī—Final *Naivedya*-of *Pāyasa* (Rice-pudding) with a cocoa-nut and *Dakṣiṇā* to be offered to a Brāhmaṇa—Feeding of Brāhmaṇas—Breaking of fast along with one's kinsmen but with control over speech.

There are minor variations with each *Dvādaśī* but the outline is the same. After observing this *Vrata* for full one year, there is its *Udyāpana* (concluding rite).

It is found that this *Vrata* is the same as given in *Mbh. Anuśāsana* Ch. 109 and is called there *Viṣṇor dvādaśakam* or twelve days dedicated to god Viṣṇu. *AP*. Ch. 188 gives a number of *Dvādaśī Vratas* different from that in the NP. Out of fifty such *Vratas*, *Kṛtya Kalpataru* (*Vrata kāṇḍa*) describes 26 Vratas, Hemādri in CC (Vratakhaṇḍa I, pp. 1162—1222) describes these various

Vratas. This has been a very popular *Vrata* as it is described in various *Dharma-Śāstra* digests.

2. *Vratāni*—The *Purāṇic* concept of *Vrata* implies "any undertaking, religious or ascetic performance or observance, vow or religious duty and thus seems to be an amalgam of *ṛta*, *dharman* and *Vrata* concepts of the Vedic period. Later on, *Vrata* became *Vrata-dharma* and had a strong hold on the public.

3. These verses describe how to observe the *Dvādaśī-Vrata* (from the month of and) for the month of Mārgaśīrṣa. As is wellknown, Lord Kṛṣṇa declares himself to be Mārgaśīrṣa among the months of the year (*māsānām Mārgaśīrṣo-'ham*) in BG. X. 35. Hence, the propriety of beginning this *Viṣṇu-Vrata* from Mārgaśīrṣa.

4. These verses describe the observance of *Dvādaśī-Vrata* in the month of Pauṣa.

5. *Tṛṇaiḥ* is most probably a misprint for *Tūryaiḥ* 'with trumpets.' The Veṅkaṭeśvara Press edition of this Purāṇa has a number of such misprints. But as the corresponding verse in The *Bṛhan Nāradīya* XVI.17 is *nṛtyaiḥ* and that suits better in this context, I have translated 'dances.'

6. *Kṛśara* according to Skd. is as *Tulya-tilānnam*, but *Kṛśarā* is what is known as *Khicaṛī* (खिचड़ी) in Hindi and Marathi. If *Kṛśarānnam* is dissolved as *Kṛśarā+anna* 'the spicy preparation of rice and pulse (*dāl*)' gives a better meaning.

7. Name of a *Soma* sacrifice. Sacrifices are divided into *iṣṭi*, *paśu* and *Soma*. There are seven forms of the *Soma* sacrifices, viz. *Agniṣṭoma*, *Atyagniṣṭoma*, *Ukthya*, *Ṣoḍaśin*, *Vājapeya*, *Atirātra* and *Āptoryāma*. The Agniṣṭoma is the model of all *Soma* sacrifices. The Agniṣṭoma is of one day duration (*ekāha*) and is an integral part of *Jyotiṣṭoma* and hence both are many times identified. (For details of this sacrifice vide HD. Vol.II. Ch. XXXIII pp. 1133-1203).

8. *Vājapeya*—Though this is a form of *Jyotiṣṭoma* and though it follows the procedure of the Soma sacrifice called *Ṣoḍaśin*, it has many special features which may claim the class of an independent sacrifice. The characteristic feature is that the number seventeen has a special significance in this sacrifice. For example : there are 17 *Stotras*, 17 *Śastras*, 17 objects as sacrificial fee, etc. It gives sovereignty or post of Indra to the sacrificer (For details HD II.ii. pp. 1206-1214).

9. *Atyagniṣṭoma*—a variety of *Agniṣṭoma* (see note above). Here only the *Ṣoḍaśī Stotra* and *Soḍaśin* cup are added (vide S.B.E. 41, p. XVII).

10. *Nara-medha* though literally translated as 'human sacrifice' in the bracket, actually involves no killing of human beings. This point is generally overlooked by its critics. It is only a symbolism.

11. *Hunet* is obviously an *ārṣa* form of Pot 3 P. sg. of $\sqrt{}$*hu*-'to offer oblations, perform a sacrifice.'

12. *Brahma-medhas* is *Brahma-yajña* or recitation of Vedas. Its earliest description is given in *Śatapatha* Br. XI.5.6.3-8. It defines *Svādhyāyo vai brahma-yajñaḥ*—'Recitation of Veda, etc. is *Brahma-yajña*.

It is a daily duty, but now-a-days, it is formally recited in a nut-shell on the Śrāvaṇī day in the Deccan. The reference in the NP. shows the great importance given to the recitation of the Vedas in those days.

Note 13, p. 295 (on I.17.92, p. 291) *Sarvato-Bhadra* (a cross-section)

B=Black; *G*=Green; *R*=Red; *W*=White; Y=Yellow.

Y	Y	Y	Y	Y	Y						
Y	R	R	R	R	Y						
Y	R			R	Y						
Y	R			R	Y	W	W	W	W	W	W
Y	R	R	R	R	Y	G	W	W	W	W	R
Y	Y	Y	Y	Y	Y	G	G	W	W	R	R
			W	G	G	B	G	G	R	R	R
			W	W	G	G	B	G	G	R	R
			W	W	W	G	G	B	G	G	R
			W	W	W	R	G	G	B	G	G
			W	W	R	R	R	G	G	B	W
			W	R	R	R	R	R	G	W	W

13. *Sarvatobhadra* literally means 'auspicious on all sides?' It is a *Maṇḍala* (a geometrical design) common to all worships. As the *Śāradātilaka* III.131 states :

maṇḍalaṁ sarvato-bhadram etat-sādhāraṇaṁ smṛtam /

The same work instructs that the *maṇḍala* should be drawn with five coloured powders, viz. yellow with turmeric powder, white produced from husked grains of rice, red with *Kusumbha* powder, black with the fine powder of half-burnt inferior cereals, sprinkled with milk and greenish with powder of the leaves of *bilva* tree (*ibid* III 122-24). cf. *AP.* 3-19-20. There appear to be some differences about the figures to be drawn. For example the quotation of SKP in CC as quoted in the *Vrata rāja* p. 9 is different from that in the *Jñānārṇava Tantra* 26.15.16.

It is enough to note that it is a special design in five colours and was regarded auspicious in all worships.

14. There is a difference of opinion about the 'five jewels' (*pañca ratnas*) to be deposited in the jars. According to *Āditya Purāṇa* quoted in CC *Vrata Khaṇḍa* I.47, they are gold, silver, pearl, coral and *rājāvarta* (Lapis Lazuli) but, according to *Kālikā Purāṇa* quoted in CC on *Kāla* p. 413 they are : gold, diamond, sapphire, ruby and pearl. *Vrata rāja* p. 6 quotes these and adds one more from the *Viṣṇudharmottara* as follows :

It gives the list of nine precious stones :

muktāphalaṁ hiraṇyaṁ ca vaidūryam padmarāgakam /
puṣpa-rāgaṁ ca gomedaṁ nīlaṁ gārutmakaṁ tathā /
pravāla-yuktānyuktāni mahāratnāni vā nava //

They are pearls, gold, lapis lazuli, ruby, topaz, *gomeda* (a gem found in the Himālayas. It is of four different colours, viz. white, pale, yellow, red and dark blue), a sapphire, an emerald and corals.

CHAPTER EIGHTEEN

The Holy Observance Pertaining to Lakṣmī-Nārāyaṇa[1]

Sanaka said :

1. O excellent sage, listen. I shall tell you another holy observance that removes all sins, destroys all miseries and is very sacred and meritorious.

2. It bestows all desired objects to the Brāhmaṇas, Kṣatriyas, Vaiśyas, Śūdras and the women folk. It yields the benefits of all other holy rites.

3. It is conducive to righteousness; it destroys bad effects of evil dreams; it wards off (the influence of) evil planets. It is the excellent *Pūrṇimā Vrata* (observance of the full Moon day), well-known in all worlds. If it is performed, a ten million heaps of accumulated sins perish.

4. On the full moon day, in the bright half of the month of Mārgaśīrṣa, the devotee should, after duly washing the teeth, perform the rite of ablution according to the prescribed procedure, and be self-restrained and pure.

5-6. He should return home and wear pure and white garments. With restrained speech (i.e. silence), he should wash the feet and sip water as *Ācamana*. Remembering Lord Nārāyaṇa, he should perform his usual daily worship of gods. He should, thereupon, worship Lord Lakṣmī-Nārāyaṇa devoutly with the solemn vow.

7. The performer of this *Vrata* (observance) should devoutly worship saying, "Obeisance to Nārāyaṇa". After invoking the deity and offering him a seat, etc., he should worship the Lord with scents, fragrant flowers, etc. with full concentrated mind.

8. The observer of the holy rite should propitiate the Lord with songs, musical instruments, dances, hymns, readings of *Purāṇas*, etc. also.

9. The devotee should make a raised platform of an *Aratni* (about 45 cms.) square, in front of the Lord and place fire

thereon, in accordance with the rules laid down in *Gṛhya Sūtras*. Repeating the *Puruṣa sūkta* upto *Ājya* hymns he should propitiate the Lord by performing the *Homa* with ghee, *Caru* and sesamum seeds.

10. In order to dispel all sins he should assiduously perform the *Homa* once, twice or thrice, according to his capacity.

11. After completing the *Homa* duly, in accordance with the injunctions laid down in one's own *Gṛhya sūtra* including all expiatory rites and other rites, the intelligent person should mutter the *Śānti sūkta*.[2]

12. Afterwards he should approach the deity and perform the worship again. With piety, he should dedicate the observance of the fast unto the Lord.

13. Observing fast on the full moon day, he should pray "O Lotus-eyed God, I shall partake of food, the next day. Be pleased to be my refuge."

14. After submitting thus to the Lord, the devotee should take white flowers and raw rice grains in his hand, kneel on the ground and offer *Arghya* to the Moon.

15-16. "O lord of Rohiṇī, born in the family of Atri, and in the milk ocean (as well), (kindly) accept the *Arghya* offered by me, O Lord." After offering *Arghya* thus to the moon, he should stand facing the east. Looking at the moon with palms joined in reverence, he should pray thus.

17. "Obeisance to you, of white rays; salutations to you to the lord of the stars, and to the lord of Rohiṇī; obeisance be to you, to the brother of Lakṣmī."

18. Thereafter, he should keep awake during the night by listening to the *Purāṇas* and other pious activities. He should control his sense-organs and be pure. He should avoid the very sight of heretics.

19. Thereafter, he should perform the routine and conventional duties in the morning, in accordance with the prescribed injunctions. Again he should perform the worship of the Lord befitting the extent of his riches.

20. He should feed the Brāhmaṇas according to his capacity. With purity and restrained speech (silence), the man should take food along with kinsmen and servants as well as others.

21. In the same manner, he should observe fast on the full moon days of Pauṣa and other months and with due devotion should worship the infallible Lord Nārāyaṇa.

22. Performing thus for one year, he should perform the ritualistic concluding ceremony on the full moon day in the month of Kārttika. I shall tell you the procedure for the same.

23. He should construct an exquisite pavilion (*Maṇḍapa*) extremely auspicious in nature and square in shape, beautified with flower garlands and shining with a canopy and a row of banners.

24. Many lamps and tinkling bells should brighten its splendour. It should be decorated on all sides with mirrors, chowries and water-pots all round.

25. O Brāhmaṇa, in the middle, there should be a *Sarvato-Bhadra* shining with five colours. Thereon the devotee should place a jar full of water.

26. The jar should be covered with a cloth of very fine texture. O Brāhmaṇa, an image of lord Lakṣmī-Nārāyaṇa should be made in gold, silver or copper and placed over it.

27-28. The image should be bathed in *Pañcāmṛta* and worshipped in the serial order, by scents, etc., and food offerings of various kinds. With due devotion and restraint over the sense-organs, he should keep awake during the night with due faith. On the morning of the next day, he should worship Viṣṇu as per procedure prescribed for it.

29. The image should be presented to the preceptor accompanied by the usual *Dakṣiṇā*. He should feed the Brāhmaṇas in accordance with his capacity. If one is affluent enough one should feed the Brāhmaṇas unobstructedly without any restriction on their number.

30. With proper attention and purity of mind, he should perform the *Dāna* of sesamum seeds befitting his capacity. The clever devotee should perform *Homa* rites in the fire duly, with sesamum seeds.

31-32. If a man performs this holy vow—*vrata* properly, he will enjoy all pleasures here in the company of his sons and grandsons. He will be liberated from his sins. Accompanied by ten thousand members of his family, he will go to Viṣṇu's abode, difficult of access even to the *Yogins*.

CHAPTER EIGHTEEN

Lakṣmī-Nārāyaṇa Vrata
(of Mārgaśīrṣa Pūrṇimā)

1. *Lakṣmī-Nārāyaṇa-Vrata* :

This *Vrata* is different from that given in *CC. Vrata*.II.164 and also other about 38 *Pūrṇimā vratas* given therein (pp.160-245). The *Vrata-rāja* also is silent about this. This *vrata* is to be observed from the Full Moon day in the month of Mārgaśīrṣa ending it on the Full moon day of Kārttika,—Thus completing one full year i.e. 12 *Pūrṇimās*. The *Vrata* can be undertaken even by women and Śūdras.

2. *The Śānti sūkta*—

The belief that some calamities or effects of ill omens, bad dreams, evil influences of stars, unprecedental or unnatural happenings, etc., can be prevented or mitigated by the recitation of some Vedic Sūktas is found since the later Vedic times and the *Sūtra* period. The following *Sūktas* are regarded as *Śānti Sūktas*, the recital of which is beneficial :

(1) *Ā no bhadrāḥ* (RV.I.89.1-10)
(2) *Svasti na Indro* (RV. I.89.6-10)
(3) *Śaṁ na Indrāgnī* (RV.VIII.35.1-11) This is regarded as *Śāntikādhyāya* (Mt.P.274.56).
(4) *Yata Indra bhayāmahe* (RV.VIII.61.13-18).
(5) *Bhadraṁ no api vātaya manaḥ* (RV.X.20.1)
(6) *Āśuḥ śiśāno* (RV.X.103.1-13).
(7) *Muñcāmi tvā* (RV.X.161.1-5).
(8) *Tyam-u ṣu* (RV.X.178-1-3).
(9) *Mahi trīṇām* (RV.X.185-1-3).
(10) *Rātrī Vyakhyat* (RV.X.127.1-8).

A reference to Bloomfield's *Vedic Concordance* shows that these verses are repeated in other Vedic texts like TS., AV. etc.

The belief in the auspicious and protective effects of recital of holy texts is found in Buddhists of Laṅkā and countries of the South East Asia. There are 30 such *suttas* such as *Mahā maṅgala sutta*, *Metti sutta*, *Dasa-dhamma sutta* and others in Pali *Sutta Piṭaka* and they are used for similar purpose as the Vedic Sūktas in Brahmanism. These *suttas* are called *Parittas* 'Protectors' and they are the most popular in Burma (M. Bode—*The Pali Literature of Burma*, pp. 3-4).

CHAPTER NINETEEN

Installation of the Banner

Sanaka said :

1. "I shall expound to you another holy *Vrata* which dispels all sins and causes delight to Viṣṇu. It is named *Dhvajāropaṇa*[1] (installation of the banner).

2. He who installs an excellent banner on the temple of Viṣṇu is honoured by Brahmā and others. What more need be spoken (in praise of it) ?.

3. The gift of a thousand *Bhāras*[2] of gold to a man burdened with a large family is but equal in benefit to the rite of installation of the banner.

4. The excellent ablution in the Gaṅgā or the service unto the Tulasī plant or the adoration of Śiva-Liṅga is on a par with the installation of the banner.

5. O Brāhmaṇa, unprecedented it is ! Rare and unequalled it is ! It is unprecedented ! It is a rite that dispels all sins, the rite called *Dhvajāropaṇa*.

6. I shall describe all those rites ancillary to the installation of the banner. Even as I recount it, listen.

7. On the *Daśamī* (tenth) day in the bright half of the month of Kārttika,[3] a man in complete self-restraint, should assiduously perform the rite of ablution beginning with the cleaning of his teeth.

8. The Brāhmaṇa devotee should take food only once. He should observe the vow of celibacy. Remembering the lord Nārāyaṇa, he shall sleep in front of the deity. He should be pure and be clad in white robes.

9. He should get up early in the morning and perform the rites of *Ācamana* and ablution duly. After finishing the daily routine of prescribed duties, he should worship Viṣṇu.

10. Causing the *Svastivācana* (the utterance of benediction) along with four Brāhmaṇas, the devotee should perform the *Nāndī Śrāddha*[4] (Śrāddha, preliminary to *Saṁskāras* and festive occasions) in the holy rite of the installation of the banner.

11. Repeating the Gāyatrī, he should sprinkle the banner

and the flag-staff along with the cloth. Devoted to them, he should worship the sun, moon and Vainateya (Garuḍa).

12. He should worship Dhātṛ and Vidhātṛ (gods Viṣṇu and Brahmā) on the staff of the flag, with turmeric, raw rice grains, scents and other things and particularly with white flowers.

13. Thereafter, he should get a small plot measuring a *Gocarman*[5] (scrubbed, cleaned and smeared well. The sacrificial fire should be placed there. One should oblate ghee and other things in the prescribed order[6] in accordance with the injunctions in one's own *Gṛhya Sūtra*.

14-15. He should offer a hundred and eight oblations of milk pudding and ghee in the *homa*. At the outset, the *Puruṣa Sūkta* (RV.X.90) is repeated, then the Sūkta *Viṣṇornu kam* (RV.1.154) etc. and then The *Irāvati* (RV.VII.99) (should be repeated). Thereafter, he should give eight *Āhutis* (in the fire) saying *Vainateyāya svāhā*. Thereafter, O Brāhmaṇa the Sūktas *Somo Dhenum* (RV.I.91.20) and *U du tyam* (RV.I.50.1) should be repeated and oblations be offered.[7]

16. There, he should repeat the *sūkta* pertaining to the Sun (viz. RV.I.50) and the *Śānti Sūktas* in accordance with one's capacity. With purity, he should keep awake during the night in the vicinity of Hari.

17. Thereafter, he should get up early in the morning and complete the daily routine activities. As before, he should worship the Lord with scents, sweet smelling flowers and other things in due order.

18. Thereafter, the splendid auspicious flag should be taken to the shrine of Viṣṇu, to the accompaniment of auspicious musical instruments, chanting of the *Sūktas*, dances and singing of hymns.

19. O Brāhmaṇa, the joyous devotee should firmly plant the flagstaff (with the hoisted flag) either at the entrance to the shrine of the Lord or on the top of it.

20. Then, he should worship Lord Hari with scents, flowers, raw rice grains, charming incense and lamps and *Naivedya* offerings consisting of various dishes.

21. After installing the excellent and splendid banner in the temple, he should circumambulate it and chant this song of prayer.

22. "Obeisance to you, O Lotus-eyed Lord, the Conceiver and creator of the Universe; O Hṛṣikeśa, salutations to you, O earliest-born great Puruṣa.

23. I resort to Keśava by whom all this universe has been created, in whom everything is established and in whom the universe will get dissolved.

24. I salute that Lord, the embodiment of perfect knowledge, whose supreme nature even Brahmā and other gods do not know and whom even the Yogins do not perceive.

25. I salute that Lord whose form consists of the entire universe,[8] whose umbilical region is the firmament, whose head is the heaven and whose feet are the Earth.

26. I salute that Lord who is Brahmā incarnate whose ears are all the quarters, whose eyes are the sun and the moon, and by whom the mantras of *Ṛk*, *Sāman* and *Yajus* have been uttered.

27. I salute that Lord from whose mouth the Brāhmaṇas originated, from whose arms the kings came forth, from whose thighs the Vaiśyas were born and from whose feet were born the Śūdras.

28. I salute that unborn Lord whom they call *Puruṣa* only on account of the contact with Māyā, but who is naturally free from impurities, who is pure, who is free from modifications or change and is unsullied.

29. I salute that god Viṣṇu who reposes in the milk-ocean, who is the infinite and unvanquished Lord, and is favourably disposed towards good devotees and who is attainable only through devotion.

30. I salute that omnifaced Lord from whom originated the earth and other elements, the *Tanmātrās*, the sense-organs and both the subtle and gross substances.

31. Again and again I bow unto that attributeless, subtle supreme being which is the *Brahman*, the highest resort that is the supreme-most and the most excellent in all the worlds.

32. I bow down to that unborn pure Lord who is not subject to modification or change and who has arms all round and whom the leading *Yogins* consider the cause of the cause of all.

33. May that Viṣṇu be propitiated unto me—Lord Viṣṇu who is the immanent soul in all living beings, who is identical with the universe, and who is the attributeless great *Ātman*.

34. May that Viṣṇu be pleased with me—the Lord who though stationed within the heart, is yet staying far off to those whose Ātmans had been deluded by Māyā but who is omnipresent to persons endowed with spiritual knowledge.

35. May that Viṣṇu be pleased with me, Viṣṇu, the Lord whose *homa* is performed by set of four, set of four, with a set of two, set of five and again by a set of two.[9]

36. May that Viṣṇu be pleased with me, the lord who is the bestower of salvation to those men possessing perfect knowledge (i.e. followers of *Jñāna-yoga*), meritorious deeds (performers of *Karmas* or followers of karma-*mārga*) and devotional feelings (followers of the path of devotion) and who is sought by the whole universe.

37. May that Viṣṇu be gracious unto me—Lord Viṣṇu whose persons assumed sportively for the well-being of the world, are worshipped by gods.

38. May that Viṣṇu be propitious unto me—the Lord whom the saintly persons consider to be the embodiment of existence, knowledge and bliss, the attributeless support of the attributes."

39. After eulogising thus, he should bow down to Viṣṇu and worship the Brāhmaṇas richly. Afterwards, he should adore the preceptor with the offerings of religious fees, raiments, etc.

40-41. In accordance with his capacity, he should feed the Brāhmaṇas, with devotional feelings. O Brāhmaṇa, devoted to Nārāyaṇa he should perform *Pāraṇā*—the ritualistic break of the fast—along with his sons, friends, wives and other kinsmen. I shall mention the meritorious benefits to the person who performs this excellent rite of *Dhvajāropaṇa*. Listen with attention.

42. Undoubtedly, as many accumulations of his sins perish, O leading Brāhmaṇa, as there are flutters in the banner cloth due to the wind.

43. Whether one is vitiated by great sins or by all kinds of sins, one is absolved of them all by installing a banner in the shrine of Viṣṇu.

44. O Brāhmaṇa, he enjoys *Sārūpya* (similarity of form) with Hari for as many thousands of Yugas as the number of days that the banner stands aloft in Viṣṇu's abode.

45. If righteous men take delight and praise on seeing the banner installed, all of them are liberated from crores of great sins.

46. The banner installed in Viṣṇu's abode shakes off within half wink of eye, the sins of the man who had installed it, even as it flutters its cloth.

47. He who installs a banner in the abode of Viṣṇu and looks after it every day, goes to heaven by means of *Devayāna* (the divine path) like king Sumati of good intellect."

CHAPTER NINETEEN

The Vrata of Installation of the Banner

1. Although the principal Gṛhya and Dharma Sūtras are silent about the installation of an image (*Devatā-Pratiṣṭhā*) in a temple, the custom of installing a banner with the sign of Garuḍa on it (*Garuḍa-dhvaja*) in honour of Vāsudeva seems to be pretty old. In an inscription of the 2nd Cent. B.C., the Greek Bhāgavata Heliodorus is recorded to have erected a *Garuḍa-dhvaja* (D.C. Sircar—*Select Inscriptions*, pp. 90-91).

In the Gupta Age, temple-building activity and installation of images became popular and we find in an early *Purāṇa* like the Mt.P. (Chs. 264-66), a detailed procedure of such installation. Later on, even the installation of a flag at the entrance of or over the shrine became so important that it came to be regarded as a *Vrata* (religious observance). Hemādri in the *Caturvarga Cintāmaṇi* (CC)—*Vrata Khaṇḍa* (pp. 829-30 Bib. Ind. 1879) gives *Dhvaja-Vrata* (The observance of raising a flag on the temple of Viṣṇu) from the *Viṣṇudharmottara.* But that seems to be a part of Pāñcarātra cult, as the colour of the banner was to be yellow, blue, white and red. The figures on them are to be Garuḍa, the Palm-tree, the Alligator, etc. according to the *Vyūha* (Vāsudeva, Saṅkarṣana and others). The *Vrata* is to start from the month of Caitra when the flag of Vāsudeva is to be worshipped, Saṅkarṣaṇa's banner to be adored in Vaiśākha and so on.

This vow is observed for twelve years and thereby, the devotee attains the *Sāyujya* type of liberation.

The above outline from Hemādri's CC will show how the NP. differs from the *Viṣṇudharmottara,* though the flag in the NP., is to be planted at the door or above the temple of Viṣṇu. It is to be noted that no *Vyūha* is brought in the NP., though the influence of the Pāñcarātra cult on the NP. is undeniable.

2. *hema-bhārasahasram.*

Gold weighing one thousand *bhāras.*

1 *bhāra*=8000 *Tolas* of gold—SKD III.499.

3. This *Vrata* is to begin on the 11th day of the bright half of Kārttika. Contrast *CC,* where it is said to begin in the month of Caitra.

4. Normally *Nāndī-Śrāddha* is a necessary preliminary in the *Upanayana* (Investiture of the sacred thread) Ceremony, and other *Saṁskāras* (Haradatta on *Āpastamba Gr.* S.10.5). But its prescription before undertaking this *Vrata,* shows its elevation to the status of a *Saṁskāra.*

5. *Go-carma-mātraṁ sthaṇḍilam*

A *Sthaṇḍila* is a square with each of its sides 18, 16, etc. finger-breadths. The term *go-carma* seems to be flexible. Here its area is limited to the altar or the ground levelled, squared and prepared for the sacrifice.

6. *ājya-bhāgādikaṁ kramāt.*

Ājya-bhāgas mark the limits, as it were, of oblations. The northern limit is with *Agnaye Svāhā* (accompanied with oblation of ghee, etc.) and the Southern limit is with *Somāya Svāhā* and other oblations are in between these two limits.

7a. *Pauruṣa Sūkta* is the *Puruṣa Sūkta* RV. X.90, *Viṣṇor nu kam* is the *Viṣṇu Sūkta* in RV.I.154 and *Irāvatī* is the mantra *Irāvatī dhenumatī*, etc. in RV.VII.99.3. This mantra is found in *Tai. Saṁ* I.2.13.1, *Vāj.Saṁ.* V.16 and other Vedic works.

7b. *Somo dhenum* is RV. I.91.2 while *udu tyam* is the 1st *Mantra* of the famous *Saura* hymn RV.I.50.

8. An echo of the famous *Puruṣa Sūkta* (RV.X.90).

9. This famous verse containing numerals to represent the number of the syllables to be uttered is wellknown to all *Agni-hotrins*. The syllables are to be pronounced in the serial order as given in the verse. While uttering these syllables (*mantras*) one is to offer oblation to the sacrificial fire (in the *Homa*).

The literal meaning of the verse is as follows :

Caturbhiḥ : With the four syllables, viz. *ośrāvaya* (*Tait. Āraṇyaka* VII.8.1)

Caturbhiḥ : The next four syllables are : *astu śrauṣaṭ* (*Tait. Saṁhitā.* I.6.11, 1, 2 etc.)

After these the two syllables to be pronounced are :

yaja (*Tait. Saṁhitā* I.6.11, 1, 2, 3 etc.)

These two syllables are followed by the five syllables, viz. *ye yajāmahe* (*Tait. Saṁhitā* I.6.11.1, 2, 3, etc). This is to be concluded with the two syllables *Vauṣaṭ* (*Aitareya Br.* III.6.5).

The whole expression to be recited is :

Ośrāvaya, astu śrauṣaṭ, yaja, ye yajāmahe vauṣaṭ |

CHAPTER TWENTY

The Legend of King Sumati

Nārada said :

1. O holy sir, the knower of all *Dharmas*, the master of all scriptural topics, the most excellent of all holy rites (or observances), the installation of the banner (on Viṣṇu shrines) has been recounted by you.

2. O sage, narrate to me in detail, the anecdote of Sumati[1] who is mentioned by you as one devoted to the installation of banners.

Sanaka said

3. Listen with single-minded attention to this ancient meritorious mythological anecdote that is destructive of all sins. It has been narrated to me by god Brahmā.

4. Formerly, there was a king named Sumati, in the Kṛta yuga. He was born of the lunar race. He was (then the sole) glorious sovereign ruler of all the seven continents.

5. A scion of the Lunar race, he was pious-souled, truthful and fond of guests. Endowed with all auspicious characteristics, he was embellished with all kinds of wealth.

6. He always resorted to (listening to) the stories of Hari, and was always absorbed in the worship of Hari. Devoid of arrogance, he was eager to render service to those who were absolutely absorbed in devotion to Hari.

7. He was devoted to the worship of those who are worthy of adoration. He was impartial in outlook. He was endowed with all good qualities. He was a benefactor of all living beings, quiescent, grateful and glorious.

8. O sage, his wife was a highly blessed lady named Satyamatī. She was richly endowed with all auspicious characteristics. She was chaste, and to her, her husband was her very vital breath.

9. That couple were always engaged in the adoration of

Hari. Those highly blessed persons could remember their previous births. Knowers of the truth as they were, they were absorbed in what was Reality.

10. They were always engaged in offering charitable gift of food and cool water. They built and dug innumerable bunds, tanks and parks.

11. The pure and chaste lady Satyamatī, the charming, sweet-voiced queen used to dance delightedly in the temple of Viṣṇu.

12. On every *Dvādaśi* day, the highly blessed king also used to instal a wide and charming banner (on the shrine of Viṣṇu).

13. Even the Devas always eulogised the king who was perpetually devoted to Hari, and was an expert in *Dharmas*, and his beloved queen Satyamatī.

14. On coming to know that the couple were well-known in the three worlds as adepts in Dharmas, sage Vibhāṇḍaka[2] who was desirous of seeing them, came there along with a number of disciples.

15. On hearing that the sage was coming, the king accompanied by his wife, went out to greet the sage Vibhāṇḍaka with extensive material of honouring the *guru*.

16. When the rites of hospitable reception had been completed and when the sage had taken his seat, the king, seated on a lower seat, spoke to the quiescent sage with palms joined in reverence.

The King said :

17. O holy sir, I feel satisfied by your visit. Good men praise the arrival of saintly persons as pleasing.

18. Learned men say that all riches are where great men offer their affection. Brilliance, renown, wealth and progeny also do abide there.

19. O holy lord, O sage, all good fortunes and welfare flourish day by day where good men bestow their great mercy.

20. There is no doubt in this that he who wears on his head the dust and the water that has washed the feet of great men is a meritorious soul.

He has the benefit of having bathed in all sacred rivers, O Brāhmaṇa.

21. O leading Brāhmaṇa, my sons, my wife, my riches—all these are dedicated to you. Kindly command me what shall I do, by way of pleasing you?

22. On seeing the king full of modesty, the leading sage was much delighted. Lovingly he stroked him with his hand and said as follows :

The sage said :

23. O king, what has been said by you is fully befitting your family. Every one who bows down with humility, attains great wealth.

24. O excellent king, it is due to humility, that a man obtains virtue, wealth, love and liberation (i.e. all the four *Puruṣārthas*). What is it that is difficult to attain in the case of a noble-souled person?

25. O protector of the Earth, I am pleased with you inasmuch as you follow the path of the good. May welfare bless you perpetually. May what I ask you, be very kindly related.

26. There are various types of worship causing satisfaction to Hari. But among them, you abide always by the installation of banners. You are always attempting that alone.

27. This chaste lady, your wife, is always engaged in dancing before the deity. How has this come about? It behoves you to relate it to me precisely.

The king said :

28. Listen, O holy sir, I shall tell you everything that you ask. The conduct of life of both of us is surprising and astonishing to all worlds.

29. O excellent one, formerly I was a Śūdra named Mālinī. I was always engaged in evil ways. I was absorbed in the acts of injury to all worlds.

30. I was a slander-monger, a hater of righteousness. I used to plunder the wealth of deities (in shrines), and to kill cows and Brāhmaṇas—nay—all living beings. I was a thief (also).

31. I was always harsh in speech and a sinner devoted to the dalliance with prostitutes. Thus I continued for sometime, disregarding the words of the great.

32. Later on, I was abandoned by my kinsmen. In

misery I went to a forest subsisting myself on the perpetual diet of venison and other flesh. I used to rob the way-farers.

33. Isolated and extremely miserable, I stayed there in the tenantless forest. Once I was extremely oppressed by the heat of the summer. I was utterly famished with hunger. I was thirsty.

34. In the lonely forest, I saw a ruined dilapidated temple of Viṣṇu. There was a great lake near it, teeming with swans and ducks called Kāraṇḍava.

35. O prominent sage, it was covered with clusters of flowers from the surrounding forest. I drank water therefrom. On its banks, I alleviated my tedium.

36. By eating fruits scattered here and there, my hunger was satiated. I resided in that dilapidated temple of Viṣṇu.

37. Every day, I repaired the decaying ruined place, joining together the broken parts. With leaves, grasses and assemblages of twigs and wood, an abode (a shrine of the god) was duly erected.

38-39. O leading sage, to increase my own happiness and comfort, the whole area was scrubbed and smeared well by me. Killing various kinds of animals and maintaining the practice of hunters, I maintained my livelihood, for full twenty years there. Then came this chaste lady hailing from the lands adjoining the Vindhya mountains.

40. O Brāhmaṇa, she was born of the family of Niṣādas (hunters). She was known by the name Avakokilā. She too had been abandoned by her kinsmen. She was very miserable with shattered body.

41. She was overwhelmed with fatigue. She repented for the sins committed by herself. Wandering in the lonely forest, it was only by chance that she came there.

42. Externally she had been oppressed by the summer heat. Internally she was afflicted with worries and anxieties. On seeing her affected by miseries, great sympathy surged in me.

43. Water, wild fruits and raw flesh were given to her by me. O Brāhmaṇa, when her exhaustion subsided, she was asked by me as to the real state of affairs.

44. She told me about her history. O great sage, listen to that; (She said :) "I am born of a Niṣāda family and (am known) by the name Avakokilā.

45-46. I am the daughter of Dāruka. I was a resident of the Vindhya mountains. I was forsaken by my kinsmen condemning me—"She is an unchaste woman. She always loots wealth and assets of others. She is a perpetual back-biter.". Though censured by the world, I was maintained by my husband for some time.

47. Unfortunately, he too went to the world of Yama, leaving me here. In the lonely forest, I am roaming about alone and am afflicted by misery.

48. By chance, I have come near you. I have been brought back to life by you now. Thus, she recounted to me all of her activities.

49. Thereafter, for ten years, we two stayed in that temple as husband and wife, with flesh and fruits constituting our diet.

50-51. Once, O sage, we became much intoxicated due to the drinking of wine. At night, there in the temple, we were so overjoyed by eating meat that we began to dance, utterly deluded and (blissfully) unconscious of our bodies and garments. At that time, the last stage of our experiencing the fruits of our past acts, the activities that had begun to bear fruits, befell us both at the same time.

52. Even as we were absorbed in our dance, the terrible emissaries of Yama came there, armed with their nooses in order to take us to the terrible torturesome hell of Yama.

53-54a. O bestower of honour, thereafter, the Lord who was pleased with our services, namely the scrubbing and cleaning of the lord's abode, and who was always interested in protecting his own devotees, sent his angels.

54b-56a. Each of those emissaries of the Lord of Devas wielded a conch, a discus and a mace (in their hands). All of them resembled a thousand suns in refulgence. All of them had four splendid arms. Wearing crowns, ear-rings necklaces and garlands of sylvan flowers, they made all the quarters free from darkness by means of their lustre, O Brāhmaṇa.

56b-57. The followers of Kṛṣṇa spoke to the servants of Yama who were terrible with their curved fangs, had nooses in their arms and were attempting to capture us.

Viṣṇu's Emissaries said :

58. O ruthless ones, O wicked ones devoid of discrimi-

nation, leave off the sinless couple who are beloved of Hari.

59-60. In the three worlds, it is discrimination that is the first cause of riches and prosperity. Know him to be the meanest of person, who regards a non-sinner to be sinner. Know that person to be the meanest of the mean, that person who considers a sinner to be a non-sinner.

Yama's Emissaries replied :

61. Truth has been mentioned by you all. But these two are the most notorious among sinners. Sinners must be punished by Yama. Hence, we shall take them away.

62. That which has been enjoined in the Śrutis is the *Dharma*. *Adharma* is the opposite of the same. This is the way to distinguish between *Dharma* and *Adharma*. Hence, we will take them to Yama's presence.

63. On hearing this, the exceedingly powerful emissaries of Viṣṇu became infuriated. They spoke in reply to the soldiers of Yama who were considering *Adharma* to be *Dharma*.

Viṣṇu's Emissaries said :

64. Alas ! It is pitiable that *Adharma* affects the assembly of the seers of *Dharma*. The diagnosis of those lacking in discrimination is a great calamity.

65. Why do you, who have been reduced to preside over hells, still exert to commit more sins by means of a special argument today ?

66. Even the great sinners remain in the terrible hell till their sins have been exhausted as long as the sun, the moon and the stars shine.

67. Without seeing the expiation of sins accumulated before, why do you commit sins again and again ?

68. What is enjoined in the *Śrutis* is the *Dharma*. True. Undoubtedly it is true. But we will relate precisely the virtuous acts performed by these two.

69. These two are absolved from sins because they were engaged in serving Hari. They are being protected by Hari. Hence, without any more delay leave them off.

70. At the time of death, she performed a dance (before Lord Viṣṇu) and he installed the banner in the abode of Viṣṇu. Hence, they have attained freedom from sins.

71. Either by bearing or by uttering his name even for once, at the time of death, one attains the greatest abode. What then if one is engaged in service of that Lord ?

72. Though he be vitiated with great sins or minor sins, a man who serves Kṛṣṇa, attains the greatest goal at the end.

73. O messengers, those who are engrossed in the service of ascetics or the devotees of Viṣṇu instantaneously attain the supreme goal, even though they be sinners.

74. He who stays in the temple of Hari even for a *Muhūrta* (48 minutes) or half that time, goes to the geatest abode (Vaikuṇṭha). What then of a person who has stayed for thirty-two years ?

75. These two had been engaged in sweeping and cleaning and smearing in the abode of Hari. They had been looking after its maintenance by repairing the decay and the ruins.

76. They had been sprinkling water and they had lighted lamps in Hari's abode. How can these blessed ones deserve the experience of tortures in the hell ?

77. After saying this and cutting off our bonds, the emissaries of Viṣṇu took us in an excellent aerial chariot and went to the greatest region of Viṣṇu.

78. O leading sage, there we attained the *Sāmīpya* (nearness) of the discus-bearing Lord of Devas. We enjoyed the exquisite divine pleasures throughout that period.

79. After enjoying the divine pleasures there, we came back to this earth. Here also, our wealth is incomparable due to the grace of service to Hari.

80. O sage through services rendered to Hari without entertaining any special desire for return, such a fruit has been attained which is difficult to access even to Devas, O Brāhmaṇa.

81. We shall attain the greatest elegance and welfare by propitiating Mahādeva the Lord of the Universe (by offering service for some object) willingly and with devotional feelings. For this purpose, the cause (of our prosperity etc.) is explained.

82. If any holy rite, performed by one due to helplessness, bears great fruit, O leading Brāhmaṇa, what doubt is there that a rite performed with faith becomes so ?

83. On hearing what has been thus narrated, the leading

sage Vibhāṇḍaka[2] praised the couple and went back to his penance grove.

84. Hence, O celestial sage, know that the service of the discusbearing lord of Devas is remembered as something comparable to the wish-yielding cow.

85. To those who are devoted to the worship of Hari, it is eternal Hari himself who grants the highest beatitude. He is the bestower of all desired benefits.

86. He who reads or listens to this meritorious narrative, that is destructive of all sins, attains the greatest goal.

CHAPTER TWENTY

The Legend of King Sumati

1. Sumati (a person with excellent intellectual capacity) is a popular name in Purāṇas. The *Puranic Encyclopaedia* records Sumatis, male, female, kings, sages, demons (p. 763) but this Sumati in the NP. is a different person. As this legend is given to illustrate the efficacy of the merit in hoisting a flag on the temple of Viṣṇu and is not found elsewhere, it is presumably a new contribution of the NP.

2. Vibhāṇḍaka—A sage born in the family of Kaśyapa; a member of Indra's assembly. He was the father of the Vedic scholar Ṛṣya-Śṛṅga who married Rāma's sister Śāntā. (*Mbh. Vana,* ch.110-113; *VR.I. Sarga* 9 & 10).

CHAPTER TWENTY-ONE

The Pañca-rātri-Vrata

The Holy Rite of Five Nights

Sanaka said :

1. I shall tell you another *Vrata* which is the excellentmost in all worlds. It is well known as *Hari-Pañcamī*.[1] Listen accurately to its essential nature.

2. O excellent sage, it is conducive to the removal of all miseries of men and women. It is the primary cause of righteousness, wealth, love and liberation.

3-4. It is the bestower of all desires and it grants the benefit of all *Vratas*. On the *Daśamī* (tenth) day in the bright half of the month of Mārgaśīrṣa, the devotee, keeping under control his sense-organs, should take his bath after brushing his teeth. After performing the worship of the Lord duly, he should perform the five great *Yajñas*.[2]

5-6. On that day he should observe all the rules (of religious discipline) and take food only once. O leading sage, on the *Ekādaśī* (eleventh) day, he should get up early in the morning and take his bath. According to the prescribed manner, he should worship Hari in his abode. He should bathe the Lord the chiefs of Devas, in *Pañcāmṛta* duly.

7. With great devotion he should worship him, according to the prescribed order, with scents, fragrant flowers and other things, incense and lamps, food offerings, betel leaves and circumambulations.

8-9a. After worshipping the Lord of the chiefs of Devas, he should utter the following *Mantra* : "Obeisance to you, the embodiment of perfect knowledge. Salutations be to you, the bestower of knowledge. Bow to you, abiding in all forms, to one who bestows all *Siddhis*. (Super-human powers).

9b-11a. After bowing thus to Vāsudeva, Janārdana, the Lord of Devas, he should dedicate the fast to the Lord with the following *Mantra*, "At thy behest, O Keśava, I shall observe fast for five days beginning from today. O Lord of the universe, be the bestower of my desires."

11b-12a. After dedicating the fast thus, he should control his sense-organs. O Brāhmaṇa, on the night of the *Ekādaśī* day, he should remain awake.

12b-13. O sage, the worship of Viṣṇu must be conducted thus, on the Twelfth, Thirteenth, Fourteenth and on the full-moon days. He must keep awake during the nights of *Ekādaśī* and the full moon day.

14. The worship by means of *Pañcāmṛta*, etc. is common to all five days. On the full moon day, he should bathe Viṣṇu in milk according to his capacity. *Homa* should be performed with sesamum seeds. Gift of the sesamum seeds should also be made.

15. On the sixth day, he should perform all rites befitting his stage in life (i.e. householders'), take in *Pañcagavya* and duly perform the worship of Hari.

16. He should then feed the Brāhmaṇas without any restriction, if he has the means. Thereafter, restrained in speech, he should take his food along with his kinsmen.

17. O Nārada, men should thus perform the holy *Vrata* in accordance with the injunctions mentioned before, in the bright halves of the months from Pauṣa to Kārttika.

18. Thus the *Vrata* which is destructive of sins, should be performed for one full year. When the month of Mārgaśīrṣa comes again, the performer of the *Vrata* should perform the *Udyāpana* (concluding) rites.

19. On the *Ekādaśī* day, he should fully abstain from taking food as before. O Brāhmaṇa, with due reverence and attention, he should take in *Pañcagavya* on the *Dvādaśī* day.

20. After duly worshipping the Lord of Devas with scents, fragrant flowers and other things, the devotee who has conquered his sense organs should offer the following present to a Brāhmaṇa.

21-22. (The present is :) Milk-pudding mixed with honey and ghee. It should be accompanied with fruits, O leading sage, to a Brāhmana who is a learned scholar in spiritual topics; he should offer a jar filled with scented water along with the usual Dakṣiṇā. The water-jar should contain five precious stones within it and be covered with a cloth.

23. (Mantra) "O *Ātman* of everything, O Lord of all living beings, O Omnipresent and eternal deity Mādhava, be pleased with this gift of *Paramānna* (rice boiled in milk)."

24. Repeating this Mantra, he should present the milk pudding. Thereafter, according to his capacity, he should feed the Brāhmaṇas. Restrained in speech, he should himself take food in the company of his kinsmen.

25. He who performs this *Vrata* called *Hari Pañcaka* never returns from Brahmaloka.

26. O Brāhmaṇa, this excellent *Vrata* must be performed by those who wish for salvation. It is like the conflagration unto the forest of all sins.

27. From this *Vrata* of fasts, men obtain that benefit which one attains after giving thousands and crores of cows.

28. He who is devoted to Nārāyaṇa and listens to this narrative, is liberated from millions of extremely terrific sins."

CHAPTER TWENTY-ONE

Hari-Pañcaka Vrata

1. *Hari-pañcamī* or *Pañca-rātri-vrata* as stated in the colophon, is not recorded in Kane's HD.V.1 in the list of *Vratas* (ch.XIII pp.251-462). It is called Hari-Pañcaka as it extends for five days from the Daśamī day to the Full-moon day. One should start to observe it from the month of Mārgaśirṣa on the 10th day of the bright half. The usual procedure of fast, worship, keeping awake (on the 11th and 15th day of the bright half) are common to all such fasts. It is to be observed every month for one year. In the concluding rite (*Uddyāpana*), a pitcher of water with five precious stones deposited in it, is to be given to a Brāhmaṇa, expert in spiritual knowledge. Rice-pudding mixed with honey and fruits are also to be offered. As usual, Brāhmaṇas (the number to be limited according to one's financial capacity) are to be fed after which one is to break fast (in silence) in company of one's kinsmen.

2. *Pañca-mahāyajñas*

Five 'great sacrifices'—The term is applied to the five daily 'sacrifices' or acts of piety to be performed by a householder. They are : *deva-yajña* (offerings in fire), *pitṛ-yajña* (*Tarpaṇa*, etc. to ancestors), *bhūta-yajña* (offering of *bali*—a ball of food to beings). *manuṣya-yajña* (giving food to a Brāhmaṇa) and *Brahma Yajña* (study or recital of Veda or at least one *mantra* (*Tait. Āraṇyaka* II.10). They are called 'great *yajñas*' or 'great sacrificial sessions' eulogistically. The term *yajña* as applied to these five daily duties, is figurative and the term *mahā* is laudatory (*Āpastamba Dh.S.*I : 4.12.13-1 also *Baudhāyana Dh.S.* II.6.1-8).

CHAPTER TWENTY-TWO

The *Māsopavāsa*[1] *Vrata* (Fast for a month)

Sanaka said :

1. I shall describe another excellent *Vrata* which is destructive of all sins, meritorious and rendering benefitial service to all worlds. Listen to it, attentively.

2. O Brāhmaṇa, one should perform this holy observance in the month of Āṣāḍha or Śrāvaṇa or Bhādrapada or Āśvina.

3. In one of these months, during the bright half, the devotee who has subdued his sense-organs, should take in *Pañcagavya* and sleep in the vicinity of Viṣṇu.

4. Getting up early in the morning and finishing the daily routine tasks, he should worship Viṣṇu with due faith and full control of his sense-organs, eschewing all forms of anger.

5. In the company of learned man, he should worship Viṣṇu in the proper manner. Thereafter, after invoking the blessings by the recital of *Svasti-sūkta* (RV.V.51.11-15), in the specific religious rite, he should perform the rite of *Saṁkalpa* (revelation of intention).

6. O Keśava, from this day onwards, I shall observe fast for a month. I shall perform *Pāraṇā* (breaking the fast) rite at the end of the month, O Lord of Devas, at thy behast.

7. Obeisance to thee, O embodiment of penance, O bestower of the benefit of austerities. Bestow what fulfils my desires. Ward off all obstacles.

8. After dedicating thus, the splendid *Māsa Vrata* (i.e. *Māsopavāsa*) to Lord Viṣṇu, he should stay in the shrine of Hari, till the end of the month.

9. Everyday he should bathe the Lord in *Pañcāmṛta* in accordance with the injunctions. During that month he should continuously retain the light of the lamps in the shrine of Hari.

10. Everyday he should chew the tooth-brush twig taken from the *Apāmārga* plant (*Āghāḍā* in Marathi). Then he should take his bath as per prescribed injunctions and be devoted to Nārāyaṇa duly.

11. Thereafter, he should bathe the Viṣṇu image as before. Exerting himself as described before, he should worship the Lord. Endowed with piety, he should feed the Brāhmaṇas according to his capacity and offer the usual *Dakṣiṇā*.

12. With his sense-organs under proper control, he should take food along with his kinsmen. Thus, the performer of the Vrata should complete thirteen monthly fasts.

13. At the end of the year, he should make the charitable gift of a cow along with the usual Dakṣiṇā, to a Vedic scholar. Therein, he should feed twelve Brāhmaṇas in accordance with the injunctions. He should offer Dakṣiṇās according to his ability. Ornaments also should be given to the Brāhmaṇa lady.

14. He who performs three-monthly fasts with full restraint on the sense-organs attains twice the benefit of "Aptor-yāma" sacrifice (a Soma sacrifice).

15. O excellent sage, if four times the monthly fasts are performed successfully to their concluding break-fasts called a **Pārāka*[2], he shall attain the great merit usually derived from eight *Agniṣṭoma* sacrifices.

16. If this *Vrata* is performed five times by any noble devotee, that man shall attain twice the merit accruing from Atyagniṣṭoma sacrifice.

17. He who performs six monthly fasts with great concentration of mind and mental purity attains eight times the benefit of *Jyotiṣṭoma* sacrifice.

18. Remaining without food, a person who deserves the vow of monthly fasts, seven times, attains eight times the benefit of a horse-sacrifice (*Aśvamedha*).

19. O leading sage, he who performs the monthly fasts eight times, shall attain five times the benefit of sacrifice called *Naramedha* (Human sacrifice).

20. The man who performs monthly fasts nine times, derives three times the merit accruing from *Gomedha* sacrifice (cow sacrifice).

21. O excellent sage, he who performs the monthly fasts

*A misprint for *Parāka*. *Bṛhan-Nāradīya* XX.19 has the following verse on this topic (the same as in NP.) *catuḥ-kṛtvaḥ kṛtaṁ yena parākam muni-sattama / sa labhet Paramam puṇyam agniṣṭomāṣṭa-sambhavam //*

(called) *Parāka* ten times, enjoys three times the benefit of sacrifice called *Brahmamedha*.

22. He who, with controlled sense organs, performs eleven Parākas attains *Sārūpya* (identity of form) with Hari, along with the enjoyment of all pleasures.

23. The self-controlled person who performs thirteen *Parākas*, attains the greatest bliss after reaching which no one suffers any grief or misery.

24. Those who are engaged in monthly fasts, those who are devoted to ablutions in the Gaṅgā and those who expound the paths of *Dharma* are undoubtedly the liberated ones.

25. The monthly fasts must be observed by women having no husbands and sons, recluses, religious students and particularly by forest-dwellers (hermits).[3]

26. Whether a woman or a man, whosoever observes this excellent *Vrata*, attains salvation which is difficult to attain even by the Yogins.

27. On hearing this, everyone, whether he is a householder or a forest-dweller, or an observer of a vow or a mendicant, a fool or a scholar attains salvation.

28. He who, devoted to Nārāyaṇa, listens to or reads this meritorious narrative shall be liberated from all sins.

CHAPTER TWENTY-TWO

Māsopavāsa Vrata

1. *Māsopavāsa Vrata*

The observance of fast for a month is the greatest of all *Vratas*. The *Viṣṇu-rahasya* as quoted by Hemādri, in *CC* II, pp. 776-783 states that "The merit that accrues from observing all *Vratas*, from ablutions in all sacred waters, from all religious gifts and performance of all sacrifices like *Agniṣṭoma* and others with rich sacrificial fees, is gained by this *māsopavāsa* (Fast for one month). Before undertaking it, one should have performed all the Vaiṣṇava Vratas like Dvādaśī and other difficult penances like *Ati-kṛcchra*, *Cāndrāyaṇa* and others.

The NP., in its enthusiasm for extolling this *Vrata* commends even thirteen such fasts without taking into account the physical capacity of a human being to undergo sustained continuous fasting. The *Viṣṇurahaṣya*, however, wants to save the life of the observer of this Vrata first.

amṛtam pāyayet kṣīraṁ...yatheha na viyujyet prāṇaiḥ
Kṣut-pīḍito Vratī /

God Brahmā further ordains that when the observer of the *Vrata* faints or is very weak or in danger of life, he should be given milk, fruit juice, etc. and such in-take does not nullify or adversely affect the *Vrata*—

evaṁ māsopavāsastham ārūḍham prāṇa-saṁśaye
avrataghna-guṇair divyaiḥ parīpsed Brahmaṇājñayā /
naite vrataṁ vinighnanti /

This was such a popular *Vrata* that it is eulogised in *AP*. 204-1-18, *GP*.I.122. 1-7, *Pd.P*. VI.121.15-54. Though the main outline of the Vrata is practically the same in all Purāṇas, there are slight differences. Thus A P. prescribes its commencement on the 11th day in the bright half of Āśvina, but NP. states that it should be undertaken in Āṣāḍha, Śrāvaṇa, Bhādrapada or Āśvina (I.22.2-3). The remaining procedure : To sip *Pañcagavya*, sleep in the vicinity of the Viṣṇu image, *svasti-vācana*, *Saṅkalpa* (declaration of undertaking the vow) and prayer to god Viṣṇu to help the observer to complete the vow, offering worship to Viṣṇu three times with *Pañcāmṛta* every day, stay in Viṣṇu's shrine, to observe complete purity in word and deed, feeding thirteen Brāhmaṇas at the time of *Pāraṇā*, giving a bed-stead to one's preceptor, etc.—all is common in these texts.

This *Vrata* is also called *parāka* (see vv.15, 23 below).

This *Vrata* was observed even in ancient times. Inscriptions in Naneghat of the 2nd cent. B.C. records that queen Nayanika had observed it.

2. *Pāräka*

It is a misprint for *Parāka*, A kind of observance or penance—It consists of fast for twelve days (*dvādaśāhopavāsena parākaḥ*—GP.) or *dvādaśāham abhojanaṁ Parāko nāma Kṛcchro'yam* /

(*Manu* XI.215).

Bṛhan-Nāradīya XX also deals with Māsopavāsa-Vrata and has the same verses as in NP.XXII. Hence the correction as *parāka*.

3. House-holders are not eligible to undertake this fateful observance. This verse is common to other Purāṇas and the *Viṣṇu-rahasya*.

In verse 23 below the correct form 'Parāka' is used.

CHAPTER TWENTY-THREE

The Greatness of Ekādaśī Vrata

Sanaka said :

1. I shall describe another *Vrata* well known in all the three worlds, which subdues all sins and which bestows all the desired benefits.

2. O Brāhmaṇa, to those who perform this rite with devotion to Viṣṇu, (whether they are) Brāhmaṇas, or Kṣatriyas, or Vaiśyas or Śūdras or women, it bestows salvation. It is very pleasing to Viṣṇu.

3. The holy vow called *Ekādaśī Vrata*[1] (holy rite on the eleventh day) verily bestows everything that is desired by men. O Brāhmaṇa, it should be performed by all means, since it is very pleasing to Viṣṇu.

4. One should not take food on the Ekādaśī (eleventh) day in either of the fortnights (of a month). He who takes food, is a sinner in this world. In the other world, he shall fall into hell.

5. One who is desirous of attaining the benefit of the fast, should not take four meals, viz. the night meals on the previous (Daśamī day) as well as following (Dvādaśī day) and both the meals on the (*Ekādaśī*) day in the middle. (*vide* V.7 below).

6. The man who desires to take food on the *Ekādaśī* day is one who seeks the enjoyment of all sins. There is no doubt about this.

7. If anyone desires salvation, O leading sage, let him take only one meal on the *Daśamī* (tenth) as well as on the *Dvādaśī* (twelfth) day (in each fortnight). He shall fully abstain from taking food on the *Ekādaśī* (Eleventh) day (in both fortnights).

8. O Brāhmaṇa, whatever sins are there, such as Brāhmaṇa-slaughter, etc., they abide in the cooked food on the day of Hari (i.e. the *Ekādaśī* day).[2]

9. To sins of Brāhmaṇa-slaughter, etc., there may be some means of expiation (with difficulty). But there is no redemption for one who takes food on the *Ekādaśī* day.

10. If one is defiled by great sins or even if he is defiled by all types of sins, he attains the greatest salvation by refraining from food on the *Ekādaśī* day.

11. *Ekādaśī* is a highly meritoricus day, the most pleasing to Viṣṇu. By all means, it must be resorted to by Brāhmaṇas desirous of liberation from the worldly existence.

(*The Procedure of Ekādaśī Vrata*)

12. On the *Daśamī* (tenth) day, the devotee should get up very early in the morning (and should take bath) after duly washing the teeth. With purity and control over the sense-organs, he should duly bathe Viṣṇu and worship him (according to the prescription of the Śāstras).

13. On the *Ekādaśī* day, one should go without food and put curbs on the sense-organs. Devoted to Nārāyaṇa, he should go to bed in the vicinity of Viṣṇu.

14. On the *Ekādaśī* day, the devotee should take bath and worship Janārdana duly with scents, fragrant flowers and other things. Then he should repeat as follows :

15. "O Puṇḍarīkākṣa (Lotus-eyed God) after refraining from food today, the *Ekādaśī* day, I shall take food the next day, O Acyuta, be my refuge."[3]

16. After uttering properly this Mantra of the Discus-bearing lord of Devas, he should be contented in the mind, with emotional feelings and devotion, dedicate fast (unto the Lord).

17. Maintaining the observances and the holy rites, the devoted one should keep awake in front of the Lord, singing songs, playing on instruments and listening to *Purāṇas*.

18. Then, he should get up in the morning on the *Dvādaśī* day. After taking the bath duly, he should worship Viṣṇu keeping sense-organs under control.

19. After bathing Janārdana in *Pañcāmṛta* on the *Ekādaśī* day and in milk on the *Dvādaśī* day, O Brāhmaṇa, the devotee shall attain Sārūpya (sameness of form—a kind of liberation) with Hari.

20. "O Keśava, be pleased with the observance of this holy vow. Be pleased to be gracious-looking. Please be the bestower of the vision of spiritual knowledge to me, blinded as I am by the darkness of ignorance."[4]

21. O leading Brāhmaṇa, after requesting thus to Mādhava with attention and purity, he should feed the Brāhmaṇas according to his ability. He should then give the usual *Dakṣiṇā.*

22. He should thereafter perform the five sacrifices and devoted to Nārāyaṇa, restrained in speech, he should take food along with his kinsmen.

23. He who thus, with purity and self restraint, performs the observance called the holy *Ekādaśī* goes to Viṣṇu's abode, the return from which is rare.

24. A person engaged in the holy fast and absorbed in religious activities should never even cast a glance at *Cāṇḍālas* and fallen persons.

25. A person engaged in the holy observance of fast should never converse with atheists, with those who break the bounds of convention, the censurers and the back-biters.[5]

26. The observer of the holy rite should never talk to one who nourishes his progeny through a Śūdra woman, to the husband of a Śūdra woman and to one who performs sacrifices on behalf of those who are not eligible for the same.

27-28. One devoted to the holy observances of this fast should never honour the following even with words, viz.—the pander and the pimp, the professional musicians, one who partakes of the food of a professional worshipper of idols, the physician, the composer of poems, the opposer of Devas and the Brāhmaṇas, one who covets after other men's food and one who is interested in other man's wives.

29. Thus remaining pure by these restrictions and other means, the devotee maintaining the *Vrata* of fast should control himself and be devoted to the well-being of all. He shall then attain the highest *Siddhi.*

30. There is no other sacred water equal to that of the Gaṅgā; there is no other preceptor equal to one's own mother; there is no other deity equal to Viṣṇu and there is no greater austerity than the observance of fast.

31. No mother is equal to forbearance; no wealth is equal to renown; no acquisition is equal to perfect knowledge and no father is equal to righteousness.

32. No kinsmen is equal to the power of discrimination; no holy observance is superior to *Ekādaśī.* In this connection they cite this ancient ancedote.

33a. This is in the nature of a dialogue between Bhadraśīla and his father Gālava.[6]

33b. Formerly, there lived on the banks of the Narmadā, a sage named Gālava who was absolutely devoted to Truth.

34-36. He was a quiescent, self-controlled and a storehouse of austerities. He made his residence for a long time on the bank of the Narmadā which was full of many trees and was frequented by elephants and beers, and was attended by Siddhas, Cāraṇas, Gandharvas, Yakṣas and Vidyādharas. The place was full of bulbous roots, roots and fruits and was resorted to by groups of sages. Gālava had a son named Bhadraśīla who was self-controlled.

37-38. He was highly blessed and could remember his previous births. He was so devoted to Nārāyaṇa that even at the time of playing with boys, the highly intelligent Bhadraśīla used to make an image of Viṣṇu out of clay and used to worship it. He used to urge and enlighten his playmates saying, "Viṣṇu must always be worshipped by men.

39-40. The observance of the vow of *Ekādaśī* should be performed even by learned men". O leading sage, even those children, thus enlightened by him, made idols of Hari out of clay. Collectively and severally, those blessed ones, absorbed in Viṣṇu's devotion, used to worship that image joyously.

41. Making obeisance to Viṣṇu the all-pervading Lord, that boy of good intellect prayed : "May there be the well being of all the worlds."

42. In the course of the play, he used to allot a *Muhūrta* or half of it, conceiving that it was the *Ekādaśī* vow and used to dedicate it to Keśava.

43. On seeing his son with such a good conduct of life, sage Gālava, the storehouse of austerities, embraced him and asked him with great surprise.

Gālava said :

44. O highly-blessed Bhadraśīla,[7] a good observer of religious vows, you are (as implied in your name) a real *Bhadraśīla* (of auspicious conduct) since your conduct is auspicious and un-attainable even to the Yogins.

45-46. You are always devoted to the worship of Hari and are interested in the welfare of all living beings. Devoid of all forbidden activities, you are engaged in the observance of *Ekādaśī Vrata.* You are free from *Dvandvas* (mutually opposed pairs, such as pleasure, pain). You are devoid of the sense of 'My-ness'. You are serene and absorbed in the meditation on Hari. How did such an inclination originate in you, though you are but a child ? Hari's devotion is difficult to acquire without rendering service to the great ones.

47. O dear one, naturally the mind of the people is diverted towards *Avidyā* (Ignorance), *Kāma* (Passion) and *Karmans* (other activities). How is it that your activity has become extra-ordinary and supra-mundane ?

48. It is, due to the superabundance of previous merits, that men become attached to the saintly people and also devoted to the Lord. Hence I am surprised.

49-50. It is out of filial affection that I am asking you. It behoves you to explain it to me. On being urged by his father with these conjectures, Bhadraśīla, the leading sage, remembered his previous births. The meritorious soul, being delighted and with his countenance beaming with a smile, narrated to his father everything as it took place and was experienced by him.

Bhadraśīla said :

51. Listen, O dear father. I know what has been experienced before by me, O excellent sage, because of the faculty of remembering the previous birth. I understand what had been mentioned by Yama.

52. On hearing this, the highly blessed Gālava who was surprised said thus with delight to the highly intelligent Bhadraśīla.

Gālava said :

53. O blessed one, it behoves you to explain everything as to who you were formerly, what was told to you by Yama and what was its reason and basis.

Bhadraśīla said :

54. O dear father, formerly I was a king born of the lunar race. I was well known by the name Dharmakīrti.[7] I have been educated by Dattātreya.

55. For nine thousand years, I ruled over the entire Earth. Many evil deeds and virtuous acts were committed by me.

56. Thereafter, becoming intoxicated with the arrogance of wealth, I committed many sins. Due to association with heretics, my conduct became heresy-oriented.

57. Formerly many meritorious activities were pursued by me, but when influenced by heretics I gave up the Vedic path.

58-59. All the sacrifices were destroyed by me who was well-versed in fraudulant arguments. On seeing me engaged in evil and impious deeds, the subjects of my land pursued in wicked deeds continuously. One sixth of those demerits clung to me. Thus I was engaged in sinful deeds and was always indulgent in inordinate addictions.

60-61. On one occasion, engaged in hunting, I entered a forest. I was accompanied by my army. I killed different types of animals. Overwhelmed by hunger and thirst, I reached the banks of the river Revā. Exhausted and oppressed by the severe heat of the sun, I took bath in the Revā.

62-64. The army was not seen anywhere. I was alone and was much afflicted by hunger. In the evening some of the residents on the banks of the Revā who came there were engaged in the *Ekādaśī Vrata*. They were seen by me. I was without food. Unattended by the army, I was alone but in the company of those people, I kept awake that night.

65. I was fatigued due to a long journey. I had been afflicted with hunger and thirst. O father, hence after keeping awake that night I died.

66. Then I was bound by the soldiers of Yama who looked very terrific due to their huge curved fangs. Through a path rendered tedious and painful in many ways, I reached the presence of Yama. I saw *Samavartin* (god of Death) whose face was terrible due to the curved fangs.

67. Then Kāla (the god of Death) called Citragupta (the Chief Accounts Officer of human merits and sins) and spoke thus, "O learned one, tell me precisely, the learning and other attainments as well as the activities of this man".

68. O excellent one, Citragupta who was thus commanded by Dharmarāja, thought for a long time and then spoke as follows :

69. It is true that this man had been engaged in sinful activities. Still, listen, O king of righteousness, one who abstains from food on the *Ekādaśī* day is liberated from all sins.

70. On the day of Hari (*Ekādaśī*), on the charming banks of the Revā, he abstained from taking food. By observance of rites of fasting and keeping awake at night (on the *Ekādaśī* day), he became free from sins.

71. Whatever sins had been committed by him, though numerous, all of them have been abolished by the power of the fast.

72. Dharmarāja who was informed thus by the intelligent Citragupta prostrated himself before me like a staff. He was full of sympathy.

73. With devotional feelings, Dharmarāja worshipped me. Then he called all his soldiers and commanded them thus.

Dharmarāja said :

74. Listen to my words, O my emissaries, I shall tell you what is excellent and wholesome unto you. Do not bring those men who are engaged in the path of virtue anywhere near me.

75. Let go those persons who are engaged in the worship of Viṣṇu, are self-controlled and grateful, are devoted to the observance of *Ekādaśī Vrata*, have conquered their sense-organs and those who serenely pray thus continuously—"O Nārāyaṇa, O Acyuta, O Hari, be my refuge". Avoid them immediately.

76. O soldiers, avoid from a long distance those persons who repeat the names of God thus—"O Nārāyaṇa, O Acyuta, O Janārdana, O Kṛṣṇa, O Viṣṇu, O Lord of goddess Lakṣmī, O father of the lotus-born deity, O Śiva, O Śaṅkara". They are the benefactors of the entire world. They are quiescent. My jurisdiction does not cover them.

77. O emissaries, avoid always those who have dedicated all their actions to Nārāyaṇa, cherish devotion to Hari; those who are strictly confined to their conventional duties; those who serve their preceptors; those who grant gifts to the good and the deserving; who protect the indigent and are attached and engaged in the repetition of names of Hari.

78. O emissaries, avoid those who have no association with heretics, who are deeply devoted to Brāhmaṇas, covet

association with the saintly persons, those who render services to guests (*atithis*) (those who entertain the same conception of Śambhu and Hari) or those who consider Hari and Śambhu equal and those who render obligations to the people.

79. O soldiers, bring those sinners to my abode—those who have no taste for the nectar of Hari's stories, whose minds are not directed to the remembrance of Nārāyaṇa and those who are not delighted with the sprinkling with the water from the feet of leading Brāhmaṇas.

80. O emissaries, bring here those persons who are in the habit of reviling their parents, hate the people, whose activities are injurious to their own benefactors, who are greedy of temple-property and whose activities are detrimental to the public.

81. O emissaries, bring here the person who is averse to the observance of the holy vow of *Ekādaśi*, of fierce temperament, is engaged in slandering the world, who censures others, brings about the ruin of the village, is inimical to excellent men and is greedy of the riches of Brāhmaṇas.

82. Forcibly bring those big fools who turn their faces away from devotion to Viṣṇu, who never bow to Nārāyaṇa the protector of those who seek refuge in him and those men who never go to Viṣṇu's shrine and indulge in sins extremely."

83. When what had been recounted by Dharma thus was heard by me, I who was as if burning within myself due to remorse, remembered the despicable activities.

84. Due to my repentance for the evil actions, and listening to righteous ones, all my sins were completely wiped out there automatically.

85. Yama too bowed to me, since I was liberated even from the last traces of sins, and had attained similarity of form with Hari and was refulgent like a thousand suns.

86. On seeing this, the extremely terrible emissaries of Yama were astonished. They completely believed in what was related to them by Yama.

87. Thereafter, worshipping me duly, Kāla (god Yama) immediately despatched me to that greatest region of Viṣṇu, (teeming with hundreds of aerial cars).

88. O Brāhmaṇa sage, thanks to that holy observance,

I stayed in Viṣṇu's region along with crores of aerial chariots equipped with all objects of enjoyment.

89. After residing in Viṣṇu's region for thousands and hundreds of crores of *Kalpas,* I came down to Indra's region.

90. There too, I who enjoyed richly all pleasures, was bowed to by all Devas. After staying that much time (equal to that spent in Viṣṇu's region) in the heaven I came to the Earth.

91. Here too, I am born in the family of Viṣṇu's devotees, like you. O great sage, since I have the faculty of remembering previous births, I know all these events.

92. That is why I attempt to worship Viṣṇu along with the children. Formerly, I did not know that this was *Ekādaśī Vrata.*

93. Due to the faculty of remembering previous births, it has been understood by me now. In this world, this is the fruit of that act which has been done by me here.

94. O Lord, what doubt is there then in the case of those who perform *Ekādaśī Vrata* with great devotion? Hence, O leading Brāhmaṇa, I shall also observe this auspicious *Ekādaśī Vrata.*

95-96a. Everyday, I shall perform the worship of Viṣṇu too with a desire for attaining the greatest abode. Those men who devoutly perform *Ekādaśī Vrata* will find Viṣṇu's abode which bestows the greatest bliss."

96b-97a. On hearing thus the words of his son, sage Gālava was delighted. He attained the greatest satisfaction. He was extremely delighted in his heart.

97b-98a. (He said :) "My birth is fruitful. My family has been sanctified since you, one deeply interested in devotion to Viṣṇu, have been born here, in my house."

98b-99a. Thus delighted in mind, thanks to his son's activity, he enlightened him in the procedure of the worship of Hari.

99b-c. Thus, O excellent sage, everything has been precisely narrated to you by me succinctly (at some places) or in detail (at other parts). What more do you wish to hear?

CHAPTER TWENTY-THREE

The Greatness of Ekādaśī Vrata

1. This is one of the most important *Vratas* elaborately discussed in various Purāṇas and mediaeval digests on Dharma Śāstra such as *CC.* Kāla (pp.145-288), Mādhava's *Kālanirṇaya* (pp. 233-275), *Vratarāja* (pp. 361-475) and others. The *NP.* is quoted as an authority by most of them. Being one of the early texts, the procedure of this *Vrata* as given from verse 12 onwards is important. It is interesting to note that the rules of Ekādaśī followed by Gauḍīya Vaiṣṇavas and summarised from *Haribhaktivilāsa* by Prof. S. K. De in *Vaiṣṇava* Faith and Movement (pp. 371-75) have a close resemblance to those given in the NP. here. As is wellknown the *Nārada* is a Vaiṣṇava Purāṇa.

2. Quoted by Hemādri in *CC—Kāla,* p. 153, in Mādhava's *Kālanirṇaya,* p. 235.

3. Quoted in *CC* (on *Vrata*) I.P.1000, *Kālanirṇaya* quotes it from VP. (prob. *Varāha P.* 39.32) and instructs, "after uttering this *mantra,* the knower (devotee) should offer flowers from the cavity of his palms (*Puṣpāñjali*).

4. Quoted in *CC* (*Vrata*) I.P.1001 and *Dharma Sindhu,* p. 20.

5. Quoted in *CC* (*Vrata*) I.P.1008, cf. *Hārīta* : *Patitapākhaṇḍi-nāstikādi-sambhāsaṇānṛta-dyūtādikam upavāsadine varjanīyam* |

6. Gālava—sages of this name are mentioned in the *Aitareya Brāhmaṇa, Bṛhadāraṇyaka Up., Va.P., Br.P., Mbh., HV.* but none of them record that he had a son called Bhadraśīla (vide *P E* & Chitrava's *Prācīna caritra kośa* under Gālava.) This legend is probably a contribution of the NP. to illustrate the importance of the *Ekādaśī Vrata.* In NP. II. Chs. 3 ff, we have a long story of Rukmāṅgada about the importance of this *Vrata.* PE. also has no entry on 'Bhadraśīla'.

7. The episode of Bhadraśīla to illustrate the great efficacy of the Ekādaśī Vrata, seems to be an original contribution of the NP., as the legend is not found in other Purāṇas (*vide* P.E.).

CHAPTER TWENTY-FOUR

The Conduct of the Good and Approved usages[1]

Sūta said :

1. On hearing what was said by Sanaka regarding the merit accruing from Hari's day (i.e. Ekādaśī) which is incomprehensibly meritorious, the best of all Vratas, that subdues host of sins, the delighted son of Brahmā spoke again.

Nārada said :

2. O sage, expert in the interpretation of principles, everything concerning the narration of holy Vratas has been mentioned by you. It is highly meritorious and it bestows devotion to Hari.

3. O sage, now I wish to hear the rules of conduct prescribed for all castes and stages of life as well as the procedure for expiation.

4. O highly blessed one, adept in the interpretation of all principles, it behoves you please to explain it to me precisely and with great compassion and favour."

Sanaka replied :

5. "O prominent sage, listen how the immutable Hari who is affectionate to the devotees, is worshipped by those who are devoted to the conduct of life befitting different castes and stages in life.

6. I shall relate to you the arrangement of castes and stages of life as explained duly by Manu and others, as you are a devotee of Viṣṇu.

7. Those castes are said to be four, viz., the Brāhmaṇas, Kṣatriyas, Vaiśyas and Śūdras. Among these the Brāhmaṇa is the foremost.

8. The Brāhmaṇas, Kṣatriyas and Vaiśyas — these three are called *Dvijas* (the twice-born), because at first they are born of their mothers and later on, they are consecrated by means of sacred thread with due repetition of the *Mantras*

(which constitute the second birth). Thus twice-born-ness is attained by these three classes.

9. All holy rites and duties must be performed by these castes in accordance with the specific duties prescribed for their castes. By failing to perform the holy duties prescribed for one's own caste, one is called a heretic by learned men.

10. A twice-born, performing the holy rites and duties enjoined by his own *Gṛhya Sūtra* becomes blessed and contented. Otherwise, he will be fallen and excluded from all righteous activities.

11. The *Yuga dharma*[2] (virtuous activities specially pertaining to the particular *Yuga*) must be pursued by these castes according to propriety and relevancy. The customs and conventions of the different regions and lands must be followed as long as they are not repugnant to the rites and duties enjoined in the *Smṛtis*.[3]

12. One must strive to practise prescribed religious duties physically, mentally and verbally. One shall never do anything repugnant to the public and not securing the heaven, even if it is of a righteous nature.

13-16. There are certain activities righteous (in other Yugas) but learned men say that they are to be avoided in the *Kaliyuga*[4] viz. undertaking a sea voyage, carrying a (wooden or earthen) jar of water (by a householder i.e. renunciation of that stage of life), the marriage of the twice-borns with girls not belonging to their caste, begetting of sons through (dead) husband's brother, the slaughtering of animals in *Madhuparka* (respectful offering to a guest), offering flesh in *Śrāddhas*, the stage of life called *Vānaprastha* (forest-hermit), remarriage of a married girl when the marriage was not consummated, *Naiṣṭhika Brahmacarya* (life long celibacy), human sacrifice, horse-sacrifice, *Mahāprasthānagamana* (undertaking a long journey to end in death) *Gomedha* (cowsacrifice) as well as *Makhas* (sacrifices). These activities, though righteous in other *Yugas*, are declared as fit to be avoided in the Kaliyuga.

17. The peculiar conventions of the different lands must be followed by men of respective lands. Otherwise he (the dissenter) should be known as a fallen man, excluded from all religious activities (or social intercourse).

18. O excellent *Brāhmaṇa*, I shall mention in general

the holy rites of the Brāhmaṇas, Kṣatriyas, Vaiśyas and the Śūdras. Listen to it with attention.

19. (The duties of a Brāhmaṇa are :) He should offer charitable gifts to the Brāhmaṇas; he should worship the gods by means of sacrifices; for the sake of livelihood he may beg for alms; he should teach others.

20. He should perform sacrifices on behalf of those who are eligible for the same; he should perpetually offer water libations; he should learn the Vedas and maintain sacrificial fires.

21. He should have impartial conception of the acceptable wealth and that intended for others and should do what is conducive to the welfare of the world; he should speak softly.

22. The sexual intercourse of a Brāhmaṇa with his wife is commended only on the prescribed nights after the menstruation; he should never utter anything unwholesome and injurious to anyone; he shall be devoted to the worship of Viṣṇu.

23. (The duties of a Kṣatriya are) : O excellent Brāhmaṇa, a Kṣatriya should give charitable gifts to Brāhmaṇas, he should learn the Vedas; he should worship Devas by performance of sacrifices.

24. He should maintain himself by means of weapons (i.e. military profession); he should rule over the Earth righteously and should chastise and curb the wicked; he should protect the disciplined (the good).

25. O excellent Brāhmaṇa, breeding of cattle, commerce, agriculture and study of the Vedas are glorified as the duties of the Vaiśya also.

26. He should marry duly and practise righteous activities through wealth earned by means of business transactions or industrial activities.

27. A Śūdra also should give charitable gifts, but he should not perform domestic sacrifices involving cooking. He should render service to the Brāhmaṇas, Kṣatriyas and the Vaiśyas.

28-29. The following duties are common to all castes : every one should indulge in sexual intercourse with his own wife only on the prescribed nights after the menstruation; sincere desire for the welfare of all worlds, always speaking auspicious and pleasing words, absence of fool-hardiness, joyous temperament, forbearance, absence of over-arrogance, all these have been glorified as attributes common to all castes.

30. By performing the rites befitting one's own stage of life, everyone attains the status of a sage, O Brāhmaṇa. In times of emergency[5] a Brāhmaṇa may take to the conduct of life of a Kṣatriya.

31. In times of grave emergency, a Kṣatriya also may take to the activities of a Vaiśya. Even in times of very grave emergency, a twice-born person should not take to the activities of a Śūdra.

32-34a. If a twice-born person in a confused state of mind takes to it, he shall become a Cāṇḍāla. O excellent sage, in the case of the three castes, the Brāhmaṇas, the Kṣatriyas and the Vaiśyas, four *Āśramas* (stages of life) have been mentioned. There is no fifth stage of life. They are : (the stages of) the religious student, the householder, the forest-hermit and the mendicant, O good one. Excellent Dharma is achieved through these four *Āśramas*.

34b-35. O leading Brāhmaṇa, Viṣṇu is pleased with a person who is engaged in the path of action, whose mind is quiescent, free from desire, and is absorbed in his own duties. Thereafter, he goes to the greatest abode from which he does not return to this world.

CHAPTER TWENTYFOUR

The conduct of the Good and Approved Usages

1. The term *Sadācāra* is used in the sense of 'customs and usages'. The customs in Brahmāvarta were looked upon with great respect in Smṛtis and Purāṇas. But here the term means 'the conduct of the good'. VP. III.11.3 defines it :

Sādhavaḥ Kṣīṇa-doṣās tu sac-chabdāḥ sādhu-vācakāḥ |
teṣām ācaraṇaṁ yat tu sadācāras sa ucyate ||

This is attributed to Hārīta in *Parāśaramādhavīya* I.i.,p.144.

This topic is treated in many Purāṇas e.g. VP.III.Chs. 11 & 12, KP.II. chs. 16 and 19, AP.Chs. 155, 165, 253, Bh.P. VII.11, XI.17 & 18 to mention a few. In the NP. it is later described again in ch. I.43; overlapping and repetition of verses is expected in such a work, but a number of verses are common to many of these Purāṇas and are found in Smṛtis as well.

2. According to *Mbh. Śānti* 232.28, the principal aspects of religious life were : penance (*tapas*) in the Kṛta age; metaphysical knowledge in the Tretā, performance of sacrifices in the Dvāpara and *Dāna* (religious gifts) in the Kali age.

tapaḥ paraṁ Kṛta-yuge, Tretāyāṁ jñanam ucyate |
Dvāpare yajñam evāhur, dānam ekaṁ Kalau yuge ||

This verse is repeated in *Manu* I.86, *Parāśara* I.23 and *Va.P.* 8.65 substitutes *dhyānam* 'meditation' for *tapas* in the Kṛta age.

3. This sanction to customs is granted in the Sūtra period. For example, the Āśvalāyana sūtra gives its sanction to different customs belonging to different regions and villages in celebration of marriages :

(*Uccāvacā vai jānapadadharmā grāmadharmās tān vivāhe pratīyat |*

Aśv.Gr. S.

4. The general principle of *Sadācāra* is that if a religious practice though sanctioned by *Dharma Śāstra* is found abhorrent to the public taste, it should be avoided. (Verse No.12). Thus the sea-voyage involved pollution through contact with Mlecchas and hence was forbidden. The moral sense of the public abhorred the idea of *niyoga*, marrying a girl from a lower class, killing an animal for *madhuparka* (receiving a guest), offering meat or non-vegetarian diet to Brāhmaṇas at the time of Śrāddha, etc. and it came to be prohibited in the Kali Age. These four verses from the NP. (Nos.13-16) enumerate what acts are to be avoided in the Kali age. *Kali-varjya* are quoted in the *Nirṇayasindhu*, p. 367, *Aparārka*, p.15, CC.III.2, p.666, Sc.I.p.12, Parāśara Mādhavīya I.i p.133. The number of such forbidden acts differ with different texts. P.V. Kane in H.D.III.pp.930-966 enumerates 55 *Kali Varjya* acts—one-fourth of which are against the institution of sacrifice, ten are due to the public insistence on purity of women and two, viz., the prohibition against *Vānaprastha* and *Sannyāsa* give a blow to the ancient *āśrama-dharma*. The

wording "though righteous in other yugas" (verse 16) is just to show respect to the authorities which prescribed them. Kane's view that '*Kalivarjya* lists were put together at the earliest in the 10th and 11th century A.D.' needs modification in view of its occurrence in the NP.—unless we regard these verses as later interpolations.

5. Verses 30-33 deal with the *Āpad-dharma* The principle is that in times of emergency one should resort to the means of livelihood prescribed for the caste (*Varṇa*) which is immediately below one's own, *vide* Manu X.81-82. Yājña-valkya III.35, Viṣṇu Dh.S.54.28, but NP. insists that one should never follow Śūdra's vocation. When the emergency is over, the person following a 'lower' avocation should undergo expiation and follow his profession (Manu XI.193-194, Yājñavalkya III.35).

CHAPTER TWENTYFIVE

Vedic Studies and other Religious Duties Defined

Sanaka said :

1. I shall tell you specifically the precepts governing the disciplined conduct of life of the different castes and stages. Listen to it with attentive mind, O excellent sage.

2. He who eschews his own prescribed course of duties (*Dharma*) and pursues that of others should be known as a heretic and be excluded from all *Dharmas*.

3. Such purificatory ceremonies as *Garbhādhāna* (rite of religious consummation of marriage-impregnation) should be performed with due chanting of Mantras at the proper time and in accordance with the injunctions. To women these rites do not require the chanting of Mantras.

4. The first holy rite of *Sīmanta*[1] (ritualistic parting of the hair upwards, as a part of the purificatory rite during pregnancy) should preferably be performed in the fourth month. It can be performed in the sixth or the seventh or the eighth month also.

5. When the son is born, the father should take his bath along with the cloth worn and perform the post-natal holy rite. He should perform *Nāndī Śrāddha* with the formal prescribed utterance of benediction.

6. One should perform the *Vṛddhi-Śrāddha* (*Śrāddha* at the time when one has acquired special prosperity and glory) either with gold or with silver. He who performs it with cooked food shall be on a par with a Cāṇḍāla.

7. At the end of the *Sūtaka* (i.e. the period of pollution due to the birth of a child) the father should perform the *Abhyudayika Śrāddha* (i.e. *Śrāddha* due to prosperity) for the son, observing restraint in speech. He should indicate the name also.[2] (i.e. the naming ceremony is to be performed).

8. O leading Brāhmaṇa, the name given shall not be unclear, meaningless, or one with many long syllables. Nor shall it contain letters difficult to pronounce.

9. He shall perform the *Caula*[3], the rite of keeping locks

of hair—in accordance with the injunction in the *Gṛhya sūtras* in the third, fifth, sixth, seventh or eighth year.

10. If due to unavoidable situations, the *Garbhādhāna* and other rites are not performed in due course, the expiatory rite of one fourth *Kṛcchra* shall be performed. In the case of the *Caula* rite, it should be half a *Kṛcchra*.

11. The investiture with sacred thread for the boy should be in the eighth year after conception or birth.[4] Any time upto the sixteenth year is permitted as a subsidiary period (for the same rite in the case of a Brāhmaṇa).

12. The investiture with sacred thread in the case of a Kṣatriya is in the eleventh year after conception. (If not done in the eleventh year due to circumstances), learned men permit any time upto the twentysecond year.

13. The *Upanayana* rite of a Vaiśya is to be performed in the twelfth year after conception. Learned men say that the period (though allowed) upto the twentyfourth year, is subsidiary.

14. If the twiceborn is not invested with the sacred thread within these limits of time, know him to be *Sāvitrīpatita* (fallen from the sacred *Gāyatrī* or *Sāvitrī mantra*. No one should even converse with him.

15. O Brāhmaṇa, if the chief time limit is transgressed in the Upanayana of a twice-born, *Kṛcchra* penance should be performed for twelve years. Afterwards he should perform the *Cāndrāyaṇa* and two *Sāntapana Prāyaścittas* (expiations) and thereafter perform the original holy rite (i.e. *Upanayana*).

16-21a. Otherwise know him to be a fallen person. He who does so shall be on a par with a slayer of a Brāhmaṇa. The girdle of a Brāhmaṇa should be of the Muñja grass, that of Kṣatriya should be the bowstring and that of a Vaiśya should be woollen. May the deerskin (for wearing) be stated thus:—The skin of the *eṇa* deer should be used by a Brāhmaṇa; that of a ruru deer should be used by a Kṣatriya. A Vaiśya should use the skin of a goat. I shall describe the staff in due order:—The Palāśa stick is prescribed for a Brāhmaṇa; the Udumbara stick for a Kṣatriya and that of Bilva for a Vaiśya.

Now listen to their size :—The staff of a Brāhmaṇa should come upto his hair on the head; that of a Kṣatriya should come upto the forehead. Learned men say that the staff of a Vaiśya should come up to the tip of his nose.

I shall now describe the clothes of Brāhmaṇa and others in due order. They are ochre-coloured, madder-coloured (red) and turmeric-coloured (yellow) (respectively).

21b-22a. O Brāhmaṇa, the Brāhmaṇa who has been invested with the sacred thread should be devoted to the service of his preceptor. He should stay in the house of his preceptor till he learns the Vedas.

22b-23a. The (Brāhmaṇa) religious student should take bath in the morning. O leading sage, for the sake of the preceptor, the student should bring sacrificial twigs, *Kuśa* grass, fruits and other things, everyday in the morning.

23b-24a. O excellent sage, whenever the sacred thread, the deer-skin or the staff is lost, soiled or broken, a new one should be used with due repetition of the *mantras*. The soiled ones should be thrown into the water.

24b-25a. They (the religious authorities) prescribe that the means of livelihood of the religious student is only through alms begged and received by them. The student with controlled sense organs should bring the alms from the houses of Brāhmaṇas well-versed in Vedas.

25b-26a. When the Brāhmaṇa begs for alms he should say, *bhavati bhikṣām dehi* (O madam, give me the alms); the Kṣatriya should say, *bhikṣām bhavati dehi* (Alms, O madam, give me). When the Vaiśya begs, he should say *bhikṣāṁ dehi bhavati* (Give me alms, O madam).

26b. The religious student should conquer his sense organs and perform the rites of fire-worship both in the morning and in the evening according to convention.

27. The religious student should perform the *Brahmayajña* and the *Tarpaṇa* rite every day. He who forsakes the ritualistic fire-worship is called a fallen fellow by the learned.

28. He who does not perform *Brahmayajña* is called a slayer of a Brāhmaṇa. After rendering service to the preceptor, he should perform the worship of the deities.

29. Every day he should partake of the food got as alms only. Never should he take food given by a single man. The student who has conquered his sense-organs should bring alms from the houses of Brāhmaṇas of irreproachable character.

30a. After offering alms first to the preceptor, he should, with his permission, partake of it, remaining restrained in speech.

30b-32a. He should avoid wine, women, meat, salt, chewing the betel-leaves, cleansing the teeth, eating the leavings of foods of others, sleep during the day, use of the umbrella, wearing of shoes, scents and unguents, garlands, sports in water, dance, vocal music, instrumental music.

32b-33a. He should abstain from slandering, distressing others, prattling (grumbling), application of collyrium, contact with heretic people, association with the Śūdras, etc.

33b. As to elders, he should habitually bow to and salute them in due order.

34-35. The elders are of three types, viz.—Elders in knowledge, elders in piety and austerity and elders in age. He who removes spiritual misery and the like is the (bonafide) *guru*. He does it through the instruction in the Vedas and the scriptural texts. The student should salute him at the outset. While saluting, the Brāhmaṇa should say *Asau aham* (I am he—so and so).

36-39a. The Kṣatriyas and others are by no means to be bowed to by a Brāhmaṇa. The following should not be saluted : An atheist, a person who breaks the bounds of decency, an ungrateful person, the common priest of the village, a thief, a rogue, a heretic, the fallen fellow, the *Vrātya* (one of the three castes fallen from his caste-position due to non-performance of holy rites), a professional astrologer, a sinner, who shall never be saluted, a mad man, a gambler, an unclean person, a person (who is) running, a person who has applied oil to his head and a person performing *Japa*.

39b-40. He should never salute a person always given to arguing, a fierce man, a person vomiting, a person standing in water, a person holding the alms and a person lying down. He should never salute a woman who had killed her husband, a woman in her menses, a woman with a paramour, a woman who has recently delivered of a child, a woman who had an abortion, an ungrateful woman, and a fierce woman.

41-42a. If individual salutation is made in an assembly, a sacrificial hall or a temple, it destroys the merit earned before.

42b-43a. He should not bow to a person who is performing a *Śrāddha, Vrata, Dāna,* worship of the deities, *Yajña* or *Tarpaṇa.*

43b-44a. If anyone does not salute in return when he is saluted, he is on a par with a Śūdra. He should not be considered worthy of being saluted.

44b-45a. The student should wash his feet and perform the *Ācamana* rite. Sitting face to face with the preceptor and touching his feet, the clever student should begin his study.

45b-50a. A Brāhmaṇa who is eager to attain the benefit of all holy rites should not pursue the study of the Vedas on the following days : during the holidays: viz. the first and eighth day (*Aṣṭakas*), the fourteenth day, the *Pratipats* (first day of a fortnight), the *Parvan* days, *Mahābharaṇī* day (when the moon is in Bharaṇī Nakṣatra in Pītṛ Pakṣa), on the twelfth day in the month of Śrāvaṇa, on the second day in the latter fortnight of the month of Bhādrapada, on the seventh day in the bright half of the month of Māgha, on the ninth day in the month of Āśvina, when the sun is encircled by a halo, when a Vedic scholar comes to the house, when a Brāhmaṇa is bound, when a quarrel increases, during the dusk, when the cloud rumbles, when there is an untimely heavy down-pour, when a comet or thunderbolt falls, when a Brāhmaṇa is insulted, O celestial sage, on the *Manvādi* days (i.e. on the days on which Manvantaras started) and the four *Yugādi* days (i.e. on the days on which the four yugas commenced)—these foregoing occasions are to be treated as holidays.

50b-51 The third day in the bright half of the month of *Mādhava* (i.e. Vaiśākha), the thirteenth day in the dark half of the month of Bhādrapada, the ninth day in the bright half of the month of Kārttika and the full moon day in the month of Māgha —these are said to be *Yugādi* days. Whatever is given in these days becomes everlasting in its benefit.

52-55. I shall mention the Manvādi days. Listen to it attentively; the ninth and the twelfth days in the bright half of Kārttika ; the third day of the Caitra month, as well as of the month of Bhādrapada; the tenth day of the bright half of Āṣāḍha, the seventh day in the bright half of Māgha, the eighth day in the dark half of Śrāvaṇa, the full moon day in the month of Āṣāḍha, the new moon day in the month of Phālguna, the eleventh day in the bright half of Pauṣa, the full moon days in the months of Kārttika, Phālguna, Caitra, and Jyeṣṭha—these are the first days of the *Manvantaras*; whatever is given on these days becomes everlasting in its benefit.

56-57. On the Manvādi and Yugādi days, Śrāddha should be performed by the twice-born; one should never study the Vedas during these days[5] — when one is invited to a Śrāddha, during the eclipse of the sun and the moon; on the two *ayana* days, when there is earthquake; on the *Galagraha* days (some days in the dark fortnight) and on *Durdinas* (when the sun is invisible due to clouds).

58-59. O Nārada, if a foolish person pursues the study of the Vedas during these holidays, Yama himself will destroy his progeny, intellect, renown, prosperity, longevity, strength and health. Know the person who studies the Vedas during the *Anadhyāya* days (holidays) to be *Brahma-ghātaka* (the slayer of a Brāhmaṇa).

60-65. O Brāhmaṇa, no one should hold conversation with him; no one shall reside with him; O Nārada, some persons say that even *Kuṇḍas* and *Golakas* (bastards) and the sluggish etc. should be invested with sacred thread; some say that their sons etc. should be invested with sacred thread. One who does not study the Vedas but puts forth effort elsewhere should be known to be on a par with a Śūdra; he is the beloved guest in hell. Even if a Brāhmaṇa who has not learned the Vedas follows the conventional conduct of life, he does not attain the benefit of the *Ācāras*. He is just like a Śūdra. In the case of a Brāhmaṇa who has not learned the Vedas the *Nitya*, *Naimittika*, *Kāmya* and all other *Vedic* rites are futile. Viṣṇu is identical with the *Śabda Brahman* (the supreme Soul in the form of Sound) ; hence Veda is Hari Himself. Hence, a Brāhmaṇa who studies the Vedas will attain his desires.

CHAPTER TWENTYFIVE

1. *Sīmanta-karma, Sīmanta* or *Sīmantonnayana* is really a rite of a social and festival nature expressing joy felt by the family and the woman concerned at the prospect of a child. Literally it means 'parting the hair of the woman, upward.' The Saṁskāra is treated in many *Gṛhya sūtras* like that of Āśvalāyana (I.14.1-9), Baudhāyana (I.10), Gobhila (II.7.1-12), Vaikhānasa (III.12) and others, but there is a great divergence in the details of this *Saṁskāra* showing the difference in the geographical region where they were composed. The garlanding of the pregnant girl and playing of lute and singing of ballads prescribed in the *gṛhya sūtras*, shows its festival nature. The month of pregnancy in which it is to be celebrated differs. NP. seems to follow Khādira Gr.S. in prescribing the 4th, 6th or the 8th month out of which the 4th is supported by Āśvalāyana and Āpastamba. In prescribing the 7th month, NP. follows Śāṅkhāyana Gr.S. (I-22-1) indicating NP.'s affinity if not location.

2. NP. is much removed in time from the *Bṛhadāraṇyaka Up.* and *Gṛhya Sūtras* of Gobhila, Khādira and others which prescribe that the name should be given to the boy on the day of his birth. It was to be the *Nakṣatra-nāma* which was to be kept a secret till the thread-ceremony of the boy and the name for common use was given on the 10th day.

3. *Caula or Cūḍākaraṇa* :

Most writers recommend the 3rd year for this rite but Āśvalāyana, Pāraskara, Yājñavalkya allow the family usage for the time of performance of this, though they don't disapprove of the 3rd year.

4. This is clearly an exposition of *Āśvalāyana Gr.S.* regarding the usual and the final limit of the age of the thread ceremony of the three varṇas :

aṣṭame varṣe Brāhmaṇam upanayet |
Garbhāṣṭame vā | ekādaśe Kṣattriyam |
dvādaśe Vaiśyam | ā ṣoḍaśād Brāhmaṇasyānatītaḥ Kālaḥ |
ā dvāviṁśāt Kṣattriyasya | ā caturviṁśād Vaiśyasya |

Āśva Gr.S. I.19.1-6.

5. The topic of holidays or days on which the Veda should not be taught, is discussed in the Gṛhya and Dharma Śūtras and most of the Smṛtis. A reference to SC. on *Anadhyāya* (I.pp.56-61) shows the difference of opinion among these authorities. Many of the verses in NP. are found in VP.III.14.13 ff, *Mt.P.*17.4-8, *M. Nṛsiṁha P.* ch.56. The list of holidays is stupendous. But the *anadhyāya* is limited to learning (new) Vedic *mantras* and not to their application or self study (*Jaimini* XII.3.18-19, *Āpastamba Śrauta Sūtra* 24.1.37. Hence, normal studies of other lores were not affected.

CHAPTER TWENTYSIX

The Statement of the Dharma of the Householder[1]

Sanaka said :

1. As long as the Vedas are being learned, he (the religious student) should remain with the preceptor, rendering service to him with purity invariably. After being permitted by him (to return to his house), he should take up the sacrificial fires.

2. A twice-born person should study the Vedas, the Dharma-śāstras (i.e. Smṛtis, etc.) and the Vedāṅgas (accessories to Vedic studies)[2] and give *Dakṣiṇā* to the preceptor and then enter the householder's life.

3. A twice-born should marry a virgin who is endowed with good features and beauty, who is born of a good family, who possesses good qualities,[3] whose conduct and habits are good and who practises righteous activities.

4. The intelligent Brāhmaṇa should marry a girl beyond the seventh remove from his father and fifth remove from his mother; otherwise he is on a par with the defiler of the preceptor's bed.[4]

5. A sensible man should not marry a girl who is sickly, whose eyes are round, who is born in a family of ailing persons (i.e. with unhealthy heredity), who has too much of hair or who has no hair at all or who is garrulous.[5]

6. A wise person should not marry a girl who is hot-tempered, too short or too tall (in stature), who is wanting in any limb, who has an extra limb (i.e. physically handicapped or abnormal), who is mad, or slanderous.

7. One should not marry a girl with heavy, big ankles or long shanks or has masculine features with traces of moustache and beard and is hunchbacked.

8. A prudent person should not marry a girl who laughs without reason, who stays in others' houses always, is habitually contentious, wayward and ruthless.

9. A sensible man should not marry a voracious girl, whose teeth and lips are too large and thick, who snorts and

grumbles, who is very dark or red in complexion, or who is cunning and mischievous.

10. One should not marry a girl who is always given to weeping, is of pallid complexion, who is despicable, a chronic patient of cough and Asthma or of somnolent nature.

11. A sagacious man should not marry a girl who habitually speaks worthless and meaningless words who is interested in antagonizing the world, who is in the habit of scandalising others or is a thief.

12. A worldly-wise man should by no means marry a girl whose nose is too long, who is a liar and a cheat, whose body is covered with hair, who is arrogant or a religious hypocrite.

13. If the marriage had taken place during childhood when the real nature had not been realised and if her defect is realized after maturity, he should by all means forsake her.[6]

14. If any woman is always harsh and ruthless to the husband and children but is favourably disposed towards others, he (the husband) should by all means forsake her.

15. O excellent sage, it should be known that marriages are of eight types such as the *Brāhma*,[7] etc. The previous one should be understood to be better than the latter one; if the preceding form of marriage is not possible the latter one may be adopted.

16. The eight types of marriages are : the Brāhma, Daiva, Ārṣa, Prājāpatya, Āsura, Gāndharva, Rākṣasa and Paiśāca which is considered the eighth one.

17. O Brāhmaṇa, an excellent Brāhmaṇa should be united in wedlock by means of the *Brāhma* form of marriage or by means of *Daiva* type. Some recommend the *Ārṣa* type also.

18. O Brāhmaṇa, the five types of marriage beginning with the *Prājāpatya* are censurable. If the earlier types are not possible, (then only) a wise person should adopt the latter ones.

19. (After marriage) he should wear two sacred threads, the upper garment and two golden ear-rings. The two clothes (he wears) should be well washed and white.

20. He should smear his limbs with unguents. Hair and nails must be well cut. He should remain pure and clean. He shall hold a bamboo stick and a *Kamaṇḍalu* filled with water.

21. He should appear neat and pleasing. He should put

on a clean turban, an umbrella and two neat sandals or shoes. He should wear flower garlands too and apply sweet scents.

22. He should regularly read and study the Vedas and maintain the religious and prescribed (or conventional) conduct of life. He should not subsist on others' food. He should avoid rumour-mongering.

23. He should not keep one leg mounted over another nor should he step across the leavings of food. He should not scratch his head with the combined pair of his hands.[8]

24-25. A twice-born person should not go anticlockwise round a temple worthy of worship. He should not keep his tresses untied during the worship of deities, *Ācamana* rites, ablutions and Śrāddha and other holy rites. Nor shall he be in a single cloth on these occasions. He should not ride in a vehicle drawn by a camel and he should avoid vain and groundless arguments.

26. He should not carnally approach another man's wife, and should avoid backbiting. O Brāhmaṇa, he should never go anticlockwise round cows, holy fig-trees, fire and mountains.

27. Nor should he go round the four-cross roads, a holy fig-tree standing on a sacred spot, a natural lake or a king, in that manner. He should avoid jealousy, rivalry and diurnal slumber.

28. He should not speak about other men's sins nor should he boast about his own merit. (He should not reveal his merit). He should keep his own name, the constellation (at the time of his birth) star and honour well-protected.

29. A twice-born should never live in the company of wicked men nor should he pay heed to anything contrary to the scriptural texts. He should never be interested in wine-drinking, gambling and low music.

30. If he touches a wet bone, leavings of food, a Śūdra, a fallen man, a serpent or a dog, he should bathe along with the clothes he is wearing.

31. After touching the funeral pyre, a piece of wood thereon, the sacrificial pole, a Cāṇḍāla and a professional worshipper of idols, he should plunge into water along with the clothes he is wearing.

32. The shadow of the lamp, cot or a body (one's own body ?), the water dripping from the hair, clothes, or a mat

and the dust particles kicked up by a goat or a cat or blown off from a broom—all these remove auspicious fortune.

33. One should avoid even from a distance, the wind from the winnowing basket, the smoke from the burning corpse, eating the cooked food of a Śūdra and the contact with the paramour of a Śūdra woman.

34. He should always avoid musing over heterodox doctrines, biting the nail and hair and going to sleep in a nude state.

35. He should not apply over the body the oil that is left over after applying on the head; he should not chew unclean betel leaves; he should not wake up a sleeping person.

36. No unclean person should perform rites in (sacrificial) fire or worship the preceptor and deities. No one should drink water with the left hand only applied to the mouth.

37. O leading sage, no one should tread on the shadow of his preceptor, nor should one transgress the command of his preceptor or censure the Yogins, the Brāhmaṇas, the ascetics and those who observe sacred vows.

38. Brāhmaṇas should not expose or speak of mutual defects and weaknesses. He should duly perform the sacrifice on the new moon and full moon days.

39. The worship and Homa should be performed by the twice-born both in the morning and evening. He who eschews *Upāsanā* (worship) is called a wine-addict by the learned.

40. A twice born house-holder should perform *Śrāddha*[9] during the tropical[10] and equinotical transit[11] of the sun, the four *Yugādi*[12] days, the new moon day and the *Pretapakṣa* (the fortnight of the dead i.e. the dark half of Bhādrapada).

41. O Nārada, a householder should perform *Śrāddha* on the *Manvādi*[13] days, on the day of death, during the *Aṣṭakā* days* (of the parents, etc.) and after the newly harvested grain had been brought home.

42. A householder should perform *Śrāddha*, when a person

---

*7th, 8th, 9th beginning from the seventh day after the full moon day or the 8th day of the dark half of Mārgaśirṣa, Pauṣa and Māgha on which Manes are to be propitiated). (HD, IV, p. 354).

well-versed in the Vedas visits the house, during the lunar and the solar eclipses and in holy centres and at pools of sacred waters.

43. If performed without the *Ūrddhva puṇḍra* (the vertical castemark on the forehead) the *Yajñas*, *Dānas*, (charitable gifts), austerities, *Homa*, study of the Vedas and the *Tarpaṇa* rite to the manes become futile.

44. Some people do not like to have *Ūrddhva puṇḍra* and *Tulasī* at the time of Śrāddha.[14] It is a futile convention and hence, it should be avoided by the Brāhmaṇas who seek welfare.

45. All these and similar holy rites enjoined in the path of Smṛtis shall be performed by the twice-born duly. They bestow the benefits of all holy rites.

46. Viṣṇu is pleased with those who are devoted to the conduct of good people. O excellent Brāhmaṇa, what is it that cannot be achieved if Viṣṇu is pleased.

CHAPTER TWENTYSIX

Dharmas of the Householder

1. Since the days of ancient Sūtra and Smṛti periods, the stage of householder (*Gṛhasthāśrama*) has been considered as the best *Āśrama*, as it is the support or source of all other *Āśramas* (Gautama III.3); also *vide* Manu (III. 77-78). *Mbh. Śānti.* (270.6-7) observes that like a mother, it helps other *Āśramas* to subsist; elsewhere (*ibid.*12.12) it states that it is equal in weight to all other *Āśramas* put together. Hence, Smṛtis, Purāṇas, digests on Dharma Śāstra deal in details with the duties of the house-holder. For example, Manu IV, Yājñavalkya I. 96-127, KP. II. Chs. 15 and 16, Mbh. Anuśāsana 97, SC. I. pp. 88-232.

2. This shows that the course of studies of the twice-born emphasized 'Humanities', viz. the study of the Veda (of his particular Śākhā) and its six accessories like phonetics, grammar, etymology (or Nirukta), Prosody and Astronomy (-cum-Astrology) and the Smṛtis or Dharma-Śāstra. Vocations and professions being hereditary, trades, commerce, technology or manual skills were learnt at their own homes, farms, work-shops or guilds.

3. Cf. *Buddhi-rūpa-śīla-lakṣaṇa-sampannām arogāṇīm upayaccheta* |

—*Āśvalāyana Gṛ. S.* I.5.3.

Echoed in Āpastamba Gr. S. III. 20.

Vātsyāyana quotes Ghoṭakamukha, "One should marry a girl who would give him a feeling of blessedness and compliments from his friends—*Kāmasūtra* III. 1-3.

4. This restriction on Sapiṇḍa marriage is an echo of *Nārada Smṛti* (xii. 7 Gurumandal edt.) :

ā saptamāt pañcamāc ca bandhubhyaḥ pitṛ-mātṛtaḥ |
a-vivāhyāḥ sagotrāḥ syuḥ samāna-pravarās tathā ||

The restriction indicates that the NP. was not written by a Southerner among whom cross-cousin marriages have been in vogue (even among the *Śiṣṭas*) as noted by *Baudhāyana Gr. S.* I. 1.19-26. Southern writers on Dharma-Śāstra like Devaṇṇa Bhaṭṭa (SC.I. pp. 70-74) and Mādhava (*Parāśara Mādhavīya* (I.2. pp. 63-68) stoutly defend and support marriage with maternal uncle's daughter.

5. VV.5-14 enumerate the defects of girls and advises against marrying them. A reference to Manu (III.8 and 10), Viṣṇu Dh. S. (24. 12-16), VP. III. 10.18-22 etc. shows that there was a consensus about the *doṣas* (defects) to be avoided in selecting a girl. Strangely enough, NP. does not quote from the *Nārada Smṛti* where the defects of girls are described (*Strī-puṁ-saṁyoga* 36) but echoes VP.III.10.16-22 quoting lines and phrases.

6. VV. 13 and 14 allow a husband to forsake his wife under certain circumstances.

But that is not a divorce—*a vinculo matrimonii* was not known to Hindu society in ancient and medieval times, though some low-castes had this custom.

7. VV. 15-18 describe the eight forms of marriage. They are : *Brāhma*, *Daiva*, *Ārṣa*, *Prājāpatya*, *Āsura*, *Gāndharva*, *Rākṣasa* and *Paiśāca*. These are mentioned in Gṛhya Sūtras, Dharma Sūtras, Smṛtis and Purāṇas (e.g. *Āśvalāyana Gr. S.* I. 6, *Baudhāyana Dh. S.* I. 11, Manu III. 21, *Nārada Smṛti Strī-Pum*-38-39, *VP*.III.10-24).

It is significant to note that NP. *differs* from the *Nārada Smṛti* in the arrangement of the list of these forms and follows the VP.

The *Nārada Smṛti* gives the following order of the forms of marriage : *Brāhma*, *Prājāpatya*, *Ārṣa*, *Daiva*, *Gāndharva*, *Āsura*, *Rākṣasa* and *Paiśāca*. NP. quotes VP.III.10.24. This further brings out the difference that the Smṛti approves of the *first four* forms as *dharmya* (sanctioned by or acceptable to Dharma) but NP. calls *Prājāpatya* as censurable (vide verse 18). *It indicates that Nārada, the writer of the Smṛti is not the author of the NP. who differs from him in many important respects.*

The description of the forms of marriage is given in Manu III. 27-34 and there is a general consensus on the characteristics of these forms of marriage which may be briefly indicated here.

(1) *Brāhma* : A daughter decked with ornaments is gifted to a Vedic scholar of good conduct after respectfully inviting him.

(2) *Daiva* : A daughter duly ornamented is given to a priest who officiates the performance of one's sacrifice (*Baudhāyana* I. 11.5 and Aparārka regards the girl as a part of *dakṣiṇā*.

(3) *Ārṣa* : Gift of a daughter in formal exchange of one or two pairs of cattle. (This is not a sale or barter but a legal formality).

(4) *Prājāpatya* : The gift of a daughter after duly honouring the boy (bride-groom) and addressing the couple, "May both of you practice religion".

(5) *Āsura* : Gift of a daughter in return for payment of maximum wealth to her and to her relatives.

(6) *Gāndharva* : Love-marriage. Marriage by the mutual consent of the girl and the bride-groom.

(7) *Rākṣasa* : Forcible abduction of a girl from her house while she weeps and cries and her kinsmen are defeated.

(8) *Paiśāca* : Intercourse with a girl while she is asleep, intoxicated, unconscious or mentally deranged.

8. The prescriptive and prohibitive rules of conduct in these verses (VV.23ff) reflect the then social tastes and etiquettes and as such are interesting from the sociological point of view. Some of these etiquettes and beliefs have survived till our times for over a millenium or so.

9. Verses 40-42 state the days and the times when Śrāddha should be performed. Here what were treated auspicious for *dāna* in ch. 25 above are recommended for Śrāddha :

10. *Ayana* days :

Days marking the beginning of the summer and winter solstice.

Viṣuva days :

11. *Viṣuva days*

The first point of *Aries* or *Libra* into which the sun enters at the vernal or autumnal equinox. Days marking these entries of the sun are called *Viṣuva days.*

12. Yugādi days—*vide supra* I.25.50-51.

13. *Manvādi days*—vide Supra I. 25.52-55.

Aṣṭakā days—*vide* footnote to the verse.

14. *The Smṛtyarthasāra* prescribes that *Tulasī* should be avoided at the time of Śrāddha. Devaṇṇa Bhaṭṭa notes it in *SC. Śrāddha*, p. 435, but he remarks that this dictum of prohibiting *Tulasī* in *Śrāddha* has no basis in *Smṛtis* (*prasiddha-Smṛti-samuccayeṣu Tulasī-niṣedhasyādarśanāt* |

CHAPTER TWENTYSEVEN

The Religious Duties of the Householders, Forest-Hermits and Sannyāsins

Sanaka said :

1. "O excellent sage, I shall describe to you the good conduct of life of the householder on observing which all his sins definitely perish.

Āhnika (Daily routine of duties)

2. O Brāhmaṇa, the householder should get up in the *Brāhma Muhūrta*[1] (i.e. within an hour and a half before the dawn). He should then arrange his tresses properly. He should then think about the means of livelihood that is not contrary to the aims of life.

3. He should pass urine or evacuate the bowels with the sacred thread placed on the ear. If it is during day or the two junctions of dawn and dusk, he should face the north and if it is in the night time, he should face the south (for answering calls of nature).

4. (While answering calls of nature)[2] the man should keep his head covered with a cloth, he should spread grass on the ground where he is going to answer calls of nature; he should hold a stick or a wooden piece in his hand and be silent during the whole period.

5-7. Neither urine nor fecal matter should be discharged in the following places : on the high way, in a cow pen, on the banks of a river, near lakes and houses, in the shade of a tree, in a dense forest, near fire, in a temple, in a garden, in a ploughed field, at the place where four roads meet, in the presence of Brāhmaṇas, cows and women, over husks, burning coal or broken mudpots and in water. No one should answer calls of nature in these and similar places.

8. Effort should always be made for the sake of purity; a Brāhmaṇa is remembered as one whose root is in cleanliness; every holy rite of one devoid of cleanliness and prescribed conventional conduct of life is in vain.[3]

9. Cleanliness is said to be of two kinds—the external and the internal. The external cleanliness is through clay and

water and the internal cleanliness is the purity of thoughts and emotions.[4]

10-11. After answering the call of nature he should hold the penis and get up. For the purificatory process he should bring good mud.[5] It should not be from holes dug up by rats and other rodents, nor from the ploughed field. No one shall take the mud from wells, tanks and lakes. One should carry out the purificatory process after bringing with effort good earth.

12. Learned men say that the cleaning process after passing urine is as follows : One part of the mud is applied to the penis and three parts over each of the testicles.

13. The mud is divided into many parts. One part is smeared over the penis, five parts at the anus and seven over the left leg and three over the right leg. Thus ten parts should be applied over the legs separately.

14. This is the purificatory process on discharging fecal matter so that the bad odour and the sliminess can be removed. Moreover this rite of cleansing is for the householder. In the case of religious students twice this is to be applied.

15. In the case of forest-hermits thrice this is to be applied and four times in the case of recluses (*Sannyāsins*). In one's own abode the full purificatory process is applicable. O excellent sage, while on a travel, half of this will do.

16. There is no hard and fast rule in regard to an ailing man; so also in times of grave emergency. A wise man should perform the *śauca* rite that dispels bad odour and sliminess.

17. To women without initiation, the purificatory rite is as long as the odour and sliminess are removed; but to every one who is observing a religious vow, the purificatory rite is like that of an ascetic.

The Ācamana rite

18-19. O leading Brāhmaṇa, in the case of widows too the same is prescribed. After finishing the purificatory rite with great attention, he should sit facing the east or the north and perform the *Ācamana* rite,[6] maintaining the purity of the sense organs, three times or four times he should drink water that has no odour, foam, etc.

20. O excellent one, he should wipe off the checks twice

with the palm and also the two lips. He should touch the two nostrils with the index finger combined with the thumb.

21. He should touch the eyes and the ears in order, with the thumb and the ring finger. The Brāhmaṇa should touch the umbilical region with the little finger in combination with the thumb.

22. The wise man should touch the chest with the palm and the head with the tips of the fingers. He should touch the shoulders with the palm or the tips of the fingers.

Brushing the Teeth

23. O leading Brāhmaṇa, after performing the *Ācamana* rite thus, he attains excellent purity. Thereafter, he should chew the tooth brush twig of some good tree.[7] It must have the bark in tact.

24-25. It may be taken from any of these trees : Bilva, Asana, Apāmārga, Nimba (Margosa), mango, or the sun plant. First he should wash the twig with water and then chant the following mantra : "O Vanaspati (tree), you instil in us longevity, strength, renown, splendour, progeny, animals, wealth, Vedic knowledge, intellect and sharp-wittedness."[8]

26-27a. The twig chewed by a Brāhmaṇa should have the thickness of the little finger and the length of ten *aṅgulas*, that of the *Kṣatriya's* tooth-brush should be nine *Aṅgulas* in length and in the case of a Vaiśya it should measure eight *aṅgulas*. O leading sage, the Śūdra should chew a tooth brush twig four *aṅgulas* in length, and so much in the case of a woman also.

27b-29a. If the tooth-brush twigs are not available, the purification of the mouth is effected through the process of gargling twelve times. Grasses and leaves also can be used. He should hold the twig with the left hand and chew at the outset with the teeth on the left side. He should scrub the teeth as long as the time taken to milk a cow. He should then wash it and split it into two pieces.

29b-30. The householder with the control of sense organs should scrape the tongue with those pieces. He should wash them and cast them off. Again he should perform the *Ācamana* rite as before and take his bath in clear water in a river, etc.

The rite of taking bath

31-32. He should wash the bank and place the Darbha grasses there before entering the water. He should bow down and invoke the holy waters from the solar sphere. O son of god Brahmā, he should make a mystic diagram with scents (sandal-paste), etc. and meditate upon Lord Janārdana. Remembering the holy Mantras and the sacred rivers, he should take this bath.[9]

The Mantra :

33-34. "O Gaṅgā, Yamunā, O Godāvarī, O Sarasvatī, O Narmadā, O Sindhu, O Kāverī, be present in this water. Always, at the time of my ablution, may the blessed sacred waters of Puṣkara, etc. and the rivers Gaṅgā, etc. come here.

35. The following seven cities should be known as the bestowers of salvation: viz. Ayodhyā, Mathurā, Māyā, Kāśī, Kāñcī, Avantikā and Dvārāvatī."

36. He should then perform the Japa of the Mantra, *Aghamarṣaṇa* (RV.X.190). After performing the *Prāṇāyāma* rite, he should plunge into the water. He should perform the *Tarpaṇa* rite as ancillary to ablution and then sip water in the *Ācamana* rite. Thereafter, he should offer *Arghya* to the Sun.

Sandhyā-Vandana (*The Twilight Prayer*)

37-38. O Nārada, meditating on the sun, he should come out of the water. He should wear a cloth that is fresh from the loom[10] (literally—unwashed) and cover himself with a second one that is washed. Sitting on a seat or mattress of Darbha grass, he should begin his Sandhyā rite.[11] He should face the north-east. O Brāhmaṇa, after the Ācamana rite, he should repeat the Gāyatrī.

39. The learned person should repeat the *Mantra* beginning with *Ṛtam* etc. (RV.X.190.1) and then perform the *Ācamana* rite. Thereafter, he should take some water in his hand, and encircle himself with it and sprinkle it up.

40-41. He should then perform the *Saṅkalpa* rite (viz. I perform morning/noon/evening *Sandhyā* for absolution of sins and grace of God). At the end of the *Praṇava,* he should remember the Vedic seers and (Vedic) metres and the deities. He should sprinkle water over his head while uttering the seven *vyāhṛtis* (mystic words) beginning with *bhūḥ* (and *bhuvaḥ*, *svaḥ*, etc. each to be preceded by *Om* (such as *Oṁ bhūḥ*, *Oṁ bhuvaḥ*). He should perform *Nyāsa* (or mental invocation of a deity and of the holy text to occupy a certain part of the body and to render it pure for worship and meditation). It should be performed separately for hands and the limbs. (of his body). He should fix the *Tāra* (syllable *Om*) in the heart and the *vyāhṛti Bhūḥ* on the head.

42. He should place (the *vyāhṛti*) *Bhuvaḥ* on the tuft of his hair, (the *vyāhṛti*) *svaḥ* on the *Kavaca* and *Bhūr* and *Bhuvaḥ* on both of the eyes. Similarly, he should utter the *vyāhṛtis Bhūr*, *Bhuvaḥ* and *Svaḥ* and making thrice a clapping sound (of hands) in (all directions, say *Astrāya Phaṭ*.)

43-46a. (*Invocation of the Gāyatri*)

43-44a. Then he should invoke the *Sandhyā* of the morning as seated on a white lotus—"O Gāyatrī of three syllables ! O Goddess granting boons ! O expounder of the Brahman (or the Vedas), do you come. O mother of metres ! O the source of the Brahman ! Obeisance to you."

44b-45a. At mid-day, he should invoke Sāvitrī seated on a bull and clad in white garments. She is the goddess, the source of the origin of Rudra and expounder of Rudra.

45b-46a. In the evening, she is seated on Garuḍa and is clad in yellow garments. She is goddess Sarasvatī and the origin or the source of Viṣṇu and the expounder of Viṣṇu. The householder should invoke her thus (as propounded above).

46b-47. *Prāṇāyāma* (*Breath-control*)

While uttering the syllable *Om* and the seven *vyāhṛtis* (i.e. uttering *Oṁ bhūḥ*, *Oṁ bhuvaḥ*, *Oṁ Svaḥ*, *Oṁ mahaḥ*, *Oṁ Janaḥ*, *Oṁ tapaḥ* and *Oṁ satyam*) and the three-footed Gāyatrī mantra (viz. *Om tat savitur vareṇyam*, *bhargo devasya dhīmahi*, *dhiyo yo naḥ pracodayāt*) and the *Śiras* (head) of the Gāyatrī (viz. *Om āpo jyoti rasó mṛtam*, *etc.*), he should inhale (take in the breath) and retaining it (for the same duration as inhaling), he should exhale it (while muttering the same mystic syllables as at the time of inhaling it). In this (exercise of) breath-control, the air is to be breathed through the left nostril and breathed out of the other (i.e. the right nostril. This is the rite of breath-control.

48. Thereafter, he should perform the *Ācamana* rite twice

and recite the *mantras* as follows : In the morning the mantra is :

Śūryaś ca mā etc. (TA X.25.1). In the mid-day : *Āpaḥ punantu pṛthivīm*, etc. (TA.X.23.1). In the evening the mantra is *Agniś ca mā*, etc. (TA X.24.1)

49-50. He should perform the rite of *Mārjana* (sprinkling one's body with water by means of hand or a blade of Kuśa grass) reciting the three *mantras* from *Āpo hi ṣṭhā* etc. (RV. X.9.13 VS.11.50). He should ritualistically dismiss (destroy) the host of enemies with the water touching the nose after repeating the *mantra Sumitriyā naḥ*, etc. (VS.6.22).

He should then sprinkle water over the head with the *mantra Drupadād iva*, etc. (VS.20.20; AV.6.115.3)

With the *mantra Ṛtaṁ ca satyam* etc. (RV.X.190.1-3 he should perform the *Agha-marṣaṇa rite** ("Driving out sin).

51. Repeating the *mantra Antaś carasi* etc. (TA.10.31.1), he should drink the water once. Then he should duly offer scents, flowers and handful of water to the Sun.

52-53. O celestial sage ! He should thus worship the Sun. During the morning and the evening he should raise his hand and perform *Svastikāñjali* (joining palms together in prayer). At mid-day, he should keep the hands lowered down. (At this time of *sūryopasthāna*—worship of the Sun), the three *mantras* viz. *Udu tyam* etc (RV.I.50.1), *Citraṁ devānām* etc. (RV.I.115.1) *Tac cakṣuḥ* etc. (RV.VII.66.16) should be repeated. O Nārada, he shohld repeat other *mantras* also pertaining to the Sun, Viṣṇu or Śiva.

54. He should pray to the splendour of the Sun with the *mantra Tejo si*† etc. (VS. 22.1) "You are the brilliance", *Gāyatryasi*‡ (*Śat. Br.* 14.8.15.10) (also *Bṛhad. Up.* 5.14.7). "You are Gāyatrī". He should then turn round himself thrice and meditate on the Śaktis (potencies) pertaining to him.

---

* This consists in taking water in the right palm formed in the shape of cow's ear, holding it near one's nose, breathing out (one's sins as it were) from the nostril on the water while one is repeating the three verses under reference (RV.X.190 1-3) and then casting the water to one's left on the ground — Kane : *HD*.II.i. P.317.

†. The *mantra* used in the *Mādhyandina Sandhyā is Tejo'si Śukram amṛtam*, etc.

‡. This *mantra* in the *Mādhyandina Sandhyā* is given as *Gāyatryasyekapadī dvipadī* ...

55. Gāyatrī is the wife of Brahmā, surrounded by the circle of eyes of the four-faced Lord. She is holding a jar, *Sruk* and *Sruva* (sacrificial ladles) in her own hands. Her face has the brilliant lustre of the moon. She is of the form of Ṛgveda. She is a young girl. She sportively rides on the swan. She is worshipped by the lustrous jewel of the firmament (the Sun). She is bedecked by means of his orb. May Gāyatrī, conceived thus be for our ever-flourishing prosperity.

56. Sāvitrī of the form of Yajus must be meditated upon like this : She is the consort of god Rudra; she is in the fresh prime of youth. She has three eyes. She is clad in the tiger's hide. She holds the *Khaṭvāṅga* (the club with a skull at the top), the trident, the *Akṣa-sūtra* (rosary) and the girdle. She is embellished with the crescent moon on her crest which resembles a forked lightning streek in the midst of her matted hair. Sāvitrī has the bull for her vehicle and is fair (white) in complexion. May she be conducive to our fearlessness and prosperity.

57. She is to be meditated upon as the divine goddess Sarasvatī, decorated in yellow robes. Dark in complexion, she is known as Śyāmā. She is beautiful in the radiating old *Vaiṣṇava* (belonging to Viṣṇu) form. She is seated on Tārkṣya (Garuḍa). She is brilliant with ornaments such as anklets set with gems and jewels, bracelets and the shining necklace. Her hands are embellished with a conch, a discus, a mace (*gadā*) and a lotus. May she be for our prosperity.[12]

58. Meditating thus he should perform the *Japa*, standing in the morning and at midday, and seated in the evening. With great devotion his mind he must be concentrated on the deity.

59. The Tripadā (three-footed) (i.e. the Gāyatrī Mantra) must be repeated a minimum number of ten times and a maximum number of a thousand times. The average should never go below a hundred. The Mantra is to be accompanied by the *Praṇava* (the syllable OM) and inaugurated with *Bhūrbhuvaḥ svaḥ*.[13]

60. The *Japa* (repetition of the Gayatrī mantra) of an observer of a religious vows (*vratin*) or of a recluse (*yati*) should be accompanied with six repetitions of OM followed by three *Vyāhṛtis* and the same (*OM*) repetition at the end (*ṣaṭ-tāra*) or commencing with OM followed by *Vyāhṛtis* (*bhūr bhuvas svaḥ*) and ending with the same repetition (*sampuṭa*).[14] The

Japa of a householder should be accompanied with OM and *Vyāhṛtis* (*Sa-tāra*).

61. He should thus perform the *Japa* according to his ability and dedicate the same to the Sun-god. He should then offer two water-oblations with cavity formed by joining together both the palms of hands (*añjali*), to Gāyatrī and the Sun-god.

62. With the Mantra *Uttame Śikhare* (TA.10.30.1) etc. he should ritualistically bid good bye to her (Gāyatrī). (He should say) "Do go respectfully on being permitted by Brahmā, Iśa and Hari."

63. With palms joined in reverence, he should bow down to the quarters and the guardian deities of the quarters.[15] Thereafter, he should perform the other rites prescribed for the morning in accordance with the injunctions.

64. A householder should take bath both in the morning and at midday. O celestial sage, the forest dwelling hermit and the ascetic should take ablutions at three times (in the morning, the noon and the evening).

65. Those who are ailing due to chronic illness, etc. and the wayfarer need take bath once only. O leading sage, with *Darbhas* in the hand, he should then perform the rite of *Brahma Yajña*.

66. If the rites enjoined for the day are left unperformed due to oversight or negligence, he should perform them in due order in the first *Yāma* (three-hour-period) of the night.

67. The twice-born person of knavish disposition who does not perform Sandhyā worship even when there is no emergency, should be known as a heretic. He is excluded from all Dharmas.[16]

68. If a person, an expert in fraudulent arguments neglects and ceases to perform the *Sandhyā*-worship and other rites, know him to be the foremost among the great sinners.

69. Those twice-born ones who hold *tete-a-tete* with the neglectors of Sandhyā-worship and other rites fall into terrible hells and stay there as long as the sun, the moon and the stars shine.

70. Thereafter, he should worship the deities and perform the rite of *Vaiśvadeva* (offerings in the fire to all *devas* collectively) in accordance with the injunction. He should duly honour the guest thereat, by means of food, etc.[17]

71. Sweet words must be spoken to them and to the other guests. He should worship them and propitiate them with water, food, bulbous roots and roots. He should honour him with the charitable gift of a house as well.

72. If any guest returns disappointed from the house of anyone, he gives the latter all his sins and goes away taking his (host's) merits.

73. Learned men say that *Atithi* (guest) is that person who has come from another village and whose name and lineage are not known. The householder shall worship him like Viṣṇu.

74. O Brāhmaṇa, everyday he should propitiate with cooked food, etc. a resident of his own village who is well-versed in the Vedas and is devoted to Viṣṇu. He should propitiate him with the Manes in view (i.e. with a view to propitiate the *pitṛs*).

Five Great Sacrifiices

75. A person who neglects to perform the five *Yajñas*[18] is called a Brāhmaṇa (the slayer of a *Brāhmaṇa*) by learned men. Hence, one should assiduously perform the five *Yajñas* everyday.

76. They call the following as the five *yajñas* : *Devayajña*, *Bhūtayajña*, *Pitṛyajña*, *Nṛyajña* (yajna for men)and Brahmayajña.

77. Remaining restrained in speech, he should himself take food accompanied by servants, friends and others. He should take only such food as Brāhmaṇas take, he should never miss the opportunity of serving a deserving person.[19]

78. While taking food if one places one's feet in the seat or if one wears half the clothes (i.e. only one cloth) or if one swallows again what is vomited out of the mouth, learned men call him the wine-addict.

79. If anyone eats sweets, fruits, etc, some part of which is already eaten before, or if one takes salt directly, he is called the eater of raw beef.

80. While drinking water (at the conclusion of meals) or while performing the *Ācamana* rite or while eating solid food-stuffs, a Brāhmaṇa should not make sounds. The Brāhmaṇa who makes such noise, shall fall into hell.

81. He should take in wholesome cooked food with restrained speech. He should not speak contemptuously of the food. Before taking food, water is ritualistically sipped, repeating the

mantra *Amṛtopastaraṇam asi* [TA.10.32.1] (Thou art nectar spread out).

82. He should then perform the rite of *Prāṇādi āhuti* (i.e. he should take in six bits of food one by one repeating *Prāṇāya Svāhā, Apānāya Svāhā*, etc.) : and after the *Ācamana* rite he should begin the meal. At the end of the meal, he should sip water once again saying *Amṛtāpidhānam asi* [TA 10.35.1] (Thou art the covering lid with nectar).

83. O leading Brāhmaṇa, he should then perform the *Ācamana* rite and thereafter be engaged in pondering over the scriptural topics. At night too, he should go to bed, sit and take food in accordance with his ability.

84. O sage, thus the householder should practise the conventional conduct of the good every day. Whenever he commits any breach in the conventional conduct of life, he should immediately perform expiatory rites.

Rules for Forest Hermits

85. O excellent one, on seeing the body defiled by greying of hairs, etc., he should entrust the care of his wife to his sons and go to the forest. Or he should go there along with her.[20]

86. He should bathe three times every day.[21] He should not pare off the nails or cut off the moustache or beard. He should keep matted hair. Maintaining celibacy, he should be devoted to the five *Yajñas*.[22] He should sleep on the bare ground.

87. He should perpetually devote himself to the study of the Vedas[23] and take to the diet of fruits and roots. He should be merciful towards all living beings and devoted to Nārāyaṇa.

88. He should avoid flowers and fruits produced in the village. He should eat only eight morsels of food, and should not take food during the night.

89. A person who follows the *Āśrama* of the forest-hermits should completely avoid oil. He should abstain from sexual intercourse. He should not be lethargic nor should he sleep too long.

90. A forest dweller should always remember Nārāyaṇa who wields in his hands a conch, a discus and a mace and perform *Cāndrāyaṇa*[24] and other austerities.

91-92a. He should endure chillness and scorching heat. He should always maintain the holy fire. When utter detachment develops in his mind in regard to all objects of senses, he should immediately renounce.[25] O Brāhmaṇa, otherwise he will be a fallen fellow.

The Duties of a Sannyāsin.

92b-93. The ascetic should be engaged in the study of Vedantic principles.[26] He should be quiescent and self-controlled. He should subdue the sense organs. He should be free from the *Dvandvas* (natural opposed pairs, e.g. pleasure and pain) and devoid of arrogance. Never should he entertain the sense of "my-ness". He should possess all attributes such as quiescence, etc. He should be absolutely free from desires, passion and anger.

94. The Brāhmaṇa ascetic may remain naked or wear only a ragged loin cloth. He should keep his head completely shaven.[27] He should be impartial to an enemy or a friend and view honour and dishonour with equanimity.

95. The ascetic should stay in a village only for a night and in a town, for three nights. He should maintain himself through alms, but should not take food from one person.

96. The ascetic should beg for alms only in an uncensured Brāhmaṇa household where there is no burning coal and where the people have finished taking food and where there is no quarrel.

97. He should take bath thrice a day and be devoted to Nārāyaṇa. He should always repeat the *Praṇava.* (The syllable OM). He should subdue the sense-organs and keep his mind under control.

98. If at any time the ascetic becomes greedy or dissolute and becomes the regular partaker of the cooked food of a single individual, no prospect of redemption for him is in view, even after ten thousand expiatory rites.

99. O Brāhmaṇa, if out of greediness an ascetic becomes interested in developing his body, he should be known as some one equal to a *Cāṇḍāla.* He is the most despicable among the people of all castes and stages of life.

100-102. He should meditate on Lord Nārāyaṇa, who is the Ātman, free from ailments, above mutually opposed pairs;

and the sense of 'myness', who is quiescent, beyond the pale of Māyā, and absolutely free from jealousy; who is perfect and immutable, the very embodiment of eternal bliss and existence; whose form is that of perfect knowledge; who is devoid of impurities and is the eternal light; who has no aberrations; who is beginningless and endless, the cause of the sentience of the universe; who is free from attributes, and is greater than the greatest.

103. He should regularly read the passages of the Upaniṣads, ponder over the Vedāntic topics. Conquering the sense organs, he should always meditate on the thousand-headed Lord.

104. The ascetic who is habituated to meditating thus, and is devoid of rivalry or jealousy, attains the greatest bliss, the eternal and supreme light.

105. The twice-born one who practises the conventional code of conduct in the different stages of life, goes to the greatest abode after reaching which no one regrets (i.e. there is no sorrow).

106. Those who strictly abide by the discipline of the castes and stages of life, those who are devoted to Nārāyaṇa, those who are devoid of all sins, go to that highest region of Viṣṇu."

CHAPTER TWENTYSEVEN

Religious Duties of the Householders, forest-hermits and samnnyāsin

1. Cf. Manu IV.92, Yājñavalkya I.115 who enjoins a Brāhmaṇa to get up from bed at the *Brāhma muhūrta* i.e. 4 *ghaṭikas* before the sunrise (*Br. Vaivarta P.*) SC. (I.p. 88) quotes Pitāmaha who says that the last watch of the night is the *Brāhma muhūrta.* /

2. VV.4-7 contain rules regarding answering calls of nature. Detailed rules regarding this act are laid down in ancient Dh.S., Smṛtis etc. For example, Manu IV.45-52, Vāyu P. 78. 59-64, Vāmana P. 14.30-32. The detailed instructions regarding the direction in which to go to answer the call of nature, keeping the sacred thread on the ear, covering the ground with grass, etc. quoted in SC.I., pp. 88-90 tally with those in the NP.

3. VV. 8-19 give the details of cleaning those parts (the penis, anus, etc.) with lumps of earth and water. As SC.I., pp. 91-94 shows there have been some differences in details but as Devala rightly states, it is not the number of times (of cleaning with mud and water) that matters but cleansing should be carried on till one feels it is all right.

yāvat sādhviti manyeta tāvac chaucam vidhīyate /

(quoted in SC. I. 93) vide V.16b also.

The present verse (No. 8 in NP.) is a quotation form *Dakṣa Sm. V.*3.

4. Quoted from *Dakṣa Sm. V.* 3.

5. Cf. Vasiṣṭha Dh. S. VI. 17.

6. Very elaborate rules for *Ācamana* (sipping of water) are prescribed in digests like SC (I. P.95-103) NP. seems to follow VP.

7. VV.23-30 deal with brushing the teeth (*Danta-dhāvana*) which is regarded as an integral yet independent part of *Āhnika* (daily routine of duties) and not a subordinate part (*aṅga*) of bath or *Sandhyā*—morning Prayer (*Āhnika prakāśa,* p. 121). The practice is mentioned in old Vedic works like the *Tait.* S.II.5.1.7. Digests like SC.I., p. 104-107 give quotations from different Smṛtis and Purāṇas (including NP.) which show minor differences about the choice of trees for twigs to be used as a brush and the length and thickness of the twigs to be so used. It shows the insistence of ancient law-givers on the importance of brushing the teeth. NP., however, does not give the quotation of *Nārada Smrti* :

sarve kaṇṭakinaḥ puṇyāḥ kṣīriṇaś ca yaśasvinaḥ /

As Dakṣa observes brushing the teeth should precede the morning bath.

8. This *mantra* i.e. prayer to the tree, the twig of which is used for brushing the teeth, is found in the *Gobhila-Smṛti* and is quoted in the SC. and other digests on Dharma Śāstra.

9. VV.31-36 describe a usual (*nitya*) brief procedure of bathing, consisting

of invocation of water (VV.33-34) *mārjana,* bath and citing *Aghamarṣaṇa* and offering *Arghya* to the sun (V.36)—a procedure recommended in *Brahmokta-Yājñavalkya Saṁhitā II.* 16-22 (Gurumandal Edt). which probably is quoted as *yogi-yājñavalkya* by Aparārka, p. 134.

10. Though the usual meaning of *a-hata* is given in the translation, it also means a cloth or a garment which is practically new—unwashed for many days (vide Pulastya quoted in SC.I.P.113).

11. The *Sandhyā* means a 'Twilight prayer' and is to be performed at dawn and dusk, though prayer at mid-day came to be known as *madhyāhna sandhyā.* Originally *sandhyā* consisted of *arghya* (offering of water as worship to the Sun God) and *japa* of *Gāyatrī* (*Tait. Ar.* II.2. also *Āśvalāyana* Gr.S.III. 7.3-6). We find elaborate *sandhyopāsanā* consisting of *ācamana, prāṇāyāma, mārjana* (sprinkling oneself with water thrice), *aghamarṣaṇa, arghya* (offering water to the sun), *japa* of Gāyatrī, *upasthāna* (recitation of *mantras* with reference to the sun in the morning and Varuṇa in the evening). We perform *ācamana* with three names of Viṣṇu, viz. Keśava, Nārāyaṇa and Mādhava thus *Oṁ Keśavāya namaḥ* and repeat the remaining 21 names (uttering in all 24 names) of Viṣṇu, each preceded by *Oṁ* and followed by *namaḥ.*

A comparison of the procedure of *Sandhyā* as given in the N P. with the *Sandhyā* of the Mādhyandinas of Kātyāyana Sūtra in Maharashtra shows a substantial agreement in the *mantras*, etc. But the sequence of constituents or procedure of *Sandhyā* in the NP. differs to some extent from the present day Sandhyopāsanā of Madhyandinas (vide the *Nitya-Brahma-Karma Samuccaya* edt. by Shridhar Shastri Pathak, Poona, Śaka 1851 (1929 A.D.) The difference may be due to the age and region of the NP.

Instead of giving literal translation of these verses it is necessary to explain technical terms in the *Sandhyā*, the details of procedure regarding acts to be performed as *Arghya, Aghamarṣaṇa,* etc. and the exact reference of the *mantras* to be recited during the Sandhyā prayer along with the translation itself. Hence, the explanation of these terms, etc. is not repeated here.

12. Verses 55-57 give the description of the Gāyatrī to be invoked at the morning, at the mid-day and in the evening. These verses are the elaboration of the similar couplets in the Sandhyā of Mādhyandina Brāhmaṇas. (vide *Pathak's NBK Samuccaya,* p. 8).

13. In plain words the *mantra* to be muttered is :

> *Oṁ bhūr-bhuvaḥ svaḥ—Oṁ tatsavitur vareṇyam, bhargo devasya dhīmahi, dhiyo yo naḥ pracodayāt* /

14. *Sampuṭa*—enclosed in two *praṇavas,* viz. *oṁ bhūrbhuvaḥ svaḥ / oṁ tatsavitur etc. pracodayāt oṁ / Yogi-Yājñavalkya* as quoted in SC I P.149.

The quarters and their guardian deities to whom respects are to be paid are as follows :

15. The East—Indra; the South-East—Agni, The South—Yama; the South-West—Nir-ṛti; the West—Varuṇa; the North-West—the Wind god; the North—Kubera; the North-East—Īśvara (God Śiva); the upper (Skywards)—god Brahmā; the lower direction—god Viṣṇu; the remaining direction—Ananta.

16. Verses 67-69, censure a shirker of Sandhyā-prayers. SC.I.139 quotes KP., Gobhila and Dakṣa, advising his (the shirker's) ex-communication. Gobhila

states that such a person is Śūdra while alive and after death he becomes a dog (*jīvamāno bhavec chūdro mṛtaḥ śvā cābhijāyate*).

17. Out of 'Five great sacrifices (*Pañca-mahā-yajñas*) *manuṣya-yajña* (feeding an unknown guest) is described in VV.70-74. The *atithi* is defined in verse 73.

18. From early Vedic times great importance was attached to the following daily observances, viz., *Devayajña* (sacrifice of gods), *pitṛyajña* (sacrifice—offering of water to ancestors by way of *Tarpaṇa*), *bhūta-yajña* (offering at least a ball of food to living beings), *manuṣya-yajña* (receiving and feeding at least one guest) and *Brahma-yajña* (*svādhyāya* or recitation of at least one mantra from the Veda). They are emphasized in *Śat.Br.* (XI.5-6.1), *Tait.Ār.* (II.10), Gṛhya sūtras and Smṛtis (*vide* SC.I., pp. 208-211) and pp. 217-220 for the importance of receiving an *atithi* (unexpected guest).

19. VV.77-82 lay down rules (and indirectly confirm the social etiquettes) at the time of taking meals. SC.I., pp. 221-225 show that there was a sort of standardization about the rules or conventions to be observed at the time of taking meals.

20. VV.85-91, give an epitome of the life and rules of the forest-hermit.

21. *Vide* Manu VI. 22 & 24; Yājñavalkya III. 48.

22. Five yajñas—The five *Mahā-yajñas* mentioned above : *vide* Manu VI. 5 & 7; Yājñavalkya III.46.

23. *Vide* Āpastamba Dh.S. 11.9 and Manu VI.8.

24. *Vide* Manu VI.2—. But this is a part of penance in general and not expiation for a particular sin.

25. VV.91-104 describe the stage of life known as *sannyāsa*.

26. Although Manu recommends the recitation of Vedic texts referring to gods or Yajñas along with these metaphysical texts called the Vedānta (VI.83), NP. insists on the recitation of Vedāntic or Upaniṣadic texts only, vide verse 103 below.

27. Though NP. gives nudity as an option to Sannyāsins—an option according to 'some' in Āpastamba Dh.S.II. 9.21.11-12, Smṛtis are lukeworm about it. Manu VI.52 prescribes the paring of nails and complete shaving of the head and beard.

CHAPTER TWENTYEIGHT

The Description of the Rite of Śrāddha

Sanaka said :

1. O leading sage, listen to the excellent procedure in the performance of *Śrāddha*,[1] on hearing which one is undoubtedly liberated from sins.

2. On the day previous to the *Kṣayāha* (day of the Death-anniversary) the householder should take his bath. He should take only a single meal on that day. He should duly invite the Brāhmaṇas (for the next day). In the night he should observe celibacy and lie on the ground.

3. The performer of *Śrāddha* should avoid cleaning of the teeth, chewing the betel leaves, anointing the body with oil, and foodstuffs of an aphrodisiac nature.

4. The performer of *Śrāddha* and the partaker of food therein should avoid long journey, quarrel, fury, sexual intercourse, bearing of burdens and sleep during the day.[2]

5. If he, who is invited for a *Śrāddha* indulges in sexual intercourse, incurs the sin of Brāhmaṇa-slaughter and falls into hell.

Qualifications of the Brāhmaṇa Invitee for Śrāddha:

6. The Brāhmaṇa who has the following characteristics can be invited for a *Śrāddha*[3] : He should be well-versed in the Vedas and devoted to Viṣṇu. He should be an abider by his own conventional conduct of life. He should be born of a good family and be of quiet nature.

7. He should be devoid of passionate attachment and hatred. He should be an expert in the interpretation of the Purāṇas. He must be conversant with the *madhu* verses (viz. RV.I.90.6-8, Vāj. S.13.27-29 in which the word *madhu* occurs) and must have studied the *Tri-suparṇa*, (viz. the three *anuvākas* beginning with *Brahmametu mām* etc. (*Tait. Āraṇyaka* X.48-50).

8. He should be engaged in the worship of the deities and be an adept in the principles of Smṛtis. He must be a past-

master in the knowledge of the principles of the Upaniṣads. He must be interested in the welfare of all worlds.

9-10. He should be grateful and richly endowed with all good qualities. He must be engaged in serving his preceptor. He must be engaged in advising others by recounting the good scriptural texts. These are the Brāhmaṇas, O leading sage, who can be employed in a *Śrāddha*. I shall mention those who should be excluded from the *Śrāddhas*. Listen with great attention.

Disqualifications of an Invitee[4]

11-18. One who is physically a deformed being wanting in a limb or by having a superfluous limb, a miser, a sickly person, a leper, one with deformed nails, a person with long suspended ears, one who has broken his religious vows, a person whose livelihood is the reading of the stars (i.e. astrology), he who (professionally) burns corpses, a person indulgent in heretical arguments, the younger brother who marries when the elder brother is yet a bachelor; a professional worshipper of idols, a rogue, a person who speaks ill of others; a hot-tempered person, a knave, the village priest, one who is interested in unholy scriptures, one who is devoted to (and dependent on) other men's food, one who supports the son of a Śūdra woman, the paramour of a Śūdra woman, Kuṇḍas and Golakas (i.e. bastards born of adultery when the husband is alive or when the husband is dead), one who performs the *Yajña* of those who are not eligible to perform it, a man of fradulent conduct, a man who shaves off his head without purpose, one who is enamoured of another man's wife or wealth, one who is devoid of devotion to Viṣṇu; one who turns his face away from devotion to Śiva, those who sell the Vedas (i.e. accept fee for recitation and teaching of the Vedas), the sellers of *Vratas*, those who sell *Smṛtis*, and *Mantras* (who charge fees for these), professional musicians, composers of poems, those who maintain themselves by means of practising medicine (for money), one who is engaged in decrying the Vedas, arsonists of villages and forests, one who is over-passionate, one who sells intoxicating beverages and one who indulges in deceitful arguments. All these should be excluded scrupulously from the *Śrāddha*.

19. He should invite the Brāhmaṇa the previous day or

on the same day. The Brāhmaṇa who is invited should maintain celibacy and conquer his sense organs.[5]

20. With his sense-organs duly subdued, a householder should take *darbha*-grass in his hands and invite an intelligent Brāhmaṇa with the following words : "O excellent Sir, you should do me a favour and accept my invitation for *Śrāddha*".[6]

21. He should get up early in the morning and perform the daily morning routine. The learned man should perform the *Śrāddha* at the hour called *Kutapa*[7] (i.e. the eighth *muhūrta* or five hours and thirty six minutes after the sunrise).

22. That hour in the eighth Kāla (*Muhūrta*) of the day when the sun begins to be less fierce is called the *Kutapa*. That which is given to the Pitṛs at that time is of everlasting benefit.

23. The afternoon is the time granted to the *Pitṛs* by the self-born deity (god Brahmā). Hence, the Kavya (oblations to Pitṛs) should be given by excellent Brāhmaṇas only at that time.

24. O excellent sage, if the Kavya is offered along with the monetary gifts at the wrong hour it should be known as belonging to the *Rākṣasas*. It never reaches the *Pitṛs*.

25. The *Kavya* offered in the evening too becomes something pertaining to the Rākṣasas. The giver as well as the partaker of food falls into the hell.

Decisions about Śrāddha-Tithis[8]

26. If the duration of the Tithi of the annual *Śrāddha* be of only one *ghaṭikā* (*daṇḍa*=24 minutes) on the previous day, O Brāhmaṇa the Śrāddha must be performed on the *Tithi* the afternoon of which is affected (touched) by another *Tithi*, by a person knowing (the required religious rite).[9]

27. If the *Tithi* (lunar-day) of the death anniversary spreads over the afternoons of two (consecutive) days, the *Śrāddha* should be performed on the previous day if there be the *Kṣaya* (less duration, loss) of the (particular) *Tithi* and on the next day if that *Tithi* has extended duration (*Vṛddhi*).

28. If the *Tithi* of the death-anniversary is for two Muhūrtas (i.e. one hour and thirtysix minutes) in the previous day and spreads till evening on the next day, the latter is recommended for *Śrāddha*.

29. Some opine that when the *Tithi* (of the death-anniversary is of the duration of two *muhūrtas*, the *Śrāddha* should be performed on the previous day, but O chief of sages, this is not a universally held view about the performance of *Śrāddha*.

30. O excellent Brāhmaṇa, when the invited *Brāhmaṇas* have all assembled together, the householder with his sons purified through expiation, should formally solicit their permission.

31. On being formally permitted to perform the Śrāddha, he should invite the Brāhmaṇas again in accordance with the injunctions—two for the purpose of Viśve-devas and three for the *Pitṛs*.

32. Or he should invite one for each, i.e. for Devas and the *Pitṛs* respectively; when he has been permitted to perform Śrāddha, he should make two mystic diagrams called *Maṇḍala*[10] (on the ground).

33. The diagram of a Brāhmaṇa (performer of Śrāddha) should be square or four-cornered; that of the Kṣatriya triangular; that of a Vaiśya should be known as circular. As for a Śūdra the consecration by sprinkling is enough.

34. If Brāhmaṇas are not available, one should engage even one's own brother or son or the *Ātman* himself but he should never engage a Brāhmaṇa devoid of the Vedas.

35. He should wash the feet of the Brāhmaṇas. After they had performed the *Ācamana* rite, they must be seated. Remembering Lord Nārāyaṇa, they should be suitably worshipped.

36. Repeating the ṚK *mantra Apahatāḥ* (RV. X.76.4, V.S. II.29) etc., the householder should strew gingelly seeds in between the Brāhmaṇas and at the threshold.

37. He should offer the seat to the *devas* by means of barley grains and Darbha grass, saying "This is the seat unto the Viśve-Devas". After giving this he should offer *Kṣaṇa-pratīkṣaṇa* (a formality of invitation).

38. For the expression of imperishability and the offering of seat, Ṣaṣṭhī (the genitive case) is used; in invoking *Dvitīyā* (the accusative case) is used; in offering food Caturthī (the Dative case) is used; all the rest are addressed as *Sambuddhis* (the Vocative case).[11]

39. He should take up two vessels joined together by

means of the Darbha grass. Repeating the *ṛk* *Śanno Devī* (Vaj.S. 36.12, (RV.X.9.4)—(May the divine waters be for our happiness, etc.), he should sprinkle water on it.

40. Restrained in speech he should offer scents and flowers after putting barley grains repeating the Mantra *Yavosi* (V.S.5.26) etc. Thereafter, he should invoke Devas by means of the *ṛk Viśve devāsaḥ* (RV.I.3.7,V.S.7.34)—"Come, Ye all gods, listen to this my call and sit on this darbha grass."

41. With great attention he should offer *Arghya* repeating the Mantra *Yā Divyā* (TB.II.7.15.4a), etc. Thereafter, he should worship by means of scents, leaves, flowers, incense and lamps.

42. After being permitted by the Brāhmaṇas representing Devas, he should worship the groups of the *Pitṛs*. He should offer them good seats by means of Darbhas mixed with sesamum seeds.

43. He should take up three vessels. The Brāhmaṇa should place them as before for the purpose of *Arghya*. Reciting the Mantra *Śanno Devī* (RV.X.9.4) etc. he should pour water and then put gingelly seeds repeating *Tilosi* (*Āśvalāyana Gr.S.*4.7.11), etc.

44. With great attention the Brāhmaṇa should invoke the *Pitṛs* by means of the *ṛk Uśantaḥ* (RV.X.16.12) etc. He should offer *Arghya* as before by means of the Mantra *Yā Divyā*, etc. (TB.II.7.4a).

45. O excellent one, he should honour and worship them in accordance with his capacity, by means of scents, leaves, flowers, incense and lamps as well as garments and ornaments.

Agnau-Karaṇa[12]

46. The intelligent householder should take up a portion of the cooked rice soaked in ghee and say, "I shall consign it to the fire", and solicit their formal permission.

47. O sage, on being asked by him saying, "May I do ?", "Let me do", those Brāhmaṇas should say, "Please do", "It may be done", "You may do".

48. After kindling the fire for worship in accordance with the injunctions mentioned in his own *Gṛhyasūtras*, he should utter thus—"Svadhā and obeisance to Soma accompanied by the *Pitṛs*.

49. Or he should utter—"Svadhā and obeisance to Agni the conveyor of the Kavya". Or as in the *Pitṛ Yajña*, the intelligent householder can perform Homa by means of *Svāhā* endings as well.

50. The satisfaction of the *Pitṛs* shall be everlasting even, thanks to these two *Āhutis*. If the fire is not available, Homa can be performed in the hands of the Brāhmaṇa.

51. O Brāhmaṇa, he should perform it in the hand or in the fire according to the conventional practice. When the *Pārvaṇa* rites are to be performed, fire cannot be kept far off.

52. O Brāhmaṇa, if the Agni is far off, when the *Pārvaṇa* rites are in vogue, he should kindle the fire (ordinary fire, not the hereditarily kept one) perform the rite and be contented after ritualistically dismissing it.

53-55. When the day of death-anniversary arrives but the hereditary fire is not available, he should make his brothers duly perform the Śrāddha, those brothers who are Brāhmaṇas with the sacrificial fire (duly maintained). When the Upāsanā fire (traditionally kept fire or *gṛhyāgni*) is far off, but the brother is nearby and the brothers are maintaining only ordinary fire, if the Homa is performed in the worldly fire or in the hand (of the Brāhmaṇas) he would be a sinner; when the *Upāsanā* fire is far off, some Brāhmaṇas wish for this (i.e. they recommend it).

56. The balance of that he should strew into the dishes of the Brāhmaṇas duly remembering Hari. He should propitiate the Brāhmaṇas with various kinds of edibles, tasty dishes and lambatives.

57-58. With due attention on either side, he should perform the rite of *Annatyāga*—"Eschewal of the food". He should then pray to Devas—"O Viśve Devas, O powerful ones, O blessed ones, come ye all. Be alert in your respective places wherever you have been enjoined and he should repeat the *ṛk Ye Devāsaḥ* (RV.I.139.11, etc.)

59-61. By means of the *ṛk Ye ca ha* (RV.X.15.13) he should request the Brāhmaṇas, "Among them embodied and the unembodied *Pitṛs* of illuminating splendour, I bow down always to them who meditate and those who have the Yogic vision." After bowing to the *Pitṛs* thus, he should be devoted to Nārāyaṇa and offer the rite, and *havis* that had been offered to Viṣṇu. Thereafter, all the Brāhmaṇas should be restrained in speech and partake of the food.

62. If any one speaks out or laughs, the *Havis* offering shall become one pertaining to the Rākṣasas. According to convention wine and meat can be served.

63-65a. Those persons of restrained speech and occupying the (place near) the plates (dishes), should praise the cooking, etc. If any Brāhmaṇa engaged in the Śrāddha, sets aside his dish, he should be known as the destroyer of Śrāddha. He is fit only for the hell. If the Brāhmaṇas taking food touch one another, they should continue their meal, but after completing it, they should perform one hundred and eight *Japa* of the *Gāyatri mantra*.

65b-67. While Brāhmaṇas partake of their food, he should remember Lord Nārāyaṇa with great faith. He should remember the infinite Lord, the unvanquished deity. He should repeat the hymns pertaining to Viṣṇu, the Rakṣoghnī hymns (viz. RV.IV. 4. 1-15, RV.X.87, VII.104,X.118 and 162). He should specially recite the hymns pertaining to *Pitṛs* (viz. RV.X.15. 1-13). He should perform the *japa* of (or recite) the Puruṣa Sūkta (RV.X.90), the three Naciketa hymns[13], the Tri-madhu[14] (RV.I. 90-6-8),Trisuparṇa[15] (RV. V. 57.2), Pavamāna Sūkta and hymns from the Yajur-Veda.

68. He should repeat the *Uktha* and other *Sāman Mantras* that bestow merit. He should also recite verses from *Itihāsas*, *Purāṇas* and *Dharma śāstras*.

69. As long as the Brāhmaṇas continue their meal, he should repeat these *mantras*, etc. O Brāhmaṇa, when the Brāhmaṇas have completed their meal, he should strew (two lumps of rice called) *Vikira*.

70-71. He should enquire "What should be done about the remaining food?" He should repeat *Madhu Sūkta* O Nārada, then he should wash his own feet and perform the *Ācamana* rite. When the Brāhmaṇas have finished their meals and performed the *Ācamana* rite, he should offer the *Piṇḍas*. He should then perform the rites of *Svasti Vācanaka* (utterance of benediction) and *Akṣayyodaka* (getting the blessing that food and water be inexhaustible).

72-74. After offering the same, with great concentration he should offer salutations to the Brāhmaṇas. If the Brāhmaṇas utter benediction without stirring the vessel, their *Pitṛs* will be the partakers of *Ucchiṣṭa* (leavings of food) for a full year. With these utterances of the Smṛti, viz. "May our donors flourish..." (Yājñavalkya I.245-46), etc. he should receive the blessings from them and then prostrate himself before them. According to his ability, he should offer *Dakṣiṇā* and the betel-leaves mixed with sweet scents.

75. He should then bring the vessel that had been placed with face downwards and repeat the *Svadhā-kāra* (the word *Svadhā*). With the *ṛk Vāje vāje* (RV.VII.38.8) etc. he should ritualistically dismiss the *Pitṛs* and Devas.

76. The performer of the Śrāddha and the partaker of the food thereat should avoid sexual intercourse that night. He should assiduously refrain from the study of the Vedas and undertaking a long journey on foot.

77. A wayfarer, a sick man and a person devoid of funds should perform *Amāśrāddha* (*Śrāddha* with uncooked rice). One whose wife cannot be touched (i.e. is in her monthly courses) shall perform Śrāddha through the offer of gold.

78. If funds are not available, or if the Brāhmaṇas are not available he should prepare the food alone. The wise man should then perform the*Homa* repeating the Sūkta belonging to the *Pitṛs*.

79. If one cannot afford the *Havya* offerings at all, he may offer grass unto the cows according to his ability. O Brāhamaṇa, as an alternative, let him take his bath and duly perform the *Tarpaṇa* rite with gingelly seeds.

80. Or he may go to a lonely forest and lament very loudly. The wise man should proclaim "I am indigent. I am a great sinner".

81. If a performer of Śrāddha does not perform the rite of *Tarpaṇa* for the *Pitṛs*, the next day that family will perish. He will incur the sin of Brāhmaṇa-slaughter.

82. O leading sage, those faithful persons who perform Śrāddha do become rich. Their line is never extinct.

83. Virtually, Viṣṇu has been worshipped by those who worship the *pitṛs*. If the Lord of the Universe is pleased, the deities are also pleased.

84. It is eternal Hari himself who manifests as the Pitṛs, deities, Gandharvas, Apsaras, Yakṣas, Siddhas, and human beings.

85. Hence, the person who performs the Śrāddha and he who partakes of it—everyone is Viṣṇu, the eternal Lord, from whom the entire universe including the mobile and immobile beings, has originated.

86. O Brāhmaṇa, whatever exists, what does not exist, the visible and the invisible—everything should be known as identical with Viṣṇu. There is nothing else other than that.

87. He is the being that supports the universe; He is the *Ātman* of all living beings. He comprises all beings in himself; He is unchanging and of incomparable nature. He is the Lord who partakes of *Havya* and *Kavya*.

88. Janārdana is the only Lord who can be called *Parabrahman* (the Supreme Brahman). The eternal Viṣṇu does everything himself and makes everyone do so.

89. Thus, O excellent sage, the excellent procedure of the Śrāddha rite has been narrated to you. The sins of those who perform it, perish instantaneously.

90. If any excellent Brāhmaṇa reads this with piety and devotional feelings at the time of Śrāddha, the Pitṛs are delighted, his progeny flourishes.

CHAPTER TWENTYEIGHT

The Rite of Śrāddha

1. *Śrāddha*

This is an important topic as it forms an integral part of Hindu Dharma Śāstra. The belief in the after-death survival of deceased ancestors and their separate world (*Pitṛ-loka*) belongs to the Indo-Iranian period and as such is pre-Vedic (*vide* S.B.E. Vol.IV, p. 262 for the Iranian Fravarshis of Yima-Yama). Ancestor-worship for one's prosperity, continuation of one's race is as old as the Ṛg-Veda. It is not only NP. but several other Purāṇas deal with the ritual of *śrāddha*, e.g. AP.163.2-42, GP.I.210, KP.II.22.20-62, Pd.P. (*Sṛṣṭi-Khaṇḍa*) 9.140-186, VP.III.15.13-49, MP.17.12-60. Most of them prescribe practically the same procedure as given in the Gṛhya Sūtras and Smṛtis of Manu and Yājñavalkya. If the author of a Purāṇa follows a particular Sūtra, he prescribes the procedure of his Sūtra. For example, in the present case, the procedure of Śrāddha given in the NP. shows much resemblance to the details given in the Śrāddha Sūtra of Kātyāyana (which by the way has so much similarity with the procedure of Śrāddha given in the Yājñavalkya Smṛti).

We find that NP. and Kātyāyana use the same full *mantras, tilo'si, yā divyā* prescription of the repetition of the word *madhu* thrice (in addition to the Gāyatrī and *Madhumatī* verses) and recital of the following texts while the Brāhmaṇas are being fed :

The Gāyatrī (once or thrice), the five Rakṣoghnī verses (RV.IV.4.1-5); the Puruṣa Sūkta (RV. X.90), the Apratiratha hymns (RV.X.103.1-13), the *Svadhā-vācana* relates both to paternal and ma ternal ancestors (cf. *Yājñ. Smṛ*.I.244).

In addition to the blessing recorded in Yājñavalkya I.246-47, Kātyāyana requires the performer to pray for and receive from Brāhmaṇas the following blessings :

(i) "May the *Pitṛs* be not terrible to us and

(ii) May our family prosper.

The Mādhyandina Brāhmaṇas of Bengal follow Raghunandana's *Yajurvedī-Śrāddha-tattva* which is based on the *Śrāddha-sūtra* of Kātyāyana. Possibly the author of the NP. who prescribes the rules of Kātyāyana's *Śrāddhasūtra* might be an East Indian.

2. These restrictions are both on the invitee and the inviter. Kātyāyana prescribes that from the time of giving invitation by the performer of Śrāddha to the time of completion of the Śrāddha ritual marked by the final *ācamana*, Brāhmaṇas should remain pure, free from anger, hurry, negligence, should speak the truth, avoid journey, sexual intercourse, hard work, study the Veda

and control speech and the Brāhmaṇas invited should observe the same rules (*Śrāddha sūtra* I)

akrodhano'tvaro'mattaḥ satyavādī samāhitaḥ |
bhāram maithunam adhvānaṁ śrāddhā-kṛd varjayed japam ||
compare also Mt.P.16-27-28. —KP.II.22.6.

3. The qualities and qualifications required of a Brāhmaṇa invitee for Śrāddha. Cf. *Smṛ.C.* (*Smṛti Candrikā*) III (*Śrāddha-Kāṇḍa*) pp. 389-394. *Mt.P.* 16:8-10 state the same qualities as in NP. The ancient Smṛtis insist on the pure character and not so much on the scholarship of the invitee. As Manu says (II.118) "A Brāhmaṇa who knows only the Gāyatri but is self-controlled, is preferable to a Brāhmaṇa who knows three Vedas but lacks in self-control, eats every thing and sells anything (prohibited by Dharma)". He insists on the close enquiry of the antecedents of such an invitee. Later Purāṇas slackened these restrictions.

4. Disqualifications of a Brāhmaṇa rendering him ineligible for invitation to *Śrāddha*: This is an echo of Manu III. 150-169. Manu's list of disqualified Brāhmaṇas is very comprehensive as it includes Ninety-three disqualifications. It includes physically defective or handicapped persons e.g. a person with deformed nails, black teeth or a squint-eye or a scabby person, an epileptic, a leper, a person with scrofulous swelling of gland, a blind man, a lunatic, an impotent or a consumptive person.

It excludes Brāhmaṇas of the following professions : a physician, a temple-priest, a vendor of meat, a shop-keeper, a paid servant (of a village or the king), a usurer, a tender of cattles, an actor or singer, a seller of Vedas and Smṛtis, a teacher of Śūdras, a navigator, an oilman a manufacturer of weapons, a trainer of animals, a bird fancier, an architect, a messenger, a falconer, a carrier of dead bodies. Brāhmaṇas with immoral character (such as a thief, gambler, a debauchee, etc.) Brāhmaṇas with good heredity were eligible but not socially unacceptable ones such as marrying before elder brothers or bastards like Kuṇḍas or Golakas. A reference to SC.III., pp. 394-403 will show how writers on Dharma Sūtras, Smṛtis and Purāṇas gave importance to the selection of Brāhmaṇas for a Śrāddha. As Manu puts it one may not put Brāhmaṇas to test for work pertaining to gods but in the case of *Pitṛs* (Śrāddha) one must be scrupulously careful (III. 149)—an opinion endorsed by most other writers on *Dharma Śāstra*.

5. *brahmacārī*, etc. 'The invited Brāhmaṇa should abstain from sexual intercourse, etc. Some Purāṇas (e.g. Mt.P. 16-20) and some Smṛtis (Prajāpati 63) state that the invited Brāhmaṇa should be requested with the traditional verse

akrodhanaiḥ śaucaparaiḥ satatam brahmacāribhiḥ |
bhavitavyam bhavadbhiś ca mayā ca Śrāddha-kāriṇā ||

6. The procedure of invitation to Śrāddha as detailed in Mt. P. 16-17-20 is as follows :

The inviter should respectfully invite the Brāhmaṇas on the previous day or in the morning of the day of Śrāddha. He should (with *darbha*=grass in his hand) touch the right knee of the invitee and extend the invitation. *SC—Śrāddha* (p. 406) quotes *Pd.P.Sṛṣṭi* 9.85-88 which are the same as Mt.P.

7. *Kāle Kutapa Saṁjñite* : 'In the period of the day called *Kutapa*', Although

SC. (*Śrāddha*), p. 433 gives eight meanings of *Kutapa*, here 'The 8th *muhūrta* from the sunrise' is applicable. Its derivation is from *Ku* (bad, a sin)+*tapa* (that which burns). The *muhūrta* begins from five hours and thirty six minutes after the sun-rise. Prajāpati states that out of the fifteen *muhūrtas* comprising a day, *Kutapa* is the 8th and a *Śrāddha* should begin from the 8th *muhūrta* and should not extend beyond the *Rauhiṇeya* (12th) *muhūra.*

ārambhaṁ kutape kuryād rauhiṇaṁ na tu laṅghayet /
etat pañca muhūrtā'ntaḥ śrāddha-kāla udāhṛtaḥ / /

Prajāpati Smr. 158.

8. VV. 26-29 give decisions regarding the *Tithi* (lunar-day) acceptable for *Śrāddha*. When the particular *Tithi* is not full (covering the civil day) but spreads over two days, etc. (for discussion of *Tithis* vide the next chapter).
9. Verses repeated in Saura P. 19.13-14.

P.V. Kane states that two *maṇḍalas* are to be drawn in front of the performer's residence to receive the Brāhmaṇas. Of the two Maṇḍalas one should be on the northern side sloping towards the north for Brāhmaṇas representing *devas* and the second on the southern side sloping towards the south for Brāhmaṇas representing *Pitṛs*.

(H.D.IV. pp. 456-57).

10. There is nothing mystical here but application of the rules of SK. grammar : The use of genitive case : *asmat-pitṛ-pitāmahaprapitāmahānām—idam āsanam* / (This seat is for my father, grand-father, great-grand-father).

The use of the accusative case : *pitṛ-pitāmahān āvāhayāmi* (I invoke my father...great grand sire). RV.X.16.12 uses the same case wherein Agni is requested to invite the ancestors.

11. The use of the Dative case : *pitre idaṁ arghyaṁ dattaṁ na mama* / 'The *Arghya* is given to my father'...saying this the performer is to offer water mixed with sesamum seed on the palm of the invited Brāhmaṇa.

12. VV 46-51 describe what is technically known as *agnau-karaṇa*. When domestic sacrificial fires are not maintained (as is the case of majority of homes now-a-days), the right hand of the Brāhmaṇa is regarded as fire and the oblations are offered in his hand as if it is the sacrificial fire, with the *mantras* mentioned in these verses.

13. Though the translation follows the text *tri-nāciketaṁ*... (*Japet*), the term *tri-nāciketa* is variously explained : *Tri-ṇāciketa* is a person who knows the Nāciketa fire or a person who has thrice kindled the Nāciketa fire or a person who has studied the *Anuvāka* called virajas. *Tait. Br.* (III. 11.7-8) describes the Nāciketa fire and the story of Naciketas.

14. *Tri-madhu*—The three Vedic verses (RV.I.90.6-8; VS. 13-27-29, TS.IV. 2.9.3) in which the word *madhu* occurs three times.

15. *Tri-Suparṇa*—Haradatta applies the name to the three *Anuvākas* beginning with *Brahmametu mām* (*Tait. Ar.*X.48-50). *Paitrika* hymns are RV. X.15.1-13.

There has been some difference of opinion about the texts to be recited : *vide Pd. P. Sṛṣṭi* 9.165-69 also *Mt.P.* 17.37-39.

CHAPTER TWENTYNINE

Determination of Tithis (Lunar days)

Sanaka said :

1. I shall recount how the *Tithis*[1] (lunar days) can be decisively fixed. I shall relate also the mode of expiation, O excellent sage, listen to that from which the holy rites, bear fruit.

2. O Brāhmaṇa, the *Vratas*, charitable gifts, etc. enjoined in the Śrutis or Smṛtis, nay all the other Vedic rites, do not bear fruits if performed on Tithis other than what have been fixed.

(Decision about tithis for observance of fasts)

3-4a. For the observance of a fast or undertaking a *Vrata* (religious vow), if the *tithis* (lunar days), viz. the eleventh, eighth, sixth, the Full Moon day, the fourteenth, the New Moon day and the third *tithi* are pierced (contacted) by the next *tithi* (lunar day) [that is the eleventh *tithi* spreads into the twelfth....the third lunar day into the fourth. etc.] they become commendable, but not so when they are combined with their (immediately) previous *tithi*[2] [as when *Ekādaśi*, the eleventh *tithi* is combined with the *Daśami*, the tenth *tithi*....the *tṛtiyā*, the third *tithi* with the second, etc.]

4b-5a. If the sixth *tithi* is 'pierced' by i.e. combined with the fifth *tithi* (*nāga-viddhā*)[3] or the seventh tithi is combined with the eighth and the tenth *tithi* is contacted by the eleventh, these days are never to be observed as fasts.

(Decisions about Śrāddha-tithis)

5b-6a. A person performing Śrāddha on the new Moon day, the Full Moon day, the seventh *tithi* when these are combined with their respective immediately preceding *tithi*, goes to hell.

6b-7a. Some, however, have stated that if in the dark half of the month, the seventh and the fourteenth *tithis* are contacted by their (respective) previous *tithis*, those (*tithis*) are commendable; the same is the case with the third and the ninth *tithi* (in the dark half) [for the performance of śrāddha.]

7b-8a. For all *Vratas* and similar undertakings, the bright half of the month is specially preferable and the first half of the day is superior to the second half of the day.

8b-9. If the particular *tithi* for the sake of *vratas*, etc. is not possible (available) in the first (full) half of the day (but is available for the first two *muhūrtas* immediately after the sunrise) that pair of *muhūrtas* should be accepted (for undertaking the *Vrata*). In the cases of Vratas special to night-time (e.g. (*Śiva-rātri*), the *tithi* which spreads the *pradoṣa* periods (i.e. 3 *muhūrtas* or two hours and twentyfour minutes after the sunset) should always be accepted.

10-11a. In the case of a *Vrata* (holy observance) where the combination of a particular *tithi* and a constellation is enjoined, the constellation is acceptable if the sun sets while the period of the constellation continues. And the *tithi* is acceptable if it spreads for a period of three *muhūrtas* (two hours and twentyfour minutes) after the sunset. Otherwise it won't yield the fruit (of the Vrata).

11b-12a. In the case of a *Vrata* based on (i.e. for which it is enjoined) a particular constellation, it is acceptable if the particular constellation and *Tithi* coexist upto the midnight.

12b-13a. If the (period of the) same constellation covers two midnights in the course of two (consecutive) days, the constellation whose combination with a particular *tithi* is enjoined (as in the case of Rohiṇī constellation and Aṣṭamī in Kṛṣṇa-Janmāṣṭamī) is meritorious (and hence suitable for the *Vrata*).

13b-14a. If both the (period of the) constellation and the *tithi* spread from midnight to midnight (and are available on both the midnights), the former is recommended if its duration is shorter and the latter if its duration is longer (the preference thus depends on the length of duration available of a particular *tithi*)

14b-15a. If the *tithi* in combination with the constellation extends over two midnights and there is neither increase or decrease (i.e. they are of equal duration on both the *tithis*), then both former as well as the latter is acceptable.

15b-16a. The combinations of the constellation Jyeṣṭhā with Mūla, of Rohiṇī with the constellation Kṛttikā and that of Anurādhā with Jyeṣṭhā are destructive of progeny.

16b-17a. If the *Vratas* are to be performed during the day-time, the *tithis* should be auspicious. In case of all rites to be performed at night (e.g. *Śiva-rātri*) the combination for that period of night is of special importance.

17b-18a. That *Vrata* (religious observance) should be performed on that *Tithi* which is glorified as meritorious (for that *Vrata*) due to the combination of the particular tithi and constellation. That particular *Vrata* must be performed on that very *tithi* by clever persons.

18b. In the case of the *Vrata* called *Śravaṇa Dvādaśi* (also called *Vāmana dvādaśi*) in the bright half of Bhādrapada) it must have the combination at the time of the sun-rise.

Puṇyakāla (Auspicious period) re : eclipses and Saṅkrama (Transit of the Sun).

19-20a. The whole duration of the eclipse of the sun and the moon should be taken as *Puṇyakāla* (Auspicious period) for *Japa*, etc. The *Puṇyakāla* in all the *Saṅkrāntis* (transit of the sun) is being recounted. The benefit is inexhaustable in the case of those who perform ablutions, charitable gifts, *Japas*, etc. during this period.

20b-21a. The *Karkaṭaka Saṅkrama* (the transit to the zodiac of Cancer) is called the *Saṅkrama* (transit) of *Dakṣiṇāyana* [The winter solstice when the sun appears to move from the north to the south.] Learned men know that the *Puṇyakāla* starts thirty *Ghaṭikās* (i.e. 12 hours) before (the actual transit).

21b-22a. In the case of the *Saṅkramas* (transits) to the zodiacal signs of Vṛṣabha (Taurus), Vṛścika (Scorpio), Siṁha (Leo) and Kumbha (Aquarius), eight *Muhūrtas* previous (to the actual transit) are acceptable for ablution, *Japa*, etc.

22b-23a. In the case of the transit to *Tulā* (Libra) and Meṣa (Aries), ten *Ghaṭikās* both before and after should be known as conducive to the imperishability of what is given as gift.

23b-24a. O Brāhmaṇa, in the case of the transits to Kanyā (Virgo) Mithuna (Gemini), Mīna (Pisces) and Dhanus (Sagittarius) sixteen *Ghaṭikās* after (the transit) should be known as bestowing merit.

24b-25a. They say that the transit to Makara (Capricornus) is Uttarāyaṇa (the summer solstice marking northward movement of the sun). Here, forty *ghaṭikās* before and thirty *ghaṭikās* after (the transit) are auspicious.

25b-26a. If the sun and the moon set during their respective eclipses, O leading Brāhmaṇa, he must see the clear sphere the next day, take his bath and only then can he take food.

26b-27a. Amāvāsyā (New Moon) is said to be of two kinds by scholars desirous of acquiring piety. (1) *Sinīvālī* when the moon is slightly visible (i.e. *amāvāsyā* is mixed up with its previous—14th-*tithi*) and (2) *Kuhū* when the moon is entirely invisible (i.e. when *Amāvāsyā* is mixed with the first *tithi* of the next first night).

27b-28a. *Sinīvālī* should be accepted by the Brāhmaṇas who maintain their sacrificial fires, for the purpose of the Śrāddha rite, while Kuhū is to be accepted by women, Śūdras and the Brāhmaṇas who do not maintain sacrificial fires.

28b.-29a. If the *tithi* of *Amāvāsyā* (the New Moon day) spreads over two afternoons, the former is accepted if its duration is short and the latter, if its duration is longer on that day.

29b-30a. If the New Moon day (*Amāvāsyā*) is found to begin from the mid-day only, it is known as *Bhūta-viddhā* (pierced or contacted by the fourteenth-*caturdaśī-tithi*.)

30b-31a. If there is absolute loss of the *tithi* (i.e. when it is not available for the purpose *Śrāddha* as it is not available either in the afternoon on the first day nor does it reach the post-midday period the next day), the 'sinīvālī' which spreads over the evening upto sunset (i.e. *sāyāhna*) should be accepted.

31b-32a. If the *tithi* is available for a short duration but extends upto the sunset (and as such is *sāyāhna-vyāpinī*) the *sinīvālī* on the next day is always acceptable for performance of *Śrāddha*.

32b-33a. If the *tithi* is extremely extended (i.e. it is available for the after-noon period for both consecutive days), the *amāvāsyā* which is 'pierced' or contacted by *Caturdaśī* should be avoided.

In rites connected with *manes* (*pitṛs*), *Kuhū* type of *Amāvāsyā* if available in the after-noon should be accepted.

33b-34a. Just as in the case of Amāvāsyā which is slightly extending, the Amāvāsyā connected with the *Caturdaśī* is to be rejected and the Kuhū extending over the after-noon of the next day is to be accepted (for Śrāddha) by eminent scholars (or wise men).

34b-35a. If the new moon day spreads over two mid-days, either the former or the latter day be accepted for *Śrāddha*, according to one's wish.

(*Decisions about the* tithi *for performance of* Iṣṭis)

35b-36a. Now I shall explain (the decision of *tithis*) regarding *Anvādhāna* (depositing fuel of sacred sticks on the sacrificial fire. This precedes the day on which *Iṣṭi* is to be performed) when the *Parvan* (the day of the new or full moon, the days of opposition or conjunction) are fully available. The *Yāga* (*Iṣṭi*-fortnightly sacrifice) be performed on the *pratipad* (the first *tithi*), O excellent sage.

36b-37a. If one (last) quarter of the *parvan* day and the first three parts of the *Pratipad* are available, the morning time is said to be proper for performing the sacrifice according to the learned ones.

37b-38. If the New Moon day or the Full Moon day spread over the two (consecutive) mid-days, the second day is regarded as the day for performing *anvādhāna* and *iṣṭi* (such combination of *anvādhāna* and *iṣṭi* on the same day is called *sadyaḥ kāla*).

39. If the previous two continue after the *saṅgava*[4] part of the day (from six to twelve *ghaṭis* after the sunrise) on the next day, the *sadyaḥ kāla* shall be on the next day. The same holds good when there is 'loss' (*kṣaya*) of the *tithi* (i.e. unavailability of the proper time of the *Tithi*, for performance of the rite).

(*Decisions about the observance of Ekādaśī vrata*)

40. All should accept the *Ekādaśī*[5] (the eleventh) *tithi* (for observance of fast) if it is not connected with *Daśamī*. If it is combined with the *Daśamī*, (tenth) *tithi* (the observance of fast on such contaminated *Ekādaśī*) destroys the merit accumulated during the last three births.[6]

41. If *Ekādaśī* is known to be present for the duration of a *Kalā* on the *Dvādaśī* day and if *Dvādaśī* is present in *Trayodaśī*, the latter one (i.e. Dvādaśī) is remembered (as acceptable) for fasting.

42. In case pure[7] and perfect Ekādaśī is known (to be

present) in Dvādaśī also and Trayodaśī is only at the end of the night, I shall tell you my decision in the matter.

43. The earlier *Ekādaśī* is to be accepted by householders and the latter one by ascetics, since, householders wish for *Siddhi* (or prosperity) and the prominent ascetics wish for salvation.

44. If the *tithi* called *Ekādaśī* is pierced by (i.e. touched by) the *Daśamī* (tenth) day, fast should be observed on that (*viddha*) *Ekādaśī*, if a duration of one *Kalā* is available for Pāraṇā on the *Dvādaśī* day.

45. Whether in the bright half or in the dark half, if the *Ekādaśī tithi* falls on two days, the householders should follow the earlier one and the ascetics the latter one.

46. If the *Ekādaśī* day is slightly mixed with by *Daśamī* but extends to (or is spread over) in *Dvādaśī*, (and thus there is *dina-kṣaya*), the second Ekādaśī only is prescribed for all (i.e. householders and ascetics).

47. If there is no subsequent *Dvādaśī*, the Ekādaśī is acceptable even if it is mixed (with Daśamī). If there is subsequent *Dvādaśī* even the unmixed *Ekādaśī* is forbidden.

48. If it happens like this, viz.—*Ekādaśī* is overlapped by *Dvādaśī* and at the close of the night there is *Trayodaśī*, the merit acquired is that of twelve *Dvādaśīs*, should the fast be broken on the *Trayodaśī* day.

49-50. In the following case, viz.—There is *Ekādaśī* on the day of Dvādaśī for the duration of a Kalā and it is doubtful whether there is *Dvādaśī* on the *Trayodaśī* day—the earlier Ekādaśī even if it is mixed should be acceptable to householders. The latter one is to be accepted by ascetics and *Avīrās* (i.e. women without sons and husbands).

51. The whole of the *Ekādaśī* is pure, (i.e. extending from sunrise to sunset). It does not overlap on *Dvādaśī*. But *Dvādaśī* overlaps *Trayodaśī* what should be done then?

52. The earlier one should be utilized by householders for the observance and the latter *tithi* by the ascetics. Some opine that the second day should also be used for fasting devoutly.

53-54. When the *Viddhā* (pierced) *Ekādaśī* is not known (to be present) on the *Dvādaśī* day; but *Dvādaśī* spreads into *Trayodaśī*—in these circumstances. Others say that the pure *Dvādaśī* is to be undoubtedly used for observance of fast by all. Some say that the previous one must be used for fast. Their opinion is not logically tenable.

55. A householder who has sons should not observe fast or break one during Saṅkrānti that falls on a Sunday or during the solar and lunar eclipses due to Rāhu (or is *gaṇita-gamya* i.e. astronomically present).

56. If one takes food on a Sunday at day and *parvan* days at night, on the eighth and the fourteenth days during the day time, or either during the day or during the night on the *Ekādaśī* day he should perform the expiatory penance called *Cāndrāyaṇa*.

57. On the day of the solar eclipse one shall not take food for three *yāmas* (1 yāma = 3 hours) before the eclipse. If he takes food, he will be on a par with the liquor-addict.

58. O excellent sage, if there is an eclipse of the Sun or the Moon in between *Anvādhāna* and *Iṣṭi* (which is on the subsequent day), expiation should be performed by the performers of *Yajñas*.

59. During the lunar eclipse they should perform Homa repeating the ṚK *Daśame soma* etc. or *Āpyāyasva* (RV.I.19.16, IX.31.4, VS.12.11.2, TS. 3.2.5.3 (RV.I.21.3) etc. or *Somapāste*, etc. O Brāhmaṇa.

60. Three mantras are cited for the performance of Homa during the solar eclipse—Viz. *Udu tyam Jātavedasam* (RV. I.50.1. AV.XIII.2.16, VS.VII.41) etc. or *Āsatyena* TS.III. 4-11-2 (RV.I.35.2) etc. or *Udvayaṁ tamasaḥ* (RV.I.50,.10, VS XX.21), etc.

61. The benefit shall be inexhaustible to that scholarly person who performs *Vratas*, etc. after deciding the *Tithi* as laid down in the path of *Smṛtis*.

62. *Dharma* is that which is enjoined in the Vedas. Keśava is delighted through *Dharmas* (holy rites). Hence, those who are devoted to the *Dharmas* attain that greatest region of Viṣṇu.

63. Those who wish to perform holy rites are indeed ones whose form is identical with that of *Kṛṣṇa*. Hence, the sickness of worldly existence never harasses them."

CHAPTER TWENTYNINE

Determination of Tithis

1. *Tithi* is the time or period required by the moon to gain twelve degrees on the sun to the east. As the motion of the moon is irregular, it takes some times 60 *ghaṭikās*, some-times more upto 65 *ghaṭikās* and some times less upto about 54 *ghaṭikās.* Since Kane wrote this in HD. IV. p. 68, there has been some change in opinion which holds *Saptavṛddhir daśa Kṣayaḥ* i. e. the maximum *ghaṭikās* of a *tithi* are 60+7=67 and the minimum 60-10=50 *ghaṭikās.* It is obvious that a *tithi* is not co-terminus with a "civil day". Hence the need to determine *tithis* exactly, as every Vedic or *Smārta* rite or *Vrata* must be begun and observed on the exact Time or *Tithi.* Otherwise, it becomes fruitless (vide the next verse).

Tithis are either *Pūrṇā* (complete or of 60 full *ghaṭikās*) or *Sakhaṇḍā* (mutilated or broken) *Sakhaṇḍa tithis* are either *Śuddhā* (extending from sunrise to sunset or in the case of *Śivarātri* extending to midnight) or *Viddhā* (pierced i.e. intermixed or contacted by another *tithi*). This intermixture or *Vedha* is of two kinds : morning—*Vedha* when six *ghaṭikās* after the Sun rise a *tithi* becomes merged with the next *Tithi,* while evening-*Vedha* generally occurs when a *Tithi* contacts another *Tithi* six *ghaṭikās* (or more) before the Sunset.

The knowledge of these technical terms is taken for granted by the author of the NP.

The discussion is essential, as *Kāla* or time prescribed for an act is a point or occasion (*nimitta*) and must be seized for gaining the fruit of the act.

2. This is technically known as *yugma-vākya.* AP.175.36-37, GPI.12 B.16-17. and CC on *Kāla* p. 67 give the approved and disapproved pairs of such contacted *tithis* in technical terms. NP. is more plain. According to the principle of *yugma-vākya,* the following combinations of *tithis* are favourable, viz. of the 2nd and 3rd *tithi,* of the 4th and 5th, of the 6th and 7th, of the 8th and 9th, of the 11th and 12th, of the 14th and the *Paurṇimā* (the Full Moon day), of the *Amāvāsyā* (The New moon day), with the next 1st *tithi.* The reverse i.e. the combination of other *tithis* e.g. when the Ekādaśī is combined with the Daśamī or the examples given in the next verse(s), these are not recommended for fast or *Vrata.*

Here two terms are used : When a *tithi* is combined with the previous *tithi* or 'pierced' by the previous *tithi* it is *purva-viddhā* (e.g. the 6th with the 5th) and when contacted or 'pierced' by the next *tithi* (e.g. (the 6th *tithi* combined with the 7th *tithi*), it is *para-viddhā.*

3. These works on Astronomy-cum-Astrology use the following terms to symbolize the following numbers e.g. *yugma*=two, *Agni*=three, *Yuga*=four, *Nāga*=five, *muni*=seven, Rudra=eleven, etc.

4. In the Vedic period a day was divided into five parts : *Prātaḥ, Saṅgava, madhyāhna* or *madhyandina, aparāhṇa* and *sāyāhna* or *astamaya* (*Śat.Br.*II.3.2.9; RV.V.76.3 for the 1st three parts). Roughly each part gets six *ghaṭikas* (start-

ing from the Sun-rise). Hence *saṁgava* is a period from six to twelve *ghaṭikas* after the Sun-rise.

5. This is one of the most important Vratas and in addition to the discussion of this *Vrata* in Purāṇas, we have extensive discussion of this *Vrata* in medieval digests like *CC Kāla* (pp. 145-288), Mādhava's *Kāla-nirṇaya* (pp. 233-75), *Vratarāja* (pp. 361-475) and independent works like Raghunandana's *Ekādaśī-tattva*. NP. has devoted a number of chapters on this Vrata *vide* the story of Rukmāṅgada from Ch. 2 ff in the II part. Here the *Tithi-nirṇaya* or decisions on the day on which the fast should be observed are given. These have special importance as the NP., being a Vaiṣṇava Purāṇa, decides for Vaiṣṇavas, the day on which the Ekādaśī should be observed (as under certain conditions they are advised to observe fast on the Dvādaśī day in the name of Ekādaśī), Moreover, these decisions are found to be observed in the Vaiṣṇavas of Bengal indicating the probable region of the author of the NP.

6. GP.I.125.2 states that the combination of Daśamī with Ekādaśī should be avoided for fasting as Gāndhārī lost all her hundred sons by observing such a fast :

Daśamyekādaśī-viddhā Gāndhāryā sumupoṣitā /
tasyāḥ putraśataṁ naṣṭam tasmāt tāṁ parivarjayet //

I think it is due to *yugma-vākya* (as explained previously) that this combination of Daśamī and Ekādaśī is not approved. Vaiṣṇavas would prefer fasting on the Dvādaśī day even if one *Kalā* of Ekādaśī is available at Sun-rise and the rest is a Dvādaśī day.

7. Śuddhā—from Sunrise to Sunset.

CHAPTER THIRTY

The Mode of Expiation

Sanaka said :

1. O Nārada, I shall now explain the rules regarding the expiatory rites.[1] Listen. One who has purified his soul by means of expiatory rites shall attain the benefit of all holy observances.

2. O sage, all the rites performed by those who are devoid of (i.e. do not perform) expiatory rites are said to be futile. They are resorted to by Rākṣasas.

3. Brāhmaṇas must be consulted about *Dharma* by those who are desirous of the benefits of all *dharmas*, are devoid of lust and fury and are experts in the scriptures on *Dharma*.

4. O leading Brāhmaṇa, the expiatory rites performed by those who are averse to Nārāyaṇa do not sanctify the people even as the rivers cannot purify the pot of wine.

Prāyaścittas for Mahā-Pātakas

5. These are the five great sinners[2] — the slayer of a Brāhmaṇa, the wine addict, the thief, the defiler of the preceptor's bed and those who associate with any or all of these sinners.

6. If any one associates oneself with them by sharing their beds, seats or foodstuffs for a year, he shall be known as *Patita* (a fallen man) in regard to all holy rites.

7. If anyone slays a Brāhmaṇa unknowingly,[3] he should wear bark garments and matted hair. He should also hold the skull of the Brāhmaṇa killed by him.

8. If that skull, or any other article belonging to this man is not available, he should roam the forest holding up that material on a staff like a banner displaying his crime.

9. He should take to things available in the forest for his diet. He should stay there on limited diet for one time per day. He should take bath thrice a day and perform *Sandhyā* rite duly.

10. He should give up study and teaching of the

Vedas, but should all the time remember Hari. He should observe the vow of continuous celibacy and avoid wearing scented garlands, etc.

11. He should visit and stay at holy places and sacred hermitages. If he cannot maintain himself by means of the articles available in forests, he should beg for alms in the villages.

12. He should perform the expiatory rite thus for twelve years and be devoted to Hari. The slayer of a Brāhmaṇa then attains purity and becomes worthy of and eligible to perform holy rites.

13-14. The slayer of a Brāhmaṇa should perform any of the following rites and attain purity : viz. should he be killed by animals or die due to ailments while observing the expiatory penance, he attains purity. Or he should sacrifice his life to save a cow or a Brāhmaṇa or make a gift of ten thousand excellent cows to leading Brāhmaṇas.

15. On killing a kṣatriya who has been consecrated (for the performance of sacrifices, etc.[4]), the sinner should perform the expiatory rite of a Brāhmaṇa-slayer, or enter the funeral pyre or jump off a lofty cliff.

16. On killing a Brāhmaṇa who has been so consecreted, the sinner should perform twice the expiatory rites. In the event of killing a preceptor and others, the expiatory rites cited are four times the former.

17. On killing an ordinary Brāhmaṇa (by birth only who has not studied the Vedas, etc.), he should perform the expiatory rite for one year. O Brāhmaṇa, thus the mode of expiation for killing a Brāhmaṇa has been stated.

18. The expiation for a Kṣatriya is twice this and that for a Vaiśya is thrice : Learned men know that the Śūdra who kills a Brāhmaṇa is to be pounded to death with a club.

19. The decision in the scriptural texts is this that this punishment is to be meted out by the king himself. If Brāhmaṇa women are killed, half the expiation is to be performed and one-fourth in the case of the slaying of a girl.

20-23a. By killing a Brāhmaṇa boy not invested with the sacred thread, one should perform one-fourth of the expiatory rite. A Brāhmaṇa who kills a Kṣatriya should perform the *Kṛcchra*[5] penance for six years, for three years if it is a Vaiśya who is killed and for one year if a Śūdra is killed. On killing the wife of a consecrated one, a Brāhmaṇa woman, he should perform the expiatory rite for Brāhmaṇa-slaughter for eight years. He should certainly become pure. O excellent sage, the expiatory penance enjoined on old men, sick men, women and children in all cases is said to be half as related by learned men.

Expiatory rites for wine-drinking[6]

23b-24a. Wine (spirituous liquor) is of three kinds, *Gauḍī* (that which is prepared from molasses), *Paiṣṭī* (that which is prepared from grain meal) and *Mādhvī* (that which is prepared from honey). O Nārada, this should not be drunk by any of the four castes as well as by women, O Nārada.

24b-26. O sage, he should take bath and remain pure wearing the wet clothes. Remembering Nārāyaṇa, he should make one of these, viz., milk, ghee or cow's urine resemble red-hot iron and drink the liquid then. Then he should pour it into any metallic vessel, iron or copper, and drink it like water and meet death.

27a. It is by this that a wine-addict gets purified. There is no other way of purification.

27b-28a. A Brāhmaṇa who drinks wine due to inadvertence or deliberately (due to the belief that it is for his own good) should perform penance enjoined for Brāhmaṇa-murder with the difference that the exhibition of a skull on a staff and such symbols of *Brahmahatyā* should be absent.

28b-29a. If a Brāhmaṇa drinks liquor as an antidote for some ailment, he should undergo the rite of investiture with the sacred thread[7] once again. Moreover, he should perform two *cāndrāyaṇa* penances.

29b-30a. They say that any vessel which comes into contact with the spirituous liquor (is also defiled). Even if water is taken from the liquor pot it is on a par with drinking of liquor. So is the eating of camphor.

30b-31. Spirituous liquor is of eleven varieties, viz. *Tāla*, (extracted from palmyra), *Pānasa* (taken from the jack fruit), (*Drākṣa* (prepared from grapes), *Khārjūra-sambhava* (prepared from date fruits), *Āriṣṭa* (fermented liquor), *Mādhuka* (prepared from honey), *Maireya* (specially concocted from Ariṣṭa and Surā), *Nālikeraja* (prepared from coconut palm), Gauḍī prepared from molasses), *Mādhvī* (prepared from honey) and *Surā* (prepared from grain meal).

32-33a. No Brāhmaṇa should at any time drink any of these spirituous liquors. If any Brāhmaṇa drinks any of these due to ignorance, he is to be invested with the sacred thread once again. He should perform the expiatory penance called *Tapta-Kṛcchra*.[8]

(*Theft*) :

33b-34a. Whether directly or indirectly whether forcibly or clandestinely, the (illegal) taking of other people's wealth is called *Steya* (theft) by learned men.

34b-35a The magnitude or (the scale of the weight) of gold has been specified by Manu and others. O leading Brāhmaṇa listen. I shall detail it which is the means of relating it to the mode of expiation.

35b-36. The dust particle that is seen in the middle of the beam of the sun coming through the window is called the magnitude of *Trasareṇu* by learned men.[9] Eight *Trasareṇus* make one *Niṣka*. Three such *Niṣkas* make one *Rājasarṣapa*.

37-38a. Three *Rājasarṣapas* make one *Gaurasarṣapa*. Six *Gaurasarṣapas* make what is called *Yava*. Three *Yavas* make one *Kṛṣṇala* and five *Kṛṣṇalas* make one *Māṣa*. O Nārada, sixteen *Māṣas* shall make the mass of one *Suvarṇa*.

38b-39a. If out of ignorance one steals the wealth of a Brāhmaṇa, one should perform *Brahma-hatyā* expiatory penance without the skull on the staff as the banner (symbol of *Brahmahatyā*).

39b-40a. On stealing the gold of preceptors, performers of *Yajñas* and pious Brāhmaṇas well-versed in the Vedas, the expiatory rite is as follows:

40b-41a. He should repent and apply ghee all over his body. He should then cover himself with dried cowdung (and get himself scorched by fire). If he is thus burned he is liberated from the sin of theft.

41b-42a. If a Kṣatriya steals the wealth of a Brāhmaṇa, he should repent for it and return it to the owner. Listen to its procedure from me.

42b-43a. He should perform the expiatory penance called *Sāntapana* and observe fast for twelve days. O celestial sage, he shall then attain purity, otherwise he will become fallen.

43b-44a. Half the expiation is enjoined in the case of thefts of articles resembling gold, viz : jewels, seats, men (servants), womenfolk, cows, plots of lands, etc.

44b-45. A man who steals gold equal to a *Trasareṇu* should perform two *Prāṇāyāmas* duly.[10] He thereby becomes pure. On stealing gold of the size of a *Niṣka* he should perform three *Prāṇāyāmas*.

46-47a. For stealing gold of the size of a *Rājasarṣapa*, he should perform four *Prāṇāyāmas*. On stealing gold of the size of *Gaurasarṣapa* the shrewd man should take bath and duly perform the Japa of a thousand and eight *Gāyatrīs*.

47b-48a. On stealing gold of the size of a *Yava*, the sinner should begin to perform the Japa of Vedic mother (i.e. Gāyatrī) in the morning and continue it till the evening. The Brāhmaṇa sinner should then be purified.

48b. On stealing gold of the size of *Kṛṣṇala*, he should perform the expiatory rite of *Sāntapana*.

49. The expiation for the theft of gold of the size of a *Māṣa* is now enjoined. He should regularly eat barley cooked in cow's urine. He will be purified of his sin in a year.

50. O leading sage, on stealing gold of the complete size of *Suvarṇa*, he should perform the *Brahma-hatyā* expiatory rite with great attention for twelve years.

51. If the act of stealing silver is of a quantity less than a *Suvarṇa* magnitude,[11] the sinner should duly perform the expiatory penance called *Sāntapana*. Otherwise, he shall be fallen.

52. O sage, a person who knowingly steals between four and ten *Niṣkas* of silver should perform the *Cāndrāyaṇa* penance.

53. If any one steals silver of the size ranging from ten to hundred *Niṣkas*, two *Cāndrāyaṇas* constitute the expiation for his sin.

54. Between a hundred and a thousand *Niṣkas*, he should perform three *Cāndrāyaṇas*. If the stolen quantity exceeds a thousand *Niṣkas* he should perform *Brahmahatyā* expiatory penance.

55. If the stolen quantity is upto a thousand *Niṣkas* and

the material is mainly bell-metal, iron or load stones, the expiatory rite is stated to be *Parāka.*[12]

56. In the case of theft of jewels, the expiation is the same as that of silver. Now the expiatory penance of persons who defile the preceptors' bed is being stated.

Adultery

57. If due to inadvertence one cohabits with one's mother or her co-wife one should cut off one's own testicles proclaiming one's own sin[13].

58. He should hold the testicle in his hand and proceed towards the South west. While going, he should never consider what is pleasant or what is miserable.

59. He should go ahead without seeing the other persons who go about here and there. He who walks thus till death becomes purified. Or he should fall from a promontory proclaiming his own sin.

60. On cohabiting with a woman of a higher caste unthinkingly the sinner should with great attention perform *Brahma-hatyā* expiatory rite for twelve years.

61. O excellent Brāhmaṇa, either unthinkingly or as a regular practice if one cohabits with a woman of his own caste or a higher caste one attains purity on being burned in the fire of dried cow dung balls.

62. If after the sexual intercourse with his mother, the sinner withdraws before the discharge of the semen virile, he should perform the *Brahmahatyā* expiatory rite. If he discharges the semen virile, he should burn himself in the fire.

63. If any one withdraws before the discharge of semen virile in a woman of his own caste or of a higher caste he should perform *Brahmahatyā* expiatory rite for nine years and be devoted to Viṣṇu.

64. If one cohabits with the Vaiśya wife of one's own father, one should perform the expiatory rite for six years. On cohabiting with the Śūdra wife of the preceptor, one should perform the expiatory rite for three years.

65-66. If due to infatuation one is deluded and cohabits with mother's sister, father's sister, preceptor's wife, wife of the father-in-law, paternal uncle's wife, maternal uncle's wife or one's own daughter, he should duly perform the *Brahmahatyā* expiatory rite if the sin continues for two days; if the sin is committed for many times on a single day, the expiatory rite should be performed for three years.

67. If the sin is committed only for once, he becomes purified after performing the rite of expiation for a year; if the sin is committed for three days, he should become pure only if he is burnt in fire and not otherwise.

68-69. He who passionately cohabits with a Cāṇḍāla or Puṣkasa woman, daughter-in-law, sister, friends' wife, or disciple's wife, should perform *Brahma-hatyā* expiatory rite for six years, O leading sage. He who cohabits without passion should perform *Kṛcchra* rite for a year.

Expiation for Associates of great sinners

70. The expiatory rite for associating with great sinners is being mentioned.[14] A person whose soul is sanctified, thanks to the expiatory rite, should attain the benefit of all religious rites.

71. Persons who associate with the great sinners have to perform the respective expiatory rites of those sinners, to be undoubtedly free from those impurities.

72. He who associates with these unknowingly for five days, should perform physical *Kṛcchra* rite. Otherwise, he becomes fallen.

73. If the association lasts for twelve days, the expiatory penance called *Mahā-sāntapana* must be performed. If the association continues for half a month he should observe fast for twelve days.

74. If the association lasts for a month the expiatory rite is *Parāka* and if the association is for three months the rite of *Cāndrāyaṇa* has to be performed. If the association is for six months, two *Cāndrāyaṇa* penances are to be performed.

75. If the association lasts for a period slightly less than a year he should perform the expiatory rite for six months. All these expiatory rites are to be performed three times if the association is knowingly pursued.

Expiation for Miscellaneous sins

76-77. If a Brāhmaṇa kills a frog, a mongoose, a crow, a boar, a rat, a cat, a goat, a sheep, a dog or a fowl, he should perform the rite of half a *Kṛcchra*.[15] The slayer of a horse should perform *Atikṛcchra* rite. In the event of killing an elephant he should perform *Taptakṛcchra* expiation and *Parāka* if he kills a cow.

78a. No mode of purification is enjoined by learned men in the event of wanton killing of a cow.

Minor sins

78b-82. If any beverage, quilt, seat, flowers, fruits, roots or foodstuffs and edibles are stolen the atonement is through *Pañcagavya*. If dried wood, grass, trees, jaggery, hides, garments and meat are stolen, he should fast for three nights. On killing any of these, viz.—the sparrow, the ruddy goose, the swan, the Kāraṇḍava bird, owl, crane, dove, webfoot, parrot, blue jay, white crane, the Gangetic porpoise or the tortoise, the sinner should abstain from food for twelve days. If semen virile, feces or urine is taken in, *Prājāpatya* rite is to be performed.

83-84. Three *Cāndrāyaṇas* are enjoined (as expiatory rites) in the event of taking in the leavings of the Śūdra's food. On touching a woman in her menses, a Cāṇḍāla, a great sinner, a woman recently delivered of a child, a fallen fellow, a man defiled by *Ucchiṣṭa* (left-over of eaten food) or a washerman and others one should take bath along with the clothes one is clad in. He should take in ghee also.

85-86a. O Brāhmaṇa, the man of purified soul should perform the Japa of *Gāyatrī Mantra* one hundred and eight times. On touching any of the above-mentioned persons unwittingly at the time of taking food, one should observe fast for three nights and take in *Pañcagavya*. He should then be purified, O Nārada.

86b-87. If at the time of ablution, charitable gifts, Japas, Bhojana (meal), etc., if anyone hears the voice of anyone of these or talks to any of them, he should vomit the food taken in. He should take bath again and observe fast.

88-89a. O Nārada, he should take in ghee on the next day after which he shall attain purity. If in the midst of holy rites, even the sound of these is heard, he should perform the Japa of the *Gāyatrī Mantra*, a thousand and eight times.

89b-90a. Censuring Brāhmaṇas and the deities is the vilest of all sins. O Nārada, no expiation for this is found in any scripture.

90b-91a. In the case of those sins mentioned by the learned ones to be on a par with great sins, one should duly perform expiatory rites.

91b-92a. If anyone performs the expiatory rites with devotional feelings to Nārāyaṇa, all his sins perish. Otherwise, he shall be a fallen fellow.

92b-94a. A person who is free from passions, etc. and is endowed with (i.e. fully feels) repentance and is possessed of mercy and kindness to all beings and is alertly devoted to the remembrance of Viṣṇu, he is absolved of all sins whether he is defiled by great sins or by all sins, as he is devoted to Viṣṇu.

94b-95a. He who remembers Nārāyaṇa devoid of beginning and end, the man who remembers the embodiment of the universe and free from ailments, is liberated from crores of sins.

95b-96a. On being remembered, worshipped, meditated upon or bowed to, Viṣṇu who is stationed in the hearts of the good, does destroy all sins.

96b-97. He who worships Hari in virtue of his association or even delusion, becomes liberated from all sins. He goes to Viṣṇu's region. All the accumulated heaps of pain and distress perish by remembering Viṣṇu even once.

98-101a. O Brāhmaṇa, his attainment of heavenly pleasures and the like can be inferred. O leading sage, rarely indeed is human birth obtained. There too, the devotion to Hari is said to be rarer still. Hence, after attaining the rare human birth, as fleeting and transitory as the streak of lightening, one must devoutly worship Hari who liberates the *Paśus* (individual Souls) from bondage. All the obstacles perish; purity of the mind is generated and salvation is achieved when Janārdana is worshipped.

101b-102a. The eternal Puruṣārthas (aims of life), viz., virtue, wealth, love and liberation are realized by those who are devoted to Hari's worship. There is no doubt about this.

102b-103a. O ye men ! Do not be arrogant after attaining the human existence consisting of fickle entities namely, sons, wives, houses, fields, wealth and grain.

103b-104. Eschew your lust and fury, greed and delusion, inebriety and slandering and censure. Cherish the pious feelings towards Hari. Leave off all your activities and worship Janārdana.

105-106. The trees in the city of Kṛtānta (god of Death) are seen close at hand. As long as death does not overtake one, so long as old age has not come, even before the sense organs become incapacitated, one should worship Hari. No sane man should put any faith in the body that is of a perishing nature.

107. Death is ever near; riches are too unsteady and fickle and the death of the body is imminent. Hence, leave off pride and arrogance.

108. All unions end in separation; everything is transitory and transient. Knowing this, O blessed one, worship Janārdana.

109-110a. One only increases one's miseries by hopes. Liberation is too rare and inaccessible. Even the great sinner who worships Viṣṇu with devotion attains the greatest abode on reaching which none is subjected to affliction.

110b-111a. O excellent one, all holy centres, all sacrifices (*Yajñas*), and the Vedas with their ancillary subjects are not worth even a sixteenth part of the worship of Nārāyaṇa.

111b-112. If people are devoid of devotion to Viṣṇu, of what use are the Vedas, scriptures, sacrifices and pilgrimages to holy centres. Of what avail are austerities and holy rites?

113. Those men who worship Viṣṇu of infinite forms, comprehensible through Vedāntas, attain the region of Acyuta. Those who see the excellent deity as pervasive as the firmament, who is the plysician that cures the illness of worldly existence, attain the region of Acyuta.

114. On remembering the primordial Ātman who possesses infinite power, who is the support of Universe, who is worthy of being worshipped by Devas, whose form is brilliant and who is called Acyuta, a man attains to his true friend.

CHAPTER THIRTY

Mode of Expiation

1. The term *prāyaścitta* is variously derived but most digest-writers and commentators of Dharma-Śāstra regard it a combination of *prāyas* (Penance)+*citta* (Resolve). Plainly it means "A resolve to undergo penance" (in the belief that it will absolve one of sins). Hemādri thinks that the term cannotes a special act in atonement of sin (*prāyaścittatśabdaḥ pāpakṣayārthe naimittike karmaviśeṣe vartate / CC—Prāyaścitta*, p. 989). Bālambhaṭṭi on *Yājñ. Smṛ.* III. 206 regards *Prāyaḥ* (a sin)+*citta* (purification) and quotes an authority to support the view that *prāyaścitta* is purification from sins :

prāyaḥ pāpaṁ vinirdiṣṭaṁ cittaṁ tasya viśodhanam /

The NP. regards faith in Nārāyaṇa as the condition precedent, without which all expiatory acts will be futile (see V. 4).

2. Sins are classified in three categories (1) *Mahā-pātakas* (Great sins), (2) *Ati-pātakas* (Super-sins) and (3) *Upa-pātakas* (minor sins). This verse enumerates the *mahā-pātakas*. It is worth noting that wine drinking is a 'great sin' and association with the sinners is also a great sin.

The general expiation for these *mahā-pātakas* requires the following penance : (1) Three baths per day; (2) stay in a thatched cottage alone in a forest; (3) sleep on bare ground; (4) subsistence on roots, fruits and leaves (5) eating only once a day; (6) if the sinner enters a village for begging, he should proclaim his sin.

This penance is to be practised for twelve years.

—*Śaṅkha Smr.* 17-1-3; cf. NP. vv 7-12 below.

3. VV. 7-17 deal mainly with the homicide of a Brāhmaṇa. The act can be expiated if done unknowingly. VV 7-12 refer to slaying a Brāhmaṇa whose death affects the continuity of the Vedic lore. For killing an ordinary Brāhmaṇa, the expiation is for one year only, i.e. 1/12 of the expiation of killing a knower of a Veda. This is the precaution taken by the society, to preserve our literary and cultural tradition by prescribing a deterrent punishment. Dharma Sūtras of Gautama, Āpastamba, Viṣṇu and Smṛtis of Manu (XI.72-82), Yājñavalkya (III.243-50) and AP. 169.1.4, 173. 7-8 prescribe practically the same type of penances for slaying a Brāhmaṇa and cover the penances given in the NP., though he (Manu) gives some other penances as well.

4. It is noteworthy that a Kṣattriya who has been consecrated for performance of a sacrifice is equated with a Brāhmaṇa.

5. *Kṛcchra*—

A kind of penance, for details vide *Yājñavalkya Smṛti*, Prāyaścitta Adhyāya.

6. VV. 23b—33a deal with the expiations for the second *Mahāpāpa*—wine-drinking. The varieties of wines are detailed in Verses 23b-24a and 30b-31. It appears that wine-drinking was regarded worse than Brāhmaṇa-slaughter, and death-penalty in a painful way is prescribed for it. For drinking spirituous liquor inadvertently, the penance of a Brāhmaṇa-slaughter is laid down in VV. 24-28.

Here NP. is repeating this way of death penalty for wine-drinking which has been already prescribed in Dh.Ss of Āpastamba (I.9.25.3), Gautama (23,1) Baudhāyana (II.1.21) and the Smṛtis of Manu (XI.90-91) and Yājñavalkya (III.253).

7. The second *upanayana* (investiture of sacred thread) seems to be symbolic. Āśvalāyana Gr. S. (I.22.22-26) prescribes cutting of hair and *medhājanana* as optional; there is no mention of rules regarding time of this *upanayana* and the verse to be recited as Sāvitrī is RV.V.82.1 and not the regular *Gāyatrī Mantra* (RV.III.62.10.)

8. Vide Supra fn.

9. VV 35b-38a give the weights used for weighing gold. It is the same as in Manu VIII. 132-135.

Trasareṇu	=A particle of dust seen in the Sun-beam coming through a window
8 *Trasareṇus*	=1 *niṣka* (called *likṣa* by Manu)
3 *Niṣkas*	=1 *Rāja sarṣapa*
3 *Rāja sarṣapas*	=1 *Gaura sarṣapa* (A white mustard-seed)
6 *Gaura sarṣapas*	=1 *Yava*
3 *Yavas*	=1 *Kṛṣṇala*
5 *Kṛṣṇalas*	=1 *Māṣa*
16 *Māṣas*	=1 *Suvarṇa*

Some of these terms are found in some other Smṛtis and the Kauṭalīya *Artha-Śāstra*, the difference in terms and their equation (if any) is due to difference of Time and region.

10. The NP. (VV. 44b-50) has decided the punishment or *Prāyaścitta* for stealing gold according to its weight.

weight of the stolen gold	*Prāyaścitta*
1 *Trasareṇu*	1 *Prāṇāyāma*
1 *niṣka*	3 *Prāṇāyāmas*.
1 *Rājasarṣapa*	4 *Prāṇāyāmas*
1 *Gaurasarṣapa*	Bath and Japa of Gāyatrī 1008 times.
1 *yava*	Japa of Gāyatrī from morning (Sun-rise) to evening (Sun-set).
1 *Kṛṣṇala*	A Sāntapana
1 Māṣa	Subsistence on barley cooked in a cow's urine, for one year
1 *Suvarṇa*	Expiation meant for Brahmahatyā (for 12 years).

11. VV. 51-54 declare the Prāyaścitta to be performed by a thief of silver depending on the weight of the metal as follows:

Weight of the stolen silver	*Prāyaścitta prescribed*
Less than 1 *suvarṇa* in weight	One *Sāntapana*.
Between 4 to 10 *niṣkas*	One Cāndrāyaṇa.
From 10 to 100 *Niṣkas*	Two *Cāndrāyaṇas*.
from 100 to 1000 *Niṣkas*	Three *Cāndrāyaṇas*.
More than 1000 *Niṣkas*	Expiation meant for *Brahmahatyā*.

12. *Parāka* :

A penance requiring continuous fast for twelve days and observance of self-control (vide Manu XI.215, Yājñavalkya III. 320 A.P.171-10).

13. Incest with one's preceptor's wife or one's mother or step-mother is to be expiated with the incision of the organ and to go on walking with his testicles in one's hand and proclaiming the sins till one falls dead. This has been prescribed since the days of Dharma Sūtras. For example :

Gautama states :

liṅgaṁ vā savṛṣaṇam utkṛtyā' ñjalāvādhāya dakṣiṇapratīcīṁ vrajed ajihmam ā-śarīra-pātāt /

Manu XI.105 repeats the same. But the NP. does not lay down the other punishment, viz. lying on a red-hot iron bed or embracing a red hot iron image of a woman, though the Dharma Sūtras and Manu prescribe that alternatively. But the NP. prescribes leap from a precipice, which is its special view.

The *prāyaścittas* for other cases of incest vary in various Smṛtis. NP.'s views are stated in vv. 60-69.

14. As stated above, association with the four types of grave sinners mentioned above, is regarded as a serious sin and Manu XI. 181, Yājñavalkya III. 261 provided that a person associating with a person guilty of serious sins (*Mahāpātakas*) should undergo the same *Prāyaścitta* as is prescribed for the *Mahāpāpa*. NP. voices the same view but he takes a lenient view and prescribes milder *prāyaścittas* of shorter duration as compared with those for the original sinners. Kullūka, Vijñāneśvara and other commentators state that the *Prāyaścitta* in such cases is a *Vrata* and as such should not be extended to or involve death of the performer of the *Vrata*.

(*maraṇasya ca Vrataśabdavācyatvā'bhāvāt* /

—*Mitākṣarā* on *Yājña. Smṛ*. III. 261.

15. VV 76-92a deal with miscellaneous sins. Smṛti-writers (e.g. Manu XI. 133-37, Yājñ III. 269-74) have prescribed various expiatory rites for them. The NP. agrees with some. The NP. emphasizes that slandering gods and Brāhmaṇas is a great sin from which there is no absolution (89b-90). The main point is that if one is devoted to Lord Nārāyaṇa and undergoes expiatory rites, he becomes free from sins. In extolling devotion to Viṣṇu, NP. asserts that all sins are destroyed by remembering (or worshipping or meditating on) Hari. He concludes : All heaps of miseries instantly disappear if Lord Viṣṇu is remembered but once (V. 97).

CHAPTER THIRTYONE

The Duties of the Emissaries of Yama

Nārada said :

1. O sage, the rules governing the discipline and conduct of life of the different castes and stages of life have been duly narrated by you. Now I wish to hear the extremely impassable path of Yama.

Sanaka said :

2. Listen O Brāhmaṇa, I shall recount to you the impassable path of Yama that bestows happiness to men of meritorious deeds and that is awe-inspiring unto the sinners.[1]

3. It has been mentioned by the earlier sages (i.e. philosophers) that the extent of the path of Yama is, O leading sage, eightysix thousand *Yojanas*.

4. O Brāhmaṇa, men who habitually give charitable gifts go through it with great pleasure and happiness. Men devoid of righteous activities go through it miserably as they are pounded and thrashed roundly on the way.

5. Extremely terrified, devoid of garments and with their throats, lips and palates parched up, the sinners traverse that way crying bitterly and pitiably.

6. Yama's soldiers strike them with whips, goads and other weapons.

7. They run about here and there along that path with great pain and misery. In some places there is deep mud; in some places there is fire; in some places there is red-hot sand; at some places there is forest-fire; while there are sharp-edged rocks elsewhere.

8. In some places there are thorny trees and rocky mountains very difficult to climb; there are many caves with pitch darkness, there are great covering hedges of thorny bushes.

9. In many places, people have to climb to the top of steep bunds and mounds and enter long caves. The path is strewn with gravels, pebbles and clods, as well as thorns pointed like needles.

10. Some places on the way are made slippery with mosses; in some places there are rows of bamboos; tigers roar in some places; in some places paroxysms of fever (overwhelm the people).

11. O Nārada, the sinners undergo much distress and move ahead slowly. Crying loudly and weeping they fade and languish.

12. Some of the sinners are bound with nooses; some are dragged with goads and hooks; some are beaten and hit with diverse weapons on their backs—in this way the sinners wend their way.

13. Some are dragged with nooses at the tip of their noses, some are bound with entrails. Some go ahead bearing weighty iron mass with the tip of their penis.

14. Some sinners bear two weighty iron balls by means of the tips of their noses; some sinners bear the same with their ears and go ahead.

15. Some falter at every step and plod on. Others, on being struck, slip down. Some leave deep sighs and some keep their eyes closed.

16. Along the path that contains no shady place to rest nor water to drink, they miserably plod on lamenting their sins committed knowingly or unknowingly.[2]

17. O Nārada, those who are pious and righteous, those who are habitual givers of gifts, those who are of good intention, go to the palace of Dharma (god of death) with great pleasure and happiness.

18-19. Those who had given the gifts of cooked food (on the Earth), O excellent sage, go along that path eating tasty things; the bestowers of water go happily, drinking excellent milk; the givers of buttermilk and curds obtain similar kinds of pleasures (correspondingly). O excellent Brāhmaṇa, those who give ghee, honey or milk (on the earth), go to the mansion of Dharma (god of Death) imbibing nectar on the way. He who has given green vegetables, goes ahead tasting milk pudding and he who has gifted lamps, goes there illuminating the quarters.

20. O leading sage, the giver of robes and cloth goes clad in divine garments. He who has given a mine previously goes along the path eulogised by the immortal ones.

21-22a. Thanks to the gift of a cow, a man goes there endowed with all means of happiness on the way; a giver of plots or houses goes riding in an aerial chariot filled with all riches and luxuries. He sports about in the aerial chariot filled with groups of celestial damsels and goes to the abode of Dharma (god of Death).

22b-23. O excellent sage, the giver of horses, vehicles, or elephants goes to the abode of Dharma by means of an aerial chariot equipped with all means of enjoyment. O excellent sage, the giver of bullocks goes riding on a vehicle.

24. The giver of fruits and flowers goes with great contentedness. The man who gives betel-leaves to chew goes to the abode of Dharma with great delight.

25. The excellent man who had rendered service to his father and mother (while on the Earth), walks ahead with a delighted soul honoured and worshipped by the heaven-dwellers.

26. He who renders great service to ascetics who perform great holy rites, and to leading Brāhmaṇas, goes (to Dharma's palace) with great pleasure.

27. A Brāhmaṇa who is endowed with compassion to all living beings is worshipped along the path by the immortal ones and he goes riding in an aerial chariot endowed with all means of pleasures.

28-29a. A person engaged in the gift of learning goes ahead while he is being worshipped by lotus-born deities. The regular reader of the *Purāṇas* goes ahead as he is being eulogised by leading sages. Thus, those who are engaged in righteousness go to the abode of Dharma with great pleasure.

29b-30a. Yama assumes a form with four faces and holds a conch, a discus, an iron club and a sword. He honours the person engaged in meritorious rites duly with great love and affection like a friend.

30b-31a. He says—"O, ye excellent ones among the intellectuals, ye who are afraid of distress in hells, the merit that yields happiness both on Earth and in heaven, has been earned by you all.

31b-32a. He alone who, after attaining a human life, does not perform meritorious deeds, is the vilest of sinners. He is the slayer of his own *Ātman*.

32b-33a. He, who, after obtaining the transient human life does not achieve the permanent one, goes to the terrible hell. Who can be a more senseless person than he ?

33b-34. The body is torture itself; it is defiled by impurities (like feces) and the like. Know that the person who places his reliance on it, is one who slays his *Ātman*. Among all things, the living beings are the most excellent and among them the intellectual beings.

35. Men are most excellent among the intellectual beings; among men the Brāhmaṇas are most excellent; the scholars are most excellent among the Brāhmaṇas; really wise ones are most excellent among scholars.

36. Among the wise ones the performers of holy rites are most excellent, the expounders of the Brāhmaṇa (or the Veda) are most excellent among them. The person who has no feeling of myness is said to be most excellent among the expounders of *Brahman*.

37. He who is perpetually interested in meditation should be known as greater than all these. Hence, by all means, piety and righteousness must be accumulated.

38. There is no doubt that a righteous creature is worshipped everywhere. Go, you, to my abode endowed with all means of enjoyment and pleasure. Go there, thanks to your own merits.

39. If at all, there is any sin, you shall experience the fruit thereof here itself afterwards". Thus Yama greets and honours the meritorious one and enables him to attain the goal of the good.

40. Having summoned the sinners, he would threaten them with his *Kāladaṇḍa* (rod of punishment or the Black baton). (Now he assumes a terrible form). He roars loudly like the cloud at the time of dissolution. His lustre is like that of the mountain of collyrium.

41. He appears terrific due to his weapons glittering like lightning. He has thirtytwo arms and his girth is three *Yojanas*. His nose is long and his eyes are red.

42. His face is terrific due to the curved fangs. His fierce eyes resemble (two deep) wells. Citragupta (the accountant of deeds of all men) accompanied by *Mṛtyu* (Death), *Jvara* (Fever), etc. is also terrible.

43-44a. All the emissaries roar. They too are as terrible as Yama. Thereafter, Citragupta addresses at the behest of Yama all sinners who quake with fear and who bewail their own sinful fate.

44b-45a. "O ye sinners, O wicked ones defiled by arrogance, why was so much of sin accumulated by you, the thoughtless ones devoid of discrimination?

45b-47a. With a lofty mind defiled by lust and fury you have committed every conceivable form of sin. O people why have you done so? Formerly, at the time of committing sins you were extremely delighted. So the tortures too must be borne by you. Why are you unnecessarily worried too much?

47b-48. As sins had been committed for the sake of servants, friends and wives, so, you have come here drawn by your own sinful acts weighed down with extreme distress and dejection. But those sons and others nourished by you have gone elsewhere.

49-50. The sin has befallen you alone. Is that the cause of your misery? Since too many sins have been committed by you, the miseries too have befallen you. Why do you feel sorry for it? Ponder over what has been committed by you before.

51-52a. Why did you not consider before that Yama would mete out punishment? Yama is equal and impartial to the rich and the poor, the fool and the learned, the daring one and the dastard."

52b-53a. On hearing this statement of Citragupta, those sinners bewail their actions and their lot. Utterly frightened, they keep quiet.

53b-54a. The ruthless and terrific emissaries such as Cāṇḍālas and others, the executors of the behests of Yama, throw them forcibly into hells.

54b-55a. They experience the fruits of their sinful actions. In the end, as a result of the residue of their sins they come down to the Earth and become immobile and other beings."[3]

Nārada said :

55b-56a. 'O holy Lord, O storehouse of mercy, a doubt has occurred in my mind, which you are competent to eradicate, since you are our eldest brother.

56b-57a. Many kinds of holy rites and duties have been narrated by you. Many sins too have been related by you. You, the knower of many things stated that the fruits (of the sins, etc.) have to be enjoyed by them for a long time (till eternity).

57b. The destruction too of the three worlds at the end of a day of Brahmā has been mentioned by you.

58-59a. At the end of two *Parārdhas*, the annihilation of the whole Cosmic egg (is going to take place as mentioned by you). O son of Brahmā, it has been mentioned by you yourself that the enjoyment of the pleasures of the merits, thanks to the charitable gifts of villages, etc., is great and lasts for thousands and crores of Kalpas.

59b-60a. In the *Prākṛta-laya* (the dissolution into the *Prakṛti*) the destruction of all worlds (has been mentioned by you). It has been said by you that the only one who survives is Janārdana.

60b-61a. The doubt that there cannot be any end to the enjoyment of the fruits of merits and sins before the dissolution of the universe, has arisen in my mind. It behoves your honour to dispel it.

Sanaka said :

61b-62a. Well done, O highly intelligent, one, well done. What you have now asked is the greatest of all secrets, I shall recount it to you. Listen with great attention.

62b-63. Nārāyaṇa is infinite and imperishable. He is eternal and the supreme splendour. He is the purest one and devoid of attributes. He is perpetually devoid of delusions due to Māyā. Although, in reality, he is devoid of Guṇas, he is the greatest bliss and appears like one endowed with Guṇas.

64. He appears to be differentiated through the forms of Brahmā, Viṣṇu, Śiva, etc. The eternal lord appears to be differently conditioned by these three different Guṇas.

65-66a. By employing the entire Māyā-power, He performs the function of the universe. He creates (the universe) in the form of Brahmā and protects it in the form of Viṣṇu. It is certain that in the end he swallows everything in the form of Rudra.

66b-67a. At the end of the *Pralaya* (Dissolution), Janārdana gets up in the form of Brahmā, and creates everything in the whole universe consisting of the mobile and immobile beings as before.

67b-68a. O leading Brāhmaṇa, Brahmā makes even the immobile beings positioned in the same manner and place as they were before.

68b-69. Hence, O excellent one, the fruit of the actions meritorious or sinful must, compulsorily be experienced. The fruit of an action is inexhaustible or inevitable and must be enjoyed. Even in the course of hundreds of crores of Kalpas, no action perishes without being borne and experienced.

70. The action performed, whether auspicious or inauspicious must, of necessity, be enjoyed. He who is the lord of all worlds is the immanent soul of all and is identical with the universe. He is perfect and eternal and he enjoys through all the fruits of all actions.[4]

71. The God who pervades all universe and who is endowed with different Guṇas, creates, protects and swallows up everything. The immutable Lord is the enjoyer of everything.

CHAPTER THIRTYONE

The Duties of the Emissaries of Yama

1. This horrible description of the journey of the departed soul to the capital of Yama has little basis in the *Vedic* literature. The medieval authors of the *Purāṇas* used this deterrence against immoral tendencies to maintain a certain standard of morality in the public and their success can be gauged from the fact that the illiterate Hindu masses are still under the Purāṇic influence of Yama and his emissaries.

2. VV 5-16 graphically depict the crude tortures of those times. But this Purāṇic author seems to be unaware that the departed soul has no physical body of gross elements as the two gross elements, viz. the earth and water are left behind and the body that goes ahead consists of fire, wind and ether and as such many of the tortures are not applicable to such a body.

3. Cf. Manu XII.54 ff and Yājñavalkya. III.206 ff which state that sinners after serving their term in hells are born as lower animals, insects, trees, shrubs, etc.

4. The doctrine of *Karmavipāka* is common to all Indian religions—Brāhmaṇism, Jainism and Buddhism (despite their doctrine of 'No Soul'—*Anattā*). The Buddhist *Avadāna Śatakas* and the Jain *Vipāka Sūtra* (*Vivāga Suya*) testify to their belief in sufferings due to evil deeds. The *Mitākṣarā* on Yājñavalkya III.216 regards this as an *arthavāda*, i.e. it should not be taken literally but is an attempt to persuade people to undergo expiations for their sins. The relieving feature of the Indian (Jain, Buddhist and Brahmanical) doctrine of *Karma-vipāka* is the hope it offers to fallen persons of their redemption from sin and the possibility (nay their birthright) to secure liberation from *Saṁsāra*).

CHAPTER THIRTYTWO

The Forest of Worldly Existence

Sanaka said :

1. Thus all the creatures curbed and controlled by their respective *Karmas* (Actions, the fruit whereof they have to reap) enjoy the pleasures of their *Puṇyas* (merits) in heaven and other places of merits and undergo extremely painful sufferings, as the result of their sins, in hells. With the residue of their dwindled *Karmas,* they come to this world. They are born as immobiles and other beings infested with all fearsome things and subject to the harassment of death. Trees, bushes, creepers twining plants, grass and the mountains are well known as *Sthāvaras* (Immobile beings). They are enveloped by great delusions.[1]

2. In the course of their state of being immobile (the development is as follows) : The seeds sown in the ground become well cooked (as it were) through the reproductive faculty (that had been dormant) immediately after being watered. They become swollen and assume the form of the main shoot and its root. It germinates into a sprout from which the leaves, stem and tubular vessels develop. Buds come out from the stalk and blossom into flowers.

3. Among the flowers some do not yield fruits. Some of the flowers produce fruits. When the flowers mature the chaffs develop at their bottoms. Thanks to the residual impressions of the *Karmans* of the living beings destined to enjoy, the cool snowy beams of the moon and the lymphatic juice of herb plants penetrate the husks and the chaffs. They assume milklike form and in course of time become grains. Thanks to the dormant impressions of destiny for enjoyment belonging to the living beings, they fructify in the course of a year (the crop is ready for reaping the harvest).

4. In the course of their state of life as immobile beings that continues for a long time, they experience misery in many ways. For example, they are munched and crunched by monkeys and other animals; they are cut off by men; they are destroyed by forest fire; they endure chilliness, scorching

heat of the sun and similar miseries. Finally, they perish. Thereafter, they become worms experiencing many miseries continuously. Their span of life is but half a moment. Some live, some die. They are unable to ward off the attack of other powerful creatures. They undergo a great deal of sufferings due to chill, wind, etc. which (miseries) are also severe and prolonged. They endure perpetual hunger. They move about in urine and fecal matter. They thus experience misery.

5. Then they take to *Paśuyoni* (birth as animals). They are agitated and tormented forcibly. They suffer immense agony in vain. They are overwhelmed with hunger. They perpetually move about in the forests. They are afflicted with passionate sensual attachment even to their mothers. They undergo many sufferings due to gusts of wind, etc. During some births they are herbivorous. During other births they are carnivorous, some swallowing even fecel matter; some live subsisting on bulbous roots, fruits and roots. They are bent upon inflicting pain on weaker animals. They too suffer miseries.

6. In their state of oviparous living beings (i.e. birds), they take in gaseous, flesh, fecal and other matter, they are prone to injure others and they themselves suffer. After being born as domestic beasts (such as cattle) and other animals, they endure all sorts of miseries such as separation from their own kindred, bearing heavy loads, bondage in nooses and tethers, hitting with whips, etc., dragging the ploughs and similar agonies.

7. After wandering thus through various births, they gradually attain human life. Some of them enter human life as a result of special merit.[2]

8. As human beings too, they suffer no less when they are born as cobblers, *Cāṇḍālas*, hunters, barbers, washermen, potters, blacksmiths, goldsmiths, weavers, tailors, *Siddhas* with matted hair, launderers and dyers, scribes and painters, servants, errand boys, menial servants, slaves, indigent fellows etc.[3] Some have surplus limbs while others are wanting in some limbs (and physically handicapped). Their distresses are numerous. They suffer from fever, phlegmatic attack, enlargement of the spleen, pain in the legs, eyes, head, sides and womb and other distress as well.[4]

9. In the birth as human beings (there are other sufferings

as well). After the sexual intercourse between a man and a woman the semen virile enters the womb.[5] At the same time, as a result of his own *Karmas* the creature (i.e. the soul) too enters the womb along with the semen virile. The semen virile mixes with the blood and develops into the foetus.

10. The semen virile becomes a foetus within five days of the entry of the soul. Within half a month it becomes a fleshy man. Within a month it attains the size of a *Pradeśa* (the span measured with the forefinger and the thumb).

11. From that time onwards it begins to move within the belly of the mother, thanks to the action of the wind. Although it has no consciousness, it is unable to stay in one single place within the belly of the mother, due to the unbearable heat and pain.

12. When the second month is complete it takes human shape; when three months are over, the hands, legs and other limbs are formed; when four months elapse, the knots and joints of all limbs are clearly developed; when five months pass away, the nails appear; when six months pass off, the nail-joints become distinct. The body of the newborn is nourished through the umbilical cord; it is defiled by feces and urine (present within the mother's body); it is tied up with the embryo; it is vitiated by the blood, bone, germs, suet, marrow, sinews, hair, etc.; it is scorched amidst the intake of the food of the mother whether pungent or sour or saline but hot (to the touch). The soul observes that its body is in such a defiled place. At that time it has the faculty of remembering its previous birth. It remembers the miseries in hells it has experienced before; it burns within itself due to excessive agony on being scorched by the stringent urine (and other secretions) within the mother's body. It begins to lament as follows :

13. "Alas I am extremely sinful. In my previous birth I was too fond of servants, children, friends, womenfolk, houses, fields, wealth, grains, etc. In order to maintain my wives (and others) I used to rob others of their wealth, fields, etc. in their very sight. Since I was blind due to lust, I had abducted other men's wives. Thus, I have committed many sins. As a result of it I underwent sufferings in hells. I was then born as immobile being and experienced great miseries. Now, enveloped in this embryo, I burn within myself as well as without.[6]

14. The wives and others maintained by me have gone elsewhere according to their own *Karmas*.

15. O How miserable is the lot of embodied beings!

16. The body is born of sin. Hence, one must not commit sins. For the sake of my servants, friends and wives wealth belonging to others had been taken away by me.

17. Due to that sin, I burn within myself enveloped by this (outer skin of the) embryo. Formerly, I had been distressed by jealousy on seeing another man's wealth and glory.

18. Even now, the sinner that I am, I am being burned by the fire (heat) of this womb. I had inflicted pain on others physically, mentally and verbally. I am being burnt by that sin. I am lonely and extremely distressed."

19-20. The creature in the womb laments thus, in diverse ways. He consoles himself and mentally decides as follows : "After my birth I will become one of the pure mind, thanks to the association with saintly people and to the listening to the stories of Viṣṇu. I shall perform holy rites. With great devotion, I will worship the pair of feet of Nārāyaṇa who is the immanent soul of the universe, identical with truth, knowledge and bliss; who has created all worlds through the power of his Śakti, who is the lord of Lakṣmī, and whose lotus-like feet are duly worshipped by all Devas, Asuras, Yakṣas, Gandharvas, Rākṣasas, serpents, sages, Kinnaras and other groups of people. I shall meditate within my heart upon the lord who is the cause of destruction of the unbearable worldly existence, who is engaged in the protection of the universe and who becomes clearly visible through the secret *Upaniṣads*. I shall then go beyond this prison of worldly existence that is excessively miserable."

21. O sage Nārada, at the time of the confinement of his mother, the soul within the womb is afflicted by the wind. Urged by his *Karmas* he is forced out through the vaginal passage. Inflicting pain on his mother also, he simultaneously experiences all tortures.

22. Due to this excess of pain he is afflicted in the vaginal passage as though within a mechanical device. As soon as he comes out of the womb, he becomes unconscious.

23. The external wind enlivens him. Immediately after the contact with the external wind, he loses all his memory.

Since he has lost all wisdom, he does not realise the miseries experienced before as well as what are the current ones. He thus experiences the excess of misery.

24. The creature that is now born as a baby experiences many sufferings during the infancy. He is smeared with his own fecal matter and urine. He is unable to utter even when he suffers from bodily pain. If he is oppressed by hunger and thirst, he cries, when others think that the boy must be breast-fed and do accordingly.

25. He experiences bodily pains, etc. of various types and he does so only through subservience to others. It is impossible for him to ward off even the flies.

26. After becoming a slightly bigger boy he experiences all these things :—He is beaten by his mother, father and preceptor. He gets the habit of listless wandering here and there. He plays about in dust, ashes and mud. He is always quarrelsome. He is dirty. He engages himself in many futile tasks. When those do not fructify he feels sorry. Thus, he undergoes sufferings.

27. Then in his youth (he experiences various other sufferings:) there is misery in earning wealth; there is misery in preserving what is earned. He is very miserable when the earned wealth is lost or spent. The young men are deluded by Māyā; their minds are defiled by lust and fury and similar emotions; they are always engrossed in jealousy, and in devising means of knocking off other men's wealth and abducting other men's wives; they are always worried over the ways of sustenance for their sons, friends and wives; they are puffed with vain arrogance. When their sons or other kinsmen are bedridden due to ailments, they cancel all their engagements and sit beside the patients. They are too remorseful and begin to muse as follows :

28. No action regarding the house, fields, etc. has been contemplated by me. How is the increasing family to be maintained ?

29. I have no capital with me. We do not get timely showers of rain. Where has the horse run away ? How is it that my kine have not yet returned ?

30. My wife is burdened with an infant son. I am sick and indigent. Due to lack of thought and care, the farm has perished. All the sons are now crying.

31. My house is in bad repairs. It is in ruins. All my kinsmen are far off. I am not able to get any job. The tyranny of the king is unbearable.

32. My enemies rush at me. How can I conquer them ? I am incompetent to pursue any vocation. These guests have come now !

33. Thus, he is much agitated and worried. Unable to ward off his miseries, he blames the destiny saying—"Fie upon Fate. Why has it rendered me unfortunate ?"

34-36. When he attains old age (his miseries are equally terrible). His strength decreases. Greying hairs, old age, etc. have asserted themselves all over his body; he is oppressed by sickness; all his limbs begin to quiver; he is afflicted by sneezing and asthmatic trouble; his eyes are tremulous and clouded; lumps of phlegmatic secretion choke his throat; he is being cursed and rebuked by his sons, wife and others. He then begins to worry over every thing.... "O when shall I die ? After my death how can my sons and others preserve the house, fields and other property that I have earthed ? To whom shall they belong? When my wealth is taken away by others, how can my sons and others maintain themselves ?" Thus, the old man is afflicted with the misery of my-ness. He heaves deep sighs. He begins to recollect various things committed by him at different periods of his life. Within a moment he forgets every thing. His death is now imminent. Afflicted by sickness as well as by mental agony, sometimes he moves on the bare cot, sometimes on the bed. Oppressed by hunger and thirst, he pleads, "Please give me some water to drink !" Even when he implores pitiably they say, "Water is not congenial to the health of those who are afflicted by fever". The old man chafes extremely in the mind and lapses into unconsciousness.

37. Thereafter, he becomes incapable of even making any movement of (drawing back) his hands and feet. He is surrounded by weeping kinsmen. He is unable to speak. His worry now is, "to whom will the wealth earned by him go ?". Tears begin to well up in his eyes and cloud them. There is a snorting-like sound in his throat. The vital breaths leave off his body. He is then rebuked by the emissaries of Yama. Bound and fettered by them, he falls into the hells as before.

38. Just as metals are cast into fire and blown with the

bellows till the impurities are removed, so also the living beings are tortured in the hells till their Karmans are completely destroyed (by suffering the fruits of acts.)

39. Hence, O excellent Brāhmaṇa, one who is distressed by the scorching heat of the forest-fire of worldly existence shall practise the perfect (spiritual) knowledge. Through knowledge one should attain liberation (from *Saṁsāra*).

40. Those men who are devoid of knowledge are said to be brutes. Hence, for the liberation from worldly existence, one shall practise perfect knowledge.

41. Who is more senseless than that person who does not serve Hari even after attaining human birth that enables one to accomplish all rites (and holy acts).

41A* Surprising, very strange, O leading sages, this is indeed extremely astonishing that men undergo torture even when Viṣṇu, the bestower of desires, stands by.

42. Alas ! even when Nārāyaṇa, the lord of the universe, the bestower of all desired benefits, stands by, men devoid of perfect knowledge are cooked in the hells !

43. Ignorant persons enveloped by great delusions, consider this transient body permanent—the body that exudes fecal matter and urine.

44. After attaining the body that is rendered despicable due to (its contents of) flesh, blood, etc., the man who does not worship Viṣṇu who puts an end to the cycle of worldly existence is a great sinner.

45. Alas it is a pity ! Alas it is a pity ! It is sheer foolishness. O Brāhmaṇa, even a Cāṇḍāla who is engaged in the meditation on Hari, is extremely happy.

46. How is it that the foolish sinful men do not get nauseated (lit: alarmed and excited) on seeing the bane of fecal matter, urine, etc. issuing out of their own body ?

47. Rare and inaccessible human birth is sought for even by Devas. A clever man on getting the same, must indeed strive for attaining the greatest of the worlds.

48. Those who are richly endowed with spiritual knowledge, those who are engaged in the worship of Hari attain the greatest abode, a return from which is difficult to get.

*Verse No 41A is really No. 42, but No 41 is wrongly repeated in the Printed text.

49. He is the liberator from the worldly existence, he from whom the universe is born; from whom it attains consciousness and in whom it is dissolved.

50. A person is liberated from the worldly existence on worshipping that Lord of Devas who appears to be one endowed with attributes, though he is really devoid of them, who is the supreme and the infinite deity.

CHAPTER THIRTYTWO

The Forest of Worldly Existence

1. An echo of Manu XII.54 ff & Yājñavalkya III.206 ff. Curiously enough here, both Manu and Yājñavalkya are textually very similar to each other pointing thereby to an earlier common source.

2. The ancient theory of evolution. Before a *Jīva* reaches the stage of human beings they undergo the following stages of evolution : immobile beings, trees, grass → animal-world (wild beasts) → oviparous beings and domestic animals → human beings.

3. The idea that people are born in lower castes as a result of their sins in previous birth is traceable to the *Dharma Sūtra* period. Thus *Āpastamba* (Dh. S. II.1.2.6-7) states that after undergoing the torments of the hell, the sinner is born as a Cāṇḍāla, Paulkasa and Vaina and outcaste. Cf. Manu's explanation for birth as a goldsmith (Manu XII.61).

4. Since ancient times diseases are believed to be the consequences of sins. Thus *Viṣṇu Dh.* S. Ch. 45, Manu XI.49-52, Śātātapa I. 3-11, Gautama (versified *Smṛti*) Ch. 20 (to mention a few) state the diseases and bodily defects from which sinners suffer after they are born as men. Not that all of these authors agree in their pronouncements of such defects and diseases as the result of a particular sin. Thus Brāhmaṇa-slaughter causes leprosy according to Vasiṣṭha 20.44 but Phthisis according to Manu XI.49, Yājñavalkya III. 209 Vijñāneśvara in *Mitākṣarā* on Yājñavalkya III. 216 gives a list of births in lower species and diseases and deformities suffered for various sins.

5. This chapter is in prose. Paragraphs 9-12 give the ancient ideas of embryology—the development of the foetus since its inception from sexual intercourse. For want of space it is not possible to quote the relevant portions from Suśruta or Vāgbhaṭa but the quotations on *garbha* in SKD.II-pp 312-313 show how the NP depends on the old works on Āyurveda. Other Purāṇas also do the same. Thus the *Garuḍa Purāṇa* I.146-167 corresponds to Vāgbhaṭa's *Aṣṭāṅgahṛdaya* (Ramshankar Bhattacharya—Intrd. to *Garuḍa Purāṇa* pp. 29-30.).

Modern medical Science however differs in its findings about the development of the foetus. Thus in C. S. Dawn's *Text book of Obstetrics* (Calcutta, 1967) we are told that it is the union of spermatozoon which is united with the ovum and for the first eight weeks is in 'embryo stage' after which it is called foetus. The Sk. dictionaries make a confusion between 'embryo' and 'foetus by using them as synonyms (*vide* Apte's *Sk-Eng. Dict.* p. 183 at 2). NP.'s description of the development of foetus and the process of delivery reflects the state of knowledge in the medieval India.

6. The soliloquy in paragraphs 13-20 is of course imaginary. But these very words have been repeated (as the prayer of the foetus) by saint poets of Maharashtra.

CHAPTER THIRTYTHREE

A Discourse on Yoga

Nārada said :

1-2. Whatever has been asked by me has been recounted by you of scholarly attainments. A great many miseries of those who are bound by the noose of *Saṁsāra* (worldly existence) also have been described by you). Who is remembered as the person who severs the noose of worldly existence? O sage, rich in penance, kindly enlighten me in the means whereby liberation from *Saṁsāra* is achieved.[1]

3. O excellent sage, series of actions are being performed by living beings every day and are enjoyed also. How can they (*Karmas*) be destroyed?

4. The embodied soul takes up the body as a result of his *Karman*; he is bound by lust. As a result of lust he is overwhelmed by avarice and avarice makes him prone to anger.

5. Due to anger, Dharma perishes and the destruction of Dharma leads to misapprehension. A man of confused intellect commits sin again.

6. Hence, the body has its root in sins. It is always engaged in sinful activities. Narrate to me how one attains liberation after eschewing the misconception about the body.

Sanaka said :

7. Well done, O highly intelligent one, well done. Your mind is noble and free of impurities, since you desire to know from us the means of liberation from the misery of worldly existence.

8. O strict observer of religious vows, indeed, it is only that Deity who is the bestower of salvation—the deity at whose behest Brahmā creates the entire universe; Hari protects it and Rudra annihilates it.

9. Know Viṣṇu[2] to be the bestower of salvation. He is Nārāyaṇa free from ailments. Thanks to his prowess, are born the principles beginning with *Ahaṁkāra* (the Ego) and ending with *Viśeṣa* (particularities).

10. All this (visible universe) consisting of the mobile and immobile, is not different from him. One is liberated from misery of *saṁsāra* by meditating on the mighty Lord, devoid of old age.

11. Verily they call him the Liberator (lit. the means of liberation from *Saṁsāra*), one above modifications and aberrations, who is unborn, the purest, the self-luminous, the unsullied embodiment of perfect knowledge and of eternal bliss.

12. The groups of deities the first of whom is Brahmā, worship the incarnations and manifestations of that lord. Know him to be Hari the bestower of the eternal abode.

13. Those who have conquered their *Prāṇas* (vital breaths), those who have controlled their diet, those who are always absorbed in meditation, see him in their hearts. Know him to be the Reality that accords happiness.

14. Though he is devoid of attributes, he is the receptacle of good qualities; he assumes the forms that bless the worlds. He is perfect and is stationed in the middle of the firmament. They call him the bestower of salvation unto men.

15. He is the presiding deity and the observer of all activities; he is enthroned in the heart of the embodied soul; he is simply incomparable; he is the support of all. With such a Lord, one should seek refuge.

16. At the end of the Kalpa, he withdraws everything and lies down on the cosmic water. Sages, the perceivers of the truth, call Viṣṇu, the bestower of salvation.

17. The *Karmajñas* (the knowers of the path of *Karmans*), who know the meanings of the Vedic passages, worship him through various kinds of sacrifices. He alone is the bestower of the fruits of holy rites to them and salvation to those who perform holy rites without desire of their fruits.

18. They call him the lord, the bestower of salvation—the lord who is unmanifest and who partakes of oblations (offered in sacrificial fire) by assuming the forms of deities and the oblation of food and other offerings to the manes by assuming the forms of *Pitṛs* (ancestors).[3]

19. One should worship that merciful Lord who on being meditated upon, or bowed to or worshipped with devotion, bestows the permanent abode (*Mokṣa*).

20. That immutable Hari, the Supreme Person, the only

support of all beings, one free from old age and death, is the bestower of liberation from *Saṁsāra*.

21. O leading sage, after worshipping his lotus-like feet, the embodied souls immediately attain to immortality (i.e. *Mokṣa*). They know him to be the Supreme Person.

22. The Brahman is bliss.[4] He is the greatest splendour, devoid of old age. He is eternal, greater than the greatest. That is the highest region of Viṣṇu.

23. They know him to be one without a second, devoid of attributes, non-dual and matchless, eternal, incomparable and perfect embodiment of knowledge. He is the deity who enables one to achieve salvation.

24. The Yogin who always worships this Supreme entity of such a nature, through the rites of the Yogic path, attains the greatest region.

25. The Yogin who has eschewed all contacts and associations, who is endowed with *Śama* (self-control) and other good qualities and who is devoid of lust and similar bad qualities attains the highest region.

Nārada said :

26. By what holy rite is the achievement of the Yoga attained by the Yogins? O sage the most excellent among the eloquent ones, tell me precisely the means for the same.

Sanaka said :

27. Those who ponder over the meanings of principles (or the Reality) say that the greatest salvation is attainable through perfect knowledge. This perfect knowledge has its root in devotion. Similarly this devotion is engendered in those persons who perform holy rites.

28. Devotion to Hari is generated in that person by whom, in the course of thousands of births, charitable gifts, different kinds of sacrifices and pilgrimages, etc. have been performed.

29. The highest and inexhaustible Dharma is produced even through the slightest of devotion and piety. All sins perish through the deepest faith.

30. When all the sins are quelled, the intellect becomes free from impurities. That same intellect is declared by wise sages by the word *Jñāna* (knowledge).

31. They say that knowledge bestows salvation. It is the Yogins who acquire that knowledge. Yoga is said to be of two kinds, differentiated by holy rites and by perfect knowledge.

32. The *Jñāna Yoga* (path of knowledge) cannot be accomplished without the *Kriyā Yoga* (path of holy rites). Hence, one who is engaged in the *Kriyā Yoga* should worship Hari with deep faith.

33. With devotion the following idols of Keśava are to be worshipped; the idols termed as *Dvija* (Brāhmaṇa), *Bhūmi* (Earth), *Agni* (fire), *Sūrya* (Sun), *Ambu* (Water) *Dhātu* (metals or the essential ingredients of body), *Hṛt* (the heart) and *Citra* (Picture).

34. Hence, becoming completely averse to (i.e. abstaining absolutely from) inflicting pain on others in thought, word and deed, one, endowed with devotion, should worship Lord Viṣṇu who pervades everything.

35. The following good qualities are common to both types of Yogas—viz. nonviolence, truthfulness, absence of anger, celibacy, non-acceptance of gifts (and non-possession of property), absence of jealousy and mercifulness.

36. Firmly determining mentally that "the eternal Viṣṇu is identical with the universe consisting of the mobile and immobile beings", one shall practise the two types of Yogas.

37. The learned men who consider all living beings their own *Ātman* realise the supreme nature of the discus-bearing lord of Devas (viz. Viṣṇu).

38. If a person whose soul is defiled by fury, etc. becomes devoted to worship and meditation, Viṣṇu is not pleased with him, since he is the lord of Dharma.

39. If a person whose soul is defiled by lust, etc. becomes devoted to worship, he should be known as a hypocrite. He is on a par with all sinners.

40. If a person full of envy and jealousy becomes absorbed in austerities, worship and meditation, his austerities, worship and meditation—everything is futile.

41. Hence, a man, eagerly engaged in practising the good qualities of *Śama* (self-control), etc. and who is absorbed in *Kriyā-Yoga*[5] should duly worship Viṣṇu who is the Soul of all (and is one with them), for the purpose of liberation (from *Saṁsāra*).

42. If a person interested in the welfare of all worlds, mentally, verbally and physically, devoutly worships the lord of Devas, it is called *Kriyā Yoga*.

43. The person who eulogises through hymns, etc. Lord Nārāyaṇa, the source of the origin of the universe, Viṣṇu, Hari, the immanent soul of everyone, through hymns, etc., he is called, a *Karma Yogin*.

44. The worship of Viṣṇu through flowers, etc., by means of observance of fasts, etc. as well as listening to *Purāṇas* (and other forms of devotion), etc., is declared as *Kriyā Yoga*.

45. All the sins accumulated in the course of previous births of those who are devotionally attached to Viṣṇu and whose minds are absorbed in *Kriyā Yoga*, perish completely.

46. One whose intellect is purified through the destruction of sins, desires the excellent knowledge. Perfect knowledge should be known as the bestower of salvation. I shall narrate to you the means thereof.

47. In the company of saintly persons who are adepts in the interpretation of scriptural texts, the intelligent man shall deeply ponder over what is permanent and what is non-permanent in the world consisting of the mobile and immobile beings.

48. All the sense objects are evanescent. Only Hari is eternal. One should eschew the non-eternal objects and resort only to the eternal one (viz. Hari).

49. He should also be unattached to the pleasures of this as well as of the other world. He who is not detached becomes involved in the cycle of worldy existence.

50. Never can he be severed from the bond of worldly existence,—the man who is passionately attached to non-eternal objects.

51. Only he who is richly endowed with self-control and other good qualities and who is desirous of liberation can practise knowledge. One who is wanting in self-control never realizes the spiritual knowledge.

52. He who is devoid of lust and hatred, is richly endowed with self-control and is perpetually absorbed in the meditation on Hari, is called a *Mumukṣu* (one who is desirous of liberation).

53. One who possesses these four means is called a man of pure intellect. One who is absorbed in the feelings of

compassion towards all living beings should ponder over Viṣṇu who is omnipresent.

54. O Brāhmaṇas if any one realises this that Nārāyaṇa abides pervading the universe consisting of the perishable and the imperishable, they say, it is the knowledge arising from Yoga.

55. Henceforth, I shall recount the means for the acquisition of Yoga, the means that makes this metempsychosis recede. The knowledge that is pure is Yoga. The wise know that this knowledge is the bestower of salvation.

56. They say that the *Ātman* is two-fold as differentiated as the *Para* (Higher) and the *Apara* (lower). The Atharva Veda says—" Two Brahmans are to be known"[6]

57. That which is devoid of attributes (*Nirguṇa*) is spoken of as *Para*. The *Apara* is that which is combined with the *Ahaṁkāra* (Ego). The realization of their non-difference is called Yoga.

58. That which is stationed in the heart as *Sākṣin* (the witness) in the body constituted by the five elements, is called *Apara* while the Supreme *Ātman* is remembered as *Para* by the saintly people.

59. The body is called Kṣetra (field) that which is stationed therein is called *Kṣetrjña*) (The individual soul). He is said to be unmanifest, Supreme, pure and perfect.

60. O excellent sage, when the non-difference between the individual soul and the Supreme Soul is realised, the bonds of the *Apara Ātman* (the lower i.e. the individual soul) are snapped.

61. The *Paramātman* (the Supreme Soul) who is pure, imperishable, eternal and identical with the universe appears like one differentiated, in view of the difference of perception among men.

62. That which is the greatest and eternal Brahman is the only one without a second (*Chāndogya Up*. 6.2.1) O Brāhmaṇa, it is thus sung about by the Vedāntic passages. There is nothing greater than that.

63. That attributeless great *Ātman* has no function or rite to perform. It has neither form nor colour. It is neither an agent nor an enjoyer.

64. That which is the cause of all causes, that splendour which is greater than every other brilliance, that without which nothing exists, should be known for the sake of salvation.

65. O Brāhmaṇa, that which is *Śabda Brahman* (Brahman in the form of sound) is the *Mahā Vākya*[7] etc. (the great statements such as *Tat Tvam Asi* 'That Thou art'. The perfect knowledge arising out of meditating over the same great statement is the greatest means of salvation.

66. O Brāhmaṇa, the universe appears to be of diverse kinds to those who are devoid of perfect knowledge. To those endowed with the supreme (spiritual) knowledge, it is one with the greatest Brahman.

67. The only greatest bliss, the attributeless one, the greater than the greatest, the unchanging one, appears to be assuming many forms due to difference in perception.

68. O excellent one among the Brāhmaṇas, people perceive difference in the *Parama Ātman* due to the Māyā of the wielder of the Māyā. Hence a *Mumukṣu* (one desirous of liberation) should eschew the Māyā through the Yogic power.

69. The Māyā is neither of the form of the non-existence nor of that of the existence nor is it of the form of both. Hence it should be understood as being unspecifiable. It gives (creates) the idea of difference.

70. O excellent sage, it is the Māyā alone that is understood by the word *Ajñāna*[8] (ignorance). Hence, only those who have conquered Māyā can have the riddance from *Ajñāna*. (Only they can get rid of it).

71. The greatest eternal Brahman is denoted by the word *Jñāna* (the spiritual knowledge). Indeed the greatest *Ātman* shines continuously in the hearts of those endowed with *Jñāna*.

72. O excellent sage, the Yogin must destroy ignorance through Yoga. The Yoga is achieved through eight ancillaries. I shall mention them factually.

73-74. O leading sage, O excellent sage, the ancillaries (aids) of Yoga are these : viz. : *Yamas* (Restraints), *Niyamas* (observances), *Āsanas* (physical postures), *Prāṇāyāma* (control of breath), *Pratyāhāra* (withdrawal) of senses, *Dhāraṇā* (fixed attention—Retention), *Dhyāna* (meditation and *Samādhi* (Trance).[9] I shall succinctly relate the characteristics of these in order, O excellent sage.

75. The *Yamas* (Restraints) are in brief the following : *Ahiṁsā* (non-violence), *Satya* (truthfulness), *Asteya* (non-stealing), *Brahmacarya* (celibacy), *Aparigraha* (non-acceptance of

monetary gifts), *Akrodha* (absence of fury) and *Anasūyā* (absence of jealousy).[10]

76. Abstention from inflicting pain on all living beings is called *Ahiṁsā* (Non-Violence) by good men. It is the bestower of Yogic achievements.

77. O excellent sage, statement of the actual fact after discriminating between *Dharma* (righteousness) and *Adharma* (unrighteousness), they call *Satya* (truth). Now listen to *Asteya* (non-stealing).

78. Taking away the wealth of others through force or stealth is called *Steya* (stealth) by good men. The opposite of the same is non-stealing (*Asteya*).

79. Eschewal of sexual intercourse in regard to every-one is glorified as *Brahmacarya* (celibacy). Due to the abandon-ment of celibacy, even a person endowed with knowledge, becomes a sinner.

80. He who professes to be one refraining from intimate contact with all, but continues to indulge in sexual intercourse, should be known as one on a par with a Cāṇḍāla. He is excommunicated from all castes.

81. O Brāhmaṇa, if anyone engaged in the practice of Yoga harbours a craving for sensuous objects, other men are affected by the sin of *Brahmahatyā* (Brāhmaṇa-slaughter) even by talking to him.

82. If a person who eschews all intimate contacts resumes the contacts once again, one attains the defect of a great sin (*Mahāpāpa*) even by means of contact with those who touch them.

83. O leading sage, non-acceptance of moneys even in emergencies, is called *Aparigraha*. It leads to the achievement of Yogic power.

84. If as a result of one's own superior position one indul-ges in harsh speech, knowers of Dharma call it *Krodha* (fury). *Akrodha* is its opposite.

85. Severe heart-burn and mental agony that one suffers, on seeing others superior to him in wealth, etc. is called *Asūyā* (jealousy) by good men. Its abandonment is *Anasūyatā* (absence of jealousy).

86. O Nārada, the most excellent among enlightened ones, the *Yamas* (Restraints) have thus been succinctly

recounted. I shall narrate, *Niyamas* (observances) also to you. Listen.

87. Austerities, self-study (of Vedas), contentment, purity (cleanliness), worship of Hari and the offering of Sandhyā prayers—these are mentioned as main observances (*Niyamas*).[11]

88. Where the body is desicated through Cāndrāyaṇa and other (expiatory rites), it is called *Tapas* (Austerity) by good men. It is an excellent means of Yoga.

89-90. The *Japa* (prayerful repetitions) of *Praṇava*, the Upaniṣad passages, the twelve-syllabled or eight-syllabled Mantras (viz. *Oṁ namo bhagavate Vāsudevāya* / *Oṁ Namo Nārāyaṇāya* and the *Japa* (repeated recitation) of the collections of great statements (*Mahāvākyas* such as *Tat tvam asi*, etc.) is called Svādhyāya (self-study). It is an excellent means of Yoga. The foolish one who abandons *Svādhyāya* does not achieve Yogic power.

91. Even without the (other ancillaries of) Yoga, men's sins are quelled through *Svādhyāya.* On being propitiated through *Svādhyāyas*, the deities become delighted.

92. *Japa* (Prayerful repetition) is said to be of three types : *Vācika* (verbal and voluble), *Upāṁśu* (indistinct or mumbling) and *Mānasa* (mental). O leading Brāhmaṇa, the later ones in these three types are better than the earlier ones.

93. If the *Mantra* is uttered well making the syllables and words clearly articulated, the *Japa* is called *Vācika* (Verbal). It bestows the benefits of all *Yajñas.*

94. When the *Mantra* is uttered, if the words are only slightly distinct from one another, that *Japa* is said to be *Upāṁśu.* It is twice more beneficial than the previous one.

95. If the respective meanings of the series of syllables (in the *Mantra*) are pondered over, that *Japa* is said to be *Mānasa* (mental). It bestows all Yogic achievements.

96. The deity becomes delighted with one who eulogises continuously through *Japa.* Hence, one who is richly endowed with the practice of *Svādhyāya* realises all his desires.

97. Satisfaction with obtaining what comes spontaneously is called *Santoṣa* (contentment). A disgruntled man does not get pleasure anywhere.

98. Never does lust subside by the enjoyment of the pleasures of lust.[12] The lustful desire "When will I get more than this ?" ever goes on increasing.

99. Hence, one should leave off lust that causes the desiccation and dissipation of the body. One should be contented with the effortless spontaneous acquisitions and be absorbed in Dharma.

100. Cleanliness is of two types as differentiated by its external and internal applications. The external cleanliness is through clay and water. The internal cleanliness is emotional purity.

101. O leading sage, the different kinds of sacrifices performed by those who are devoid of internal purity, do not bear fruit like the sacrificial oblation poured on ashes.

102. All the rites of those who are devoid of emotional purity are futile. Hence, one should eschew passionate attachment and similar emotions and be happy.

103. A man whose soul is defiled is one similar to a Cāṇḍāla, though be might have externally washed himself with ten million potful of water and thousands of Bhāras (1 Bhāra = 20 Tulas or 2000 Palas) of clay.

104. If a person devoid of internal purity becomes engaged in the worship of a deity, he vitiates that deity and falls into a hell.

105. He who is devoid of internal purity but strives for external cleanliness does not attain calmness like an embellished liquor pot (which remains impure internally).

106. Holy centres do not sanctify those who perform pilgrimages without mental purity, just as the river cannot purify the liquor pot.

107. If a person mentally yearns for a sinful thing even as he expatiates on righteousness, O excellent sage, know him to be the most villainous among the great sinners.

108. If those persons whose minds are pure perform only their excellent duties, know that the benefit thereof is imperishable and pleasure-bestowing.

109. If devotion to Hari is stabilised by means of worships, eulogies and listening (to Purāṇas, etc.) mentally, verbally and physically, it is called the real *Haripūjā* (worship of Hari).

110. The *Yamas* and the *Niyamas* have been taught succinctly. They (the knowers) know that salvation is within the reach of those whose minds are purified by means of those (observances).

111. One who has conquered his sense-organs and stabilised his intellect through the observance of *Yamas* and *Niyamas* should begin the practice of *Āsanas* (postures) duly. It is an excellent means of achieving Yoga.

112-115. The *Āsanas* (postures) mentioned by leading sages are thirty in number.[13] They are—Padmaka, Svastika, Pīṭha, Saiṁha, Kaukkuṭa, Kauñjara, Kaurma, Vajrāsana, Vāräha, Mṛga, Cailika, Krauñca, Nālika, Sarvatobhadra, Vārṣabha, Nāga, Mātsya, Vaiyāghra, Ardhacandraka, Daṇḍavāta, Śaila, Śvabhra, Maudgara, Mākara, Traipatha, *Kāṣṭha*, Sthāṇu, Vaikarṇika, Bhauma and Vīrāsana. These are instrumental to the achievement for Yoga.

116. The follower of Yoga with full faith and devotion to his spiritual preceptor should bind (fully stabilise himself) in one of these postures and transcending the *dvandvas*[14] (opposite pairs like pleasure and pain) and eschewing jealousy (from his mind) should attain control over his vital breaths.

117. He should sit facing the east, north or the west. He should control the vital breaths by means of practice in a quiet place unfrequented by people.

118. *Prāṇa* is the wind stationed within the body. Its *Āyāma* means restraint. Thus *Prāṇāyāma* means breath control. It is of two types.

119. Out of the *Agarbha* and the *Sagarbha* types of breath-control the latter is the better of the two. The *Agarbha* is the curbing of the breath without *Japa* and meditation while in the *Sagarbha* control of breath, we have them (i.e. *Japa* and *Dhyāna*) both.

120. The restraint of breath has been mentioned by learned men to be of four kinds : *Recaka* (exhalation of air), *Pūraka* (inhalation of air), *Kumbhaka* (retention of the inhaled air), and Śūnyaka (a breathless stage) (see below 124-126).

121. The tubular organ or artery (the channel of the vital air) on the right hand side of the creatures is mentioned as *Piṅgalā*. The sun is its deity. It is well known as the source of the origin of the *Pitṛs*.

122. The artery or the channel of the vital air well known as the source of the origin of Devas is on (flows through) the left (nostril). It is the vein called Iḍā. O excellent sage, know that the moon is its presiding deity.

123. In the middle of these two is the vein Suṣumnā. It is very subtle and the most mysterious one. It should be known as having Brahman for its deity.

124. The breath should be expelled through the left nostril. *Recana* means exhaling and hence this is called *Recaka*. The intake of breath must be through the right nostril. *Pūraṇa* means filling up. Hence .this is called *Pūraka*.

125. One restrains the wind that fills the body and does not exhale it. He stands like a pitcher filled with water. Hence, it is well known as *Kumbhaka*.

126. If there is neither inhalation nor exhalation of the external or the internal wind, know that to be the *Prāṇāyāma* of the name of *Śūnyaka*. There is a perfect standstill.

127. The vital breaths are to be conquered slowly, like lordly elephants in their rut that have to be tamed slowly. Otherwise, terribly great ailments are bound to effect.

128. The Yogin devoid of sins shall make use of the wind gradually. He should be liberated from all sins. He shall attain the region of the Brahman.

129. O leading sage, if one withdraws the sense-organs involved in the sensuous objects and restrain them, it is called *Pratyāhāra*[15] (withdrawal of senses).

130. O Brāhmaṇa, noble-souled men though devoid of meditation, but who have conquered their sense organs attain the greatest Brahman from which it is difficult to return.

131. If anyone tries to get absorbed in meditation before completely conquering the sense-organs, know him to be stupefied in mind. Even his meditation cannot be successfully accomplished.

132. Whatever he sees he sees to be like his self within his *Ātman*. The retention of the withdrawn sense-organs is *Dhāraṇā*.

133. One who has conquered the groups of sense-organs by means of Yoga shall completely withdraw them from the field of operation. He should then deeply meditate in the heart on the Supreme *Ātman*, Acyuta, the creator and supporter of all.[16]

134-137. In the lotus of the heart that extends to twelve *Aṅgulas* and that has eight petals, he should meditate on lord Viṣṇu, the embodiment of entire universe, the sole cause of all worlds, His eyes resembling the petals of the blooming lotus;—Lord Viṣṇu who is bedecked with charming earrings, whose arms are long, limbs elegant; who is embellished with all ornaments; who wears yellow robes, and a golden sacred thread, *Tulasī* garlands; who shines with the Kaustubha jewel; who bears the Śrīvatsa mark on his chest; who is bowed to by Devas and Asuras; who is the unmanifest *Ātman* and the lord greater than the greatest.

138. It has been stated by saintly men that *Dhyāna* (meditation) is perception with attention[17] and concentration. By performing meditation even for a *Muhūrta*, a man attains the highest salvation.

139. Sins perish, thanks to meditation, one attains liberation (from *Saṁsāra*) due to meditation; Hari becomes pleased through meditation; all objects are realised through meditation.

140. With great concentration one should meditate on every form of Mahāviṣṇu. Delighted with that meditation, Hari shall indeed bestow salvation.

141. O excellent one, one should make the mind steady in the object of meditation so that the state of being the meditator, the object of meditation, and the act of meditation every thing ceases to be completely.

142. Then immortality is achieved by resorting to the nectar of knowledge. The nondifference is realised by continuous meditation.

143. If the devotee (who meditates) feels the greatest bliss as in sleep, if all his sense organs become subdued, if he stands steady like the flame of the lamp in a place devoid of wind in motion, it is called *Samādhi* (trance).

144. O excellent one, in the state of *Samādhi* (trance) the Yogin neither hears nor sees, neither smells nor touches nor does he utter anything.

145. The *Ātman* is free of impurities, it is pure; it is Existence, Knowledge and Bliss incarnate. It is devoid of all conditioning factors; it appears steady to Yogins.

146. The Supreme Lord, though devoid of attributes, appears, due to ignorance, to be endowed with attributes. He appears steady and attributeless as before, when ignorance disappears.

147. The immeasurable *Ātman*, that supreme brilliance appears to be deflected by Māyā to those affected by Māyā.

O scholar, when the Māyā (illusion) is destroyed, the Brahman free from impurities shines resplendent.

148. It is one without a second; is the Supreme unsullied light. It is abiding in all living beings as the immanent soul.

149. He is minuter than the minutest atom;[18] he is greater than the greatest being; he is the eternal *Ātman*; he is the cause of the entire universe; those who are the most excellent among the possessors of perfect knowledge observe him who is greater than the greatest and very pure.

150. That primordial beginningless ancient *Puruṣa* is sung about as the *Śabdabrahman* comprised within the letters of the alphabet beginning with 'A' and ending with 'Kṣa'.

151. It is sung about as the greatest Brahman that is extremely pure, imperishable, eternal, perfect, situated in the middle of the firmament, and as the bliss devoid of impurities and quiescent.

152. The Yogins perceive the eternal Supreme *Ātman* in their hearts. It is changless, unborn, pure and is sung about as the greatest *Brahman*.

153. O excellent sage, listen. I shall narrate in details another type of meditation. It is as though like a shower of nectar to the men scorched by the distress of worldly existence.

154. One should contemplate upon Nārāyaṇa, the greatest Bliss stationed in the *Praṇava Oṁ* in the form of *Nāda* (the spiritual sound) incomparable and as situated over half the *Mātrā*.

155. The syllable '*A*' is the form of Brahmā; the letter '*U*' is the form of Viṣṇu; the letter '*M*' is the form of Rudra and half the Mātrā is of the greatest *Ātman*.[19]

156. O Brāhmaṇa, three Mātrās (of Oṁ) are mentioned as having Brahmā, Viṣṇu and Śiva as their deities. Their collective form indicates the greatest *Brahman*.

157. The Supreme *Brahman* is the *Vācya* (that which is to be expressed), the *Praṇava* is called the *Vācaka* (the expression). O Brāhmaṇa, their relation as *Vācya* and *Vācaka* is a formality.

158. Those who continuously perform the *Japa* of *Praṇava* are liberated from all sins. Those who have its constant practice, attain the greatest salvation.

159. Performing the *Japa* of the *Praṇava Mantra* of the form of Brahmā, Viṣṇu and Śiva, one shall meditate on a pure brilliance like that of ten million suns in the *Ātman*.

160. Or one should ponder over any holy object that quells sins—such as the Śālagrāma stone or an idol.

161. O leading sage, what has been mentioned to you is the perfect knowledge pertaining to Viṣṇu. On knowing this, the prominent Yogin attains excellent salvation.

162. He who listens to this or reads it with concentration shall be freed from all sins. He shall attain the *Sālokya* (having the same world) with Hari.

CHAPTER THIRTYTHREE

A Discourse on Yoga

1. After the terrible description of *Saṁsāra*, Nārada naturally asks Sanaka the way out of this terrific cycle of births and deaths. It is on the background of the last chapter that this *Vaiṣṇava-Jñāna* is explained by Sanaka. Though the heading of the chapter is 'A discourse on Yoga', the Yoga path of Patañjali finds a secondary place here. It is a synthesis of spiritual knowledge, *Bhakti* & *Karma*. Yoga is the means of realization of the identity between the individual soul and the Supreme soul. It is this realization which relieves a person from *Saṁsāra*.

2. Here Viṣṇu is identified with the Brahman and Hari the protector of the Universe only as one of the dieties in the Trinity alongwith gods Brahmā and Śiva, and is thus regarded on a lower level (vide V.8 above). All the epithets in VV. 8-23 describe Viṣṇu as being the *Para Brahman* and as such a bestower of *Mokṣa*.

3. *Havya* is the oblation or offering (generally poured in the sacrificial fire) to gods while *Kavya* is the oblation of food to the deceased ancestors. But it is Lord Viṣṇu who is the real recipient of both these offerings.

4. VV.22.23 echo the Upaniṣadic epithets of the *Brahman, vide Tait.Up*. 3.6.1, *Bṛhadāraṇyaka* 4.4,25, etc.

5. VV 41-44 emphasize that devotion to and worship of Viṣṇu is the *Kriyā-Yoga* and it absolves one of all accumulated sins.

6. This refers to the *Maitrāyaṇī Up*. and not to the *Maitrī Up*. as given in Jacob's *Concordance*. But the *Maitrāyaṇī* 6.22 states that *Śabda* and *Para* are two *Brahmans* and one who is expert in *Śabda brahman* attains to *Para Brahman* :

dve brahmaṇī Veditavye Śabda-brahma paraṁ ca yat |
Śabda-brahmaṇi niṣṇātaḥ paraṁ brahmādhigacchati ||

VI-22.

But the NP. (VV 57-60) states that *apara brahma* is that which is combined with *ahaṁkāra* (ego) i.e. it is the individual soul or *Kṣetrajña* and *NOT Śabda-brahman* as stated in the *Maitrāyaṇī* above.

7. *Mahāvākya* literally means 'a sentence conveying great import' (*mahad= mahadartha—prakāśakaṁ vākyam*). And the term is used according to the main interest of the user. Thus to Viśvanātha (in the *Sāhitya darpaṇa*) it connotes 'any long continuous composition or literary work.' The NP., however, implies the 12 sacred utterances of the *Upaniṣads*, e.g.

tat-tvamasi (*Chāndogya Up*. VI.8.7 and
aham brahmāsmi (*Br.Up*. I.4.10)
Satyaṁ jñānam anantam brahma (Tai-Up. II-1, 1) and others.

8. In translating this term I emended the text of the NP. as *māyaivajñā-*

naśabdena by māyaivājñāna-sabdena, etc. The Venkat press text of the NP. is obviously wrong and a probable misprint as can be seen from its context. NP. ch.33 and Brn.ch. 31 are textually identical. And Brn. 31.71 reads:

māyaivājñāna-śabdena śabdyate muni-sattama /

Hence the validity of my emendation. The textual identity between NP. Part I and Brn. is too well known to need elaboration here.

9. vide YS.II.29.

10. YS.II.30 gives only five *Yamas* to which the NP. adds two more, viz, *akrodha* (absence of anger) and *anasūyā* (non-jealousy).

11. Cf. *Śauca-santoṣa-tapaḥ-svādhyāyeśvara-praṇidhānāni niyamāḥ*, YS.II.32. The NP. adds here 'performance of *Sandhyā* prayers' as a *niyama*.

12. An echo of king Yayāti's famous words of repentance :

Na jātu kāmaḥ kāmānām upabhogena śāmyati /
Haviṣā kṛṣṇa-vartmeva bhūya evābhivardhate //

Mbh-Ādi.85.12

13. The bodily postures mentioned here are described (sometimes under different names) in hand books on yogic practice like the *Yoga-pradīpikā* and others and as such their description here is superfluous. It is interesting to note that Vyāsa in his com. on YS.II.46 recommends most of these.

14. Cf.YS.II.48 which states that as a result of mastering the postures, he is unassailed by extremes (like heat and cold).

15. Cf. YS.II.54 : "The withdrawal of the senses is, as it were, the imitation of the mind-stuff itself on the part of the organs, by disjoining themselves from their objects."

As the Commentator Vyāsa explains : "When there is no conjunction with their own objects, the organs in imitation of the mind-stuff, as it is in itself, become as it were restricted."

16. VV 133-137 describe what form of god Viṣṇu should be the object of meditation.

17. Cf. YS.III.2. *tatra pratyayaikatānatā dhyānam* /

18. Cf. *Kaṭha* Up.2.20, *Śvet*.3.20, *Mahānārāyaṇa Up*.8.3.

19. The identity of the trinity of gods (Brahmā, Viṣṇu, and Śiva) with the three *mātrās* of *Om* has been a popular concept in later Upaniṣads like the *Nṛsiṁha Uttara-Tāpanīya* and in Purāṇas.

CHAPTER THIRTYFOUR

The Characteristics of Devotion to Hari

Nārada said :

1. O great sage, all the ancillaries of the Yoga have been recounted by you. Now once again, O ominiscient one, what I ask may be narrated to me.

2-3. It has been mentioned by you that Yoga is realised only by the devotees. That person with whom the lord of all is pleased has perpetual devotional feelings. O omniscient sage, O ocean of mercy, kindly recount to me how Janārdana, the lord of Devas, the lord of all, is satisfied (and becomes gracious).

Sanaka said :

4. O Brāhmaṇa, if you desire to attain liberation from *saṁsāra* worship (with your heart and soul) the great lord Nārāyaṇa whose body is constituted of existence (*sat*), consciousness (*cit*) and Bliss (*ānanda*).

5. The enemies do not molest him; the planets do not affect him adversely; the Rākṣasas do not look at the man devoted to Viṣṇu.

6. He whose devotion to Janārdana, the lord of Devas, is firm and unswerving, realises all welfare and happiness. Hence, those who are devotees are superior to all.

7. Those two legs which proceed towards the abode (temple) of Viṣṇu are fruitful. Those two hands which are engaged in the worship of Viṣṇu should be known as the most fruitful.

8. Those two eyes of men which perceive Janārdana are the most fruitful; that tongue which is engaged in (repeating the) names of Hari is mentioned by good people (as the real tongue).

9. With upraised arm it is emphatically proclaimed that it is the truth, (and nothing but) the truth again, that there is no entity equal to the spiritual preceptor and there is no other God who is geater than Keśava.

10. I am speaking the truth. I am telling you the most

wholesome thing. I am repeating the essence again and again. In this world which is vain and worthless, the only true thing is Hari's worship.

11. Be supremely happy by cutting off with the axe of devotion to Hari, the extremely strong entangled noose of worldly existence which causes great delusion.

12. That mind which is attached to Viṣṇu, that speech which is absorbed in him (i.e. Viṣṇu) and those ears which are filled with the essence of his stories—all these are honoured in the world.

13. O Nārada, worship continuously the imperishable Bliss that is devoid of the three forms of *Avasthās* (states),* the lord who is stationed in the middle of Ākāśa (the firmament).

14. O leading sage, it is not at all possible to see or point out his abode or form to persons who are not self-possessed.

15-18. When he remains endowed with the (external) *Karaṇas* (sense-organs and organs of activity), the eternal immanent soul is called *Jāgrat* (in the waking state). When he moves about, out of his own will and is endowed with all the internal *Karaṇas* (senses) the *Ātman* is called Dreaming, when he is not in deep slumber. When he has neither the external *Karaṇas* nor the internal *Karaṇas,* when the *Ātman* is devoid of form, when he is freed from both merits and sins, when he has the form of Bliss, when the lord is devoid of all conditioning factors, when he is without attributes, the lord identical with the great *Brahman*, is sung about as *Suṣupta* (sunk in slumber).

19. O leading Brāhmaṇa this universe consisting of the mobile and immobile beings is merely the product of imagination. It is as unsteady as the lightning. Hence worship Janārdana.

20. The lord of the worlds is pleased with only that person who practises non-violence, truthfulness, celibacy and *Aparigraha* (Abstention from accepting monetary gifts or non-possession of property).

21. If a person is endowed with the quality of mercy towards all living beings, is engaged in the worship of Brāhmaṇas, the lord of the universe, the suppressor of demons Madhu and Kaiṭabha, is pleased with him.

22. If a person takes delight in the stories of the good, if

* The three states are waking, dreaming, and sound sleep. These states are described in VV 15-18 below.

he narrates the stories of the good, if he associates with saintly persons and if he is devoid of egotism, the lord of goddess Lakṣmī (i.e. Viṣṇu) is pleased with him.

23. On the occasions of hunger, thirst and commission of blunders, if anyone always repeats the names of Viṣṇu incessantly, Viṣṇu becomes pleased with him.

24. If a woman loves her husband like her own *Prāṇas* (vital breath), if she is engaged in the worship of her husband, O sage, the lord of the universe becomes pleased with her and bestows his own region on her.

25. Keśava is satisfied and delighted with those who are devoid of jealousy and egotism and those who are engaged in the worship of Devas.

26. Hence, O celestial sage, listen. Always worship Hari. Do not be egotistic and arrogant in vain, due to the prosperity and glory that are as unsteady as the lightning.

27. The body is in contact with death; the life is very fickle; wealth is always liable to be affected (confiscated) by kings and others; riches are transitory.

28. Don't you see, O celestial sage, half the span of life is wasted in sleep? How much of life is lost in such activities as taking food, etc. !

29. How much of life is wasted in vain in infancy and old age ! How much (is spent) by way of enjoyment of pleasures of the sensuous objects. When will he then perform holy rites ?

30. The worship of Acyuta may not be possible in childhood or in the old age. Hence, you perform the holy rites during the period of youth itself, refraining from egotistic feelings.

31. O sage, do not suffer destruction by being submerged in the deep cavity of worldly existence. The body is the abode of ruination (and death), the greatest receptacle of adversities.

32. The body (which is supposed to be the seat of enjoyment) is much defiled by feces and other impurities. Why should a man commit sins in vain by mistaking it to be permanent ?

33. No faith or belief should be placed in this worldly existence that is worthless, that is accompanied by various kinds of miseries, and that is definitely rendered more disorderly through death.

34-35. Hence O leading Brāhmaṇa, listen. What I am telling you is the truth. In order to prevent the recurrence of the advent of body in the next birth, eschew false prestige and covetousness, be devoid of lust and fury and continuously worship Viṣṇu. For the birth as a human being is extremely difficult to get.

36. O excellent one, human birth is somehow achieved with great difficulty by one who has wandered through thousands and crores of births as an immobile being, etc.

37. Even there, O excellent one, the inclination of the intellect towards the (worship, etc. of) deities, charitable gifts and enjoyment of pleasures is the fruit of austerities performed by men in the course of previous births.

38. Who can be more stupid than he who after attaining the rare human life (i.e. birth as a human being) does not worship Hari even once? He is insentient and of sluggish intellect.

39. Where is the sense of discrimination in those bloody fools who do not worship Hari even after attaining the human birth?

40. The lord of the universe, if propitiated, grants the desired benefits. O Brāhmaṇa which person who is being scorched by the fire of worldly existence, shall not worship him?

41. O excellent sage, even a Cāṇḍāla who is a devotee of Viṣṇu, is superior to a Brāhmaṇa. Even a Brāhmaṇa devoid of devotion to Viṣṇu is the worst king of Cāṇḍāla (who cooks dog's flesh for food).

42. Hence, one should eschew lust and other (base emotions) and worship the unchanging Hari. If he is pleased everything is pleased, since Hari is omnipresent.

43. Just as all other foot-prints get merged in the big foot-print of an elephant so also the universe consisting of the mobile and immobile beings gets merged in Viṣṇu alone.

44. Just as the universe consisting of the mobile and immobile beings is pervaded by the firmament, so also it is pervaded by Hari.

45. Death of men is due to birth, and death is the cause of the subsequent birth. Know, that both of them are near at hand and their destruction is brought only by service to Hari.

46. If meditated upon, remembered, worshipped or bowed-to, Janārdana severs the bondage of worldly existence who then would not worship him?

47. O Brāhmanical sage, by the mere utterance of his names, great sins are destroyed; on worshipping him a man attains salvation.

48. Still, O Brāhmaṇa, it is surprising; it is astonishing! It is simply astounding that all people undergo the sufferings of recurring worldly existence even when the name of Hari is present.

49. O ascetic, I shall aver you the truth again and again. As one is being led by the soldiers of Yama, one is incapable of achieving Dharma.

50. If one wishes for salvation, one should worship Viṣṇu as long as there is no defect in the sense organs and as long as no sickness harasses one.

51. *Mṛtyu* (the God of Death) is present near the creature from the very moment of its coming out of its mother's womb. Hence, one should be engaged in Dharma.

52. Alas! It is a pity. Ah! How pitiful it is! It is a pity that even after realising that the body is perishable, he (the worldly-minded man) does not perform holy rites.

53. Raising up the arm it is proclaimed: ..."It is truth. It is the truth, that after eschewing religious hypocrisy and arrogance, one should worship Vāsudeva".

54. O Nārada, I raise my arm and repeatedly proclaim what is beneficial. Eschewing completely envy and false-hood, Viṣṇu should be worshipped with heart and Soul.

55. The root of mental distress is anger. It is wrath which binds one to the worldly existence. Fury causes destruction of Dharma. Hence, one should avoid it.

56. The birth has its root in lust; lust is the cause of sin; lust causes the destruction of fame. Hence, one shall shun it.

57. It is remembered that malicious spite is the cause of all sorts of miseries; it is the way (lit. cause) of attainment of hell. Hence, one should eschew that also.

58. The cause of bondage and liberation of men is their mind itself. Hence, one should be happy after dedicating it to the Supreme *Ātman*.

59. O the dare-devilry of men! O the fool-hardiness of

men ! O the mindless arrogance of the people. Even when Viṣṇu, the lord of the universe, is present, those haughty fellows do not worship him.

60. Without propitiating Acyuta, the lord of all worlds, the creator of everything, how do they who are submerged in the ocean of worldly existence, cross the same ?

61. I solemnly assert the truth repeatedly that all ailments perish, thanks to the medicine in the form of uttering the Names of the Lord like Acyuta, Ananta, Govinda.

62. "O Nārāyaṇa, O Jagannātha, O Vāsudeva, O Janārdana." Those who continuously utter these names of God are honoured everywhere.

63. O leading sage, seek refuge in that deity whose prowess, Brahmā and other deities have not understood even till to-day.

64. Alas, the foolishness of the wicked-minded ones ! Alas, the stupidity ! O the idioticness (of people), O Nārada, they do not know that Viṣṇu is stationed in the lotus of the heart (and nowhere else).

65. O leading sage, listen to what I repeatedly say. Hari is delighted with those who possess faith. He is not pleased with or enamoured of riches or kinsmen.

66. O excellent one, in every birth, men endowed with devotion to Viṣṇu, shall possess the good fortune of having plenty of kinsmen, riches and sons.

67. This body is the root of sins. It is engaged in sinful activities. On realising this, Janārdana should always be worshipped.

68. There is no doubt at all in this, that those who are engaged in the worship of Hari, shall be blessed with many sons, friends, womenfolk, etc. as well as all riches.

69. He who is desirous of attaining happiness here and hereafter, shall worship Hari continuously. He who is desirous of unhappiness here and hereafter may engage himself in censuring others.

70. Fie upon the life of those who are devoid of devotion to Janārdana, the lord of Devas. Again and again fie upon that wealth (which is not donated in the charitable gift to the deserving persons).

71. O excellent sage, that body should be known as the

mine of sins, the body that does not bow down to Viṣṇu, the destroyer of *Karmans*.

72. If anyone hoards and preserves wealth that has not been distributed among deserving persons, know that it is certainly like that wealth which is preserved by a thief in the world.

73. Those who are proud and arrogant due to the wealth that is as unsteady as lightning, and that is momentary do not propitiate the lord of the universe, the deity who separates the *Jiva* from its bonds of *Saṁsāra*.

74. The creation is said to be of two kinds as differentiated by the Divine and Demoniac. That creation which is endowed with devotion to Hari is the Divine one. That which is devoid of it is considered to be demoniac.

75. Hence, O leading Brāhmaṇa, listen. Those who are absorbed in devotion to Hari are the excellent ones and are well known everywhere since *Bhakti* is extremely rare.

76. Keśava is delighted with those persons who are devoid of envy, are engaged in the protection of the Brāhmaṇas and are devoid of lust and other base emotions.

77. Those who are engaged in serving Viṣṇu by sweeping (the premises of the temple) and other activities and those who are eager to bestow charitable gifts on the deserving persons attain the greatest region.

CHAPTER THIRTYFIVE

A Disquisition on Spiritual Knowledge[1]
(*The Anecdote of Vedamālī.*)

Sanaka said :

1. Again I shall recount the greatness of the discus-bearing Lord of Devas. Heaps of sins of those who read and listen shall perish thereby.

2. Those who are quiescent, have conquered the group of six enemies, viz. lust, fury, covetousness, delusion, arrogance and malice and have not become arrogant even due to their Yogic power, and worship the unchanging deity of the form of *Jñāna* (spiritual knowledge) through *Jñāna Yoga* (the path of knowledge).

3. Those who are purified by means of ablution in holy waters, observances of holy vows, charitable gifts, austerities and sacrifices, worship Acyuta, the creator of all, by means of *Karma Yoga*, the path of holy rites.[2]

4. Greedy persons, ignorant ones, those who indulge in vices—do not worship the lord of the universe. Those men of confused intellect think they are devoid of old age and death. They are worms of men who continue to remain so.

5. Those who are proud due to their prosperity and glory that is as evanescent as the streak of lightning, those who are vainglorious and defiled by arrogance, do not worship the lord of universe who creates and lays down all sorts of welfare.

6. In this world, fortunately, a few are born who are engaged in Hari's Dharma, are quiescent, serve the lotuslike feet of Hari and who take interest in blessing all worlds.

7. He who worships Hari with devotion mentally, physically, and verbally, attains the greatest abode which is the most excellent of all excellent things in the universe.

8. In this context, they cite this ancient mythological anecdote which destroys the sins of those who read and listen.

9. I shall (now) recount that narrative of Yajñamāli and Sumāli, by merely listening to which one may attain the benefit of a horse-sacrifice.

10. O Brāhmaṇa, formerly in the Raivata Manvantara[3] there was a Brāhmaṇa well-known as Vedamāli.. He was a master of the Vedas and the Vedāṅgas (the six ancillaries like *Śikṣā*, *Chandas*, etc.).

11. He was kind-hearted and merciful towards all living beings. He was absorbed in the worship of Hari. He became interested in amassing wealth for his sons, friends and wife.

12. He regularly sold those things which are forbidden; he regularly conversed with Cāṇḍālas and others. He accepted monetary gifts from them.

13. He sold his austerities; he sold his *Vratas* (holy rites) (i.e. performed them in return for monetary consideration), he went on pilgrimage on behalf of others. He did (all those) for the sake of his wife.

14. O Brāhmaṇa, as time passed on, two sons were born to him. They were Yajñamāli and Sumāli. They were twins of great splendour.

15. Then, out of affection, the father who was full of too much of affection, nourished them by means of many articles.

16. After strenuously amassing wealth by many means, Vedamāli began to count it in order to understand how much it amounted to.

17. After counting his treasure which amounted to many billions, he was much delighted. He wondered at the thought of so much of wealth.

18. (He thought :—) "This wealth has been earned and accumulated by me through the acceptance of monetary gifts from bad people, through selling prohibited goods and through such other means such as selling of austerities.

19. My unbearable thirst (for gold) has not been pacified till now. It covets to possess innumerable gold pieces as huge as the mount Meru.

20. Alas, I consider it as one (involving) great pain and the source of all strenuous means. One attains all desires, but again one covets still other things.[4]

21. As one grows old his hairs (turn grey); the teeth become old (and feeble); the eyes (sight) and ears (power of listening) become feeble but his longing and yearning for more grow young.

22. All my sense-organs have become feeble and weak; my strength has been subdued (and dwindled) by old age but my longing has attained its prime of youth.

23. Only he is a real scholar and a learned man, the man whose *Āśā* (yearning, hope) has been quelled. (If it is not quelled) the quietest man will be the most furious and the most intelligent one will have extremely confused mind.

24. *Āśā* (longing) causes frustration and disappointment among men. It is like an invincible enemy. If an intelligent man desires permanent happiness he must eschew *Āśā*.

25. With great force, *Āśā* destroys strength, brilliance, fame, learning, honour, prosperous state and nobility of birth.

26. This is being mentioned to the dismay of men overwhelmed with *Āśā* (yearning, hope) that even a Cāṇḍāla who gives away something is superior to them.

27. Those who are in the vicious grip of *Āśā* (yearning) are men of great delusion and of too much arrogance. Alas ! they are never conscious of the pangs of being miserably) disrespected, etc.

28. This enormous wealth has been hoarded by me after undergoing many hardships. The body has been rendered old and emaciated. Old age has taken away the energy.

29. Henceforth, I shall endeavour eagerly (and earnestly) for the sake of the other world". After deciding thus, O leading Brāhmaṇa, he became absorbed in the path of righteousness.

30. At the very same time, he divided his assets into four parts. He kept two parts of his accumulated wealth for himself.

31-32. The two remaining parts he gave his two sons. Thereafter, with the intention of destroying the sins accumulated by him, he built water sheds and parks, got lakes dug up, and built many temples.[5] He distributed cooked food and other charitable gifts on the banks of the Gaṅgā.

33. After having distributed his entire possessions thus, he became imbued with devotion to Hari. He went to the forest-abode of Nara and Nārāyaṇa for performing penance.[6]

34. There he saw a very beautiful hermitage frequented by sages and embellished with groups of trees bearing fruits and flowers.

35. Its splendidness had been heightened by old sages who eulogised the great Brahman, who were engaged in

pondering over the topics in the scriptural texts and who were absorbed in service to the lord.

36. There he saw a sage named Jānanti[7] who was surrounded by his disciples, who was eulogising the great Brahman, and who appeared like a mass of splendour.

37. On seeing the sage who was devoid of passionate attachment and other similar base feelings, who was endowed with the good qualities of *Śama* (self-control), etc. and who subsisted only on dry decaying leaves, Vedamāli bowed to him.

38. O sage, with bulbous roots, roots, fruits and other things, sage Jānanti greeted the guest taking him to be Nārāyaṇa himself.

39. On being hospitably received and honoured by him, Vedamāli bowed down with humility, kept his palms joined in reverence and spoke to the sage who was the most excellent among fluent speakers.

40. "O holy Sir, O learned one, I am contented. My sin is removed. O blessed one, uplift me by imparting me (the gift of) perfect knowledge."

41. Thus requested by him, the excellent sage Jānanti the eloquent speaker laughingly spoke to Vedamāli endowed with good qualities.

Jānanti said :—

42. O leading Brāhmaṇa, listen : I shall succinctly enunciate the way of severance from worldly existence. It is very difficult to get (bring into practice) indeed for those who are not self-possessed.

43. Perpetually worship Viṣṇu, the greatest deity; continuously remember lord Nārāyaṇa. Never indulge in slandering others or backbiting.

44. O highly intelligent one, be always engaged in helping others and in worshipping Hari. Avoid close contact with the fools.

45. By avoiding lust and fury, covetousness and delusion, haughtiness and malicious spite and by viewing (considering) the whole world like your own *Ātman*, you will attain peace and quietude.

46. Never be envious. Never blame others. Avoid hypocritical conduct of life, egotism and ruthlessness.

47. Show kindness to all living beings. Render service to the good. Even to those who enquire, do not reveal the righteous actions performed by you.

48. Do not overlook if you see people engaged in evil ways of life. Worship guests every day in accordance with your capacity and without detriment to your family.

49. Without any (specific) desire, worship Nārāyaṇa, the lord of the universe, by means of flowers and leaves, *Dūrvā* grass, sprouts or fruits.[8]

50. In accordance with the injunctions, propitiate Devas, pitṛs and sages. O Brāhmaṇa, be interested in the due maintenance of holy fire.

51. Every day, with great concentration be engaged in the sweeping and scrubbing of the temple (of Viṣṇu) with due care. Smear it also duly.[9]

52. Join the broken parts and always repair the decaying sections in a temple. Beautify the path of and illuminate the temple of Viṣṇu.

53. Always worship Mādhava at least with bulbous roots, fruits and roots. Worship him by means of circumambulations, obeisances and recitals of prayers.

54. Every day, according to your capacity listen to or read the *Purāṇas* as well as the Vedāntic texts.

55. If this is strictly followed, you will have the most excellent knowledge. Certainly one is absolved of all sins, through perfect knowledge.

56. Thus enlightened by him, Vedamāli, of great intellect, became absorbed in the (path of) knowledge continuously and attained a small quantum of perfect knowledge.

57. On one occasion, urged by the quantum of perfect knowledge, Vedamāli began to think to himself like this. "Who am I? What is my duty?

58. How was I born? Of what nature is my form?" Thus, he began to think and muse by day and night alertly.

59. Unable to come to any decision, Vedamāli, the excellent Brāhmaṇa, came again to Jānanti, bowed to him and said thus :—

Vedamāli said :

60. O preceptor, O foremost one among the knowers

of Brahman, my mind is much confused. Who am I ? What is my rite ? How am I born ? Tell me.

Jānanti said :—

61. O highly blessed one, true. It is certainly true that your mind is confused. The mind is the abode of Avidyā (ignorance). How will it attain good nature ?

62. When you say the word 'My' it is certainly a misconception. O learned one, the egotism is a quality of the mind and not of the *Ātman*.

63. Moreover, O Vedamāli, it has been mentioned by you thus : "who am I ?" How can I ascribe a name to one who is devoid of name and nativity ?

64. How can I mention the name of the deity devoid of form, of the deity who is incomprehensible ? His nature is incomparable. He is the supreme *Ātman*, devoid of attributes.

65. How can the activity of the *Ātman* who is the embodiment of Supreme Splendour, perfect, immutable and of indiscernible nature be described.

66. O Brāhmaṇa, the *Ātman* is the self-luminous, eternal, infinite, Supreme Soul. How can the action and the birth of that *Ātman* be spoken of ?

67. The great eternal Brahman is devoid of age, is comprehensible only through perfect knowledge. O Brāhmaṇa, there is nothing else that is fuller and more blissful than that.

68. The knowledge through the statements such as 'That thou art' etc. is the means of achievement of salvation. When the unobstructed knowledge is achieved, everything becomes identical with Brahman.

69. O excellent sage, thus enlightened by him, Vedamāli realised the *Ātman*, Lord Acyuta, in his own soul and rejoiced.

70. He came to the conclusion...."I alone am the self-luminous Brahman, unsullied and unlimited by the conditioning factors", and he attained the deepest calmness and peace.

71. Thereafter, Vedamāli bowed down to his preceptor Jānanti, the leading sage, for the sake of formality and became absorbed in the meditation for ever.

72. After a lapse of time, O leading sage, Vedamāli reached the city of Vārāṇasī and attained salvation.

73. He who reads or listens to this chapter with great attention shall be severed from all bonds of *Karman* and attain happiness.

CHAPTER THIRTYFIVE

1. Although the chapter is called "Disquisition on Spiritual knowledge (*Jñāna-Nirūpaṇa*) in its colophon, it is the story of a Brāhmaṇa called Vedamāli who after earning wealth by unscrupulous means repented in after-life and after giving half of it to his sons, spent his share in public welfare-works and under the spiritual guidance of sage Jānanti, performed austere penance, was enlightened about the nature of the *Ātman* and ultimately reached *Mokṣa* at Vārāṇasī.

This Vedamāli does not appear in any other Purāṇa (*vide* V. Mani's P.E.-*Purāṇic Encyclopaedia*). Obviously this narrative is the special contribution of the NP. to illustrate how charity, spiritual knowledge and penance lead to Liberation from *Saṁsāra.*

This chapter and the subsequent ones give the story of two generations of the Vedamāli family.

2. The NP. prescribes both *Jñāna-yoga* and *Karma-yoga* for attaining *Mokṣa* but as emphasised in V.7 below, the path of devotion is the best one to illustrate which the narrative of Yajñamāli and Sumāli is told (in the next chapter and this chapter is limited to the story of their father Vedamāli.)

3. This is the fifth *Manvantara* of the present era. According to the Bh.P., Vikuṇṭha is Viṣṇu's incarnation, Vibhu is the Indra and Hiraṇyaroman, etc. are the seven sages in this *Manvantara.*

4. Such wise sayings (*Subhāṣitas*) as recorded in VV. 20ff are common to many *Purāṇas* and other works like *Vairāgya-Śataka* (vide Index to *Subhāṣita-ratna-bhāṇḍāra*). Their counter-parts in Pāli (e.g. in the *Dhamma Pada, Thera* and *Therī gāthās*) and in Prakrits show that this fund of wisdom was the common legacy of ancient Indians.

5. Such acts come under *Pūrta-dharma* and include works of public utility. In the Upaniṣads the compound *Iṣṭāpūrta* is used to include sacrificial performances as well (*vide Praśna* I-9, *Muṇḍaka* I.2.10, but there these are denigrated as not leading to *Mokṣa* but to *Svarga* after which the person falls to lower worlds). But Varāha Purāṇa declares that the *Pūrta-dharma* leads to *Mokṣa*

iṣṭena labhate svargam pūrte moksaṁ ca vindati /

—*Varāha P.* 172.33

Cf. *Yama-Smṛti* 68, *Atri Saṁhitā* 145.

6. i.e. Badari-Vana in the Garhwal, U.P.

7. The Sage Jānanti is untraced in other Purāṇas (vide *Purāṇic Ency.* under J). Like Vedamāli this is a creation of the NP. The Prakrit √Jāṇa—'to know' (<Sh.√Jñā) seems to have influenced the author in coining this name :

8. An echo of *Patram puṣpam phalaṁ toyaṁ yo me bhaktyā prayacchati*, etc. in the BG. IX.26.

9. The NP. lays great stress on the repairs, maintenance, etc., of old (Viṣṇu) temples; *vide* the story of Yajñamāli in the next chapter.

CHAPTER THIRTYSIX

The Efficacy of Service Unto Viṣṇu. The Story of Yajñamāli and Sumāli

Sanaka said :

1. O excellent sage, the story of the two sons of Vedamāli who had been mentioned before, viz. Yajñamāli and Sumāli, is being narrated now.

2. The elder of the two, viz. Yajñamāli divided the assets accumulated by his father, into two parts and gave one of the parts to his younger brother.

3-4. O Brāhmaṇa, Sumāli always indulged in all vices. He was absorbed in singing and playing on musical instruments. He was addicted to liquor. He was enamoured of the coquetry of prostitutes. He was interested in other men's wives. Removing (i.e. spending away) the wealth thus, Sumāli squandered all the wealth.

5. When all the gold hoarded by his father had been squandered, he continued to be interested in harlots by stealing other men's wealth.

6. On seeing the (evil) conduct of Sumāli, Yajñamāli of great intellect became distressed much and spoke to his brother thus :—

7. "O younger brother, enough of this wrong and evil conduct. In our family, you alone are interested in this great sin. You are the only wicked-minded fellow born in our family.

8. When the elder brother thus tried to wean him (from evil ways) by diverse methods on many occasions, Sumāli took a sword in his hand and caught hold of his elder brother by his tuft of hair on his head deciding to himself, "I will kill him".

9. Thereafter, a terrific uproar took place in the city. The infuriated citizens bound Sumāli.

10. But Yajñamāli, (the depth of feelings in) whose heart could not be measured, became distressed. He was deluded by fraternal affection. He implored the citizens and got his brother liberated from the bondage.

11. Again Yajñamāli split his (remaining) wealth into

two parts. He took half of his assets and gave the other half to his younger brother.

12. But Sumāli who was haughty and whose soul was excessively confounded, O Nārada, squandered that wealth too by enjoying it along with fools, heretics and Cāṇḍālas.

13. The riches of wicked men are for the enjoyment of men of evil ways. The Neem (Margosa) tree laden with plenty of fruits is enjoyed only by crows.

14. O sage, Sumāli wasted that wealth also given by his brother. He became inebriated by drinking liquor. He (unhesitatingly) ate beef and other forbidden foodstuffs.

15. He was excommunicated by his kinsmen along with his Cāṇḍāla women. O Brāhmaṇa, he was arrested (and punished) by the king.

16. O Brāhmaṇa, Yajñamāli of good intellect was always absorbed in righteous activities. All his sins were wiped off, thanks to his association with the good. He distributed cooked food without restriction.

17. O excellent one, he strenuously maintained all the lakes and other things erected by his father. He was always engrossed in pious rites.

18. All the wealth of Yajñamāli of great *Ātman* was distributed among good men. He was a follower of the righteous path and he abided by his principle of giving charitable gifts to the deserving.

19. O ! The riches of good men are for the enjoyment of the good. All the fruits of the wish-yielding tree are enjoyed only by the immortal Devas.

20. After distributing his wealth in pious and charitable acts (for the sake of piety), Yajñamāli of great intellect engaged himself in the continuous service in the abode of Viṣṇu.

21. As time passed on, Yajñamāli and Sumāli who attained old age died simultaneously.

22. Hari despatched his aerial chariot filled by his attendants to the noble-souled Yajñamāli who was engaged in the regular worship of Hari.

23-25. Yajñamāli of great intellect got into the divine chariot. He was being worshipped by the groups of Devas; he was being eulogised by leading sages. Gandharvas sang about him. Groups of Apsaras served him. He was being nourished by the divine wish-yielding cow Kāmadhenu. He was bedecked in various kinds of ornaments. He adorned himself with tender garlands of Tulasī leaves. He shone as the storehouse of brilliance. As he was going to the divine region of Viṣṇu, he saw his younger brother on the way.

26-27. He was being beaten by the soldiers of Yama. He was afflicted with hunger and thirst. He had become a ghost. He was naked, miserable and bound by nooses. He ran about here and there. He was crying helplessly. He was weeping and lamenting. On seeing him, he (Yajñamāli) was excessively distressed in his mind.

28. Overwhelmed by sympathy, Yajñamāli asked the emissaries of Viṣṇu who were near him, with his palms joined in reverence. He asked :—"Who is this man harassed by the soldiers of Yama ?"

29. Then those emissaries of Hari spoke thus to Yajñamāli of great power. "This is Sumāli, the sinful soul, your brother".

30. O Nārada, on hearing what was explained by the servants of Viṣṇu, Yajñamāli was mentally depressed. He asked them again :

31. "Please tell the remedy by means of which his liberation from the hoarded heaps of sins may become possible. Indeed you are my kinsmen.

32-33. Those who are adepts in Dharma say that friendship originates in seven words spoken or seven steps walked together. The friendship of good men is based on (exchanging) seven words (or accompanying seven steps). But that of very good men (the friendship) is contracted in three words (or steps). Those who are very very good men have friendship at every step (word).

34. Hence, you are my kinsmen. You have come to take me (to heaven). How is my brother to be liberated ? May this be kindly explained".

35. On hearing the words of Yajñamāli, the sympathetic emissaries of Viṣṇu spoke to Yajñamāli who was a favourite of Hari. They spoke with their faces beaming with smiles. Viṣṇu's emissaries said :

36. "O highly blessed Yajñamāli, absorbed (in the devotion) to Nārāyaṇa, we shall mention to you the means that will accord living liberation to Sumāli.

37. We shall succinctly recount to you the great work that had been performed by you in your previous birth.[1] Listen to it with great attention.

38. Formerly, you were born of a Vaiśya family. You were remembered by the name Viśvambhara. Countless and great sins were committed by you.

39-40. You were devoid of even traces of good deeds. You opposed even your parents. Once, when you were forsaken by your kinsmen, you were afflicted by grief and distress. You were oppressed by the fire of hunger. Thus you reached a temple of Hari. There had been a downpour and the whole place became marshy.

41. The mud was removed by you, since you desired to stay there. This became the service of smearing in the temple of Viṣṇu.

42. O Brāhmaṇa, you stayed in that temple during that night. You were bitten by a serpent and you died.

Thanks to the power of your meritorious deed of smearing and scrubbing, the birth as a Brāhmaṇa was attained by you. Your devotion to Hari was steady.

43. You will reach the presence of Hari and stay there for a hundred crores of *Kalpas*. Afterwards you will acquire spiritual knowledge and attain the great salvation.

44. You desire to uplift your younger brother who is the greatest sinner. We shall tell you the means thereof. O highly intelligent one, understand it.

45. You donate to your brother the benefit of smearing an area extending to a *Gocarma*. O highly blessed one, thus kindly uplift your brother."

46. Thus urged by the emissaries of Viṣṇu, the highly intelligent Yajñamāli gave that much merit to his brother for the sake of liberation from sins.

47. Through the merit bestowed by his brother, Sumāli became free from sins. The emissaries of Yama left him off and fled.

48. An aerial chariot that contained all means of enjoyment of pleasures came there immediately. O sage, Sumāli then stepped into the heavenly vehicle and rejoiced.

49. O Brāhmaṇa, both the brothers were bowed to by groups of Devas. By embracing each other they attained great pleasure.

50. Being eulogised by great sages and sung about by Gandharvas, Yajñamāli and Sumāli went to Viṣṇu's world.

51. Attaining *Sālokya* (stay in the same region) with Hari, O excellent sage, Sumāli and Yajñamāli lived there joyously for the period of a Kalpa.

52. After enjoying many pleasures there, Yajñamāli of great intellect, became richly endowed with perfect knowledge and attained the great salvation (*Mokṣa*).

53. The highly blessed Sumāli rejoiced in the Viṣṇuloka (region of Lord Viṣṇu). (Afterwards) he came to the Earth again and was born as a Brāhmaṇa.

54. He was born in a very pure family. He had all good qualities. He was a master of the Vedas. He was endowed with all riches. He was devoted to Hari.

55-56. Repeating the names of Hari, he reached the banks of the Gaṅgā. He took his bath in the Gaṅgā. After seeing lord Viśveśvara he attained the greatest abode, difficult of access even to the Yogins. O leading sage, the great merit accruing from smearing Viṣṇu's temple, has been recounted to you.

57-59a. Hence, the lord of the worlds should be, with best possible efforts, worshipped. Those who worship Viṣṇu even for once, without any specific desire, never get entangled in the worldly existence. Those who worship people engaged in the devotion of Hari thinking them to be Hari himself, are delightedly blessed by Brahmā, Viṣṇu and Maheśvara.

59b-61. Even a great sinner is liberated from all sins by the mere contact with those who came into contact with those devoted to Hari.

Those who are engaged in the service of those who are devoted to Hari and of those who are engaged in the repetitions of the names of Hari, attain the greatest goal, even if they happen to be sinners.

CHAPTER THIRTYSIX

1. As mentioned above, all names in this story of Vedamāli family are fictitious. Thus Sumāli a demon mentioned in the Brahmāṇḍa P.3.7.99 and in the *Yuddha Kāṇḍa* of the Kamba Rāmāyaṇa have no connection with this son of Vedamāli.

2. This chapter is intended to describe the efficacy of even menial service rendered to a shrine of Viṣṇu without intending any service to the deity. Thus the wicked Vaiśya Viśvambhara who had committed countless sins and who after ex-communication was driven to the temple of Viṣṇu for refuge due to the downpour of rain, became a holy Brāhmaṇa called Yajñamāli, the son of Vedamāli simply because he, in that birth, removed the mud in the temple of Viṣṇu for his night-stay there but he was bitten by a serpent and he died.

CHAPTER THIRTYSEVEN

The Greatness of Viṣṇu : The Story of Gulika,[1] *The Hunter*

Sanaka said :

1. O leading Brāhmaṇa, listen once again to the greatness of the lord of Lakṣmī. What person is not delighted to hear the nectarine stories of Hari ?

2. To men blinded by sensual objects, to those whose minds are agitated by the feelings of 'mine-ness', the only thing that destroys all sins is the name of Hari.

3. If anyone, even for once, does not bow to Viṣṇu the destroyer of the sins of men, know him to be a Cāṇḍāla (one who cooks dog's flesh for food). Never shall anyone converse with him.

4. O excellent Brāhmaṇa, if no worship of Hari is performed in any house, know that to be on a par with the cremation ground. Never shall one enter it.

5. Those who are devoid of the worship of Hari, those who hate the Vedas, and those who are engaged in the hatred of cows and Brāhmaṇas are said to be Rākṣasas

6. O leading Brāhmaṇa, if anyone is engaged in the hatred of the Brāhmaṇas—no matter who he is—and he worships Govinda, that worship is futile.

7. O highly blessed one, if any one were to worship Janārdana for the destruction of another man's welfare, the very same act of worship immediately kills the worshippers.

8. If a worshipper of Hari commits a sin, he alone is the hater of Viṣṇu, so say the persons who are experts in the interpretations of principles.

9. Those who are engaged in the worship of Viṣṇu and are interested in blessing (and obliging) the world, and those who are always engaged in the righteous activities are considered to be persons in the eternal form of Viṣṇu.

10. Devotion to Viṣṇu is the result of the merits accumulated in the course of ten million births. How can they who have steady devotion to Viṣṇu be sinfully inclined ?

11. Within a moment the sins accumulated in the course

of crores of births, perish, if people are engaged in the worship of Viṣṇu. How can they have sinful intentions ?

12. Those who are devoid of devotion to Viṣṇu are said to be Cāṇḍālas. If the Cāṇḍālas are devotionally engaged in the worship of Hari, they are verily excellent persons.

13. Service to Hari is reputed to be the destroyer of all miseries of men blinded by sensuous objects. It yields both worldly pleasures and salvation.

14. If a man worships Viṣṇu as a result of his association, or due to real love, or due to fear, or out of covetousness or due to ignorance, he enjoys inexhaustible happiness.

15. He who drinks even a drop of the water that has washed the feet of Hari, becomes a great favourite of Viṣṇu. He is equal to one who has taken his ablutions in all the sacred waters.

16. The water that has washed the feet of Hari is remembered as something that subdues premature death, that destroys all ailments and that removes all miseries.

17. Nārāyaṇa is the greatest splendour (or the Supreme abode), the most excellent of all luminaries. Salvation is perpetual to those noble-souled ones who seek refuge in Nārāyaṇa.

18. In this context, they cite the following ancient mythological anecdote. It is destructive of all sins of those who read and listen to this.

19. Formerly, in the *Kṛta Yuga*, there was a hunter named Gulika. He always attempted to abduct other men's wives or to take away other men's wealth.

20. He was always engaged in censuring others. He regularly tortured all creatures. He killed Brāhmaṇas and cows in hundreds and thousands.

21. O Brāhmaṇa, this lord of demonic fellows was always eager to rob godly assets and other men's wealth.

22. So many great sins were committed by him, that it is impossible to enumerate them even in the course of crores of years.

23-24. Once this great sinner who could be compared to the god of death in regard to his dealings with creatures, went to the capital city of the King of Sauvīra. It was filled with all kinds of riches. It was richly decorated with well-adorned women and lakes of translucent water as well as trading centres. It was comparable to the city of gods.

25. There was a beautiful temple of Keśava situated in the middle of a park therein. On seeing that it was covered with golden domes resembling pots, the hunter was very much pleased.

26. The hunter who resembled god of Death and who was ardently longing for stealing, made up his mind thus "I shall take away much of the gold from here" and he went into the temple.

27. There he saw Uttaṅka, the storehouse of austerities, the quiescent excellent Brāhmaṇa, an adept in the interpretation of the principles, and engaged in rendering service to Viṣṇu.

28-29. The Brāhmaṇa who was devoid of desire, was alone. He was eager to meditate. O sage, yet, the hunter regarded him as one who would put obstacles in his act of stealing. Desirous of taking away the collected treasures of the lord, the dare-devil who was very haughty, took out his sword and began to kill Uttaṅka.

30. The hunter pressed down his chest under his foot and caught hold of his matted hair with his hand. On seeing that the hunter had decided to kill him, Uttaṅka spoke thus:—

Uttaṅka said :—

31. O my good man, in vain do you try to kill me, utterly sinless. O intelligent man, tell me in what way I have offended you.

32. My gentle friend, powerful persons in the world chastise the offenders and teach them a lesson. But good men do not kill even the sinners in vain.

33. Good men of calm minds perceive the good qualities present even in the offending fools. And they do not offend them in return.

34. They call him the excellent man, the person who continues to be forbearing even when he is being harassed.* He is the favourite of Viṣṇu for ever.

35. Even at the time of death, a good man thinks of the welfare of others, but he does not become inimical (to his offender). Even when cut, the sandal tree renders the face (i.e. edge) of the hatchet fragrant.

**Bodhyamāna* in the text is obviously a misprint for *bādhyamāna*.

36. Alas! fate is very powerful. It afflicts people in many ways, for even a man who has eschewed all intimate contacts (with worldly affairs) is being harassed by the wicked-minded.

37. Alas! (many) in the world oppress the people in many ways without reason. Even a man who has eschewed all intimate contact (with worldly affairs) is harassed by back-biters and calumniators. There too they harass the good men and never their equals.

38. In this universe, the hunter, the fisherman and the calumniator are the causeless (unreasonable) enemies of the deer, the fish and the good people who maintain themselves with grass, water and contentment.

39. Alas ! the Māyā is very powerful. It deludes the entire universe and makes all people miserable for the sake of sons, friends and women.

40. By looting other people's wealth you have maintained your wife and women dependents. In the end, you have to leave everyone and go alone.

41. "My mother", "My father", "My wife," "My sons" "This is mine". Thus the feelings of 'My-ness' of all creatures harass them in vain.

42. One has (the benefits of having) the kinsmen only as long as one earns wealth. It is the *Dharma* and *Adharma* (merits and sins) that remain with one both here and hereafter and not anything else.

43. (Defective) Men who are nourished by means of wealth earned through *Dharma* as well as *Adharma* by a person, consign him (that very person) to flames and enjoy rich food soaked in ghee.

44. Only the *Dharma* and the *Adharma* follow the man who goes to the other world, not his wealth, nor his sons, nor any of his kinsmen.

45. Lust of men indulging in sinful activities increases (day by day). Lust of men of meritorious deeds becomes reduced and quelled.

46. All people are always unnecessarily worried and agitated over the problem of earning wealth, etc.

47. "What is destined to happen does definitely happen. What is not to occur shall never occur".[2] If people come to this decision, no anxiety worries them at all.

48. The whole of this universe consisting of the mobile and immobile beings is under the control of fate. Only fate and none else can know the happening of birth and death.

49. Wherever one may stay, whatever is destined to happen certainly happens. Being ignorant and unaware of it, the whole world exerts itself in vain.

50. Alas ! the misery of men who are worried due to the feelings of 'My-ness' ! Even by committing great sins (those people) assiduously go on feeding others.

51. It is the kinsmen who enjoy all wealth earned by one. Alone and perplexed, one experiences the adverse effects of all one's sins."

52. As the sage said this, Gulika, the hunter became frightened. He let off the sage and with palms joined in reverence repeatedly begged of the sage to forgive him.

53. By the mere presence of Hari and thanks to the power of the association of the good, the hunter became free from sins. Repenting for his misdeeds he said thus :—

54. "O leading Brāhmaṇa, many great sins have been committed by me. All of them have perished at your very sight.

55. Alas ! I have been sinfully inclined. I have continuously committed great sins. O holy lord, how is my redemption possible ? To whom shall I approach for refuge ?

56. I have been born as a hunter due to the sins accumulated in the previous births. By committing sins here too (I do not know) what state I shall attain ?

57. Alas ! My span of life gets reduced quickly. Many sins have been accumulated. I have not atoned for them. What will be my state after death ? What will be my next birth ?

58. Alas! Why did the creator make me one defiled by hundreds of sins ? I am perpetually becoming more and more sinful. How shall I reap the adverse effects of those sins ? For how many births am I to be one committing terribly fierce deeds ?"

59. Thus censuring his own self, the hunter became scorched by means of the fire of his own mental agony. He died instantaneously.

60. On seeing the fallen hunter, the kind-hearted highly intelligent (sage) Uttaṅka sprinkled him with the water that had washed the feet of Viṣṇu.

61. Thanks to the contact with the water from the feet of Viṣṇu the hunter became free from his sins. Seated in a divine aerial car, he spoke to the sage thus :—

Gulika said :

62. O leading sage Uttaṅka of holy rites, you are my preceptor. I have been freed from the slough of great sins. Thanks to your favour.

63. O leading sage, thanks to your instructions, my distress has gone. Similarly, all sins have been quelled quickly.

64. O sage, since the water from the feet of Viṣṇu has been sprinkled on me by you, I have been enabled to attain the greatest region of Viṣṇu.

65. O Brāhmaṇa, I have been redeemed from this sinful body by you. Hence, O learned one, I bow down unto you. Forgive the misdeed committed by me (or the maltreatment given by me to you)".

66. After saying this he showered the leading sage with divine flowers. After circumambulating him thrice, he prostrated himself before him.

67. Thereafter, he got into the aerial chariot equipped with all desirable things and occupied by the groups of celestial damsels. He then went to the abode of Hari.

68. On seeing this, Uttaṅka, the storehouse of austerities, became surprised. Keeping the palms joined over his head in reverence, he eulogised the lord of Kamalā (Goddess Lakṣmī).

69. Eulogised by him, Mahāviṣṇu granted him an excellent boon. Thanks to that boon Uttaṅka attained the highest region (*Mokṣa*).

CHAPTER THIRTYSEVEN

1. The story of Gulika, the wicked hunter is given to illustrate how even the worst sinners attain to *Mokṣa* by seeking refuge in Lord Nārāyaṇa. The story resembles the Vālmīki episode in which Nārada reminds Vālmīki that he alone and none of his relatives should have to answer for his sin. The hunter Gulika repented so deeply due to this admonition that he fell down dead at the shock of the consequences of his sins. The Brāhmaṇa Uttaṅka immediately sprinkled him with water touching Viṣṇu's feet and the wicked hunter, being absolved of all sins paid homage to his *Guru* Uttaṅka and attained *Mokṣa.*

In the NP. Gulika is a fictitious figure and Uttaṅka is in no way related to the sage of the same name in *Mbh.Ādi.ch.*3 or of the Uttaṅkopākhyāna in *Mbh. Āśva.* chs. 53.58 or the sage who urged King Kuvalayāśva to kill demon Dhundhu (*Mbh. Vana.* chs. 201-204).

2. Cf. the famous *Subhāṣita* in the *Hitopadeśa* :

Yadabhāvi na tad bhāvi bhāvi cenna tadanyathā |
iti cintā-viṣaghnoyam agadaḥ kim na pīyate ||

CHAPTER THIRTYEIGHT

Uttaṅka's Eulogy of Viṣṇu : Uttaṅka Liberated

Nārada said :

1. O blessed one, what is that hymn? How was Janārdana propitiated? What sort of a boon did Uttaṅka, the meritorious person, attain?

Sanaka said :

2. Uttaṅka, the Brāhmaṇa engrossed in the meditation on Hari, saw the great efficacy (greatness) of the water from the feet of Lord Viṣṇu and eulogised him devoutly.

Uttaṅka prayed :[1]

3. I bow down unto Nārāyaṇa, the primordial deity, the supporting abode of the universe, the sole kinsman unto the whole universe. I seek refuge in the great deity holding the discus, the lotus, the Śārṅga bow and the sword and who destroys the distress of anyone immediately after being remembered.

4. I bow down to Viṣṇu, that primordial deity, from whose umbilical lotus was born god Brahmā who creates the aggregation of worlds and from whose fury was born Rudra who annihilates the universe.

5. Suppliantly, I betake myself to Viṣṇu who is the lord of Padmā (goddess Lakṣmī), whose eyes are as large as the petals of a lotus, whose prowess is of mysterious and miraculous nature, who is the sole cause of all, who is the ancient Puruṣa comprehensible through the Vedānta texts and who is the store-house of brilliance.

6. He is the imperishable *Ātman*, the omnipresent deity named Acyuta who is of the nature of perfect knowledge and is worthy of being the refuge of those who possess perfect knowledge. May the primordial lord, comprehensible only through perfect knowledge, be propitious unto me—The Lord

who is of the form of *Vyaṣṭi* (Distributive pervasion)and *Samaṣṭi* (aggregate collective)—as well be pleased.

7. He is of infinite prowess, devoid of attributes and births, of the nature of *Guṇas*, the most excellent among the possessors of perfect knowledge. He is eternal and he removes the distress of those who seek shelter in him. May that great *Ātman*, the ocean of mercy, be the bestower of boons unto me.

8. You have precisely pervaded the universe created by you, entering it through the special qualities of subtlety and grossness. O great *Ātman*, you alone are identical with all those, as there is no other infinite essence excepting you.

9. Your pure form is invisible; it is devoid of *Māyā*, and of attributes and births; it is unsullied; free from impurities and unmeasurable. Good men observe that pure form which is termed the true and the great entity.

10. All ornaments are identical inasmuch as the same gold is present in all of them. They assume different forms due to the conditioning factors. Similarly, the same lord of all, the *Ātman* of everyone, though single appears as different due to conditioning factors.

11. Those whose minds are deluded by his Māyā do not perceive even the well-known *Ātman*. Those very persons when freed from Māyā, perceive the same as their ownself being the self of all.

12. I bow down to the lord named Viṣṇu, the incomparable brilliance, from whom all this visible world has originated and in whom that has been established.

13. Obeisance to that lord whose form is consciousness; and from whom sentience has originated. Obeisance to that lord who is incomprehensible, who has nothing to support and who is of the form of both the supporter and the supported.

14. I bow down to Vāsudeva who is the embodiment of pure bliss and knowledge. I bow down to that Lord whose abode is the cavity of the heart and who is served by Yogins.

15. I bow down to that deity who has become the first among the Yogins and who abides in the *Praṇava* (Oṁ). I bow down to that unchanging deity of the nature of *Nāda* (mystic sound) who is the *Bija* (seed) of the *Nāda* and who is of the nature of *Praṇava*.

16. I bow down to that deity who has the nature of Being

(or Existence) and who is Existence, knowledge and Bliss, the possessor of that fiery sharpedged discus; who is the unageing cosmic witness and who is beyond the ken of speech and mind.

17-19. I bow down to the form of Viṣṇu that is called *Ananta* (Infinite) and is unsullied. They say that the sense organs, the mind, the intellect, the inherent power, the brilliance, the strength, fortitude, the *Kṣetra* (the body) and the Kṣetrajña - (the Soul)—all these are of the nature of Vāsudeva. They call him one who is of the form of both *Vidyā* and *Avidyā* (knowledge and Nescience). They call him greater than the greatest. Perpetual is the salvation of those great noble souls who seek refuge in the quiescent Acyuta who has neither beginning nor destruction and who is the creator of every thing.

20. Repeatedly, I bow unto him who is the most excellent, a bestower of boons who is the ancient and eternal deity identifying with everything and pervading all.

21. I worship that incomprehensible *Puruṣa*, the water from whose feet is an antidote for the ailment of worldly existence (*Saṁsāra*), the dust of whose feet is conducive to the achievement of purity and whose name is efficacious to ward off evil rites.

22. I worship him who is of the form of *Sat* (Existent) and who is of the form of *Asat* (non-Existent) and who is of the form of both *Sat* and *Asat*; who is unchanging, and different from all these. He is the excellent one, more excellent than the most excellent.

23. He is unsullied, formless, perfect and stationed in the midst of firmament. He is beyond both *Vidyā* and *Avidyā*; and is abiding in the lotus of the heart.

24. He is self-luminous, unspecifiable, greater than the greatest, and minuter than the minutest. He is devoid of all conditioning factors.

25. I sought refuge in that supporting abode of the universe termed Viṣṇu, which is eternal, the greatest bliss and which is the greatest eternal Brahman.

26. I sought asylum in that quiescent Lord whom, those who strictly adhere to holy rites, worship, whom the Yogins perceive and who is more worthy of being worshipped than anyone else.

27. I bow down to the unchanging Lord who is eternal

and superior to all, whom even learned men do not perceive and who stands pervading this entire universe.

28. It is he who is called *Jiva* (the individual Soul) due to the contact with internal sense-organ (i.e. the Mind). It is he who is sung about as the greatest *Ātman* when he is devoid of *Avidyā* and the physical body.

29. I bow down to that deity who is identical with every thing, is the cause of all; who is the bestower of the benefits of all holy rites and is the most excellent of all; who is unborn and greater than the greatest.

30. I worship Hari who is omniscient, omnipresent and quiescent; who is the immanent soul of all and is identical with perfect knowledge; who is the storehouse of perfect knowledge and the Lord stationed in perfect knowledge.

31. I bow down to the receptacle of the Vedas, the slayer of demon Mura (Viṣṇu) whose import is well decided by the sound knowledge of the *Vedānta* (contained in upaniṣads) who is the Lord with the shining eyes in the form of the Sun and the Moon, and who has the form of the bird, viz., that of Vipati (lord of the birds).

32. I worship that Puruṣa who is the great lord of all, omni-present; who is identical with the *Vedas* and is the most excellent of all knowers of the *Vedas*; who is beyond the ken of speech and the mind; is incomprehensible, of infinite power and knowable only through perfect spiritual knowledge.

33. I seek refuge in that incomprehensible and unmeasurable Lord, who possesses the perfect nature and who protects the worlds through Indra, Agni, Kāla (i.e. Yama), Asura (i.e. Nirṛti), Pāśin (Varuṇa), Vāyu, Soma (the Moon) Īśa, Mārtaṇḍa (the Sun), Purandara and others.

34. I bow down to that deity who has thousand hands, thousand feet, thousand arms and thousand eyes, who is served by means of Yajñas, and who is the primordial deity of fierce valour, the bestower of contentment and pleasure.

35-36. I worship the deity who is identical with Kāla (Time, Death); who is the cause of the division of Time, who is beyond the three *Guṇas*, but is the knower of attributes; who is the appreciator of good qualities, the bestower of desired objects, contactless and unknowable through the sense-organs; who is the enjoyer of the universe yet is devoid of thirst (i.e.

desire for worldly things); who is devoid of desire, the foremost (one), who cannot be approached even mentally; who is inherent in the vestures (*Kośas*) constituted of the mind and food (mental) and physical vestures, who is discerned through spiritual wisdom and attained through *Kalpas* (sacred precepts?) and who is not identical with either speech or *Prāṇas* (vital breaths).

37. How can I eulogise that deity of the form of *Ātman* about whom the lotus-born deity and other Devas (deities) do not know anything? They do not know his form, or strength or prowess, or activities or valid means of knowing him (or his magnitude).

38. O ocean of mercy, protect me! I am fallen into the ocean of worldly existence; I am miserly and deluded; I am bound by hundreds of lustful entanglements, I am infamous slanderous, ungrateful. I am always impure, engaged in sinful activities and extremely furious. I am frightened as well. I seek refuge in you again and again. Save me".

39. Thus propitiated by him, the sympathetic lord of Kamalā (Lakṣmī), the lordly receptacle of all brilliance became visible to him directly.

40-43. He resembled the *Atasī* (blue) flower (in complexion). His eyes were like full-blown lotuses. He was bedecked in coronet, ear-rings, necklaces and bracelets. He was wearing the Kaustubha jewel and the golden line of hair on the chest called *Śrīvatsa.* He had golden sacred thread. The beauty of his body was hightened by the lustre of the pearl placed at the tip of his nose. He was clad in yellow robes. The lord was adorned with garlands of sylvan flowers. His feet were worshipped with the tender leaves of *Tulasī* plant. He had a great lustre. He was adorned with tinkling ornaments and anklets, etc. On seeing the Garuḍa-emblemed deity, the leading Brāhmaṇa bowed down and prostrated himself like a staff, on the ground.

44. With tears of delight, Uttaṅka sprinkled the feet of Hari. Without his mind turning to anyone else he said, "O Murāri, save me, save me".

45-46. Raising him up, Mahā-Viṣṇu, the merciful deity, embraced the leading sage and said, "O dear child, choose your boon. O excellent one, when I am delighted, there is nothing which cannot be achieved by you".

On hearing this uttered by the discus-bearing deity, Uttaṅka again bowed to Janārdana, the lord of Devas and said :

47. "O Lord, why do you delude me ? O Lord, of what use are other boons unto me ? May my devotion to you be firm and stable in everyone of my births.

48. Among the worms, birds, animals, reptiles, Rākṣasas, Piśācas or human beings—wherever I may be born, O Keśava ! may my devotion to you alone be steady and unswerving through your grace".

49. Saying "May it be so", the Lord of the worlds touched him with the tip of his conch. He granted him the divine knowledge difficult to be attained even by Yogins.

50. As the leading Brāhmaṇa began to eulogise again, Janārdana, the lord of Devas, said thus with a beam of smile flickering on his face and placed his hand on his head.

Śrī Bhagavān said :

51. O excellent Brāhmaṇa, propitiate me always by means of holy and Yogic rites. Go to the abode of Nara and Nārāyaṇa. You will attain salvation.

52. The man who always reads the song of prayer composed by you, attains all desires and in the end he shall attain salvation".

53. O sage, after saying this to the Brāhmaṇa, Mādhava (Viṣṇu) vanished there itself. Thereafter, Uttaṅka went to the abode of Nara and Nārāyaṇa.

54. Hence, devotion to the discus-bearing lord of Devas should always be practised. *Bhakti* (devotion) towards Hari is said to be the greatest means that yields all desired benefits.

55-56. O sage, engaged in the Yogic and holy rites with great devotional feelings, Uttaṅka worshipped Mādhava continuously in the hermitage of Nara and Nārāyaṇa. He was richly endowed with wisdom and perfect knowledge. All his dualistic doubts were quelled.[2] He attained the greatest region of Viṣṇu difficult to be attained by all.

57. Worshipped, bowed to or well-remembered, Nārāyaṇa, the lord of the universe, bestows salvation. He increases the honour of devotees.

58. Hence, one who desires to attain happiness here and hereafter should worship with great devotion, Lord Nārāyaṇa who is infinite and unvanquished.

59. He who listens to or reads this narrative with great attention becomes liberated from all sins. He goes to the abode of Hari.

CHAPTER THIRTYEIGHT

1. NP. being a Vaiṣṇava Purāṇa takes every opportunity to eulogize Viṣṇu who is the Supreme Brahman. The Viṣṇu in the trinity of gods entrusted with the protection of the Universe, is on a lower plane. This glorification of Viṣṇu the *Para-brahman* is full of Vedāntic ideas contained in the Puruṣa Sūkta and reminds one of Upaniṣads and Śaṅkara's *Vedānta stotras* like *Parā Pūjā*.

This eulogy shows little textual influence of Uttaṅka's praise of Viṣṇu in the *Mbh. Vana.* 201, 14-23, though the commonness of Vedāntic ideas is inevitable.

2. This again confirms the mission of the NP.—to propagate *Bhakti* based on Advaita.

CHAPTER THIRTYNINE

The Greatness of Viṣṇu : The Story of Raivata

Sanaka said :

1. O leading Brāhmaṇa, listen, once again, to the greatness of Parameṣṭhin. It is meritorious and destructive of all sins. It yields worldly pleasures and salvation to men.

2. Lo! The story of Hari is destructive of sins in the world. It bestows merits upon those who listen to the same or narrate it particularly so to his devotees.

3. I bow down to those excellent men who rejoice after tasting the exquisite juice of devotion to Hari. Thanks to association with them, a man attains salvation.

4. Obeisance, obeisance for ever to those men who are absorbed in repeating the names of Hari, irrespective of whether they are of good conduct or evil-minded.

5. O leading sage, he who wishes to cross the ocean of worldly existence should worship the devotees of the devotees of Hari.

6. Seen, remembered, worshipped, meditated upon or bowed to, Govinda uplifts people from the ocean of worldly existence which is very difficult to cross.

7. Salutations for ever to that man who thinks of Hari's name even while he is sleeping or eating or walking, or standing or sitting or talking.

8. O how wonderful ! Wonderful is the good fortune of those who are engrossed in devotion to Viṣṇu since salvation which is inaccessible even to the Yogins is as if in their hand (within their reach).

9. In this context they cite the following mythological anecdote which is destructive of all sins of those who speak about and listen to this.

10. Formerly, there was a king born of the lunar race. He was known as Jayadhvaja.[1] He was devoted to Nārāyaṇa.

11. He was regularly absorbed in the activities of scrubbing and cleaning in the temple of Viṣṇu. He used to be engaged in offering lights as well. He sympathised with all living beings.

12. Once, that king built a temple of Viṣṇu on the beautiful banks of the river Revā. It consisted of wonderful flowers of various colours.

13. The leading king was always engaged in sweeping and cleaning in the temple. He was particularly fond of Hari and regularly lighted lamps there.

14. He was deeply interested in repeating the names of Hari. His mind was always drawn towards Hari. He was engaged in worshipping and bowing to Hari. He was fond of persons devoted to Hari.

15. His priest was famous by the name of Vītihotra.[2] On observing the conduct of Jayadhvaja, he was surprised.

16. Once Vītihotra who was a master of the Vedas and the ancillaries to Vedas, asked the king who was devoted to Viṣṇu while he was leisurely seated (somewhere).

Vītihotra said :

17. O king, the knower of the great Dharma, engaged in devotion to Hari, O leading member of the family of Bharata, you are the most excellent among men endowed with devotion to Viṣṇu.

18. You are constantly engaged in sweeping and cleaning as well as in lighting the lamps (in the shrine of Viṣṇu). Hence, O blessed one, tell me what benefit by this has been known by you.

19. O gentle Sir, you are always engaged in collecting wicks and oil as well as in cleaning the abode of Viṣṇu.

20. There are other activities pleasing to Viṣṇu. Still, O blessed one, why are you engaged only in these two activities continuously ?

21. O lord of men, if you have any love towards me, tell me the secret of the same which is highly meritorious in every respect and known to you.

22. On being requested thus by his priest, Jayadhvaja laughingly spoke these words. He bowed down with humility and kept his palms joined in reverence.

Jayadhvaja said :

23. O leading Brāhmaṇa, listen. Thanks to my faculty of remembering previous births, I know what had been

performed by me formerly. It is conducive to the surprise of those who listen.

24. Formerly, in the *Svārociṣa Manvantara* of the *Kṛtayuga*, O Brāhmaṇa, there was a prominent Brāhmaṇa named Raivata. He was a master of the *Vedas* and the *Vedāṅgas*.

25. He used to perform *Yajñas* on behalf of those who were not eligible for the same. He was a common priest for the whole village. He was a ruthless backbiter. He even sold forbidden goods.

26. He was abandoned by his kinsmen because he used to perform forbidden rites. Hence, he became indigent and miserable. He became sickly with shattered limbs.

27. For the purpose of wealth, he was wandering over the Earth. Once the Brāhmaṇa was afflicted by Asthma and hiccough. He died on the banks of the Narmadā.

28. O sage, when he died, his wife named Bandhumatī became a wayward wanton woman. Hence, she was forsaken by her kinsmen.

29. I was born of her as a *Cāṇḍāla*, popularly known as Daṇḍaketu. I was always engaged in great sins and was a habitual hater of Brāhmaṇas.

30. I was covetous of other men's wealth and enamoured of other men's wives. I killed many creatures. Many cows, Brāhmaṇas, birds and animals were killed by me.

31. Many huge pieces of gold like the Meru mountain were stolen by me. I was always engaged in drinking liquor. Many times I had been a highway robber too.

32-33. I was comparable to the god of death for animals, birds, deer and other creatures. Once I was overwhelmed by lust and was desirous of having sexual intercourse with my wife. On seeing a lonely abode of Viṣṇu I entered it in the company of my wife. In order to enjoy my wife during that night, I lay there lustfully.

34-36. O Brāhmaṇa, by my clothes some space in the temple was swept by me. The sins committed by me in the course of so many births as the number of dust particles swept, were quelled immediately. O excellent Brāhmaṇa, a lamp had been kept there by me for the sexual intercourse. On account of this also my evil actions were entirely wiped off.

When such was the situation, the city guards came there to the temple of Viṣṇu.

37. They caught hold of her and me saying "Here is an adulterer" and killed us. After killing us both, the city guards returned.

38. Immediately the emissaries of Viṣṇu came there. All of them had four arms. They were wearing crowns and earrings. They were bedecked in garlands of sylvan flowers.

39. Directed by those sinless emissaries of Viṣṇu, we both entered a divine aerial car, equipped with all means of enjoyment.

40. We ourselves assumed divine forms and went to Viṣṇuloka. O excellent Brāhmaṇa, we stayed there for a period of a hundred *Kalpas* of Brahmā and more.

41. For a similar period, we stayed in the heaven too, equipped with all divine pleasures. Then by turns we lived on the Earth as well as in the Deva regions.

42. As a result of that meritorious activity I was born as a scion of the family of Yadus. For the same reason my riches never dwindle and my kingdom is devoid of thorns (i.e. enemies and other turbulence).

43. O Brāhmaṇa, after doing something for my own enjoyment, such welfare has been attained by me. I do not know the extent of the benefit and merit of those good men who perform these things with devotion.

44. Hence, O excellent one, with great devotion I endeavour to fulfil my duties of sweeping the floor and lighting the lamps, since I have the faculty of remembering the previous birth.

45. He who worships the lord of the universe with single-minded attention and absence of desire (for any fruit therefrom) becomes free from all sins and goes to the greatest region.

46. I have attained this much of prosperity after performing the holy rites helplessly. What then will not be attained by quiescent and devout persons by worshipping perfectly ?".

47. On hearing the words of the king, the excellent Brāhmaṇa Vītihotra was infinitely contented. He became absorbed in the worship of Hari.

48. Hence, listen, O Chief of Brāhmaṇas! The unchanging lord Nārāyaṇa is the bestower of salvation to those who worship him with or without perfect knowledge.

49. All the kinsmen are casual and unsteady, wealth is never permanent. God of death is continuously near at hand. Hence, *Dharma* (religious and pious acts) must be accumulated.

50. It is the ignorant people who in their extreme arrogance, are vainglorious. Even the body is near (in the very shadow of) dangers. What needs be spoken about riches, etc.

51. Pure devotion unto Janārdana, the God of gods, will be generated only in those people who have accumulated merit during the course of thousands of crores of previous births.

52. The ablution in the Gaṅgā is easily accessible; so also is the worship of guests; all the *Yajñas* too can be easily performed but devotion towards Viṣṇu is very difficult to obtain.

53-54. The service to the *Tulasī* plant is difficult to get; intimate contact with the saintly people is also inaccessible; but the merciful nature towards all living beings may be easy to some. But contact with the good, service to the *Tulasī* plant and devotion towards Hari—every thing is difficult to get.

55. A sensible man should not waste it in vain, after attaining the rare birth as a human being. He should worship the Lord of the universe. This is essential, O excellent Brāhmaṇa.

56. If any man wishes to cross the impassable ocean of worldly existence, let him be devoted to Hari. This is the only panacea.

57. O brother, seek the support of Govinda. O beloved one, do not delay. The city of *Kṛtānta* (God of death) is seen nearby.

58. O leading Brāhmaṇa, if you wish to attain liberation, worship Nārāyaṇa, the source of the origin of the universe, the cause of the cause of all.

59. Undoubtedly only those noble-souled ones who have resorted to the Lord, the support of all, the source of origin of all, the immanent soul of all, have attained their goal in life.

60. Those who worship Mahā-Viṣṇu, the destroyer of the distress of those who bow down to him, are worthy of being saluted, worshipped and especially bowed to.

61. Those devotees of Viṣṇu who worship the Supreme Lord without any specific desire, go to the abode of Hari along with twenty-one generations of his family.

62. Only he becomes the beloved favourite of the Lord—he who gives water or fruit to a noble-souled devotee of Viṣṇu, who is devoid of any desire.

63. Those who render service to the devotees of Viṣṇu go to Viṣṇu's world and stay there till the final dissolution of all living beings takes places.[4]

64. Only those can purify the universe with the dust of their feet who worship Hari and Hari's devotees, without any specific desire (in return).

65. If anyone devoted to the worship of the Lord stays in a house, Devas as well as Śrī Hari also stay there.

66. O Brāhmaṇa, welfare and happiness increase day by day in that house where *Tulasī* is planted and worshipped.

67. Evil planets, goblins, Vetālas, etc., do not harass anyone in that place where Keśava stays in the form of Śālagrāma stone.

68. That spot is a holy centre, that place is a penance grove, where the Śālagrāma stone stands, since lord Madhusūdana is present there.

69. O celestial sage, know that house to be devoid of auspiciousness and on a par with the cremation ground, if there is no worship of the Śālagrāma stone.

70. The *Purāṇas*, *Nyāya* (texts), *Mīmāṁsā* (texts), *Dharmaśāstras*, *Vedas* along with their *Aṅgas*—all these are glorified as the form of Viṣṇu.

71. The persons who circumambulates Viṣṇu four times with devotion, goes to the highest abode that quells all *Karmans*.

CHAPTER THIRTYNINE

1. This Jayadhvaja is a different person from the fifth son (of the same name) of Kārttavīrya Arjuna and the father of Tālajaṅgha and who became the ruler of Avanti, although both of them belonged to the Lunar race (AIHT. p.146). This Vijayadhvaja belonged to the Bhārata clan (see. v.17).

2. P.E. (*Purāṇic Encyclopaedia*) p.878 records four Vītihotras but all of them are Kṣattriya kings and not Brāhmaṇas.

3. Obviously the story of Jayadhvaja or rather that of a sinful bastard Cāṇḍāla called Daṇḍaketu who swept a part of a temple of Viṣṇu and lit up a lamp for sexual intercourse, was absolved of all sins by that unintended meritorious service to god Viṣṇu and after enjoying heavenly life was born as King Jayadhvaja with the woman of his previous birth as a legitimate queen, is a creation of the author of the NP., as it has no basis in any Vedic or Purāṇic work. The NP. wants to emphasize the covetable fruit of the slightest unintentional service of Lord Viṣṇu (vide vv. 48, 55, 56-61).

4. VV 63 ff. describe the importance of services rendered to the devotees of Viṣṇu and the sanctity of the *Tulasī* plant and of *Śālagrāma* stone.

CHAPTER FORTY

The Greatness of Viṣṇu

(*The Story of Sudharmā*)[1]

Sanaka said :

1. O sage, henceforth I shall tell you the *Vibhūti* (greatness and Super-human powers) pertaining to Viṣṇu. If people listen to it or narrate it, their sins are reduced immediately.

2. Formerly, in the Vaivasvata Manvantara, a lengthy dialogue between Indra and Bṛhaspati took place. I shall narrate it; listen to it attentively.

3. Once Indra who was richly endowed with the enjoyment of all pleasures and was surrounded by all Devas and the celestial damsels, spoke to Bṛhaspati.

Indra said :

4. O lord, O highly blessed Bṛhaspati, O expert in the interpretation of all principles, of what nature was the creation in the *Kalpa* of Brahmā which had gone by.

5. How was Indra as narrated by them ? How were Devas as remembered by them ? Of what nature was their holy rite ? It behoves you to recount this precisely.

Bṛhaspati said :

6. O Indra, the conduct of Brahmā on his previous day is not known to me. Even that of his present day appears to be very difficult to comprehend.

7. Many Manus have gone by. Even to recount them I am not competent. I shall tell you who knows it to day, listen.

8. There is some one in your city well-known as Sudharmā. He has come here from Brahmā's world and is now enjoying the divine pleasures.

9-10. I shall tell you. Listen. Indeed he knows this. When he was informed thus by his preceptor, Indra went to the abode of Sudharmā accompanied by the preceptor (Bṛhaspati) and surrounded by groups of Devas.

11. O celestial sage, on seeing the lord of Devas arrived in the company of Bṛhaspati, he (Sudharmā) received him and worshipped him respectfully.

12. When he was greeted and honoured by Sudharmâ, Indra observed his excellent glory. He was surprised in his mind. Then he respectfully addressed him thus :

Indra said :

13. "O learned one, if you know the conduct of life and other details in the *Kalpa* of Brahmā which had gone by, narrate it. I have come here accompanied by my preceptor in order to enquire about this.

14. O sage of holy observances, since you know Devas too who have no sleep, tell us who is the greater ? How are they greater than we, the residents of heaven ?

15. O lord, O tormentor of enemies, how were they in brilliance, fame, renown, perfect knowledge, charitable gifts or penances ?"

16. On being requested thus by the king of Devas, Sudharmā who was endowed with humility, laughingly recounted what happened before, duly.

Sudharmā said :[2]

17. "O Indra, a thousand cycles of four Yugas are said to constitute a day of Brahmā. In one day, O Indra, there are fourteen Manus.

18-19. (During that period) Indras are also said to be fourteen; Devas are separate and of different kinds. O Vāsava (Indra), all the Indras, Manus and others, are equal in brilliance, glory, prowess and strength. I shall mention their names. Listen with great attention.

20-21. The Svāyambhuva Manu was the first (one), then Svārociṣa. Thereafter, Uttama, Tāmasa, Raivata, Cākṣuṣa and Vaivasvata (the son of the Sun) and Sūrya Sāvarṇi was the eighth. The ninth Manu was Dakṣa Sāvarṇi who was engaged in the welfare of all Devas.

22-23a. The tenth was Brahmasāvarṇi and Dharmasāvarṇi was the next. Thereafter, Rudrasāvarṇi, and Rocamāna is remembered as the next. Bhautya is said to be the fourteenth (Manu). These are the Manus.

23b. O leading Deva, listen, I shall recount Devas and Indras.

24. In the *Svāyambhuva Manvantara* those who were well known as Yāmas were Devas. Their Indra was the highly intelligent Śacīpati.

25. In the *Svārociṣa Manvantara*, Devas were Pārāvatas and Tuṣitas. The lord of Devas was one named Vipaścit who was endowed with all riches.

26. In the third *Manvantara*, the set of Devas were the Sudhāmans, Satyas, Śivas and Pratardanas. Their Indra was glorified as Suśānti.

27-28. In the *Tāmasa Manvantara* Devas were Sutas, Pārāharas, Sutyas and Asudhis.* O Indra, their Indra is said to be Śiva. One named Vibhu is glorified as the fifth *Devapati* (Indra) and Devas are Amitābha and others.

Listen to them in the sixth (*Manvantara*). Āryas and others are said to be Devas and their Indra is Manojava.

29. In the *Vaivasvata Manvantara*, Devas are the Ādityas, Vasus, Rudras and others. Purandara is said to be Indra. He is equipped with all desirable things.

30. The Aprameyas, beginning with Sutapa are glorified as Devas in the eighth *Manvantara*. Thanks to the power of the Pūjā of Viṣṇu, Bali is remembered as their Indra.

31. In the ninth (*Manvantara*) Pāra and others are Devas. Adbhuta is said to be Indra.

In the tenth (*Manvantara*), Suvāsana and others are glorified as Devas.

32-33. Their Indra was named Śānti. He was equipped with all means of enjoyment.

In the eleventh (*Manvantara*), Devas were Vihaṅgama and others. Vṛṣa is remembered as their Indra. Understand the details in the twelfth *Manvantara*. I shall narrate the Indra is one named Ṛbhu and Devas are Hari-Nābhas.

34. In the thirteenth *Manvantara*, Sutrāmās and others are Devas, Divaspati of great prowess is glorified as their Indra.

---

* *Sutyāścāsudhiyaḥ* is probably a misprint for *sutyāśca sudhiyaḥ*.

35. In the fourteenth *Manvantara*, the Cākṣuṣas and others are Devas. Śuci is remembered as Indra. Thus the Manus, Indras and Devas have been recounted to you precisely.

36. In the course of one day of Brahmā, all these enjoy their rights.

37. In all worlds, in the course of all creations, the manner of creation is remembered to be of one type.[3] The makers are many. Only an expert knows their number.

38. O excellent Brāhmaṇa, while I was staying in the Brahmaloka many Brahmās came and went away. I am unable to enumerate them.

39. Listen, how much time I had spent after reaching the heaven. Four Manus have come and gone and my glory is still very extensive.

40. O lord, for the period of a hundred crores of Yugas, I have to stay here; thereafter, I will go to the *Karmabhūmi*. Listen to me.

41. O observer of holy rites, I shall describe the holy rites performed by me formerly. It is destructive of all sins of those who talk and listen.

42. O Indra, formerly, I was a vulture who was particularly sinful. I was stationed on the surface of the Earth with fecal matter and raw flesh as my diet.

43. On one occasion, I was perching on the rampart of a Viṣṇu temple. O lord, I was hit by the weapon of a hunter in the evening. I died and fell in the courtyard of a temple of Viṣṇu (from its rampart).

44. Even as I was having the vital breath reaching my throat (i.e. when my death was imminent), a dog covetous of my flesh caught hold of me by means of its jaw. It was hotly chased by the other dogs.

45. O lord, carrying me in his jaw, the dog, frightened of the other dogs, went round that temple of Viṣṇu.

46. The Lord who is identical with the universe and who is the immanent soul, became delighted with that act. He gave me and the dog the greatest of his region.

47. O leading Deva, such was the benefit for one who went in the form of a circumambulation. What then would not be attained by worshipping him properly?"

48. Thus addressed by Sudharmā, the noble-souled one, the king of Devas was mentally delighted. He became engaged in the worship of Hari.

49. Still all Devas are desirous of taking birth in the Bhārata land. They worship Nārāyaṇa, the lord of Devas, devoid of ailments. Brahmā and other groups of Devas worship them* (Probably : him) for ever.

50. How can there be the bondage of the terrible worldly existence for those noble souls, who endeavour to remember Nārāyaṇa and who have eschewed acceptance of monetary gifts even when those coveting their association attain salvation ?

51. Those men who have eschewed contact with worldly affairs and worship the Garuḍa-vehicled Nārāyaṇa every day, are liberated from all sins and delightfully attain the auspicious region of Viṣṇu.

52. Those men who are devoid of passionate attachment, those who know the greater and the smaller entities, and those who always remember Nārāyaṇa, the preceptor of the gods, get their sins quelled through meditation. Having died once, they do not imbibe again the tasty juice from the breasts of their mothers, i.e. they are not born again.

53. Those men whose blemishes have been dispelled through listening to the stories of Hari, those whose minds are engaged in worshipping the lotus-like feet of Kṛṣṇa, sanctify the worlds through the contact of their bodies or through their talks. Hence, it is Hari alone who is to be worshipped.

54. O Brāhmaṇa, even as it is true that water flows down and remains at a lower level, so also all welfare and happiness stay gathered together only where there are great men who are devoted to the worship of Hari and who possess pure intellects.

55. Hari alone is the greatest and the closest kinsman. Hari alone is the highest goal. Therefore, Hari alone should be worshipped since he is the cause of sentience.

56. O leading sage, worship the deity of perpetual bliss, the bestower of heavenly benefits and salvation, the deity free from ailments. Great happiness and welfare will befall you.

57. Lord Viṣṇu becomes delighted with those people

**tān arcayante* is probably a misprint for *tam arcayanti* as god Viṣṇu alone is meant.

who becoming devoid of lust and desires worship him with purity of mind and he grants them all their desires (desired objects).

58. O the best one among prominent sages, he who listens to this or reads this with great attention, attains the benefit of a horse-sacrifice.

59. O Brāhmaṇa, thus the benefit of the worship of Hari has been recounted to you partly in detail and partly in brief. What else shall I recount to you ?"

CHAPTER FORTY

1. This dialogue between Indra and Bṛhaspati is intended to bring out the importance of circumambulation around the shrine of Viṣṇu.

2. VV. 17-37 describe the fourteen *Manvantaras* which form one day of god Brahmā. Sudharmā enumerates the office-bearers—Manus, Indras, gods, etc. —in each of the *Manvantaras*, cf. Bh.P.VIII chs. 13 & 14, VP III 1 & 2. The only difference is that Rocamāna and Bhautya are the last two Manus given here for Devasāvarṇi and Indrasāvarṇi in the Bh.P. But of these V.P. gives Ruci for NP.'s Rocamāna and Bhautya of the NP. is supported by Mk. Chs. 94, 97.

3. This is the real reply to Indra's query and is based on *dhātā yathāpūrvam akalpayat* |

CHAPTER FORTYONE

The Glory of the Lord's Name

Nārada said :

1. O sage, expert in the interpretation of principles, everything has been narrated by you. Now, I wish to hear the situation and the characteristics of different Yugas.[1]

Sanaka said :

2. Well done, O sage, well done, O highly intelligent one who render service to the worlds, I shall explain the *Yuga-Dharmas* (the specific righteous activities in different *Yugas*) helping all worlds.

3. O excellent one, on certain occasions, *Dharma* flourishingly) increases and on other occasions *Dharma* undergoes destruction on the surface of the Earth.

4. There are four Yugas, viz. Kṛta, Tretā, Dvāpara and Kali. O excellent one, it should be known that all together they consist of twelve thousand divine years.

5. All these Yugas, fully consisting of *Sandhyās* (intermediary period) and *Sandhyāṁśas* (such subsidiary periods) are equal in every cycle. They must be known as extending to the same period. So it has been mentioned by the seers of the true principles.

6. They call the first, the *Kṛtayuga*, then comes the *Tretā Yuga*. Then they say is the *Dvāpara* and the last one they know to be the *Kali Age*.

7. O Brāhmaṇa, there were no separate Devas, Dānavas, Gandharvas, Yakṣas, Rākṣasas and the serpents in *Kṛtayuga*.[2] All were remembered as equal to Devas.

8. All were always full of delight and righteousness. There was neither buying nor selling. There was no classification of the Vedas in the *Kṛtayuga*.

9. The Brāhmaṇas, the Kṣatriyas, the Vaiśyas and the Śūdras were interested in their respective duties and conduct of life. They were always engrossed in penance and meditation and were devoted to Nārāyaṇa.

10. They were free from lust and other defects. They were endowed with good qualities, such as Śama, (selfcontrol). etc. Their minds were engaged in seeking the means of *Dharma*; they were devoid of envy and jealousy; they were not arrogant or hypocrites.

11. All were engaged in speaking truthful words; all practised the respective holy rites of their stage in life; they were richly endowed with Vedic study and were clever in all scriptural texts.

12. Those who are not in communion with lustful benefits, attain the greatest goal by means of holy rites pertaining to the four *Āśramas* (stages in life) and originating at the proper time.

13. In the *Kṛta Yuga*, Nārāyaṇa is of white complexion and is perfectly free from impurities. I shall declare the peculiar features of Tretā. Listen with great attention.

14. O excellent sage in the Tretā Yuga, *Dharma* assumes pale white colour. Hari attains red colour. People undergo slight sufferings.

15. All are absorbed in the path of holy rites; they abide by the holy performance of *Yajña*; they hold steadfastly to truthfulness; they are devoted to meditation, they are always engaged in meditation.

16. O leading sage, in the Dvāpara, *Dharma* stands on two legs, Hari assumes yellow colour; the Vedas are classified.

17. At that time even some excellent Brāhmaṇas are absorbed in untruths. Among the Brāhmaṇas and the people of other castes, some possess the evils of passionate attachment to worldly objects.

18. O Brāhmaṇa, some of them perform *Yajñas* for the attainment of heaven and salvation; some are desirous of wealth etc., and some have their minds affected by sin.

19. O excellent Brāhmaṇa, in Dvāpara, *Dharma* and *Adharma* are equal mutually and balanced. Due to the power of *Adharma* the subjects dwindle in power and glory.

20. O leading sage, some are short-lived. O Brāhmaṇa, on seeing some engaged in meritorious rites, some men begin to envy them.

21. I shall describe the situation in the Kali Yuga. Listen to it with attention. At the advent of Kali Yuga, *Dharma* stands on one leg.[3]

22-23. Entering the *Tāmasic Yuga* (i.e. Kali Yuga) Hari assumes blackness of complexion. Some righteous soul performs *Yajñas* and conventional religious routines. Some meritorious soul may be engaged in the path of holy rites. On seeing a man absorbed in *Dharma*, all people are afflicted with jealousy.

24. Holy rites and good conduct perish. Similarly do perfect knowledge, Yajña, etc., owing to the prevalence of *Adharma* calamities shall befall.

25. In the Kali Yuga, all people are engrossed in envy and jealousy; they are devoted to arrogant conduct of life; the subjects will be short-lived.

Nārada said :

26. O sage, the characteristic features of the different Yugas have been succinctly mentioned by you. Kindly recount Kali in detail as you are the most excellent among the knowers of *Dharma*.

27. O excellent sage, what will be the diet and conduct of life of the Brāhmaṇas, Kṣatriyas, Vaiśyas and Śūdras in the *Kali Yuga* ?

Sanaka said :

28. O leading sage rendering service to all worlds, I shall recount the characteristics of the *Kali Yuga* precisely and in detail.[4]

29. When Kṛṣṇa assumes black complexion all *Dharmas* perish. Hence, Kali is extremely terrible; it is the mixture of all sins.

30. The Brāhmaṇas, Kṣatriyas, Vaiśyas and Śūdras are averse to righteousness. At the advent of the terrible *Kali Yuga*, the Brāhmaṇas turn their faces away from the Vedas.

31. All people are engaged in the pretence of righteousness; they are engrossed in jealousy and envy. Learned men are vainglorious and wicked as well as devoid of truthfulness.

32. Everyone begins to argue. "I am superior to all"; all people ardently love to perform sins; all men are captious and disputatious.

33. Hence, in the *Kali Yuga* all will be short-lived. O Brāhmaṇa, as the span of life is short, men do not grasp enough learning.

34. As the understanding of different lores diminishes, sin increases. All subjects die to the reverse order (young men die and are survived by the elders). People are engaged in sins.

35-36. The Brāhmaṇas and other castes get mixed with other castes mutually; all castes will be more or less like the Śūdras, overwhelmed by lust and fury, confounded and afflicted by unnecessary distress. In the Kali Yuga the excellent men become mean and the base men rise to excellence.

37. The kings are greedily absorbed in wealth; they are tyrannous; imposing heavy taxes they inflict pain on their subjects.

38. Brāhmaṇas become the pall-bearers of the Śūdras; husbands approach their legally wedded wives in the manner of paramours.

39. Sons hate fathers; women begin to hate their husbands; men are enamoured of other men's wives; people misappropriate other men's wealth.

40. O Brāhmaṇa, in the terrible *Kali Yuga*, the people are engaged in sins; they maintain themselves by means of fish and flesh; they milk even goats and sheep* (Reading *Ajāvikam* not Ajīvikām).

41. Those who are jealous begin to ridicule good men; on the banks of rivers they dig with hoes and spades and grow medicinal herbs. (?)

42. The Earth loses its fertileness (lit. fruitfulness). The seed and the flower perish; women desire to imitate the make-up and the coquetry of prostitutes.

43. Brāhmaṇas sell their *Dharmas*, women resort to prostitution; others sell the Vedas; Brāhmaṇas are absorbed in the conduct of life of the Śūdras.

44. Brāhmaṇas (priests), greedy for money, take away the wealth of good men and pious widows, but do not perform the holy observances.

45. Brāhmaṇas abandon righteous conduct; they are well-equipped with modes of unnecessary arguments; it is mostly out of religious hypocrisy that they perform such rites as the *Śrāddha*, etc., for the *Pitṛs*.

**ajīvikām* in the text is probably a misprint for *Ajāvikām*.

46. Base men give charitable gifts to the undeserving persons; covetous of the milk, they (pretend) to love cows.

47-48. Brāhmaṇas do not perform ablutions and other purificatory rites properly. The vilest Brāhmaṇas become absorbed in holy rites at the improper time. They are engaged in blaming good men and the Brāhmaṇas. O Brāhmaṇa, the mind of none becomes devoted to Viṣṇu.

49. When Kṛṣṇa assumes the dark colour, the wicked servants of the king begin to beat Brāhmaṇas who perform *Yajñas*. They do so for extorting money out of them.

50. O sage, in the terrible *Kali Yuga*, men are devoid of (i.e. abstain from giving) charitable gifts. Brāhmaṇas accept monetary gifts even from fallen men.

51. Even in the first quarter of *Kali Yuga*, men begin to censure Hari; towards the end of the *Yuga* none will repeat the name of Hari.

52. In the *Kali Yuga*, Brāhmaṇas will be indulging in sexual intercourse with Śūdra women. They will be craving for union with widows; they will be engaged in the enjoyment of the cooked food of the Śūdras.

53. Giving up the good Vedic path, they will be pursuing evil ways and manners. They will become heretics and censure the system of the four *Āśramas* (stages in life).

54. The *Śūdras* will not serve the twice-born. Assuming the airs of heretics, the base-born assume and practice holy rites of the Brāhmaṇas.

55. The Śūdras will clothe themselves in ochre-robes; they will have matted hair; they will smear ashes all over their bodies. Thus equipped and employing deceptive arguments, they will begin to expatiate on *Dharma*.

56. The Brāhmaṇas will give up their conventional activities and duties and will partake of other's cooked food; wicked-minded Śūdras will renounce and become wandering recluses.

57. O sage, people will take up bribes as their means of livelihood in the *Kali Yuga*; heretics without piety, the mendicant Kāpālikas and base men will be in plenty in the *Kali Yuga*.

58. Occupying excellent seats, Śūdrás will expatiate on *Dharma*—religious duties—to Brāhmaṇas who habitually destroy *Dharma*.

59. These and many other heretics such as nude ascetics

(*Digambaras*), red-roled mendicants, will roam about; most of whom will be decrying the Vedas.

60. In the *Kali Yuga*, the men who generally destroy *Dharma* will be adept in singing and playing on musical instruments; they will resort to petty and insignificant holy rites.

61. People will be extremely vile. They themselves not possessing much wealth but defiled by vain-gloriousness will be exhibiting for nothing a false show of symbols of piety.

62. They are always dependent on monetary gifts; they practise treading the wrong path in the world; all of them are fond of boasting about themselves and decrying others.

63. O Brāhmaṇa, in the *Kali Yuga*, men will be cruel, treacherous, merciless and devoid of piety; they will be the kinsmen of the sinning ones.

64. Then the maximum expectation of life will be sixteen years. O Brāhmaṇa, in the terrible *Kali Yuga*, a girl of five years will give birth to children.

65. Men of seven or eight years will be the so-called youths and beyond that age is old age. All will abandon their holy duties. They will be ungrateful and breakers of codes of discipline in the society.

66. In the *Kali Yuga*, the Brāhmaṇas will always be beggars. They will not mind being disrespected by others. They will be delighted to stay in other men's houses.

67. There itself, they will entertain vain faith and will be engaged in censuring. They will be censuring in the presence of their fathers, mothers and sons.

68. They will be expatiating verbally on *Dharmas* but in their heart of heart, they will be indulging in sins. They will be proud due to their wealth, learning or age; they will be experiencing all miseries.

69. They will be afflicted by sickness, famine and robbers. Without minding the sinful nature of the act, they will be employing deceptive means and nourishing (their dependents) for nothing.

70. Sinners slight and dishonour the person who points out the righteous path. Those who are vainly self-complacent disrespect one who is engaged in holy rites.

71. After the advent of the *Kali* age, Śūdras and outcastes

will become kings and the Brāhmaṇas will be engaged in rendering service to them. They will be begging for alms.

72. No one will be the true disciple, preceptor, son, father, wife or husband in this confused mixture of castes.

73. When *Kali Yuga* advances, even rich persons will become beggars. The twice-born will be selling liquid beverages.

74. The Brāhmaṇas will be covered with their cloak of piety. They will be assuming the guise of sages. They will be engaged in selling forbidden goods and indulging in sexual contacts with forbidden women.

75. O sage, the Brāhmaṇas who desire to be thrown into hell will maintain themselves through the activities befitting Śūdras; they will invariably hate the Vedas and the *Dharma Śāstras*.

76. In the *Kali Yuga*, men will be terribly afraid of hunger. Frightened of drought, they will be continuously gazing at the sky.

77. Extremely distressed by absence of rain, men will somehow sustain themselves by eating bulbous roots, leaves and fruits like the ascetics.

78. In the *Kali* age, all the people will be distressed through lust, greed and be engaged in sinful activities. They will be short in stature, deficient in good luck and prolific in their progeny.

79. Women will be self-supporting. They will be using the beauty aids like prostitutes; they will disobey their husbands' behests and will be interested in staying in other people's houses.

80. Women of wicked nature entertain a lustful design for men of wicked nature. Even women of noble families will be unfaithful to their husbands through evil activities.

81. Being panick-stricken with the fear of robbers, etc., people will adopt wooden-contrivances as a security measure. People will be extremely harassed by droughts and overtaxation.

82. Being distressed, they will be going to such lands as are full of wheat and barley. Offering the people pleasing tasks, they urge them with auspicious pleasing words (?)

83. People will maintain fraternal relationships till their purpose is achieved. Even mendicants are restrained by friendly relationships.

84. With food as a conditioning factor, disciples will be taken by mendicants.

85. Women scratch their heads with their hands and disobey the behests of their husbands and other elders.

86. When Brāhmaṇas become absorbed in talks on heresy, when they cultivate the company of heretics, the age of Kali will be advancing.

87. That the *Kali Yuga* has advanced should be inferred by clever people at the very same time when people cease to perform *Yajñas* and the twice-born do not perform *Homa* rites.

88. When the *Dharmas* perish, the whole universe becomes inglorious; infant-mortality is bound to occur and there will be growth of *Adharma* (absence of virtue), O Brāhmaṇa.

89. Thus, O excellent Brāhmaṇa, the general features of Kali have been narrated to you. But nowhere does the dark age of Kali affect those people who are devoted to Hari.

90. *Tapas* (penance) is the greatest thing in the *Kṛta Yuga. Dhyāna* (meditation) in the *Tretā Yuga,* and *Yajña* in the *Dvāpara.* They say that *Dāna* (charitable gift) alone is the greatest in the *Kali Yuga.*

91. What is acquired in *Kṛta* in ten years, in the *Tretā* in a year, and in the Dvāpara in a month, is acquired in the course of a day and a night in the *Kali* age.[5]

92. What one achieves by meditating in the *Kṛta Yuga,* by performing *Yajñas* in the *Tretā* and by worshipping in the *Dvāpara,* one obtains in the *Kali Yuga* by repeating the name and glorifying Keśava.

93. Kali does not oppress those persons who perform the worship of Hari or who repeat his names and glorify Hari day and night.

94. Kali does not affect those men who with or without desire for the fruits there-of glorify the deity saying "Obeisance to Nārāyaṇa."

95. O Brāhmaṇa, in the terrible *Kali Yuga,* only those are contented and blessed, those who are absorbed in the names of Hari. Kali does not harass them.

96. Those who are engaged in the worship of Hari, and are devoted to the repetition of the names of Hari, are equal to Śiva. No doubt need be entertained in this respect.

97. After the advent of the terrible *Kali Yuga,* if one

meditates on Viṣṇu whose form is real and who is the support of the entire universe, one does not go to ruin or distress.

98. After the advent of the terrible Kali age that is devoid of all virtue, those who worship Keśava even once, are extremely fortunate.

99. In the Kali age, the holy rites enjoined in the Vedas are likely to be defiled by deficiency or superfluity. Only the remembrance of Hari is conducive to the perfection or completion of the same.

100. Kali does not harass those who always utter the names of Viṣṇu, thus—"O Hari O Keśava, O Govinda, O Vāsudeva, the embodiment of the universe."[6]

101. Kali does not harass even those who utter the names of Śiva, thus—"O Śiva, O Śaṅkara, O Rudra, O Īśa, O blue-necked one, O Three-eyed God !"

102. O Brāhmaṇa, those who speak or utter the names of God thus "O Mahādeva (O great God), O Virūpākṣa (three-eyed one), O Gaṅgādhara (the bearer of the Gaṅgā on the head), O immutable Mṛḍa", have undoubtedly their objects achieved and are happy.

103. Or, those who utter the name of the Lord, thus : "O Janārdana, O Jagannātha, O yellow-robed Acyuta," need not be afraid of Kali.

104. O Brāhmaṇa, in this world, sons, wives, riches and other things are easily accessible to men. But devotion to Hari is difficult to get.

105. Those who are devoid of faith in holy rites, those who are heretics and censure the Vedas and those who are engaged in *Adharma* (sinful activities) do not desire hell, should they remember Hari.

106. It is only through the repetition of the names of Hari that redemption is attained by the people who commit sins, who are beyond the pale of Vedic path and who are wanting in mental purity.

107. O Brāhmaṇa, this entire universe is submissive to *Daiva* (fate, destiny). The mobile and immobile beings do only as they are directed by this destiny.

108. After performing according to one's capacity all the holy rites prescribed in the Vedas, a person devoted to God Nārāyaṇa should dedicate them to Lord Mahāviṣṇu.

109. Holy rites dedicated to Mahāviṣṇu, the Supreme *Ātman*, become complete merely by the remembrance of Hari.

110. Sins do not bind those who are engaged in devotion to Hari. Hence, devotion to Hari is difficult to be attained by the wicked-minded in the world.

111. O ! In the frightful and terrific *Kali Yuga*, those who are devoted to Hari are very fortunate and noble-souled even if they are not in close contact with saintly persons.

112. O Brāhmaṇa, it is true that all the holy rites of those who are engrossed in the remembrance of Hari and those who are absorbed in the repetition of Śiva's names attain perfect completion.

113. O how fortunate are those who are engaged in the names of Hari ! What a good luck ! They are worthy of being worshipped even by Devas. Of what use is much talk ?

114. Hence, only what is beneficial to the worlds, is being proclaimed by me. Nowhere does Kali harass those men who are fond of the names of Hari.

115. My very life is only the name of Hari, only that name and nothing but that name. I emphatically declare that in the *Kali Yuga* salvation is never possible otherwise, not at all."

Sūta said :

116. O Brāhmaṇa, thus enlightened by Sanaka, Nārada attained great delight. He again submitted thus :—

Nārada said :[7]

117. O holy lord, O knower of all scriptural texts, the splendour of the universe, the great eternal Brahman has been revealed by you who are extremely merciful at heart.

118. This is the greatest merit. This is the greatest penance that one remembers the lotus-eyed lord who destroys all sins.

119. O Brāhmaṇa, this universe is manifold. It has been mentioned by you to have been evolved out of this knowledge alone. How can I understand it without an illustrative example ?

120. Hence elucidate that thing by the enlightenment of which the Brahman can be known. Tell it to me so that the depressed mind can steady itself.

121. O Brāhmaṇa, on hearing these words of the noble-souled Nārada, Sanaka remembered the great Nārāyaṇa and replied thus :

Sanaka said :

122. O Brāhmaṇa, I am going to perform meditation. Ask Sanandana as you please. He is an adept in the *Vedānta Śāstra.* He is worthy of being revered and saluted by the noble. He will clear your doubts.

123. On hearing these words uttered by Sanaka, Nārada began to ask Sanandana about the *Mokṣa Dharmas* i.e. holy rites leading to salvation.

CHAPTER FORTYONE

1. The theory of Yugas may appear fanciful but the underlying idea is the time-less-ness of the Universe. The period of Yugas may be four years according to Āryabhaṭa, five years according to Kauṭilya (*Arthaśāstra* XX-*Deśa-Kāla-māna*), but Purāṇas follow Manu I 61-74, 79-86. According to him *Kṛtayuga* extends over 4000 years of gods with a twilight period (*Sandhyā*) of 400 Divine years before it and a transitional period, to the next *yuga* (*Sandhyaṁśa*) of 400 divine years (1-divine year=360 human years). The three other yugas *Tretā*, *Dvāpara* and *Kali* have respectively a period of 3000, 2000, 1000 celestial years and the preceding *Sandhyā* and following *Sandhyaṁśa* together of respectively 600 (300×2), 400 and 200 gods' years. This theory is generally accepted in Purāṇas e.g. VP I.3, Mt.P.142-145, Vāyu P. chs. 21, 22, 57, 58, KP. chs. 51 and 53. Cf *Mbh. Vana* P. chs. 149, 188. So the total number of years in all *yugas* is 12000 divine years.

2. Ancient Indians believed in the existence of an ideally perfect community in hoary past and that it was followed by gradual degeneracy and decline in morals, physique and longevity (*vide Mbh. Śānti* P. ch.59, Manu. I.81, and other Purāṇas also).

3. Cf. Manu I. 81-82 wherein he states that *Dharma* was four-footed and perfect in the *Kṛta Yuga* and that in the successive yugas *Dharma* declined successively by one foot and vices went on increasing. Manu's identification of *Dharma* with a bull (Manu VIII.16) seems at the basis of the four-footedness of *Dharma*.

4. This terrible description of the Kali Age in VV-28-89 is common to many Purāṇas e.g. Vāyu (ch.58), Mt. P. ch. 144, BH.P. XII.2, VP.VI.1, KP.I.29, All these depict a society in which the rules of caste and Āśramas were neglected and non-Brahmanical and anti-Brahmanical ideas and beliefs prevailed. R.C. Hazra in PRHRC (*Purāṇic Records on Hindu* Rites and Customs) pp.208-214 shows that the disintegration of the social fabric and Brahmanism described in the Purāṇas was due to the political supremacy of Śūdras as kings, officers and other elites, vigorous offensive launched against Brahmanism by Buddhist and Jains, in the invasions and settlements of "immoral, casteless, nomads, viz. Śakas, Pahlavas and Ābhiras."

This explains the Brahmanical restrictions against contacts of any kind with foreigners and non-Brahmanical faiths and harsh *prāyaścittas* for such lapses.

It is interesting to note that many verses in the description of the Kali Age are common in *Purāṇas*.

5. VV.91-92 cf. VP. VI 2.15 & 17.

> *Yat Kṛte daśabhir varṣais -Tretāyāṁ hāyanena yat |*
> *Dvāpare tac ca māsena, hyahorātreṇa tat Kalau ||*
> *dhyāyan Kṛte yajan yajñais Tretāyāṁ Dvāpare 'rcayan |*
> *Yadāpnoti tadāpnoti Kalau saṅkīrtya Keśavam ||*

6. VV 100-115 glorify the efficacy of the name of God and the importance of dedicating all our actions to God—This glorification of remembering God's name is a favourite topic of all Purāṇas dealing with Bhakti and with Indian saints.

7. VV 117-123 serve as an introduction to Part II of the NP.